Routledge International Handbook of Diversity Studies

In recent years the concept of 'diversity' has gained a leading place in academic thought, business practice and public policy worldwide. Although variously used, 'diversity' tends to refer to patterns of social difference in terms of certain key categories. Today the foremost categories shaping discourses and policies of diversity include race, ethnicity, religion, gender, disability, sexuality and age; further important notions include class, language, locality, lifestyle and legal status. The *Routledge International Handbook of Diversity Studies* examines a range of such concepts along with historical and contemporary cases concerning social and political dynamics surrounding them. With contributions by experts spanning Sociology, Anthropology, Political Science, History and Geography, the Handbook will be a key resource for students, social scientists and professionals. It represents a landmark volume within a field that has become, and will continue to be, one of the most significant global topics of concern throughout the twenty-first century.

Steven Vertovec is Director at the Max Planck Institute for the Study of Religious and Ethnic Diversity, Göttingen, Germany. He is co-editor of the journal *Global Networks*, author of four books including *Transnationalism* (Routledge, 2008) and *Super-Diversity* (Routledge, forthcoming), and editor or co-editor of over thirty volumes including *Conceiving Cosmopolitanism* (Oxford University Press, 2003), *Migration* (five volumes, Routledge, 2010) and *The Multicultural Backlash* (Routledge, 2010).

Routledge International Handbook of Diversity Studies

Edited by Steven Vertovec

Routledge
Taylor & Francis Group

LONDON AND NEW YORK

First published 2015
by Routledge
2 Park Square, Milton Park, Abingdon, Oxon OX14 4RN

and by Routledge
711 Third Avenue, New York, NY 10017

Routledge is an imprint of the Taylor & Francis Group, an informa business

British Library Cataloguing-in-Publication Data
A catalogue record for this book is available from the British Library

Library of Congress Cataloging-in-Publication Data
Routledge international handbook of diversity studies / edited by Steven Vertovec.—1 Edition.
    pages cm.—(Routledge international handbooks)
  1. Cultural pluralism. 2. Multiculturalism. I. Vertovec, Steven, editor of compilation.
HM1271.R698 2014
305.8—dc23   2014017331

ISBN: 978-0-415-81386-0 (hbk)
ISBN: 978-1-315-74722-4 (ebk)

Typeset in Bembo
by RefineCatch Ltd, Bungay, Suffolk

MIX
Paper from
responsible sources
FSC
www.fsc.org   FSC® C013056

Printed and bound in Great Britain by
TJ International Ltd, Padstow, Cornwall

Contents

Contents

Contents

Figures

Tables

Contributors

Jan Blommaert is Director of Babylon, Center for the Study of Superdiversity, and Professor of Language, Culture and Globalization at Tilburg University, the Netherlands. His work in sociolinguistics and linguistic anthropology has led him towards the study of new forms of sociolinguistic complexity in urban areas. Highlights from his publications include *Discourse: A Critical Introduction* (Cambridge University Press, 2005), *The Sociolinguistics of Globalization* (Cambridge University Press, 2010) and *Ethnography, Superdiversity and Linguistic Landscapes: Chronicles of Complexity* (Multilingual Matters, 2013).

Andrea D. Bührmann is a Professor of Sociology at the University of Göttingen, Germany, and Director of the Göttingen Diversity Research Institute. Her research interests include diversity and gender studies, research on organizations (e.g. universities and companies), qualitative methods and methodologies as well as practice theory. She has widely published within these topics and is co-editor of *Self-Controlling/Self-Regulation or Self-Caring – The Sociology of the Subject in the 21st Century* (Cambridge Scholars Press, 2010).

Colin Clarke is Emeritus Professor of Geography at Oxford University. He is a Caribbeanist and Mexicanist, and his research interests are in race, ethnicity and class in urban and rural social structures. In 2011–12 he was a Visiting Senior Research Fellow at the Max Planck Institute for the Study of Religious and Ethnic Diversity in Göttingen, Germany, where he researched Nazi racial policy and land settlement in Eastern Europe. His most recent publications include *Decolonizing the Colonial City: Urbanization and Stratification in Kingston, Jamaica* (Oxford University Press, 2006) and, with Gillian Clarke, *Post-Colonial Trinidad: An Ethnographic Journal* (Palgrave, 2010).

Thomas Hylland Eriksen is Professor of Social Anthropology at the University of Oslo and Principal Investigator of the ERC funded research project 'Overheating', a comparative study of accelerated change. His books in English include *Ethnicity and Nationalism: Anthropological Perspectives* (3rd edn., Pluto Press, 2010 [1993]), *Small Places, Large Issues* (3rd edn., Pluto Press, 2010 [1995]) and *Globalization: The Key Concepts* (Bloomsbury, 2014 [2007]). His latest book in Norwegian, a biography of Fredrik Barth, will be published in English in 2015.

Thomas Faist is Professor of Transnational and Development Studies at the Faculty of Sociology, Bielefeld University. He is director of the Center on Migration, Citizenship and Development. Formerly, he directed International Studies in Political Management (ISPM) at Hochschule Bremen. His research focuses on migration, ethnic relations, social policy, comparative politics and transnationalization. His recent book publications include *Beyond a Border: The Causes and*

Consequences of Contemporary Immigration (Sage, 2009) and *Dual Citizenship in Global Perspective: From Unitary to Multiple Citizenship* (Palgrave Macmillan, 2007), both co-authored with Peter Kivisto.

Benjamin Fell is a postgraduate researcher in the Oxford Centre for the Study of Intergroup Conflict at Oxford University. His research focus is negative intergroup contact, and he has contributed to a chapter on measures of intergroup contact in *Measures of Personality and Social Psychological Constructs* (Academic Press, forthcoming).

Nancy Foner is Distinguished Professor of Sociology at Hunter College and the Graduate Center of the City University of New York. Her many books include *From Ellis Island to JFK: New York's Two Great Waves of Immigration* (Yale University Press, 2000), *In a New Land: A Comparative View of Immigration* (NYU Press, 2005), and, most recently, *One Out of Three: Immigrant New York in the Twenty-First Century* (Columbia University Press, 2013) and *New York and Amsterdam: Immigration and the New Urban Landscape* (NYU Press, 2014) (edited with Jan Rath, Jan Willem Duyvendak and Rogier van Reekum).

Allison Harell is Assistant Professor at the Université du Québec à Montréal. Her research focuses on social capital and ethno-racial diversity, support for immigration in Canada and the USA and perspectives toward trust and tolerance. She is the co-director of the Laboratoire d'analyse de communication politique et d'opinion publique (LACPOP). Professor Harell's research has appeared in the *Canadian Journal of Political Science*, *Political Research Quarterly* and *Political Studies*.

Peter Heather is the Chair of Medieval History at King's College in London. Prior to joining King's, he worked at University College London, Yale University and Worcester College, Oxford. Professor Heather has published widely on the later Roman Empire and its successor states, with a focus on the Goth and Visigoth kingdoms of the Medieval period and with publications including *The Goths* (Wiley-Blackwell, 1996) and (with D. Moncur), *Politics, Philosophy, and Empire in the Fourth Century* (Liverpool University Press, 2001).

Tilmann Heil is a social and cultural anthropologist at the University of Konstanz. His doctoral research at the University of Oxford and the Max Planck Institute for the Study of Ethnic and Religious Diversity was on the discourses, practices and transnational experiences of diversity, difference, conviviality and migration in Casamance (Senegal) and Catalonia (Spain). He has authored *Are Neighbours Alike? Practices of Conviviality in Casamance and Catalonia* (Sage, 2014) and is currently preparing his manuscript for the forthcoming book *Comparing Conviviality, Cohabitation and Convivencia*.

Kristin Henrard is Professor of Fundamental Rights and Minorities at the Erasmus University Rotterdam (EUR). Her publications touch on a broad range of themes, including the right to equal treatment, religious rights and participatory rights. Between March 2005 and March 2010 she was a member of The Young Academy of the Dutch Academy of Science. In addition to being an editor for several international journals, she is the co-editor of the Brill *Studies in International Minority and Group Rights* series.

Professor Hewstone is Professor of Social Psychology at the University of Oxford and Fellow of New College. He has published widely in the field of experimental social psychology, focusing on prejudice and stereotyping, intergroup contact, the reduction of intergroup conflict, sectarianism in Northern Ireland and segregation and integration. He is co-editor of *The European Review of Social Psychology*, and he has published two books and edited or co-edited nineteen. These include *The Sage Handbook of Prejudice, Stereotyping, and Discrimination* (Sage, 2010), *Minority Influence and Innovation: Antecedents, Processes and Consequences* (Psychology Press, 2010) and *Advances in Intergroup Contact* (Psychology Press, 2013).

Surinder S. Jodhka is Professor of Sociology at the Jawaharlal Nehru University, New Delhi. He has published widely on the subjects of rural and agrarian change; caste in contemporary India; and social/cultural identities. His publications include *Interrogating India's Modernity* (ed. OUP 2013); *Caste: Oxford India Short Introductions* (OUP 2012); *Village Society* (ed. Orient Blackswan 2012); *Community and Identities: Contemporary Discourses on Culture and Politics in India* (ed. Sage 2001). He is also editor of the Routledge India book series on 'Religion and Citizenship'.

Kim Knott is Professor of Religious and Secular Studies at Lancaster University, UK. She is author of *The Location of Religion: A Spatial Analysis* (Equinox, 2005) and, with E. Poole and T. Taira, *Media Portrayals of Religion and the Secular Sacred* (Ashgate, 2013) and editor, with S. McLoughlin, of *Diasporas: Concepts, Intersections, Identities* (Zed Books, 2010).

Nora Lafi is a French and Algerian historian. She was born in 1965 near Marseille; she graduated in Arabic Language and History at Aix-Marseille University, where she also received her PhD in 1999 and her Habilitation in 2011. Her research focused first on the urban history of Tripoli (Libya) during the Ottoman period (*Une Ville du Maghreb*, L'Harmattan, 2002) and then on the question of urban governance in the Ottoman Empire. Before moving to Berlin in 2004, she worked in Cairo, Tunis, Tripoli, Tours and Paris. Among her publications are *Municipalités Méditerranéennes* (ed., K. Schwarz, 2005); *The City in the Ottoman Empire* (co-ed., Routledge, 2010) and *Urban Governance Under the Ottomans* (co-ed., Routledge, 2014). Nora Lafi is also the co-founder and co-editor of H-Mediterranean (H-Net, Michigan State University).

Keith Lowe is a freelance historian, living in London, UK, whose books have been translated into 16 languages. He is the author of *Inferno: The Devastation of Hamburg, 1943* (Viking, 2007) and the international bestseller *Savage Continent: Europe in the Aftermath of World War II* (Viking, 2012), which won the 2013 Hessell-Tiltman Prize for History.

Helma Lutz is Professor of Women's and Gender Studies in Sociology at Goethe University Frankfurt, Germany. She previously worked at several European universities in the Netherlands, France and Sweden. Her research is concerned with gender, migration, nationalism, racism, citizenship and intersectionality. Her latest books in English are: *The New Maids. Transnational Women and the Care Economy* (Zed Books, 2011) and *Framing Intersectionality: Debates on a Multi-Faceted Concept in Gender Studies* (Ashgate, 2011) (co-editor with Maria Teresa Herrera Vivar and Linda Supik). She is the author of the forthcoming monograph *Behind Europe's Care Curtain: Migration and the Global Market of Care* (2015, in preparation).

Ruth Mandel teaches anthropology at University College London. She is the author of the book *Cosmopolitan Anxieties: Turkish Challenges to Citizenship and Belonging in Germany* (Duke University Press, 2008). She is currently completing a book, *At Crossroads in Kazakhstan*, based on her research about a British development aid project soap opera. With Caroline Humphrey she co-edited *Markets and Moralities: Ethnographies of Postsocialism* (Berg, 2002). She has held numerous awards and honours, including Berlin Prize Fellow at American Academy Berlin, Fulbright Grants, and was a fellow at the Woodrow Wilson International Center for Scholars, Washington D.C.

Lydia Morris is Professor of Sociology at the University of Essex, UK, and a member of the Human Rights Centre. She has a background in sociology, politics and anthropology, and has researched and published on the topics of inequality, gender, migration, welfare and human rights. She is the author of six books, including *Managing Migration: Civic Stratification and Migrants Rights* (Routledge, 2003); *Asylum, Welfare and the Cosmopolitan Ideal: A Sociology of Rights* (Routledge-Cavendish, 2010); and *Human Rights and Social Theory* (Macmillan, 2013). She is also the editor of *Rights: Sociological Perspectives* (Routledge, 2006).

Brendan O'Leary is Lauder Professor of Political Science at the University of Pennsylvania and visiting Professor of Political Science at Queen's University Belfast (2012–14). Recent books include *How To Get Out of Iraq With Integrity* (University of Pennsylvania Press, 2009), *Courts and Consociations: Human Rights versus Power-Sharing* (Oxford University Press, 2013) (with C. McCrudden), *Power-sharing in Deeply Divided Places* (University of Pennsylvania Press, 2013) (co-edited with J. McEvoy) and *Divided Nations and European Integration* (University of Pennsylvania Press, 2013) (co-edited with T.J. Mabry, J. McGarry and M. Moore). In 2009–10 he was Senior Advisor on Power-Sharing with the Standby Team of the Mediation Support Unit of the United Nations.

Jenny Phillimore is Director of the Institute for Research into Superdiversity and Professor of Migration and Superdiversity at the University of Birmingham. She is co-author of *Community Research for Community Participation* (Policy Press, 2012), *New Migrants in the UK* (Trentham, 2008) and *Delivering Welfare in an Era of Superdiversity* (Routledge, forthcoming). She has published extensively on migrant integration and migrants' access to welfare.

Deborah Phillips is Visiting Professor in the School of Geography and Environment at Oxford University and Visiting Research Fellow in Geography at the University of Leeds. She has published widely on aspects of 'race', segregation, integration, citizenship and belonging. Recent publications include *Linking Integration and Residential Segregation* (Routledge, 2012), with G. Bolt and S. Ozuekren, 'Towards inter-cultural engagement: building shared visions of neighbourhood and community' (*Journal of Ethnic and Migration Studies*, 2014), with B. Athwal, D. Robinson and M. Harrison and 'Claiming spaces: British Muslim negotiations of urban citizenship in an era of new migration' (*Transactions of the Institute of British Geographers*, 2014).

Momin Rahman is an Associate Professor of Sociology at Trent University, Canada, and a Fellow of the Mark S. Bonham Centre for Sexual Diversity Studies at the University of Toronto. He has written extensively on the politics of sexuality and was on the board of the 2014 World Pride Human Rights Conference. Books include *Homosexualities, Muslim Cultures and Modernity* (Palgrave Macmillan, 2014); *Gender and Sexuality: Sociological Approaches* (Polity, 2010, with Stevi Jackson); and *Sexuality and Democracy: Identities and Strategies in Lesbian and Gay Politics* (Edinburgh University Press, 2000).

Vincent J. Roscigno is Distinguished Professor of Arts & Science in Sociology at Ohio State University. His books include *The Voice of Southern Labor* (University of Minnesota Press, 2004) and *The Face of Discrimination* (Rowman & Littlefield, 2007). His research on work, bullying, discrimination and inequality has appeared in the journals *American Sociological Review, American Journal of Sociology, Social Forces, Work & Occupations* and *Human Relations*. He is a past editor of the *American Sociological Review* and a current editor of *Social Currents*.

Jens Rydgren is Professor of Sociology at Stockholm University, Sweden. He is working within the fields of political sociology and ethnic relations. He is the author and editor of several books on the radical right in Europe – most recently *Class Politics and the Radical Right* (Routledge, 2013) – and his works have appeared in leading journals such as the *American Journal of Sociology* and the *Annual Review of Sociology*.

William Safran is Professor Emeritus of Political Science at the University of Colorado Boulder. He has published widely on French and comparative politics as well as on ethnicity, the politics of language and diaspora. His recent books include *Politics in Europe* (6th edn., Sage, 2014), *The French Polity* (7th edn., Longman, 2009), *Transnational Migrations* (Routledge, 2009), *Language, Ethnic Identity and the State* (Routledge, 2005) and *The Secular and the Sacred: Nation, Religion and Politics* (Cass, 2003).

Katharina Schramm is a Senior Lecturer in Social Anthropology at the Martin-Luther-University in Halle (Saale), Germany. She has published widely on race, heritage and identity politics as well as science and technology. Her book *African Homecoming: Pan-African Ideology and the Politics of Heritage* came out with Left Coast Press in 2010. She is co-editor of four books and special issues, including *Identity Politics and the New Genetics: Re/Creating Categories of Difference and Belonging* (Berghahn, 2011) and *Technologies of Belonging: Making Race in Europe* (Science, Technology and Human Values, 2014).

Ayelet Shachar is Professor of Law and Political Science at the University of Toronto, and holder of the Canada Research Chair in Citizenship and Multiculturalism. She has published and lectured widely on citizenship theory, immigration law, multiculturalism and women's rights. She is the author of *Multicultural Jurisdictions: Cultural Differences and Women's Rights* (Cambridge University Press, 2001), *The Birthright Lottery: Citizenship and Global Inequality* (Harvard University Press, 2009) and *Olympic Citizenship: Migration and the Global Race for Talent* (Oxford University Press, forthcoming in 2015). Beyond academia, her work has also proved influential in public policy and legislative debates. It was cited, most recently, by the Archbishop of Canterbury and the Supreme Court of Canada.

Sarah Spencer CBE is an Open Society Fellow at the Centre on Migration, Policy and Society (COMPAS), University of Oxford, and a Visiting Professor at the Human Rights Centre, University of Essex. She has researched and published widely on migration, human rights and equality issues, including a critical analysis of UK migration policy *The Migration Debate* (Policy Press, 2011); 'Equality for all? The relationship between immigration status and the allocation of rights in the UK', co-author, in the *European Human Rights Law Review*, 2012; and 'Advancing human rights and equality: assessing the role of commissions in the UK and Ireland', co-author, in the *Fordham International Law Journal*, 2012. Dr. Spencer is a former Deputy Chair of a statutory body, the Commission for Racial Equality, and former Director of Liberty, the UK's leading NGO in the human rights field. She has twice been seconded into the strategy unit in the Cabinet Office to contribute to studies on future migration policy.

Contributors

Charles Stewart is Professor of Anthropology at University College London. Together with Rosalind Shaw he edited *Syncretism/Anti-Syncretism* (Routledge, 1994) and then branched out to consider creolization in the edited volume *Creolization: History, Ethnography, Theory* (Left Coast Press, 2007). His latest book is *Dreaming and Historical Consciousness in Island Greece* (Harvard University Press, 2012), and he continues to work on the anthropology of history.

Melissa Steyn is Professor in Sociology, and Director of iNCUDISA of the University of the Witwatersrand. She has published on many aspects of diversity, including race, gender, culture and sexuality. She is best known for her work on whiteness and white identity in post-apartheid South Africa, an interest on which she is often asked to speak in the media and at conferences. Her book on this topic, *Whiteness Just Isn't What it Used To Be: White Identity in a Changing South Africa* (State University of New York Press, 2001), won the 2002 outstanding scholarship award from the National Communication Association (USA) in International and Intercultural Communication.

Dietlind Stolle is Associate Professor in Political Science at McGill University, Montréal, Canada. She conducts research and has published on voluntary associations, trust, institutional foundations of social capital, political mobilization and new forms of political participation, particularly political consumerism. Recent edited books include *Politics, Products, and Markets: Exploring Political Consumerism Past and Present*, co-edited with Michele Micheletti and Andreas Follesdal (Transaction Publishers, 2003 and in paperback 2006) as well as *Generating Social Capital*, co-edited with Marc Hooghe (Palgrave, 2003).

Carol Thomas is Professor of Sociology at Lancaster University, UK, based in the Faculty of Health and Medicine. She is best known for her publications in Disability Studies - including her books *Female Forms: Experiencing and Understanding Disability* (1997, Open University Press) and *Sociologies of Disability and Illness: Contested Ideas in Disability Studies and Medical Sociology* (2007, Palgrave Macmillan). She has also researched and published widely on patients' and carers' experiences of living with cancer, and has developed an interest in illness narratives. Publications on narrative analysis have followed – notably in debate context in *Sociology of Health and Illness, 32 (4)*. Carol is currently Director of the Centre for Disability Research (CeDR) at Lancaster University.

Jelena Tosic is an anthropologist currently based at the University of Konstanz (Junior Professorship of Political Anthropology) and the University of Vienna. Her research interests include socio-cultural and religious diversity, (forced) migration studies, anthropology of morality/justice/human rights, Europe (the Balkans in particular) and the Middle East. Her books include *Refugee Studies and Politics* (WUV, 2002) and *Anthropologie der Migration* (Facultas, 2009).

John Vincent was trained as a social anthropologist at the University of Sussex, UK. Following professional, political and voluntary association activity related to the condition of old people, he started academic research and publication in social gerontology in the 1980s. He has published books and journal articles on the social, cultural, political and economic impact of age and ageing societies. In the twenty-first century he has specialised in extending his critique of ageism to the anti-ageing movement. His book publications include *Inequality and Old Age* (1995), *Politics, Power and Old Age* (1999), *Politics and Old Age* (2001) and *Old Age* (2003). He retired from the position of Associate Professor in the Department of Sociology and Philosophy at the University of Exeter in 2009. He is a great-grandfather and beekeeper.

Rupa Viswanath is Professor of Indian Religions at the Centre for Modern Indian Studies, Göttingen, Germany. Her work concerns caste subordination, national minorities and practices of minoritization, comparative secularisms, the relations among religions and forms of democratic practice, and political theory and the global south. Her most recent book is *The Pariah Problem: Caste, Religion and the Social in Modern India* (Columbia University Press, 2014).

Alex Wafer is a Postdoctoral Research Fellow at the Max Planck Institute for the Study of Religious and Ethnic Diversity, Göttingen, Germany. As part of the GlobaldiverCities project, he is studying superdiversity in public spaces in a neighbourhood in Johannesburg, South Africa. He holds a PhD in geography from Open University, Milton Keynes, UK. The subject of his thesis was 'Informality, infrastructure and spaces of citizenship in post-apartheid Johannesburg'. His research interests include public services, education and governance. Alex has worked as a researcher at the Centre for Applied Legal Studies, University of the Witwatersrand, Johannesburg, South Africa.

Natasha Kumar Warikoo is Associate Professor of Education at Harvard Graduate School of Education. During 2013–14 she was a Visiting Scholar at Russell Sage Foundation. She is the author of *Balancing Acts:Youth Culture in the Global City* (University of California Press, 2011) and the forthcoming *What Merit Means: Admissions, Diversity, and Inequality at Elite Universities in the United States and Britain*. She holds a PhD in Sociology from Harvard University, and previously was a school teacher in New York City.

Jessica S. Welburn is a President's Postdoctoral Fellow in the Department of Sociology at the University of Michigan, USA. Her research interests include race and ethnicity, racial attitudes, social mobility and stratification, cultural sociology and qualitative research methods. She is currently working on a book manuscript exploring how African Americans understand opportunities for social mobility since the election of United States President Barack Obama. She is also conducting research on how African Americans in Detroit, Michigan conceptualize their social mobility prospects in the midst of the city's financial crisis. Her work has been published in a number of journals, including *Ethnic and Racial Studies* and *DuBois Review: Social Science Research on Race*. Beginning in August 2014, Dr. Welburn will be an Assistant Professor of Sociology and African American Studies at the University of Iowa, USA.

John Wrench is Senior Scientific Officer at the European Union Agency for Fundamental Rights (FRA) in Vienna, currently on leave of absence from the Norwegian University of Science and Technology, Trondheim, where he is Professor at the Centre for Migration and Refugee Studies. He has researched and published for many years in the area of ethnic discrimination and inclusion in the labour market at a European comparative level, first at the Centre for Research in Ethnic Relations, University of Warwick, and later at the Danish Centre for Migration and Ethnic Studies, University of Southern Denmark.

Jill Yavorsky is a PhD candidate of sociology and an affiliate of the Institute of Population Research at Ohio State University. She is also the managing editor of *Social Currents*, the official journal of the Southern Sociological Society. Her research focuses on hiring discrimination and gendered social interactions and status hierarchies at work. In addition, she studies the division of housework and child-rearing practices of new parents. Her research has been published in *Sociological Quarterly*.

Junjia Ye is currently a Postdoctoral Research Fellow in Urban Geography with the Max Planck Institute for the Study of Religious and Ethnic Diversity, Göttingen, Germany, as part of the GlobaldiverCities project. She received her PhD in Geography at The University of British Columbia, Canada, in 2011. Her research interests lie at the intersections of cultural diversity, critical cosmopolitanism, class, gender studies and the political-economic development of urban Southeast Asia. Her work has been published in journals, including *Geoforum, Gender, Place and Culture* and the *Singapore Journal of Tropical Geography*. She is currently finishing her first book, entitled *Inequality in the Global City: The Division of Labour and the Politics of Cosmopolitanism in Singapore*.

Dariuš Zifonun is Professor of Sociology at Alice Salomon University of Applied Sciences, Berlin, Germany, and Associate Research Fellow at the Institute for Advanced Study in the Humanities (KWI), Essen, and Lecturer at TU Berlin. At the KWI he is currently working on the research project 'Spheres of intercultural contact. Societal patterns of dealing with the consequences of migration. Japan, China, Singapore and Germany compared'. His research interests include migration, ethnicity, intercultural studies and sociology of knowledge.

Sami Zubaida is Emeritus Professor of Politics and Sociology at Birkbeck, University of London, Research Associate of the London Middle East Institute and Professorial Research Associate of the Food Studies Centre, both at the School of Oriental and African Studies. He has held visiting positions in Cairo, Istanbul, Beirut, Aix-en-Provence, Paris, Berkeley CA and New York, written and lectured widely on themes of religion, culture, law and politics in the Middle East, with particular attention to Egypt, Iran, Iraq and Turkey. His other work is on food history and culture. Books include *Islam, the People and the State: Political Ideas and Movements in the Middle East* (revised and updated edition I. B. Tauris, 2009); *A Taste of Thyme: Culinary Cultures of the Middle East* (ed., with R. Tapper and C. Roden, 2nd edn., Tauris Parke Paperbacks, 2000); *Law and Power in the Islamic World* (I. B. Tauris, 2003) and *Beyond Islam: A New Understanding of the Middle East* (I. B. Tauris, 2011).

Introduction
Formulating diversity studies

Steven Vertovec

It is both a stimulating and a challenging time to be engaged in what might be called 'diversity studies'. It is stimulating because there is currently an outpouring of academic work surrounding diversity. Contemporary scholarship on diversity condenses and builds upon decades of significant empirical and theoretical work surrounding key concepts like race, gender and sexuality as well as subjects such as discrimination, social movements and social inequality. Diversity is undoubtedly a hot topic in the social sciences and humanities.

For academics, it is also a challenging time because 'diversity' is, simultaneously, a hot topic in the public sphere too. Within businesses and corporations, state agencies, universities and a variety of public institutions, 'diversity' is an essential reference point within mission statements, strategy frameworks and staffing structures. Indeed 'diversity' is to be found across broad areas of public policy and discourse. Consequently, real challenges arise when academics attempt to probe such a term critically and analytically while public bodies are using it normatively or instrumentally. Confusion and miscommunication are bound to arise.

This introduction commences with an outline of some issues surrounding the idea of 'diversity' in the public sphere. It follows with a discussion of the meanings, potential scope and thought-provoking approaches to the concept of 'diversity' in social science. Thereafter, I propose possible ways of modelling research and theory-building within the field. Given that a broad area of interest and scholarship around social difference – what most mean by 'diversity' – is emerging, it is time to think about what could comprise diversity studies, and how it might be formulated.

Public discourses of 'diversity'

Why is there so much interest in 'diversity' now? There have been many reasons offered (see, for instance, Faist 2009; Salzbrunn 2012; Vertovec 2012). Perhaps the foremost reason is the success, increasingly and cumulatively since the 1960s, of key identity-based public/political campaigns among women's, African American, lesbian and gay, age- and disability-based movements. Their respective calls for an end to discrimination, equality of treatment, more positive images, respect of rights and symbolic recognition have brought about a sea change in laws, policies and attitudes in numerous societies around the world. To be sure, life is not now entirely rosy for people within these categories – but there is no doubt that the public attention and legislative changes wrought by these movements are monumental (especially considering the state of affairs and levels of discrimination surrounding each category just fifty years ago). While stemming largely from the United States, Europe and other Western countries, such movements for categorical rights and recognition have contributed to numerous parallel movements elsewhere (such as anti-apartheid struggles in South Africa and Adivasi movements in India).

Just how these separate movements became amalgamated as 'diversity' – including not just anti-discrimination measures but also normative and celebratory rhetoric – is another story (see Vertovec 2012). It has often had to do with firms or government departments taking a negative motivation (such as fear of lawsuit) and – cynically or not – turning it into a positive value (promoting a range of attributes for the benefits they might bring). The shift from identity-based politics to an amalgamated 'diversity' agenda has entailed a vast opening-up of categories of 'difference' (often presuming 'difference' from a white, male, middle-aged, able-bodied hetero-sexual). Drawing from a wide range of sources (campaigns, brochures, websites, job descriptions, etc.) that invoke 'diversity', we can observe that many public or corporate understandings of 'diversity' include categories of difference such as: race, gender, ethnicity, culture, social class, religious belief, sexual orientation, mental ability, physical ability, psychological ability, veteran or military status, marital status, place of residence, nationality, perspectives, insights, background, experience, age, education level, cultural and personal perspectives, viewpoints and opinions (ibid.: 295–6). It is clear: in many people's (and institutions') thinking, 'diversity' and 'difference' can refer to practically anything.

This expansive view of 'difference' has also been reflected in the range of policy types developed in the name of 'diversity'. Elsewhere I have suggested that 'the corpus of "diversity" seems marked by its elusive multivalence (speaking or having meanings to many audiences), if not outright vagueness. This is not only because of uncertainty with regard to its subjects, but also with regard to its purpose' (ibid.: 296–7). Much of this elusiveness stems from the fact that across a range of public institutions the goals of 'diversity' policy are mixed. We can identify at least six facets of 'diversity' discourses, policies and practices derived from a range of programmes, mission statements, campaigns and guidelines within institutions:

> *Redistribution.* This facet includes policies intended to redress historical discrimination against groups, especially 'economic harm'. Here, the purpose of 'diversity' is largely akin to Affirmative Action, with goals toward helping minorities gain better access to scarce economic and societal goods – especially jobs, equitable income, housing and education.

> *Recognition.* 'Diversity' policies for recognition are also directed toward a kind of historical redress, but here with respect to 'cultural harms'. Measures here are to foster dignity and esteem among minorities, promote positive images, and facilitate their fuller participation in social interaction and political processes . . .

> *Representation.* This facet of 'diversity' can be characterized as a politics of presence. Here the goal is to create an institution – a company workforce, teaching faculty, student body, health service, civil service, military, police, or chamber of political representatives – that looks like the population it serves. This may include the use of monitoring or quotas . . .

> *Provision.* Public services today often employ this facet of 'diversity'. It entails identifying, developing skills around, sensitizing staff to, and responding adequately to the specific requirements of customers with reference to their myriad group and individual differences (variously and broadly defined) . . .

Competition. Often known as the 'business case for diversity', this facet takes in strategies to improve a company's marketing and, ultimately, market share. . . . Promotion of 'diversity' and a diverse workforce is to gain a better understanding of customers, spot market opportunities and thereby increase competitiveness, improve product quality, appeal to a wider consumer base and increase sales. . . . The promotion of 'diversity' in a company's public relations is also meant to influence customer perceptions by improving its image (or at least deflecting image damage by not having a visible 'diversity' commitment). It is also, at the same time, a measure to avoid grievances and discrimination lawsuits.

Organization. 'Diversity' management policies, training programmes, structures and staff positions within corporations or other institutions serve the purpose of developing and delivering many of the facets listed above. Additionally, they are undertaken with the aim of maximizing the performance of teams or workforces. . . . The premise, drawing from a large body of management and human relations materials, is that more diverse teams outperform less diverse ones.

(ibid.: 297–9)

In public discourse and policy, then, 'diversity' has no clear content or overall aim (except perhaps to underline the view that 'difference is OK'). Apart from a seemingly benign interpretation, there are some who are strongly critical of the rise of loose talk and normative programmes surrounding 'diversity'. Loïc Wacquant, for example, believes 'the term diversity is very often used to obfuscate marginality' (personal communication). Other critiques of 'diversity' discourse and policy are that:

- It is instrumentalist, conceiving that some people comprise 'the diverse' who are to be managed by someone else.
- It reinforces normativity, with the white, male, able, sexually straight person as the model from which others are different.
- It is patronizing, claiming to function for the benefit of some purported downtrodden group.
- It amounts to social engineering, attempting to artificially create a (normatively conceived) perfect team, company or society.
- It equalizes differences by way of assuming that, in terms of experiences of discrimination (and, following this rationale, measures for anti-discrimination), race is like gender is like disability, and so on.
- It dissipates politics (esp. of group-based movements), carrying a divide-and-rule logic to extremes of individuals and their innumerable attributes.
- It shifts attention from inequality, placing emphasis on esteem and 'feel-good' measures rather than real improvement of structural conditions.
- It is just a 'formality' or façade for companies or other institutions to make it look like they are doing something positive for minorities.
- It is easily cut-off from other programmes within a company or public institution – that is, just something for the minorities rather than for all.
- It is little more than 'counting people who are different', which some – especially those deemed 'different' – might find offensive.

(Vertovec 2012: 300)

From the standpoint of academics, all these meanings and critiques of 'diversity' discourse and policy themselves signify why these should be studied critically, including the structures of power in which they are embedded, their discursive formation, their outcomes in affecting real social structural change and the ways they reflect (or not) the views and desires of the identity-based movements that have propelled them. To do this, social scientists need to keep a conscious conceptual 'distance' between their uses and those circulating in the public sphere. The latter must not be reified by the former (Wacquant, personal communication). As Rogers Brubaker puts it, 'diversity' is

> ... not only a zeitgeist term, a policy catchphrase, or a corporate tool, though it is indeed all of these. It's important to distinguish between categories of analysis – the categories that social scientists use – and categories of practice that are used in everyday social and political life. And 'diversity' is clearly both a category of analysis and a category of practice. As a category of practice, it's used in the corporate world, in universities, in advertising, in public policy discourse, and so on. So if we are going to use the term in social science, we have to give the term a specific analytical meaning, otherwise we risk simply conflating the analytic category with the practical category.
>
> *(Brubaker 2012)*

How can the social sciences and humanities productively conceive and utilize 'diversity'? Exploring the potential meanings and scope of the concept is an essential start.

Thinking about 'diversity': prospects for social science

Despite its vagueness and other problematic aspects of the term, 'diversity' nevertheless holds potential as an organizing concept in the social sciences and humanities. This potential was clearly expressed in numerous interviews with senior scholars, who were specifically asked about the prospects and pitfalls of the concept of 'diversity' for social scientific research and theory (these interviews are posted in full on the website of the Max Planck Institute for the Study of Religious and Ethnic Diversity (MPI MMG), www.mmg.mpg.de). Several significant statements from these interviews, provided in the following, help us contemplate the concept of 'diversity' and how it might shape a field of 'diversity studies'.

For many of the interviewed scholars, one advantage of the concept is that 'diversity', at present, 'comes without baggage'. That is, there is to date not much conceptualization, theory-building or methodological reflection surrounding it. It is still to be shaped (particularly, again, if it can be distanced from some of the public and policy uses of the term).

For a start, a sharpened conceptualization of 'diversity' can help break certain assumptions, both in the public mind and in certain social scientific quarters. In this way, Thomas Blom Hansen conjectures,

> maybe diversity opens for the possibility of thinking of any group of human beings as being fundamentally diverse; maybe it opens for thinking about people who are otherwise defined as white or 'non-ethnic' – the supposedly neutral ground on which the nation stands – as actually not homogeneous, as always shot through with differences.... I think diversity can be an advance, especially if used to dissolve or challenge some of the hidden presuppositions about the homogeneity of the native populations in Europe. We need to get beyond the notion that minorities 'have' diversity whilst the natives do not.
>
> *(Blom Hansen 2009)*

It follows that ideas about, and studies focused on, 'diversity' must not start with pre-conceived notions of difference – or, as Hansen says, of homogeneity. Such advice to break with assumptions was pressed by most of the scholars interviewed.

Another kind of break with assumptions was underscored by Josh DeWind. His opinion reiterates some of those abovementioned caveats about maintaining a distance between social scientific and public discourse categories:

> ... whether the concept of 'diversity' is useful will depend on how it is used to identify categories of diversity. An issue that has plagued immigration studies, is that most of the social identity categories that are used analytically, are also categories that are used or have their origin in usage by states to manage populations. Many studies are limited to such categories of state censuses, for example, to define racial and ethnic groups that often use more nuanced, overlapping, and contextually distinct categories ...
>
> Academics then have used state categories to frame studies of immigrant group incorporation and mobility, even if members of the groups define themselves as distinct on the basis of language, religion, class or the like. Measuring the 'mobility' of Latinos, for example, compared to that of 'Asians' is for many members of those groups meaningless, as these categories obscure significant differences between rich and poor, and educated and uneducated members of the groups. ... What is good for administration may not be good for explanation.
>
> So if studies of 'diversity' begin with given categories, rather than utilizing categories that are directly appropriate to the analysis, then the categories end up being more of a problem than being useful or they get in the way of understanding.
>
> *(DeWind 2009)*

DeWind's views underline the point that academics must not only deconstruct the categories of difference used by minorities or public bodies, but also be aware of how their own categories and presumptions surrounding difference are both informed by, and serve to reproduce or reify, state-based or other types of classification.

The issues encapsulated by 'diversity' are not altogether new to social science. Rather, some of them lay at the core of the social scientific endeavour. As Brubaker suggests, 'in a sense "diversity" is just a more recent term for concepts that have been central to sociology from the very beginning – the idea of differentiation, for example, or the notion of heterogeneity. "Modern" societies have been defined precisely by their heterogeneity, by being differentiated societies' (Brubaker 2012). Since at least the time of Durkheim, social science has been addressing the question of how differentiated or complex societies are held together. 'Diversity' can provide a particular kind of entry or perspective on the question. Matthias Koenig importantly reflects upon the relation of 'diversity' to such fundamental sociological concerns:

> The term thus draws attention away, at least initially, from normative controversies and encourages the sustained empirical analysis of the ways in which people from different cultural backgrounds actually live together. Having said this, I would like to stress that the term diversity hasn't yet achieved the degree of technical elaboration as other established concepts in the social sciences. So the danger of conceptual vagueness that you are mentioning does exist. Perhaps we should therefore conceive of diversity as a sensitizing concept rather than as a term which already comes along with an articulated theory. Actually, many of the questions underlying research on diversity relate to old theoretical problems in the social sciences. Think of the following core questions of sociological

theory: Does social interaction require shared horizons of meaning? Does social integration depend on common value commitments or is a consensus on formal procedures for collective action and conflict-resolution sufficient? What the concept of diversity does is sensitize for a range of new phenomena in contemporary societies, notably the struggles for recognition by various sorts of minorities that might challenge us to rethink some of the received wisdoms on these theoretical problems.

(Koenig 2009)

This notion of a 'sensitizing concept' is a key one. In this way, despite certain drawbacks, the concept of 'diversity' can help scholars think about modes of difference, their differentiated qualities, the processes that surround them and the ways that they are negotiated in social practice. Once more, these are core concerns of social science.

Observing how 'diversity' is currently 'in the air', Arjun Appadurai also points to some core theoretical concerns that the concept raises:

This is a very good moment to have diversity as an organizing topic, and the two main reasons for this are quite different from each other. One is that it is a pressing public policy issue, whether under the rubric of immigration or under the rubric of tolerance or under the rubric of multiculturalism or under the rubric of reconciliation when there has been severe conflict or ethnocidal violence. On the other hand, I also think that diversity remains a basic feature of human societies, and of how human societies organize difference itself. In this sense, I would say that diversity is a lens on the idea of culture itself. So you might say diversity – though it sounds like a very neutral and very innocent term – actually forces us to re-examine older ideas of culture and rethink some of the following questions: how does it work? How is it organized? What is culture as a system? How does its symbolism work? How do people get socialized into it or out of it? These are perennial questions ... So, we have a chance here to examine several interesting and fundamental social science questions.

(Appadurai 2009)

Appadurai further thinks that the concept of diversity is also 'a lens and a medium, in which and through which we can approach other forces and processes' (ibid.). This is an important line to bear in mind: that by studying 'diversity' we can both re-examine longstanding sociological questions and look at other broad phenomena and trends with a transformed view. In this way, moreover, significant understandings can arise through comparison and generalization. However, generalization about social differentiation should not be the sole purpose of invoking 'diversity'. 'Clearly,' Brubaker says, '"diversity" is doing more work than simply referring to this extremely general notion of differentiation or heterogeneity. But there are limits to what one can do by talking about diversity in general. Different forms of diversity work in different ways, in everyday interaction and in political life' (Brubaker 2012).

By way of referring to such variable forms and respective mechanisms of difference, Loren Landau also wishes to emphasize both potential drawbacks, as well as advantages, of adopting 'diversity' as a social scientific concept:

Diversity's strength is the focus on difference – however defined – within a particular space or globally. But that is also one of its greatest weaknesses. Without clarification, we risk speaking past each other when we think we are speaking of the same thing. Take for example, gender diversity which is fundamentally different in many ways from diversity based on class. By lumping these together as a common category or phenomenon, we can hide the fact that there are often very different processes that are associated with creating those differences or come into play when they interact.

(Landau 2011)

The view that 'diversity' can refer to numerous forms and modes of difference is also highlighted by Andreas Wimmer, who believes the concept is rather worthless if it's too indiscriminate. However, he sees the 'diversity' concept as potentially opening up a methodological terrain. 'I think it's largely a descriptive term,' Wimmer says,

> that captures different dimensions of social differentiation: ethnic, religious, gender and so on. And, as such, it is useful because it implies multi-perspectivity; it is not focused exclusively on ethnicity or exclusively on gender or exclusively on social class. So, it brings together all of these differentiations, mode of distinctions and categorizations together and forces us to think about the relationship between them. It thus runs against the tendency to see these different modes of differentiation and categorization as separate domains that are unrelated to each other. It forces us to adopt a holistic perspective on social processes looking from different angles. That is the potential, I think, of using 'diversity' as a concept.
> …It avoids the overspecialization that comes from looking at gender, or at ethnic differentiations and so on exclusively, and forces you to think about the relationship between the different dimensions of diversity. It has also the advantage of avoiding essentialization, because diversity is a concept that describes a plurality of modes of categorizations and differentiations that are internally complex etc. So, it avoids all of the more problematic and essentialized notions of gender or sexuality or ethnicity.
>
> *(Wimmer 2009)*

In and of itself, however, Wimmer notes that 'diversity' 'doesn't offer any analytical leverage to solve the many questions that this interrelatedness of different dimensions of differentiation and categorization is posing' (ibid.). That work has to be done by careful theory-building.

Nina Glick-Schiller raises another set of cautions that also relate to the problem of essentialization raised by Wimmer. She insists that scholars in this field must recognize, and promote the view, that:

> Every individual has multiple positionings that lead to multiple identities. If you use the word 'diverse' without the concept of multiplicity, it is essentialized difference and it ends up as a naturalizing discourse in the same way that multiculturalist discourses sometimes project fixed difference.… Diversity as fixed difference and diversity as overlapping multiplicities are two very different views of how social life works. So it is an important research strategy to look at the underlying multiplicities, when they are taken for granted and when one aspect of those experiences is made primarily and contrasted to somebody else's experience.
>
> *(Glick-Schiller 2009)*

Again, an advantage of 'diversity' is that it can immediately refer to several, concomitant modes of social differentiation. In this way, the term can also underscore the nested nature, permeability and intersectionality of coexisting categories of difference. This is stressed by Thomas Hylland Eriksen, who observes that 'when you say diversity, you remind yourself that there is diversity within any designated group and that boundaries are not absolute.… [S]uddenly you discover other distinctions which are just as imperative and situational and grouplike.... Sometimes the groups in question are not ethnic at all. I mean they're gendered or they are based on class or residence or other things' (Eriksen 2009). John Eade also takes this perspective toward the diversity concept, suggesting that 'given the multiplicity of our identities, we are constantly moving across group boundaries and negotiating the competing demands of group identities' (Eade 2009).

Yet another point about multiplicity and permeability is raised by Ulrich Beck, who first takes aim at 'an important prerequisite that is often considered to be obvious when dealing with plurality, with identity, etc. I am referring to the prerequisite that clear boundaries and boxes exist between Us and the Others: one is either this or that' (Beck 2009). Condemning such a view, he proposes that 'the classification according to "either/or" is no longer valid in many cases, but rather, as a result of the successes of modernization, this classification must be expanded by and replaced with a new logic of "not only/but also"' (ibid.).

Following Beck and the other scholars quoted so far, 'diversity' should help break down a sense of rigid categories and groups. This is because, as Melissa Steyn stresses in her chapter in this volume, 'difference is always (inter)relational, inessential, incomplete, fluid and destabilized'. Ash Amin develops this perspective further to suggest that 'diversity' can play a part in shaping a broader, more open approach to contemporary forms of social complexity:

> In the present political moment, which is suspicious of heterogeneity, the word is an invitation to think about the value of living with difference, and more generally, the open society. As publics and politicians deepen their suspicion of the open society, scholarship becomes clearer about the properties – largely positive – of complex open systems. ... The normative challenge, one that progressives need to shout over the heads of those who fear or vilify pluralism, is to fashion arguments and policies for the society of strangers and cosmopolitan engagement that take us beyond the currently narrow language of multiculturalism versus assimilationism. Diversity, for me, therefore is a way of widening the debate on managing complex and uncertain environments.
>
> The concept of diversity started out as a kind of Zeitgeist term to manage a pluralism considered by some to be a dirty word, something to be avoided. It still retains these qualities for those who wish to make a virtue or necessity out of living with difference. But equally, as I have intimated, the term also signals a particular turning point in social scientific thinking away from the world of specialisms, linear thinking, linear dynamics, towards a sense that we need a new social science that is able to grasp the world in both its complexity and its everyday evolution. In this attempt to renew and rethink the social sciences, I think diversity can play a more interesting role as part of a new social science lexicon.
>
> *(Amin 2010)*

This is a strong call, and hopefully the nascent field of diversity studies can meet the challenge raised by Amin.

Finally, by thinking about 'diversity' in these kinds of ways, significant perspectives might be opened – in the public eye as well as in social scientific approaches to research and theory. Here, Manuel Vásquez ponders that 'if by diversity is meant a systematic effort to really come out of one's own perspective and understand otherness or at least attempt to extend one's hand, to be open to the surprise of the other, then I like that notion of diversity. That would be the notion of diversity I would work towards' (Vásquez 2009). Like many scholars who are unhappy about utilizing the term while it is also employed in public policy, advertising and corporate development, Vásquez is nevertheless optimistic about the prospects of adopting 'diversity' as a conceptual tool:

> The category of diversity can still be useful provided that we know when we're using it, how we're using it, who is using it; provided that we understand the discursive regime in which the term is being used. And we strategically place ourselves in ways that allow us to maximize this openness to otherness. If we are open to otherness, if we're open to the fact that we're limited, that we are partial, that we're embodied and emplaced beings and recognize that therefore our perspectives are by definition biased and that there are other perspectives, then I think it's a very useful tool.
>
> *(ibid.)*

To summarize, these senior scholars have advocated a number of positive ways of thinking about 'diversity'. To rephrase some of the key points they raise, it is suggested that, via the concept of 'diversity', social science can gain new potential to:

- question notions of homogeneity (Blom Hansen);
- break from, challenge or at least be cognizant of social scientific categories versus public categories (DeWind);
- re-examine core questions in social science, particularly around differentiation and the nature of society (Brubaker and Koenig);
- provide new insights on the social organization of difference (Appadurai);
- provide an alternative lens for looking at a variety of longstanding social and cultural issues (Appadurai);
- examine the discrete workings of different kinds of difference (Brubaker), avoid lumping together dissimilar types of difference (Landau) and instead explore the relations or parallels between them (Wimmer);
- interrogate purported fixed differences and overlapping multiplicities (Glick-Schiller and Beck);
- understand, appreciate and explore the intersectionality, multiplicity and boundary-crossing dynamics of social categories (Eriksen and Eade);
- develop a path-breaking social science of complex open systems (Amin); and
- adopt a perspective on otherness grounded in recognizing the partiality and emplacement of categories (Vásquez).

With such a rich compendium of potentiality surrounding the concept of 'diversity', what might a scholarly field of 'diversity studies' actually entail?

Toward diversity studies

Migration studies, gender studies and sexuality studies are just three academic fields that have been established in order to open up broad yet related areas of interdisciplinary research and theory-building. Surrounding each, there are substantial literatures (including field-specific journals, book series and handbooks). Each field includes work on a variety of connected topics; within each field, these topics are interdependent or bear enough 'family resemblance' to be advantageously combined for new insights on field-specific processes and their outcomes. Along these lines, for instance, by linking sociological, anthropological and geographical analyses within the field of migration studies, we can learn a great deal about migrants' motivations, adaptations, community dynamics and patterns of transnational linkage; similarly, through a range of works across disciplines within gender studies we can understand more about the social construction of masculinities and femininities, gender roles in relation to biological and cultural traits and the reproduction of patriarchies; and through the interdisciplinary linkage of research in sexuality studies we can gain a better comprehension of historically emergent norms of sexual behaviour and their social control, the social conditioning of desires and intimacies and the relation between sexual preferences and social identity.

Similarly, an emergent field of diversity studies can be seen as such an overarching rubric that enables cross-fertilization of topics and disciplines concerned with the study of social differentiation. This should ideally be done to include the approaches to 'diversity' suggested by the scholars in the preceding section. Moreover, through diversity studies we might analytically distil and comparatively combine theoretical lessons gained from migration studies, gender studies, sexuality studies and other fields that focus on particular modes of differentiation.

Diversity studies should not be about celebrating, empowering, recognizing, promoting self-esteem or valorizing particular modes of difference – or creating some cheery picture of unity-in-difference. It should not represent an exercise in privileging, reifying or validating any particular categories of difference, but rather in social scientifically scrutinizing social categories, processes of differentiation and outcomes in social, political, economic and geographical spheres. This includes the interrogation of presumptions and taken-for-granted categories, units, traits and variables of 'difference'. In addition, it should not be based on a premise contraposing white, male, heterosexual Europeans/Americans to others. Further, a field of diversity studies should underline the importance of including historical and non-Western contexts in order to build better theory concerning contexts, process and consequences of variable modes of social differentiation.

A condensed definition of diversity studies might be the one offered by Vincent J. Roscigno and Jill E. Yavorksy in this volume: they suggest such a field should investigate 'the extent and manner in which categorical distinctions, such as race and sex, are meaningful and enacted within organizational contexts and in the course of everyday interactions'. In his contribution to the *Handbook*, Darius Zifonun echoes such an approach: stressing that 'diversity' implies a multiplicity of different possible units and dimensions of difference, he suggests we should study the 'set of everyday-life typifications that are being used to manage interaction.' Here, 'to manage interaction' could refer to state or corporate attempts to influence social activity, as well as to group-, setting- and individually-centred ways that action and behaviour are guided or conditioned by social categories of difference.

Hence we can conceive of diversity studies as a field of social science concerned with understanding modes, mechanisms and outcomes of social differentiation. The rubric opens up possibilities for compiling, across disciplines, conceptual, methodological and theoretical tools for this purpose. In what follows, I compile a few key concepts and approaches that might help in formulating the emergent field of diversity studies.

With that broad definition in place, I suggest that diversity studies should entail two distinct, but inherently related, topics of investigation. The first topic concerns studies of diversity as *modes of social differentiation*: how categories of difference are constructed, manifested, utilized, internalized, socially reproduced – and what kinds of social, political and other implications and consequences they produce. This approach to diversity – surrounding subjects such as gender, race, disability and sexuality – has received a considerable amount of scholarly attention. The second topic relates to diversity as *complex social environments*: this includes studies of how social relations evolve in a context that comprises multiple classifications across a single mode of difference (e.g. a neighbourhood that is home to numerous ethnicities) or research on how a

"How would you like me to answer that question? As
a member of my ethnic group, educational class, in
come group, or religious category?"

Figure I.1 Reproduced with the permission of Condé Naste

multiplicity of modes of difference interact to condition social relations in a single site (e.g. class and sexuality, race and gender). In this sphere, there has been far less social scientific inquiry to date.

The study of modes of social differentiation

A classic cartoon in *The New Yorker* (above) conveys the fact that any single individual can be classified in a range of possible ways, each potentially offering a distinct perspective or set of interests surrounding almost any topic. How do such classifications arise? How are they conveyed, shared (or contested) and reproduced – by individuals and institutions? How do they affect interpersonal interactions – with persons deemed members of the same classification, and with those who are not? How do the perspectives and interests associated with certain classifications combine, and how or when do they conflict? How do certain classifications become embedded in social, economic and political structures?

These are among the key questions asked within the field of diversity studies (see Rosenblum and Travis 2008). Once again, they are by no means new questions. Within a variety of disciplines – sociology, anthropology, social psychology, political science and geography – these questions, and many arising from them, have been engaged through several concepts, methods and theories. These have largely arisen around many of the following key words or phrases (the following list is not intended to be exhaustive, but only suggestive of pertinent ways of thinking about social differentiation generally):

Categorization. Sociological and social psychological works on categorization often concern the ways that certain classifications – otherwise described as modes of difference: race, gender, sexuality, etc. – come to carry with them (pre-) judgments, valuations and perceptions that create or reproduce group belonging and symbolic status (see e.g. Tajfel *et al.* 1971). An accumulated set of status-ranked categories comprises a system of social stratification – which, in turn, tends to have explicit material or political outcomes.

Social inequality. As Thomas Faist describes in his contribution to this volume, 'such categorizations generate unequal access to resources (redistribution), to status (recognition), and to decision-making (power)'. This combination of social categories and orders of stratification – what Charles Tilly (1998) calls 'categorical inequality' – creates remarkably durable systems that are socially and institutionally reproduced across generations. Just how these categories and systems of unequal distribution are created, maintained and manipulated is a question at the heart of much sociological inquiry.

In-group/out-group. These concepts – referring to a group that a subject considers his or her own versus one that is not – have been at the heart of much work in social psychology for generations (see e.g. Tajfel 2010). This includes research about what kind of affinities one has for the former, anxieties about the latter and how these can both be breached.

Self-ascription and ascription by others. Social scientific thought along these lines considers both the subjective view of classification – 'to which group do I belong and what do I share with them?' – and the outsider's view – 'I consider that person to belong to such a group because of these attributes . . .' – as well as the connections and contestations between them (see e.g. Barth 1998). The recognition of 'internal' versus 'external' classification of difference runs through many concepts and approaches across the social sciences.

Group and category. These terms represent two significant modes of collective identification, also resting on the 'internal/external' distinction. A common way of distinguishing group from category is that 'the first exists inasmuch as it is recognized by its members; the second is constituted in its recognition by observers' (Jenkins 2008: 104). Both are prone to give rise to what Rogers Brubaker describes as '*group-ism*', 'the tendency to take discrete, sharply differentiated, internally homogeneous and externally bounded groups as basic constituents of social life, chief protagonists of social conflicts, and fundamental units of social analysis' (Brubaker 2002: 164). Such assumptions also problematically surround ideas about '*community*' (see Amit and Rapport 2002). Related to group-ism, social scientists tend to be wary of any kind of difference *essentialism*, or the presumption that inherent attributes permanently imbue all members of a presumed bounded category or group (see e.g. Sayer 1997).

Symbolic and social boundaries. Work on these topics generally surrounds the ways people enact their differences and similarities. Here, Michèle Lamont and Virág Molnár make a conceptual distinction: on the one hand, they consider that 'symbolic boundaries are conceptual distinctions made by social actors to categorize objects, people, practices, and even time and space ... [and] separate people into groups and generate feelings of similarity and group membership' (Lamont and Molnar 2002: 168); on the other hand, 'social boundaries are objectified forms of social differences manifested in unequal access to and unequal distribution of resources (material and nonmaterial) and social opportunities' (ibid.). For either or both kinds, research has examined the role of cultural or physical markers of boundaries, their purported limits and the enforcement of the kinds of social closure they instill (see Wimmer 2013).

Identity. This is certainly one of the most ubiquitous and slippery terms in social science, which 'tends to mean too much (when understood in a strong sense), too little (when understood in a weak sense), or nothing at all (because of its sheer ambiguity)' (Brubaker and Cooper 2000: 1). Despite many problems with the concept, it remains one of critical interest – not least because of its central importance to many ordinary people themselves. Studies in this field include both group and personal meanings of the concept, usually with an emphasis on a subjective sense. Related notions take in multiple and overlapping identities as well as situational identity – adopting one's sense of belonging, or highlighting a particular categorical belonging, by way of particular social circumstances. The latter is related to the idea of instrumentalism, or emphasizing a specific identity according to self-interest. In any case, relevant themes include the distinction between presumed innate, natural or biological determinants and what are assumed to be chosen, acquired or socially constructed characteristics and senses of belonging. In more recent years, much attention has been devoted to the study of hybrid or hyphenated identities, as well as to social identity complexity (how people comprehend and manage their multiple senses of categorical belonging).

Intersectionality. As mentioned repeatedly, individuals can be classified (by themselves and by others) into a number of categories, each with a set of perspectives, interests, affiliations and social rankings. The concept of intersectionality represents the compound effects of categorization and concomitant mechanisms of stratification (especially oppression and discrimination; see Lutz, this volume). Following on from the development of this concept, it is important to examine what Thomas Faist (this volume) describes as '*de-intersectionalization*'; that is, when the variety of possible relevant categories are ignored and people are treated by way of one, usually essentialized, category only.

Recall Brubaker's quote earlier in this introduction: 'different forms of diversity work in different ways, in everyday interaction and in political life' (Brubaker 2012). Each set of difference categorizations (such as race, ethnicity, gender, sexuality) entails its own modes of definition and expression, processes of affinity or discrimination and outcomes in social, economic and political spheres. Accordingly, these also often require quite different conceptual approaches and research techniques. However, the concepts listed here might be considered as those of a basic theoretical and methodological toolkit for diversity studies. There are certainly many more that can be added, particularly within specific social science disciplines. With some common notions and approaches, social scientists will be in a better position to understand more about just how different forms of diversity work in different – and in similar – ways.

The study of complex social environments

The mechanisms surrounding modes of social differentiation comprise a major field of study. Much has been learned about such mechanisms and modes within specialized subjects and disciplines; much theoretical synthesis remains to be done. However, a noticeably understudied field that can both draw from and add to the study of modes of social differentiation is that of complex social environments.

Mechanisms of classification and processes determining their outcome do not play out in a vacuum. Rather, these are played out within historically produced conditions comprising: social fields, structures of power, discursive idioms, institutional frameworks, systems of access and denial, economic and material inequalities and spatial arrangements. Each of these conditions is inherently – and one could argue, increasingly – marked by multiple modes of difference, i.e. diversity. Just how does such complexity itself affect the ongoing dynamics of different modes of social differentiation? This contextual question has barely been addressed anywhere within the social sciences.

The contextual question immediately raises the issue of scale. Are we examining modes of social differentiation, and the conditioning context of diversity, on the macro-, meso- or micro-scale? National, urban or neighbourhood scale? On each scale, each set of conditions just listed will likely entail their own histories, processes, influences and (linear, path-dependent or chaotic) dynamics. What, thereafter, is the conditioning relationship between scales as they affect social differentiation and its outcomes? Following Appadurai's comments, these questions represent one way in which 'diversity' can provide a lens to look anew at perennial concerns of social science.

The fact that social scientists have not devoted enough attention to complex environments of diversity is noted by Thomas Blom Hansen. Also emphasizing the importance of comparison – and, by implication, the potential it holds for theoretical development – he states,

> I think there would be a lot to be learned from places like India, like South Africa and many other parts of the world that have a very, very long experience in dealing with multiethnic societies and multiracial coexistence. We often tend to focus on conflicts in these societies – that's also been part of my own work – but what is also true is that such societies build on the daily coexistence and interaction between many different groups. We have not really started to record and explore how people live with difference, how people draw many different lines around aspects of their private life, their public life, and how people are able to deal with many different kinds of publics and audiences. These are also multi-lingual societies, which is very often forgotten. The average urban Indian uses at least three languages on a daily basis because one needs that in order to exist in a major Indian city. South Africa is pretty much the same thing certainly for any person of color. Urban dwellers in such spaces have developed a kind of agility and ability to live simultaneously in many different spheres. It doesn't mean that it is always pretty or friendly or that people do harbor hostile feelings vis-à-vis other groups, by no means. There is undoubtedly a capacity and a tolerance for difference that is completely different from a European sensibility.
>
> *(Blom Hansen 2009)*

In order to conduct research, undertake comparison and build theory surrounding modes of social differentiation and their conditioning contexts, it may be useful to employ a conceptual framework that can take into account relations between structural, discursive and social phenomena. The following is offered as one possible model.

Configurations – representations – encounters

Each of the terms, configurations – representations – encounters, can be considered as a discrete analytical domain; however, the three domains should nevertheless be considered together in order to have any explanatory function in addressing modes of social differentiation and their relation to complex social environments. Ideally, the conceptual triad should also facilitate comparison between contexts.

The conceptual framework is derived from J. Clyde Mitchell's and Max Gluckman's methods for situational analysis (Gluckman 1940; Mitchell 1983). Their task was first to abstract conceptually and then to interrelate analytically: a set of events (the actual social encounters which happen); what they called 'the situation' (how the people involved themselves give meaning to what happens); the setting (the structural or institutional environment encompassing what happens) (see Mitchell 1987; Rogers and Vertovec 1995). Through such a technique of analytical interrelation, a rich and more comprehensive set of factors could be accounted for, not least in terms of understanding what influences what (social relations, the individual's classifications and structural conditions) in which way. This pioneering mode of analysis was mainly used for anthropological analysis of general patterns of socio-cultural change in southern Africa – but in one classic study it was indeed applied to the analysis of modes of social differentiation in a complex social environment (namely, Mitchell's (1959) *The Kalela Dance*). Here, I take these three analytical domains and re-interpret them as configurations – representations – encounters.

Configurations. This domain refers to structural conditions within which people carry out their lives. Especially relevant structures include those of an immediate political economy, political and economic geography, institutions of governance (policies, laws and legal structures) and other external arrangements that enable or constrain people's opportunities for action and social or physical mobility. In every society, these structural conditions clearly change through time.

Representations. This domain refers to the conceptual ordering of the social world. It includes social concepts and categories, terminology and discursive frames, cultural idioms, media images, public discourse, ideological regimes and hegemonic narratives, census categories, shared memories, normative schemes and what is often constructed as commonsense knowledge. Foremost, it refers to embedded understandings stemming from and reflecting power relations in a society.

Encounters. This domain refers to actual human interactions. These entail a range of contacts from fleeting to sustained exchanges, relations and communications, social networks, processes of negotiation and varieties of conflict. In this schema, the domain especially concerns the micro-sociological level, but encounters and their effects can of course be accrued into meso- or macro-sociological patterns.

Once more, these domains are for the purpose of methodological abstraction and analytical interrelation. I refer to this schema as a conceptual triad because, particularly in order to investigate phenomena such as mechanisms of social differentiation – through whatever methods – all three domains must be taken into account. Even if a research focus concerns phenomena in just one domain, the conditioning effects of the other two should be taken into account. Accordingly, we can examine how a specific event or set of interactions is conditioned both by the categorical representations the actors carry in their head and by the overarching set of conditions (including legal status, political recognition or representation, access to resources and socio-economic position) affecting the actors. This type of analysis was what Mitchell and Gluckman intended through situational analysis. But the triad works in other directions too. That is, we can also use it to understand how representations are modified (or reified) through actual social interactions as well as by changes in policy or governance; similarly, the conceptual triad can serve to demonstrate how political and other structures are informed by historically produced representations and by public concerns, claims and activities arising from everyday social phenomena.

Relating the three domains, moreover, we can observe how class stratification emerges from the compound functions of configurations – representations – encounters: this entails the combined workings of a political-economic system characterized by a spectrum of institutional rewards and penalties as well as material outcomes, a classification system that carries symbolic value and a set of social interactions that both draws from and contributes to both the economic system and classification modus. Processes and dynamics of diversity, as multiple modes of social differentiation, operate in the same, mutually reinforcing way.

Political-economic systems, sets of classifications and commonplace social interactions co-evolve. The co-evolution of the three domains is well demonstrated, for instance, in Part II of the *Handbook*. In chapters on historical change within social orders, such as the Roman and Ottoman Empires, Balkan societies, fascist Europe and the recent Middle East, we clearly see the mutually conditioning patterns of change in governance structures, the ways diversity was conceived and the nature of everyday social relations between people (often by way of changing policies and classifications differentially leading to group formation or disbanding, upward or downward social mobility, privilege, persecution or conflict). However, as such studies also show, the co-evolution of phenomena within the three domains is not necessarily an even process: changes in one domain might develop long before transformations are felt in either of the other domains. For instance, policy changes regularly take a considerable period to modify social relations, and shifting social relations might not be reflected in public or political discourse for some time. In such cases we might consider the nature and implications of what can be called 'domain lag'.

For the purposes of theory-building, the necessary interweaving of these analytical domains – the structural, discursive and interactional – has been discussed for some time in various ways within social science. With particular relevance to diversity studies, Brubaker has advocated a corresponding approach to studying categories like ethnicity (what I am calling modes of social differentiation):

> From above, we can focus on the ways in which categories are proposed, propagated, embedded in multifarious forms of 'governmentality' ... From below, we can study the 'micropolitics' of categories, the ways in which the categorized appropriate, internalize, subvert, evade or transform the categories that are imposed on them ... And drawing on advances in cognitive research, ethnomethodology and conversational analysis, we can study the sociocognitive and interactional processes through which categories are used by individuals to make sense of the social world; linked to stereotypical beliefs and expectations about category members; invested with emotional associations and evaluative judgments; deployed as resources in specific interactional contexts; and activated by situational triggers or cues.
>
> *(Brubaker 2002: 170)*

This approach usefully incorporates different scales of analysis, which should characterize the model of configurations – representations – encounters too.

Wimmer also advocates an analogous approach to mutually conditioning factors that can cross or combine scales. He suggests that one needs to adopt

> the adequate theoretical tools that allow you to link macro-level social processes and developments, such as individualization and globalization, with meso-level processes of institutionalization, processes of group formation and political mobilization and so on, with the micro-level aspects of individual practices of classification and categorization, of social networking and distancing, of discriminating against certain kinds of people and favoring others. Then these micro-level processes need to be linked back up to meso-level institutional consequences that they have in the aggregate. So we need a complex theory of social classification and closure that go from the macro-level to the meso- and the micro-level and then back up again to the meso- and macro-level.
>
> *(Wimmer 2009)*

On a similar tack, Matthias Koenig suggests the following approach to the study of diversity:

> Patterns of diversity are here characterized by several properties of boundaries, e.g. their degrees of stability, politicization or cultural differentiation. Explaining these properties requires reconstructing the boundary making strategies of various actors whose action is, in turn, enabled and constrained by situational conditions, institutional frameworks, power relations and the like. A specific challenge in this context is to grasp the situation-specific salience of various cultural distinctions such as ethnicity or religion. When and why are latent differences activated in social interaction and become constitutive of potentially conflicting groups? Or how can manifest differences be de-activated through institutional design and policy-making? Understanding these dynamics of nested diversities is crucial for the more general question that lurks behind most research about diversity, i.e. the question how political communities are formed and how political allegiances are sustained which in liberal democracies by necessity require a minimum degree of commonality.
>
> *(Koenig 2009)*

Hence there are a number of common approaches for analysis and theory-building that, I suggest, can bring together the study of modes of social differentiation and the study of complex social environments. The intellectual model of configurations – representations – encounters represents one way that social scientific research can be organized to facilitate comparative and explanatory analysis, across scales, concerning the entangled or mutually influencing conditions and dynamics that link these domains. The model can perhaps serve as a kind of formula for the development of diversity studies itself.

Outline of the *Handbook*

The *Handbook* contains forty-one articles. This certainly seems a lot, but in each section many more themes, topics and cases could have been included. Therefore, the volume is by no means intended to be comprehensive; it is supposed to be suggestive of the kinds of issues, instances, conditions, outcomes and theoretical matters that can and should be addressed with the field of diversity studies.

In Part 1 – Dimensions of diversity – a sample range of some key modes of social differentiation (including gender, race and ethnicity, age, sexuality, language and more) are discussed by a range of experts. To be sure, a number of other modes could be added, such as indigeneity, itineracy, nationality, locality, lifestyle and subculture. Moreover, there are modes of difference – namely, class – that, like gender, seem importantly to intersect, run through or add inflection to practically every other mode. The authors here have provided excellent views on their respective modes of difference, with important lessons for understanding the social mechanisms involved in others.

A set of significant case studies are provided in Part 2 – Historical geographies of diversity. Here, especially, we can observe how configurations – representations – encounters have co-evolved over time. This includes looking at how various groups (here, mostly ethnic and religious) have been conceived especially for purposes of governance and maintenance of hierarchy – particularly to maintain the position of the powerful. Most chapters show the extraordinary multiplicity and malleability of policies, categories and practices. The cases also clearly demonstrate how certain categories are not only socially and politically constructed, but also institutionalized with profound effects. In these ways, regimes – and the common people they govern – have undertaken repression and persecution, provided protection and largesse, celebrated, included, excluded or exterminated large parts of the society. And as Keith Lowe powerfully demonstrates in his chapter, there have been times and situations in which people had to choose one from among a variety of possible identifications in order to survive.

Following the section on historical case studies of contestation and institutionalization of difference, Part 3 – Policies and politics of diversity – takes a step back to look at fundamental issues surrounding the public and institutional treatment of difference. Here we have a group of articles probing questions concerning group and individual rights, notions of equality and fairness, recognition and belonging, citizenship, access and participation. Perspectives on the themes are developed through considering philosophy, political theory, law and legal institutions, social policies and corporate strategies.

What kind of themes and concerns arise through the engagements, conflicts and negotiations of interpersonal experiences of difference? Part 4 – Encounters and diversity – addresses this question with articles that examine both processes that shape encounters and the consequences of encounters with difference. Here are works concerning discrimination, prejudice and inequality, so-called social cohesion and conviviality, xenophobia and local identity politics. Again, these selected contributions represent a small set of relevant topics within this theme; however, each provides a critical snapshot of meaningful social mechanisms at work.

Finally, Part 5 – Fusions of diversity – represents a general approach to how we might be able to consider ways in which several processes of social differentiation operate together. This might entail ways of merging categories of difference – as in assimilation and creolization; interconnecting them – as in intersectionality; or thinking critically about their co-presence – as in cultural complexity. These chapters are among the most theoretical and (particularly the final chapter on 'critical diversity literacy') methodologically driven pieces in the *Handbook*. They serve as a fitting conclusion to a volume, which, it is hoped, can serve to amalgamate and develop diversity studies as a field of burgeoning, multidisciplinary scholarly interest.

Acknowledgements

I wish to convey my gratitude to several people who have helped considerably in the production of this *Handbook*. Christiane Kofri, Jutta Esser, Bettina Voigt and Wiebke Unger have undertaken a range of tasks in the preparation of the manuscript; numerous staff members of the MPI MMG have provided critical discussions; and Gerhard Boomgaarden and Alyson Claffey at Routledge have helpfully guided the entire publication process.

References

Amin, A. (2010) 'Diversity Interview', MPI MMG. Online. Available HTTP: <http://www.mmg.mpg.de/diversity-interviews/amin/> (accessed 29 May 2014).

Amit, V. and Rapport, N. (2002) *The Trouble with Community: Anthropological Reflections on Movement, Identity and Collectivity*, London: Pluto Press.

Appadurai, A. (2009) 'Diversity Interview', MPI MMG. Online. Available HTTP: <http://www.mmg.mpg.de/diversity-interviews/appadurai/> (accessed 29 May 2014).

Barth, F. (ed.) (1998) *Ethnic Groups and Boundaries: The Social Organization of Culture Difference*, Oslo: Universitetsforlaget.

Beck, U. (2009) 'Diversity Interview', MPI MMG. Online. Available HTTP: <http://www.mmg.mpg.de/diversity-interviews/beck/> (accessed 29 May 2014).

Blom Hansen, T. (2009) 'Diversity Interview', MPI MMG. Online. Available HTTP: <http://www.mmg.mpg.de/diversity-interviews/blom-hansen/> (accessed 29 May 2014).

Brubaker, R. (2002) 'Ethnicity Without Groups', *European Journal of Sociology*, 43(2): 163–89.

—(2012) 'Diversity Interview', MPI MMG. Online. Available HTTP: <http://www.mmg.mpg.de/diversity-interviews/brubaker/> (accessed 29 May 2014).

Brubaker, R. and Cooper, F. (2000) 'Beyond "Identity"', *Theory and Society*, 29(1): 1–47.

DeWind, J. (2009) 'Diversity Interview', MPI MMG. Online. Available HTTP: <http://www.mmg.mpg.de/diversity-interviews/dewind/> (accessed 29 May 2014).

Eade, J. (2009) 'Diversity Interview', MPI MMG. Online. Available HTTP: <http://www.mmg.mpg.de/diversity-interviews/eade/> (accessed 29 May 2014).

Eriksen, T.H. (2009) 'Diversity Interview', MPI MMG. Online. Available HTTP: <http://www.mmg.mpg.de/diversity-interviews/hylland-eriksen/> (accessed 29 May 2014).

Faist, T. (2009) 'Diversity – A New Mode of Incorporation?' *Ethnic and Racial Studies* 32(1): 171–190.

Glick-Schiller, N. (2009) 'Diversity Interview', MPI MMG. Online. Available HTTP: < http://www.mmg.mpg.de/diversity-interviews/glick-schiller/> (accessed 29 May 2014).

Gluckman, M. (1940) 'Analysis of a Social Situation in Modern Zululand', *Bantu Studies*, 14(1): 1–30.

Jenkins, R. (2008) *Social Identity*, London: Taylor & Francis.

Koenig, M. (2009) 'Diversity Interview', MPI MMG. Online. Available HTTP: <http://www.mmg.mpg.de/diversity-interviews/koenig/> (accessed 29 May 2014).

Lamont, M. and Molnár, V. (2002) 'The Study of Boundaries in the Social Sciences', *Annual Review of Sociology*, 28(1): 167–95.

Landau, L. (2011) 'Diversity Interview', MPI MMG. Online. Available HTTP: <http://www.mmg.mpg.de/diversity-interviews/landau/> (accessed 29 May 2014).

Mitchell, J.C. (1959) *The Kalela Dance; Aspects of Social Relationships among Urban Africans in Northern Rhodesia*, Manchester: Rhodes–Livingstone Institute/Manchester University Press.

—(1983) 'Case and Situation Analysis', *The Sociological Review*, 31(2): 187–211.

—(1987) *Cities, Society, and Social Perception: A Central African Perspective*, Oxford, UK: Clarendon Press.

Rogers, A. and Vertovec, S. (1995) *The Urban Context: Ethnicity, Social Networks and Situational Analysis*, Oxford, UK: Berg.

Rosenblum, K.E. and Travis, T-M.C. (eds.) (2008) *The Meaning of Difference*, 5th edn, New York, NY: McGraw-Hill.

Salzbrunn, M. (2012) 'Vielfalt/Diversity/Diversité', *Soziologische Revue*, 35(4): 375–94.

Sayer, A. (1997) 'Essentialism, Social Constructionism, and Beyond', *The Sociological Review*, 45(3): 453–87.

Tajfel, H. (2010) *Social Identity and Intergroup Relations*, Cambridge, UK: Cambridge University Press.

Tajfel, H., Billig, M.G., Bundy, R.P. and Flament, C. (1971) 'Social Categorization and Intergroup Behaviour', *European Journal of Social Psychology*, 1(2): 149–78.

Tilly, C. (1998) *Durable Inequality*, Berkeley, CA: University of California Press.

Vásquez, M. (2009) 'Diversity Interview', MPI MMG. Online. Available HTTP: <http://www.mmg.mpg.de/diversity-interviews/vasquez/> (accessed 29 May 2014).

Vertovec, S. (2012) '"Diversity" and the Social Imaginary', *European Journal of Sociology*, 53(3): 287–312.

Wimmer, A. (2009) 'Diversity Interview', MPI MMG. Online. Available HTTP: <http://www.mmg. mpg.de/diversity-interviews/wimmer/> (accessed 29 May 2014).

—(2013) *Ethnic Boundary Making: Institutions, Power, Networks*, Oxford, UK: Oxford University Press.

Part I
Dimensions of diversity

1

Gender – a central dimension of diversity

Andrea D. Bührmann

As we enter the twenty-first century, modern differentiated societies are characterised by fundamental social transformations. Particular mention must be given here to the progressive globalisation of economic activities, the transnationalisation of social environments, advancing individualisation and, at the same time, the resurgence of social movements and the increased digitalisation of transport, information, organisation and production technologies. Within social science debates, those processes and developments are accorded different weights and interpretations. Informed by a structural functionalist and systems theoretical orientation, one observes modern industrial societies changing to become post-modern knowledge-based or information societies (Stehr 2001); from a regulation theory or neo-Marxist perspective, one detects a transformation from Fordism to post-Fordism (Jessop 2001); and in the tradition of critical social theory, processes of cosmopolitanisation are diagnosed (Beck 2006). Notwithstanding all their differences in the interpretation of those developments, within the specialised discourses of the social sciences there is a general consensus that the seemingly rigid institutional arrangements of western industrial societies are coming increasingly under pressure such that ongoing processes of diversification are now underway, resulting in an increasing diversity of form, style and mode in relation to living and working arrangements.[1]

Gender – a central dimension of diversity

Societal processes of differentiation and thus also diversification have been discussed ever since the birth of modern social sciences. However, it was not until 1978 that the term 'diversity' expressly came to light. In the lawsuit *University of California* v. *Bakke*, US universities defended their right to engage in affirmative action in favour of minorities that had experienced discrimination (on grounds of race). Crucial to the subsequent rise and propagation of diversity as a relevant notion for the social sciences were the activities of various social movements, above all the civil rights movement, the women's and lesbian movement and also the labour movement (Salzbrunn 2012). Today, the issue of diversity features in many disparate areas of society and at different levels. The spectrum stretches from discussions at the micro level on the identity politics of individual social groups, tending to involve, in particular, women, members of ethnic minorities and also lesbian, gay, bisexual and transgender (LGBT) activists, to the macro level with the central axes of social inequality, for example, hierarchical gender relations, class relations or migration regimes, and also encompasses, at the meso level, approaches to diversity in the workplace in the form of organisational diversity management policies. Further, at the level of the symbolic order, discussions are taking place on the possible consequences of diversity. Indeed, many of the important positions in that discourse are included in this handbook. What is at issue in those discussions is the recognition of historical discrimination and privilege and the redistribution – primarily – of economic and cultural resources (Fraser 2007). A further area of controversy is whether diversity management policies should be seen as the appreciation or simply the economisation of the 'other'.

Notwithstanding the multiplicity of discussions in relation to diversity and the exploration of diversification processes, diversity consultants and researchers have identified that the greatest attention has been paid to the following categories: race, gender, ethnicity/nationality, organisational role/function, age, sexual orientation, mental/physical ability and religion. Of these 'big 8' (Plummer 2003: 25), three are particularly prominent. In the United States, diversity is associated primarily with the category of race, whereas in Europe it is identified above all with cultural and ethnic differences (Wrench 2007: 5). However, 'in both contexts gender remains highly associated with the term, too' (Vertovec 2012: 296). In the debates in German-speaking countries, diversity is generally linked first and foremost with the category of gender and only subsequently with cultural and ethnic identities and, in addition, with socio-economic background.[2] Thus, gender is one of the central dimensions with which to describe diversification processes and diversity. At the same time, gender itself must be regarded as the product of discursive processes of differentiation.

In that connection, much of the current research in diversity studies builds upon findings from gender studies showing that gender must be understood both as a process and a structural category. In other words, the category of gender is produced through specific practices of differentiation and, at the same time, serves alongside race and class as one of the central axes of inequality in modern societies. Taking that as my starting point, in the following sections I will first reconstruct the processes – identified in gender studies – by which the category of gender came to be differentiated. I will then present certain key findings from gender studies illustrating the relevance of gender as a social category in modern societies. In a third section, I will sketch future research perspectives for the gender dimension of diversity and, at the same time, propose several cautionary directives that should be taken into consideration when researching further dimensions of diversity and the interplay between those dimensions.

The differentiation of gender

The genealogy of the processes by which gender became differentiated is characterised by several different stages. The starting point for the following reconstruction of those processes of differentiation must be to consider not only the very notion of gender itself, but also the processes of differentiation between and within genus groups as sedimented and thus persistent effects of dispositive construction processes and practices (Bührmann and Schneider 2012).[3] Consequently, although gender identities and differences between and amongst the sexes appear, ultimately, unstable, variable and historically contingent, in an empirical sense, they cannot be freely chosen or simply altered at will. Instead, they are formed through the interplay of discursive practices with existing social structures of power and dominance, which, in turn, provides the basis for possible modifications.

The differentiation of two biological genus groups

Historical research has shown that well into the early modern period a biological 'one-sex model' prevailed. Only since the eighteenth century has it been presumed that the female body differs fundamentally from the male body in terms of its physiological and psychological 'nature' (Laqueur 1990). In this system of two sexes, man is regarded as the natural representation of all that is human whereas woman is considered to be the 'other', 'special' and 'lesser' form. This knowledge about the 'natural' order of the sexes was disseminated via encyclopaedias, journals and also literary texts to the middle-class public. As a consequence, from the nineteenth century onwards a 'polarisation of the character of the sexes' (Hausen 1976) became regarded as a given, according to which a woman was required to act within the family as housewife, wife and mother, and, on the other hand, a man had to act in the public sphere as the breadwinner for 'his' family. Whereas the masculine represented culture, rationality and activity, the feminine stood for nature, irrationality and passivity. This 'natural' division of labour and the resulting hierarchical order(ing) of the sexes was challenged subsequently by the women's movement and women's studies and, since the mid-1990s in particular, has been intensely scrutinised within the mainstream of the social sciences.

The differentiation between sex and gender

Since the 1970s, women's studies have ascribed the observed differences between men and women primarily to processes of socialisation. In that context, a distinction was drawn between 'sex', understood as an inborn biological embodiment that may also be culturally shaped, and 'gender' in the sense of behaviours and characteristics mapped onto a specific sex (see e.g. Rubin 1975). It was presumed that in the framework of gender-specific socialisation processes individuals learn and adopt a feminine or masculine gender identity and develop certain characteristics or behaviours. Whereas some wished to recognise the psychological and physiological differences resulting from those processes, and indeed this position can be found in many diversity management concepts (e.g. Loden and Rosener 1991), others considered those differences to be due to the effects of deforming socialisation processes.

Differentiation within the genus groups

In this phase, attention turned to the differences within genus groups. Above all, discussions focused on the need to take account of the interests not only of white heterosexual middle-class women, but also of black women, lesbians and working-class women. Research showed that not all women were equally affected by discrimination. For example, in the late 1970s in the United States, members of the Combahee River Collective drew attention to the multiple discrimination of black women both as black people and as women and called for different and interlocking forms and situations of discrimination to be understood from an integrational perspective (Combahee River Collective 1982). Since the late 1980s, starting from the notion of hegemonic masculinity, men's studies has sought to explore the differences amongst men. According to Robert Connell (1987), hegemonic masculinity – and its beneficiaries[4] – are characterised by a dual form of dominance. First, it dominates all other forms of masculinity, in particular marginalised masculinity, considered 'too' feminine and thus often embodied by homosexual men, and also the subordinate masculinity of the lower social classes. Second, in order to dominate, hegemonic masculinity requires a certain type of femininity that Connell describes as 'emphasised femininity' (ibid.: 183). In western societies, hegemonic masculinity is embodied, as a rule, by successful men from educated families with a Christian background holding a suitable (professional) qualification and having a wife and housewife at their side who, in turn, embodies emphasised femininity. In other words, this hegemonic masculinity continues to be based on the 'polarisation of the character of the sexes' popularised in the nineteenth century.

In fact, both in women's studies and in men's studies, efforts began in the 1980s to carry out research on an intersectional basis, that is, to examine the links and interplays between various dimensions and categories of inequality (see Lutz, this volume). In this context, the term 'intersectional' was coined by Kimberlé Crenshaw, who wrote:

> Consider an analogy to traffic in an intersection, coming and going in all four directions. Discrimination, like traffic through an intersection, may flow in one direction, and may flow in another. If an accident happens in an intersection, it can be caused by cars travelling from any number of directions and, sometimes, from all of them. Similarly, if a black woman is harmed because she is in the intersection, her injury could result from sex discrimination or race discrimination.
>
> *(Crenshaw 1989: 149)*

Questioning the practices of differentiation

Since the early 1990s, the very practices by which the genus groups are differentiated have been subject to close investigation. In that context, recourse has been had in particular to ethnomethodological and constructivist approaches. Building on earlier research on transsexuals, ethnomethodological studies in the 1970s examined the everyday performance and, thus, production of femininity and masculinity, in other words, doing gender. It became clear that individuals are not per se feminine or masculine, but have to perform a specific gender identity in a manner that is competent and appropriate to the situation if they are to be identified as masculine or feminine (Goffman 1977). For example, in his study of the male-to-female transsexual Agnes, Garfinkel (1967) examined the practices of day-to-day performance and interactive production of gender identity. In order to understand how in interactions gender is produced as a function of sex, West and Zimmermann (1991: 15) coined the term 'sex category', i.e. a person's assumed sex.

If, in principle, from an ethnomethodological perspective, the existence of gender difference is presumed, something which must then be produced through performance, constructivist approaches go one step further and question how the knowledge on gender differences and the category itself came into being and how they are continuously reproduced. In that context, the distinction between sex and gender itself is seen as culturally constructed. For that reason, the interest of researchers no longer focuses simply on transsexuals, who, in principle, actually confirm the two-sex system, but now includes individuals who refuse to be categorised in a particular sex. In particular, intersex people and the growing community of transgender people have encouraged thinking to develop around flexible and fluid sexual identities (e.g. Wilchins 2004). The person most closely identified with this deconstructivist perspective is Judith Butler (1990). Taking as her starting point the notion of the heterosexual matrix, she questions the two-sex system and the associated fixed categorisations of identity and, drawing on the work of Michel Foucault and Pierre Bourdieu, draws attention to the role of specialist academic discourses in the reification of sex(ed) identities. Namely, if researchers are looking to find differences between sexes or disagree on their relevance, they are, at the same time, continuing to confirm the relevance of gender as a category (see Bührmann 2010). Nonetheless, figures, data and facts demonstrate that, in practice, gender matters.

Gender as a category of social structures

Individuals are excluded, marginalised and encounter discrimination on grounds of their sex in many different ways and to varying extents. The shocking nature of this can be seen, for example, in the latest Human Development Report of the United Nations (2013). In western societies, the notion of sex discrimination is generally associated with the oppression of women. However, men, too, can experience discrimination, for example if they do not conform to the demands of hegemonic masculinity and are considered 'too' feminine or not sufficiently successful. In recent years, awareness has grown that individuals can experience discrimination because they refuse to conform to the two-sex system. However, representative findings are scarce on the discrimination experienced by transgender individuals.

Discrimination at the macro level

On the other hand, there is plenty of evidence that, in the EU27 Member States, in central aspects of their living and working conditions, women are disadvantaged in relation to men. Admittedly, they are no longer confined to their roles as housewife, mother and wife. In recent years, the proportion of women in employment has risen continuously across the European Union (EU), with 62.4 per cent of women in employment in 2012. However, across the EU, the employment rate of women is still lower than that of men (74.6 per cent) (EU 2013a). In addition, women are overrepresented in precarious, fixed-term or part-time forms of employment and are threatened by or experience poverty or social exclusion more often than men. In 2010, some 24.5 per cent of women (62 million) were affected in that way, whereas this applied to only 22.3 per cent of men (54 million). Women aged over 65 or who are single parents feature heavily in that group. The fact that so many women are threatened by poverty and social exclusion is closely linked to their lower average earnings. The gender pay gap, that is, the difference between the average hourly wage of men and women, was 16.2 per cent in 2013. This was an improvement of 0.8 percentage points in comparison with the previous year. However, the slight narrowing of the pay gap does not result primarily from improved wages and working conditions for women. Instead, it is men's working conditions that have changed. The proportion of men working part-time has increased, and in sectors in which large numbers of men are employed (for example, construction and mechanical engineering) wages have fallen (EU 2013b). However, the EU labour market is segregated not only on a horizontal basis, but also vertically. This is particularly evident in relation to the proportion of women in executive and board-level positions in industry. Although progress is being made across the EU, it remains the case that 86.3 per cent of board members are men and 96.8 per cent of board chairs are men (EU 2012: 5). Thus, it is men who take the important and strategic decisions in industry. The same is true – but to a less pronounced extent – in the areas of politics and academia (Dahlerup and Freidenvall 2011, EU 2013c).

Discrimination at the micro level

Women continue to experience discrimination despite considerable research efforts, the commitment of many activists and targeted support measures – such as the introduction of gender mainstreaming as regards employment, earnings and standard of living – and also their ability to influence strategic decisions. In addition, they are increasingly exposed to sexual threats and physical violence and are disproportionately at risk of being forced into human trafficking and prostitution.[5] Whereas in the abovementioned situations the discrimination women experience arises because of belonging to a particular sex, at the same time transgender people experience marginalisation and discrimination because of their very refusal to conform to the two-sex system and fit in or adapt to become feminine or masculine. They are stigmatised as cross-dressers, drag queens or kings and transgender, and are continuously challenged to adopt a particular sex. Unlike transsexual people, many intersex people have been, and even today continue to be, forced to undergo cosmetic genital operations in order to ensure that their biological sex as a man or woman is unambiguous. For that reason, intersex people in particular have been calling for years to be recognised as human beings who are neither masculine nor feminine.[6] Their demands are not focused on economic redistribution but on greater social recognition. However, in a certain way, men appearing 'too' feminine or women appearing 'too' masculine experience the same form of stigmatisation. Precisely this form of stigmatisation can be seen in the comments of Regine Stachelhaus, senior executive at E.ON (the German power and gas multinational) in 2010. In a newspaper article, she is quoted as saying:

> If you believe in the idea of diversity, in other words that the success of a company depends on having as many different talents and personalities as possible working there, you do not want to have any women who act in a masculine way, hang around in shapeless trouser suits, and have super short hairstyles.
>
> *(Stachelhaus in Banze 2010)*[7]

Discrimination at the meso level

Recent research shows that organisations must be regarded as key locations for the production and reproduction of differences between genus groups. First, it is argued that organisations are gendered. By reason of their culture and structure, they provide continuing support for the distinction between paid employment and family work (Acker 1991). In that context, not only gender-specific task allocations and job descriptions, but also gender-specific expectations and ascriptions with regard to abilities and knowledge play an important role (e.g. Ely *et al.* 2003; Herring 2009). Second, it is argued that within organisations – understood as networks of social interactions and relations – by their everyday actions, individuals are engaged in doing gender (e.g. Britton 2000). From this perspective, gender is both a component and a consequence of constant processes of differentiation. Conversely, this also means that gender does not always have to be prioritised as a relevant category, and in certain situations and contexts its relevance may be surpassed, for example, by class or race. Viewed in this way, the crucial questions to be resolved can be formulated thus: When is a particular category relevant? And to what extent? And when is it not relevant? Thus, we are no longer simply concerned with 'doing gender' but also with 'doing differences' (West and Fenstermaker 2002). In diversity studies, this is precisely the issue being examined in relation to the concepts of diversity management.

Future research perspectives

Taking as a starting point these findings from gender studies, the task for diversity research is to examine the interplay between the different dimensions of diversity.

The need at the macro level is to identify the central processes of diversification in modern societies and to determine their relevance for and between one another. In this context, it does not suffice simply to conclude that black women experience discrimination more frequently than white women or that heterosexual men are generally less likely than homosexual men to encounter discrimination. Instead, clarification is needed of the commonalities that exist (or could exist) between members of the different sexes and other dimensions of diversity and whether changes can be observed in this area in recent years. Of particular interest in this connection is the finding from gender studies that gender relations are becoming increasingly differentiated and less clearly structured. Increasing numbers of men are now in precarious forms of employment and, at the same time, increasing numbers of women are achieving senior management positions. In this regard, therefore, instead of concentrating the analysis on exploring the differences between and within genus groups, it would appear more productive to adopt an intersectional approach to establish on a systematic basis the commonalities between individuals who are successful in their professional lives and those who find themselves in precarious forms of employment (see also Bührmann 2013). Taking the dimensions of diversity as a starting point, the objective then is to establish a systematic social structure analysis which allows conclusions to be drawn in relation to workforce diversity. If the specific power relations can be documented in this way, a key issue from another perspective is to examine the interventions launched by social movements to counter these existing social inequalities. What activities are successful and what is the extent of that success? What alliances can be forged? These are important questions here.

Research is needed at the micro level to establish how individuals, in fact, describe themselves and the importance they attach to different dimensions of diversity. It should not restrict itself to the question of which descriptive rules are used in particular empirical situations. Instead, what happens at the boundaries of dimensions of diversity such as gender, where those boundaries are drawn, what areas are enclosed by them and how they are justified should also be examined. A key question here is to examine how, for example, by means of the stigmatisation of certain groups as 'other', notions of normality and deviance are produced and, further, how those practices are supported in institutional and organisational terms.

At the meso level, in light of the increasing phenomenon of workplace diversity, the processes of differentiation in an organisational context deserve investigation. From research on gendered organisations, we know that ever fewer principles of gender differentiation may be observed to qualify as comprehensive, cardinal and consistent. For that reason, it is all the more interesting to determine the locations of diffusion and, further, perhaps, to clarify whether particular types of organisation have an important role to play in the practices of differentiation. Is it the case that differences in relation, for example, to gender are produced in a different manner in commercial organisations than in universities? And, if so, does it make any difference whether these are traditional research universities or modern institutions founded in the 1960s? Another important area of research concerns the transition from gender mainstreaming to diversity management. Questions arise in this area in relation to the management of observed inequalities. If certain other groups are 'encouraged' or 'supported', does this mean that women receive reduced attention and, as a result, does the proportion of women in senior management decrease or will it, in fact, increase? This question has already been raised in relation to ethnic minorities (e.g. Schönwälder 2007). A further issue to be considered is whether and, if so, to what extent diversity management is actually of benefit to individual companies and the workforce as a whole or whether, in fact, only to certain groups, (Wrench and Modood 2000; see also Wrench, this volume). However, in this area, research is in its infancy. Finally, there is also the question whether diversity management measures do not, in fact, simply reify socially constructed differences between genus groups. Indeed, the comment by the senior executive Regina Stachelhaus is a compelling illustration of that risk.

Consequently, at the level of the symbolic order, it is important to investigate whether, and if so to what extent, specialist academic discourses have contributed to the fact that in modern societies there is a greater tendency to detect diversification processes and register the existence of diversity. In the second section of my analysis above, I reconstructed how since the Enlightenment the conceptualisation of sex has changed considerably and, as a result, other differences have been detected. For that reason, it is essential to examine also the performative consequences of conceptual differentiation in specialist academic discourses. However, equally important is the need to clarify the social philosophical arguments by which diversity can be recognised without having to accept social inequalities.

In researching these connections and implications at the different levels, it is crucial, however, to pay regard to the following cautionary directives.

- *Intersectional perspective*: It is important to adopt an intersectional perspective and not transform an individual dimension of diversity into the master category. What is crucial is to determine the discreteness of the individual structures and their relationships between one another. This is paramount as categories are neither additive to one another nor can they be multiplied with one another, let alone reduced.
- *Transdisciplinary orientation*: Research should adopt a transdisciplinary orientation in order to profit from the findings and methods of numerous disciplines and fields of practice. The categories observed through that lens must be understood as historically constructed and, thus, by their very nature, contingent. In that analysis, it must be remembered that in different contexts categories (can) entail different impacts and effects. Connecting factors should be determined in order to permit an integrated perspective along axes of inequality that differ but, at the same time, are mutually linked by reason of societal structures. It should be borne in mind, however, that inequalities not only generate discrimination and experiences of oppression, but also create chances and privileges.
- *Dispositive approach*: It is important to regard dimensions of diversity as dispositive effects and thus not to reify existing empirical processes of diversification and their consequences and thereby, for example, reproduce affirmative recognition strategies, but instead to (re-)construct them in the sense of a 'critical ontology of the present' (Foucault 1984). However, it appears appropriate in that connection – on a provisional basis – to regard race, class and gender as the central axes of inequality in modern differentiated societies.

These directives have been developed on the basis of findings from gender studies. They are intended to guide research into the societal processes of differentiation, and thus also of diversification, and the consequences thereof set out in the introduction to this chapter. Naturally, in the course of that process, it is likely that they will be expanded and developed further.

Notes

1 Whether, in fact, the incidence of empirical processes of diversification has increased or whether those processes are simply more often observed remains to be determined. I shall return to this point later.
2 On this see also Aretz and Hansen (2003), Bendl *et al.* (2006), Heitzmann and Klein (2012), Koall and Bruchhagen (2005) and Krell and Sieben (2007).
3 On the notion of the dispositive (or apparatus) in the work of Foucault see Bührmann (2005).
4 Only a few men incorporate all the elements of hegemonic masculinity. However, the majority of men profit from the dominance of patriarchy.
5 For further information see e.g. www.terre-des-femmes.de.
6 In Germany, following an amendment to the law on personal status (Personenstandgesetz), it has been possible since 1 November 2011 to belong to an 'indeterminate sex'. However, the consequences for the registration of individuals with municipal authorities, in relation to passports and also for other areas of the law, have not yet been determined.
7 I am grateful to Gertraude Krell for drawing my attention to this comment.

References

Acker, J. (1991) 'Hierarchies, Jobs, Bodies', in J. Lorber and S. Farell (eds) *The Social Construction of Gender*, Newbury Park, CA: Sage.

Aretz, H.J. and Hansen, K. (2003) 'Erfolgreiches Management von Diversity: die Multikulturelle Organisation als Strategie der Verbesserung einer Nachhaltigen Wettbewerbsfähigkeit', *Zeitschrift für Personalforschung*, 17(1): 9–36.

Banze, S. (2010) 'Interview with Regine Stachelhaus', *Süddeutsche Zeitung Magazin*, 2010(41).

Beck, U. (2006) *The Cosmopolitan Vision*, Cambridge, UK: Polity.

Bendl, R., Hanappi-Egger, E. and Hofmann, R. (eds) (2006) *Agenda Diversität: Gender- und Diversitätsmanagement in Wissenschaft und Praxis*, München: Hampp.

Britton, D. (2000) 'The Epistemology of the Gendered Organization', *Gender & Society*, 14(3): 418–34.

Bührmann, A.D. (2005) 'The Emerging of the Enterprising Self and its Contemporary Hegemonic Status', *Forum Qualitative Social Research*, 6(1): Art. 16.

—(2010) 'The Death of the Subject and its Sociological Rebirth as Subjectivation: Future Research Perspectives' in A.D. Bührmann and S. Ernst (eds.) *Self-controlling / Self-regulation or Self-caring – The Sociology of the Subject in the 21st Century*, Cambridge, UK: Scholars.

—(2013) 'Lessons from Previous Research on Women on Boards for Future Research', in S. Machold, M. Huse, K. Hansen and M. Brogi (eds) *Getting Women on to Corporate Boards: A Snowball Starting in Norway*, Cheltenham: Edward Elgar.

Bührmann, A.D. and Schneider, W. (2012) *Vom Diskurs zum Dispositiv: Einführung in die Dispositivanalyse*, Bielefeld: Transcript.

Butler, J. (1990) *Gender Trouble: Feminism and the Subversion of Identity*, New York, NY: Routledge.

Combahee River Collective (1982) 'A Black Feminist Statement', in G.T. Hull, P. Scott and B. Smith (eds) *All the Women are White, All the Blacks are Men, but Some of Us are Brave: Black Women's Studies*, New York, NY: Feminist Press.

Connell, R. (1987) *Gender and Power: Society, the Person and Sexual Politics*, Cambridge, UK: Polity.

Crenshaw, K. (1989) 'Demarginalizing the Intersection of Race and Sex: a Black Feminist's Critique of Antidiscrimination Doctrine', *University of Chicago Legal Forum*, 1989: 139–68.

Dahlerup, D. and Freidenvall, L. (2011) 'Electoral Gender Quota Systems and their Implementation in Europe', Brussels: European Parliament. Online. Available HTTP: <http://www.europarl.europa.eu/document/activities/cont/200903/20090310ATT51390/20090310ATT51390EN.pdf> (accessed 21 August 2013).

Ely, R.J., Foldy, G. and Scully, M.A. (eds) (2003) *Reader in Gender, Work, and Organization*, Oxford, UK: Blackwell.

European Union, EU (2012) 'Gender Balance in Business Leadership: A Contribution to Smart, Sustainable, and Inclusive Growth', Brussels: European Commission. Online. Available HTTP: <http://ec.europa.eu/justice/gender-equality/files/womenonboards/communication_quotas_en.pdf> (accessed 21 August 2013).

—(2013a) 'Erwerbstätigenquote nach Geschlecht, Altersgruppe 20–64', Luxembourg: Eurostat. Online. Available HTTP: <http://epp.eurostat.ec.europa.eu/tgm/refreshTableAction.do?tab=table& plugin= 1&pcode=t2020_10&language=de> (accessed 21 August 2013).

—(2013b) 'Equal Pay Day: Frauen in Europa Arbeiten 59 Tage Unentgeltlich', Brussels: European Commission. Online. Available HTTP: <http://europa.eu/rapid/press-release_IP-13-165_de.htm> (accessed 21 August 2013).

—(2013c) 'She-figures 2012: Gender in Research and Innovation', Luxembourg: Publications Office of the European Union. Online. Available HTTP: <http://ec.europa.eu/research/science-society/document_library/pdf_06/she-figures-2012_en.pdf> (accessed 21 August 2013).

Foucault, M. (1984) 'What is Enlightenment?', translated by Catherine Porter from an unpublished French original, in P. Rabinow (ed.) *The Foucault Reader*, New York, NY: Pantheon, 1985, 38–51.

Fraser, N. (2007) 'Feminist Politics in the Age of Recognition: A Two-dimensional Approach to Gender Justice', *Studies in Social Justice*, 1(1): 23–35.

Garfinkel, H. (1967) *Studies in Ethnomethodology*, Cambridge, UK: Polity.

Goffman, E. (1977) 'The Arrangement Between the Sexes', *Theory and Society*, 4(3): 301–31.

Hausen, K. (1976) 'Die Polarisation der "Geschlechtscharaktere": Eine Spiegelung der Dissoziation von Erwerbs- und Familienleben', in W. Conze (ed.) *Sozialgeschichte der Familie in der Neuzeit Europas: neuere Forschungen*, Stuttgart: Klett.

Heitzmann, D. and Klein, U. (eds) (2012) *Diversity Konkret Gemacht: Wege zur Gestaltung von Vielfalt an Hochschulen*, Weinhein: Juventa.

Herring, C. (2009) 'Does Diversity Pay? Race, Gender, and the Business Case for Diversity', *American Sociological Review*, 74(2): 208–24.

Jessop, B. (2001) *Regulation Theory and the Crisis of Capitalism*, Cheltenham: Edward Elgar.

Koall, I. and Bruchhagen, V. (2005) 'Zum Umgang mit Unterschieden im Managing Gender and Diversity: eine Angewandte Systemperspektive', in G. Hartmann and M. Judy (eds) *Unterschiede machen: Managing Gender and Diversity in Organisation und Gesellschaft*, Vienna: Edition Volkshochschule.

Krell, G. and Sieben, B. (2007) 'Diversity Management und Personalforschung', in G. Krell, B. Riedmüller, B. Sieben and D. Vinz (eds) *Diversity Studies: Grundlagen und Disziplinäre Ansätze*, Frankfurt/Main: Campus.

Laqueur, T. (1990) *Making Sex: Body and Gender from the Greeks to Freud*, Cambridge, MA: Harvard University Press.

Loden, M. and Rosener, J. (1991) *Workforce America: Managing Employee Diversity as a Vital Resource*, New York, NY: McGraw-Hill.

Plummer, D. (2003) 'Overview over the Field of Diversity Management', in D. Plummer (ed.) *Handbook of Diversity Management: Beyond Awareness to Competency Based Learning*, Lanham, MD: University Press of America.

Rubin, G. (1975) 'The Traffic in Women: Notes on the "Political Economy" of Sex', in R.R. Reiter (ed.) *Toward an Anthropology of Women*, New York, NY: Monthly Review Press.

Salzbrunn, M. (2012) 'Vielfalt/Diversity/Diversité', *Soziologische Revue*, 35: 375–94.

Schönwälder, K. (2007) 'Diversity und Antidiskriminierungspolitik', in G. Krell, B. Riedmüller, B. Sieben and D. Vinz (eds) *Diversity Studies: Grundlagen und Disziplinäre Ansätze*, Frankfurt/Main: Campus.

Stehr, N. (2001) *The Fragility of Modern Societies: Knowledge and Risk in the Information Age*, London: Sage.

United Nations (2013) 'Human Development Report 2013: The Rise of the South: Human Progress in a Diverse World', New York, NY: United Nations Development Programme. Online. Available HTTP: <http://hdr.undp.org/en/reports/global/hdr2013> (accessed 9 April 2014).

Vertovec, S. (2012) '"Diversity" and the Social Imaginary', *European Journal of Sociology*, 53(3): 287–312.

West, C. and Zimmerman, D.H. (1991) 'Doing Gender', in J. Lorber and A. Farrell (eds) *The Social Construction of Gender*, Newbury Park, CA: Sage.

West, C. and Fenstermaker, S. (2002) 'Doing Differences', in S. Fenstermaker and C. West (eds) *Doing Gender, Doing Differences*, New York, NY: Routledge.

Wilchins, R. (2004) *Queer Theory, Gender Theory: an Instant Primer*, Los Angeles, CA: Alyson.

Wrench, J. (2007) *Diversity Management and Discrimination: Immigrants and Ethnic Minorities in the EU*, Aldershot, UK: Ashgate.

Wrench, J. and Modood, T. (2000) *The Effectiveness of Employment Equality Policies in Relation to Immigrants and Ethnic Minorities in the U.K.*, Geneva: International Labour Office.

2

Age, ageism and social identity in later years

John Vincent

Age seems so ubiquitous that when teaching sociology of old age my students were often incredulous that there were many people in the world who do not know how old they are. When I asked them how they knew how old they were, the answer was easy, as they live in the West where birthdays are a major annual ritual. However, when we dug a little deeper, they would identify how they lived in a highly bureaucratised society in which they were registered at birth and had to certificate their age at many points to validate access to age regulated rights: legal rights such as voting, social rights such as marriage and economic rights such as minimum wages. Moreover, their educational careers had been structured around progression up an annual certification ladder within an age specific cohort. As many of these students were teenagers they were very aware of the transitions to adult identities with attendant rights and duties – who can drive, who can buy alcohol, who is a legal sexual partner. They were, of course, much less familiar with the bureaucratisation of age in later years which, as a recent retiree, I have a raised consciousness – pension entitlements, bus pass regulations, driving licence renewal at 70, end of jury service duties. In other societies with other cultures and in different times, people neither celebrated birthdays nor bureaucratised age in the way British people currently do. Hence, many could not have put a number to their years since birth. Age is not irrelevant in such societies, but people are differentiated from each other using different criteria, perhaps birth order or reference to key historical or life course events. They coalesce into categories and groups through other methods of marking 'age' than chronological time, most frequently through rituals of initiation and other symbolically marked transitions to new statuses such as spouse or elder (Vincent 2005, 2013).

This chapter will discuss the cultural and political aspects of age difference but will concentrate on examples of old age transitions and resistance rather than youth cultures and movements. The relevent social science conceptual frameworks and terminology – 'age', 'historical generation', 'familial generation', 'cohort', etc. – are not exclusive to old age. This could legitimately be seen as neglecting a whole area of literature and concern; there are fascinating histories of childhood and development of categories such as 'teenager' (Jenks 1996). Interestingly, there is very little literature on 'middle age'. The dominant category is seldom self-reflective, while other categories tend to image themselves in opposition to, and thus articulate the taken for granted attributes of, the 'prime of life'. In this chapter, while acknowledging the extent of 'age' in all its social manifestations, I will concentrate on issues around difference and identity in people's later years.

There are radically different approaches to the study of ageing within academia. So different are the premises, theories, methods and points of attention that there is no over-arching paradigm which integrates all the different kinds of knowledge. There are a variety of medical and biological sciences which see ageing as a biological process – the curse of creatures who have sexual reproduction (Arking 2006). There are those in psychology and allied disciplines who observe the impact of age on personalities and adaptive behaviour by individuals (Eriksen 1982). There are those who see age in cultural and societal terms – from the institutionalisation of age criteria to the cultural construction of the meanings of age (Gubrium and Holstein 2000;Vincent 1995).This essay takes this latter approach and sees the first two as primarily data that describe the way contemporary society has built on earlier cultural concepts and has come to formulate its understanding of the nature of ageing.

Appreciating that age is a socially constructed method of differentiating people can direct our attention to all the diverse possibilities afforded by the segmentation of time.These segments of time may be seen as fixed by calendars, clocks and ritual cycles. Alternatively they might be relational, as for example with relationships of older to younger – even twins, in some situations, differentiate themselves by birth order, or the 'sandwich generation' caring for both children and parents. Social and cultural science uses a number of concepts to articulate different kinds of collective experience as opposed to the perspective of the individual actor. For the individual, getting older can be experienced as a single undifferentiated process, although awareness is sparked by specific cues and experiences (Oberg 2003). However, when viewed from a societal perspective, ageing covers a number of very distinct processes.These are usually listed as 'age', 'cohort' and 'history' effects (Hardy 1997).'Age' can refer to the passing of the years through the life course; we leave school, we gain experience of dealing with others, our hair grows grey (if we let it) and we can change the tick boxes we enter when being grouped into age categories by questionnaires.Thus social differentiation can take place based on 'age' groups and culturally derived attributes assigned to them.

In addition, being born at the same time as a set of other people has social effects, and social generations can be identified. For example, those who were teenagers in the 1960s often self-identify themselves as a specific generation with distinctive attitudes (Blaike 2006). Men born after 1939 in Britain avoided compulsory conscription and didn't learn to march in step. Mannheim (1997) in his seminal exposition on generations uses the example of the group of people born about 1810 that experienced an awakening sense of German identity in opposition to Napoleon's conquests.The term 'generation' is widely used but there is considerable debate about its meaning. It can mean a socially recognised group of people born in a particular historical era with common experience and cultural identifiers as a result. In a familial context generation refers to the succession of parents and children, but is used rhetorically in other contexts, for example as in 'fathers of the nation' or 'future generations'. In other specific knowledge contexts the term can also be used to describe a succession of cohorts, for example different generations of computer programmes, hybrid crosses in seed propagation or questionnaire samples in a repeated wave survey.

Historical change also needs to be understood as a social variable distinguished from 'age'. For example, the older people are, the less likely they are to have academic qualifications, but this is due to change in the education system through modern history not because they have got older or have a taste for particular forms of popular music. Less frequently discussed as a component of 'age' is the effect of duration on social relationships and group loyalties.While strictly independent of age as either chronology, history or generation, duration matters in social and interpersonal contexts. Relationships that last sixty years are different from those that last six months. Older people can form new relationships but in the nature of things they are more likely to have very long-standing relationships than are younger people. These can be interpersonal relationships, but can also be meaningful attachments to (or indeed alienation from) such things as landscape, technology and institutions (Gubrium and Holstein 2000).

Age and identity

Having established that there is nothing simple or 'commonsense' about what 'age' means in social science, we can examine the social dynamics of how 'age' becomes relevant to social difference. By comparing how age differences are conceptualised in various ways within different historical and cultural contexts, we can illuminate contemporary practice (Cole 1992; Daatland and Biggs 2005). In the context of modern Western culture, science is the dominant knowledge creation institution. The 'science of ageing' proceeds as if its subject is a fundamental life process to be understood through biological analysis (Kirkwood 1999). This is the dominant mode for constructing the meaning of old age in contemporary society (Lafontaine 2008). From this perspective age is essentially a feature of the body and its mechanisms and thus potentially something which can be understood and manipulated by science (Estes and Binney 1989). This plays into social difference in a number of ways, not least within the social movement around 'anti-ageing' (Mykytyn 2006). Within this perspective there are at least four ways in which old age as a phenomenon can be understood; each of them can be articulated into social difference in a variety of ways (Vincent 2006a,b).

Age can be considered to be the appearance of the body – how old you look. Age is, in this context, a feature of the body's surface. Enormous effort is put into manipulating the inscription of age on the body. It produces a form of metric as in 'looking ten years younger', and science is used to validate claims to cosmetic effectiveness of 'rejuvenating' procedures (Hurd Clarke 2011).

Age can be considered as part of the interior of the body (Moreira and Palladino 2008). Hence old age is seen as sickness and loss of vitality of different organs of the body. Metrics here suggest different organs age at different rates. There are popular quizzes and ratings which purport to rate biological age as opposed to chronological age. The brain, the heart, the bones, etc., are given indices of 'age'; but in practice these numbers merely rehearse the normative distributions of medical or fitness data.

Age can be considered to be a biological process which happens to all living things (although this statement is more controversial for unicellular or small life forms), and is in essence a biochemical process located at the intra-cellular level. Modern genetic science and bio-chemistry have been able to analyse and shed light on these processes (Carey 2003). But there remains a range of competing theories as to the significance of the different processes and problems in understanding the complex interactions involved. What is clear is that there is no single gene, or set of genes, which is responsible for ageing. In the model species predominantly used in laboratory experiments on ageing (yeast, fruit-flies and mice) many gene associations with life span have been found. In humans, it remains the case that the biochemical elixir of life remains as elusive as any of the other techniques envisaged in the long history of attempts to avoid ageing and death (Boia 2004). There have been many attempts to create reliable bio-markers to indicate 'age', and such scientific endeavours continue. People are not usually differentiated by such bio-markers, but there are concerns that such tests could be used to allocate people to groups assessed on the basis of risk, with consequences for their social rights and obligations.

The meaning of 'old age' can also be constructed through its position as the life stage next to death, whereby its essential defining features stem from the recognition of the proximity of life's end. This construction is manifest in the ideas of post-humanism and various attempts, with greater or lesser scientific validity, to enhance longevity to the point of immortality (Turner 2007). From the understanding of the body as merely a biological machine, its demise is failure and oblivion, with implied culpability from those who did not prevent it happening. This perspective poses many ethical dilemmas about the end of life with which medical staff and carers have to struggle (Gott and Ingleton 2011; Schermer and Pinxten 2013). Further, it places responsibility on individuals to discipline their bodies and avoid life threatening or 'risky' behaviours. Health and lifestyle thus become part of the age based construction of identity and difference (Dumas and Turner 2007; Rose 2007).

It is possible to take a sceptical approach to 'age' existing at all within an unreconstructed empiricist perspective. Bio-gerontology contains many, often incompatible, theories of ageing, often reflecting the high degree of specialisation and fragmentation of scientific endeavour. If by 'age' we mean some single fundamental force of nature open to scientific measurement – which is a popular conception of 'age' – then it proves very difficult to pin down (Hall 2003). Just as there is human genetic variability which has no relationship to the social category of race, so there is biological variability, including human variability, with the passage of time, but this has little or nothing to do with the social categorisation of people by 'age' (Jones and Higgs 2010). Years since birth are of course, along with class and gender, powerful predictors of social phenomena. But those effects are not the consequence of cell reproduction, accumulation of anti-oxidants or 'antagonistic pleiotropy', but rather of specific social and cultural processes (Lock and Farquhar 2007).

Life courses and historical change

Over the last two centuries the transition to old age in industrial societies has become related to employment and retirement. There are good historical accounts of how modern industrial society developed a three-fold life course of pre-work, work and post-work (Vincent 1995). The stability of this model is questioned by the post-modern view of the plasticity of roles in the contemporary world (Gilleard and Higgs 2000). Britain no longer has a legally enforceable retirement age (BIS 2011). Anthropology can offer alternative perspectives to British and Western understanding of ageing. For example, there is great interest in Asia in the impact the dramatic economic changes over the last 50 years have had on family structures and values, particularly focussing on the role and destiny of 'filial piety' (Mehta 1997), while work on globalisation has looked at the impact of migration, urbanisation and rural depopulation on age differentiation (Phillipson and Vincent 2007).

Even within the culture of the West there is enormous variation in the criteria for marking difference and the social mechanisms of inclusion and exclusion. Solomon (2013) explores the fascinating world of families where a child has a radically different identity to that of the parents. Differences explored included deafness, dwarfism, homosexuality, criminality, etc. He uses the conceptual device of horizontal, distinguished from vertical, identities. Vertical identities are those which come from or are inherited through family upbringing – ethnicity, religion, language, etc. Horizontal identities are seen as achieved or acquired, rather than ascribed, or at least as ones which the younger generation enter independently, and perhaps despite of, their family of origin. Age is neither vertical nor horizontal; rather, it differentiates those kinds of identity. Thus people can be differentiated into language groups but language usage can be different amongst different age groups (Coupland et al. 1991); people may share a religion but cannot simultaneously be both an elder and a novice. Similarly, horizontal identities have different meanings for different age groups: homosexuality is different if you are 17 or 70 (Rosenfeld 1999), and criminality is treated differently by age (Wahidin and Cain 2006). So, although these identities are seen to represent some important essence of a person which fixes them into one social category as opposed to others, with age identity that fixity is tempered by the perceived inevitability of the march of time. Generations may acquire labels or stigma from involvement in historical events which in some sense are fixed through time. However, even the meaning of historical or generational social markers of difference change their salience with the passage of time (Blaike 2006).

Importantly, identities are not pre-existing slots into which people are simply ascribed – identities are forged, changed and respond in particular historical and political circumstances. So Solomon's account of his growing up into a gay identity despite his family is specific to his context of New York at that historical moment. People actively engage in inclusion and exclusion activity and create and elaborate cultural categories.

The dynamics of age identity

'Age' clearly exists because people believe it to exist and act accordingly. Social constructionist approaches to age differentiation look at how such differences are represented in symbol, ritual and behaviour and made manifest in interaction and institutionalisation. These are frequently explored through language use – how different discourses image sameness or otherness. The English language has a plethora of aphorisms which can be used either to deny ('we are only as old as we think we are'; 'you are as old as you feel') or affirm ('the ravages of time'; 'you have to grow older but you don't have to grow up'), the salience of age as an identity marker. Younger people may strive to be treated as having adult status as part of growing up, even though the institutionalisation of full adult status is being pushed later by wage and benefit legislation.[1] Older people can also struggle to maintain an adult identity, infantalisation is a problem in care settings; a respondent to an Exeter AgeUK questionnaire said of her advice and information interview, 'I came away feeling like a human being not an old woman with a problem.'[2]

A comparison of different identities can be made by asking how they are transformed or transgressed – become the opposite of, or supersede, the category. In terms of gender and sexuality, there is a whole literature about transgender, and some babies have ambiguous gender assignment. Racial passing is also documented in anthropology and literature; moving from one racial group to another is a historical reality. With age one can envisage some sort of passing – people attempt to appear younger on a daily basis (Gimlin 2002). Can you be any age, gender or race you wish to be? The key distinction with age is that you clearly can if you wait long enough; what is more problematic is going backwards – reversing the ageing process. Of course, many people attempt this and the anti-ageing movement is a strong cultural tide. However, it is possible to say of 'age', in contradistinction to the other major sources of social difference, that all humans will experience social transitions across the boundaries between age based identities.

Old age identities are constructed like other identities in opposition. Minorities define themselves against the majority. Youth cultures define themselves by not being of their parents' culture. This creates interesting issues for old age; reaction against the authority and seriousness responsibility of middle age and parenthood: 'recycled teenager spending the kids' inheritance'; red-hat ladies subverting the gentility of the retired afternoon tea brigade; or raging grannies subverting images of passive acceptance and withdrawal by direct action and political activism (Vincent 1999; Vincent *et al.* 2001).

Ageing population and its meaning

The proportion of older people in the world's population is growing, and many, but not all, national population profiles are also changing in this way. There is a variety of reasons for this. Overwhelmingly it is to do with declines in fertility experienced across the world. It is also due to falls in infant mortality leading to longer average length of life. To some extent, and concentrated in the richest nations in the world, it is to do with increased life expectancy at age 60 or above (United Nations 2011).

These changing demographics are reflected in changes to people's experience of the life course. People do not now expect their children to die in infancy; the experience of being a grandparent is more frequent, lasts longer and has a different character than previously. Many more older people are privileged to be great-grandparents like myself. This changing demographic structure provides the opportunity for new and more complex social solidarities. Family inclusion and exclusion and retirement migration are two areas where these new social dynamics are manifest (Vincent 2006a).

Strangely these changes have aroused many scare stories in the media, in political discourse and in academia about the consequences of an older population. These are based around fears about the cost of medical and social care to welfare states (seldom to family carers) and the cost to public pension provisions (Gee and Gutman 2000). The rising average age of the population has been used to suggest that public pension provision is unsustainable (World Bank 1994). Many governments have picked away at terms and conditions of pension rights. In particular, the UK has abolished the legal retirement age and is raising the age of eligibility for the state pension – from 65 for men and 60 for women to 67 for both.

Although it is sometimes acknowledged that increased life expectancy represents a success for modern society, more often it is discussed in terms of loss of working age population and economic dynamism, and even by some in geo-political terms as loss of military personnel and willingness to enter military confrontations (CIA 2001; World Bank 1994). The demography on which these discourses are conducted is often flawed, showing no appreciation of the 'life expectancy' as a statistical measure or the greater significance of fertility rates to the shape of age distribution pyramids (Bourdelais 1998). In terms of constructing social difference around age criteria, the significance of changing demography lies in the way that it is imaged and contextualised. The tropes used to characterise demographic change and the increasing proportion of older people in the population concentrate on negative stereotypes (Gee and Gutman 2000; Vincent 1996).

Ageing populations are frequently imaged in swarm, swamping and rising tide images and also in epidemic tropes. These metaphors position older people as a large growing undifferentiated mass which pose a threat to the wellbeing of 'us', taken for granted, normals. They reflect similar tropes used to characterise other kinds of difference and processes of social exclusion. There are similarities with the way in which issues of race and immigration are constructed using swamp and rising tides rhetoric. The increasing number of older people is also imaged as a growing wave of illness and disease and dependency. Similarly epidemic images, particularly around AIDS, have been used in the stigmatisation of some sexualities and play a part in demonising some ethnic and disability identities. The alienation of one demographic category from another can also be expressed in terms of generation; hence the literature on intergenerational equity and greedy baby-boomers (e.g. Williamson et al. 1999). However, the distinctive nature of age differentiation makes this trope ambiguous, as we all age and will become part of the stigmatised age category. Further, the dominant form of intergenerational social intercourse, that of the family, exerts a powerful rhetorical effect: exclusionary tactics are difficult to institutionalise when the consequences are intra-familial. The key questions to ask are by whom and why are such tropes expounded. They clearly form an essential part of the arsenal of those who wish to favour private over public provision and emphasise individual responsibility over collective provision. They erroneously position the dismantling of public welfare as a demographic inevitability rather than a political choice.

There is a long history of political activism around old age issues and identities. Much of this has been centred around pensions (Macnicol 2006; Vincent et al. 2001). The establishment of national pension systems in the USA and in Britain was, at least in part, the consequence of mass publicly supported campaigns for state provision of financial support in old age – in the form of some scheme of national insurance. In the last third of the twentieth century there has also been the articulation of identity politics to mirror activism which sought to revalue racial, gender and sexual identities. Iconic among such movements were the Grey Panthers, but more broadly the 'third age' social movement has sought to re-evaluate post-retirement life (Laslett 1989). In recent times there have been pensioner activism, pensioner political parties seeking to prevent the roll-back of the welfare state and anti-ageing campaigns in health and employment.

In contemporary UK politics, age based parties or political movements are not absent but are less conspicuous than some other modern democracies (cf. Goerres 2009). Although there is much rhetoric about the older vote, there is a lack of articulation between age interests and political institutions, and old age is seen as a handicap to political leadership. Older people vote in higher proportions than younger people so are often seen as having political clout; the Conservative pledge at the 2009 UK general election not to take away universal age benefits such as a bus pass can be cited as an example (Chambers 2013). However, older people's real interests in the NHS, pensions and annuities have not been protected. In Britain, charities such as AgeUK (2009), or even the specialist supplier of products for older people, Saga, take the voice of older people rather than single interest parties. There are significant differences between the UK and the US, where the American Association of Retired Persons is a powerful single interest lobby group. The issues of pension funds and how older people's interests relate to the global financial crisis are scandalously under-researched areas (Blackburn 2002).

The politics of pensions is played out in part around the ambiguity of the term 'generation'. As discussed above, generation can have a familial referent or mean a particular birth cohort. Thus those seeking to undermine universal and state provision seek to undermine its legitimacy by identifying pension recipients as a specific cohort, people who have benefitted at the expense of others, specifically the golden generation feather bedded by passing debts to their children; and worse, tainted by the link with the 1960s as a hedonistic generation into sex, drugs and rock and roll and therefore undeserving of such privileged status (Williamson et al. 1999). However, generation as the familial image of grandparents is a powerful political force – 'compassionate ageism' (Vincent et al. 2001). Those seeking to demonise welfare recipients struggle to include older people in the category 'scroungers' because it is the nature of the identity that we all should love our grandparents. The symbolic salience in the UK of the bus pass as a badge of old age presents a challenge to those who wish to end universal age based benefits.

Conclusion

There are a number of suggestions as to why ageism is so prevalent in contemporary society. Unlike racism or sexism, it is still socially acceptable to express ageist attitudes in public (AgeUK 2011; Macnicol 2006). There are psychological explanations which link fear of old age with fear of sickness and death – hence the tendencies to remove older people and their images from sight and mind (Elias 1985). There are class explanations which locate the need in capitalist society to coerce or incentivise people to work to the detriment of the status and living standards of those at the post-work stage of life (Formosa and Higgs 2013; Vincent 1995). Of course, some older people live from capital. However, although pension funds are highly significant sources of capital in the modern economy, the nominal owners of rights in them have no significant control over them and so they may be better understood as deferred wages rather than return on capital (Clark 2000). Ageism has been associated with cultural values of the body and of individualism – values at the forefront of contemporary culture (Gagnier 2010; Tulle 2008). But simple single cause explanations do not do justice to the complex social dynamics and the contemporary social narrative by which 'third age' values contest with the marginalisaton and exclusion of older people (Laslett 1989). C. Wright Mills (1970) suggests that one of the most powerful insights social science can offer is to link large scale societal change with individual personal experience. The range of emotions and feelings when, for the first time, I was proffered a seat on the London Underground by a young Chinese student, has to be understood in the context of a society which regards older people as different and the status of old age as undesirable, as well as my rucksack being heavy.

Notes

1   For example, from 1 January 2012 you have to be 35 or over to be entitled to housing benefit, which does not assume as a single person you are sharing your accommodation with others (DWP 2011).
2   Quotation from a respondent in an internal quality control report that the author co-produced as a Trustee of Exeter AgeUK.

References

AgeUK (2009) *One Voice: Shaping our Aging Society*, Online. Available HTTP: <http://www.ageuk.org.uk/documents/en-gb/for-professionals/research/one%20voice%20%282009%29_pro.pdf?dtrk=true> (accessed 10 September 2013).

—(2011) *A Snapshot of Ageism in the UK and across Europe*, Online. Available HTTP: <http://www.ageuk.org.uk/Documents/EN-GB/ID10180%20Snapshot%20of%20Ageism%20in%20Europe.pdf?dtrk=true> (accessed 10 September 2013).

Arking, R. (2006) *The Biology of Aging*, 3rd edn, Oxford, UK: Oxford University Press.

BIS (Department for Business, Skills and Innovation) (2011) 'Default Retirement Age to End this Year', Online. Available HTTP: <http://www.bis.gov.uk/news/topstories/2011/Jan/default-retirement-age-to-end> (accessed 10 September 2013).

Blackburn, R. (2002) *Banking on Death Or, Investing in Life: The History and Future of Pensions*, London: Verso.

Blaike, A. (2006) 'Visions of Later Life: Golden Cohort to Generation Z', in J.A. Vincent, C.R. Phillipson and M. Downs (eds) *The Futures of Old Age*, London: Sage.

Boia, L. (2004) *Forever Young: A Cultural History of Longevity*, London: Reaktion.

Bourdelais, P. (1998) 'The Ageing of the Population: Relevant Question or Obsolete Notion?', in P. Johnson and P. Thane (eds) *Old Age from Antiquity to Post-modernity*, London: Routledge.

Carey, J. (2003) *Longevity: The Biology and Demography of Life Span*, Princeton, NJ: Princeton University Press.

Chambers, M. (2013) 'To Win, Cameron Must Make a Game-changing Offer to the Young Middle-classes', Online. Available HTTP: <http://conservativehome.blogs.com/majority_conservatism/2013/06/max-chambers.html> (accessed 10 September 2013).

CIA (2001) *Long Term Global Demographic Trends: Reshaping the Geo-political Landscape*. Online. Available HTTP: <https://www.cia.gov/library/reports/general-reports-1/Demo_Trends_For_Web.pdf> (accessed 11 September 2013).

Clark, G. (2000) *Pension Fund Capitalism*, Oxford, UK: Oxford University Press.

Cole, T.R. (1992) *The Journey of Life: A Cultural History of Aging in America*, Cambridge: Cambridge University Press.

Coupland, N., Coupland, J. and Giles, H. (1991) *Language, Society and the Elderly: Discourse, Identity and Ageing*, Oxford, UK: Blackwell.

Daatland, S.O. and Biggs, S. (eds) (2005) *Ageing and Diversity: Multiple Pathways and Cultural Migrations*, Bristol: Policy.

Dumas, A. and Turner, B.S. (2007) 'The Life-extension Project: A Sociological Critique', *Health Sociology Review*, 16(1): 5–17.

DWP (Department of Work and Pensions) (2011) 'Housing Benefit is Changing From 1 January 2012 for Single People aged 25 to 35 and Rent From a Private Landlord', Online. Available HTTP: <http://www.dwp.gov.uk/docs/sar1.pdf> (accessed 10 September 2013).

Elias, N. (1985) *The Loneliness of Dying*, Oxford, UK: Blackwell.

Eriksen, E. (1982) *The Life Cycle Completed*, New York, NY: Norton.

Estes, C.L. and Binney, E. (1989) 'The Biomedicalisation of Aging: Dangers and Dilemmas', *Gerontologist*, 29(5): 587–96.

Formosa, M. and Higgs, P. (eds) (2013) *Social Class in Later Life: Power, Identity and Lifestyle*, Bristol: Policy.

Gagnier, R. (2010) *Individualism, Decadence and Globalization: On the Relationship of Part to Whole, 1859–1920*, Basingstoke, UK: Palgrave Macmillan.

Gee, E.M. and Gutman, G.M. (eds) (2000) *The Overselling of Population Aging*, New York, NY: Oxford University Press.

Gilleard, C. and Higgs, P. (2000) *Cultures of Ageing*, Harlow, UK: Prentice Hall.

Gimlin, D. (2002) *Body Work: Beauty and Self Image in American Culture*, Berkeley, CA: University of California Press.

Goerres, A. (2009) *The Political Participation of Older People in Europe*, Basingstoke, UK: Palgrave Macmillan.

Gott, M. and Ingleton, C. (2011) *Living with Ageing and Dying: Palliative and End of Life Care for Older People*, Oxford, UK: Oxford University Press.

Gubrium, J. and Holstein, J.A. (eds) (2000) *Aging and Everyday Life*, Oxford, UK: Blackwell.

Hall, S.S. (2003) *Merchants of Immortality: Chasing the Dream of Human Life Extension*, Boston, MA: Houghton Mifflin.

Hardy, M. (ed.) (1997) *Studying Aging and Social Change*, London: Sage.

Hurd Clarke, L. (2011) *Facing Age: Women Growing Older in Anti-Aging Culture*, Plymouth, UK: Rowman and Littlefield.

Jenks, C. (1996) *Childhood*, London: Routledge.

Jones, I.R. and Higgs, P.F. (2010) 'The Natural, the Normal and the Normative: Contested Terrains in Ageing and Old Age', *Social Science and Medicine*, 71(8): 1513–19.

Kirkwood, T. (1999) *Time of Our Lives: The Science of Human Ageing*, London: Weidenfeld & Nicolson.

Lafontaine, C. (2008) *La Société Post-Mortelle*, Paris: Seuil.

Laslett, P. (1989) *A Fresh Map of Life: The Emergence of the Third Age*, London: Weidenfeld & Nicolson.

Lock, M. and Farquhar, J. (eds) (2007) *Beyond the Body Proper: Reading the Anthropology of Material Life*, Durham, NC: Duke University Press.

Macnicol, J. (2006) *Age Discrimination: An Historical and Contemporary Analysis*, Cambridge: Cambridge University Press.

Mannheim, K. (1997) The Problem of Generations, in Hardy, M.A. (ed.) *Studying Aging and Social Change*, London: Sage.

Mehta, K. (1997) 'Cultural Scripts and the Social Integration of Older People', *Ageing and Society*, 17(3): 253–75.

Mills, C.W. (1970) *The Sociological Imagination*, Harmondsworth: Penguin.

Minois, G. (1989) *History of Old Age*, Cambridge, UK: Polity.

Moreira, T. and Palladino, P. (2008) 'Squaring the Curve: The Anatomo-politics of Ageing, Life and Death', *Body and Society*, 14(3): 21–48.

Mykytyn, C.E. (2006) 'Anti-aging Medicine: A Patient/Practitioner Movement to Redefine Aging', *Social Science and Medicine*, 62(3): 643–53.

Oberg, P. (2003) 'Images versus Experience of the Aging Body', in C.A. Fairclough (ed.) *Aging Bodies: Images and Everyday Experience*, Oxford, UK: AltaMira.

Phillipson, C. and Vincent, J.A. (2007) 'Globalization and Aging', in J. Birren (ed.) *Encyclopedia of Gerontology*, Boston, MA: Academic Press.

Rose, N. (2007) *Politics of Life Itself: Biomedicine, Power and Subjectivity in the Twenty-first Century*, Oxford, UK: Princeton University Press.

Rosenfeld, D. (1999) 'Identity Work among Lesbian and Gay Elderly', *Journal of Aging Studies*, 13(2): 121–44.

Schermer, M. and Pinxten, W. (eds) (2013) *Ethics, Health Policy and (Anti) Aging: Mixed Blessings*, Dordrecht: Springer.

Solomon, A. (2013) *Far from the Tree: A Dozen Kinds of Love*, London: Chatto and Windus.

Tulle, E. (2008) *Ageing, the Body and Social Change*, Basingstoke: Palgrave Macmillan.

Turner, B.S. (2007) 'Culture, Technologies and Bodies: The Technological Utopia of Living Forever', in C. Shilling (ed.) *Embodying Sociology: Retrospect, Progress and Prospects*, Oxford, UK: Blackwell.

United Nations (2011) *World Population Prospects: The 2010 Revision*, New York, NY: United Nations. Online. Available HTTP: <http://esa.un.org/unpd/wpp/Documentation/pdf/WPP2010_Volume-II_Demographic- Profiles.pdf> (accessed 10 September 2013).

Vincent, J.A. (1995) *Inequality and Old Age*, London: University College London Press.

—(1996) 'Who's Afraid of an Ageing Population?', *Critical Social Policy*, 16(2): 3–26.

—(1999) *Politics, Power and Old Age*, Buckingham: Open University Press.

—(2005) 'Understanding Generations: Political Economy and Culture in an Ageing Society', *British Journal of Sociology*, 56(4): 579–99.

— (2006a) 'Anti-Ageing Science and the Future of Old Age', in J.A. Vincent, C. Phillipson and M. Downs (eds) *Futures of Old Age*, London: Sage.

—(2006b) 'Ageing Contested: Anti-ageing Science and the Cultural Construction of Old Age', *Sociology*, 40(4): 681–98.

—(2013) 'The Anti-Aging Movement', in M. Schermer and W. Pinxten (eds) *Ethics, Health Policy and (Anti-)aging: Mixed Blessings*, Dordrecht: Springer, 29–40.

Vincent, J.A., Patterson, G. and Wale, K. (2001) *Politics and Old Age: Older Citizens and Political Processes in Britain*, Basingstoke, UK: Ashgate.

Wahidin, A. and Cain, M. (2006) *Ageing, Crime and Society*, London: Willan.

Williamson, J.B. Watts-Roy, D.M. and Kingston, E.R. (eds) (1999) *The Generational Equity Debate*, New York, NY: Columbia University Press.

World Bank (1994) *Averting the Old Age Crisis: Policies to Protect the Old and Promote Growth*, Oxford, UK: Oxford University Press.

3

Disability and diversity

Carol Thomas

Whilst this book is testimony to the importance that the concept *diversity* has attained in recent years, it is necessary to explore a relatively unanswered question: what does diversity mean in relation to disability and disablism? In addressing this question this chapter touches on matters of numerical diversity, theoretical diversity and the relevance of contemporary diversity debates. As in other fields – for example, explorations of gender, 'race' and sexuality – questions about diversity connect with related debates about social divisions and intersectionality (see Lutz, this volume).

The title of this chapter may conjure up images of bodies whose diversity resides in the need for mobility aids such as wheelchairs or crutches, or assistive technologies such as white canes and hearing aids. Or perhaps readers' thoughts turn toward elite disabled athletes who display their bodies' trained capacities at the Paralympic Games. Either way, the diversity invoked concerns matters of embodied *difference* associated with *impairment* – that is, those variations in body and mind that biomedicine has classified as degrees of *abnormality*, whether life-long or acquired. However, this chapter is primarily about *disability* and diversity, not impairment and diversity. This distinction is important because, in the tradition of disabled people's movements across the globe, disability is first and foremost about the disadvantaged *social* status and inequitable life opportunities experienced by people whose bodies and minds are designated *impaired* by representatives of scientific medicine and other professions. Their non-disabled counterparts, who make up the majority in any society, are people defined as *normal* – at least temporarily. These non-disabled social actors wield *relative* authority and power over those designated impaired, and the former's practices toward disabled people – whether individual or collective – have given rise to the concept *disablism*:

> **Disablism:** refers to the social imposition of avoidable restrictions on the life activities, aspirations and psycho-emotional well-being of people categorised as 'impaired' by those deemed 'normal'. Disablism is social relational in character and constitutes a form of social oppression in contemporary society – alongside sexism, racism, ageism, and homophobia. As well as enacted in person-to-person interactions, disablism may manifest itself in institutionalised and other socio-structural forms.
>
> *(Thomas 2010: 37)*

This paves the way for greater accuracy in outlining the topic of this chapter: *disablism and diversity*. As noted at the start, the discussion will touch on matters of numerical diversity, theoretical diversity and the relevance of contemporary diversity debates. However, and despite bringing the concept disablism to the fore, it is necessary in a multi-topic book such as this to begin with *impairment*.

Impairment: numerical diversity

Medically defined categories of *impairment* (physical, sensory, intellectual, emotional) cannot be simply set aside here, because these are the *marked categories of social difference* that attract disablism. Types of impairment are unevenly distributed across the globe in a numerical sense, and carry meanings that bring forth particular forms of disablism in time and space. For example, people with learning disabilities in rich nations such as the UK are sometimes victims of *hate crime* (Thomas 2013) – because their behavioural differences, vulnerability and social isolation have attracted the attention of individuals who inflict harm upon those perceived to be less than human and 'easy targets'.

Moreover, categories of impairment continue to determine how the numbers of *disabled* people in any population are estimated and counted; these are what are enumerated by authorities charged with producing statistics on disability (Abberley 1992). For example, current estimates from the *World Health Organization* (WHO) are as follows:

> Over a billion people are estimated to live with some form of disability. This corresponds to about 15% of the world's population. ... Furthermore, the rates of disability are increasing in part due to ageing populations and an increase in chronic health conditions.
>
> *(WHO and The World Bank 2011: 1)*

In terms of the severity and prevalence of disability:

> [T]he *Global Burden of Disease* estimates that 190 million (3.8%) have 'severe disability' – the equivalent of disability inferred for conditions such as quadriplegia, severe depression, or blindness. Only the *Global Burden of Disease* measures childhood disabilities (0–14 years), which is estimated to be 95 million (5.1%) children, of whom 13 million (0.7%) have 'severe disability'.
>
> *(WHO and The World Bank 2011: 8)*

> Results from the World Health Survey indicate a higher disability prevalence in lower income countries than in higher income countries. People from the poorest wealth quintile, women, and older people also have a higher prevalence of disability (World Health Statistics 2012). People who have a low income, are out of work, or have low educational qualifications are at an increased risk of disability. Data from the Multiple Indicator Cluster Surveys in selected countries show that children from poorer households and those in ethnic minority groups are at significantly higher risk of disability than other children [UN Children's Fund].
>
> *(WHO and The World Bank 2011: 8)*

Aside from genetic risks, these data tell us that individuals' vulnerability and exposure to the determinants of *impairment* are much higher: in war-torn regions; in low-income countries; in locations blighted by industrial hazards; amongst the socio-economically challenged in any society; and amongst systematically disadvantaged groups such as women, homeless children and unsupported elders (WHO 2012). In the global South, the impairments involved are typically: infectious and chronic diseases (especially HIV and AIDS), injuries, violence, malnutrition and other causes closely related to poverty; 'accidental injuries' are regular occurrences – typically traffic accidents, drowning, falls, burns or poisoning.

In addition to the primary risks of impairment, it has now been established epidemiologically that people with impairments are at higher risk of developing *secondary* health problems than their non-disabled counterparts – that is, health problems such as circulatory diseases *not* aetiologically associated with the original or main impairment. This is because of poor living conditions and the cumulative effects of encounters with disadvantage and disablism (Emerson *et al.* 2012).

Finally, it is important to distinguish between impairments per se (medically defined categories) and what I have termed *impairment effects*:

> **Impairment effects:** the direct and unavoidable impacts that 'impairments' (physical, sensory, intellectual, emotional) have on individuals' embodied functioning in the social world. Impairments and impairment effects are always bio-social and culturally constructed in character, and may occur at any stage in the life course.
>
> *(Thomas 2012: 211)*

Disablism: theoretical diversity

Turning to disablism, the definition cited above noted its social relational character: that is, the existence of relationships (at individual and institutional scales) between those designated *normal* and those designated *disabled* in any social arena. The non-disabled occupy positions of relative power and authority, for example within: family settings; health and social services; occupational hierarchies; institutions of governance; or leisure arenas. The challenge is to theorise these relationships, as previously occurred in the social sciences with regard to gender, 'race', sexuality and age – where markers of *difference* also have somatic links with individuals' appearance and/or behaviours. As Iris Marion Young (1990) argued some decades ago, the concept *social oppression* has been mobilised to capture these types of social relationships. She summarised the meaning of this much used concept as follows:

> In [an] extended structural sense oppression refers to the vast and deep injustices some groups suffer as a consequence of often unconscious assumptions and reactions of well-meaning people in ordinary interactions, media and cultural stereotypes, and structural features of bureaucratic hierarchies and market mechanisms – in short, the normal processes of everyday life. We cannot eliminate this structural oppression by getting rid of the rulers or making some new laws, because oppressions are systematically reproduced in major economic, political, and cultural institutions.
>
> *(Young 1990: 41)*

Theorising social oppression has proven to be an enormous challenge in disability studies, and writers have been particularly influenced by ideas developed in the study of class, gender and in critical race studies. The two theoretical traditions that have assumed dominance in disability studies since the 1980s are as follows – both with strong feminist components (Garland-Thomson 2005; Thomas 2007).

Materialism/Marxism/materialist feminism

In this tradition, disablism is understood to be rooted in economic systems and relationships of production and exchange. Capitalism, and particularly its industrial phase of expansion in Europe, created the foundations for the social exclusion of people with impairments – overturning their *relative* social integration in feudal and other agrarian-based economies (Gleeson 1999; Oliver 1990). For example, in Britain's late eighteenth and early nineteenth centuries, the developing system of generalised commodity production required that non-owners of the means of production sold their labour-power as a commodity – to be consumed in fast-moving and exhausting industrial labour processes, or in the relentlessly busy domestic service sector. Those who could not labour according to employment norms were excluded, and thus denied independent access to the means of subsistence and survival. Coupled with the break-up of extended families in rural settings, people with impairments were cast adrift – suffering a profound loss of connectivity and social status. With the assistance of an ascendant medical profession, an ideology of *abnormality* took hold in all quarters of society from the mid-nineteenth century, and authorities grappled with what to do with 'cripples', 'imbeciles' and 'the mad'. In later decades, these diverse communities of 'abnormal people' were grouped together with the war-wounded, to constitute *the disabled* (Campbell and Oliver 1996).

Across many continents, the institutional and other practical solutions to the unwelcome presence of disabled people persisted well into the twentieth century ('solutions' still found today in many countries): workhouses, enforced dependency, sterilisation, 'special' education, 'sheltered' workshops, community care 'homes'. In other words, the solutions involved invoked the whole paraphernalia of so-called *care and welfare services*, exercising philanthropic and professional control over disabled people's lives (Borsay 2005; Gleeson 1999).

In resource-poor regions in the global South, living with disablism was, and continues to be, a matter of basic subsistence and perilous survival for millions of disabled children and adults – especially in war-torn countries and depleted rural locations (Barnes and Sheldon 2010; Priestley 2001). Today, priority needs are for access to basic health and rehabilitation services, followed by access to education and employment; but these services and life-course opportunities are often minimal or almost entirely absent, especially in rural areas (Tomlinson *et al.* 2009). Where health care and rehabilitation services are available in middle-income countries with developed urban centres, disabled people find that their access to services is disadvantaged by physical blocks and attitudinal barriers among service providers, together with a shortage of mobility devices and other assistive technologies (Officer 2010; Tomlinson *et al.* 2009). Additional social barriers operate forcefully in more favourable economic circumstances in relation to education, employment, transport systems, housing and the built environment (Barnes and Sheldon 2010). Nonetheless, wherever possible disabled people have actively resisted their degradation in the resource-poor world.

Indeed, the rise of disabled people's movements across the globe from the last quarter of the twentieth century have called for dramatic changes in the position of disabled people in society – under the banner of *the social model of disability*. These movements have formed wherever conditions permit, and are now international in scope; see, for example, the websites of the *Disabled People's International* and the *International Disability Alliance*. Once unleashed, the *disability rights* campaigns began to make tangible progress in richer nations, especially with regard to deinstitutionalisation, *independent living* and service accessibility (Campbell and Oliver 1996). These developments were certainly assisted by economic developments, especially material and electronic innovations (Roulstone 2012; Roulstone and Barnes 2005). However, the twenty-first century soon witnessed vigorous attacks on the so-called *welfare dependency* of disabled people in richer nations – fuelled by economic crises and governmental retrenchment. Now, neo-liberal solutions to the *problems* posed by the 'burden' of disabled people point toward 'work not welfare' under the guise of policies on *equality and diversity* (Roulstone and Barnes 2005; Soldatic and Meekosha 2012).

Poststructuralism/postmodernism – and feminist variants[1]

Since the 1990s, materialist perspectives on what brought disability and disablism into being have been rejected as modernist and misconceived by some writers in disability studies. Those informed by postmodernist and poststructuralist theoretical perspectives – for example, the late Mairian Corker, Dan Goodley and Margrit Shildrick – reject the materialist focus on socio-structural determinants of disablism and have turned instead to cultural and linguistic theory for answers (Corker and Shakespeare 2002; Goodley *et al.* 2012; Shildrick 2012). Many have been drawn to the French philosophical ideas of writers such as Foucault (1973), Deleuze (1990) and Derrida (1978), and in recent years have begun to locate their contributions in what they prefer to term *critical disability studies*. From these perspectives, disability has no 'fixed', 'absolute' and 'essential' qualities; rather, disablist practices and relationships stem from the operation of power-ful systems of knowledge in society – particularly biomedical knowledge. Following Foucault's (1973) ideas about social power, biomedical surveillance provides the authoritative reference points for what is deemed *normal* and *acceptable* in society – and gives rise to widespread cultural practices that assume normativity and reject and/or despise the *abnormal other*. Thus, those who wield power through the authority and status of their specialist knowledge – doctors, state administrators and legislators – construct and impose the category *disabled* upon selected indi-viduals in their purview. The person who is socially constructed as 'disabled' in this way may often come, in turn, to view him or herself as 'abnormal'. That is, people with embodied features and differences marked out as impairments come to see themselves as 'pitiable' and 'useless' – hence 'disabled' – and to self-regulate themselves as such. Any hope for resistance – and it is a slim hope – lies in a disabled person's ability to reject and resist the medical and associated cat-egories imposed upon them, that is, to break free from the discursive bonds by which they are tied. From this perspective, the disability rights agenda exercised by disabled people's movements across the globe from the 1970s is viewed, in the main, as the result of changes in patterns of discursive governance. Put another way, the narrative of the social *inclusion* of disabled people could be accommodated by those in power (for example, via anti-discrimination legislation), because doing so served the interests of the state and bio-power in the twenty-first century. Finally, the concept of disablism has been replaced in critical disability studies with *ableism* (Goodley *et al.* 2012; Kumari Campbell 2009) – because the latter redirects attention toward the exclusionary practices of *the normative*, that is, those in the unmarked category:

> [Ableism refers to] a network of beliefs, processes and practices that produces a particular kind of self and body (the corporeal standard) that is projected as the perfect, species-typical and therefore essential and fully human. Disability then is cast as a diminished state of being human.
>
> *(Kumari Campbell 2009: 9)*

Diversity debates: how does disablism fit in?

As the twenty-first century has moved ahead, politicians and policy makers in many nations and regions have swung around to supporting the rhetoric of *full citizenship* and *inclusion* of disabled people, and have introduced or tightened up anti-discriminatory legislation. Such developments have been increasingly accompanied by *diversity and equality* policy agendas. For example, the UK's *Disability Discrimination Acts* (1995, 2005) have been followed by the *Equality Act 2010* and the related *Equality Duty*, now in force in England, Scotland and Wales. The *Equality and Human Rights Commission* (EHRC, formed in 2007) laid the foundations for this Equality Act 2010 by acknowledging and celebrating social diversity *and* bringing sectional interests (associated with gender, race, disability, age, etc.) into alignment via a singular/unified piece of legislation designed to protect the human rights of all. This legislation required fresh thinking about the meaning of social diversity, divisions and interconnections, and the recognition that disadvantaged social groups have many equity needs in common. On the international scale, unifying thinking was also underway on the disability question, and it was acknowledged that – despite diversity – there were common needs/rights evident in disabled people's lives across the globe. This resulted in the *United Nations Convention on the Rights of People with Disabilities* (United Nations 2006) – now signed up to by many governments. These positive national and inter-national developments highlight the fundamental rhetorical and discursive shifts that have occurred on disability rights in policy-making and official circles.

So, how much beneficial change has actually been experienced by disabled people in their everyday lives? The answer from most writers in disability studies across the globe is 'not much' – but their interpretations of the mismatch between *rhetoric* and the *reality* have varied according to the theoretical stance adopted on the nature of disablism/ableism. The two dominant theoretical traditions at work in disability studies were discussed above: materialism and poststructuralism. Not surprisingly, there is conceptual consistency in their adherents' engagements with the failure of the *diversity and equality* agenda.

Materialism/Marxism/materialist feminism

It is a disappointment, but not a surprise, to materialists that the diversity and equality agenda has only made a limited number of marginal improvements in the lives of disabled adults and children. Indeed, the full force of neo-liberal governmental retrenchment in the capitalist heartlands since the 2008 financial crisis blocked any opportunities for advancement (Barnes 2012; Roulstone and Barnes 2005). Indeed, in both the global North and South large sections of the disabled population have reported *worsening* living standards in recent years, as well as diminished life-chances (Soldatic and Meekosha 2012).

The argument has been that politicians, state officials and leading industrialists *appropriated* the language of empowerment, inclusion and individual rights – because this served their shared neo-liberal political and economic agendas (Roulstone 2012). That is, encouraging self-management and independent living among disabled people has suited politicians' calls to curtail state welfare provision and to free-up market mechanisms; disabled people have thus been instructed to consolidate their 'individual responsibilities' by coming off benefits and joining the ranks of the employed. A good example of this perspective is found in the words of Jenny Morris (2011) – a leading feminist writer and activist in the disabled people's movement who reflects on the time she spent working within the UK's governmental corridors of power during the 2000s and 2010s, trying to further the interests of disabled people *from the inside*:

> [T]here are aspects of the arguments made by disability organisations which have been capitalised on by the politics and ideology driving recent and current policies in ways that are significantly to the disadvantage of disabled people. These concern, in particular, the social model of disability and the concepts of 'independent living', and 'user involvement' or

'co-production'. I want to look at the way governments have colonised and corrupted these ideas, and to start to identify some possible responses which may help with future progress on disability policies.

(Morris 2011: 3)

Morris goes on to conclude that 'there is little room for making progress in the context of the ideological framework which is driving the government's disability policies' (ibid.: 18).

Thus, adherents to variants of this theoretical perspective have focused on capitalist economic crises and the responses – ideological and practical – of the state apparatus and the industrial ruling class. Politicians' talk of *diversity and equality* is viewed as a key dimension of the ideological theatre involved in their appropriation of the disabled people's movement's agenda. However, revolutionary solutions are no longer advocated in this theoretical tradition. Rather, hope lies in economic recovery, left-leaning social democratic politics and reform – as well, of course, in the political resurgence of disabled *people's* movements and their allies (Oliver 2009).

Poststructuralism/postmodernism – and feminist variants

Given the summary of this theoretical tradition provided earlier, it follows that the *diversity and equality agenda* pursued by politicians and officials in the twenty-first century is viewed as a discursive means of governance of those 'others' who constitute *the diverse* (Goodley *et al.* 2012). A good example of how *diversity discourses* are understood to have constructed both *disability* and *abnormality* and, as a result, disadvantaged disabled people is found in a paper by Marta D. Infante and Claudia Matus (2009) in the journal *Disability & Society.*

Using a Foucauldian lens, Infante and Matus (2009) have explored how the Chilean government has used international *diversity discourses* as the rationale to move disabled children into mainstream schools (closing 'special schools') – an apparently radical act in support of disability rights. But, in so doing, the authorities have *reproduced exclusionary practices of the body* (ibid.: 438), by constructing children with special educational needs as *unruly bodies* and *the developmentally delayed.* This, in turn, has created *regimes of truth* that perpetuate and apparently justify the second-class treatment of 'the abnormal' (Infante and Matus 2009: 442). By these means, the governance of disabled people is assured, and practices of *self-regulation among disabled people are easy to instil. In this theoretical perspective, therefore,* diversity discourses have the effect of deeply embedding notions of *abhorrent difference* in the cultural imaginary. Sara Ahmed (2009) has captured this well in her discussion of black feminism: 'Diversity becomes both a problem and a paradox for those who embody diversity' (ibid.: 42).

Summary

This chapter has engaged with disability and diversity in a variety of ways. First, the meaning of the concept *disablism* – the key concept – was clarified. This was followed by discussions about: impairment and numerical diversity; theorising disablism in diverse ways; and how disablism relates to contemporary diversity debates.

The conclusion, whichever theoretical perspective is adopted, is that disabled people have not been the beneficiaries of contemporary eulogies about *diversity and equality* in national and global policy circles.

Note

1   As well as Marxist/materialist and postmodernist/poststructuralist perspectives in disability studies, there are others in use, especially those drawing on phenomenology (Goodley *et al.* 2012) or critical realism (Watson *et al.* 2012); and all traditional and contemporary theoretical perspectives have strong feminist variants (Thomas 2007).

References

Abberley, P. (1992) 'Counting Us Out: A Discussion of the OPCS Disability Surveys', *Disability, Handicap and Society*, 7(2): 139–55.

Ahmed, S. (2009) 'The Language of Diversity', *Ethnic and Racial Studies*, 30(2): 235–56.

Barnes, C. (2012) 'Understanding the Social Model of Disability: Past Present and Future' in N. Watson, A. Roulstone and C. Thomas (eds) *Routledge Handbook of Disability Studies*, London: Routledge.

Barnes, C. and Sheldon, A. (2010) 'Disability, Politics and Poverty in a Majority World Context', *Disability & Society*, 25(7): 771–82.

Borsay, A. (2005) *Disability and Social Policy in Britain Since 1750*, Basingstoke, UK: Palgrave Macmillan.

Campbell, J. and Oliver, M. (1996) *Disability Politics: Understanding our Past, Changing our Future*, London: Routledge.

Corker, M. and Shakespeare, T. (eds) (2002) *Disability/Postmodernity: Embodying Disability Theory*, London: Continuum.

Deleuze, G. (1990) *The Logic of Sense*, London: Athlone.

Derrida, J. (1978) *Writing and Difference*, Chicago: University of Chicago Press.

Emerson, E., Brandon, V., Graham, H., Hatton, C., Llewellyn, G., Madden, R., Rechel, B. and Robertson, J. (2012) 'Disablement and Health', in N. Watson, A. Roulstone and C. Thomas (eds) *Routledge Handbook of Disability Studies*, London: Routledge.

Foucault, M. (1973) *The Birth of the Clinic: An Archaeology of Medical Perception*, London: Tavistock.

Garland-Thomson, R. (2005) 'Feminist Disability Studies', *Signs: The Journal of Women in Culture and Society*, 30(2): 1577–87.

Gleeson, B. (1999) *Geographies of Disability*, London: Routledge.

Goodley, D., Hughes, B. and Davis, L. (eds) (2012) *Disability and Social Theory: New Developments and Directions*, Basingstoke, UK: Palgrave Macmillan.

Infante, M.D. and Matus, C. (2009) 'Policies and Practices of Diversity: Reimagining Possibilities for New Discourses', *Disability & Society*, 24(4): 437–45.

Kumari Campbell, F. (2009) *Contours of Ableism: The Production of Disability and Abledness*, Basingstoke: Palgrave Macmillan.

Morris, J. (2011) *Rethinking Disability Policy*, Viewpoint paper, Joseph Rowntree Foundation. Online. Available HTTP: <http://www.jrf.org.uk> (accessed 20 April, 2014).

Officer, A. (2010) *Research and Policy Working Together to Improve the Lives of Disabled People Worldwide*, Plenary Paper delivered to the Disability Studies Conference, Lancaster University, September 2010. Online. Available HTTP: <http://www.lancs.ac.uk/cedr/> (accessed 20 April, 2014).

Oliver, M. (1990) *The Politics of Disablement*, London: Palgrave Macmillan.

—(2009) *Understanding Disability: From Theory to Practice*, 2nd edn, Basingstoke, UK: Palgrave Macmillan.

Priestley, M. (ed.) (2001) *Disability and the Life Course: Global Perspectives*, Cambridge, UK: Cambridge University Press.

Roulstone, A. (2012) 'Disabled People, Work and Employment', in N. Watson, A. Roulstone and C. Thomas (eds) *Routledge Handbook of Disability Studies*, London: Routledge.

Roulstone, A. and Barnes, C. (2005) *Working Futures: Disabled People and Social Inclusion*, Bristol, UK: Policy.

Shildrick, M. (2012) 'Critical Disability Studies: Rethinking the Conventions for the Age of Postmodernity' in N. Watson, A. Roulstone and C. Thomas (eds) *Routledge Handbook of Disability Studies*, London: Routledge.

Soldatic, K. and Meekosha, H. (2012) 'Disability and Neoliberal State Formations', in N. Watson, A. Roulstone and C. Thomas (eds) *Routledge Handbook of Disability Studies*, London: Routledge.

Thomas, C. (2007) *Sociologies of Disability and Illness: Contested Ideas in Disability Studies and Medical Sociology*, Basingstoke, UK: Palgrave Macmillan.

—(2010) 'Medical Sociology and Disability Theory', in G. Scambler and S. Scambler (eds) *New Directions in the Sociology of Chronic and Disabling Conditions: Assaults on the Lifeworld*, Basingstoke, UK: Palgrave Macmillan.

—(2012) 'Theorising Disability and Chronic Illness: Where Next for Perspectives in Medical Sociology?' *Social Theory and Health*, 10(3): 209–27.

Thomas, P. (2013) 'Hate Crime and the Criminal Justice System', in J. Swain, S. French, C. Barnes and C. Thomas (eds) *Disabling Barriers: Enabling Environments*, 3rd edn, London: Sage.

Tomlinson, M., Swartz, L., Officer, A., Chan, K.Y., Rudan, I. and Saxena, S. (2009) 'Research Priorities for Health of People with Disabilities: An Expert Opinion Exercise', *The Lancet*, 374(9704): 1857–62.

United Nations (2006) *Convention on the Rights of People with Disabilities (CRPD)*, Online. Available HTTP: <http://www.un.org/disabilities/default.asp?navid=14&pid=150> (accessed 1 March 2012).

Watson, N., Roulstone, A. and Thomas, C. (eds) (2012) *Routledge Handbook of Disability Studies*, London: Routledge.

WHO (2012) *World Health Statistics 2012*: World Health Organization. Online. Available HTTP: <http://www.who.int/gho/publications/world_health_statistics/2012/en/> (accessed 25 April, 2012).

WHO and The World Bank (2011) *World Report on Disability: Summary*, Geneva: World Health Organization.

Young, I.M. (1990) *Justice and the Politics of Difference*, Princeton, NJ: Princeton University Press.

4

Thinking about race in an age of diversity

Katharina Schramm

At the dawn of the twentieth century, W.E.B. Du Bois made his famous prediction that the problem of the coming age was going to be 'the problem of the colour line' (Du Bois 1903: vii). Consequently, he spent his long lifetime thinking about race and racism, arguing vehemently against discriminatory practices that defined racial groups in order to privilege one against the other. For Du Bois, race was first and foremost a political category, yet with a strong emotional appeal.[1] He was also well aware of the slipperiness of the concept, which made it irreducible to a clear-cut entity. Thus he argued in 1940 that race was not so much an ontological given or a concept as such, but rather was constantly made and remade through 'a group of contradictory forces, facts and tendencies' (Du Bois 1940: 133). Many of these contradictions lay in the simultaneity of the violence inherent in dominant regimes of racial classification and the emancipatory power of self-identification and solidarity among all those who 'must ride "Jim Crow" in Georgia' (Du Bois 1996 [1923]: 68). Moreover, ambiguity was inscribed in the classificatory practices themselves, which made up racialized bodies between biological taxonomies and other forms of dividing practices (see Foucault 1982).

Race was indeed a major issue throughout the twentieth century – and not only in the United States, where Martin Luther King would speak about his dream of equality a day after Du Bois' death in Ghanaian exile in 1963. The end of apartheid in 1994 marked the official demise of legitimate state racism, announcing formal equality under the roof of common citizenship. The iconic imagery of the rainbow nation that was meant to replace the old racial regime in South Africa stands exemplarily for a new discourse of cultural diversity that has gained global currency.[2] As Steve Vertovec indicates in his article on diversity and the social imaginary, there is little doubt that 'we are living in the age of diversity' (Vertovec 2012: 2). Does that mean that race has simply vanished? Has it become less of a central problem, but rather a policy issue of how to deal with right-wing extremists and die-hard racists? Or has it even been turned from a negative and vicious discriminatory category into a positive label of difference and playful consumption? And what has happened to the entanglement of nature/culture that was constitutive of race from the beginning? What about the oppressive regimes of hierarchical difference associated with it?

The political move from race to diversity had its predecessor in the development of the life-sciences post-World War Two. After the experience of Nazi eugenics and racial genocide, the paradigm of racial typology, which had been the obsessive preoccupation of a large number of scientists from the nineteenth century onwards, was declared obsolete and marked down as scientific racism, from which proper science would seek its distance (Reardon 2005; UNESCO 1969). From the 1960s onwards, scientific interest turned more and more to the investigation of *diversity within* as well as *gradual variation* (instead of clear-cut boundaries) *between* populations (cf. Lewontin 1972). In many respects, race became an anathema.[3]

And yet race has not disappeared completely – neither from the epistemological practices of the life sciences nor from the political realm. In genomics, there has even been what some authors have called a race revival, i.e. a growing preoccupation with genetic differences at group level. In this expanding field of medical and basic genomic research, ethnicity and racial proxies often feature as influential factors that are called upon to mark biological diversity (see Duster 2003; Koenig *et al.* 2008; Schramm *et al.* 2011). Here, as in other cases, race needs not to be explicitly referenced in order for racial effects to manifest. To take an example from politics: an emphasis on colour-blindness in political debates may rest on normative (though invisible) assumptions about whiteness and thus contribute to a racializing effect (see Bonilla-Silva 2003).[4]

In my contribution I seek to develop an analytical framework with which to grasp this ongoing and troubling presence of race and the methodological and theoretical challenges that go along with it. This calls for a critical theoretical questioning of race itself. In an essay on critical race theory, Patricia H. Collins (2011) calls for a theoretical engagement with race that is cognizant of its own location. I share this dialectical approach to knowledge and knowledge production that also informs feminist science and technology studies and anthropology (e.g. Haraway 1988; Strathern 2004). Collins, however, goes a step further by calling for academic projects to be politically transformative in order to be considered critical. My work is not activist in that immediate sense – rather I seek to draw attention to some common lapses in the discourse about race. As I will argue in this chapter, it is not sufficient to announce that race does not exist as a biological reality, i.e. that it would be a social construction *instead* – in order to undermine its effects. Rather, race needs to be analyzed as an intricate phenomenon that cannot be meaningfully assigned to either the realm of 'biology' or of 'society', but is constantly coproduced between them. I therefore suggest a topological approach that pays attention to the performance and articulation of race as a relational object.[5]

Towards a topological understanding of race

Topology is a concept that is helpful when thinking about the amorphous and slippery character of race (and other complex matters, see Mol and Law 1994). It provides a spatial model with which we can conceive of fluidity and concreteness concurrently.[6] Against the linearity of time (or a teleological take on history) and the fixity of coordinates in Euclidean space, it offers a dynamic understanding of relational ontologies. A narrative of progress would suggest that race, as a false and dangerous concept, would gradually disappear the more we know and understand about biological diversity on the one hand, and the more we act against social inequality on the other. Obviously, this is not quite the case: race disappears and reappears in ever-changing and surprising constellations. Race cannot be pinpointed to one thing that is already known in advance. It is therefore important to pay attention to the nodes, holes and fissures through which the multiple connections between different sectors and their racializing effects become visible. We should thus make an effort to investigate the epistemic genealogies and multiple references through which race is 'gaining in reality' (Latour quoted in Hartigan 2008: 166) in concrete practices.

This topological view goes along with an understanding of diversity that is non-descriptive and not normatively loaded as 'good' (or even 'neutral') in itself. The topological approach allows us to pay critical attention to political and scientific projects that aim to monitor, manage or explore diversity – often understood in terms of 'natural' groups (of 'cultures', 'minorities', 'migrants', 'ethnicities', 'populations' or the like). The diversity that is the subject of such projects is 'not a given but made' (M'charek 2009: 422) – like race, it is the product of a specific and contingent configuration of social, material, technical and political elements. Talking about race in the singular (that is, *not* races), but racial effects in the plural, enables me to pay attention to the multiplicity of components that situationally and relationally produce race. If the concept of diversity connotes this fluidity, it can be turned into a useful methodological tool to think about race in the twenty-first century.

In the remainder of this essay, I will attempt to set a possible direction for this debate. I will mainly focus on recent debates on race in the life-sciences, and genomics in particular. It is here that diversity has featured prominently, also as a way of disproving the biological reality of race, while at the same time race has emerged as a matter of concern in and through the associated scientific practices, material base and political reverberations.

Race and the limits of social construction

As John Hartigan Jr. has put it bluntly and poignantly 'saying "socially constructed" is *not enough*' (Hartigan 2006, 2008; my emphasis) if we want to understand how race is being made and unmade in our post-genomic times. The issue that is at stake here is the common proclamation of race as a *social* construct that is put in opposition to claims of it to constitute a *natural* reality. This line of argumentation is sometimes accompanied by references to scientific evidence to verify the non-existence of race as natural kind. Once this fact has been established, our role as social scientists would be to deal with the realities of racial oppression in society. This assertion, however, reproduces a problematic dichotomy of biology (as nature) and society (as culture and politics) – as if these were independent and self-contained categories.[7] It also simplifies the ways in which race is actually performed. Increasingly, racialization occurs without an explicit reference to biology. A sole focus on the production and naturalization of biological differences fails to acknowledge the various intersections and overlaps of biological references with class, citizenship, religion, morality, lifestyle, etc. In certain constellations these seemingly unrelated aspects, which in themselves do not signify race, come together and produce racial effects. In a similar vein, it is also important to note that contemporary biological research on human differences does not *automatically* re/produce race science or race for that matter (Abu El-Haj 2012). In order to understand how racialization occurs in these settings, one has to go beyond mere analogies. As Michael Montoya (2007) has argued, it is through subtle processes of bioethnic conscription, a mix of descriptive and ascriptive practices, that race may come to the fore in contemporary genetic studies that investigate genetic dispositions for diseases in ethnically or racially defined populations.

A topological analysis of race goes further than that, however. It not only considers the nature/culture of biological fact-making between observation and ascription of meaning (Marks 2013: 250), but also necessarily pays attention to extra-scientific, or seemingly unrelated, aspects that play a role in the performance of race – without falling into the trap of reducing the discussion to these. The debate about BiDil, which became the first 'racial drug', marketed exclusively to African Americans, is a good case in point (see Kahn 2013). As African Americans suffer disproportionately from heart failure and other cardiovascular diseases, and BiDil apparently 'works better' in African Americans, the suggestion was that the susceptibility to heart failure, as well as

African Americanness and the correlation between the two were mere biological, i.e. genetic, facts that could be targetted by a pharmaceutical solution. However, other factors, such as the effects of racism on African American bodies, as well as the specific conditions under which the data of the medical trial were produced or the patenting interests of the company which is marketing BiDil, were largely ignored in the reasoning behind the licensing of the drug by the Food and Drug Administration (FDA). These latter arguments focused solely on efficacy. Issues of racism and inequality found their way back into the debate through the enthusiastic embrace of BiDil by the National Association for the Advancement of Colored People (NAACP) who saw it as a positive step towards the improvement of the general health of African Americans. It is thus not sufficient to criticize BiDil for being 'racial'. We rather need to ask *how exactly* race is brought about in this specific configuration – not as an objective fact among others (as the licensing seems to suggest), nor as a mirror of the race science of old (as some critics have argued), but instead as a result of the specific material-semiotic configuration called BiDil.

Race and the politics of science

With regard to a discussion of race it is also important to recognize that the strict separation of science and politics was upheld during the high-time of race science – even if it is evident now that the scientific practice was largely informed by ideological assumptions. This is not to say that race scientists were simply trapped in the politics of the day – surely, there were also contemporaneous critics who articulated their stance against scientific racism. Nevertheless, the majority of the involved scientists declared unanimously that they had no explicit interest in politics, or that their work had been 'abused' by politicians (see Lipphardt 2008). The official goal of race science was to prove that race, and white supremacy for that matter, were a biological reality that could be objectively assessed – through meticulous practices of measurement, association and comparison. Even if they hardly reached a consensus about the exact qualities of the various racial types, the degree of variation within or the correct distinction between them, race science and eugenics were widely regarded as serious work. And it was precisely through its claim to independence and objectivity that race science could serve as a powerful legitimation of regimes of racial oppression.

With the unravelling of the eugenic perversions in Nazi Germany and the demise of the typological paradigm, the scientific practices that were employed in the determination of racial difference were shown to be tainted by racist suppositions; moreover, they were unmasked as bad science (Gould 1981). In his seminal work *The Mismeasure of Man*, Stephen Jay Gould clearly argued against 'the myth that science itself is an objective enterprise, done properly only when scientists can shuck the constraints of their culture and view the world as it really is' (Gould 1981: 21). While Gould's argument refers to scientific practice in general, the association of race science or scientific racism is often that of a *pseudo*science. This connotation also has a side-effect, especially for the popular understanding of the social construction of race. It produces the image of a complete break with the past, leaving the claim to scientific objectivity and the underlying distinction of politics, nature and science largely untouched.

In many anti-racist fora, the proclamation that race is a fiction or a myth, yet with profound repercussions in the lives and experiences of real people, is one of the basic assumptions in the struggle for transformation. It partly relies on the scientific disproof of the biological value of conventional racial groupings. Likewise, population geneticists, most prominently perhaps Luigi Luca Cavalli-Sforza, have not ceased to announce publically that their research on human diversity has contributed fundamentally to the dismissal of race as a relevant factor in human evolution and thus to the demise of racism. This has been willingly taken up, for example in post-apartheid South Africa, where the scientific evidence of common human origins and the accompanying rhetoric of unity in diversity have been marketed as important steps towards a post-racial society (see Bystrom 2009; Schramm 2014b). During a symposium on 'The Human Genome and Africa', which took place in 2003 on the initiative of the South African Genome Education Institute, Cavalli-Sforza was celebrated as 'the "honest man" who aims to eliminate racism' (Morris 2003a). He is quoted as follows:

> The real message that I want to put across is that difference, genetically between continents and races – which correspond – are really a small part of human variation. . . . It is ridiculous that we are racist because we are merely different for having adapted to different climates.
>
> *(Cavalli-Sforza quoted in Morris 2003b)*

Criticizing diversity and acknowledging the complexity of race

So far, so good. But does this really help us to understand the ongoing significance of race-trouble? Cavalli-Sforza locates racism and the corresponding lay concepts of race solely in the overvaluation of somatic differences between people and groups. Once this misunderstanding is overcome, so goes the logic, racism will lose its foundation and an appreciation of diversity will take its place (see also Soodyall 2003). And yet Cavalli-Sforza's own work has been not only utilized in anti-racist discourse (as in the quote just given), but also heavily criticized as racist practice in other contexts, most notably through the highly contested Human Genome Diversity Project (HGDP) (cf. M'charek 2005, 2009; Reardon 2005).[8] How is that possible? The HGDP was meant to balance the apparent euro-centrism of the Human Genome Project – and to demonstrate the richness of human genomic variation. The main concern was the documentation of so-called indigenous groups that were thought of as biological (and cultural) isolates, whose genomes would provide valuable information on human evolution. Supporters argued for the urgency of the sampling, because with increasing globalization and the accompanying 'interbreeding' and 'admixture', indigenous people were about to vanish – they were conceived of as being on the edge of extinction.

The critics of this project, of which there were many, including indigenous activists, lawyers, historians of science, anthropologists, etc., have highlighted the problematic linkages of the HGDP to colonial practices of science and governance, and to the racial effects that went along with it. These connections were by no means straightforward – the HGDP did not simply mirror the assumptions of scientific racism – on the contrary, it aimed in an opposite direction. Race did not come to the fore in genetic sequences or through a biological hierarchy of difference. Neither was it simply a matter of old-fashioned nomenclature. Instead, it was produced via a combination of strands: the conceptualization of indigeneity outside of historical and political circumstances (including colonial violence and contemporary struggles, cf. Gordon 2009; TallBear 2013); the juxtaposition of stasis and mobility for different people ('traditional'/indigenous vs. 'modern'); the rhetoric of salvage anthropology, reminiscent of the large-scale sampling efforts of the early twentieth century; the connected reverberations of colonial violence in the gathering of scientific data (cf. Hoffmann 2009); ethical concerns about benefit sharing and informed consent; the political histories inscribed in the materiality of samples (cf. Schramm 2014a), etc. Consequently, the critique of the HGDP and its successors concentrated on the analysis of concrete practices of sampling, comparison and meaning-making as well as the interactions between scientists, subjects, materialities (such as blood samples and other specimens), representations and technologies as well as economic and legal issues.

Concluding remarks

'Staying with the trouble', Donna Haraway's (2010) catchy phrase for addressing the role of companion species in contemporary (posthumanist) biopolitics, helps me to summarize the approach that I have laid out in this essay. The trouble with race, indeed, is manifold. First of all, race-trouble connotes the violence that went along with racial classification and the accompanying regimes of oppression. It reverberates through various channels, whenever race is referenced – though not always in the same way. This brings me to the second point, which also links up to the topological approach that I have suggested: the contemporary trouble with race cannot always be anticipated – since race is not this one fixed entity that can be easily known or dismissed. Staying with the trouble means precisely to pay attention to the intersections and relations through which race becomes articulated. Thirdly, race, as a troubling object, calls into question the very possibility of neutral description or analysis. It shows how closely nature, culture and politics are entwined. The trouble cannot be fully resolved; it can only be transformed.

Notes

1   Kwame Anthony Appiah (1992) has argued that Du Bois was nevertheless 'trapped' in biological notions of race. I disagree with Appiah on two grounds. First, Du Bois always analyzes race in a political framework; even if he speaks about the black body and soul this is never detached from social relations and historical circumstances. Second, as I will demonstrate, Appiah's implicit suggestion that one could neatly distinguish between biological (denoting racism) and social (denoting emancipation) notions of race is misleading – even if it is still widespread and was sometimes followed by Du Bois himself.
2   In the political realm, this is, of course, a qualified diversity; see the onslaught on so-called multiculturalism (which both German and British politicians have declared to be 'dead' or 'have utterly failed') plus the ever more restrictive, even deadly, politics of European border regimes designed to keep the undesired 'other' at bay (see M'charek et al. 2013).
3   This narrative, of course, is a simplification – debates on race and human variation in the field of biology took many turns; for a brief discussion, which also pays attention to the co-constitution of race as a social formation, always combining 'biological' and 'social' categories, see Outlaw (1990).
4   Obviously, the 'racial state' as a complex social formation has not vanished either, even if its particular forms of articulation have changed. For a careful analysis of such re-articulations of race, the United States post-civil rights and Black Power, see Omi and Winant (1994).
5   My thinking around this issue has evolved through joint conversations with Amade M'charek and David Skinner (M'charek et al. 2013); see also M'charek (2014).
6   In mathematics, topology describes the consistency of an object under conditions of constant plasticity and transformation.
7   The division between these realms also reflects distinct (and often fiercely opposed) disciplinary debates, especially between biological and social/cultural anthropology. For attempts at bridging these gaps, see Mukhopadhyay and Moses (1997), Goodman and Leatherman (2001) and recently Ingold and Palsson (2013).
8   In the meantime, with increasing sequencing and computational capacity, there has been a large proliferation of such projects – from the HapMap to the Genographic Project to various national genome projects, for example the Mexican IMMIGEN or the South African Human Genome Project (SAHGP). I will stick to the HGDP because it has been so iconic and therefore helps to illustrate the dynamic relationship between concepts of race and diversity.

References

Abu El-Haj, N. (2012) *The Genealogical Science: The Search for Jewish Origins and the Politics of Epistemology*, Chicago, IL: Chicago University Press.

Appiah, K.A. (1992) *In My Father's House: Africa in the Philosophy of Culture*, Oxford, UK: Oxford University Press.

Bonilla-Silva, E. (2003) *Racism Without Racists: Color-Blind Racism and the Persistence of Racial Inequality in the United States*, Lanham, MD: Rowman & Littlefield.

Bystrom, K. (2009) 'The DNA of the Democratic South Africa: Ancestral Maps, Family Trees, Genealogical Fictions', *Journal of Southern African Studies*, 35(1): 223–35.

Collins, P.H. (2011) 'What is "Critical" about Critical Race Theory?', in G. Delanty and S.P. Turner (eds) *Routledge International Handbook of Contemporary Social and Political Theory*, London: Routledge.

Du Bois, W.E.B. (1903) *The Souls of Black Folk*, Chicago, IL: McClurg.

—(1940) *Dusk of Dawn*, Millwood, NY: Kraus-Thomson.

—(1996) [1923] 'The Superior Race', in E.J. Sundquist (ed.) *The Oxford W.E.B. Du Bois Reader*, Oxford, UK: Oxford University Press.

Duster, T. (2003) *Backdoor to Eugenics*, London: Routledge.

Foucault, M. (1982) 'The Subject and Power', in H. Dreyfus and P. Rabinow (eds) *Michel Foucault: Beyond Structuralism and Hermeneutics*, Chicago, IL: University of Chicago Press.

Goodman, A.H. and Leatherman, T.L. (2001) *Building a New Biocultural Synthesis: Political-Economic Perspectives on Human Biology*, Ann Arbor, MI: University of Michigan Press.

Gordon, R. (2009) '"Dirty Words": Nomenclature and the African Human Genome Project', in K. McKenna (ed.) *The Proverbial Pied Piper: Festschrift for Wolfgang Mieder*, Frankfurt/Main: Lang.

Gould, S.J. (1981) *The Mismeasure of Man*, New York, NY: Norton.

Haraway, D. (1988) 'Situated Knowledges: The Science Question in Feminism and the Privilege of Partial Perspective', *Feminist Studies*, 14(3): 575–99.

—(2010) 'When Species Meet: Staying with the Trouble', *Environment and Planning D*, 28(1): 53–5.

Hartigan Jr., J. (2006) 'Saying "Socially Constructed" is not Enough', *Anthropology News*, 47(2): 8.

—(2008) 'Is Race Still Socially Constructed? The Recent Controversy over Race and Medical Genetics', *Science as Culture*, 17(2): 163–93.

Hoffmann, A. (ed.) (2009) *What We See: Reconsidering an Anthropometrical Collection from Southern Africa: Images, Voices, and Versioning*, Basel: Basler Afrika Bibliographien.

Ingold, T. and Palsson (eds) (2013) *Biosocial Becomings: Integrating Social and Biological Anthropology*, Cambridge, UK: Cambridge University Press.

Kahn, J. (2013) *Race in a Bottle: The Story of BiDil and Racialized Medicine in a Post-Genomic Age*, New York: Columbia University Press.

Koenig, B.A., Lee, S.J.S. and Richardson, S.S. (eds) (2008) *Revisiting Race in a Genomic Age*, New Brunswick, NJ: Rutgers University Press.

Lewontin, R.S. (1972) 'The Apportionment of Human Diversity', *Evolutionary Biology*, 6: 381–98.

Lipphardt, V. (2008) 'Das "Schwarze Schaf" der Biowissenschaften: Marginalisierungen und Rehabilitierungen der Rassenbiologie im 20. Jahrhundert', in D. Rupnow (ed.) *Pseudowissenschaft: Konzeptionen von Nichtwissenschaftlichkeit in der Wissenschaftsgeschichte*, Frankfurt/Main: Suhrkamp.

Marks, J. (2013) 'The Nature/Culture of Genetic Facts', *Annual Review of Anthropology*, 42(1): 247–67.

M'charek, A. (2005) *The Human Genome Diversity Project: An Ethnography of Scientific Practice*, Cambridge, UK: Cambridge University Press.

—(2009) 'Extravagance, or the Good and the Bad of Genetic Diversity', in P. Atkinson, P. Glasner and M. Lock (eds) *Routledge International Handbook of Genetics and Society: Mapping the New Genomic Era*, London: Routledge.

—(2014) 'The HeLa Error: On Race, Time and Folded Objects', *Theory Culture and Society*. Published Online. Available HTTP: <http://tcs.sagepub.com/content/early/2014/01/24/0263276413501704> (accessed 16 April 2014).

M'charek, A., Schramm, K. and Skinner, D. (2013) 'Topologies of Race: Doing Territory, Population, and Identity in Europe', *Science, Technology and Human Values*. Published Online. Available HTTP: <http://sth.sagepub.com/content/early/2013/11/13/0162243913509493> (accessed 16 April 2014).

Mol, A. and Law, J. (1994) 'Regions, Networks and Fluids: Anaemia and Social Topology', *Social Studies of Science*, 24(4): 641–71.

Montoya, M.J. (2007) 'Bioethnic Conscription: Genes, Race, and Mexicana/o Ethnicity in Diabetes Research', *Cultural Anthropology*, 22(1): 94–128.

Morris, M. (2003a) 'The "Honest Man" Who Aims to Eliminate Racism', *The Daily Genome*, 21 March.

—(2003b) 'Emphasis on Races "Absolutely Ridiculous"', *The Daily Genome*, 23 March.

Mukhopadhyay, C.C. and Moses, Y.T. (1997) 'Reestablishing "Race" in Anthropological Discourse', *American Anthropologist*, 99(3): 517–33.

Omi, M. and Winant, H. (1994) *Racial Formation in the United States: From the 1960s to the 1990s*, London: Routledge.

Outlaw, L. (1990) 'Toward a Critical Theory of "Race"', in D.T. Goldberg (ed.) *Anatomy of Racism*, Minneapolis, MN: University of Minnesota Press.

Reardon, J. (2005) *Race to the Finish: Identity and Governance in an Age of Genomics*, Princeton, NJ: Princeton University Press.

Schramm, K. (2014a) 'From the Kalahari to the Mitochondrial Eve: Travelling Samples, Race and Representation in Genomic Research', Paper delivered at the Conference 'Mapping Science and Technology in Africa: Traveling Technologies and Global Dis\orders', 12–15 February 2014, WISER, Johannesburg.

—(2014b) 'Vom Horror des Hybriden zur Zelebrierung genetischer Vielfalt: Rasse und Genealogie in Südafrika', in C. Bender and M. Zillinger (eds) *Handbuch der Medienethnographie*, Berlin: Reimer.

Schramm, K., Skinner, D. and Rottenburg, R. (eds) (2011) *Identity Politics and the New Genetics: Re/Creating Categories of Difference and Belonging*, Oxford, NY: Berghahn.

Soodyall, H. (2003) *A Walk in the Garden of Eden: Genetic Trails into our African Past*, Cape Town: Human Sciences Research Council.

Strathern, M. (2004) *Partial Connections*, updated edn, Walnut Creek, CA: AltaMira.

TallBear, K. (2013) 'Genomic Articulations of Indigeneity', *Social Studies of Science*, 43(4): 509–34.

UNESCO (1969) *Four Statements on the Race Question*, Paris: UNESCO.

Vertovec, S. (2012) '"Diversity" and the Social Imaginary', *European Journal of Sociology*, 53(3): 287–312.

5

Racing diversity

Ethnicity, euphemisms, and 'others'

Ruth Mandel

How does diversity articulate with ethnicity and race?[1] Where and what are the borders, and how are they delimited? Where does one start and the other stop? Are there overlapping spheres? This chapter attempts to address these questions, giving examples of the ways in which these terms are used in popular discourse, and offering some anthropological ideas about how to approach these questions.

Countless trees have been felled in the quest for producing debates about and definitions of "ethnic," "ethnicity," and "race." Anthropologists, sociologists, political scientists, demographers, and novelists, to name a few, have all got their feet wet (and often muddy) trying to address the questions raised by these problematic and often shifting, inconsistent terms.

Over the last couple of decades, much of the anthropological literature on race approaches it as a social construction, albeit one that has very powerful consequences in everyday life. Whiteness, for example, is a "structural position conferring privilege and power" (Frankenberg in Hartigan 1999: 185). Similarly, it is seen as an "organising principle in social and cultural relations" (Lipsitz in Hartigan 1999: 185). The same definitions could easily be applied to "ethnicity." Comaroff (1996) writes of ethnicity in terms of the structuring of inequalities. But we could posit the same for race, and processes of racialization.

We know that ethnicity and race play out differently in different historical, geographic, and social contexts. The ethnic or racial hierarchies of one place are not necessarily those of another. Sometimes this is due to differences in the way social class is organized. This very fact leads us to the conclusion that the categories themselves are far from fixed, and any attempt to pin them down ultimately results in reifications that are not particularly useful to think with. Instead, one way to explore this is by thinking of the terms and concepts to which they refer as attempts to deal with different notions of difference and the process of perceiving and creating marked and unmarked categories.

But is this the same as diversity: a seemingly neutral term, implying variety and difference? What does this – diversity – imply when grappling with ethnicity and race? It might be useful to consider the equation: *race : ethnicity :: multiculturalism : diversity.*

It is arguable that once race assumed a veneer of political incorrectness, ethnicity arose to euphemize the same referent. Often the two are used interchangeably, both in academic writing as well as in popular everyday speech. Likewise, with the increasing criticisms of multicultural-ism, diversity seems to have replaced it in colloquial usage.

When considering notions of markedness that underlie the processes of ethnicization and racialization, does this then transpose to diversity, but meaning instead an absence of markedness, where diversity simply is an observable neutral descriptor? Or, is diversity merely the latest of a series of concepts crafted to deal with the discomfiture of multicultural markedness?

A brief genealogy

In the USA, once the assumptions informing the assimilationist melting pot theories were seen to have failed, the discourse then shifted to civil rights, integration, and hyphenated identity poli-tics. Following this, multiculturalism moved into center stage, with ethnicity as the side-show. Now, with the advent of diversity, is it a coincidence that the diversity industry is emerging (arguably as a conceptual loss leader) at the same time that multiculturalism is widely deemed to have failed? Has diversity become the politically more correct iteration of multiculturalism, side-stepping ethnic awkwardness?

Ethnic awkwardness arises when folk theories of ethnicity, conforming to classifications that are ostensively referential, slide into social science discourse. Taxonomically anomalous, the laundry list approach always left much to be desired when reproducing the rigid and ultimately circular ethnic models: "to be an ethnic group there must be these 11 shared characteristics . . ."; because one is an ethnic x, y, or z, one is therefore a, b, or c. Barth's watershed moment, a genera-tion ago, inspired a spate of scholarship. It has been taken on board by many, but not all who deal unselfconsciously with what is simply "assumed" to be "ethnic" – particularly not all the diversity theorists. Barth's (1969) insight was that the "cultural content of ethnic consciousness may be a product, rather than the constitutive basis, of 'ethnic group organisation'" (Barth 1969: 11). Thus, for our purposes, the process of ethnicization rather than the reified ethnic group is often what is absent in the diversity discourse.

When considering these terms along with the ideas and ideologies that generated them, we cannot help but reflect on questions of identity and otherness. For is this not the common denominator of these amorphous, contradictory, elusive concepts? In other words, these conceptual debates actually revolve around the implicit threat to a putative homogeneity (see Williams 1989); the responses came to be labeled ethnicity[2] multiculturalism and its successor, diversity.

Diversity, Inc.[3]

A simple online search reveals the almost random plethora of events, programs, policies, publica-tion, and images of diversity – even a diversity scorecard. All of them share one key element: the underlying value is that diversity is "good." Many mission statements about diversity treat it as an aspirational public good, and see it as forward-looking and progressive. But what is the "it"? To misquote Gertrude Stein, is there any there, there? Moreover, there usually is an assumption that we all implicitly know what it is; this is as convenient as it is sloppy, since rarely is it defined in any consistent way. Take, for instance, the claim of a large US university (the University of Washington) on its diversity policy: " . . . diversity is integral to excellence. We value and honor diverse experiences and perspectives, strive to create welcoming and respectful learning environ-ments, and promote access, opportunity and justice for all."

Echoing the closing words of the USA Pledge of Allegiance ("with liberty and justice for all"), by substituting opportunity and access for liberty, we learn that diversity is integral to excellence. Since no one could dispute the desirability of excellence, by a syllogistic property diversity is, therefore, equally and indisputably desirable. The statement affirms that diverse experiences and perspectives are honored and valued. These lofty words are followed by descriptions of the array of programs falling under the diversity rubric.

The first image illustrating the university's diversity is of Native Americans building a longhouse, to become a "learning and gathering place for Native American students, faculty and staff." Scrolling down, in search of other diversity programs, a confusing set of categories appears. Apparently diversity comes in many shapes and sizes: it is the provision of internet technology for members of the university community with disabilities; social work students are supported in another diversity program, in their efforts to fight oppression and work to build social justice; the diversity "dream project" is part of bridging social and economic class disparity, as university students are paired with low-income high school pupils to help prepare them for their dream of attending college; women, minorities, and people with disabilities are targeted by the diversity programming in engineering, aimed at encouraging these under-represented groups in science, technology, engineering, and mathematics. Furthermore, rounding out the diversity programming are the Native American Law Center, the Global Health and Justice Project, and a handful of others.

When considering these worthy projects, one is hard-pressed to derive a coherent definition of diversity based on these juxtaposed programmatic initiatives. Still, is it possible to identify any sort of common denominator that informs the university's Chief Diversity Officer's strategy, and the Diversity Blueprint the Diversity Office produces? I would suggest that the subtextual denominator connecting all of these is a negative definition; in other words: those who are not from the able-bodied male heterosexual white (presumably WASP) upper middle-classes.

This becomes clear when examining the areas the university's diversity fund-raising efforts target. Specifically, they solicit private donations to support a range of programs to support "underrepresented racial and ethnic minorities," and to promote "cultural, racial and ethnic diversity."

As such, it is at this juncture that race and ethnicity emerge into the diversity equation. Race and ethnicity are implicated further when we examine the ways diversity is conceived and used by businesses, managers, and employers in a wide range of industries and institutions. In this age in which identity politics is often taken for granted, many institutions now self-consciously aim to incorporate diversity – variously defined and deployed – into the workplace.

An in-depth study of the diversity business in higher education was carried out by Sara Ahmed (2012) in Australia. Among other things, she found that diversity programs often obscure as much as they reveal about institutional practices and ideologies. Furthermore, the mere act of incorporating diversity programs in an institution, in some cases "proves" the absence of racism.

The ultimate contradiction

On the one hand, we assume that many share the aspiration to a race-blind society, sometimes expressed as "post-racial." This would mean, presumably, that race would no longer be the key social demarcator it is today in many contexts. It would further mean that at the workplace, race is ignored, that individuals qua individuals are considered and that their abilities are recognized along with their multilayered and unique sets of attributes. On the other hand, with the advent of the diversity industry, people are told that they must acknowledge race and take it into consideration at holidays and festivals, in making hiring and firing decisions, promotions, and so on. How can we have it both ways? As a character in a US sitcom put it: "So I am supposed to celebrate your difference while at the same time totally ignoring it, right?".[4]

Thus, the relationship between marking, celebrating, and objectifying difference, on the one hand, and the overcoming of it, on the other, is an ongoing tension not easily resolved or resolvable.

The USA spends 400–600 million dollars annually on diversity training experts, the consultants who teach the concept and practices servicing the eight billion dollar per year diversity industry. One tool that the diversity specialists often use is the Diversity Wheel.

Diversity Wheels

When businesses get into the business of diversity, often they make use of what is known as a Diversity Wheel. The Diversity Wheel, designed by Marilyn Loden and Judy Rosener in 1991, was an attempt to make explicit the social characteristics of personal identity. Their initial Diversity Wheel has been copied, expanded, and adapted countless times. The original comprised two concentric circles. The smaller, inner circle was split into six sections: race, ethnicity, age, gender, physical abilities/qualities, and sexual/affectional orientation. The outer wheel contains these characteristics: work background, income, marital status, military experience, religious beliefs, geographic location, parental status, and education (Johnson 2006). The two circles were meant to represent innate attributes (inner circle) versus acquired attributes (outer circle) of the individual, along an implicit axis of privilege versus lack thereof – or even oppression (ibid.). The underlying purpose is to make explicit not only how the different components converge to produce one's place in a social hierarchy, but also how individuals are perceived by others. It is meant as well for those using the Diversity Wheel to understand and reflect upon how they perceive and treat others and how their behavior may or may not be guided by the possession or lack of specific characteristics – or combinations of characteristics – indicated on the wheel. It is hoped that, by making these objectified elements explicit, people will be able more easily to transcend prejudice and bias.

There are a number of problems that an anthropologist might have with this approach to diversity. First, what are assumed to be assigned, inherent qualities in some cases are not at all, but represent identity attributes that can be chosen and changed. Next, the process of objectifying people through these categories risks reification, where procrustean beds of identity traits come to define individuals, locking them into stereotypes in the name of diversity training.

Some critics claim that diversity training simply does not work. Peter Bregman (2012) in the *Harvard Business Review* bases his criticism on years of working as a trainer in the field, most often with human relations departments. In the USA, in this age of proliferating litigation along with a rights-based culture and identity politics, institutions need to be mindful of lawsuits charging them with discrimination violations of a variety of sorts. Bregman claims that much of the "diversity training" is really aimed at preventative lawsuits, teaching managers in particular what they may and may not say. In other words, it is a prophylactic damage limitation exercise, bordering the realm of free speech and self-censorship. Another aspect of diversity training, he proposes, is "to create an inclusive environment in which each member of the community is valued, respected, and can fully contribute their [sic] talents. That includes reducing bias and increasing the diversity of the employee and management population." (Bregman 2012).

In other words, when tools such as the now ubiquitous Diversity Wheel sort and spin people into categories as a way of demonstrating diversity, instead they may have the opposite effect of reinforcing the categories, and thus confirming prejudices. One way to understand prejudice is as the belief in the power of categories; as Bregman puts it: "People aren't prejudiced against real people; they're prejudiced against categories. 'Sure, John is gay,' they'll say, 'but he's not like other gays.' Their problem isn't with John, but with gay people in general." (ibid.).

In other words, the category of gay-ness is the problem, not the individual who affiliates with the category. It recalls the well-intentioned claim that "some of my best friends are … [fill in the blank]" as a conversational get-out clause confirming the speaker's lack of racism, anti-Semitism, or homophobia.

Diversity, then, runs the risk of being at once too narrow and too broad. Its narrowness occludes the embedding of the individual into multilayered contexts, into a subjectivity that might not conform to the wheels or other ascribed categories. The breadth of its deployment is equally problematic, in that it does not sufficiently challenge stereotyping (and even prejudices), nor does it necessarily allow for idiosyncrasies of individuals. Diversity workers sometimes find themselves trapped into conceptual gridlock; too much terminological and categorical traffic blocks potential movement and the free flow needed for intersubjective understandings.

John and Jean Comaroff (2009) discuss the ethnocommodity produced by the commodification of culture in various ethnic incarnations. For example, commodifying responses to ethno-tourism, in some cases, offers the sole possibility of ethnic groups to re-incorporate, to define themselves, to identify as a unit, and even to survive. This notion can be extended vis-à-vis diversity, but instead of a direct "diversocommodity," a diversity linked to a legal regime, a diverso-legality, where the diversity industry has arisen to respond to the new legal classificatory regime emerging out of the affirmative action impulse over the last few decades, as well as a political correctness stemming from identity politics.

Indeed, vigorous legal arguments have been put forth to support the diversity-affirmative action nexus. Orentlicher's (2005) work does precisely this. Taking several high court decisions about affirmative action and analyzing them, he demonstrates not only the legal basis, but also the more fundamental ideological – even constitutional basis – for diversity in the USA in spheres extending far beyond higher education. Including the realms of federal politics as well as finance in the defense of the value-added attributes of diversity, this surely describes one of the broadest arrays of meanings and practices of diversity.

Final thoughts and Diversity Month

"White folks are white; other people have race" – The American Anthropological Association's (1998) statement about race expressed the conviction that "racial beliefs constitute myths about diversity in the human species." As anthropologists well know, the power and persistence of myths cannot be understated. A cynic might speak of reification of the power and effects of the diversity industry as an anti-racist myth, convincing those believers who share in it of the political correctness of the given institution, thanks to a diversity policy.

How to escape the asymmetry implied by the quotation above? Just as "others have race," some "others" have ethnicity. These observations lead to further questions, from tokenism to taxonomy, that remain to be answered. Do or can quotas define diversity – or cure its problems? Do wealthy gay men diversify an institution in a way that the white heterosexual male underclass does not? And, we are left with questions about racial and ethnic classifications. The task remains for diversity theories and practices to be put in place in a way that would allow the beneficiaries to move beyond the categorical straightjackets and prejudice, the racism and the celebratory objectifications.

In an article about a "super-diverse" neighborhood in London, Wessendorf (2013) questions the differences between groups that subscribe to the "ethos of mixing" in public and associational space and those that do not. Fascinating in that here the "ethos to mix" appears to be the unmarked norm, it is the non-mixers (in this case ultra-orthodox Jews and young hipsters) who are marked. While leading predominantly separate lives, there nevertheless is a degree of frequent cross-cultural interaction among all but the two non-mixing groups. Though the article avoids defining diversity, it does propose a "commonplace diversity" in this complex urban environment. Perhaps a model of a trajectory for diversity studies, here is a case where convergence – albeit limited – of differences are unmarked and unremarkable. A noteworthy example of grass-roots diversity, needless to say, the mixing ethos has occurred without expensive training.

While writing this essay, an email intruded onto my screen, announcing February 2014 as UCL Diversity Month. Mine is not the only university that sponsors such events; countless institutions promote annual initiatives such as "diversity month" or "diversity week." Most of them celebrate "difference" along with diversity. What are we meant to understand by the lectures, music, films, and discussion groups about women, LGBT, the disabled, Muslims, immigrants, and minorities? One lecture on offer is called "Why isn't my professor black?"

As taxonomically inconsistent, as crudely objectifying and as tokenistic as it all might sound, no doubt it is better than not having it at all; indeed, our historical moment requires such events. Perhaps they need to be seen as a step toward the day that it will no longer become necessary to make hyper-visible that which will be taken for granted, when ethnicity/race/gender/etc. markedness loses its stigma, and ultimately fades into elective subjectivities.

On another note, diversity weeks and diversity months recall Tom Lehrer's old song parodying "National Brotherhood Week," whose final verse is: "Be nice to people who are inferior to you. It's only for a week, so have no fear. Be grateful that it doesn't last all year!"

Notes

1   I would like to thank Czarina Wilpert for taking the considerable time to brainstorm around these ideas with me. Her insights are always valuable, challenging and enlightening.
2   See Brackette Williams' brilliant review article in *Annual Reviews* (1989) for an in-depth analysis of these issues.
3   This is heavily influenced by and indebted to John and Jean Comaroff's (2009) *Ethnicity, Inc.*
4   Fox TV's *Andy Richter Show*, cited in review of Peter Wood (Derbyshire 2003).

References

Ahmed, S. (2012) *On Being Included: Racism and Diversity in Institutional Life*, Durham, MD: Duke University Press

American Anthropological Association (1998) 'Statement on "Race"'. Online. Available HTTP: <http://www.aaanet.org/stmts/racepp.htm> (accessed 14 April 2014).

Barth, F. (1969) 'Introduction', in F. Barth (ed.) *Ethnic Groups and Boundaries: The Social Organization of Culture Difference*, Boston, MA: Little, Brown & Company.

Bregman, P. (2012) 'Diversity Training Doesn't Work', *Harvard Business Review* Blog Network. Online. Available HTTP: <http://blogs.hbr.org/2012/03/diversity-training-doesnt-work/> (accessed 14 April 2014).

Comaroff, J.L. (1996) 'Ethnicity, Nationalism, and the Politics of Difference in an Age of Revolution', in E. Wilmsen and P. McAllister (eds) *The Politics of Difference: Ethnic Premises in a World of Power*, Chicago, IL: University of Chicago Press.

Comaroff, J.L. and Comaroff, J. (2009) *Ethnicity, Inc.*, Chicago, IL: University of Chicago Press.

Derbyshire, J. (2003) 'E pluribus plurimum', *The New Criterion*, 21(7): 64. Online. Available HTTP: <http://www.newcriterion.com/articles.cfm/wood-derbyshire-1794www.newcriterion.com> (accessed 9 April 2014).

Hartigan, J. (1999) 'Establishing the Fact of Whiteness', in R. Torres, L. Miron and J. India (eds) *Race, Identity and Citizenship*, London: Blackwell.

Johnson, A.G. (2006) *Privilege, Power, and Difference*, New York, NY: McGraw-Hill.

Orentlicher, D. (2005) 'Diversity: A Fundamental American Principle', *Missouri Law Review*, 70(3): 777–812.

Wessendorf, S. (2013) 'Commonplace Diversity and the "Ethos of Mixing": Perceptions of Difference in a London Neighbourhood', *Identities*, 20(4): 407–22.

Williams, B. F. (1989) 'A Class Act: Anthropology and the Race to Nation Across Ethnic Terrain', *Annual Review of Anthropology*, 18: 401–44.

6

Analysing status diversity

Immigration, asylum, and stratified rights

Lydia Morris

The post-national debate

The presence on national territory of those outside of national membership has long prompted interest in both the extent and the foundation of migrants' rights, with deliberation often focussed on the balance between universal claims and national particularism.[1] Writing of the stateless persons generated in the aftermath of the First World War, Arendt (1979) remarked on the 'hopeless idealism' and 'feeble minded hypocrisy' of human rights talk (ibid.: 269) when in practice the loss of citizenship meant an absence of all rights. This juxtaposition may be termed 'Arendt's paradox', and turned on the fact that any attempt to lay claim to universal human rights broke down when states were confronted with 'the abstract nakedness of being human' (ibid.: 299). Her fear was that the promise of human rights amounted to little more than 'a right of exception . . . for those who had nothing better to fall back on' (ibid.: 293). Though the situation today is somewhat changed and there now exists a wide range of treaties and conventions which can be called upon to support the position of trans-national migrants and asylum seekers, Arendt's argument has continuing contemporary relevance. This is captured by Benhabib's (2004) reflections on a dilemma at the heart of liberal democracy: 'There is not only a tension but often an outright contradiction, between human rights declarations and states' sovereign claims to control their borders as well as to monitor the quality and quantity of admittees' (ibid.: 2).

Habermas (1998) makes a similar point in speaking of the Janus-faced nature of the nation state, manifest in: 'The tension between the universalism of an egalitarian legal community and the particularism of a community united by historical destiny . . .' (ibid.: 115).

Nevertheless, a somewhat different sentiment has emerged in a body of literature which now sees a radical reconfiguration of the nation state and the emergence of a post-national society, as characterised by: 'A new and more universal concept of citizenship . . . whose organising and legitimating principles are based on universal personhood rather than national belonging' (Soysal 1994: 1).

In effect, Arendt's paradox is thus reversed to render a different problematic: the presumption of national membership alongside the long-term presence of trans-national migrants without citizenship in their country of stay, but who nevertheless possess a significant array of rights. Sassen (1998) has made a related argument in noting the '*de facto* trans-nationalisation of immigration issues' (ibid.: 6), citing in support the expansion of international treaties and conventions which deal with migrant rights, collaboration between member states within the European Union, and the power of human rights as a means to contest the authority of the state. Meyer *et al.* (1997) have addressed a similar set of issues, albeit at the level of normative ideals, identifying an emergent world culture that can shape and constrain the actions of nation states, which in effect become enactors of 'conventionalised scripts' rather than autonomous agents of their own history. Freeman (1995) saw the force of universal human rights claims as the key driver behind an expansionary bias in the immigration policies of liberal democracies, though he also recognised a contrary dynamic in the tightening of entry controls and deterrent treatment of asylum seekers.

For attempts at a concrete assessment of the post-national argument, much rests on the amount of sovereign control a state retains over the granting of entry and stay for trans-national migrants, and the delineation of their attendant rights. Certainly, the post-war dynamic has not been all in one direction, and there has been variation between national immigration regimes, even within the member states of the European Union (Morris 2002). Indeed, national immigration regimes are not only driven by universal obligations, but also strongly influenced by national interests framed in the context of particular circumstances. So, for example, while Germany's guestworkers gradually acquired a permanent presence, this was initially driven by employer demand at the national level (Jacobson 1997). Human rights were later brought to bear in securing the entry and stay of family members through family reunification, but this has operated with tight requirements of housing and maintenance on the part of the principal migrant, though no such conditions apply to German citizens.

Conversely, in Britain many early post-war migrants arrived with a full right of abode, derived from the status of British subject, which attached to being either a Citizen of the UK and Colonies or a Commonwealth citizen. However, in an attempt to restrict immigration this right was notoriously removed from those who did not have ties with Britain through naturalisation or descent (termed partiality) by the 1971 Immigration Act, a change that was then consolidated by the definition of British citizenship in the 1981 British Nationality Act (see JCWI 1997: 319). However, the continuing presence of trans-national migrants holding citizenship in the UK has meant that (unlike Germany) family (re)unification rules are conditional for citizens and non-citizens alike. There are other common rights limitations for non-citizen residents; even once permanent residence is secured, non-citizens are commonly denied the right to vote in national elections, while absolute security from deportation still rests with citizenship status. Thus, Joppke (2010) argues 'There are intrinsic vulnerabilities to non-citizen status that Soysal glosses over too easily' (ibid.: 22), such that: 'aliens never quite reach the position of comfort allotted to them by post-nationalists' (ibid.: 84).

The European Union is a frequent reference point for those espousing the post-national position (Sassen 1998; Soysal 1994) as it uniquely establishes a multi-national citizenship, allows freedom of movement between member states, and secures a raft of rights attendant on this mobility – albeit rights which privilege EU citizens over third country nationals. However, it is also commonly acknowledged that these developments are underpinned by enhanced control over external borders, and this has been reflected in the requirements for EU membership. Other trans-national conventions have a potentially wider purchase, but can be limited in a variety of ways – by granting protection only to citizens of countries which are party to the convention, by addressing the needs of particular groups (e.g. women, children, workers), by limiting rights to those who are lawfully present, etc. Even universal human rights contain their own legitimate hierarchy of qualified, limited and absolute rights, the former permitting conditions in support of an array of national concerns, and the latter raising difficult questions of interpretation and application. The result is that rights are often negotiated on a contested terrain which brings universal rights claims into confrontation with national interests, in an ever shifting struggle over both their content and boundaries.

Normative versus empirical claims

Bosniak (2000) points to a certain ambiguity in relation to concepts such as post-national, trans-national or global citizenship, such that, while these terms ostensibly describe a process of change in the structure and operations of the nation state, they also carry a normative message, which is not always made explicit. She therefore sees post-national citizenship as a trope: 'to invert the burden of justification, so that normative nationalism may itself be interrogated' (ibid.: 453), but as having only limited empirical resonance. In particular, it is held to neglect those aspects of alien status which fall under national control – terms of entry and stay, access to the labour market, social rights for family members, etc., rather than international human rights obligations, the power of which is sometimes overstated. An interesting link can be made here to a body of work on the concept of cosmopolitanism; work that challenges the very conception of a bounded national society, but is more explicitly normative in character, actively embracing those forces which seem to be undermining national closure.

Beck (2006), for example, speaks of the 'mythic' status of the national state and identifies a network of social forces and trans-national movements which challenge any inclination to equate 'society' with the boundaries of the nation state. In formulating this argument, however, he seeks to distinguish the normative ideal of cosmopolitanism from the empirical fact of 'cosmopolitani-sation', while at the same time recognising that national sentiment persists as a potentially con-flictual force. Although the institutionalisation and application of human rights have been key reference points for attempts to elaborate the relation between the normative and empirical aspects of cosmopolitanism, many writers sympathetic to the cosmopolitan ideal adopt a tone of caution. Habermas (2001), for example, notes a tension between the universal meaning of human rights and the local conditions of their realisation, while Fine (2007) sees a dilemma for citizens confronted by their own nationally constrained interpretations and a more distant cosmopolitan view. For those seeking to grapple with what appear as contradictory tendencies towards both the institutionalisation of human rights and enhanced national closure, an additional theoretical tool is required which can do justice to both the expansive potential of universal rights and the restrictive national forces at play.

A mediating mechanism

We need therefore to look at the ways in which the universal/particular opposition is mediated, and one key mechanism which allows the state to determine the terms of entry and stay on the national territory is immigration status. An early indication of how this process functions is to be found in Hammar's (1990) distinction between citizenship, denizenship and alien status, respectively signalling full membership, permanent residence and conditional presence. Similarly, Brubaker (1989) has elaborated distinctions in relation to legal status and associated entitlements which allow the state to designate differential rights to a variety of national resources. He also argues that the process of managing access to territory and resources has become increasingly complex, such as to render a 'proliferation of statuses of partial membership' (ibid.: 5), which requires fuller theorisation.

A promising framework for such theorising can be derived from the work of David Lockwood (1996) and the concept of civic stratification – a system of inequality which operates through the differential granting and delivery of rights by the state. Lockwood's own work is concerned with inequalities generated by the functioning of citizenship, such that: 'In contemporary capitalist democracies, the ethos and practice of citizenship is at least as likely as class relations to structure group interests and thereby fields of conflict and discontent' (ibid.: 536).

His argument, however, is well suited to analysis which moves beyond citizenship to address the differential granting of rights for different categories of migrant, as in the varying terms of access to the national territory, and to rights of residence, work and welfare, whose purpose is to encourage desirable categories of migrants while discouraging others. In Lockwood's argument, civic stratification operates along two axes: the presence or absence of rights, as governed by rules of eligibility, which may be termed the formal dimension; and possession of moral and material resources, which may informally influence access to or enjoyment of particular rights.

Applying these ideas to immigration status, it may therefore be argued that the formal dimension dictates the terms of access to the national territory, while the informal dimension reflects and/or shapes the public perception or standing of a given migrant group. There is therefore an interesting possibility that these two dimensions have a dynamic interconnection – as already implied by Lockwood's framework. Thus, where there are rights without moral or material resources we find civic deficit, while civic gain occurs when existing rights are enhanced by prestige factors. Where there is an absence of rights but access to moral or material resources we might expect to find civic expansion, and where there is both a formal denial of rights and an absence of moral or material resources we find civic exclusion. I have described elsewhere (Morris 2002, 2003) the way in which this system functions, but the dynamic of these two dimensions of civic stratification may repay further study in the context of immigration. While Lockwood's schema addresses movement through the idea of civic expansion, driven by recourse to moral and material resources, we must also recognise the logical possibility of civic contraction, especially where there is an absence or erosion of moral standing for a given group.

To take the UK as an example, at the formal level there is currently a five tier system for labour migration, and there are three statuses of protection[2] for asylum seekers, while in addition there will be incoming family members for some of these statuses, and an unknown number of undocumented migrants, some of whom will be failed asylum seekers. The formal designation of varied statuses with different rights attached illustrates the way in which rights can be harnessed as a means of governance, and indeed the number and designation of statuses can shift over time, as in the UK elaboration of first four and then five tiers for labour migration (see Morris 2007; Travis 2006), and the expansion of different statuses of protection (Home Office 2002). At EU level, a growing awareness of the need for highly skilled migrants saw the creation in 2009 of a blue card which extends free movement in the EU to highly skilled non-EU workers.

Changes in the formal contours of civic stratification may also be accompanied – or more likely preceded – by a justificatory discourse, as for example when UK asylum numbers were rising and we saw a growing rhetoric of disbelief linked to assertions that a majority of claims were 'bogus'.[3] A number of restrictive measures then followed, including the selective use of visa requirements, the elaboration of carrier sanctions and the reduction or removal of welfare support for asylum claimants. Conversely, with increasing employer demand for skilled workers, the UK government rhetoric shifted from a generalised denigration of economic migrants (Home Office 2002: 7) to an emphasis on the 'disproportionate contribution' (Blunkett 2003) that migrants make to the national economy. This sentiment is currently being revised in relation to free movement within the EU, as the UK Alliance government seeks to restrict access to benefits for workers from other member states, and to deter what it terms 'benefit tourism' and 'health tourism' (*The Guardian* 2013: 6). A statement from the Council of Europe's human rights commissioner, Nils Muiznieks, notes: 'The UK debate has taken a worrying turn as it depicts lower-skilled migrants as dangerous foreigners coming to steal jobs, lower salaries and spoil the health system' (Travis and Malik 2013: 6).

The commissioner goes on to make a link between such statements and wider public perceptions insofar as they may encourage negative stereotyping and hostility towards migrants. He refers in particular to the climate of concern over the newer EU member states, whereby: 'A stigma is put on Bulgarian and Romanian citizens just because of their origin' (ibid.).

Formal and informal status dynamics

These and other developments suggest a link between the formal and informal aspects of immigration status by virtue of a distinction between 'desirable' and 'undesirable' migrant groups, which is often accompanied by attempts to shape public perceptions as a means of garnering political support. This phenomenon is addressed by Schneider and Ingram (1993) in relation to the construction of 'target groups' in policy development more generally, such that a particular public image is deployed in the course of policy formulation to convey the sense of a problem with which politicians are actively struggling. Their analysis shows some similarities with Lockwood's in that it reflects differing degrees of moral standing, as implied by their classification of advantaged, contender, dependent and deviant. These categories would correspond to immigration status as follows: highly skilled migrants – advantaged/contenders; asylum seekers – dependent; and undocumented migrants – deviant. The 'target group' framework thus adds political motivation to Lockwood's conception of civic stratification and makes the dynamic element more explicit; indeed, Schneider and Ingram refer to 'pendulum swings' in policy over time as the political climate and policy preferences themselves undergo change. The combined effect of both analyses is to raise interesting questions about the source and direction of change in relation to both the formal and informal aspects of immigration status.

The informal status of particular groups seems to play an important role in this dynamic, and there is an apparent circularity in operation. According to Schneider and Ingram, politicians construct problems which are then amenable to policy treatment, and we have already noted examples from the UK, in the form of campaigns against 'bogus' asylum seekers and 'benefit tourism'. In such cases the negative presentation of a given group seeks to shape public opinion in advance of the introduction of a policy 'solution' which then confirms the group's 'undeserving' status by the denial of a right. Indeed, such manoeuvres often alight upon issues around which there is already potential public unease that can be engaged in support, and policy can thus both reflect and heighten existing public sentiment. Conversely, and perhaps in response, target groups may seek to engage public sympathy and support to challenge both their informal denigration and the formalised policy measures which follow, but their success will, in Lockwood's terms, depend on the ability to mobilise moral and material resources. However, both Lockwood and Schneider and Ingram recognise that, once established, negative perceptions or marginal groups become difficult to dislodge and indeed may be internalised such that: 'The capacity and opportunity to engage in collective action is further diminished by the indignity of the status itself' (Lockwood 1996: 546).

These writers therefore highlight the difficulties of mobilising for improved formal status confronting groups whose informal status has been diminished, and in this context they see increasing recourse to the courts as a possible means of asserting the rights of vulnerable groups. This possibility returns us to our opening question of how far national control over the terms of entry and stay can be overridden by international conventions, and more specifically how far the claims of trans-national migrants can be pursued through the courts. Alexander's (2006) writing on the civil sphere and the potential for building solidarity around commitment to a common secular faith is relevant here, and he suggests an approach to the law that views it as a form of symbolic representation. This argument complements a civic stratification framework in recognising not only that the law can function to formalise relations of exclusion and domination, but also that such divisions may be challenged through a process of civil repair. In this context, Alexander suggests that legal interpretations on the part of judges can serve both to reflect and to initiate broader social change, such that: 'In the course of social conflicts, individuals, organisations and large social groups may be transferred from one side of the social classification to another' (Alexander 2006: 234).

This type of argument draws our attention not only to the content of change in the standing and rights of particular groups, but also to the process whereby such changes may be established or challenged, and the judiciary will often be located at the critical edge of decisions over the content and boundary of rights.

The role of judgment

Noting a massive increase in judicial activism, Jacobson (1997) has argued that: 'The state is now a forum where trans-national laws and norms are administered, mediated, and enforced' (ibid.: 106).

This is in some respects a variant of the post-national argument, which sees state legitimacy rooted less in popular sovereignty than in trans-national human rights, such that sovereignty becomes secondary to the jurisdiction of the courts. Jacobson, however, argues that this development is not necessarily driven by intrinsic normative concerns, but operates in a piecemeal way, and through a series of *ad hoc* accommodations which nevertheless reflect a shifting locus of legitimacy. He therefore concludes that these accommodations do not constitute an emergent global society, and we find an echo of the civic stratification argument in his recognition that 'social distinctions are becoming ever more multifarious' (Jackson 1997: 134). The judiciary thus comes to occupy a central position in mediating the tension between post-national universalism and national particularism, while the courts as a deliberative forum can offer a participatory space for those excluded from the national polity (see Habermas 1995). Such legal procedure, especially where universal commitments have been written into domestic law, provides support for Beck's (2006) endeavour to break with a dichotomising view that sets the global and the national in opposition, and to see the national and trans-national as interlocking and mutually constituting phenomena.

However, a focus on the judicial process as a form of procedural deliberation (Habermas 1995) draws our attention to a degree of indeterminacy with respect to the content and boundary of rights, which is especially to the fore in developing areas of law, such as universal human rights (Dworkin 2005). Judgment does not stand apart from social and political life, but may both be shaped by and seek to shape prevailing social norms and values, so there is considerable scope for deliberative disagreement to take place both within the judiciary and between the judicial and executive branches of government. An example of this three cornered dialogue can be found in extended judicial deliberation over the UK withdrawal of welfare support from in-country asylum claimants. This entailed a total of 14 legal judgments over the legitimacy of such policy, and came to turn on the interpretation of inhuman and degrading treatment as expressed by article 3 of the European Convention on Human Rights. The legal history reveals opposing interpretations of article 3 which respectively endorse a restrictive and expansive reading (see Morris 2009), though it is the latter that eventually prevailed, albeit in cautious terms, making it clear that the ruling had no purchase for the indigenous homeless or for failed asylum seekers.

The example then raises one final question in relation to status, rights and recognition, and that is whether the restitution of rights through judicial rulings can restore the public standing of vulnerable groups for whom public denigration has served to legitimate a denial of rights. A link between rights and status was present in the work of T.H. Marshall (1950), who saw the conferral of citizenship as more than the guarantee of a set of civil, political and social rights, serving primarily as a recognition of equal status. This idea is further developed by Honneth (1995), who sees the granting or denial of rights as reflecting a struggle over normative conceptions of the social community and dominant interpretations of social worth, in which we can read the 'moral grammar' of a conflict. The law and legal judgment are therefore in close interaction with broader social and cultural forces which may respond positively or negatively to attempts to expand the boundary of rights. Indeed, instead of civic expansion we may witness civic deficit, whereby the claiming of a right may provoke a backlash, and can itself confirm a group in its negative status or condition of disrespect. In other words, rights alone cannot secure recognition, but may first require 'an alteration in our cognitive orientations and normative expectations' (Kompridis 2008: 305) to bring together the respectively formal and informal character of legal and social status.

Recognising the tendencies both in social and political sentiment and in academic debate that threaten to polarise opinion with respect to conceptions and perceptions of post-national society, this essay has looked rather to the intermediate terrain on which rights actually function. In so doing, it has opened up difficult questions about the delineation of formal inclusions and exclusions with respect to rights, and the informal status judgments which formal entitlements may variously influence or mirror. The associated outcome in terms of civic stratification constitutes a complex ground of status diversity, mediated by political decisions, public sentiment and judicial rulings, all of which are in close interaction. Negotiation and contestation over rights therefore reveal their indeterminate nature, shaped on any given occasion by the mutual friction between universalism and particularism, and holding a constant scope for both expansion and contraction that may defy attempts to conclusively fix their boundaries and their content.

Notes

1 For a fuller elaboration of these ideas see Morris (2010, 2013).
2 Full refugee status, Humanitarian Protection and Discretionary Leave.
3 See, for example, HC Hansard, 20 February 1996, col. 160; Lords Hansard 17 October 2002, col. 991.

References

Alexander, J.C. (2006) *The Civil Sphere*, Oxford, UK: Oxford University Press.
Arendt, H. (1979) *The Origins of Totalitarianism*, New York, NY: Harcourt Brace.
Beck, U. (2006) *Cosmopolitan Vision*, Cambridge, UK: Polity.
Benhabib, S. (2004) *The Rights of Others*, Cambridge, UK: Cambridge University Press.
Blunkett, D. (2003) 'Managing Migration in the 21st Century', Speech to the Royal Institute for International Affairs, London, 12 November.
Bosniak, L. (2000) 'Citizenship Denationalised', *Indiana Journal of Global Legal Studies*, 7(2): 447–510.
Brubaker, W.R. (ed.) (1989) *Immigration and the Politics of Citizenship in Europe and America*, Lanham, MD: University Press of America.
Dworkin, R. (2005) *Taking Rights Seriously*, London: Duckworth.
Fine, R. (2007) *Cosmopolitanism*, London: Routledge.
Freeman, G.P. (1995) 'Modes of Immigration Politics in Liberal Democratic States', *International Migration Review* 29(4): 881–902.
The Guardian (2013) 'No 10 Targets EU Migrants for Cuts to Income and Health Benefits', 25 March.
Habermas, J. (1995) *Between Facts and Norms*, Cambridge, UK: Polity.

—(1998) *The Inclusion of the Other*, Cambridge, UK: Polity.

—(2001) *The Post-national Constellation*, Cambridge, UK: Polity.

Hammar, T. (1990) *Democracy and the Nation State: Aliens, Denizens and Citizens in a World of International Migration*, Aldershot, UK: Avebury.

Home Office (2002) *Secure Borders, Safe Haven: Integration with Diversity in Modern Britain*, London: The Stationery Office Limited. Online. Available HTTP: <https://www.gov.uk/government/uploads/system/uploads/attachment_data/file/250926/cm5387.pdf> (accessed 9 April 2014).

Honneth, A. (1995) *The Struggle for Recognition*, Cambridge, UK: Polity.

Jacobson, D. (1997) *Rights Across Borders: Immigration and the Decline of Citizenship*, Baltimore, MD: Johns Hopkins University Press.

Joint Council for the Welfare of Immigrants (JCWI) (1997) *Immigration, Nationality and Refugee Law Handbook*, London: JCWI.

Joppke, C. (2010) *Citizenship and Immigration*, Cambridge, UK: Polity.

Kompridis, N. (2008) 'Struggling over the Meaning of Recognition', in K. Olson (ed.) *Adding Insult to Injury*, London: Verso.

Lockwood, D. (1996) 'Civic Integration and Class Formation', *British Journal of Sociology*, 47(3): 531–50.

Marshall, T.H. (1950) *Citizenship and Social Class and other Essays*, Cambridge, UK: Cambridge University Press.

Meyer, J., Boli, J., Thomas, G.M. and Ramirez, F.W. (1997) 'World Society and the Nation States', *American Journal of Sociology*, 103(1): 144–81.

Morris, L.D. (2002) *Managing Migration: Civic Stratification and Migrants Rights*, London: Routledge.

—(2003) 'Managing Contradiction: Civic Stratification and Migrants' Rights', *International Migration Review*, 37(1): 74–100.

—(2007) 'New Labour's Community of Rights: Welfare, Immigration and Asylum', *Journal of Social Policy*, 36(1): 39–57.

—(2009) 'An Emergent Cosmopolitan Paradigm? Asylum, Welfare and Human Rights', *British Journal of Sociology*, 60(2): 215–35.

—(2010) *Asylum, Welfare and the Cosmopolitan Ideal*, London: Routledge.

—(2013) *Human Rights and Social Theory*, London: Palgrave Macmillan.

Sassen, S. (1998) *Globalisation and its Discontents*, New York, NY: The New Press.

Schneider, A. and Ingram, H. (1993) 'Social Construction of Target Populations', *American Political Science Review*, 87(2): 334–46.

Soysal, Y. (1994) *Limits of Citizenship*, Chicago, IL: University of Chicago Press.

Travis, A. (2006) 'Immigration Shake-up Will Bar Most Unskilled Workers from Outside EU', *The Guardian*, 8 March.

Travis, A. and Malik, S. (2013) 'EU Rights Watchdog Accuses Britain of Shameful Rhetoric on Migrants', *The Guardian*, 30 March.

7

Sexual diversity

Momin Rahman

The underlying assumptions of sexual diversity

> After decades during which the words 'sexual orientation' and 'gender identity' were rarely uttered in formal, intergovernmental meetings at the United Nations, a debate is unfolding at the Human Rights Council in Geneva on the rights of lesbian, gay, bisexual and transgender people. The discussions at the Council have focused political attention on discriminatory laws and practices at the national level and on the obligations of States under international human rights law to address these through legislative and other measures.
>
> *(United Nations Office of the High Commissioner for Human Rights 2012: 9)*

This recent report is the first by the United Nations (UN) explicitly to include sexuality within its human rights framework and detail member obligations towards lesbian, gay, bisexual, transgender, intersexed and questioning (LGBTIQ)/queer[1] individuals. As such, it represents a significant milestone in the global legitimization of queer identities and rights. Many of us living in Western countries have witnessed the rise in public visibility resulting from the gay liberation movements that emerged in the West in the late 1960s and 1970s and the consequent recent citizenship advances such as same-sex partnerships and anti-discrimination laws. No doubt we have all similarly experienced resistance to LGBTIQ politics, often from religious groups but also from those who are more broadly in favour of the traditional social organization of genders and families, exemplified most recently by the Russian Duma's outlawing of homosexual 'propaganda' in June 2013 (although same-sex acts remain legal). Nonetheless, there have been significant changes in the public visibility of sexual diversity, and in light of these the underlying assumption around sexual issues is understandably one of *progress* towards social acceptance of sexual diversity. This view is shared by both queer and mainstream individuals, political organizations and, indeed, by some prominent queer academics such as Jeffrey Weeks (2007) in his optimistic overview of queer politics since gay liberation.

In this essay I will describe the main theoretical analyses of sexuality and demonstrate how they both underscore and undermine the common-sense public idea of progress. I begin with the ways in which sexual diversity is assumed to be a 'natural' minority deviation from normative gender regimes and identities in public culture, despite the fact that the foundational academic theories of sexual stigma were anti-naturalist and based on a critique of institutionalized gender identities. The Western capitalist liberal democratic societies in which gay liberation first emerged had established models for minority politics, and I suggest that this context, together with the cultural dominance of naturalist explanations of the sexual, combines to render queer politics as one of a 'natural minority' rather than a politics of full gender and sexual diversity. I then turn to the broader sociological explanations of the conditions that are understood to permit sexual diversity, focusing here on the consequences of Western modernity for the emergence of modern sexualities. I argue that, whilst these explanations are resolutely anti-naturalist, they nonetheless contain other assumptions, primarily that modernization processes are the key trigger to sexual diversity. In the final section, I bring both preceding sets of assumptions and critiques together to consider the contemporary internationalization of LGBTIQ politics and the assumption of progress behind these recent expansions. I argue that there is an assumption of Western exceptionalism underpinning the contemporary internationalization of queer rights and that this must be challenged to deliver a more effective politics of sexual diversity.

Sexual diversity as sexual minorities *within* institutionalized gender structures

Second wave feminist critiques argued that the basis of gender inequalities was social rather than natural and hence that we could transform social institutions, laws and ideologies to challenge oppression and move towards gender equality (Rahman and Jackson 2010). These theories fundamentally challenged the culturally dominant naturalist or essentialist understandings of gender, which effectively explained the subordination of women as an inevitable function of their biological capacities compared to those of men, based on ideas of inferiority in physical strength and mental capacity and their 'natural' role in child-bearing. The success of social explanations of gender has resulted in a genuine paradigm shift whereby many countries and international organizations such as the UN have explicit protections against gender discrimination, including policies to support women's equality and access to resources. Furthermore, many different feminist theorists agree that the social construction and regulation of sexuality was a key technology of gender oppression. The strand of feminist thought known as radical feminism is largely credited with developing these insights, notably through Kate Millett's (1971) analysis of patriarchy as a social system, Adrienne Rich's (1980) critique of institutionalized heterosexuality and Catharine A. MacKinnon's (1982) description of sexuality as the 'linchpin' of gender inequality. Again, we have seen significant successes in how sexual violence and exploitation are dealt with in the public and legal realms through the broad acceptance of radical feminist critiques. More specifically, there has been a recognition that the dominant understanding of 'natural' male sexual aggressiveness is, in fact, a socialized ideology and set of behaviours that reflect the patriarchal organization of society. Both by mainstreaming the idea that gender is socially produced, therefore, and by locating sexuality within the techniques of gender, institutionalized, normative heterosexuality has largely been opened up to scrutiny in significant ways.

What has been less successful has been the translation of these theories to the public understanding of non-heterosexual identities and behaviours, despite the fact that most radical feminist theories argue that the social construction of gender has created understandings of non-heterosexual or non-normative sexualities *in relation to* the dominant view of sexuality within normative gender. As Rich (1980) argues, the institutionalization of heterosexuality as particular forms of masculinity and femininity provides the basis for the stigmatization of homosexualities. The first wave of gay liberation from the 1970s contributed similar theoretical analyses, most notably in Mary McIntosh's (1996 [1968]) argument that the social labelling of the homosexual as deviant served to police the majority into heterosexuality, Ken Plummer's (1975) identification of the broad social scripts of sexual stigma and Michel Foucault's (1981) characterization of the emergence of the homosexual as a deviant 'species' through medical, psychological and legal practices that aimed to invest normative heterosexuality with social dominance. Moreover, by drawing on Foucault's theories and cross-cultural anthropology, the academic literature since the 1980s has emphasized that the equation of sexual behaviours with specific, discrete, sexual identities was a consequence of modern ideologies of regulation and science in the West and that, in fact, historical and cross-cultural evidence demonstrated a variety of homo-erotic behaviours and potentialities in all people, which did not universally equate same-sex acts with a homosexual 'type' of person. These two major insights about the relationality of hetero/homo and the historically specific social creation of a stigmatized essentialist homosexual identity have remained at the analytical core of the gradual institutionalization of sexuality studies in most Western academies since the era of gay liberation, regardless of different theoretical or disciplinary approaches. This critique of normative gender or heteronormativity as the basis of the social stigma of homosexual identities, same-sex behaviours and non-normative gender has, however, largely transformed *academic* rather than public discourse.

The lobbying for LGBTIQ human rights has been based on a minority and ethnic identity model that fundamentally reassures the majoritarian nature of heterosexuality precisely because it is based on essentialist understandings of gender and sexuality. As the recent report from the UN cited on p. 75 puts it, we are 'born' that way and, because of that essential fact, we can have rights. Thus, the individualism central to liberal rights strategies reinforces the individualism of essentialist understandings of sexuality, so that queer identity politics compounds rather than deconstructs the dominant construction of gender that creates the oppression in the first place. This is not to deny that rights discourses and strategies based on identity politics have been successful in many contexts. Identity politics works because it provides a basis to represent experiences of oppression and for collective political participation, and we have seen the legislative and cultural impacts of queer identity politics reach a critical threshold in the last ten years or so, mostly in Western countries but also in some from the global south.[2]

Influential gay liberation theorists such as Dennis Altman (1993 [1971]) initially hoped, however, for the eventual dissolution of the binary gender framework that makes the category of homosexuality socially significant, but that has clearly not been the consequence of gay liberation, either sociologically or politically. Similarly, Weeks (2007) acknowledges that, whilst gay liberation began as a revolutionary force to end sexual categorization, its sociological reality became about asserting a specific form of self-identity, and an essentialist one at that (ibid.: 81–5). Despite the lack of actual scientific evidence for an innate 'cause' of homosexuality, the 'appalling appeal of nature' remains the dominant cultural framework for understanding gender and sexuality in 'scientific' realms and in popular culture (Jackson and Rees 2007), demonstrated by the worldwide pop hit from Lady GaGa, 'Born This Way', released in 2011 with the following lyrics: 'No matter gay, straight or bi, Lesbian, transgendered life, I'm on the right track, baby, I was born to survive'. What we have is a world of public culture that celebrates being 'born this way' and promotes rights on the basis of identifiable, stable, 'natural' sexual identities.

The Western capitalist liberal democratic societies in which gay liberation first emerged had established models for minority politics (Epstein 1992), and this combined with the cultural dominance of essentialist explanations of sexuality to create queer politics as representative of a 'natural minority'. Identity concepts such as 'lesbian', 'gay', 'trans' man or woman are now commonplace in human rights and public discourse, but, whilst these concepts emerged from sustained academic interrogations of the social organization of sexuality and gender, in their public emergence they have combined only a *partial* analysis of the social regulation of sexuality ('discrimination is socially based') with the dominant common-sense 'essentialist' understandings of these aspects of human identity. For example, the recent campaigns for marriage equality in many countries have sought equality *with* heterosexuals, confirming the dominance of hetero-normativity and seeking a place for a natural minority within that, thus reifying essentialist versions of sexual identity. Sexual diversity politics has become synonymous with sexual minority rights, rather than presenting the fundamental challenges to gender structures envisaged in the initial wave of gay liberation.

The emergence of modern sexualities in the West

The Age of Enlightenment in Europe resulted in a fundamental shift in ways of thinking about societies, politics and human nature, primarily away from faith-based frameworks towards rationalism. Enlightenment thinking framed attempts to explain fundamental changes in European societies during the sixteenth to nineteenth centuries, which was understood as a distinctly different 'modern' period that was defined by reason and progress (Callinicos 2007). Sociologically speaking, modernity is empirically defined by the expansion of Western imperialism from the sixteenth century, the advent of modern rational capitalism, and its complex divisions of labour, mass industrialization and consequent urbanization, and the application of rationalization to bureaucratic organization, particularly in the realm of government expansion (Turner 1990). This period is also identified with the development of scientific approaches to studying the physical world, subsequently applied to the study of human behaviour, as in the development of medical knowledge of the body and the emergence of psychology as a scientific discipline. There is broad agreement that these key sociological aspects of modernity have been instrumental in constructing the essentialist understanding of sexuality in the West (D'Emilio 1993; Greenberg 1988; Weeks 1989). The re-organization of gender divisions and ideologies based on wage-labour/domestic binaries during industrialization created a more rigid distinction between masculinity and femininity, and consequently a normalization of homo-social, gender segregated, work and leisure spaces. Thus we see the advent of a passive, domestic femininity idealized in the middle classes most of all, but operating in a regulatory fashion through all classes. Concurrently, the massive urbanization of industrialization led to large-scale, potentially anonymous, homo-social leisure spaces, where sexual activity was increasingly difficult to police. Historians of modern sexuality therefore argue that the need to both assert middle-class gender norms and regulate perceived working-class sexual license, produced more legal, moral and social emphasis on a rigid, marital path for sexual activity, and an increasing stigmatization of all non-normative sexual activities, including homo-erotic activity amongst men who spent much of their working and leisure lives in homo-social spaces. For example, in many Western countries, developing policing infrastructure targeted women sex-workers and homosexual activity after laws against 'sexual depravity' were introduced or bolstered (Greenberg 1988; Weeks 1989).

The consequences of modern capitalism and the resulting increase in technologies of bureaucratization and social control therefore provide the impetus to create our modern sense of homosexuality as a stigmatized behaviour, but it is the related development of medical and psychological sciences that fundamentally shifted our understanding of sexuality to an essentialist aspect of human character, creating what Foucault described as a type of person *who is* a homosexual, rather than people who might engage in homosexual acts. This medical psychological model legitimized legal and social regulation, often through studies of 'deviant' sexual behaviours; it became the dominant institutional and cultural way of understanding sexuality by the beginning of the twentieth century (Weeks 1989), and remains with us today as part of common culture, although mainstream psychology has moved away from its characterization of homosexuality as a psychological disorder. Individualized, psychologized, essentialist, sexual identity is a creation of the modern Western world and that is the first basis for understanding the emergence of contemporary sexual diversity. Moreover, this Western understanding of normative and non-normative gendered sexual identities was used to police sexuality both within 'home' nations, often creating a nationalist ideal of 'respectable' sexuality, and in the imperial sphere as part of 'civilizing' colonial ideologies (McClintock 1995). For example, Murray (1997) suggests that much of the regulation of public homosexuality in Muslim cultures is due to the impact of Christian colonialism that sought to use 'Eastern' sexual depravity to justify Western moral superiority, something that Peletz (2006) also suggests was present in colonial Southeast Asia and has been documented in India (Vanita and Kidwai 2000: 191).

Of course, for the vast majority of the modern period, non-normative sexualities have been stigmatized in the West, so we also need to understand how the shift towards the acceptance of gay rights occurred. The impact of political movements has already been discussed briefly, and the structural sociological basis to this political emergence was the increasing material independence of women through access to education and employment opportunities and the consequent de-traditionalization of family structures in advanced capitalism since the mid twentieth century. Since normative gender defines sexuality, more flexible gender led to a cultural space for non-normative sexualities. Thus, in the West we saw the rise of social justice movements based on identities other than class from the late 1960s onwards, both taking advantage of and provoking changes in these broadly democratic societies, resulting in a paradigm shift in democratic values to include multiculturalism and gender equality as part of its key criteria and, less consistently and much more recently, sexual diversity.

The role of market and consumer capitalism in creating and sustaining LGBTIQ sub-cultures has also been important to community and identity building in rich Western societies. Decriminalization and/or public visibility led to community organization for both politics and for sexual lifestyle behaviour and consumption, at first clustered in gay metropolitan ghettos, but now widened to include much of public consumer culture (Evans 1993; Hennessey 2000). The period of gay liberation in the West is also the period in which the 'Golden Age' of social democracy (Callinicos 2007) gave way to consumer societies and the withdrawal of the state from much public provision, uniformly characterized as producing ever increasing emphasis on individualist social and political forms, and in particular drawing upon the discourse of a successful sexual identity to promote goods, services and lifestyle. Sex sells not merely through titillation, but overwhelmingly because the essentialist way we understand sexual identity makes it excellent shorthand for a broader sense of lifestyle identity that is the contemporary language of consumerism (Bauman 2005). The sociological basis of gay liberation has included resistance to stigmatized essentialist understandings of sexuality, the de-traditionalization of gender divisions and their institutions and latterly the shift towards an individualist culture, overwhelmingly experienced through essentialist lifestyle consumption and compounded through individualist liberal rights strategies. Moreover, these various processes are derived from the momentum of modernity in the West or, to put it another way, modern sexual diversity has emerged from a combination of modernization processes that are first and foremost identified with Western modernity.

The contemporary internationalization of sexual diversity as Western exceptionalism?

As Altman (1993 [1971]) puts it, 'the essence of gay liberation is that it enables us to come out' (ibid.: 237). This reminds us that the political venture of sexual diversity is fundamentally dependent on the public visibility of sexual identity and the recognition of the legitimacy of political claims, both of which have emerged through modernization processes. This model of politics requires subjects who identify as queer and are able and willing to self-organize around this identity, and it requires that space exists within civil society for group association and that institutional routes are available for subsequent political demands, again, all factors that broadly comprise Western liberal democracy. The absence of public LGBTIQ identities, either through legal prohibition and/or cultural homophobia, combined with the lack of democratic institutions, are seen as fundamental obstacles to queer equality in those, mostly non-Western, countries where queer rights do not yet exist.

Sexuality has only very recently emerged as a concern for intergovernmental human rights organizations, most prominently the European Union (EU) and the UN, although the former remains the only one to have mainstreamed sexual diversity rights (Kollman 2009). This recent internationalization is, however, based largely on a Western understanding of sexuality and sexual diversity politics. Moreover, when queer rights are resisted in international contexts, the broad explanation of this resistance defaults to the 'traditionalism' of non-Western cultures, either as nations or minority immigrant populations, exemplified in academic arguments such as the World Values Surveys (Inglehart and Welzel 2005), discourses about sexuality deployed in international gay rights organizations such as the ILGA, and increasingly in Western mainstream politics. My concern is that both assumptions of a Western essentialist model of sexuality and Western experiences of modernity underlie this contemporary model of queer internationalization, combining to put forward a model of 'diffusion' of sexual diversity from the West to the (less developed) 'rest' and thus potentially positioning queer politics within a neo-colonialist project.

The broad sociological understanding of modernization processes as central to the development of sexual diversity in the West is being combined with the Western discourse of public sexual identity to put forward a claim that the presence of LGBTIQ rights indicates the exceptionalism of Western modernity. For example, Mepschen et al. (2010) argue that gay politics has undergone a 'remarkable shift' that has moved them centre-stage in the civilizational defence of European and specifically Dutch culture against the multiculturalism represented by Islam. They argue that secularism and sexual freedom have developed as key aspects of contemporary Dutch identity, and indeed that the progress of gay rights within this movement has been exceptional, resulting in a normalization of gay identity. It is this exceptionalism, however, that permits the use of homosexuality to challenge Muslim cultures as outwith modernity:

> Gay rights discourses have thus offered a language for the critique of Islam and multiculturalism – an idiom that underscores an Orientalist discourse that renders Muslim citizens knowable and produces them as objects of critique. Sexuality offers a prism through which cultural contrast comes to be perceived, temporally, as the difference between modernity and tradition.
>
> *(Mepschen et al. 2010: 970).*

Queer politics are thus being incorporated into 'homonationalist' discourses to stigmatize racialized minorities further (Puar 2007), and in particular they are contributing to Islamophobia within the West. We therefore have a dilemma for queer politics wherein the perception that sexual diversity is a Western phenomenon creates a cultural division that both permits the use of LGBTIQ in racist, orientalist discourses and, on the other side of the divide, permits a resistance to LGBTIQ public visibility based on a defence of cultural integrity against the globalization of Western culture. For example, the recent Russian ban on the promotion of homosexuality is seen as '. . . part of an effort to promote traditional Russian values over Western liberalism, which the Kremlin and the Russian Orthodox Church see as corrupting Russian youth and contributing to the protests against Putin's rule'.[3] This framing of homophobia occurs both at the national level, as in the Russian case (where most public opinion supported the law), and at the trans-national level, as in the case of Muslim resistance from both minority populations and Muslim majority states who identify themselves with a trans-national Islamic identity. Moreover, state-led homophobia is increasingly deployed as a tactic by particular governments to boost their nationalist and anti-Western credentials (Weiss and Bosia 2013).

We should therefore be aware of the fact that current human rights strategies are based not only on Western constructions of gender and sexuality, but also on Western experiences of coming out and its consequences. The trajectory of social change around sexuality in the West has been conditioned by political and social structures that have produced a particular, Western essentialist understanding of sexuality. We are therefore potentially promoting the globalized expansion of a Western, essentialist, sexual *minority* politics rather than culturally relevant forms of sexual *diversity*. The research evidence on sexual diversity from non-Western cultures demonstrates that there are significant historical and contemporary differences in understandings of sexuality that are, in contemporary times, being variously influenced by, adapting and resisting globalized Western understandings of sexual identities (Aggleton *et al.* 2012; Lennox and Waites 2013; Lind 2010; Weiss and Bosia 2013). The challenge for contemporary sexual diversity politics is to render these complex intersecting sexual formations visible in a context where both global homophobias and Western globalized sexual politics exist in a dialectical relationship. Moving beyond this dialectic will require more leadership roles for queer movements from the global south (Lennox and Waites 2013), more trans-national dialogues between West and non-West (Lind 2010) and, above all, a recognition that current Western-led sexual diversity politics is not a universal teleological project, but one that is limited to a minority accommodation model based on Western essentialism. Even in the West, these limitations are apparent in the emergence of citizenship rights that mirror and thus support heterosexuality rather than disrupt it, usefully characterized by Duggan (2002) as 'homonormativity'. If we are to see genuine sexual diversity (which must include gender diversity) around the world, we have to resist the homo-colonialist impulse to assume that Western understandings of sexuality define the totality of possible sexual diversity.

Note

1   I use LGBTIQ and queer synonymously to refer to lesbians, gays, bisexuals, transgender, intersex and questioning people and associated politics since this is common usage in academic texts, although in public texts LGBT remains most used.
2   See the annual summary of queer rights provided by the International Lesbian and Gay Association, by Lucas Paoli Itaborahy and Jingshu Zhu (2013).
3   See http://www.theguardian.com/world/2013/jun/30/russia-passes-anti-gay-law, accessed 21 August 2013.

References

Aggleton, P., Moore, H.L. and Parker, R. (eds) (2012) *Understanding Global Sexualities: New Frontiers*, London: Routledge.

Altman, D. (1993) [1971] *Homosexual Oppression and Liberation*, New York, NY: New York University Press.

Bauman, Z. (2005) *Liquid Life*, Cambridge, UK: Polity.

Callinicos, A. (2007) *Social Theory: A Historical Introduction*, Cambridge, UK: Polity.

D'Emilio, J. (1993) 'Capitalism and Gay Identity', in H. Abelove, M.A. Barale and H. David (eds) (1993) *The Lesbian and Gay Studies Reader*, New York, NY: Routledge.

Duggan, L. (2002) The New Homonormativity: The Sexual Politics of Neoliberalism', in R. Castronovo and D. Nelson (eds) *Materializing Democracy: Toward a Revitalized Cultural Politics*, Durham, MD: Duke University Press.

Epstein, S. (1992) 'Gay Politics, Ethnic Identity: The Limits of Social Constructionism', in E. Stein (ed.) *Forms of Desire: Sexual Orientation and the Social Constructionist Controversy*, New York, NY: Routledge.

Evans, D. (1993) *Sexual Citizenship: The Material Construction of Sexualities*, London: Routledge.

Foucault, M. (1981) *The History of Sexuality*, London: Pelican.

Greenberg, D.F. (1988) *The Construction of Homosexuality*, Chicago, IL: University of Chicago Press.

Hennessey, R. (2000) *Profit and Pleasure*, New York, NY: Routledge.

Inglehart, R. and Welzel, C. (2005) *Modernization, Cultural Change and Democracy*, New York, NY: Cambridge University Press.

Itaborahy, L.P. and Zhu, J. (2013) 'State-sponsored Homophobia: A World Survey of Laws: Criminalization, Protection and Recognition of Same-sex Love', ILGA – International Lesbian Gay Bisexual Trans and Intersex Association. Online. Available HTTP: <http://ilga.org/ilga/en/article/1161> (accessed 24 June 2013).

Jackson, S. and Rees, A. (2007) 'The Appalling Appeal of Nature: The Popular Influence of Evolutionary Psychology as a Problem for Sociology', *Sociology*, 41(5): 917–30.

Kollman, K. (2009) 'European Institutions, Transnational Networks and National Same-Sex Unions Policy: When Soft Law Hits Harder', *Contemporary Politics*, 15(1): 37–53.

Lennox, C. and Waites, M. (eds) (2013) *Human Rights, Sexual Orientation and Gender Identity in the Commonwealth: Struggles for Decriminalisation and Change*, London: School of Advanced Study.

Lind, A. (ed.) (2010) *Development, Sexual Rights and Global Governance*, London: Routledge.

McClintock, A. (1995) *Imperial Leather: Race, Gender and Sexuality in the Colonial Context*, London: Routledge.

McIntosh, M. (1996) [1968] 'The Homosexual Role', in S. Seidman (ed.) *Queer Theory/Sociology*, Cambridge, UK: Blackwell.

MacKinnon, C. (1982) 'Feminism, Marxism, Method and the State: An Agenda for Theory', *Signs*, 7(3): 515–44.

Mepschen, P., Duyvendak, J.W. and Tonkens, E. (2010) 'Sexual Politics, Orientalism and Multicultural Citizenship in the Netherlands', *Sociology*, 44(5): 962–80.

Millett, K. (1971) *Sexual Politics*, London: Rupert Hart-Davis.

Murray, S. (1997) 'The Will Not to Know: Islamic Accommodations of Male Homosexualities', in S. Murray and W. Roscoe (eds) *Islamic Homosexualities: Culture, History and Literature*, New York, NY: New York University Press.

Peletz, M.G. (2006) 'Transgenderism and Gender Pluralism in Southeast Asia Since Early Modern Times', *Current Anthropology*, 47(2): 309–40.

Plummer, K. (1975) *Sexual Stigma*, London: Routledge.

Puar, J.K. (2007) *Terrorist Assemblages: Homonationalism in Queer Times*, Durham, MD: Duke University Press.

Rahman, M. and Jackson, S. (2010) *Gender and Sexuality: Sociological Approaches*, Cambridge, UK: Polity.

Rich, A. (1980) 'Compulsory Heterosexuality and Lesbian Existence', *Signs*, 5(4): 631–60.

Turner, B. (1990) 'Periodization and Politics in the Postmodern', in B. Turner (ed.) *Theories of Modernity and Postmodernity*, New York, NY: Sage.

United Nations Office of the High Commissioner for Human Rights (2012) 'Born Free and Equal: Sexual Orientation and Gender Identity in International Human Rights Law', Online. Available HTTP: <http://www.ohchr.org/EN/Issues/Discrimination/Pages/LGBT.aspx> (accessed 21 August 2013).

Vanita, R. and Kidwai, S. (2000) 'Introduction to Part IV: Modern Indian Materials', in R. Vanita and S. Kidwai (eds) *Same-Sex Love in India: Readings from Literature and History*, Basingstoke, UK: St. Martin's.

Weeks, J. (1989) *Sex, Politics and Society*, 2nd edn, Harrow, UK: Longman.

—(2007) *The World We Have Won: The Remaking of Erotic and Intimate Life*, New York, NY: Routledge.

Weiss, M.L. and Bosia, M.J. (eds) (2013) *Global Homophobia: States, Movements and the Politics of Oppression*, Chicago, IL: University of Illinois Press.

8

Language

The great diversifier

Jan Blommaert

Language is one of the most immediate and sensitive indexes of diversity. Small differences in accent and speaking patterns betray someone's regional, social class, ethnic and/or gender backgrounds; hearing a different language spoken instantly provokes impressions of 'foreignness'; and seeing public signs in a language you don't read is a reliable indication that you're not in your familiar habitat. Language is also the most immediate and sensitive index of social change. Hearing or seeing languages not hitherto heard or seen in an area is a sure and immediate sign that the area has changed – 'Hey, I never heard Russian spoken here!' And language, finally, is also the key tool to organize and navigate diversity: we perpetually adjust our language repertoires to those we have to communicate with, often coming up with entirely new forms of language usage. A failure to do so would lead to something most people consciously try to avoid – misunderstanding – or can be an effect of restrictive institutional arrangements in the area of language use – as when language legislation prescribes the use of a single language and/or script. In the latter case, language also becomes a sensitive index of conflicts, contests and power in a field of diversity.

In the study of language in society – an area covered by sociolinguistics, linguistic anthropology and adjacent sciences – we like to believe that attention to the small details of language usage offers a privileged entrance into broader and less immediate social, cultural and political patterns. Spelling out the pedigree of this belief might be beyond the scope of the present essay (but see, e.g., Agha 2007a; Bourdieu 1990; Voloshinov 1973). What is more useful perhaps is to try to provide substance to the belief and discuss elements of the contemporary study of language and society that can contribute to a wider programme of diversity studies (cf. Blommaert and Rampton 2011).

The direction I shall take in this exercise is to highlight three connected sets of relatively recent significant developments in our field of study. The first one is the move from language and languages to infra-language variation, and its effects on theory and analysis. The second one is the shift in the notion of 'speaker', which has effects on notions of 'competence' and 'groupness' or 'community'. And the third development, finally, is the renewed study of societal and institutional responses to diversity. The discussion of the first development is most fundamental and will take more space than that of the others.

From language to repertoire

The study of language used to be, for a very long time, precisely that: the study of '(a) Language' – of things that have a name such as English, Bulgarian or Swahili. It fell to linguistics to determine the precise features of such Languages (the capital L signals this particular usage of the term); and to sociolinguistics to describe the relationships and contact points between such Languages (Agha 2007b; Makoni and Pennycook 2007). A term such as 'multilingualism' instantiates this hegemony: it is the co-occurrence of various Languages in the same social arena. For decades, societal diversity was sociolinguistically captured under the term 'multilingualism', and the number of Languages countable in an area was an indicator of its level of sociocultural diversity.

The co-occurrence of several Languages in one space has interesting effects. Codeswitching is one of them: people using elements from different Languages mixed in one utterance or speech event, a sure sign of societal multilingualism and of multilingual competences among speakers. Codeswitching would be studied as an exceptional, special phenomenon, challenging a widespread assumption of 'natural' monolingualism at both an individual and a societal level. A normal person speaks one Language, so people mixing several such Languages are, at least, strange and worthy of linguistic and sociolinguistic attention (so it was thought), for such Languages must fight battles in the minds of their confused speakers (hence the title of a classic in this field: *Duelling Languages*, Myers-Scotton 1993).

Careful ethnographic study of codeswitching, however, led to different results. First, the use of a 'mixed' code was not premised by individual multilingual competence. All over the world, people fluently blend English with local languages, without being capable of having an extended English-only conversation. The mixed language, in other words, is very often the *only* Language spoken by people. Second, meaning effects appear not to depend just on the mix of *Languages* but also on all kinds of other features of speech: genre, style, topic. Talking about, say, business management often triggers frequent use of English terminology in many places in the world, while talking about bicycles or birds in such places rarely provokes such mixed speech. So in order to understand what people actually achieve through codeswitching, the distinction between Languages is rarely the most salient aspect of the issue. And third, 'mixed' speech appears to be subject to precisely the same sociolinguistic variation as speech in 'one' Language. Regional and social accents, dialects, registers and so forth all occur within codeswitching as well; Auer (1998) provides an overview.

Evidently, facts of infra-Language variation were long known; in fact, dialectology can be seen as one of the sources from which contemporary sociolinguistics emerged. Historical linguistics had long established the fact that every contemporary Language is historically 'mixed'. Literary and folklore studies along with rhetoric had long before emphasized the importance of genres, styles and registers. And Hymes (1972, 1996) had provided a synthetic framework for the ethnographic study of speech attending to precisely such infra-Language variation. But the confrontation with extraordinary 'messy' data, from the mid-1990s onwards, began to trigger innovative and integrative views (e.g. Rampton 1995). The 'messy' data, often taken from what we now call globalized or superdiverse contexts, defied the clarity offered by 'Languages', as well as several foundational assumptions in (socio)linguistics. What to do, for instance, with forms such as 'w84mCU@4' (wait for me, see you at 4) widely used in various forms of mobile texting and online chatting? Using standard tools of inquiry inevitably led to crippled analysis, and scholars developed more adequate theoretical and methodological instruments (see e.g. Blommaert 2010, 2013b; Pennycook 2007; Rampton 2006).

The general theoretical orientation emerging from this wave of efforts can be summarized as follows (for surveys, see Agha 2007a; Blommaert and Rampton 2011).

1. People do not use 'Languages', they use resources for communication, driven by concerns of effect, and deployed in practices of languaging ('doing' language).
2. Specific sets of such resources are language-ideologically associated with a Language such as 'English' or 'Russian'. The Languages we know are therefore not objective units but ideological ones: we say that we write in 'English' because of the widespread association of specific features with 'English' (rather than, say, 'Russian').
3. The effects brought about by deploying specific resources are indexical: the specific ordering of resources into recognizable registers, genres and styles triggers powerful standard sociocultural interpretations operating alongside better-known 'linguistic' interpretations. Such forms of order are often labelled 'norms' or 'speech conventions', and every meaningful form of communication will be grounded in conventionalized (hence recognizable as meaningful) ordered patterns of deployed resources.
4. The collective resources available to anyone at any point in time are a repertoire; repertoires are biographically emerging complexes of indexically ordered, and therefore functionally organized, resources. Repertoires include every resource used in communication – linguistic ones, semiotic ones, sociocultural ones.

In this new view, Languages are ideological constructs but relevant ones, as we shall see on p. 88. It is not because Languages 'do not exist' that the belief in their existence cannot have powerful effects. Analytically, though, these views take us into another orbit, enabling far more precise and detailed analyses of what people effectively do with their language (the lower case 'l' stands for the real sociolinguistic object here). We can now 'enter into' Languages and find often extra-ordinarily complex and salient differences there.

We can, for instance, now determine that social trajectories of people are determined not just by access to a Language ('immigrants should learn English!'), but by access to highly *specific bits of language* such as standard orthographic literacy, control over advanced professional jargons, specific accents and so forth. And investigating the distribution of such specific resources quickly reveals a vast world of diversity *within* what used to be seen as one single 'speech community' (Blommaert 2008, 2013a applies this insight to literacy, more on this on p. 86; Rampton 1998). We also know that, given the normative aspect of communication, such forms of diversity are not neutral and equivalent but *stratified* and *unequal*. Not using the right accent or jargon in a conversation can lead to heavy sanctions, even when the Language is shared; a non-native accent or speaking style, for instance, can negatively affect crucial communicative events such as police or job interviews (Gumperz 1982; Roberts 2013). The *linguistic* diversity within a conventionally defined Language is mirrored in its *sociolinguistic* diversity, which in turn is a precipitate of the real *sociocultural* diversity that generated the repertoires of the speakers.

Seemingly innocuous details of language usage so lead us straight to wider sociocultural patterns and relationships outside of language. Changes in such details – think of, e.g., a non-prestigious accent deployed by a newsreader on TV – can point towards changes in hard and soft hierarchies 'out there'.

The speaker and the community

Evidently, in the view outlined above, few people indeed would be qualified as 'monolingual', since our repertoires invariably contain complexes of resources that are in terms of social and meaning effects often as different as 'Languages'. We know how to talk to our colleagues and we know how to talk to our loved ones; we also know that both ways of speaking should never be confused in either direction; when they are, such transgression may come with a severe social penalty. We all *have to* have widely different registers, genres and styles in our repertoires, because social life is not unified, static or homogeneous.

Equally evident is the fact that no single person could ever be qualified as the 'perfect' speaker of anything. There is not a single speaker of 'English', for instance, who could claim to possess all the resources contained under that label. Our repertoires are in reality always 'truncated', with fairly well developed parts next to poorly developed ones, and with new ones entering while obsolete ones vanish (Blommaert and Backus 2013). We are at any point of time always 'experts' of language as well as 'apprentices', depending on the specific forms of language we need to use. This, too, is an effect of the heterogeneity of social life.

Both insights sound pedestrian, and they are truisms to anyone who has had a long and hard look at the realities of actual language usage. But it is good to remember that they both disturb very deep-seated assumptions of traditional linguistics: the Chomskyan image of the perfect speaker who can generate every possible sentence in his/her Language; and the Saussurean and Bloomfieldian idea of stable and homogeneous 'speech communities' into which such perfect speakers were socialized and in which people shared a maximum of rules and norms of language usage (Agha 2007a; Rampton 1998; Silverstein 1998). Such assumptions are institutionally entrenched in language learning and testing systems based on levels or degrees of 'knowledge' of language; they also underlie widespread discourses of 'integration', as we shall see shortly.

Globalization and superdiversity effects have had a major impact on the development of the views described above. Given the fantastic spread of various forms of 'English' around the on- and offline world, for instance, how can we determine the 'speech community' of 'English speakers'? And when does one qualify as a 'speaker' of English? Is 'English' still one Language or not? And what to think of new global cultures such as those gathering around hip hop or reggae? Or members of mass online games communities, sometimes numbering millions, sharing the games' jargon? Or spectators of *The Simpsons*, scattered over the planet and picking up oneliners from such programmes?

Obviously, globalization has caused the emergence of entirely new forms of communities and forced us to think about the connections between language, individuals and collectives. We can summarize the main insights from this exercise.

1. Speech communities emerge whenever people recognize each other's deployed communicative resources as meaningful. Shared indexical orders are the key to speech communities: shared specific and functionally organized sets of resources (registers, genres, styles) explain why people can understand each other in spite of otherwise massive differences in Language, social background, age and so forth.

2. Consequently, there are more speech communities than there are speakers, because all of us are at any time included in a very broad range of speech communities: at home, among friends, in the neighbourhood, hobby clubs, professional environments, administrative contexts, as media audiences and so forth. Since our lives are characterized by several forms of mobility, we continuously move in and out of old and new communities. For each of their social arenas, we have acquired specific ordered resources: registers, genres, styles.

3. We occupy different positions in these different social arenas: we are 'old' and 'expert' members of our families but can be 'young' and 'apprentice' members of professional

communities, hobby groups and so forth. Memberships, and degrees of membership, are determined by degrees of 'enregisterment': the degree to which we have learned and acquired specific complexes of resources valid in and defining such communities.

4. The different communities we are members of are not of the same order, they are scalar. A small-scale community such as the family will demand a different set of resources than, say, a global mass online gaming community in which we spend an hour per day. We are at all times members of communities at various scale-levels, some very palpable – our families, our neighbourhoods, our job environments – others less tangible in everyday life – the administrative and police worlds in which we live; the nation-state; ethnic, age, gender, consumer and social class communities; the 'international community' into which we can be corralled at times. Here, we see how all of us belong simultaneously to tightly organized, fully integrated, enduring and dense communities as well as in loosely integrated, flexible and temporary communities.

5. We deploy certain resources only at certain scale-levels. A non-Anglophone academic, for instance, will switch into English as soon as s/he enters the scale of global academic communication, and switch back as soon as this arena is left. Mobility in a globalized world is predicated on the capacity to acquire and deploy resources needed to cross from one scale-level (say, the local) to another (say, the global).

6. The continuous presence and availability of multiple and scalar communities ensure that everyone's real social environment is at all times polycentric: we always operate in complex and potentially multi-scale situations, in which a perfectly appropriate intimate utterance to one's wife can be understood as an obscenity by overhearing audiences. Similarly: an accent in English that sounds highly educated at home in Nairobi can be turned into a stigmatized immigrant accent in New York. Mobility in the age of globalization involves movements across scales, i.e. across complexes of norms, expectations and judgments. Online environments of course complicate such forms of scale-crossing.

Obviously, memberships in speech communities are always plural, stratified, selective and dynamic. 'Full' membership will be rare, while most forms of membership will be 'by degree'. As said earlier: linguistic, sociolinguistic and sociocultural diversity are all part of one social system, and the complexity of one will be mirrored in the complexity of the other. Each of us is therefore not just 'multilingual', but also 'multicultural' – to adopt an older terminology – and one begins to get a glimpse of the highly problematic character of notions such as 'identity' and 'authenticity' these days (cf. Jacquemet 2005; Johnstone 1999; Rampton 1995; Wang 2013).

Institutional responses

The latter statement is not how governments and authorities usually perceive things. It is a striking phenomenon: while sociolinguists detect layer upon layer of diversity, institutional approaches to language in society appear to move back to the most rigorous denials of such diversity. In this move, we see several things (Hogan-Brun et al. 2009; Kroskrity 2000; Schieffelin et al. 1998; Silverstein 1996; Spotti and Detailleur 2011):

1. People and societies are seen as 'naturally' monolingual; they were born as speakers of one 'pure' Language; being multilingual is seen as an obstacle to social mobility and 'normal' identity development, unless the multilingualism includes prestigious Languages such as English.

2. The nation-state is the defining scale-level in institutional responses to diversity. There is an immense emphasis on knowledge of the 'standard' variety of the 'national Language' in connection to popular and institutional conceptions of citizenship.
3. It is assumed that particular levels of language proficiency are conclusive in determining someone's identity and social future.

Language testing has in a great number of countries become one of the central instruments in regulating immigration. The identity of refugees is investigated by means of a proficiency test in the 'native' Language of the applicant, and this Language needs to be in some way situated in the country of origin claimed by the applicant. An imagery of fully integrated nation-states shines through, in which every citizen has access to relevant national emblems such as 'standard' national language varieties; evidently this image goes with an assumption of stability, in which countries of origin of refugees have never experienced war, rebellion, famine, repression and migration. We see old, Modernist language ideologies being deployed here in contexts where none of their assumptions has much empirical purchase. The effect is often disastrous for the applicant (cf. Maryns 2006).

Similar testing regimes are frequently used in 'integration' policies designed for new immigrants. Access to certain important social benefits – official registration, social housing, welfare and education – is made conditional on immigrants taking courses in the 'standard' national Language variety and getting a certificate of language proficiency. Achievement of immigrant learners in schools is equally increasingly measured by means of standard testing tools in the national Language.

The inadequacies of such notions of language in superdiverse societies have repeatedly been emphasized (e.g. Eades 2010; Language and National Origin Group 2004; Shohamy 2001). Given our earlier remarks, the case ought to be clear too: apart from the ideological character of the 'standard' Language (who actually *speaks* the standard variety?) and the fallacy of linear models of language learning, it should be clear that the real repertoires of people never just point towards 'national' origins: they point towards an entire life, spent in various places (surely in the case of refugees) and social arenas (Blommaert 2009). Every such social arena was, and is, a learning environment in which highly specific and selected resources are made available. Consequently, somebody who grew up in a refugee camp, far from school, may be proficient in spoken vernacular varieties of the 'national' Language, but not in its 'standard' and written varieties (typically acquired at school). Likewise, a prolonged stop at one of the places in a refugee's itinerary may result in, say, a general touch of Italian accent in any Language spoken – certainly when that stop involved exposure to education and media environments. In general, the Modernist imagination of Language prevents attention to what really matters: the details of language usage, revealing the different shades and formats of people's social being in a range of contexts (Maryns 2006).

Conclusion: language and rapid social change

We begin to see how the contemporary study of language in society can become a highly developed tool for investigating rapid social change. The 'submolecular' gaze on language usage has created a panorama of differences, all relevant and all related to features of social environments. Changes in such environments will very rapidly convert to sociolinguistic changes – and the latter often stimulate or consolidate the former. Specific sociolinguistic techniques such as Linguistic Landscaping are particularly useful for monitoring rapid and unpredictable changes in social arenas, with a clear potential for interdisciplinary application (cf. Blommaert 2013b).

The shift in the study of language in society, documented in this essay, can be summarized as a shift from multiplicity to complexity (Arnaut 2013). Rather than as juxtapositions of separate Languages, sociolinguistic diversity is now seen as a complex system subject to very different and separately developing forces, with multiple historicities and scales entering in uniquely situated communicative events, and with relatively unpredictable directions of development. A more systematic and disciplined attention to diversity has, thus, shaken the robust structuralist foundations of this science. But it has made its object – language in society – vastly more attractive and relevant in the study of diversity at large.

References

Agha, A. (2007a) *Language and Social Relations*, Cambridge, UK: Cambridge University Press.

—(2007b) 'The Object Called "Language" and the Subject of Linguistics', *Journal of English Linguistics*, 35(3): 217–35.

Arnaut, K. (2013) 'Super-diversity: Elements of an Emerging Perspective', *Diversities*, 14(2): 1–16.

Auer, P. (ed.) (1998) *Code-switching in Conversation: Language, Interaction and Identity*, London: Routledge.

Blommaert, J. (2008) *Grassroots Literacy: Writing, Identity and Voice in Central Africa*, London: Routledge.

—(2009) 'Language, Asylum and the National Order', *Current Anthropology*, 50(4): 415–41.

—(2010) *The Sociolinguistics of Globalization*, Cambridge, UK: Cambridge University Press.

—(2013a) 'Writing as a Sociolinguistic Object', *Journal of Sociolinguistics*, 17(4): 440–59.

—(2013b) *Ethnography, Superdiversity and Linguistic Landscapes: Chronicles of Complexity*, Bristol, UK: Multilingual Matters.

Blommaert, J. and Rampton, B. (2011) 'Language and Superdiversity', *Diversities*, 13(2): 1–23.

Blommaert, J. and Backus, A. (2013) 'Superdiverse Repertoires and the Individual', in I. de Saint-Georges and J.J. Weber (eds) *Multilingualism and Multimodality: Current Challenges for Educational Studies*, Rotterdam: Sense.

Bourdieu, P. (1990) *Language and Symbolic Power*, Cambridge, UK: Polity.

Eades, D. (2010) *Language and the Legal Process*, Bristol, UK: Multilingual Matters.

Gumperz, J. (1982) *Discourse Strategies*, Cambridge, UK: Cambridge University Press.

Hogan-Brun, G., Mar-Molinero, C. and Stevenson, P. (eds) (2009) *Discourses on Language and Integration: Critical Perspectives on Language Testing Regimes in Europe*, Amsterdam: John Benjamins.

Hymes, D. (1972) 'Models of the Interaction of Language and Social Life', in J. Gumperz and D. Hymes (eds) *Directions in Sociolinguistics: The Ethnography of Communication*, New York, NY: Holt, Rinehart & Winston.

—(1996) *Ethnography, Linguistics, Narrative Inequality: Toward an Understanding of Voice*, London: Taylor & Francis.

Jacquemet, M. (2005) 'Transidiomatic Practices: Language and Power in the Age of Globalization', *Language and Communication*, 25(3): 257–77.

Johnstone, B. (1999) 'Uses of Southern-sounding Speech by Contemporary Texas Women', *Journal of Sociolinguistics*, 3(4): 505–22.

Kroskrity, P. (ed.) (2000) *Regimes of Language*, Santa Fe, NM: School of American Research.

Language and National Origin Group (2004) 'Guidelines for the Use of Language Analysis in Relation to Questions of National Origin in Refugee Cases', *International Journal of Speech, Language and the Law*, 11(2): 261–6.

Makoni, S. and Pennycook, A. (eds) (2007) *Disinventing and Reconstituting Language*, Bristol, UK: Multilingual Matters.

Maryns, K. (2006) *The Asylum Speaker: Language in the Belgian Asylum Procedure*, Manchester, UK: St Jerome.

Myers-Scotton, C. (1993) *Duelling Languages: Grammatical Structure in Codeswitching*, Oxford, UK: Oxford University Press.

Pennycook, A. (2007) *Global Englishes and Transcultural Flows*, London: Routledge.

Rampton, B. (1995) *Crossing: Language and Ethnicity Among Adolescents*, London: Longman.

—(1998) 'Speech Community', in J. Verschueren, J.O. Östman, J. Blommaert and C. Bulcaen (eds) *Handbook of Pragmatics*, Amsterdam: John Benjamins.

—(2006) *Language in Late Modernity: Interactions in an Urban School*, Cambridge, UK: Cambridge University Press.

Roberts, C. (2013) 'Translating Global Experience into Institutional Models of Competency: Linguistic Inequalities in the Job Interview', *Diversities*, 14(2): 49–70.

Schieffelin, B., Woolard, K. and Kroskrity, P. (eds) (1998) *Language Ideologies: Practice and Theory*, New York, NY: Oxford University Press.

Shohamy, E. (2001) *The Power of Tests: Critical Perspectives on the Uses of Language Tests*, London: Longman.

Silverstein, M. (1996) 'Monoglot "Standard" in America: Standardization and Metaphors of Linguistic Hegemony', in D. Brenneis and R. Macaulay (eds) *The Matrix of Language: Contemporary Linguistic Anthropology*, Boulder, CO: Westview.

—(1998) 'Contemporary Transformations of Local Linguistic Communities', *Annual Review of Anthropology*, 27(1): 401–26.

Spotti, M. and Detailleur, J. (2011) 'Placing Shibboleths at the Institutional Gate: LADO Tests and the Construction of Asylum Seekers' identities', Tilburg Papers in Culture Studies, paper no. 8. Online. Available HTTP: <http://www.tilburguniversity.edu/upload/d71b1a0b-bfe6-46b6-9a87-668864374505_tpcs%20paper8.pdf> (accessed 9 April 2014).

Voloshinov, V. (1973) *Marxism and the Philosophy of Language*, Cambridge, MA: Harvard University Press.

Wang, X. (2013) 'Inauthentic Authenticity: Semiotic Design for Globalization in the Margins of China', Tilburg Papers in Culture Studies, paper no. 49. Online. Available HTTP: <http://www.tilburguniversity.edu/upload/69fb8638-1adc-474f-b3a6-37e236bd0428_TPCS_49_Wang.pdf> (accessed 9 April 2014).

9

Religious differentiation and diversity in discourse and practice

Kim Knott

Religion is undoubtedly an important facet of contemporary superdiversity, influenced by migration, transnational circulations and diasporic interconnections (Knott and McLoughlin 2010; Levitt 2009; McLoughlin 2010, 2013; Tweed 2006; Vásquez and Marquardt 2003; Vertovec 2004, 2007). However, religious diversity is not solely a function of late-modern migrations and recently articulated diasporic consciousness, but has been witnessed in many times and places as a result of the predilection of religious bodies to multiply, diversify and distinguish themselves from others, and of those regulatory regimes that have sought to divide and rule them. In the second half of the twentieth century these processes were masked by the failure of Western secular social scientists and public commentators to consider and discuss the presence of religion, its importance for identity and its potential role in public life and policy making. How this changed post-2001 and the ways in which religious communities and organizations have themselves responded to new expressions of diversity will be discussed in this chapter.

Religion, differentiation, diversity

Despite the rhetoric of unity, peace, common goals and shared values, religions and those who identify with them make distinctions. They differentiate selves, groups, creatures, things, times and places, and are distinguished or set apart by others. Arguably, where religion is present, there is diversity, or at least the potential for it. The concept of 'cultural diversity' is now a political commonplace, an entailment of post-multiculturalist integration policies in which groups are to be accommodated with some if not all of their cultural differences intact. But the status that 'cultural diversity' is afforded in contemporary discourse should not be taken to mean that religious plurality and encounter is an entirely new phenomenon. Although late-modern economic, social and political globalization and urban superdiversity are clearly different from earlier processes and social formations, the movement of ethnic and religious peoples across borders is not new, and neither is religious schism or the experience of religious difference. Whether in the Roman world, along the Silk Road or trade routes of Southeast Asia, in Mughal India, Moorish Spain, colonial Africa, 1980s Japan or contemporary Canada, religious diversification has occurred, driven by migration, mission, commercial encounters or the rise of new religions in a context of social and cultural competition. Singapore and Brazil, for example, provide a striking contrast, with the former exhibiting the top-down management of post-colonial religious diversity (Ah Eng 2008) and the latter, whilst still predominantly Catholic, nevertheless witnessing the rapid growth and diversification of new grassroots Christian formations, some Evangelical Protestant, others Pentacostalist, some associated with global Churches, others highly localized and independent (Garmany 2013). One is religiously diverse by virtue of centuries of migration; the other as a result of globalization, conversion and social change.

Evidently such cases cannot be isolated from their social and political contexts, but religious 'agency' – if we can call it that – should not be ruled out. Instrumentalist, materialist, sociological and psychological arguments about the formation of religious groups, the motivations and behaviours of religious individuals, and the significance, place and movement of religious things are all the more convincing if those who make them are attentive to what separates apparently 'religious' bodies and objects from those that are not deemed 'religious'. Their special, if not unique, focus on transformation and soteriology (saving power) leads religious groups and individuals to distinguish themselves and their spiritual journeys from those of others. Through myth, theology, ritual, altered states and social organization, they make worlds, establish boundaries, sacralize people and things, times and spaces, and demarcate insiders from outsiders.

New religions and religious innovations are forged in a spirit of competition where success and superiority are identified, not solely by economic and other material measures and achievements, but also by degrees of spiritual power, piety, mystical experience, divine election, successful transplantation and new expressions, as well as by growing numbers and the capacity to sustain traditions across generations. What is important about this for thinking about diversity is that it is not simply a question of the co-presence of multiple religious identities in contemporary societies, it is about how groups and individuals in different times and places have sought to establish themselves, make meaning, forge new places, create chains of memory in order to distinguish themselves from others, cross boundaries, cope with change, dwell simultaneously in multiple locations and survive and thrive (Hervieu-Léger 2000; Knott 2005; Tweed 2006; Vásquez 2011).

Yet such endeavours, whilst being explained and articulated theologically by leaders and scholars, are also the stuff of religious people's quotidian, often unselfconscious practices, thoughts, conversations and relationships (Stringer 2013). They may be interwoven and supported by other expressions of diversity, based on nationality, ethnicity, language, gender or sexuality. Differences of a religious nature may come to the fore and be experienced as such whenever and wherever religion arises as a subject of conversation, concern, debate or public interest – in the workplace, at school, in the law court or in a local park or bar, and in relation to issues such as discrimination, marriage, security, education, ethics or human rights. Religious groups themselves have a variety of ways of dealing with religious and other forms of social and cultural diversity and their entailments. A group's theological position on an issue may be publicly stated with reference to scripture, fundamental beliefs and sacred values. Its differences from others may be highlighted, as well as its willingness – or not – to engage with them, for example, in interfaith dialogue or multi-faith spaces or events.

Colonialism, contemporary nation states and religious diversity

As Fitzgerald (2007) noted, European discourse about 'religion' and 'religions' developed from embryonic beginnings in the seventeenth century, alongside and in tension with other concepts, thus being distinguished from the non-religious domains of 'politics', 'economy' and 'society' (ibid.: 6ff.). A counter space – everything that was *not* 'religious' – emerged and was labelled 'secular' (derived from the Christian idea of the worldly or temporal). The 'crucial logic' of this development was the 'separation into two essentially different domains. It is this that makes the plural objectification of "religions" possible' (ibid.: 6). This European logic was exported globally via colonial routes and regimes, and was drawn on to distinguish other, 'traditional' and 'religious', societies from Western 'secular' ones (Chidester 1996; van der Veer 2001), as well as to identify separate 'religions' and set them apart from one another. Drawing on the Christian model, they were represented as having the same properties and dimensions, thus further essentializing 'religion' as a distinctive sphere (Fitzgerald 2000).

With such conceptual tools to hand, colonial rulers, administrators, scholars and travellers characterized and managed religion, religious identities and the requirements of different religious groups in parts of the world which never knew they needed such a concept and had no prior reason to separate out religion from other aspects of social life or from a 'secular' arena of politics and governance. In different countries within the British Empire, for example, the regulation of religious diversity was shaped not only by the colonial regime in tandem with local political structures, but also by population movements and power relations between existing and new groups. The subject of research from 2006–10 on the religious lives of migrant minorities in urban Malaysia, South Africa and the United Kingdom, these imperially connected sites were seen to provide rather different contexts of diversity, the negotiation of religious identities and religious place-making. The imperial regulation of differences was incorporated at home into the UK's secular recognition of individual religious freedom and its strained claims to tolerance of religious identities and formations, whereas, in South Africa and Malaysia, different pre-colonial and post-colonial histories and cultural traditions resulted in the adoption of somewhat more restrictive policies toward public ethnic and religious identification and mobilization (Vásquez and Dewind 2014).

In recent decades researchers have examined the place of religions and religious diversity in multiple contexts, with reference to policies of assimilation, multiculturalism and integration, the recognition and management of difference, the particular case of Islam and Muslim migrations, and comparisons between different regimes and between diverse political and academic discourses of state/religion relations and modes of accommodation. Canadian and Indian scholars, for example, have analysed and compared the state management of religious diversity in their countries, and considered how religious communities and individuals negotiate such diversity in the context of wider civil society, public policy, legislation and education. Recognising that India and Canada have exhibited varied approaches to colonialism, majority–minority relations, secularism, world religions and globalization, scholars have acknowledged the difficulties experienced as states accommodate religious identity and diversity within national frameworks whilst seeking to be fair to all and to minimize conflict (Living with Religious Diversity 2013).

Comparisons such as these depend upon the prior accumulation of knowledge about religious diversity in different national contexts. This process was hampered in some Western countries by assumptions about the progress of secularization and the decreasing relevance of religion for the secular state and public life. In the late 1970s and 1980s, when I first began to research religion, ethnicity and migration in the UK, the dominant discourse on social diversity in both policy and academic circles focused on race and ethnicity, with culture in general and religion in particular ignored. Religion was not covered by the Race Relations Act of 1976, which focused on racial discrimination, or the Commission for Racial Equality, formed soon after, which aimed to encourage integration and improve relations between people of different ethnic backgrounds. (It was not until the Equality Act 2010 that 'religion or belief' was fully incorporated into the list of protected characteristics within the UK's legal framework.) Social scientists who studied immigration, minorities and policy provision rarely mentioned religion, though anthropologists and scholars of religion recognized its significance in ethnographic studies of new migrant communities. Above all, it was *The Satanic Verses* controversy of the late 1980s – during which liberal secularist intellectuals found their position challenged by British Muslims – which saw religious identity and Islamophobia move up the public agenda (Modood 1988, 1990).

With religion re-emerging as a social force across Europe post-2001 as a result of global events and migration, it could no longer be ignored by policy makers. In the UK, public statements and policy initiatives acknowledged the role of 'faiths' and 'faith communities' and the importance of 'multi-faith' and 'interfaith' ventures and initiatives in urban regeneration, community cohesion and the prevention of terrorism (Smith 2004; Weller 2004). Across Europe, religious communities were increasingly seen to have the potential for facilitating integration, though measures to include them or draw on their resources differed from country to country (International Organization for Migration 2011).

Religions, representation and management of diversity

The marginalization of religion and its apparent re-emergence in scholarly and policy discourse has not been confined to Europe and its so-called 'Eurosecularity' (Berger *et al.* 2008). Despite major post-war studies of urban religious diversity in the United States (Herberg 1955; Glazer and Moynihan 1963), it slipped from view as attention turned to race in the 1970s. As a result, contributors to *New York Glory* (Carnes and Karpathakis 2001) saw their task as putting religion back on the public agenda. They celebrated 'one of the most diverse concentrations of religions that the world has ever seen' (Carnes 2001: 3), the result of late-twentieth-century migrations that, according to Carnes, brought 'the soul back'. The statistics he listed gave a sense of how religious diversity was constituted in this one global city:

- New York City has more Roman Catholics, Muslims, Hindus, Rastafarians, Jehovah's Witnesses, Greek Orthodox, Russian Orthodox, and religious Jews than any other city in the United States.
- More than one-half of Asian immigrants are churchgoers; 70 per cent of all immigrants to New York are Christians . . . and the fastest-growing institution in Hispanic neighbourhoods is the church.
- About one out of five school children is in a religious school . . .
- In the last ten years, Korean churches alone have founded more than a dozen local colleges and seminaries. The number of Seventh Day Adventists has grown 900 per cent . . . and the number of Mormons, 300 per cent in the 1990s.
- Eighty-two per cent of New Yorkers say that religion is very or fairly important to their lives; 90 per cent identify with a religious group and believe in God; and [46] per cent attend religious services once per month or more. . . .

(Carnes 2001: 3f.).

As these figures suggest, religious diversity in New York was not merely the sum of diverse groups for whom religion was a superficial badge of identity, but was constituted of dynamic institutions whose active participants and students could testify to the importance of religion in their lives. These issues of membership, congregation, conversion, belief, practice and religious socialization are key features around which the growth of American religious diversity is organized. Scholarly and public discourse about what it means to be religious in the United States represents and reproduces religion in terms of a dynamic congregationalism that incorporates new migrants and helps them to cope, that drives growth and attracts converts (Becker 1999; Ebaugh and Chafetz 2000).

Whilst this congregational model of religious diversity has informed some European scholarship, it is 'community' that has been the key trope (Knott 2004). As Baumann (1996) discovered in research on Southall in West London, much public and academic discourse on the settlement and organization of migrant minorities drew on the language of 'community' and 'culture', thereby contributing to the representation of 'communities of culture' and to the reification of culture and cultural boundaries. In his analysis of the discourses of identity drawn on by Southall's ethnically and religious diverse population Baumann sought to identify the demotic as well as the dominant narratives in operation as people conversed within their own groups and engaged with others. These discourses of diversity showed Southallians' ability to make appropriate judgements about 'when to use what discourse in which situation' (Baumann 1996: 204) in a fluid process whereby they were able to resort to the dominant discourse of 'community' and 'culture' when necessary and useful, but to 'switch it off' (ibid.: 195) at others and draw on demotic discourses shaped and differentiated within their immediate social groups. He summarized the latter as follows: 'Sikhs and the creation of caste *communities*[;] Hindus and the *culture* of encompassment[;] Muslims and the multi-cultural *community* of Islam[;] Afro-Caribbeans and four approaches to "finding" *culture*[;] Whites and three strategies in the absence of *community*' (ibid.: 109).

In Baumann's study, although ethnic and religious diversity was clearly apparent as a social fact, neither 'ethnicity' nor 'religion' was the principal discursive trope or unit of analysis. 'Community' and 'culture' were preferred, but shown as malleable, fluid and, at times, inter-changeable. His work highlighted the process by which certain concepts came to dominate public discourse and shape how individuals and groups were perceived and represented in the public imagination. If we return to the idea that 'religion' was erased from accounts of secular polity and society for several decades from the 1970s, but re-entered public discourse after 2001 – thus reversing its erasure – then we must question what such processes of invisibility and visibility tell us about attitudes to 'religion' and 'religious diversity' and their incorporation and management. Equally, as Baumann's focus on demotic discourse suggests, it is instructive to see how these concepts are drawn on and constituted in locally diverse but quotidian contexts.

Stringer's (2013) analysis of everyday talk about religious diversity in the English city of Birmingham revealed how ordinary people go about socially managing such diversity. Their informal discourse was very different from the formal interreligious dialogue of theologians and organized interfaith groups. It was highly contextual, sometimes used to avoid talking about race and ethnicity, sometimes to juxtapose religion and non-religion, to suggest that all religions are the same, or to express indifference (as distinct from negativity) to religion and religious diversity. In his discussion of the discourses that emerged following the deaths of three young Muslim men in August 2011, who were killed by rioters who drove into them as they sought to defend their local area, he noted that the potential to narrate the story with reference to race and ethnicity – drawing on a local history of tension between Asians and Afro-Caribbeans – was subverted. The tone was set by the father of one of the victims who offered an alternative discourse of 'interreligious commonality'. The power of demotic discourse to resist the narration of ethnic or religious differences that might lead to further violence in favour of a story of living together in diversity enabled local people to manage a potentially divisive situation.

Stringer concludes, however, that, despite this outcome, there are no simple discursive solutions to the day to day management of diversity. It is not simply a matter of ignoring or downplaying differences. Stressing positive discourses of commonality will not simply erase underlying negative, separatist discourses which have the potential to re-emerge surreptitiously or violently as circumstances change. What a case like this shows, though, is that, within contexts of diversity, there are choices to be made about how people talk about or ignore religious as well as racial and ethnic differences and commonalities that can have consequences for how people live together, and how their neighbourhoods are perceived by residents and outsiders. When and how they draw on or downplay 'religion' in the management of local diversity depends on the circumstances, their own identities and what is at stake (see also Baumann 1999).

Stringer's focus on the demotic and local is counter-balanced by an analysis for the same period of dominant discourses in the British national media (Knott *et al.* 2013) that revealed representations of religious diversity deployed variously in order to express fears about the loss of a previous national identity and heritage, the marginalization of Christianity and the Islamification of 'Britain'. However, 'Britain' was constructed in equal measure as an ethnically and religious diverse society, upheld by a secular state, with a cherished multi-faith character to be defended if attacked by outsiders. The reporting of religion revealed the tensions arising from increasing social diversity and the application of a liberal equality agenda, and was focused significantly around cases of religion and sexuality (such as clergy sexual abuse and same-sex marriage), religious dress, faith schools and the challenge of freedom of speech.

Although all people – religious and non-religious – are agents in the everyday narration and practice of diversity, they may also be involved in local and national responses to its management by government and other public bodies. Such responses include, for example, the formation of interfaith organizations charged with representing the claims and interests of religious people to government and the media and ready to respond with one voice on matters of public concern or at times of crisis. The provision by faith-based organizations of local services (e.g. advice for new migrants or help for the homeless) or multi-faith initiatives to provide rooms for worship or meditation in public places are further examples. The supply of opportunities, spaces, services and support by religious groups is a common feature of neo-liberal societies in which, to a greater or lesser extent, the state may be withdrawing from aspects of social provision.

In many cases, religious bodies have an interest in providing for their own members; in others, however, an ethic of care or welcoming the stranger may lead them to offer services for others. They may draw on 'bridging capital' as well as 'bonding capital' (Putnam 2000). In some cases, citizens eschew the conventional labels or organizing principles of religious or ethnic identity for broader coalitions in which those motivated by similar interests, irrespective of their differences, work together. For example, new initiatives grew out of the Christian ecumenical sanctuary movement which developed in Central America in the 1980s in response to the rise of those fleeing persecution and seeking asylum. New sanctuary movements, like the one in Philadelphia, are interfaith consortia of immigrant congregations and other groups established to give voice to injustices and enact policies that reflect values of hospitality, justice and dignity; the City of Sanctuary initiative in the UK is a network of both non-religious and religious people motivated to build a culture of hospitality and safe towns and cities for refugees. As diverse non-religious people increasingly articulate their beliefs, values and identities, and – in some cases – get together in like-minded groups or networks, so rainbow coalitions like the sanctuary movement shift and change.

References

Ah Eng, L. (ed.) (2008) *Religious Diversity in Singapore*, Singapore: Institute of Southeast Asian Studies and Institute of Policy Studies.

Baumann, G. (1996) *Contesting Culture: Discourses of Identity in Multi-Ethnic London*, Cambridge, UK: Cambridge University Press.

—(1999) *The Multicultural Riddle: Rethinking National, Ethnic and Religious Identities*, London: Routledge.

Becker, P.E. (1999) *Congregations in Conflict: Cultural Models of Local Religious Life*, Cambridge, UK: Cambridge University Press.

Berger, P.L., Davie, G. and Fokas, E. (2008) *Religious America, Secular Europe? A Theme and Variations*, Aldershot, UK: Ashgate.

Carnes, T. (2001) 'Religion in the City: An Overview', in T. Carnes and A. Karpathakis (eds) *New York Glory: Religions in the City*, New York, NY: New York University Press.

Carnes, T. and Karpathakis, A. (eds) (2001) *New York Glory: Religions in the City*, New York, NY: New York University Press.

Chidester, D. (1996) *Savage Systems: Colonialism and Comparative Religion in Southern Africa*, Charlottesville, VA: University of Virginia Press.

Ebaugh, H.R. and Chafetz, J.S. (2000) *Religion and the New Immigrants: Continuities and Adaptations in Immigrant Congregations*, Walnut Creek, CA: AltaMira.

Fitzgerald, T. (2000) *The Ideology of Religious Studies*, Oxford, UK: Oxford University Press.

—(2007) 'Introduction', in T. Fitzgerald (ed.) *Religion and the Secular: Historical and Colonial Formations*, London: Equinox.

Garmany, J. (2013) 'Slums, Space and Spirituality: Religious Diversity in Contemporary Brazil', *Area*, 45(1): 47–55.

Glazer, N. and Moynihan, D.P. (1963) *Beyond the Melting Pot*, Cambridge, MA: MIT Press.

Herberg, W. (1955) *Protestant, Catholic, Jew*, New York, NY: Doubleday.

Hervieu-Léger, D. (2000) [1993] *Religion as a Chain of Memory*, Cambridge, UK: Polity.

International Organization for Migration (2011) *Dialogue for Integration: Engaging Religious Communities*, Helsinki: International Organization for Migration.

Knott, K. (2004) 'The Sense and Nonsense of "Community"', in S. Sutcliffe (ed.) *Religion: Empirical Studies*, Aldershot, UK: Ashgate.

—(2005) *The Location of Religion: A Spatial Analysis*, London: Equinox.

Knott, K. and McLoughlin, S. (eds) (2010) *Diasporas: Concepts, Intersections, Identities*, London: Zed Books.

Knott, K., Poole, E. and Taira, T. (2013) *Media Portrayals of Religion and the Secular Sacred: Representation and Change*, Farnham, UK: Ashgate.

Levitt, P. (2009) *God Needs No Passport: Immigrants and the Changing American Religious Landscape*, New York, NY: The New Press.

Living with Religious Diversity. Homepage. Available HTTP: <http://www.livingwithreligiousdiversity.com/> (accessed 22 September 2013).

McLoughlin, S. (2010) 'Religion and Diaspora', in J. Hinnells (ed.) *Routledge Companion to the Study of Religion*, 2nd edn, London: Routledge.

—(2013) 'Religion, Religions and Diaspora', in A. Quayson and G. Daswani (eds) *A Companion to Diaspora and Transnationalism*, Oxford, UK: Blackwell.

Modood, T. (1988) '"Black", Racial Equality and Asian Identity', *New Community*, 14(3): 397–404.

—(1990) 'British Asian Muslims and the Rushdie Affair', *Political Quarterly*, 16(2): 143–60.

Putnam, R.D. (2000) *Bowling Alone: The Collapse and Revival of American Community*, New York, NY: Simon & Schuster.

Smith, G. (2004) 'Faith in Community and Communities of Faith? Government Rhetoric and Religious Identity in Urban Britain', *Journal of Contemporary Religion*, 19(2): 185–204.

Stringer, M.D. (2013) *Discourses of Religious Diversity: Explorations in an Urban Ecology*, Farnham, UK: Ashgate.

Tweed, T.A. (2006) *Crossing and Dwelling: Theory of Religion*, Cambridge, MA: Harvard University Press.

van der Veer, P. (2001) *Imperial Encounters: Religion and Modernity in India and Britain*, Princeton, NJ: Princeton University Press.

Vásquez, M.A. (2011) *More than Belief: A Materialist Theory of Religion*, Oxford, UK: Oxford University Press.

Vásquez, M.A. and Marquardt, M.F. (2003) *Globalizing the Sacred: Religion across the Americas*, New Brunswick, NJ: Rutgers University Press.

Vásquez, M.A. and Dewind, J. (2014) 'Introduction to the Religious Lives of Migrant Minorities: A Transnational and Multi-sited Perspective', *Global Networks*, 14: 251–72.

Vertovec, S. (2004) 'Religion and Diaspora', in P. Antes, A.W. Geertz and R. Warne (eds) *New Approaches to the Study of Religion: Textual, Comparative, Sociological and Cognitive Approaches*, Berlin: De Gruyter.

—(2007) 'Superdiversity and its Implications', *Ethnic and Racial Studies*, 30(3): 1024–54.

Weller, P. (2004) 'Identity, Politics and the Future(s) of Religion in the UK: The Case of the Religion Question in the 2001 Decennial Census', *Journal of Contemporary Religion*, 19(1): 3–21.

10

The diversity of milieu in diversity studies

Dariuš Zifonun

Milieu does not feature prominently among the analytical concepts used in diversity studies. At the same time, it plays a significant role in approaches within the social sciences that – contrary to approaches focusing on individual behaviour as isolated acts – focus either on the social organization of human life (i.e. milieu-concepts conceiving of society in terms of the things people do together) or on the subjective experience of the individual's environment (be it other individuals or 'things'). By adopting this perspective, diversity studies can benefit from the use of milieu as a supplement or substitute of concepts like group, community, culture or category.

Milieu has been conceptualized in a variety of different ways that can serve as heuristics for the study of diversity in a number of empirical research fields. Instead of limiting itself to just one way of conceptualizing milieu, this article will point at the ways four different conceptualizations of milieu go along with different ways of conceptualizing social plurality and thus shed a light on social diversity and differentiation. While differentiation is a quality of social structure – a structure thought to be irreducible to its components and one that, by way of relating its components to itself, produces the very difference of these units – diversity implies a multiplicity of different units and multiple dimensions of difference.

Along with the different ways of conceptualizing social plurality, all of the approaches conceptualize society and individuals as cultural. That is, a society is not merely a structure of positions, a system of functions or a field of competing interests to which culture is external, and individuals are not merely driven by interests. Culture is understood as a process of sense-making, by way of which society is imbued with meaning. However, the four approaches differ in the ways they conceptualize culture – holistic or fragmented, systemic or interactive.

This article will empirically focus on the question of ethnic diversity by using the fictitious but superbly portrayed milieu in Tom Wolfe's recent novel *Back to Blood* (Wolfe 2012) as a point of reference. Ethnicity takes front stage in Wolfe's account of plurality, but it will be possible to demonstrate that milieu allows for the analysis of other lines of plurality as well.

A structuralist perspective on milieus

When Emile Durkheim laid his foundations of sociology, milieu was among his key concepts, both in methodological as well as in sociological terms. Even though British and American social thought has been heavily influenced by Durkheim – from the British anthropological school to Parsons and Merton and the 'strong program' in cultural sociology – the milieu concept has not been transmitted into English-speaking sociology as French 'milieu' was translated not as English 'milieu' but as 'environment' (Durkheim 1982: 135ff., 1984: 138f.), and environment did not prove to be a very strong or compelling term.

Methodologically, Durkheim argues that sociology needs to conceptualize society as an entity in its own right, irreducible to individual will. 'Social facts' resist the will to change them. In his book *The Rules of Sociological Method*, Durkheim (1982) argues: 'Far from their being a product of our will, they determine it from without. They are like moulds into which we are forced to cast our actions.' (ibid.: 70). These 'moulds' are what Durkheim calls milieus. He distinguishes between the inner social milieu of a society and its neighbouring societies which he calls its external social milieu. The inner milieu is composed of what he refers to as particular milieus. These particular milieus are the building blocks of society. Durkheim distinguishes between three types of milieus: family, territory and profession, and argues that historically they followed each other in a process of social evolution and eventually only professional milieus will prevail (Durkheim 1984: 138f.; Rebstein and Schnettler 2014; Vester 2014). Milieus are distinct webs of social relations that are inclusive of their members, with no multiple, changing or shifting memberships. Along with this goes a holistic account of milieu-culture since these particular milieus share a 'corpus of moral rules' (Durkheim 1984: xliii) that makes possible a total incorporation of the individual. However, the 'general' milieu influences all its particular milieus: 'It is the pressure that it exerts upon these partial groups which causes their constitution to vary' (Durkheim 1982: 138).

In the prologue to *Back to Blood*, we witness Ed Topping, newspaper editor and self-declared 'member of that dying genus, the White Anglo-Saxon Protestant' (Wolfe 2012: 9) and his wife Mac as they get into an argument at a parking lot outside a fancy restaurant in Miami. The opponent, identified by Ed as a Cuban woman, took their parking spot, which leads Mac to insult her and yell: 'YOU'RE IN AMERICA NOW! SPEAK ENGLISH!', answered by her counterpart: 'We een *Mee-ah-mee* now! *You* een Mee-ah-mee now!' (Wolfe 2012: 21). Miami is the territorial milieu in which Wolfe lays out his multi-faceted account of the role of ethnicity in present-day society. Instead of disappearing in the course of modernization, we learn, there is a return to primordial attachment. Back to blood here means that 'all people everywhere' (Wolfe 2012: 22) identify as members of distinct racial groups in order to achieve a sense of meaning and stability.

Ethnic groups appear to be the societal moulds, and group classifications (such as 'WASP' or 'Cuban') display the cultural logic of any specific society's social structure. From this perspective, society is a stable national entity. Stability is the result of social structure understood as a realm of reality that exists independently of the individuals that compose any specific society. This approach conceptualizes plurality as differentiation of social structure.

In migration studies, this way of conceptualizing ethnic groups as ethnic milieus has a long and lasting tradition, reaching, for example, from Glazer and Moynihan's (1970) study on ethnic revival even to current research on transnationalism. For example,[1] Min Zhou and Rennie Lee (2013) treat immigrant organizations as key actors in immigrant incorporation in 'host societies' and immigrant communities as the building blocks of society. Immigrant communities are defined as ethnic groups with a common group culture (ibid.: 23f.). In studies of ethnic groupings, milieu might be the more applicable concept than the commonly used community concept since community refers to *Gemeinschaft* ideas whereas formal organizations (that Zhou and Lee regard as instrumental for both the maintenance of ethnic community as well as for social incorporation) are rational elements of sociation. In contrast to community, milieu is able to capture both mechanical and organic solidarity (Durkheim 1984).

Milieu, stratification and shared lifestyles

The structuralist perspective on society has been redefined by Pierre Bourdieu. In an attempt to fuse Marx, Durkheim and Weber, he views society as structured by classes, and defines classes as the moulds in which social differentiation takes form. He follows the structuralist lead by regarding social relations as objective, trans-individual units constituted by structural oppositions (such as dominant–dominated).

Society at the same time constitutes a space of social positions and a space of lifestyles (Bourdieu 1984). Classes are defined by their capital volume and by their taste. These dimensions mutually reinforce each other and work at the reproduction of class society by means of the habitus, a class specific schema that organizes the patterns of perception, interpretation and action. It operates on multiple levels: the individual, since individuals incorporate the habitus; the interactive, since the habitus is handed down in primary social relations; and the institutional, since institutions like schools and universities positively sanction the 'appropriate' habitus. In *Distinction*, Bourdieu (1984) distinguishes between proletariat, the middle classes and the bourgeoisie. However, to Bourdieu (1) this is only one possible and historically specific kind of class formation and (2) class is not the only principle of social organization:

> So the very existence of classes as containers and determinants of social life is not a brute given inscribed in the differential distributions of life chances. Rather, it is the result of a work of group-making entailing struggles to impose class as the dominant 'principle of social vision and division' over and against competing alternatives (such as locality, ethnicity, nationality, gender, age, religion, and so on).
>
> *(Wacquant 2013: 276)*

These social divisions, however, are not social groups in the sense of membership to interactive social relations, but they structurally tie together individuals by their shared position within social space. The milieu concept is not prominent in Bourdieu's work for he did not appreciate that milieu does not imply a clear social hierarchy. However, his own analysis calls for a concept to capture the type of social differentiation that has not only a vertical dimension of class inequality, but also a horizontal dimension of difference and that might go beyond class division. His successors have used the milieu concept to capture this complexity and allow for the recognition of ethnic differentiation. Based on the class model of habitus distinctions, Anja Weiß (2010) expands Bourdieu's approach by adding racist symbolic capital to the list of forms of capital. Racist habitus elements allow for the reproduction of racial hierarchy in society. Classification is the interactive ascription of status in everyday life. Ferdinand Sutterlüty and Sighard Neckel (2006) show how negative ethnic classifications establish a structure of symbolic inequality that operates independently of economic inequality.

Michael Vester (2005) elaborates a concept of social space that distinguishes between a vertical axis of domination and a horizontal axis of culture and social practice. Empirically, this concept allows Vester to distinguish between different milieus in social space. His studies of different European countries show clear differences in the structure of milieus and how it changes over time. From this perspective, it is possible to show within every nation the limited number of social milieus that exist, each with its typical mentality and morality tied together in an overall structure of inequality and diversity.

Taking a perspective similar to Vester's, Carsten Wippermann and Berthold Bodo Flaig (2009) study migrant milieus in Germany. Arguing that membership to a migrant population does not determine membership to a migrant community (in the sense of a social group with shared norms, values and interests based on their shared ethnicity), they model migrant milieus based on the immigrant status of individuals and come up with eight milieus defined by their social position and basic values. These milieus are largely similar to the milieus of the general population.

While at the outset of *Back to Blood* we learn that race is an encompassing category defining an inclusive milieu that includes individuals from all social strata as part of ethnic differentiation, the second chapter draws a different picture. We meet Nestor Camacho, a young police officer, and his girlfriend Magdalena Otero. They live with their respective families in an almost exclusively Cuban milieu in Greater Miami. Hialeah is portrayed as a middle-class ethnoburb of social climbers who came to the USA as refugees from communist Cuba. The residents share a social position and culture that results from their horizontal and vertical mobility. On the one hand, they are eager not to be mistaken as working class. Nestor's father, who runs a tiny business, owns a vessel referred to as cruiser – 'cruiser meaning it was too big to be denigrated as a "motorboat"' (Wolfe 2012: 73). He has his name written on the side of his van and parks it in front of his home. While serving as a symbol of his success and being a source of pride, this is, on the other hand, evidence of all of Hialeah's inferior social status as compared to other suburbs: 'There were parts of Coral Gables where it was against the law to park a commercial vehicle like that in front of your house' (ibid.: 72). Thus, class position is located within a social hierarchy and linked to symbolic practices that make up the corresponding habitus. It also goes along with an ethnic class lifestyle which is maintained in the local social relations within the milieu. Santería syncretized with Roman Catholicism is practised; the mothers watch over their daughters to make sure they remain within the Cuban milieu; social relations are confined to the ethnic milieu.

Milieu as subjective aura

While structural approaches (based on theoretical considerations) take certain forms of social organization as analytical starting points, the phenomenological approach to milieu starts with the subjective reality of the individual (Gurwitsch 1979) and looks at the ways in which the 'sociocultural environment' (Dürrschmidt 2000: 43) is represented in the individual's milieu.

The subject produces its milieu as that sphere in which it feels at home. It is the subjective arena of intimate persons and things in which the individual acts without problems and that appears to him as taken for granted and uncomplicated. From this perspective, each individual has one and only one milieu to occupy (Dürrschmidt 2000: 18f.), and it is a fallacy to hypostatize the existence of a milieu beyond the sphere of the subject.

Tom Wolfe allows us to participate in Nestor's milieu while we listen to his inner monologue. Nestor experiences the outer world largely in racialized terms when he interacts with his colleagues on marine patrol, when he encounters women or meets the police chief of Miami. The structure and very existence of the (otherwise implicit and self-evident) milieu becomes explicit when it becomes problematic: while on marine police duty on a safe boat, Nestor saves the life of a Cuban refugee who had climbed on the mast of a schooner. Instead of treating him like a hero, as he had expected, his father accuses him of being a race traitor and of dishonouring his family. Since the refugee had not reached land, he might be returned to Cuba instead of being granted permission to stay in the USA. Nestor loses this milieu when his father turns away from him: 'Sleep, dear God. Knock me unconscious . . . that's all I ask . . . sail me away from esta casita . . . into the arms of the Sandman . . . Take away my thoughts . . . be my morphine' (Wolfe 2012: 79). The world appears even more alien and incomprehensible to him when Magdalena tells him that she is seeing another man: 'Nestor could no longer hear a thing except for a sound that began to fill his head . . . it sounded like the steam that comes out of those big irons at the cleaners' (ibid.: 143).

Milieu as structures of interaction

While building on the phenomenological epistemology, the interactionist approach to milieu argues that reality is a subjective experience constituted in the subjective consciousness and at the same time a social construction brought about in interaction (Berger and Luckmann 1966). Milieu here refers to the social life world, that realm of reality individuals inhabit collectively. Following Weber, this approach conceptualizes social relations not as structures in their own right but as chances (and restrictions) for encounters (Schütz and Luckmann 1973: 71, 84). It focuses on everyday life as the site where society is performed in interaction. Social structure is not regarded as objective reality reproduced by classificatory practices but as a set of everyday-life typifications that are being used to manage interaction. When these typifications are institutionalized, they result in the overarching order we call society. Society is a construction that is maintained by individuals by means of communication. Social structure is not external to individuals but only exists in communication. Patterns of communication allow for the continuous reproduction of social relation. In this, memory plays a decisive role: the communicative construction of communality is achieved in interactive relations by shared commemoration. Thomas Luckmann and others refer to these societal arenas as milieus (Günthner and Luckmann 1995; Luckmann 2002).

On a similar theoretical plane, Anselm Strauss (1978) argues that society consists of relatively stable spheres of social action that he calls social worlds. Social worlds can be described as structures that are continuously produced anew and altered through processes of segmentation, intersection and legitimation. They make up 'relatively permanent, "institutionalized" spaces of perception and action, secured by relatively stable routines and a distribution of labor' (Soeffner 1991: 363).

In historical perspective, this approach argues that present-day society is characterized by a diversity of different milieus. Modern societies are composed of a multitude of milieus, at the centre of which usually lies a core activity. Modern individuals possess multiple memberships to part-time milieus (Luckmann 1978). Milieus might be locally organized or territorially scattered. What is crucial is that they develop their own language and standardized sets of behaviour in performing their activities. These are what keeps them together. Thus, this approach follows a non-holistic account of culture and society (Appadurai 1986). Milieus are not structures but processes. Segmentation, intersection and legitimation lead to boundary drawing and closure, but also to opening and the bridging of boundaries. While milieus are segmented by their activities, they are connected to other milieus by the constant move of individuals between these worlds and by conflicts that bring them in contact with neighbouring milieus. They are constantly changed by novices, by innovations and by further segmentation in sub-milieus (Soeffner and Zifonun 2008). In the face of diversity within milieus, and diversity within their individual members, they maintain the image of stability through narrative.

Not only does the interactionist approach point to a growing number of different milieus and more dimensions of diversity between these milieus, and to the fact that reality is a subjective construct, a personal reality, but also it argues that the multiplicity of communicative milieus is maintained in discourse and action. This then is the true subject of investigation (Zifonun 2014). From this interactionist perspective, ethnicity is not a question of group culture or community. Rather, ethnicity is conceptualized as a communicative construction made relevant in interaction by the use of ethno-knowledge (Müller and Zifonun 2010), i.e. the institutionalized social stock of knowledge used by actors to construct and manage ethnicity. This stock of knowledge includes everyday life as well as scientific categories, typifications of actors (or stereotypes that are being imposed on actors) and knowledge of ethnic boundaries (Brubaker et al. 2004) and is used in ways that are specific to the different milieus. Ethno-knowledge is used to construct ethnic categories that serve as mechanisms for exclusion, and ethnic milieus use ethno-knowledge to establish ethnic spheres of action, i.e. to construct self-identified ethnic groups.

The Cuban-American milieu in *Back to Blood* is based on the narration of the experience of escape and settlement. Nestor heard the story of his parents' and grandparents' escape 'many more than a hundred times' (Wolfe 2012: 74), and his father repeats the narration when he accuses Nestor of being a traitor. Nestor tries to tell him that he acted as a police officer within the executive milieu when he went on the mast of the schooner ('I was carrying out *a direct order!*', ibid.: 77), something his father is not willing to accept. On another occasion, we learn about the large degree of social distance between Cuban and WASP members of the police force. Nestor is described as wearing his uniform in a style that makes him a typical 'cool Cuban cop' (ibid.: 26). Nestor's white colleagues make use of various racial stereotypes when referring to Cubans in Nestor's presence, while he refrains from using the ethnic counter-stereotypes that are common among Cubans (ibid. 2012: 25ff.), which is evidence of both the relevance of ethnic categories within this world as well as the asymmetry between the populations. After a particularly annoying remark made by his superior, Sergeant McCorkle, Nestor responds in an aggressive manner and thus 'turns the sparring match into a real battle' (Hughes 1945: 356) and immediately knows that this was a mistake. His superior turns sarcastic and Nestor is even afraid this might end his career (Wolfe 2012: 30). When milieus are formally opened to former outsiders, ethnic classifications serve as means of symbolic closure. They prevent status climbers from being 'drawn into the informal brotherhood in which experiences are exchanged, competence built up, and the formal code elaborated and enforced' (Hughes 1945: 356). However, when Nestor saves the man on the mast, ethnicity is interactively 'undone':

> The other guys at the marina were excited for Nestor. In the eyes of cops, Cuban and non-Cuban alike, he had pulled off a super-manly feat of strength ... Sergeant McCorkle was now his pal – his pal! ... Everybody laughed and laughed, and Nestor laughed with them.
> *(Wolfe 2012: 55f.)*

What might be most compelling about Wolfe's novel is the way he introduces his readers to a large array of milieus when we follow Magdalena after her break up with Nestor as she leaves her ethnic neighbourhood milieus and enters into the part-time milieus of the medical world (Wolfe 2012: 147ff.), the sailing milieus (ibid.: 243ff.), the art world (ibid.: 323ff.), or the media milieus (ibid.: 370ff.). While at first sight it appears as though Magdalena is overwhelmed by the social logics of these alien worlds, on closer inspection there is evidence of a profound distance that Magdalena has to all these worlds. Precisely because they are so diverse and partial, she is able to limit her loyalty to any of these milieus and the roles that she is called to perform. By the end of the novel, not only has Magdalena become disillusioned, but also she has matured. Instead of a member of an ethnic group, we find an individual trying to manage the social ambivalences of diversified modernity.

Conclusions

The four approaches discussed conceptualize plurality in different ways. The Durkheimian tradition argues for a structural differentiation of societal units. Particular milieus are differentiated within the inner milieu; they are integrated in opposition to the external milieu. The second approach suggests a structural differentiation of unequal societal strata. The vertical relational structure of domination–subordination can be further differentiated along the lines of horizontal social differences. From the phenomenological perspective, milieus can be characterized as subjective differences in the ways individuals constitute their environment. The interactionist approach conceives of a diversity of social spheres of communication and praxis that are institutionalized around shared activities. While these approaches might be incommensurable on a theoretical plane, they can be combined in empirical research by using a mixed method approach as they highlight different dimensions of diversity (Zifonun 2013). Accordingly, using a life-world approach, it is possible to study an individual's participation in different interactive milieus and the ways in which they are integrated in his or her subjective milieus (Kusenbach 2003). The interactive structure of a milieu can be revealed by analyzing particular social events within this world as they bring together the participants of this milieu performing activities characteristic of the milieu (Sutterlüty 2006). The relational structure of hierarchy and influence between different milieus is a third level of investigation (Clarke 2005).

The four approaches also allow for different ways of conceptualizing ethnicity. Both structuralist approaches regard ethnicity as social structure in a way that regards social structure as a mirror image of systems of classification: ethnic categories constitute social groupings. The subjectivist approach regards ethnicity as a category that allows for everyday-life sense-making. Finally, the interactionist approach conceptualizes ethnicity as a typification institutionalized in the social stock of knowledge that is interactively made relevant in social milieus.

Note

1   See also Levitt (2012) for references to the strong program in cultural sociology.

References

Appadurai, A. (1986) 'Is Homo Hierarchicus?', *American Ethnologist*, 13(4): 745–61.

Berger, P.L. and Luckmann, T. (1966) *The Social Construction of Reality: A Ttreatise in the Sociology of Knowledge*, New York, NY: Doubleday.

Bourdieu, P. (1984) *Distinction: A Social Critique of the Judgement of Taste*, Cambridge, MA: Harvard University Press.

Brubaker, R., Loveman, M. and Stamatov, P. (2004) 'Ethnicity as Cognition', *Theory and Society*, 33(1): 31–64.

Clarke, A.E. (2005) *Situational Analysis: Grounded Theory after the Postmodern Turn*, Thousand Oaks, CA: Sage.

Durkheim, E. (1982) *The Rules of Sociological Method*, New York, NY: The Free Press.

—(1984) *The Division of Labour in Society*, Basingstoke, UK: Palgrave Macmillan.

Dürrschmidt, J. (2000) *Everyday Lives in the Global City: The Delinking of Locale and Milieu*, London: Routledge.

Glazer, N. and Moynihan, D.P. (1970) *Beyond the Melting Pot: The Negroes, Puerto Ricans, Jews, Italians and Irish of New York City*, Cambridge, MA: MIT Press.

Günthner, S. and Luckmann, T. (1995) 'Asymmetries of Knowledge in Intercultural Communication: The Relevance of Cultural Repertoires of Communicative Genres', Fachgruppe Sprachwissenschaft Universität Konstanz, Arbeitspapier 72.

Gurwitsch, A. (1979) *Human Encounters in the Social World*, Pittsburgh, PA: Duquesne University Press.

Hughes, E.C. (1945) 'Dilemmas and Contradictions of Status', *The American Journal of Sociology*, 50(5): 353–9.

Kusenbach, M. (2003) 'Street Phenomenology: The Go-along as Ethnographic Research Tool', *Ethnography*, 4(3): 455–85.

Levitt, P. (2012) 'What's Wrong with Migration Scholarship? A Critique and a Way Forward', *Identities*, 19(4): 493–500.

Luckmann, B. (1978) 'The Small Life-worlds of Modern Man', in T. Luckmann (ed.) *Phenomenology and Sociology: Selected Readings*, New York, NY: Penguin.

Luckmann, T. (2002) 'Der Kommunikative Aufbau der Sozialen Welt und die Sozialwissenschaften', in T. Luckman (ed.) *Wissen und Gesellschaft: ausgewählte Aufsätze 1981–2002*, Konstanz: UVK.

Müller, M. and Zifonun, D. (eds) (2010) *Ethnowissen: Soziologische Beiträge zu Ethnischer Differenzierung und Migration*, Wiesbaden: VS.

Rebstein, B. and Schnettler, B. (2014) 'Sozialstrukturanalyse "Feiner Körnung" oder Subjektzentrierte Lebensweltanalyse?: Ungleichheitsbezogene und wissenssoziologische Ansätze der Milieuanalyse', in P. Isenböck, L. Nell and J. Renn (eds) *Die Form des Milieus: zum Verhältnis von Gesellschaftlicher Differenzierung und Formen der Vergemeinschaftung*, Weinheim: Juventa.

Schütz, A. and Luckmann, T. (1973) *The Structures of the Life-World*, Evanston, IL: Northwestern University Press.

Soeffner, H.G. (1991) '"Trajectory" as Intended Fragment: The Critique of Empirical Reason According to Anselm Strauss', in D.R. Maines. (ed.) *Social Organization and Social Process: Essays in Honor of Anselm Strauss*, New York, NY: De Gruyter.

Soeffner, H.G. and Zifonun, D. (2008) 'Integration – an Outline from the Perspective of the Sociology of Knowledge', *Qualitative Sociology Review*, 4(2): 3–23.

Strauss, A. (1978) 'A Social World Perspective', *Studies in Symbolic Interaction*, 1: 119–28.

Sutterlüty, F. (2006) 'The Belief in Ethnic Kinship: A Deep Symbolic Dimension of Social Inequality', *Ethnography*, 7(2): 179–207.

Sutterlüty, F. and Neckel, S. (2006) 'Bashing the Migrant Climbers: Interethnic Classification Struggles in German City Neighborhoods', *International Journal for Urban and Regional Research*, 30(4): 798–815.

Vester, M. (2005) 'Class and Culture in Germany', in F. Devine, M. Savage, J. Scott and R. Crompton (eds) *Rethinking Class: Cultures, Identities and Life-Styles*, Basingstoke, UK: Palgrave Macmillan.

—(2014) 'Milieu als Soziologisches Modell oder als Historische Praxis?: Milieu- und Klassenbegriff in der Vergessenen Klassischen Soziologie von Weber, Durkheim, Marx und Geiger', in P. Isenböck, L. Nell and J. Renn (eds) *Die Form des Milieus: zum Verhältnis von Gesellschaftlicher Differenzierung und Formen der Vergemeinschaftung*, Weinheim: Juventa.

Wacquant, L. (2013) 'Symbolic Power and Group-making: On Pierre Bourdieu's Reframing of Class', *Journal of Classical Sociology*, 13(2): 274–91.

Weiß, A. (2010) 'Racist Symbolic Capital: A Bourdieuian Approach to the Analysis of Racism', in W.D. Hund, J. Krikler and D. Roediger (eds) *Wages of Whiteness & Racist Symbolic Capital*, Münster: LIT.

Wippermann, C. and Flaig, B.B. (2009) 'Lebenswelten von Migrantinnen und Migranten', *Aus Politik und Zeitgeschichte*, 5: 3–11.

Wolfe, T. (2012) *Back to Blood*, New York, NY: Little, Brown & Company.

Zhou, M. and Lee, R. (2013) 'Transnationalism and Community Building: Chinese Immigrant Organizations in the United States', *The Annals of the American Academy of Political and Social Science*, 647(1): 22–49.

Zifonun, D. (2013) 'Soziale Welten Erkunden: der Methodologische Standpunkt der Soziologie Sozialer Welten', in H.G. Soeffner (ed.) *Transnationale Vergesellschaftungen*, Verhandlungen des 35. Kongresses der Deutschen Gesellschaft für Soziologie in Frankfurt am Main 2010, Wiesbaden: Springer.

—(2014) 'Versionen: das Sonderwissen Sozialer Milieus und seine Differenzierung', in P. Isenböck, L. Nell and J. Renn (eds) *Die Form des Milieus: zum Verhältnis von Gesellschaftlicher Differenzierung und Formen der Vergemeinschaftung*, Weinheim: Juventa.

11

Caste in India

Constructs and currents

Surinder S. Jodhka

Caste has often been viewed as a peculiar social institution that evolved in India, among the Hindus, and survived for centuries because it was supported by the Hindu religious ideology. This popular view of caste presents it as a simple system of hierarchy, structured around the ideas of *varna* and *jati*. The idea of *varna* was a model or a framework of social organization that divided the Hindus into four categories: the Brahmins, the Kshatriyas, the Vaishyas and the Shudras. Beyond the four *varnas* were the *achhoots* (the untouchables). These four categories occupied different statuses in the Hindu society, with the Brahmins at the top, followed by the other three *varnas* in the order of ranking as mentioned above, with the *achhoots* occupying a position at the very bottom. The *jati* was a sub-unit of *varna*, a concrete social grouping, strictly governed by the normative frames of occupational segregation and reproduced itself through the practice of endogamous marriage. Unlike the *varnas*, *jatis* were large in numbers and their constellations varied from region to region. They were often further divided into sub-units, within the larger frame of the *varna* system. According to one estimate in each linguistic region 'there were about 200 caste groups which were further sub-divided into about 3000 smaller units each of which was endogamous and constituted the area of effective social life for the individual' (Srinivas 1962: 65).

As this popular/dominant notion of caste goes, these ideas and practices produced an internally coherent and closed system of social inequality, a hierarchical social order structured around the notions of purity and pollution. The hierarchical system of caste best survived within the frame of village life, its social and economic order, and presumably remained unchanged for centuries. As an all-encompassing institution, caste governed everything in the life of a Hindu.

Caste is also presented as a kind of traditional social and cultural system, which was gradually to weaken and eventually disappear with the processes of modernization. The development of modern industrial economy, the growth of urban centres and spread of democratic political institutions were to unleash a new social and cultural logic, which would produce a structural change in the Indian society, or so it was formerly assumed by the dominant theories of social change. The process of modernization was to give way to an open system of stratification based on the idea of individual merit and civic citizenship.

Over the past century and more, India has moved on the path of modernization. This process was pursued with much political zeal after India acquired independence from British colonial rule. After independence, the nationalist leadership was quite successful in institutionalizing a parliamentary system of democratic politics based on a Western-style liberal Constitution. India's economy has also undergone significant changes over the past five or six decades. India is no longer a traditional or pre-modern agrarian society. Even though less than one-third of India is demographically urban, the influence of city life is quite widespread. The traditional caste-based occupations have disintegrated almost everywhere. The decline of India's agrarian economy is most evident from the fact that by the first decade of the twenty-first century it contributed less than 15 per cent to the total national income of the country.

Notwithstanding these fundamental changes in India's political and economic life, caste has persisted. Many would say that its presence in the popular and political discourses in contemporary times is much more pronounced than it was during the 1950s or 1960s, when the institutional hold of caste was perhaps much stronger. One may explain this persistence of caste by attributing it to a flawed process of modernization that India has pursued. However, the persistence of caste in contemporary times also raises questions about the validity of the popular Hindu religion-centric view of caste. Further, the assumption of it being a Hindu religious institution is also questioned by the fact that caste-like hierarchies have also existed among the non-Hindu communities of India and beyond India, in the subcontinent, and not in the Hindu frame of *varna* system (see Jodhka 2012; Jodhka and Shah 2010).

How then do we make sense of the persistence of caste in today's India? This chapter tries to engage with this question by providing (i) a critical overview of the popular theorizations of caste and their flaws; (ii) a broad view of the changing dimension of caste; and (iii) alternative ways of approaching caste that could help us understand the present day realities of caste.

Conceptualizing caste

The history of the modern-day theorization of caste begins with Western and colonial engagements with Indian civilization (Cohn 1996; Dirks 2001). However, this is not to suggest that divisions that came to be described as the caste system did not exist earlier or that they were a creation of colonial rule. Categories such as *varna*, *jati* or *zat*, and the corresponding social divisions and hierarchies of status, have indeed been present in different parts (though not everywhere) of the South Asian region for a very long time. They have also been the source of contestations. For example, several social and religious movements during the 'medieval' times questioned the legitimacy of such divisions and offered alternative ways of imagining the human universe based on egalitarian ideals (see Omvedt 2008).

The Western idea of 'caste' simplified the diverse, and often contested, realities of the 'native' social order into a neatly marked out division of groups. Drawn mostly from the ancient 'Hindu' texts, these 'orientalist' writings theorized caste as a hierarchical system through the idea of *varna* as a substantive category where Brahmins were always placed at the top of the hierarchical order, followed by Kshatriya, Vaishya and Shudra. The untouchable communities were outside the formal hierarchy but their status also followed this neat hierarchical order derived from the logic of purity and impurity.

For the colonial rulers, such theorization of Indian social order was not merely an academic exercise. This helped them make sense of what seemed like an incomprehensible reality. They also deployed their notion of caste hierarchy in their administrative system for classifying the native communities and determining their qualities and traits. As Sharma points out:

> [T]he British took the existence of caste very seriously. Successive censuses of India attempted to classify the entire population by caste, on the assumption that everyone must

> belong to some caste or other and that castes were real identifiable groups. As a result, this objectification of caste actually made it more real and liable to rigidification.
>
> *(Sharma 2002: 8)*

This 'book-view' of caste also constructed India as the 'other' of the Western society, which was based on the idea of equality among individuals. The system of caste divisions was a peculiar feature of the subcontinent, where social order had been static for ages and had no possibility of change emanating from internal contradictions. Such a view presented colonial rule as being good for India. The colonized people were so completely governed by the normative order of caste that they had no agency of their own (Inden 1990: 65). Even radical thinkers like Marx and Engels were influenced by such views about the Indian social order and they affirmed in their writings the need for a colonial intervention which alone could break the equilibrium that had kept the Indian village community static for centuries.

The influence of *Colonialism and its forms of knowledge*, to use Bernard Cohn's (1996) expression, was also quite significant to the way professional sociology and social anthropology developed in India. Even when the post-colonial 'native' sociologists and social anthropologists advocated a shift away from the 'book-view' towards a 'field-view' of India, the categories through which a majority of them imagined India invariably remained the same. For example, the village typically became a convenient entry point for anthropologists interested in understanding the dynamics of Indian society (Jodhka 1998). Similarly, sociologists and social anthropologists universally assumed that the caste system was fundamental to Indian social structure, which in turn also synonymized Hindu religion with Indian culture.

More recent historical research on the subject has seriously undermined this 'common sense' about the caste system. Not only did the colonial rulers, through a process of enumeration and ethnographic surveys, raise consciousness about caste, but also they produced the conditions where 'caste became the single term capable of expressing, organizing, and above all "synthesizing" India's diverse forms of social identity, community and organization' (Dirks 2001: 5).

The dominant textbook-view of caste that emerged has continued to be based largely on the classical colonial understanding of 'Hindu India'. Putting it in a language of social science textbooks, Ghurye (1993) identified six different features of the Hindu caste system: segmental division of society; hierarchy; restrictions on feeding and social intercourse; civil and religious disabilities and privileges of different sections; lack of unrestricted choice of occupation; restrictions on marriage.

Though seemingly simple and obvious, this list represented caste as a total and unitary system. Thus, it was possible to define caste and to identify its core features which were presumably present everywhere in the subcontinent. Similarly, caste was also not merely about occupational specialization or division of labour. It encapsulated within it the features of a social structure, normative religious behaviour and even provided a fairly comprehensive idea about the personal lives of individuals living in the Hindu caste society.

Perhaps the most influential theoretical work on caste has been that of Louis Dumont. He approached the Hindu caste system from a structuralist perspective that focused on the underlying structure of ideas of a given system, the 'essential principles', which may not be apparent or visible in its everyday practice. Caste, according to Dumont, was above all an ideology, and the core element in the ideology of caste for Dumont was hierarchy. Hierarchy was not merely another name for inequality or an extreme form of social stratification, but a totally different principle of social organization. Such a principle, Dumont suggests, was 'the opposition of the pure and the impure'. Hierarchy, defined as the superiority of the pure over the impure, was the keystone in Dumont's model of the caste system (Dumont 1998 [1970]: 43). An important aspect of his theory was the specific relationship that existed between status and power in Hindu society. Unlike in the West, where power and status normally went together, in the caste system there was a divergence between the two. In caste society, status as a principle of social organization was superior to power: 'status encompassed power'.

Even social anthropologists who did not agree with Dumont's formulation subscribed to the assumption that caste was widely accepted as a frame of social organization across groups in the hierarchical system in Hindu/Indian society. For example, although the Indian social anthropologist Srinivas rejected Dumont's method of studying caste through textual sources and advocated for a field-view of caste, he appears to be underlining the ideological unity and cultural consensus in Indian society through his concept of *sanskritization*, which was a

> process by which a 'low' Hindu caste, or tribal or other group, changes its customs, ritual, ideology, and way of life in the direction of a high and frequently, 'twice-born' caste. Generally such changes are followed by a claim to higher position in the caste hierarchy than that traditionally conceded to the claimant caste by the local community.
>
> *(Srinivas 1972: 6)*

There are, however, many who completely disagree with the Dumontian view of caste. Dumont's theory was criticized for its ideological bias in favour of the Brahmins and its weak empirical groundings (Gupta 1984).

Caste and/as power and domination

As already discussed, the dominant view of caste that presented it as an integrated and harmonious system of hierarchy evolved out of the colonial and orientalist engagement with Indian society. Interestingly, the origin of an alternative view of caste can also be located in the administrative history of British colonial rule. Colonial census made the state-system a critical agent in the life of all castes. Institutionalization of the colonial census and enumeration of caste and religious communities made 'numbers' a crucial variable in the colonial administration. Along with the ritual status, the numerical strength of a group began to acquire significance, particularly when it came to the question of recognition and representation in the evolving state-system.

It was in this context that, at some time in the early decades of the twenty-first century, the caste groups located at the bottom of caste hierarchy were recognized as a separate category for their lack of basic human rights and material resources. Supported by local reformers, the colonial state clubbed together several of these caste groups into an administrative category, the 'depressed classes' (Charsley 1996; Jodhka 2012). They were so depressed that their touch was polluting for upper caste Hindus. Thus the ideas of the 'line of pollution' and 'untouchability' acquired administrative legitimacy.

In the context of the growing demand by the emergent leaders of the 'untouchable' communities for equal status and citizenship rights, the post-colonial Indian state found this classification useful and institutionalized the distinction through the introduction of a separate Schedule in the Indian Constitution that listed all the depressed caste communities. The independent Indian state also introduced an extensive programme of affirmative action in the form of quotas or 'reservations' for the Scheduled Castes in representative bodies, jobs and education. The practice of untouchability was made illegal by the new constitution (see also Viswanath, this volume).

The reservation policy became a source of social, economic and political mobility for those located at the bottom of the traditional caste hierarchy. Over the years, a new middle-class emerged from within these communities that began to speak for the common interests and experiences of the 'untouchable' caste communities and to represent them through a new political category, the Dalits (Zelliot 2001).

The process of horizontal political consolidation has not been confined to the Dalits. Even those above them have actively mobilized caste identity for political representation and consolidation. Caste proved to be a flexible institution that could easily adapt to the world of competitive electoral politics (see Kothari 1970; Rudolph and Rudolph 1967). However, while different caste groups began to use it as an easily available resource for political mobilizations, its growing participation in democratic politics also had far reaching implications for the internal logic of caste, with its political grammar woven around the idea of hierarchy and repulsion. For example, the well-known Indian political scientist Rajni Kothari argued against the popular notion that democratic politics was helping traditional institutions like caste to 'resuscitate and re-establish their legitimacy'. On the contrary, he insisted that in reality

> the consequences of caste-politics interactions are just the reverse of what is usually stated. It is not politics that gets caste-ridden; it is caste that gets politicised. Dialectical as might sound, it is precisely because the operation of competitive politics has drawn caste out of its apolitical context and given it a new status that the 'caste system' as hitherto known has eroded and has begun to disintegrate.
>
> *(Kothari 1970: 20f.)*

The gradual processes of the deepening of democratic politics, economic modernization and the policies of affirmative action have changed many aspects of caste. Empirical studies by sociologists and social anthropologists from different regions of the country have reported a loosening of the traditional structures of power/domination and disintegration of rural hierarchies (Jodhka 2002; Karanth 1996; Manor 2012; Mendelsohn 1993).

Even though the nature and extent of economic change during the post-independence period varies significantly across regions of India, rural social structures have changed everywhere. In some parts of the country the old structure of patron–client relations that bound different caste together, the *jajmani* system, has completely disintegrated. On the basis on an extensive survey of 51 villages of the northwestern state of Punjab carried out in 1999 to 2000, I proposed that the changes occurring in rural caste hierarchies could be conceptualized through the categories of dissociation, distancing and autonomy (Jodhka 2002).

Due to their social and economic mobility and the loosening of the traditional social order, a large majority of Dalits were consciously dissociating themselves from traditional 'polluting' occupations that they had been tied into for generations. Many of these occupations were no longer identified with any specific caste group in rural Punjab. For example, picking up of dead cattle became a completely commercialized enterprise. The local community now gave the work on contract to an individual contractor, who could even be from another village or nearby town. Though most of those involved in this business belonged to 'low' castes, they were poor and often lived in towns. Similarly, some degree of commercialization had taken place in the case of other low caste *jajmani* occupations. Barbers, carpenters and blacksmiths all had shops, and they came from a diversity of caste groups. Some of the barbers, for example, were the erstwhile scavengers. Relations of these shopkeepers with their clients were purely instrumental. The only 'unclean occupations', where a degree of continuity existed, was that of scavenging. But in this occupation too the traditional structure of *jajmani* relations had almost been completely changed. The cleaning of drains and toilets or sweeping of the houses was mostly done on a commercial basis.

Almost everywhere in rural India caste was closely intertwined with the local agrarian economy. The customary norms prohibited the untouchable castes from owning and cultivating agricultural lands. However, their services were needed for various agricultural operations. Many of them were tied to the landed families of the dominant and upper castes, often like bonded slaves. This was perhaps more true in agriculturally dynamic regions like Punjab. With the growing use of tractors and other modern inputs, the agrarian relations have largely been formalized. Labour in-migrations from other regions of India also played an important role in changing the local agrarian relations. One of the obvious consequences of this change was the decline of old systems of tied labour. Dalits obviously did not like getting into such arrangements and tried to withdraw from employment in agriculture wherever they could. Their attempt to distance themselves from the local agrarian economy largely depended on the availability of alternative sources of employment in the neighbouring towns or on nearby construction sites.

Political mobilizations among the ex-untouchable communities have also created a new political consciousness among them, and they have been working towards autonomizing their communities from the dominant caste controlled village institutions. Wherever they could, they constructed separate community halls, temples and *gurudwaras* of their own, sometimes with a free grant from the state, sometimes using their own resources.

While the intensity of these processes varies across regions and sub-regions of India, similar processes have also been underway in other parts of the country. The rise of autonomous politics of the Dalits in different parts of the country is an obvious evidence of this fact (see Pai 2013).

Caste today: decline and persistence

Perhaps the most fascinating aspect of the reality of caste in contemporary India is that even when the traditional hierarchies are waning, caste-based inequalities in the material and political domain continue. Notwithstanding the success of Indian democracy, the increasing participation of the historically marginalized groups/communities in the electoral process and more than six decades of development and quotas for Scheduled Castes, caste-based disparities have not disappeared. In other words, caste continues to be an important indicator of deprivation and marginality, both at the macro-level reflected in the national-level data (see Thorat 2009) and at the micro-level (see Jodhka 2002; Shah *et al.* 2006). Caste also plays an important role in the modern urban economy. For example, ownership of industry in India has historically been concentrated in the hands of a few social/cultural groups and the top jobs were always kept within the family (Munshi 2007; Rutten 2003). Recruitments to other jobs were opened to outsiders only when the required personnel were not available within the community or the wider kin-group. Caste is almost always a negative social identity for the Dalits when they wish to enter the modern/urban labour market (Jodhka and Newman 2007) or business (Jodhka 2010).

In the emerging social and economic contexts, caste appears to matter more to those who have historically been on the margins of the traditional system of hierarchy. Their position on the margin implies their lack of economic resources and social capital, which makes it harder for them to participate in the emerging neo-liberal economic system. This is happening at a time when their increased participation in democratic political process through identity-based political formations has raised their aspirations for citizenship rights and opportunities for economic mobility.

These emerging, often contradictory, trends have completely altered the discourse of caste. Since the early 1990s caste has increasingly been talked about by those who have historically been on the margins at the receiving end of the hierarchical system.

Viewed from the margins, caste needed to be talked about not because of any love for a dying tradition or as an important marker of 'cultural difference', but because it continued to be a source of deprivation and discrimination. Caste influenced development outcomes and reproduced older forms of exclusions in the emerging economic order. The continued presence of caste as a reality of the Indian society, and as a system of power and domination, thus needs to be recognized. This articulation of caste has also opened up spaces for engagements with the state for policy intervention on caste-lines.

Viewed from the margins, the caste system has three core defining features. Above all, caste is about domination. Caste has been an institutionalized form of domination, supported by a set of values, norms and institutions, some of which continue to be present even today while others have weakened or disintegrated. However, there has not been a radical break with the caste system. In the absence of a comprehensive structural change, caste asserts itself as coercive power, perhaps more often than before, because of the weakening of its ideological hold. Increase in the incidence of caste-based atrocities is an evidence of this.

The second related dimension of caste is that it refers to disparities. Caste does not simply imply power in the cultural sense of the term. It is also a structural reality where inequality is institutionalized in terms of unequal distribution of resources. Inequality, seen in terms of disparities, refers to a very different set of attributes when compared with the Dumontian notion of inequality, which refers to a cultural notion of hierarchy, something which exists only as an ideological category, derived from the dialectical opposition between pure and impure as it exists in the Hindu mind. Disparities, on the other hand, refer to inequalities in terms of entitlements and ownership of resources, closer to the Marxian notion of 'means of production'. However, the nature of disparities and inequalities in the caste society is different. They are 'graded inequalities', to use Ambedkar's (1936) expression.

The third related dimension of caste is that it is an institutionalized system of discrimination and denial. Discrimination and denial has been socially and culturally institutionalized in India and it has been group specific. It produced a pattern of disadvantages, which in turn produced deprivations and poverty among certain groups. Denial was culturally institutionalized in the sense that it had legitimacy and long term implications for the social and economic status of caste groups/communities. For example, the ex-untouchable communities were not allowed to own and cultivate land and become peasants. Such customary practices could not be explained away by referring simply to the dialectics of pure and impure. They defined and limited rights of different groups of people. More importantly perhaps, the effects of such past tradition are felt even today by a large majority of Dalits. The absence of assets, such as agricultural land, makes them much more vulnerable, economically as well as socially.

Concluding comments

Caste has for a long time been a subject of inquiry for sociologists, social anthropologists and political scientists. However, it has been invariably looked at as a traditional system of social hierarchy and culture, which would inevitably weaken and eventually disappear with the process of development or modernization. Mostly, social anthropologists and sociologists researched caste in relation to rural social order, kinship networks, religious life or traditional occupations. The economists who worked on the 'hard' questions of development rarely treated caste as a relevant area of inquiry. In the mainstream understanding of textbook economics, development or markets were essentially secular and anonymous processes. Poverty and deprivation were attributes of individuals or households, and those possessing such attributes could be classified and clubbed together using purely secular and economic categories. Using caste and community in policy discourse, the 'secular economists' argued, was akin to giving them legitimacy and strengthening hierarchical social order and traditional cultural practices.

Over the years, however, scholars have come to recognize the crucial importance of 'non-economic' factors such as caste, race, ethnicity or gender in structuring the market and determining economic outcomes. Following this realization, mainstream development studies have also undergone a complete paradigm shift over the last two decades or so with 'human' rather than 'economic' development becoming the focus and index of growth and progress.

In addition to these changes from above, the paradigm shift in the approaches to caste has also been pushed by the pressures from 'below', the social and political churning being experienced on the ground with expanding democratic political process. The autonomous Dalit movements during the late 1980s did not simply request recognition and state power, they also raised questions about the meanings of caste and how it continued to be experienced even in secular/modern spaces in contemporary life. These movements also stood (and continue to stand) for active engagement with the state system on its policies for development and its laws against discrimination.

Over the last two decades, the academic understanding of caste has also been undergoing change. There is an increasing recognition of the fact that caste is not simply a question of past tradition and Indian/Hindu culture, or that it would disappear on its own once modern forces of industrial development and democratic politics appeared on the scene. The popular understanding of caste is beginning to recognize that talking about caste means talking also about power and powerlessness, about disparities, discrimination and the denial of access to resources and entitlements. The rise of the autonomous Dalit voice also articulated a new vision of citizenship whereby recognition of community identities became essential in addressing the question of denial.

References

Ambedkar, B.R. (1936) *Annihilation of Caste*, Jalandhar: Bheem Patrika.

Charsley, S.R. (1996) '"Untouchable": What is in a Name?', *Journal of the Royal Anthropological Institute*, 2(1): 1–23.

Cohn, B. (1996) *Colonialism and its Forms of Knowledge: The British in India*, Princeton, NJ: Princeton University Press.

Dirks, N.B. (2001) *Castes of Mind: Colonialism and the Making of Modern India*, Princeton, NJ: Princeton University Press.

Dumont, L. (1998) [1970] *Homo Hierarchicus: The Caste System and its Implications*, Delhi: Oxford India Paperbacks.

Ghurye, G.S. (1993) 'Features of Caste System', in D. Gupta (ed.) *Social Stratification*, Delhi: Oxford University Press.

Gupta, D. (1984) 'Continuous Hierarchies and Discrete Castes', *Economic and Political Weekly*, 19(48): 2049–53; reprinted in D. Gupta (ed.) (1992) *Social Stratification*, Delhi: Oxford University Press.

Inden, R. (1990) *Imagining India*, Oxford, UK: Blackwell.

Jodhka, S.S. (1998) 'From "Book-view" to "Field-view": Social Anthropological Constructions of the Indian Village', *Oxford Development Studies*, 26(3): 311–31.

—(2002) 'Caste and Untouchability in Rural Punjab', *Economic and Political Weekly*, 37(19): 1813–23.

—(2010) 'Dalits in Business: Self-employed Scheduled Castes in North-West India', *Economic and Political Weekly*, 45(11): 41–8.

—(2012) *Caste*, Delhi: Oxford University Press.

Jodhka, S.S. and Newman, K. (2007) 'In the Name of Globalisation: Meritocracy, Productivity and the Hidden Language of Caste', *Economic and Political Weekly*, 42(41): 4125–32.

Jodhka, S.S. and Shah, A.M. (2010) 'Comparative Contexts of Discrimination: Caste and Untouchability in South Asia', *Economic and Political Weekly*, 45(48): 99–106.

Karanth, G.K. (1996) 'Caste in Contemporary Rural India', in M.N. Srinivas (ed.) *Caste: Its Twentieth Century Avatar*, New Delhi: Penguin.

Kothari, R. (1970) *Caste in Indian Politics*, Hyderabad: Orient Longman.

Manor, J. (2012) 'Accommodation and Conflict', *Seminar*, 2012(633): 14–18.

Mendelsohn, O. (1993) 'The Transformation of Authority in Rural India', *Modern Asian Studies*, 15(4): 805–42.

Munshi, K. (2007) 'The Birth of a Business Community: Tracing Occupational Migration in a Developing Economy', Online. Available HTTP: <www.econ.brown.edu/fac/Kaivan_Munshi/diamond10.pdf> (accessed 10 November 2008).

Omvedt, G. (2008) *Seeking Begumpura: The Social Vision of Anti-Caste Intellectuals*, New Delhi: Navayana.

Pai, S. (2013) *Dalit Assertion*, Delhi: Oxford University Press.

Rudolph, L.I. and Rudolph, S.H. (1967) *The Modernity of Tradition: Political Development in India*, Hyderabad: Orient Longman.

Rutten, M. (2003) *Rural Capitalists in Asia: A Comparative Analysis on India, Indonesia and Malaysia*, London: Routledge.

Shah, G., Mander, H. and Thorat, S. (2006) *Untouchability in Rural India*, New Delhi: Sage.

Sharma, U. (2002) *Caste*, New Delhi: Viva Books Private.

Srinivas, M.N. (1962) *Caste in Modern India and other Essays*, Bombay: Media Promoter and Publishers.

—(1972) *Social Change in Modern India*, Berkeley, CA: University of California Press.

Thorat, S. (2009) *Dalits in India: Search for a Common Destiny*, New Delhi: Sage.

Zelliot, E. (2001) *From Untouchable to Dalit: Essays on the Ambedkar Movement*, New Delhi: Manohar.

Part II
Historical geographies of diversity

12

Diversity and the Roman Empire

Peter Heather

On the face of it, it would be hard to find a more diverse political entity than the Roman Empire. The longest-lived empire that western Eurasia has ever seen, it lasted at pretty much full extent certainly for 400 years, and, in Britain aside (a minor appendage), for over half a millennium. It was also enormous. Running from Hadrian's Wall to the river Euphrates, it encompassed a huge range of diverse geographical, economic, political and cultural contexts. Indeed, when it first came into existence, there were only a few actual Romans: a small privileged group in mainly central and southern Italy who enjoyed the legal and other privileges of citizenship. In the early imperial period, the widespread human diversity which the empire encompassed at its outset was not just recognised de facto, but often licensed de jure.

The early Empire

Like most pre-modern political structures, the Roman Empire could not be run as a centralised state in the proper sense of the word. In human terms, it was far larger even than it appears on the map. The real measure of distance is how long it takes human beings to cover it, and, in the Roman period, pretty much everything (except messages carried by changes of horse) moved at about forty kilometres a day. In the modern world, ten or twenty times that speed is entirely normal for people and goods, so that, in lived human experience, the Empire was actually between ten and twenty times larger than first appears.[1] The problems of running it from a single governmental centre were thus colossal. Equally important, for much of its history the Empire possessed only limited bureaucratic capacity. As late as the mid-third century AD, when it had been in existence for over 300 years, there were only about 250 senior administrators for the entire Empire. With so little structure and so much original human variety, it is hardly surprising that diversity was a fundamental feature of the Roman imperial edifice.

On a political level, much of the Mediterranean region came pre-organised into a network of substantially autonomous local cities. Various types of organisation – leagues then monarchies – had provided a variety of political superstructure, but classical and Hellenistic Greek civilisation had put a huge cultural premium on the self-governing city (the *polis*) as a uniquely civilising form of human political institution. It had also proved a highly practical fit for Mediterranean littoral conditions in the first millennium BC. As a result, when the Roman Empire began to absorb them in the last centuries before Christ, many Mediterranean communities came with long-established traditions of self-government, which Rome lacked the capacity or will to reorganise. Especially since its own traditions were highly influenced by the cultural hegemony of the Greek polis model, imperial administrators were generally happy to relicense existing local autonomy by authorising privileges of self-government in return for designated annual payments.[2] The same was largely true in other parts of the Empire – such as northern Europe – where pre-Roman political structures took an entirely different form. Again, many existing elites and socio-political structures were often left in place with a Roman officer as political overseer.[3]

On the legal front too, pre-existing structures and identities were often respected. Possessing formal citizenship of your home polis had for centuries been the key to a place among the elite of a Greek city: a privilege not available to the majority of inhabitants. Not only did the empire largely recognise these pre-existing citizenship patterns – i.e. existing patterns of social privilege – but also, when it started recognising particular individuals by grants of Roman citizenship, it often did so via new hybrids. These gave individuals the extra benefits of Roman citizenship only insofar as they did not impinge upon the existing rights of their home cities to call upon them for priesthoods, magistracies and other administrative positions (Sherwin-White 1973).

More generally, local legal structures were largely left in place as fully operative systems, particularly in the key area of civil law. In the ancient world, capital wealth really only came in one form: land. Most ancient civil law was therefore concerned with establishing watertight mechanisms for exploiting landed wealth (tenancies, mortgages, etc.) and for passing it on between the generations (marriage settlements, inheritance, etc.). For local elites, nothing was more important than secure possession of their landed wealth (citizenship itself usually required the possession of a minimum landed portfolio), and the Empire happily left pre-existing legal structures in place. Best known, thanks to papyri, is Egypt, where the local legal system remained substantially operative for over three centuries after it became a Roman province, but there is no reason to suppose it was in any way exceptional in the survival of existing legal structures.[4]

The early Empire was also marked by wide-ranging cultural diversity, operating on various levels. Much was simply de facto. The new imperial state was just not interested in the cultural traditions of the mass of its subjects, particularly the land-working peasantry who probably made up between eighty-five and ninety per cent of its total population. So long as fiscal obligations were met, Roman administrators were content to allow life in the provinces to evolve along existing lines. Right into the late imperial period, therefore, peasants in different parts of the Empire continued to speak a vast array of languages, from Punic in North Africa to Celtic, Coptic, Illyrian and Armenian, amongst many others, across the rest of the Empire.

Sometimes, continued diversity went far beyond cultural laissez faire. In its earliest centuries, Rome had come to the fore in central and southern Italy by aggressive self-assertion against the old Greek city states of southern Italy and Sicily. Not surprisingly, therefore, an important strand in early Roman cultural self-understanding defined itself vigorously against Greek cultural patterns: portraying Romans as self-disciplined and morally virtuous where Greeks were self-indulgent and corrupt. But Greek culture was much richer, and by the last decades of the first century BC, many Greek cultural ideals came to be internalised by the Roman imperial elite. Most fundamentally, Greek grammarians provided a set of tools which were applied to the Latin language to create the fixed 'classical' Latin, which was not merely a practical exercise in taxonomy but involved accepting the grammarians' contention that possessing a language defined by clear grammatical rules was an indispensable first step for human beings who wished to develop their god-given potential for full rationality. Along with this came the absorption and mimicry of Greek philosophy, Greek science, Greek literary genres and most of the other fruits of 1000 years of cultural development, so that a Greco-Roman hybrid quickly became the characteristic cultural discourse of the Roman imperial elite.[5]

Beyond the educated elite, other cultural patterns – for instance in the realm of religion – show, again, a much greater diversity. There were some exceptions. Famously, Rome took it upon itself to suppress any religious cult – particularly that of the Druids – which practised human sacrifice. Roman officials had also periodically persecuted what they perceived as *superstitio* (worshipping non-Roman gods and magical practices of unlicensed kinds), long before early Christians found themselves categorised under the same heading. In practice, however, the Empire nonetheless tolerated rich religious diversity. Famously, a whole series of equations were made with the established Roman pantheon to legitimise the gods of new provincial populations. Aquae Sulis Minerva worshipped at Bath is only one of multiple examples. And even where such equations were impossible, as with the Empire's resolutely monotheistic Jewish populations, various types of modus vivendi were reached. Not only did the Jews function as a recognised population group within the Empire, but also, so long as various public rites were celebrated for the Capitoline Gods (Jupiter, Juno and Minerva), private cults could take many and varied forms, with new eastern cults, such as Mithraism, spreading widely through the army.[6]

In its early phases, therefore, the Empire operated as a hegemonic, bureaucratically underdeveloped superstate over such vast distances that it had no choice but to tolerate huge local diversity de facto. Much more than that, however, it also licensed much of this diversity as a matter of deliberate policy. As the Empire continued to evolve, however, and as outside conditions changed, its original diversity came under significant pressure.

Romanisation

For all its licensed and de facto diversity, the Roman Empire was a conquest state. Some petty monarchs in Asia Minor 'voluntarily' ceded their territories to Roman control, but the vast majority of Rome's territories were acquired by conquest. Not surprisingly, this hardwired a particular political dynamic into the Empire's internal politics. Because it was a conquest state run by and for Romans, the most advantageous position to occupy within it in social terms was to be a Roman citizen; even if you were – economically – a relatively poor one. Best of all, of course, was to be a prominent and rich Roman citizen, since office-holding in the new imperial structure opened up colossal opportunities for enrichment, sometimes generating the kinds of legal case in which Cicero first rose to prominence.[7] All of which posed a structural challenge to richer and more ambitious non-Romans within provincial society, who now found themselves second-class citizens within the new imperial world. How they responded to this challenge generated a significant decline in the Empire's original diversity on a whole series of levels.

The earliest manifestations of response saw prominent provincials deliberately seeking out first Roman citizenship and then opportunities to work their way into prestigious Roman cultural structures, such as the imperial cult, which began to spread at an early date (see e.g. Fishwick 1987; Price 1984). This was followed by more substantial structural shifts: most notably the replacement of originally diverse patterns of local political organisation towards an Empire-wide norm. By the third century AD, the same municipal constitution had been adopted right across the Empire, redefining local government within the Empire as the responsibility of a series of city councils with responsibility for dependent rural territories. The model was ultimately based on the Greek polis, but reworked according to imperial priorities, and, not only did the new structure quickly spread across western and northern Europe, where there had never been any *poleis*, but also was increasingly adopted by old Greek cities of the Mediterranean littoral. Equally important, the early third century saw Roman citizenship become universal for all the free inhabitants of the Empire through the *Constitutio Antoniniana* of AD 212 – and, as the third century progressed, Roman legal structures increasingly replaced older provincial traditions. Educationally, too, a much greater uniformity marked out the formation of the Empire's land-owning elites. From Hadrian's Wall to the Euphrates, a standard, private education (in either Latin or Greek predominantly, depending on which part of the Empire you were born into) at the hands of grammarians and then rhetors became the hallmark of elite status, to such an extent that not to speak the kind of educated linguistic forms these men taught was immediately to mark yourself out as a parvenu. Extending Roman citizenship and Roman legal structures obviously had broader implications, but, above all, the first two centuries AD thus saw astonishing transformations in the lives of provincial landowning elites. It expressed itself even in the kinds of houses they built and the food they ate, adding up to a new elite uniformity right across the Empire.[8]

This certainly helped to eliminate the rebellions which were a regular feature of the early Empire, Boudicca being only one example of a recurring pattern. The weight of post-conquest imperial demands was heavily enough felt to prompt serious revolts in most (especially north European) territories. Occasionally, these were successful: Arminius' rebellion led the Empire to cede land between the Rhine and the Elbe. The vast majority were unsuccessful, however, and, in general terms, such rebellions ceased by the end of the first century AD. Since this was also the moment when the lives of provincial elites were taking on a more markedly Roman character, then traditional scholarship often painted provincial elite Romanisation as a top-down process, designed to curb politically dangerous centrifugal forces.[9]

The main mechanism which expanded Roman citizenship to a wider cross-section of provincial elite society, however, was actually a specific feature of the standard municipal constitution which set up the new city councils. Under this constitution, of which a complete version was found in the 1980s inscribed on bronze tablets, one of the main perquisites of the positions was that the councils' chief administrative officers received automatic grants of Roman citizenship. Looked at more closely, moreover, it has become clear that the spread of these constitutions was not a straightforward top-down process. Local communities first put up at their own expense some of the standard stock of public buildings – temples, theatres, etc. – which signalled that they were a culturally Roman community, and then lobbied their provincial governors to persuade the Emperor to grant them a constitution. Not only did this set in motion a process which progressively made them Roman citizens, but also it gave them defined means of raising revenues – through local taxes and tolls – from the countryside which now fell under their control (Gonzalez and Crawford 1986). What the period *c.*AD50–150 (when most of the constitutions were granted) broadly witnessed, therefore, was not top-down Romanisation, but a process of provincial self-Romanisation, part of the overall response to original advantages built into the imperial system for Roman citizens.

The spread of Roman law reflects similar processes. On one level, it was a direct effect of extending Roman citizenship, since Roman citizens (as in the case of St Paul) had the right to use Roman law. But there was always a potential gap between theory and practice, and it was not until the later second and third centuries AD that we have good evidence of Roman law, as a system, becoming the dominant legal discourse across wide stretches of the Empire. And here too, the inherent advantages of things Roman, in what was indisputably a Roman Empire, played a critical role. In a world where landed wealth was so crucial to elite status, it was not sensible to take any risks with the disposition of landed assets. Using Roman law, for a Roman citizen, had the huge advantage that the Empire's premier legal system could ultimately be used to defend your assets and their distribution. In practice, therefore, provincial consumer demand spread the use of Roman legal structures, and this is firmly reflected in what became the main mechanism for updating Roman law itself in the later second and third centuries: the rescript system. This allowed citizens to write to the Emperor to clarify the law in difficult cases, and this was clearly done on a huge scale. By AD 200, the Emperor was dealing with several hundred of such petitions a year. And by the end of the third century, these clarifications had become such an important dimension of legal argument that structured collections of them had to be made for use in court (see Honoré 1994; Millar 1992).

But if self-Romanisation – an aggregate elite provincial response to the advantages of being Roman in a Roman Empire – both reduced elite diversity and brought rebellion to an end, it also generated new pressures within the imperial system. In the later Empire, these would combine with increasing pressures from the outside, and one internal cultural development of huge significance, to reduce further the Empire's original diversity.

The later Empire

By *c.* AD 250, all the profits from local taxes and tolls had been confiscated by the central Roman state. The funds were still raised by the councils, but the money had to be handed over to the imperial centre, which was trying to fund a huge increase in its armed forces. In the east, Persia had reorganised itself into a rival superpower, while new confederations beyond the Rhine and the Danube also posed a greater threat. As a direct result of this loss of funds, winning power on local city councils became a much less attractive option for provincial elites, and long-established behavioural patterns – such as making generous gifts to home cities to win influence and power – quickly disappeared. Even these confiscations were not enough, however, to pay for an army that doubled in size between AD 220 and 320, and the decades either side of the year 300 saw new Empire-wide systems of general taxation reach down into local communities. Town councils had to do the hard work of tax collection, but measuring productivity and assessing tax liabilities, checking on the collection process and passing on the sums raised were all overseen by a central bureaucracy which mushroomed in size. The 150 years before AD 400 saw a twenty-fold increase in senior administrators and countless new intermediary functionaries besides.[10]

This process certainly expanded the power of the central imperial state, but not at the expense of so much local initiative and diversity as traditional accounts suggested. In the earlier twentieth century, it was supposed that higher taxation levels bankrupted provincial landowning elites, and, based on Soviet and Nazi analogies, that the new imperial bureaucracy became a repressive, centralising force within the Empire. It is now clear, however, that the process of bureaucratic expansion was not only or indeed mainly about increasing central control. Fourth-century legislation combined with multiple letter collections (most of which are dominated by letters of recommendation) show that the process of bureaucratic expansion was quickly taken over by former city councillors who were attracted to the new positions because of the privileges attached to them. By AD 400, length of service had been reduced to such an extent (often only ten years) and privileges increased, that a brief period in the bureaucracy had become a key means of local self-advancement, since ex-bureaucrats were now tasked with most of the interesting jobs in provincial society (e.g. allocating local tax bills – a position with colossal patronage powers – and sitting with the governor to judge legal cases). In the meantime, emperors had spent much of the fourth century trying and failing to prevent ex-councillors from moving into the bureaucracy, and even to limit its overall size. Looked at closely, the rise of the ostensibly more bureaucratic late Roman state resembles earlier patterns of self-Romanisation. Once the centre implanted certain incentives into the system, provincial elites hijacked them for their own benefit, and, beyond the new tax regime, much of local society continued to govern itself as before, if under new rules and regulations (Heather 1994).

A much more substantial loss of diversity under the late Empire, in fact, was generated by the rise of Christianity. This process began with Constantine, who declared himself unambiguously Christian in the mid-320s and set in motion a process of Christianisation which was maintained by most of his successors (Julian, sole Emperor AD 361–3 being the brief exception). By AD 400, consequently, the Empire was dismantling pagan temples, and professing Christianity had become de rigueur for a career in the bureaucracy. This was not yet the end of the process. It would be another two centuries before Christian leaders came to definitive conclusions, for instance, as to how much of the old elite Greco-Roman culture was compatible with the new religion.[11] Nonetheless, by AD 400 the Empire was irrevocably committed to a close and evolving partnership with the new imperial religion.

The resulting loss of cultural diversity is most obviously visible amongst the Empire's highly literate elite. Over time, the wide range of acceptable religious cult still visible during the de facto tolerance of the Constantinian era gave way to a much narrower menu of licensed forms. Pockets of tolerated traditional elite paganism continued into the sixth century in the university schools of Athens and Alexandria in particular, but these became increasingly isolated as Christianity expanded its overall hold. That's not to say that there was one monolithic model even of Christianity in the late imperial period. Gospel-inspired renunciation of the world co-existed sometimes uneasily alongside other traditions which continued to represent the Empire as a unique, divinely supported human society which devout Christians should serve without reservation. But non-Christian traditions suffered a slow but steady eclipse as the weight of imperial favour made it clear that Christianity was now a necessary pre-condition for success in the newly Christian Empire.[12]

Some have seen in this process a qualitatively different level of political centralisation, Christianity presenting emperors with entirely new levers of power over their provincial elites. But, as the old process of self-Romanisation makes clear, the incentives for local elites to attach themselves to imperial structures in cultural terms had long had corrosive effects upon local diversity, and it is not clear that the rise of Christianity represented such a fundamental revolution in relationships.

In overall terms, the really negative impact of Christianity upon existing cultural diversity came in its entirely new imperative to interfere in the lives of non-elite inhabitants of the Empire. Before the fourth century, emperors hadn't much cared what peasants did, so long as customary revenues flowed. One hundred years later, the old temples were being demolished, and 100 years after that bishops were co-opting Roman and post-Roman state structures to replace the peasantry's traditional religious practices with Christian or at least Christianised counterparts, often with a significant element of constraint. There was still a long way to go to the thirteenth-century Inquisitions, but because Christianity prescribed that everyone possessed a soul which needed to be saved, it authorised an entirely new form of behaviour: using all the power of the state – positive and negative – to bring non-elite patterns into line with a licensed and monolithic cultural model.[13] The kind of constraint the Empire had exercised over its provincial elites for centuries was now extended to the entirety of the imperial population, and this new imperative, as much as Roman law or Latin literature, represents a powerful imperial legacy to the Middle Ages. By entrenching Christianity within its own long-established top-down structures of cultural constraint, the Empire paved the way for the domination of the Christian religion across more or less the entirety of post-Roman Europe.

Notes

1 On the speed of the imperial post, see Ramsay (1925). A good introduction to 'normal' official travel is Matthews (2006) on the Theophanes archive, published by Roberts and Turner (1952).

2 The classic treatment of relations between Rome and its Greek cities is Jones (1937); cf. Millar (1993). The deeper background can be explored through studies such as Murray and Price (1990) and Lagopoulos (2009).

3 The volumes of the Roman provinces series are an excellent place to start: Alföldy (1974); Frere (1991); Mocsy (1974); Wilkes (1969).

4 For an introduction to Greek legal structures, see Foxhall and Lewis (1996); for Egypt, see Bagnall (2006) and Bingen (2007).

5 On ideologies and practicalities of language see Kaster (1988). More generally, see e.g. Gruen (1992) on the Republican period and Bowersock (1969) for later developments (both have vast further bibliographies).

6 For a general introduction, see North and Price (2011), with Goodman (1998) on Jews and the beautifully illustrated Hattler (2013) on Mithras and other oriental cults.

7 An excellent place to start is now Steel (2013).

8 On education, see Marrou (1981); also Kaster (1988). An excellent case study in the broader process is Woolf (1998).

9 For an introduction to Arminius, see Heather (2006: 46–58). On the revolts and the chronology of Romanisation, see e.g. the studies in the Roman provinces series: Alföldy (1974); Frere (1991); Mocsy (1974); Wilkes (1969).

10 The best overall analytical introduction remains Jones (1964: 15, 16, 19), although there are of course more recent studies of all of these phenomena.

11 Sorabji (1983, 1988) explores Christianity's longer-term effects on Greek philosophy and science.

12 For pagan survivals, see Watts (2006); different dimensions of the Christianisation of upper class life and values have been explored in the different works of Peter Brown: see in particular Brown (1988, 1992, 1997, 2012).

13 An introductory bibliography would be Fletcher (1999), Hillgarth (1986) and McKitterick (1977).

References

Alföldy, G. (1974) *Noricum*, London: Routledge.

Bagnall, R.S. (2006) *Hellenistic and Roman Egypt: Sources and Approaches*, Aldershot, UK: Ashgate.

Bingen, J. (2007) *Hellenistic Egypt: Monarchy, Society, Economy, Culture*, Edinburgh: Edinburgh University Press.

Bowersock, G.W. (1969) *Greek Sophists in the Roman Empire*, Oxford, UK: Clarendon.

Brown, P.R.L. (1988) *The Body and Society: Men, Women, and Sexual Renunciation in Early Christianity*, New York, NY: Columbia University Press.

—(1992) *Power and Persuasion in Late Antiquity: Towards a Christian Empire*, Madison, WI: University of Wisconsin Press.

—(1997) *Authority and the Sacred: Aspects of the Christianisation of the Roman World*, Cambridge, UK: Cambridge University Press.

—(2012) *Through the Eye of a Needle: Wealth, the Fall of Rome, and the Making of Christianity in the West, 350–550 AD*, Princeton, NJ: Princeton University Press.

Fishwick, D. (1987) *The Imperial Cult in the Latin West: Studies in the Ruler Cult of the Western Provinces of the Roman Empire*, Leiden: Brill.

Fletcher, R.A. (1999) *The Barbarian Conversion: From Paganism to Christianity*, Los Angeles, CA: University of California Press.

Foxhall, L. and Lewis, A. (eds) (1996) *Greek Law in its Political Setting*, Oxford, UK: Clarendon.

Frere, S.S. (1991) *Britannia: A History of Roman Britain*, 3rd edn, London: Pimlico.

Gonzalez, J. and Crawford, M.H. (1986) 'The *Lex Irnitana*: A New Copy of the Flavian Municipal Law', *Journal of Roman Studies*, 76: 147–243.

Goodman, M. (1998) *Jews in a Graeco-Roman World*, Oxford, UK: Clarendon.

Gruen, E.S. (1992) *Culture and National Identity in Republican Rome*, Ithaca, NY: Cornell University Press.

Hattler, C. (2013) *Imperium der Götter: Isis, Mithras, Christus: Kulte und Religionen im Römischen Reich*, Stuttgart: Theiss.

Heather, P.J. (1994) 'New Men for New Constantines?: Creating an Imperial Elite in the Eastern Mediterranean', in P. Magdalino (ed.) *New Constantines: The Rhythm of Imperial Renewal in Byzantium, 4th–13th Centuries*, Aldershot, UK: Variorum.

—(2006) *The Fall of the Roman Empire: A New History*, London: Pan Books.

Hillgarth, J.N. (1986) *Christianity and Paganism, 350–750: The Conversion of Western Europe*, rev. edn, Philadelphia, PA: University of Pennsylvania Press.

Honoré, A.M. (1994) *Emperors and Lawyers*, 2nd edn, Oxford, UK: Oxford University Press.

Jones, A.H.M. (1937) *The Cities of the Eastern Roman Provinces*, Oxford, UK: Oxford University Press.

—(1964) *The Later Roman Empire: A Social Economic and Administrative Survey*, Oxford, UK: Blackwell.

Kaster, R.A. (1988) *Guardians of Language: The Grammarian and Society in Late Antiquity*, Berkeley, CA: University of California Press.

Lagopoulos, A. (ed.) (2009) *A History of the Greek City*, Oxford, UK: Archaeopress.

McKitterick, R. (1977) *The Frankish Church and the Carolingian Reforms, 789–895*, London: Royal Historical Society.

Marrou, H.I. (1981) *A History of Education in Antiquity*, London: Sheed and Ward.

Matthews, J.F. (2006) *The Journey of Theophanes: Travel, Business, and Daily Life in the Roman East*, New Haven, CT: Yale University Press.

Millar, F. (1992) *The Emperor in the Roman World*, 2nd edn, London: Duckworth.

—(1993) 'The Greek City in the Roman Period', in M.H. Hansen (ed.) *The Ancient Greek City-State: Symposium on the Occasion of the 250th Anniversary of the Royal Danish Academy of Sciences and Letters, July 1–4 1992*, Copenhagen: Munksgaard.

Mocsy, A. (1974) *Pannonia and Upper Moesia*, London: Routledge.

Murray, O. and Price, S. (eds) (1990) *The Greek City from Homer to Alexander*, Oxford, UK: Clarendon.

North, J.A. and Price, S. (2011) *The Religious History of the Roman Empire: Pagans, Jews, and Christians*, Oxford, UK: Oxford University Press.

Price, S. (1984) *Rituals and Power: The Roman Imperial Cult in Asia Minor*, Cambridge, UK: Cambridge University Press.

Ramsay, A.M. (1925) 'The Speed of the Imperial Post', *Journal of Roman Studies*, 15(1): 60–74.

Roberts, C.H. and Turner, E.G. (eds) (1952) *Catalogue of the Greek and Latin Papyri in the John Rylands Library Manchester*, Manchester, UK: Manchester University Press.

Sherwin-White, A.N. (1973) *The Roman Citizenship*, 2nd edn, Oxford, UK: Clarendon.

Sorabji, R. (1983) *Time, Creation and the Continuum: Theories in Antiquity and the Early Middle Ages*, London: Duckworth.

—(1988) *Matter, Space and Motion: Theories in Antiquity and their Sequel*, London: Duckworth.

Steel, C.E.W. (2013) *The Cambridge Companion to Cicero*, Cambridge, UK: Cambridge University Press.

Watts, E.J. (2006) *City and School in Late Antique Athens and Alexandria*, Berkeley, CA: University of California Press.

Wilkes, J.J. (1969) *Dalmatia*, London: Routledge.

Woolf, G. (1998) *Becoming Roman: The Origins of Provincial Civilization in Gaul*, Cambridge, UK: Cambridge University Press.

13

Diversity and the nature of the Ottoman Empire

From the construction of the imperial old regime to the challenges of modernity

Nora Lafi

The Ottoman landscape of diversity

Diversity in the Ottoman Empire, from Tunis to Baghdad and from Sarajevo to Mecca, was part of the basic features of the organization of social life. Not only were provinces of very different cultures part of this political construction, with populations of very different ethnic and religious backgrounds, but also at the local scale diversity was very often an important characteristic, with cities and villages assembling very different groups. Almost nowhere in the Empire was there what could be seen as a situation of homogeneity. Diversity was everywhere, at every scale, and this diversity of the population has been part of the very nature of the Empire since its beginning. The Ottoman Empire has been built progressively upon a heritage of diversity, with some elements taken from the Byzantine tradition and others from the Medieval Islamic, for example the Persian tradition. Coexistence was a condition necessary for the very existence of the Empire, and ethnic and religious diversity was dealt with as part of the basic elements of governance. There were in the Empire dozens of groups, like the Greeks, the Turks, the Arabs, among which a strong Christian element, the Jews, the Armenians, the Europeans in the cities of North Africa, the Maltese, the Serbs, the Bulgars, the Black Africans, the Roma, the Berbers, the Kurds, the Tuareg, the Causasians (like the Georgians or the Abkhazians), the Mongols .... Within these categories, of which one should not have a too static vision as identities were ductile, diversity also existed, such as between Coptic and Levantine Christians, Arab, Andalusian, Berber and Eastern European Jews, or even Greeks from the different parts of the Mediterranean. The Ottoman Empire was in no way a Turkish empire, and the notion of Turk itself was quite vague, covering both the descendants of migrants from Central Asia and myriad people from Anatolia. Very often someone could be perceived and described as a Turk, as he was representing the Ottoman Empire in a province, but would himself have a more complex identity, like in the case of Georgian, Circassian, Serb or even Greek governors or officers. There were also the classes of imperial servants, generally orphans or cadets from the Caucasus, who have long embodied, like the Janissaries, the Empire in the provinces. With the system of the Devshirme boarding schools, pupils from everywhere in the Empire and beyond were given an Ottoman education. Identities were also quite complex among those who converted, with religion and ethnicity not always matching automatically, for example in the case of Greek, Georgian, Armenian or Serb Muslim imperial officers. In many provinces inter-marriage also brought more complexity in diversity, with for example the Kuluglis of Algiers or Tripoli, the sons of marriages between Ottoman officers and women from local families.

Ottoman diversity was also characterized by a remarkable mosaic of languages. The Ottoman language (*Osmanlı*) was of course the dominant administrative idiom, but at the local scale local languages were always respected, even for imperial administration. Almost all Ottoman subjects, of all social *milieux*, lived in an atmosphere of pluri-linguistic realities, often using one language for family affairs, another for commerce or administration and another one again for cultural practices. For many Jews of Salonica, for example, Ladino was an everyday language, Greek and Turkish were used for business (along with other Mediterranean languages) and ancient Hebrew was used in the Synagogue. The Ottoman system was based upon the governance of hierarchized differences and not upon equality (this concept was inexistent in the contemporary political thinking of the time), and was marked by numerous episodes of conflict. Even if one overlooked the irenic visions of the coexistence between all Ottoman groups, the fact is that coexistence in the Ottoman context was the object of a complex and efficient system of regulation. The understanding of this system poses a certain number of conceptual challenges, pertaining not only to the interpretation of the nature of the Ottoman governance of diversity, but also to the nature of the Empire itself. This means that the Ottoman case is crucial to present-day studies of diversity and is worthy of renewed attention by scholars, albeit from a different angle of interpretation. The interpretation of the state of diversity in the Ottoman Empire has indeed long been made according to a conceptual dichotomy between the medieval heritage and the nineteenth-century situation. Little attention was generally given to the construction of interpretative paradigms centred on the core period of the Empire itself.

The Ottoman old regime governance of diversity

The governance of diversity in the Ottoman Empire was the result of the complex and progressive construction of a whole set of legal regulations and of locally negotiated practices. The Empire was in no way a block of bureaucratic homogeneity but was rather a complex and constantly renegotiated construction (Barkey 2008). It was in the very nature of this old regime style of governance to comprise general rules as well as local privileges or adaptations. From the very beginning, the construction of the imperial apparatus comprised a decisive acceptance of previously recognized rules, regulations and privileges. But this fact does not mean that the Ottoman Empire's approach to diversity was passive: the integration of previous negotiations was part of a dynamic renegotiation and of the construction of the imperial ideology, itself much more complex than just a mix of Byzantine and Islamic heritages. At the scale of the Empire, diversity was regulated according to a specific legal framework, based upon the system of the protection of members of religions other than Islam. Inspired by the medieval Islamic concept of *dhimmi* protection, this Ottoman interpretation comprised many dimensions, from taxation to civic rights (Masters 2004). The basic principle was that members of non-Muslim communities were subject to specific taxes, tasks or exemptions according to the community. Non-Muslims were not authorized to access the highest charges of public service. At the scale of the Empire, the system of the millet embodied the Ottoman vision of diversity: the members of a specific confessional community were affiliated by way of their judicial and legal status to this larger organization (Ursinus 1989). The main ones, besides the Islamic Millet, were the Christian Millet (*Rum*, established as early as 1453), the Armenian Millet and the Jewish Millet. Between the sixteenth and eighteenth centuries, many adaptations and corrections were made to this system, resulting from negotiations with specific groups. New millets were sometimes created in order to adapt to diversity inside a community, as well as to new political, spiritual or social stakes. But the interpretation of diversity in the Ottoman Empire should not be made only at this scale of general principles and distant institutions, even if there was always a strong symbolic and practical relation between members of single communities and their hierarchies in Istanbul. Debates are still ongoing between historians, but it seems that, for example, the Jewish *Hahambaşılık* was more the head of the Jewish community in the capital city and the symbolic representative of all the Jews of the Empire in front of the Sultan than the actual chief of all Jewish communities (Aydingün and Dardağan 2006). Most crucial were not only local interpretations of general rules on the governance of diversity, as well as the interaction with other principles of social organization, pertaining to local communities but also to professional bodies like guilds, which could be inter-confessional, to territorial entities, like villages or quarters, which could also be inter-confessional, or to specific social constructions, like tribes, which in the Ottoman Empire were not a static category pertaining to anthropology only, but also an evolving category of social regulation. Diversity was always in an Ottoman context dealt with as part of the fundamental dimensions of local societies. The Ottoman system should not be seen as something like the meeting point between general rules and local specificities, but rather as a mutual social, administrative, political and symbolic construct in which decisions resulted from both the sedimentation of acknowledged exceptions and the dynamic negotiation of equilibrium in the interpretation of this heritage for the present.

Among the most important aspects of the Ottoman governance of diversity was the delegation of imperial functions to local notables, either rural, urban or confessional. Cities were recognized as collective bodies, the governance of which was largely delegated to local notables. In this framework, confessional communities were recognized as official entities too, in charge not only of regulating social life inside the community, but also of various tasks, fiscal or pertaining to public order. Imperiality was embedded into this dimension of diversity, and functioned not just in an external or supervisory capacity. In this way, Ottoman cities, most of which were marked by a complex mosaic of confessional and ethnic identities, were an essential element in the fashioning of imperiality. Each community had its local chief, like the *sheikh al-Yahûd* for the Jews of Arab cities, but so did each quarter and each guild. As in many old regime systems, an overlap between all these dimensions was typical. For example, a Jewish carpenter living in a mixed neighbourhood could depend for the various aspects of his social life on the Chief of the Jewish community, the hierarchy of his guild and the chief of his quarter. There were as many declensions of this scheme as there were possibilities of crossing elements of diversity in cities between the confessional, sometimes the ethnic or tribal, the professional and the spatial dimensions. Those dimensions rarely matched. The capital city itself, Istanbul, was in no way a mirror of a mythical imperial homogeneous vision. The Ottoman court itself was pluri-ethnic and multi-lingual, encompassing from the very beginning of the Empire the Sultanic tradition of marrying foreign (Greek, for example) princes, or the integration of bureaucrats of various origins into the Ottoman government. In the city, the Greek element remained extremely important until the end of the Empire, and all the languages of the provinces could be heard in the streets. Outside of the cities, the delegation of local power to local tribes, nomad groups or village assemblies was most common. This resulted in daily interaction between elements of various natures, and also in the complex situation of an imperial governance of diversity in which internal hierarchies were recognized as active elements of social organization.

The coexistence of groups of various origins, religions or identities, however, should not be seen as an innate feature or as the easy result of the system described here. It was rather the result of a constant effort of social and political mediation. In the case of a flagrant injustice, all individuals or groups were entitled to petition either locally to the governor or directly to the Sultan in Istanbul. This petitioning system was also the main feature of imperial governance, with entire bureaux in the capital city dealing with the resolution of local conflicts, the degeneration of which could challenge the local declension of imperiality. The Ottoman imperial administrative old regime apparatus grew from this basis. Conflict prevention and resolution was one of the main tasks of the imperial administration. Of course, this did not always succeed, and rebellions, local wars and sometimes inter-confessional episodes of violence are not absent from Ottoman history. But there were also local features of canalization of potential expressions of violence that generally allowed dealing with inter-confessional or inter-ethnic animosity. When it happened, it was generally the sign of a rupture in the equilibrium of the local form of imperiality in the context of the negotiation of a change or of the emergence of strong internal and/or external challenges. This is what happened in the nineteenth century with the implementation of major reforms in the system of governance of diversity, in the context of the emergence of new ideas on modernity and of a new form of influence of foreign powers.

The challenges of modernity

The first great imperial reform that had a strong impact on the relationship between the Empire and the locality, with consequences on how diversity was managed, is that of the system of the Janissaries, in 1826, which followed, but also induced, several decades of troubles. The Janissaries were themselves a corps embodying the diversity of the Empire that had in old regime times had a strong local role in many provinces. The Janissaries were generally the sons of Christian families from Anatolia or the Balkans (Greeks, Armenians, Georgians, Serbs), recruited in their childhood in order to become servants of the Empire. They were given a high-level military and technical education and formed not only an elite military corps of the Sultan, but also one of the most efficient bodies of administrators and technicians working for the Empire. The defence of their privileges led them to resist all imperial efforts to reform the army. Following a series of revolts and two decades of tension, the corps of the Janissaries was violently suppressed in 1826. This not only changed the way diversity was envisaged at the scale of the Empire, but also led to a crisis of local identity in several provinces. Another challenge to the Ottoman system was the secession of Greece, which, although it had begun as a rather classical revolt, became the symbol of the emergence of a new kind of national sentiment. The growth of such national sentiments was a major challenge for the Empire, not only at the scale of its geostrategic coherence, but also at that of the very mix of diversity in almost every city and village. With nationalism increasingly becoming a category of political thought, every Greek, Armenian, Kurd, Serb, or (later) Arab or Jewish subject of the Empire faced a new identity dilemma, juxtaposing his Ottoman belonging on one side and his communal or ethnic belonging on the other. The seizure in 1830 of the Ottoman province of Algeria by France, following the Napoleonic invasion of Egypt in 1798, and in general the growth of colonial European appetites for Ottoman provinces, added another dimension to this major shift, with diversity becoming the site of a complex entanglement of stakes and scales of intimate identities, local and imperial logics and geopolitical games. All these changes, combined with the emergence of new philosophical conceptualizations of individual identity, represented profound challenges to the previous system of Ottoman governance of diversity. A new perception of the 'other', with the influence of ethnic based typologies as developed in Europe, also had an impact on how diversity was conceived. With the growing reification of categories, religious or ethnic, that were previously much more ductile and part of the old regime regulation, this system came to the point of being totally unmanageable. This situation, resulting from the complex mix of concerns – military for the defence of the most vulnerable provinces, political for the tackling of the new identity mosaic of the Empire and local relating to the tensions that emerged following the growth of adverse national or communal sentiments – explains the launch in the 1830s of a series of reforms at the scale of the Empire known as the *Tanzîmât*.

The spirit of the *Tanzîmât* was to adapt the Ottoman Empire to a new situation. As far as diversity was concerned, changes in the definition of the self and in the conceptualization of political representation induced a necessary reform of the millet system (Karpat 1982). But even if the reforms that were enacted during the 1850s and the 1860s were aimed at replacing the communal definition of the self by a more universal one creating modern citizenship, opening more widely the sphere of governance to non-Muslims, they did not totally succeed in solving all previous ambiguities. The Imperial Rescript of Gülhane of 1839 established the equality of all Ottoman subjects before the law regardless of their religion. In 1856, the Imperial Reform Rescript also improved the legal status of non-Muslims and introduced the principle of fiscal equality between Muslims and non-Muslims. Scholars have underlined how this decision on the one hand represented a path towards equality but on the other tended to deprive communal notables of part of their powers, notably those that were associated with principles of taxation inside the community (Aydingün and Dardağan 2006). The 1856 imperial Rescript also opened up government offices and administrative bureaucratic services to a more general participation of non-Muslims. In 1865, the Organic Law of the Empire confirmed these principles, and throughout the 1860s a series of decisions granted to the Greek-Orthodox, Armenian and Jewish Millets a new range of competences at the scale of the Empire, with the consequence of tending somehow to centralize communal life. The 1869 code of Ottoman nationality defined nationality as being attached to all subjects of the Sultan without consideration of religion or ethnicity. Article 8 of the 1876 constitution confirmed this important principle: 'all subjects of the Empire are called Ottoman, without distinction, whatever their religion'.

Just as it would be too simplistic to see this modernization and reform effort as a mere dynamic of 'westernization', it would not be satisfactory to examine it only at the scale of such general principles. Most of the ambiguities of the reforms and of the tensions they created are to be analyzed indeed at the local scale. In cities of the Empire, for example, the implementation of the municipal reforms was the object of strong conflicts between the Empire and the old elite who struggled to see their old regime powers transferred into the new one. At the urban scale, the reforms meant not only a redefinition of the self and of collective identities, but also a renegotiation of the power of all notables to which old regime governance had been delegated for centuries. The transitions from the old regime assemblies of notables and the mosaic of communal institutions to reformed municipalities (and reformed communal institutions, as well as reformed courts of justice) were far from easy. Even if representation was based upon property, a fact which granted Muslim old regime notables a good position in the new system, the negotiation of adaptation was an occasion for tension. The impact of modernity is thus ambiguous. This is also the case with respect to the relationship between Ottomanity and the role of foreigners. Indeed, ambiguities in many cities of the Empire derived from the fact that on the one hand a certain number of Ottoman subjects had been seeking foreign consular protection (British or French mainly) and that on the other foreign consuls pushed for modernizing reforms in order to grant new rights (notably property rights) to foreigners. The distinction between Ottoman non-Muslims, ex-Ottoman *protégés* and Europeans tended to become increasingly less obvious, a fact that undermined the spirit of equality and its local implementation. The impact of the Ottoman reforms on diversity is therefore more complex than just the clash between the imperial idea and the growth of nationalism of all sorts. The position of the various groups in the

Empire had to be redefined, from Greeks to Bulgars, Armenians to Jews and Turks to Arabs. But the clash between an incomplete form of Ottoman modernity and predation attempts by foreign powers also instrumentalized the differences. The revendication of rights for foreigners by foreign consuls interfered with the evolution of the consideration of the rights of non-Muslim Ottoman subjects. The 1858 code of property, and the local conflicts and sometimes riots it created, is an illustration of this crucial dimension. From Tunisia to Egypt, Ottoman modernization interfered with colonial stakes. This is why the crisis of the Ottoman governance of diversity that characterized the end of the nineteenth century and was marked by a series of violent incidents, including massacres in the Levant and riots in numerous Ottoman cities from the Balkans to North Africa, should be analyzed according to a complex grid of questioning that includes dimensions pertaining not only to the passage from old regime definitions of diversity to modern ones based on more universal principles, but also to the variety of challenges imperial Ottomanity itself was confronted with, from nationalism to colonialism.

Conclusion

With the fall of the Ottoman Empire after World War I, a period itself characterized by the massacre of the Armenian population in the Empire, the question of diversity in the post-Ottoman world evolved into a situation marked by a logic of segregation and separation. In what became republican Turkey, the ideological construction of Turkishness as an ethnic feature became the cement of the new regime. Exchanges of populations between Greece and Turkey resulted in the construction of both national territories as ethnically coherent entities. In the Balkans, the mosaic of populations became for a century almost the instrument of a clash of contrasting nationalisms. And in the rest of the Empire, under colonial domination (some provinces since the nineteenth century), different logics of segregation prevailed. From Algeria, where French occupation resulted in the implementation of a violent regime of segregation, with the colonial emancipation of Algerian Jews being instrumentalized in this framework, to mandatory Syria and Lebanon where the French used communal diversity as an instrument of power, or to mandatory Palestine, where Zionism as a new form of territorial and ethnic nationalism clashed both with British colonial rule and with local populations and their heritage of governance of diversity, the post-Ottoman panorama of diversity is dominated by the end of coexistence and by the growing force of separation and segregation as governance tools. The challenge for research therefore is to tackle both the historical reality of the governance of diversity in Ottoman times and its ambiguous memory. Between various forms of both neo-Ottomanism and post-colonialism, this memory is indeed subject to highly politicized interpretations. This is why any research agenda for the future should take into account a set of various considerations. First, the necessity to analyze the Ottoman period as such, and not as the mere intermediary between Islamic Middle Ages and colonization or independences, with a focus on the relationship between the imperial and the local spheres. In this framework, paying attention to the actual evolution of the participation of non-Muslim notables to urban civic life, as well as to the evolution of inner-communal life, is crucial. Second, there is today a need for research on the nature of the Ottoman reforms, mostly on the interaction between reformative impulses and the complex situation at the local scale. And third, as far as the post-Ottoman world is concerned, up to present debates in the Balkans or in Palestine, there seems to be a need to reverse the logic of genealogical research that tends to reify categories that were not necessarily relevant in Ottoman times, or at least that had a quite different meaning and content. Instead, in digging into Ottoman times from the post-Ottoman situation of fragmentation, ethnic segregation or separation, which implies certain angles of interpretation and a fragmentation of research between Jewish, Greek, Balkan, Arab or Armenian studies, what seems most important nowadays for research is to tackle the Ottoman situation as such. After decades of historical research going in the direction of understanding the logics of nationalisms, another perspective might also be, without ambiguous and naive forms of Ottomanist nostalgia, to study how the idea of Ottomanity was present in societies throughout the Empire during all the phases described here. Not everything was written in 1850, or even in 1910.

References

Aydingün, I. and Dardağan, E. (2006) 'Rethinking the Jewish Communal Apartment in the Ottoman Communal Building', *Middle Eastern Studies*, 42(2): 319–34.

Barkey, K. (2008) *Empire of Difference: The Ottomans in Comparative Perspective*, Cambridge, UK: Cambridge University Press.

Karpat, K. (1982) 'Millets and Nationality: The Roots of the Incongruity of Nation and State in the Post-Ottoman Era', in B. Braude and B. Lewis (eds) *Christians and Jews in the Ottoman Empire: The Functioning of a Plural Society*, New York, NY: Holmes & Meier.

Masters, B. (2004) *Christians and Jews in the Ottoman Empire: The Roots of Sectarianism*, Cambridge, UK: Cambridge University Press.

Ursinus, M. (1989) 'Zur Diskussion um "Millet" im Osmanischen Reich', *Südost-Forschungen*, 48(1): 195–207.

14

Race and labour, forced and free, in the formation and evolution of Caribbean social structures

Colin Clarke

Most colonial Caribbean territories after 1650 had slaves, but African slavery was not the whole of the forced labour regime, since it was replaced by Indian indentured labour in the British West Indies after slave emancipation in 1838, when a new sugar frontier was opened in the Southeastern Caribbean, notably in Trinidad and British and Dutch Guiana. Independent Cuba received huge imports of free Spanish labour after 1902, as US capital was applied to virgin sugar land in the east of the island. The cultural history of the Caribbean is bound up with forced labour imports from Africa, India (and China) and free labour imports from Europe – and the cultures (or remnants of the cultures) they brought with them centuries ago – all under the aegis of white planter regimes.

Colour-class, cultural pluralism and differential incorporation

Caribbean social science since World War II has been dominated by two indigenous models (developed by Caribbean-born sociologists and anthropologists) that identify and explain the complexities of the social structure. The first, colour-class, was originally developed by Fernando Henriques for Jamaica (1953) and Lloyd Braithwaite (1953) for the Creole segment in Trinidad and Tobago (but omitting the East Indian component) and, by extrapolation, was also applied to the British Windward and Leeward Islands (Lowenthal 1972).

These analyses had the advantage of linking Caribbean stratification to occupational/class systems in the US and Europe, while pointing to a colonial history of colour differentiation which shadowed class and reinforced it. So, the upper class was white or pass-as-white, the middle class brown with some black, and the lower class black with some brown. A number of racially or ethnically distinct groups fell originally outside this colour-class stratification, but had, over time, been accommodated within it: Jews were absorbed into the upper class, as were the Syrian professionals; Chinese, the remaining Syrians and a few East Indians were middle class; and the majority of East Indians were lower class (Lowenthal 1972).

Ideas about cultural difference were, in the 1950s, woven by M.G. Smith (like Henriques, a Jamaican-born, British-trained anthropologist) into the theory of cultural pluralism and the plural society (Smith 1955, 1960). Drawing on the ideas of Furnivall (1948), a British administrator in South-East Asia, Smith's summary volume on pluralism in the British West Indies (1965) concluded that the colonies were characterized by many cultures, assembled and ranked by colonial design. Standing at the apex of this system was European culture, with the culture of the black, formerly enslaved, population, who had lost most, but not all, of their African heritage, as the polar opposite. Between these cultural complexes was the culture of the middle-class browns and upwardly mobile blacks, who drew on elements of each of the other two cultures (Smith 1965).

What were the ingredients of these cultures? Smith argued that the basis of culture resided in the institutions that all groups needed to perform socially, and that pluralism occurs where 'there is formal diversity in the basic system of compulsory institutions' – kinship, education, religion, property, economy and recreation (Smith 1965: 85). According to his view, lower-class Jamaican culture is different (but not deviant – as the middle class often sees it) from that of the middle and upper classes. However, Smith failed to explore the extent to which education, property and economy could be seen as dimensions of class, and, in the Caribbean context, preferred to interpret property and economy as plantation and peasantry (namely, different modes of production).

Approaching culture in a relativistic way, Smith assumed that those whose institutional practices were most different would interact least well; he therefore associated pluralism with the distinction between, say, Christianity and Islam, or, in the case of Jamaica, between Christianity and Afro-Christianity – the latter comprising a creolized and syncretic set of religious sects and cults. However, recent research, drawing on evidence from Northern Ireland (Doherty and Poole 1997), for example, emphasizes that differences between branches of the same religion (in this instance Catholicism and Protestantism) may be socially constructed to be intensely divisive in terms of citizens' rights (Kymlicka 1997).

During slavery in the British Caribbean three social sections were framed by socio-legal boundaries, depicting citizens, freemen and slaves – modally white, brown and black (Smith 1974). After slavery, and prior to adult suffrage in 1944, franchise distinctions based on income and property (class) – not race or culture – framed three categories that resembled the legal estates of slavery: those who could be voted for (white and brown), those who could vote (white, brown and a black minority) and those who could not vote (the black majority, but including some who were brown). So, legal and political capacity turned cultural pluralism into structural pluralism, involving differentially incorporated and ranked cultures – the plural society par excellence according to Smith (1984, 1991, 1998). In this quintessential colonial polity, the white minority dominated the majority by non-democratic means, and relied heavily on force – or the threat of force – to maintain the unstable status quo.

Nonetheless, in my fieldwork on Kingston in 1961, at the end of 16 years of Jamaican constitutional decolonization, predicated on adult suffrage, I realized that class, colour and culture were closely correlated in the city, and together produced three social strata associated with different geographical locations, anchored by competitive bidding for real estate (Clarke 1975). I also showed that cultural difference based on education, religion and family/household composition, while crucially important and derived from differences originally created during the slave period, was insufficient to displace colour-class as an analytical framework, provided that cultural and structural pluralism were taken into account.

A typology of Caribbean societies

Combining my knowledge of the social history of the region with the various competing models that seek to explain society, I conceive of Caribbean societies as divisible into four broad types (Clarke1991; Lowenthal 1972): (1) plural stratified, where colour-class and cultural distinctions have largely coincided; (2) plural segmented, where (white, brown and black) Creole and non-Creole segments are contraposed; (3) class stratified, where occupational class predominates and other differentiators are recessive; and (4) folk, which lack stratification. Plural-stratified societies were formed during plantation slavery; plural-segmented societies were originally plural stratified, but received masses of Indian indentured labourers or Mexican immigrants from the Yucatan in the nineteenth century; class-stratified societies were a creation of the twentieth century (after weak development with slavery on the small scale), and developed with free plantation labour, most of it white; folk societies were tiny insular appendages of larger colonies during slavery, and were often marginal for sugar production.

I argue that Braithwaite and Henriques' colour-class model and Smith's ideas about pluralism and differential incorporation provide crucial insights into the first two societal types; notions of class – whether following Parsons (1952) or Weber (1947) – in the absence of colour-class stratifications, are central to the third; and social consensus (Parsons 1952) fits the fourth – although their social histories are usually closely aligned to the lower stratum of the plural-stratified societies. These are, however, only best-fit solutions, and to be comprehensive it is important to point out that cultural pluralism may have a residual part to play in explaining Afro-Christian *santería* in class-stratified societies once influenced by slavery; and that class structures are usually crucial frameworks, especially where the colour dimension of colonial colour-class may have worn thin – as it has in Jamaica.

Each category in the typology is divisible into two sub-types (Clarke 1991; Lowenthal 1972): those societies listed under (a) are the commonest variant, while those listed under (b) are racial or colour variants on the class or cultural structures that appear in (a). Plural-stratified societies (1) include those within the full stratificational range – (a) Jamaica, Barbados, the Commonwealth Leeward Islands and the French and Netherlands Antilles; and those that have had that social range truncated by the loss of white elites, for example (b) Haiti, French Guiana and the Windward Islands. Plural-segmented societies (2) encompass those with Creole-Indian contrasts, (a) Trinidad, Guyana (formerly British Guiana) and Surname (formerly Dutch Guiana), or (b) Creole-Mestizo differences as in Belize.

Class-stratified societies include those that are essentially white, but with a partial colour-class correlation – (a) (Cuba and Puerto Rico); and a society that has a miscegenated class stratification but with white-black polarization at the apex and base of the social pyramid, repectively, namely (b) (Dominican Republic). Finally, folk societies are tiny non-stratified communities with a weak resource base; either they have no major colour differences (a) Barbuda, black, and Saba, white, or they are colour differentiated (b) – Desirade, white-black, and Anguilla, brown-black (Clarke 1991).

Historically, the plural-stratified society has been key to the evolution of Caribbean social structures. Jamaica during slavery, for example, represented a classic plural society that in its origins involved ranked cultural sections, legally enshrined and largely correlated with colour and class. Haiti, Barbados and the British and French Lesser Antilles were replicas. Slave emancipation, through slave revolt, took place in Haiti in the mid-1790s, in the British Caribbean in 1838, in the French Antilles in 1848 and in the Dutch colonies over the period 1862–73, in each of the last three cases by legislative act of the imperial regime. Most other types of Caribbean society may be related to the plural-stratified Jamaican type, either as truncations or as demographic expansions of the social pyramid.

Plural-segmented societies were weakly developed as slave societies because they were neither British nor French in the eighteenth century, compared to the two great slave societies of the Western Hemisphere – Saint Domingue/Haiti (independent 1804) and Jamaica, with the

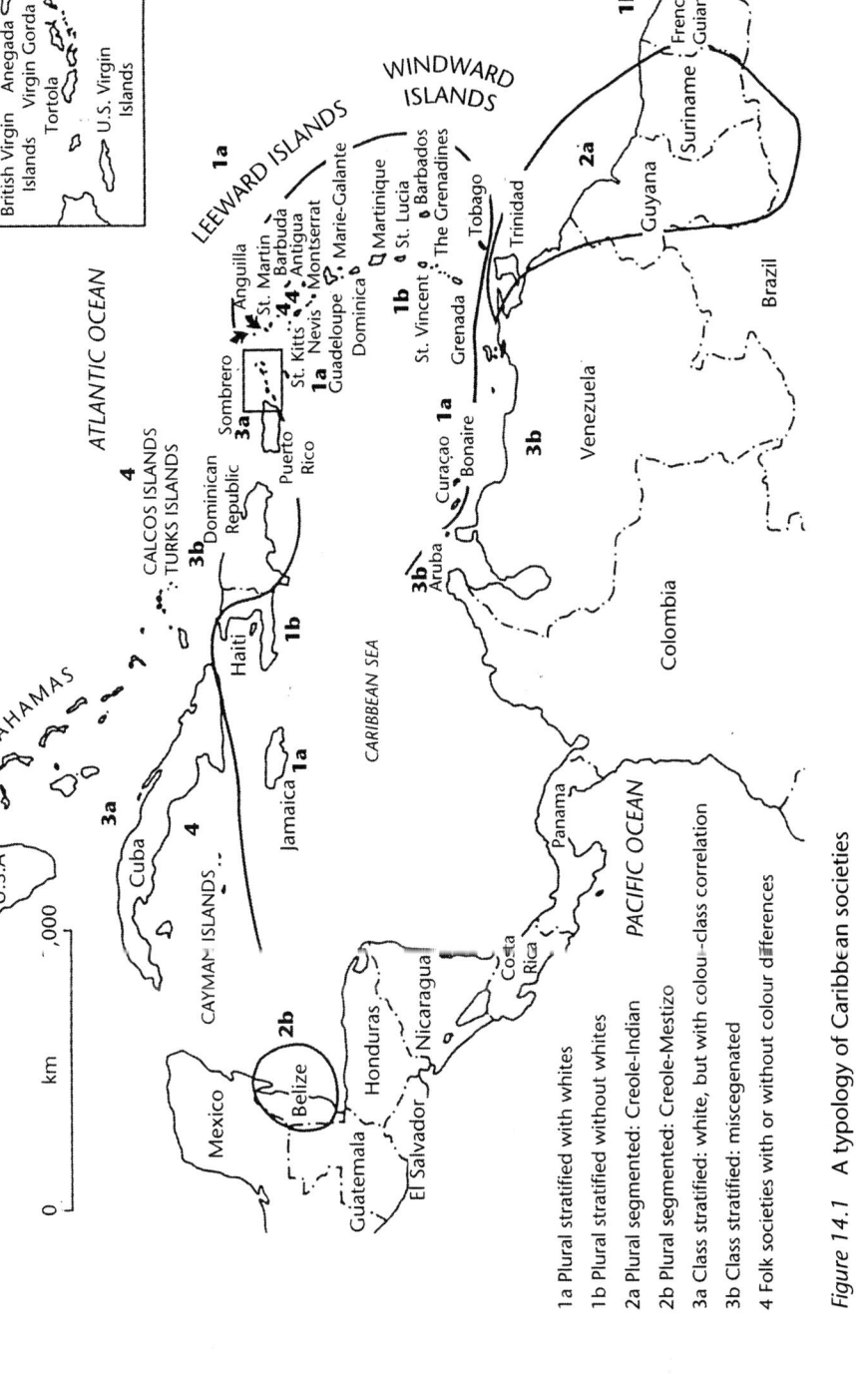

Figure 14.1 A typology of Caribbean societies

1a Plural stratified with whites
1b Plural stratified without whites
2a Plural segmented: Creole-Indian
2b Plural segmented: Creole-Mestizo
3a Class stratified: white, but with colour–class correlation
3b Class stratified: miscegenated
4 Folk societies with or without colour differences

greatest output in the world of sugar and coffee before and after 1800, respectively. Moreover, plural-segmented societies had an abundance of potential plantation land when the slave trade in the British Empire was abolished in 1808. So, once Trinidad and British Guiana were transferred to the UK in 1815, a late phase of sugar cultivation was entered using East Indian indentured labour exported through Calcutta.

The Indian communities that stayed in Trinidad, British Guiana and Dutch Guiana were so large in number that they stood outside the pre-existing social stratifications, and did not penetrate them as did their demographically smaller equivalents in Jamaica. Belize is a special case: it developed as a logwood (dyewood)-cutting enclave in Central America, and its black slaves were urban-based lumbermen, not rural cane cutters. Segmentation was reflected in urban-based, English-creole-speaking blacks and rural Spanish-speaking Mestizos and Amerindians, though some East Indians were imported later (Lowenthal 1972).

The white class-stratified Spanish colonies with their port-havens, Havana and San Juan, played a supportive role to Spanish commercial activity on the mainland until Spanish decolonization of mainland Latin America in the 1820s. Sugar plantations, based on slave and free labour, had been re-introduced to Cuba during the brief British occupation in the late eighteenth century, and were expanded by the Spanish in the early 1800s, but the proportion of the labour force that was enslaved declined from 43 to 28 per cent between 1841 and 1860, and slavery was abolished in 1886 (almost 50 years after the British Caribbean) (Knight 1970). In Puerto Rico, where tobacco and subsistence farming dominated the rural scene, slaves accounted for fewer than 12 per cent of the population in 1846, when they were most numerous, and the proportion had shrunk to well under 10 per cent before emancipation in 1873. The Dominican Republic remained detached from these circumstances, though free-labour plantations were created by US capital, using mostly local (including Haitian) labour, after 1875 (Moreno Fraginals et al. 1985).

Consequently, Cuba was a plural-stratified society in 1840, with free whites and enslaved blacks in almost equal proportions, separated by free coloureds. Yet by 1920, the modest increase of blacks and browns in contrast to the enormous influx of white labourers (750,000 arrived from Spain between 1900 and 1920 when the total population barely exceeded 2 million) had transformed Cuba into a class-based society in which browns and blacks were accorded middle- and lower-class status, respectively, but were outnumbered by whites in each class – and especially so in the elite (Clarke 1991). Similar shifts towards a white majority were recorded in Puerto Rico, where miscegenation and the gradual social incorporation of light mulattoes into the white population (as pass-as whites), as in Cuba, have played a part in the reduction of the black presence (Hoetink 1985). In the Dominican Republic, however, whites and blacks (though fortified by black immigration from Haiti) form only small minorities, and race mixing has produced a mulatto majority (Howard 2001).

Race, colour, legal estate and culture during slavery

To understand the origins and development of the plural-stratified societies, which I have argued are key to the evolution of all Caribbean societies, it is necessary to examine social conditions during the foundation period of the seventeenth and eighteenth centuries. The Caribbean developed as a colonial appendage of Europe after Columbus' first voyage of discovery in 1492. Decimation of the Amerindians under Spanish control in the sixteenth century created a green-field site for sugar cultivation on plantations in the seventeenth, but without an indigenous labour force to call upon. The islands of the Caribbean were ideal environments for the control of potentially rebellious black slave labourers recruited from Africa by European planters, who themselves originated in Britain, France and the Netherlands.

From the 1650s plantation slavery spread through the central belt of the Caribbean from Barbados, as each colony in turn took up sugar as its staple crop for export to Europe (Richardson 1992). There was no history of a class structure without an accompanying racial hierarchy of white over black, and with miscegenation between white planters and female black slaves – there were few white women in the region – a new category of coloured people started to emerge. During the first half of the eighteenth century they began to form a class of themselves, and those who were the children of men who could afford to free their offspring became the core of an emancipated group known as the free people of colour (Clarke 1975; Lowenthal 1972).

The free people of colour were not the product of the mode of production, but of the mode of reproduction. The social structure was thus composed of three legal estates: whites with full civil rights, black slaves with virtually no rights in law, and fewer in practice, and an interstitial group of coloured people, of various phenotypes ranging from light brown to black, who were not slaves, but had only limited civil rights – they could neither hold public office nor vote (Clarke 1975). Out of this socio-legal colour system evolved the colour-class structures that seized the attention of Henriques and Braithwaite, the first social scientists to study them in the Caribbean post World War II.

The three legal estates also displayed distinctive sets of cultural characteristics in family and religion. Upper-class whites usually wed, provided white women were available, and formed nuclear, male-dominated authoritarian households. The slave household was likely to be female headed, since the slave owners had no compunction about breaking up domestic units imported from Africa or formed in the Caribbean. Among the free people of colour there were few examples of endogamy, since young women were rapidly made appendages of upper-class white men, and free men of colour engaged the favours of black or brown slave women as mistresses (Clarke 1975).

Dominant Christian religions were imported into the Caribbean from metropolitan societies – Catholicism in the case of the Spanish and French colonies and Protestantism in the case of the British and Dutch. In the Catholic societies slaves were treated as beings with souls, and the plantation regime was theoretically less burdensome than in the Protestant colonies, where slaves were beyond the human pale. In reality, however, all plantation regimes at their economic peak, whether French or British, were equally inhumane, and the religions of the three social estates were distinct (Goveia 1970). Whites were nominal members of the established metropolitan religions (Catholicism and Protestantism), but led a brutalized and debauched life in keeping with their ownership of human lives. In the British islands free people of colour were abandoned by Anglicanism, and by the early 1800s were ripe for conversion to metropolitan Methodism and other non-conformist churches.

However, wherever there were slaves, syncretized Afro-Caribbean religions were created among those blacks who were deemed non-humans or, at best, lowly humans. These non-orthodox, creolized religious forms had many names – vodun (Haiti), santería (Cuba, Dominican Republic and Puerto Rico) (Moret 2008; Nicholls 1996; Palmié 2002; Scott 1985), but their core characteristics were similar to those of the Afro-Christian cults of the Protestant Caribbean (Simpson 1956). All cults syncretized African and Christian beliefs and amalgamated every-day life and the afterlife, and rituals involved ecstatic behaviour in which the spirit world was accessed by the participants. Once non-conformist missionaries entered the British West Indies after 1800, the slaves and their freed descendants began to be proselytized, only for them to turn away from orthodox Christianity and to re-embrace Afro-Christianity (Clarke 1975).

Ethnicity and religion in the post-emancipation period

After slave emancipation in the British Caribbean between 1834 and 1838, new ethnic groups were introduced to the region, at first to make good the shortage of labour – especially, but not solely, in the sugar frontier areas of the South-East Caribbean (Trinidad, British Guiana and Dutch Guiana). The first indentured labourers were Chinese, but they rapidly gravitated into the grocery trade, and Indians, known in the Caribbean as East Indians, soon became the staple of indentured immigration. Many Chinese quickly converted to Christianity, but most East Indians, where they formed large demographic components, retained ancestral commitments to Hinduism and Islam, though some Hindus converted to Catholicism or Canadian (Mission) Presbyterianism (Clarke 1986). In British Guiana, East Indians eventually became the majority of the population, but in both Trinidad and Dutch Guiana they formed large minority segments standing outside the Creole colour-class stratification of whites, browns and blacks (Richardson 1992).

In the late nineteenth century, Syrians entered the Caribbean as traders, emulating the Jews of the seventeenth and eighteenth centuries. In Jamaica in the 1950s, for example, three ethnic minorities – Jews, Syrians and Chinese – all using various branches of trade, occupied status gap positions between the two upper social strata, and had converted to the elite religions of Roman Catholicism or Anglicanism. Their upward mobility over time was contrasted with the lowly position of the ethnic groups descended from runaway slaves (such as the Bush Negroes of Dutch Guiana and the Maroons of Jamaica); the Javanese ex-indentured labourers in Dutch Guiana; and the Amerindians (where they survived in Guiana and as a miscegenated group in Dominica). The descendants of the runaways and the Amerindians, despite their long histories in the Caribbean stretching back to slavery or beyond, could be thought of, with the newer Javanese, as outcast groups (Lowenthal 1972).

Conclusion

The way in which Caribbean societies were associated (or not) historically with slavery, indenture and free labour creates the significance of the cultural difference in social stratification/ segmentation. Smith's notion of differential incorporation is crucial, because where strata or segments were distinguished into white citizens, free people of colour and black slaves, as they were in the English and French-speaking colonies (and, in the case of Trinidad, British Guiana and Dutch Guiana, into an Indian indentured segment), the cultural differences that accompanied the politico-legal framework were totally different from situations where African plantation slavery played no part in the evolution of the colony/country and miscegenation was the norm (exemplified by the Dominican Republic), or where African forced labour was superseded by white, free plantation labour (as in Cuba and Puerto Rico). Hence the focus of this chapter on the Commonwealth Caribbean, which exemplifies the extreme inequalities associated with plural-stratified and plural-segmented societies.

Smith saw plural societies, where a minority (white) ruled the majority (black, or black and Indian) undemocratically, as inherently unstable and controllable only by force (as in Jamaica and Guyana from slavery to the beginning of decolonization after the containment of the labour rebellion of 1938). The constitutional evolution of Commonwealth Caribbean colonies to independence since 1960 has removed this condition de jure through citizens' universal incorporation in sovereign states. Yet Guyana's post-independence history of black Creole hegemony (1964–92), based on electoral gerrymandering by the minority segment, shows that this condition is not settled for all time. Vigilance is required to sustain the elimination of differential incorporation de facto in the Caribbean, and especially so where Creole-Indian contraposition is endemic, and Hinduism provides an outstanding example of religious pluralism – and ethnicity.

References

Braithwaite, L. (1953) 'Social Stratification in Trinidad', *Social and Economic Studies*, 2(2/3): 5–175.

Clarke, C. (1975) *Kingston, Jamaica: Urban Development and Social Change*, Berkeley, CA: University of California Press.

—(1986) *East Indians in a West Indian Town: San Fernando, Trinidad, 1930–70*, London: Allen and Unwin.

—(1991) 'Society and Electoral Politics in Trinidad and Tobago', in C. Clarke (ed.) *Society and Politics in the Caribbean*, London: St Antony's.

Doherty, P. and Poole, M.A. (1997) 'Ethnic Residential Segregation in Belfast, Northern Ireland, 1971–1991', *Geographical Review*, 87(4): 520–36.

Fraginals, M.M., Moya Pons, F. and Engerman, S.L. (eds) (1985) *Between Slavery and Free Labour: The Spanish-Speaking Caribbean in the Nineteenth Century*, Baltimore, MD: Johns Hopkins University Press.

Furnivall, J.S. (1948) *Colonial Policy and Practice: A Comparative Study of Burma and Netherlands India*, Cambridge, UK: Cambridge University Press.

Goveia, E.V. (1970) *The West Indian Slave Laws of the 18th Century*, Barbados: Caribbean Universities Press.

Henriques, F. (1953) *Family and Colour in Jamaica*, London: Eyre and Spottiswoode.

Hoetink, H. (1985) *Caribbean Race Relations: A Study of Two Variants*, London: Oxford University Press.

Howard, D. (2001) *Colouring the Nation: Race and Ethnicity in the Dominican Republic*, Oxford, UK: Signal Books.

Knight, F. (1970) *Slave Society in Cuba During the Nineteenth Century*, Madison, WI: University of Wisconsin Press.

Kymlicka, W. (1997) *The Rights of Minority Cultures*, Oxford, UK: Oxford University Press.

Lowenthal, D. (1972) *West Indian Societies*, London: Oxford University Press.

Moret, E. (2008) 'Afro-Cuban Religion, Ethnobotany and Healthcare in the Context of Global and Economic Change', *Bulletin of Latin American Research*, 27(3): 333–50.

Nicholls, D. (1996) *From Dessalines to Duvalier: Race, Colour and National Independence in Haiti*, London: Macmillan Caribbean.

Palmié, S. (2002) *Wizards and Scientists: Explorations of Afro-Cuban Modernity and Tradition*, Durham, NC: Duke University Press.

Parsons, T. (1952) *The Social System*, London: Tavistock.

Richardson, B.C. (1992) *The Caribbean in the Wider World, 1492–1992*, Cambridge, UK: Cambridge University Press.

Scott, R. (1985) *Slave Emancipation in Cuba: The Transition to Free Labor, 1860–1899*, Princeton, NJ: Princeton University Press.

Simpson, G.E. (1956) 'Jamaican Revivalist Cults', *Social and Economic Studies*, 5(4): 321–442.

Smith, M.G. (1955) *A Framework for Caribbean Studies*, Mona, Kingston: University of West Indies.

—(1960) 'Social and Cultural Pluralism', *Annals of the New York Academy of Sciences*, 83(1): 763–77.

—(1965) *The Plural Society in the British West Indies*, Berkeley, CA: University of California Press.

—(1974) *Corporations and Society*, London: Duckworth.

—(1984) *Culture, Class and Race in the Commonwealth Caribbean*, Mona, Kingston: University of the West Indies.

—(1991) *Pluralism, Politics, and Ideology in the Creole Caribbean*, New York, NY: Research Institute for the Study of Man.

—(1998) *The Study of Social Structure*, New York, NY: Research Institute for the Study of Man.

Weber, M. (1947) *The Theory of Social and Economic Organization*, London: William Hodge.

15

Silent minority

Celebrated difference, caste difference, and the Hinduization of independent India

Rupa Viswanath

Every schoolchild in India is taught the credo of 'unity in diversity', the formula popularized by Jawarharlal Nehru, independent India's first prime minister, who instituted it as state policy. The phrase is represented, for instance, in the ubiquitous cheap posters that paper classroom walls showing colourful tableaux of Indians in regional dress, and of various religious and sectarian persuasions. The poster children of Indian diversity are India's many languages and religions. The dark horse is caste. Representative images of different castes never appear on classroom walls. The former, in short, are the kinds of diversity that Indian political leaders proudly showcase; the latter is an embarrassment, best relegated to the past as quickly as possible.[1] When scholars, public intellectuals and media figures speak of religious and linguistic diversity, the focus is almost invariably on the Indian state's protection of religious minorities, religions other than Hinduism.[2] But where languages are arguably based in pre-existing (linguistic) practices,[3] religious majorities and minorities are created entirely by the state itself. Moreover, while the focus of both official and academic diversity talk is on how *minorities* are managed, what is less noticed is how *majorities* are thereby constituted. It is this aspect of 'diversity management' – what might be called its silent partner – that this essay discusses. I will argue that although religion (a form of 'good diversity') is seen as distinct from caste (a diversity meant to be ultimately eradicated), the two are in fact inseparably linked in the processes by which the Indian state creates and maintains its Hindu majority. I begin with a brief overview of mainstream diversity talk in postcolonial Indian statecraft and in academic discourse. I then turn to how caste difference has been conceived by the postcolonial state and targeted by its policies. This will illustrate the unacknowledged processes by which an overwhelming 'Hindu' majority population was created by the Indian state.[4]

It will also demonstrate that, although state responses to religion in India are widely understood to be a form of what Nancy Fraser has called 'recognition', while policies on caste are seen to be a matter of 'redistribution', in fact *both* of these responses equally deny these groups' political autonomy.[5]

Multiculturalism avant la lettre? Diversity management as national incorporation

During the colonial period, the Indian people were represented as so deeply divided that genuine nationhood – understood to require ethnic and cultural homogeneity – was all but impossible. This view was challenged by Indian nationalists, not by denying difference, but by claiming that national identity could encompass it, though the achievement of nationhood was understood to require a concerted and programmatic effort (see Roy 2006: 19–21). Following India's independence from British rule in 1947, the recognition, protection and even cultivation of diversity have continued to be regarded by nationalist elites as essential to the success of the postcolonial polity. Drafted in the wake of an event that revealed diversity's most threatening aspect – the bloody partition of British India into India and Pakistan on the basis of religious difference – the Indian Constitution promises religious and linguistic minorities a variety of rights. 'Any section of the citizens residing in the territory of India or any part thereof having a distinct language, script or culture of its own shall have the right to conserve the same.' (Constitution of India, part III, article 29). This promise of 'conservation' includes for all 'minorities, whether based on religion or language … the right to establish and administer educational institutions of their choice' (ibid. article 30). In the parlance of the constitution – framed prior to the ascendancy of the language of multiculturalism in political theoretic discourse – all these measures were attempts to protect what was called India's 'composite culture'. Indeed, the duties enjoined upon India's citizens, the counterbalance to the rights just described, include the duty '… to promote harmony and the spirit of common brotherhood amongst all the people of India transcending religious, linguistic and regional or sectional diversities' (Constitution of India, part IVA, 51A). In short, not only the state but also its citizenry must 'value and preserve the rich heritage of [India's] composite culture' by both acknowledging and transcending subnational difference (ibid.).

The Constitution asserts that the population is naturally diverse in a way requiring a specific kind of governance and a certain type of citizen: Indian differences, then, as Srirupa Roy has observed, are most often understood as primordial: 'The interested origins and power effects … [of "diversity"] – the fact that diversity is as much of a "made" as it is a "found" formation – are removed from our line of sight' (Roy 2006: 7). A correlate of the assumption that India's 'deep diversity' must be managed by the state has been a trend in commentaries on Indian democracy to portray democracy's very existence in India as in some way an 'exceptional' phenomenon, an enduring 'paradox' or 'puzzle' requiring special explanation.[6]

Three types of difference are invoked in scholarly discussions of Indian diversity: language, religion and caste. We will focus on the latter for the bulk of this essay. Let us first briefly consider the policies framed, bearing in mind what we have seen in Constitutional rhetoric, with respect to the former two. In standard accounts of the postcolonial Indian polity, one learns that linguistic diversity has been successfully 'managed' by federalism. Power was devolved onto linguistically organized states in India primarily during the first two decades following independence. Far from strengthening centrifugal forces at play in the polity, Nehru's management of linguistic diversity, properly balanced power, strengthened the fidelity of states to the union and 'has indeed been among the more successful experiments of institutional engineering in the history of modern India' (Jayal 2006: 48). There are admitted exceptions: the union's abrogation of its promise to the United Nations in 1947 to allow Kashmir's citizenry to determine by plebiscite its national status (i.e. whether to be subsumed within India or Pakistan), and its suppression of calls for self-determination by the peoples of the northeastern states, for example (see Anderson 2012a, b; Baruah 2011). These are decried, but as egregious exceptions in an otherwise successful policy regime. Less often discussed in mainstream accounts of diversity management are initiatives in the name of development in so-called 'tribal' regions that are rich in natural resources. These have involved massive enclosures of commons and forced displacement, which more quietly and routinely violate the enshrined rights of cultural and linguistic preservation (Baviskar 2004).

What about religious difference? Notwithstanding all the unique aspects of postcolonial Indian secularism that many authors have debated (see Bhargava 2004a), it shares at least one central structural characteristic with Western secular democracies, namely that legally protected religious autonomy is exercised only in very circumscribed spheres largely corresponding to what is identified as the 'private'. While the Indian public has often been described as distinct from Western secular polities insofar as public displays of religion (including, for example, in government offices and in the symbols of state) are commonplace, citizens' religiously defined rights are confined to the private and educational domains, and primarily to the arena of the family.[7] India, since its independence, has had distinct sets of religious community-specific 'personal laws' that govern marriage, inheritance and related matters. This has been most relevant in the case of Muslims, who represent the largest religious minority, but personal laws optionally extend to Hindus, Christians and Parsis (aka Zoroastrians) as well.

The political rights held by religious minorities during the colonial period, the most significant of which was that religious minorities were permitted to have separate electorates, were denounced by Congress Party leaders (who were overwhelmingly high-caste Hindus) as an instance of the colonizer's divide-and-rule strategy. In independent India the *political rights* of religious minorities were replaced by *cultural* protections. As many have noted, this has provided manifest opportunities for the capture of community representation by conservative elements – in short, the stifling of intra-community dissent, leading to several egregious and highly publicized cases of gender injustice (see Chatterjee 2004).[8] But the more significant feature from the perspective of this essay is the replacement of political rights, especially electorally mediated representation, by non-democratically defined cultural protections.[9]

India's policies on linguistic diversity, in which major regional language groups were granted their own states, poses a contrasting case to religion with respect to the sharing of power. However, although some measure of autonomy has been granted to linguistic states, the union has done so only after having extracted the pledge to renounce for evermore any claim to independent national status. As federal systems go, India's falls squarely on the more centralized end of the spectrum, with, moreover, the central government retaining considerably more power than in comparable federal states, including the power to dissolve effectively state governments at will.[10] In short, the celebration of diversity in India is carefully framed in ways that reinforce the absolute political unity of the country by reducing internal others (non-Hindu populations and formerly distinct regional political identities) to anodyne expressions of cultural and linguistic diversity within a highly centralized federal system.[11]

The absolute foreclosure by the dominant-caste–Hindu political culture in India of independent minority political representation has been accompanied by the steady decline of a once thriving Indian Muslim population, which now ranks among the lowest of all Indian groups in terms of education, literacy and income (Jaffrelot 2012).[12] And as we will see, the situation of the lowest castes, those formerly known as untouchables and now referred to as Dalits,[13] has shown some signs of improvement in the post-independence decades, but lags scandalously behind the rest of the population. Dalits, furthermore, continue to be the victims of widespread caste-based violence in most parts of rural India.[14] Yet India's diversity policies are nevertheless frequently described in glowing terms as successful multiculturalism avant la lettre. Echoing official discourse, one prominent author writes,

India was among the first few democracies to embark on the multicultural path. At a time when Western liberalism advocated neutrality and a difference-blind approach, India acknowledged the rights of minorities and valued cultural diversity. This was an innovative and bold initiative that defied the thinking of its time.

(Mahajan 2005: 288f.)[15]

With respect to the empirical effects and specific stipulations of policy, however, India is perhaps more prosaically described as assimilationist or incorporative – and therefore somewhat less than 'bold' for its time. It was perhaps innovative in making a virtue – 'diversity' – of irreducibly political difference; India undoubtedly did not pursue nation-building in the same way as more overtly homogenizing nation-states, such as France. Yet however much the leadership of the early postcolonial nation-state may have genuinely cherished diversity, as seems to have been the case with Nehru (see Khilnani 2011; Parekh 1991), it is useful to recognize that unity-in-diversity rhetoric enabled policies that served to reinforce the hegemony of the Congress Party and the very specific set of social and cultural fractions it represented (Jaffrelot 2003).[16]

Caste difference: a distinctive mode of incorporation

I turn now to the kind of difference whose resilience is usually not celebrated in the same manner as religious and linguistic diversity.[17] It is necessary at the outset to mark a distinction between different possible meanings of caste difference that generic discussions of 'caste' tend to overlook (see also Jodhka, this volume). On one hand, there are the multiple and often trivial differences among particular castes, understood as locally or regionally specific endogamous jatis. Caste in this sense is accurately described as 'revolving around differences in tiny details'.[18] The multiplex caste differences of this sort are not of any great political significance, and do not necessarily entail systematic and intractable power differential. On the other hand, there is the singular division between Dalit castes and all others, which for clarity I will describe as 'Dalit difference'.[19]

What exactly makes Dalit difference distinctive and a special problem for both the state and nation? What defines Dalits as a class is not any shared culture, ritual or religious practices or language. Nor do they constitute a single endogamous group, or jati; Dalits, like other Indians, are subdivided into innumerable regionally and linguistically specific jatis, each with its own origin myths and traditions. Dalit difference is qualitatively distinct from all other sorts of caste difference in at least three ways. First, historically Dalits were hereditarily unfree labourers who were actively barred from acquiring land in India's major agrarian regions. Though their enslavement was made illegal in British India in 1843, and ceased to be an effective reality in most of the subcontinent by the early twentieth century (Viswanath 2014), poverty and landlessness are endemic among Dalits to the present day (Mendelsohn and Vicziany 2000), and modern forms of (largely non-hereditary) bondage remain the lot of a non-trivial minority (Breman 2013). Second, they were and still are distinguished spatially from all others in rural India. All other castes in a village, though segregated residentially from one another on different streets, nevertheless share what is seen as the village proper, the main settlement. Dalit settlements are kept at a physical distance from all others, in what has been called India's 'hidden apartheid' (Human Rights Watch 2007; Teltumbde 2010). This spatial segregation is not simply a 'superstitious' adherence to ideas of purity and impurity. It also entails differential access to all village resources: pasturage, roads and, perhaps most importantly, water sources. Finally, Dalits are regarded by most Hindus as ritually defiling, and by caste people of all religions in India as lazy, dirty, immoral and intellectually inferior.[20]

Dalits are thus a permanent, hereditary underclass comparable to a race, and their relationship to the dominant national community has always been awkward and fraught with tensions. The exclusion from temples underscores the fact that, in former times, Dalits were not considered Hindus, and this past resurfaces in ordinary language today – it is not uncommon for Dalits to refer to all other castes as 'Hindus' in contrast to themselves (see Searle-Chatterjee 1994, 2008; Roberts forthcoming). Even though Dalits worshipped gods that are today considered Hindu gods, Dalits were excluded as a matter of definition from the Hindu fold, and even in the early decades of the twentieth century one could, for example, ask of someone, 'Is he a Hindu or a Pariah?' (Viswanath 2014: chap. 1).[21] Thus, when Indian census takers in the late nineteenth century were instructed by the British to record Dalits as Hindus, they frequently balked, finding the categorization both puzzling and offensive (Mendelsohn and Vicziany 2000 quoted in Roberts, forthcoming).

But this state of affairs changed dramatically by the early decades of the twentieth century. Including Dalits within the category Hindu – administratively if not socially – came to be portrayed by Gandhi and the Congress Party as a matter of pressing national interest. This is because the British, as previously discussed, accorded political representation on the basis of religious community. Representing Dalits as *within* the Hindu fold, and thereby covering over the fact that Hindu once had a caste-specific meaning, ensured that Hindus would retain a firm numerical majority. This incorporative political strategy on the part of non-Dalit Hindus has been aptly termed a 'politics of numbers', insofar as it was driven by the new conditions instituted by the British expansion of the franchise and the introduction of forms of representative governance to the colony.[22] At first pursued primarily by those known as Hindu nationalists,[23] incorporating Dalits within Hinduism was embraced by M.K. Gandhi in the 1930s. In this way Gandhi systematically blurred the distinction between national and Hindu communal interest, though he was not the only one to do so.[24]

The larger backdrop of political activity at the time was what historian Sumit Sarkar has described as a late-colonial nationalism that subtly but unmistakably relied on Hindu imagery and modes of mobilization even while seeking to project itself as the legitimate representative of all Indians irrespective of religion.[25] The assassination of Gandhi by Hindu nationalists, who were unhappy with what they saw as his willingness to accommodate Muslims, rendered explicit appeals to Hindu majoritarianism taboo. Gandhi's assassination also helped cement Congress's long-standing attempts to project itself as a non-sectarian alternative, an effort that took more substantial form when Nehru, a staunch secularist and advocate of the 'scientific temperament', was placed at the helm of independent India's first government. But with respect to the problem of Dalit difference, the Hinduizing project of the state never flagged. The majority of Dalits in postcolonial India are now Hindu as a matter of law.

How is this so? First, the postcolonial state defined Hinduism officially as the default religion of all Indians, by deeming everyone Hindu who is born in India of Indian parents so long as they were not specifically affiliated with one of the 'minority' religions (Galanter 1971; Ludden 1996; Sen 2007). In this way, Hinduism was treated as a residual category, encompassing millions of adivasis (a.k.a. tribals), whose connection to Hinduism was ambiguous at best, and Dalits, who, as we have seen, had previously been excluded from the Hindu fold. Between this and the Partition of British India into Congress-controlled India and an explicitly Muslim Pakistan, Hinduism was constituted as the 'majority religion'. The re-definition of Hinduism according to nationalist 'blood and soil' criteria has been enshrined in the law: the legal

> test of whether a person is a Hindu ... starts with ethnic and geographical tests, which ... can be rebutted not by proof of absence of belief or presence of disbelief

but only by proof of exclusive adherence (or conversion) to a foreign (i.e. a non-Hindu) faith.

(Derrett 1968: 52)

That is, anyone practising or professing anything at all, so long as she refrains from explicitly adhering to Christianity or Islam – even a committed atheist – is, legally speaking, a Hindu. Little trace now remains in the discourse of the state that, at one time, Dalits might just as easily have been construed as another subnational minority.

What do Dalits themselves have to say about this? In the 1930s, politically active Dalits under the revered activist and intellectual Dr B.R. Ambedkar, insisted that their outsider status be recognized politically by granting them separate electorates. The idea was that they themselves, and not non-Dalits, would choose who would represent them in public office. A separate electorate was granted to Muslims as a result of the Indian Councils Act of 1909, and, although at first unhappy about this, Indian nationalists became reconciled to it (Bose and Jalal 2004: 84). In a fateful turn in the building of an anti-colonial nationalist consensus, Gandhi resolutely opposed giving Dalits similar political autonomy when the British tried to grant them this in 1932, insisting that Dalits could not be separated from the Hindu community, and that the problems they faced had to be considered as matters within the Hindu fold, which he proposed social reform and attitudinal change could 'purify'. B.R. Ambedkar, the civil rights lawyer who led the Dalits, pleaded for separate electorates to be granted for the temporary period of a decade, just long enough that Dalits could attain some measure of political equality before becoming part of the general electorate. But Gandhi's opposition to this prospect was so marked that he undertook a 'fast-unto-death' in protest. Given Gandhi's enormous stature as a national hero, his illness or death would have meant a massive retaliation against Dalits across India, so Ambedkar was forced to capitulate, and in 1932 he signed the Poona Pact. The pact foreclosed, once and for all, the possibility that Dalits could independently elect their own representatives.[26]

The Hinduizing tendencies of the postcolonial state are all the more evident in the state's proffered solution to the problem of Dalit difference. The postcolonial state has instituted what are called 'reservations', affirmative action-style policies that provide for a percentage of seats in legislatures, government employment and government-run educational establishments. In 1950 a list of Scheduled Castes (or SCs), castes that were to be named in the 'schedules', or lists that determined eligibility for reservations, was included in the Constitution. Who exactly would be considered SC for legal-administrative purposes? 'No person who professes a religion different from the Hindu [or the Sikh or the Buddhist] religion shall be deemed to be a member of a Scheduled Caste.'[27] Excluded entirely are the vast numbers of Christian and Muslim Dalit converts, who may not benefit from state-sponsored welfare schemes. Even less often publicly acknowledged is the fact that Dalits outside the definition of SC thereby also lose protection under the Scheduled Caste and Scheduled Tribes Prevention of Atrocities Act (known as the POA),[28] a piece of hate crimes-style legislation that is supposed to provide special penalties for SCs against perpetrators of caste-based violence. By excluding Dalits who opt out of Hinduism in favour of Christianity or Islam, the Indian state institutes an official disincentive to out-conversion.[29]

Over a half a century on, it is widely agreed that policies of reservation have been, if at all, only minimally successful in challenging discrimination and disadvantage (Mendelsohn and Vicziany 2000). Moreover, despite the enactment of a law in 1955 that made practising untouchability a criminal offence and punished lynching and other routine forms of violence against Dalits – primarily attacks by upper-caste employers against Dalits who appear not to 'know their place' – remain commonplace in most of rural India. Enforcement of the Act is extremely rare, and, recalling the situation of African Americans in the post-reconstruction American South, rural police, who invariably belong to the same communities as perpetrators, generally refuse to recognize even the most blatant anti-Dalit atrocities as such. Not infrequently, they are themselves among the attackers (Narula 1999; Roberts 2010). Police are answerable ultimately to the elected representatives at the state level. But due to the aforementioned depoliticization of Dalit difference, even those elected as 'Dalit representatives' are chosen by caste people, and accountability remains elusive. The most important advocate for Dalits' rights in modern India, B.R. Ambedkar, was prescient when in 1930 he unsuccessfully tried to persuade his fellow Indians that Dalits ought to be given political autonomy:

> We are often reminded that the problem of the Depressed Classes [a term for Dalit used in the early decades of the century] is a social problem and that its solution lies elsewhere than in politics. We take strong exception to this view. We hold that the problem of the Depressed Classes will never be solved unless they get political power in their own hands. ... The settlement of our problem must not be left ... to the shifting sands of sympathy and the good will of the rulers.
>
> *(Ambedkar 1982: 503–9)*

Notes

1 To cite only the most recent example of what Nicholas Dirks has described as the 'embarrassment of caste', the Indian state and prominent Indian sociologists opposed the plea by Dalit groups in India that their plight be represented before the UN's 2001 Durban Conference on Racism and Xenophobia; see discussion in Natrajan and Greenough (2009: 1–44) and Viswanath (2014). Dirks (2003: 290–6) discusses the 'embarrassment of caste' on the part of contemporary Indian intellectuals.

2 The signal distinction between official and academic discourses on diversity is that caste is absent in official celebrations of diversity, such as the Republic Day parades described by Roy (2006: 66–104). In academic discourse, caste is included among the forms of diversity that the state must manage (Jayal 2006; Mahajan 2005; Ruparelia 2008).

3 But see Crystal (1987: 25–33) on the lack of scientific support for the popular idea that languages are naturally distinct, which makes the way languages are defined inherently political. The link the state makes between languages and populations is furthermore premised on a 'folk ideology [that] assumes monolingualism to be the natural human state of affairs', and therefore 'that there should be a one-to-one mapping between languages and speakers' (Bashkow 2004: 456, n. 14).

4 The Indian state's creation of Hinduism as the majority religion completed a political project that was initiated by early Hindu nationalists in the late nineteenth century, and supported both actively and passively by the Gandhi-led Congress Party in the decades prior to Indian independence in 1947. On early Hindu nationalism and its precursors, see, respectively, Jaffrelot (2007) and Sharma (2003). On the Hinduization of Indian nationalism under a Gandhian Congress, see William Gould (2004).

5 Fraser (1995) first proposed this distinction to critique the culturalizing effects of identity politics. Kevin Olsen (2008) offers an excellent recent collection of debates on the issue.

6 An influential example of this sort of talk is Khilnani (1998). See also Lijphart (1996) and Ganguly (2007).

7 A standard scholarly position on Indian secularism, which closely approximates the Government of India's own self-description, can be found in the writings of Rajeev Bhargava (e.g. Bhargava 2004b: 1–28, 2009: 82–109). The range of existing positions on Indian secularism can be found in the latter volume, and in Rajeswari Sunderrajan and Anuradha Needham (2006). See also Amir Ali (2000), who argues that even in the public square, *pace* most observers, there has been a relative non-recognition of religious minorities.

8 The observation that India's policy of cultural protection for minorities empowers the most conservative elements in those communities is frequently seen as being exemplified in the widely discussed case of

Shah Bano, a Muslim woman whose rights to maintenance upon divorce were revoked by the Indian state in deference to the wishes of her 'community'. This has given rise to a vast literature (Ali 1987; Pathak and Rajan 1989). The intersection of patriarchy, internal minorities and group rights is also of course a mainstay in the broader theoretical literature on multiculturalism. Classic sources include Cohen et al. (1999) and Eisenberg and Spinner-Halev (2005).

9 By defining religious communities as *essentially* at odds with one another at the cultural level, the Indian state ironically reifies the very problem of 'tolerance' that it then goes on to solve (or manage) through its diversity policies. In this, India is not necessarily unique; for a parallel argument with respect to the toleration of religious difference in the contemporary United States, see Brown (2006).

10 The state governor, a position to which one is appointed by the centre, can move to dissolve the state government upon approval from the president and prime minister (Dasgupta 2001: 49–78).

11 As Srirupa Roy has put this, in the early decades of postcolonial India 'the norm of diversity' was of 'an ethnocultural, *nonpolitical* matrix organized and maintained by the state' (Roy 2006: 20, my emphasis).

12 The findings on Indian Muslims' current situation are detailed in an extensive Government of India study entitled *Social, Economic and Educational Status of the Muslims in India: A Report* (Government of India 2006). This is widely referred to as the Sachar Committee Report after Rajinder Sachar, the retired Chief Justice of the Delhi Court who headed the commission.

13 *Dalit* is the accepted scholarly term for those who were in previous times known by a wide variety of names in India. In addition to 'untouchable', terms that were used across India included 'Pariah', *panchama, avarna, chandala, achut*. They are still sometimes referred to, following Gandhian usage, as 'harijans', (meaning 'children of the [Hindu] god Hari'), but this usage has been widely rejected by Dalits as demeaning; see Natrajan and Greenough (2009: 1).

14 On ubiquitous discrimination against Dalits in education, housing and employment, see Newman and Thorat (2012), and on ongoing violence see Narula (1999).

15 Using the Constituent Assembly debates to make his case, Christophe Jaffrelot arrives at a more sceptical conclusion, parallel to the one I present, namely that 'multiculturalism' is a misleading description of Indian state policies; see Jaffrelot (2004: 126–49).

16 The absolute hegemony of Congress and the caste- and religion-specific interests it represented began to crumble at the national level only in the 1990s; the best available account of this is Jaffrelot (2003); see also note 18.

17 In a telling exception, which reflects the wider cultural stereotype that caste endogamy is beneficial to the preservation of culture, the former Commerce Minister Jairam Ramesh 'spoke proudly of India's diversity [in 2007] by including ... a glowing mention of its "4635 largely endogamous communities" – a direct reference to the approximately 3990 caste groups and 645 "tribal" groups in India.' (Cited in Natrajan 2012.)

18 Testimony of Dipankar Gupta in *Treaty Monitor Report: International Service for Human Rights*, Committee on the Elimination of Racial Discrimination, 70th Session India, p. 6

19 Since the 1990s, a larger group of lower castes who are not Dalit, falling under a new administrative category called 'Other Backward Classes', or OBC, has also been eligible for special state entitlements, and the political mobilization of such groups has radically transformed the face of parliamentary politics in India (Jaffrelot 2003). For considerations of space, I focus here on Dalit difference, which considered by itself can nevertheless provide a clear illustration of the breadth, nature and relative silence surrounding Indian assimilationism.

20 As I discuss in the following, all religious communities in India (not just Hindus) are subdivided into endogamous jatis, and the Dalit–non-Dalit division crosscuts all.

21 On terminology, see note 11.

22 In keeping with this new politics, discrimination against Dalits was then defined as a form of religious superstition internal to Hinduism (Viswanath 2010). The 'politics of numbers' is well described by Webster (1992: 93–157).

23 Hindu nationalists in colonial India comprised movements that sought to emphasize the Indian nation's putatively Hindu character (and in so doing question the legitimacy of India's large Muslim majority).

24 Gandhi's more or less explicit equation of Hindu and national interest is detailed in Roberts, *The Power of Conversion and the Foreignness of Belonging* (unpublished book manuscript).

25 William Gould details how the Congress Party consistently gave an impression of regarding India as a Hindu nation – an impression that caused considerable alarm among India's Muslims and

Dalits – despite its officially secular platform (Gould 2004). A concise discussion of these issues can also be found in Sarkar (1996: 270–93).

26 This account of the struggle over the Poona Pact is derived primarily from Anand (2014), Jaffrelot (2005) and Zelliot (2010).
27 The rules regarding Sikhism and Buddhism were amendments to the original statement, and were introduced in 1956 and 1990, respectively: Constitution of India, Scheduled Castes Order of 1950.
28 Although this law was only passed in 1989, it was based on earlier laws, the first of which was the Protection of Civil Rights Act of 1955.
29 The National Commission for Religious and Linguistic Minorities, also known as the Mishra Commission Report after the retired judge who chaired it, made for the first time an official statement that the category of Scheduled Caste should be amended to include Christians and Muslims. The Mishra Report appeared in 2007; the legal definition of SC has yet to be amended; see National Commission for Religious and Linguistic Minorities (2007).

References

Ali, A. (2000) 'Case for Multiculturalism in India', *Economic and Political Weekly*, 35(28–29): 2503–5.

Ambedkar, B.R. (1982) 'Need for Political Power for Depressed Classes', in B.R. Ambedkar and V. Moon (eds) *Writings and Speeches*, Bombay: Department of Education, Government of Maharashtra.

Anand, S. (2014) 'The Juice and the Rind: The Communal Award, the Poona Pact and its Aftermath', in B.R. Ambedkar and A. Roy (eds) *Annihilation of Caste: The Critical Annotated Edition*, New Delhi: Navayana.

Anderson, P. (2012a) 'Why Partition?', *London Review of Books*, 34(14): 11–19. Online. Available HTTP: <http://www.lrb.co.uk/v34/n14/perry-anderson/why-partition> (accessed 14 August 2012).

—(2012b) 'After Nehru', *London Review of Books*, 34(15): 21–36. Online. Available HTTP: <http://www.lrb.co.uk/v34/n15/perry-anderson/after-nehru> (accessed 14 August 2012).

Balmurli, N. and Greenough, P.R. (eds.) (2009) *Against Stigma: Studies in Caste, Race, and Justice since Durban*, New Delhi: Orient BlackSwan.

Baruah, S. (2011) 'Regionalism and Secessionism', in N. Jayal and P.B. Mehta (eds) *Oxford Companion to Politics in India*, New Delhi: Oxford University Press.

Bashkow, I. (2004) 'A Neo–Boasian Conception of Cultural Boundaries', *American Anthropologist*, 106(3): 443–58.

Baviskar, A. (2004) *In the Belly of the River: Tribal Conflicts over Development in the Narmada Valley*, Delhi: Oxford University Press.

Bhargava, R. (ed.) (2004a) *Secularism and its Critics*, Chennai: Oxford University Press.

—(2004b) 'Introduction', in R. Bhargava (ed.) *Secularism and its Critics*, Chennai: Oxford University Press.

—(2009) 'Political Secularism: Why it is Needed and What can be Learned from its Indian Version', in G. Brahm and T. Modood (eds) *Secularism, Religion and Multicultural Citizenship*, Cambridge, UK: Cambridge University Press.

Bose, S. and Jalal, A. (2004) *Modern South Asia: History, Culture and Political Economy*, New York, NY: Routledge.

Breman, J. (2013) 'On Labour Bondage', *Contributions to Indian Sociology*, 48(1): 133–41.

Brown, W. (2006) *Regulating Aversion: Tolerance in the Age of Identity and Empire*, Princeton, NJ: Princeton University Press.

Chatterjee, P. (2004) 'Secularism and Tolerance', in R. Bhargava (ed.) *Secularism and its Critics*, Chennai: Oxford University Press.

Cohen, J., Howard, M. and Nussbaum, M.C. (eds) (1999) *Is Multiculturalism Bad for Women?*, Princeton, NJ: Princeton University Press.

Constitution of India, Online. Available HTTP <http://lawmin.nic.in/olwing/coi/coi-english/coi-indexenglish.htm> (accessed 25 April 2014).

Crystal, D. (1987) *The Cambridge Encyclopedia of Language*, Cambridge, UK: Cambridge University Press.

Dasgupta, J. (2001) 'India's Federal Design and Multicultural National Construction', in A. Kohli (ed.) *The Success of India's Democracy*, Cambridge, UK: Cambridge University Press.

Derrett, J.D.M. (1968) *Religion, Law and the State in India*, New York, NY: The Free Press.

Dirks, N. (2003) *Castes of Mind: The Making of Modern India*, Princeton, NJ: Princeton University Press.

Eisenberg, A.I. and Spinner-Halev, J. (eds) (2005) *Minorities within Minorities: Equality, Rights, and Diversity*, Cambridge, UK: Cambridge University Press.

Engineer, A.A. (1989) *The Shah Bano Controversy*, New Delhi: Orient Longman.

Fraser, N. (1995) 'From Redistribution to Recognition: Dilemmas of Justice in a Postsocialist Age', *New Left Review*, 212(1): 68–93.

Galanter, M. (1971) 'Hinduism, Secularism, and the Indian Judiciary', *Philosophy East and West*, 21(4): 467–87.

Ganguly, S. (2007) 'India's Unlikely Democracy: Six Decades of Independence', *Journal of Democracy*, 18(2): 30–40.

Gould, W. (2004) *Hindu Nationalism and the Language of Politics in Late Colonial India*, Cambridge, UK: Cambridge University Press.

Government of India (2006) *Social, Economic and Educational Status of the Muslims in India: A Report*, New Delhi: Government of India. Human Rights Watch (2007) *Hidden Apartheid: Caste Discrimination Against India's Untouchables*, New York, NY: Human Rights Watch. Online. Available HTTP: <www. hrw.org/reports/2007/india0207> (accessed 16 April 2014).

Jaffrelot, C. (2003) *India's Silent Revolution: The Rise of the Lower Castes in North India*, London: Hurst.

—(2004) 'Composite Culture is not Multiculturalism: A Study of the Indian Constituent Assembly Debates', in A. Varshney (ed.) *India and the Politics of Developing Countries*, London: Sage.

—(2005) *Dr. Ambedkar and Untouchability: Analysing and Fighting Caste*, London: Hurst.

—(2007) *Hindu Nationalism: A Reader*, Princeton, NJ: Princeton University Press.

—(2012) 'The Sense of a Community', *Outlook Magazine*. Online. Available HTTP: <http://www. outlookindia.com/article.aspx?281642> (accessed 16 April 2014).

Jayal, N.G. (2006) *Representing India: Ethnic Diversity and the Governance of Public Institutions*, New York, NY: Palgrave Macmillan.

Khilnani, S. (1998) *The Idea of India*, New York, NY: Farrar Straus Giroux.

—(2011) 'Politics and National Identity', in N. Jayal and P.B. Mehta (eds) *Oxford Companion to Politics in India*, New Delhi: Oxford University Press.

Klein, H. (2007) *Treaty Body Monitor*, Human Rights Monitor Series, 70th Session India, International Service for Human Rights. Online. Available HTTP: <http://olddoc.ishr.ch/hrm/tmb/treaty/cerd/reports/cerd_70/cerd_70_india.pdf> (accessed 23 April 2014).

Lijphart, A. (1996) 'The Puzzle of Indian Democracy: A Consociational Approach', *American Political Science Review*, 90(2): 258–68.

Ludden, D. (ed.) (1996) *Contesting the Nation: Religion, Community and the Politics of Democracy in India*, Philadelphia, PA: University of Pennsylvania Press.

Mahajan, G. (2005) 'Indian Exceptionalism or Indian Model: Negotiating Cultural Diversity and Minority Rights in a Democratic Nation-State', in W. Kymlicka and B. He (eds) *Multiculturalism in Asia*, Oxford, UK: Oxford University Press.

Mendelsohn, O. and Vicziany, M. (2000) *The Untouchables: Subordination, Poverty and the State in Modern India*, New Delhi: Cambridge University Press.

Narula, S. (1999) *Broken People: Caste Violence Against India's 'Untouchables'*, New York, NY: Human Rights Watch.

National Commission for Religious and Linguistic Minorities, NCRLM (2007) Report of the NCRLM, New Delhi: Ministry of Minority Affairs. Online. Available HTTP: <http://www.minorityaffairs.gov. in/sites/upload_files/moma/files/pdfs/volume-1.pdf> (accessed 16 April 2014).

Natrajan, B. (2012) *The Culturalization of Caste in India: Identity and Inequality in a Multicultural Age*. London: Routledge.

Natrajan, B. and Greenough, P.R. (2009) 'Introduction', in B. Natrajan and P.R. Greenough (eds) *Against Stigma: Studies in Caste, Race, and Justice since Durban*, New Delhi: Orient BlackSwan.

Newman, K. and Thorat, S.K. (eds) (2012) *Blocked by Caste: Economic Discrimination in Modern India*, New Delhi: Oxford University Press.

Olsen, K. (ed.) (2008) *Adding Insult to Injury: Nancy Fraser Debates her Critics*, New York, NY: Verso.

Parekh, B. (1991) 'Nehru and the National Philosophy of India', *Economic and Political Weekly*, 26(1–2): 35–48.

Pathak, Z. and Rajan, R.S. (1989) 'Shahbano', *Signs*, 14(3): 558–82.

Roberts, N. (2010) 'Language Violence and the State: Writing Tamil Dalits', *South Asia Multidisciplinary Academic Journal*. Online. Available HTTP: <http://samaj.revues.org/2952> (accessed 16 April 2014).

—(forthcoming) 'From Village to City: Hinduism and the "Hindu Caste System"', in P. van der Veer (ed.) *Religion in Asian Cities*, Berkeley, CA: University of California Press.

Roy, S. (2006) *Beyond Belief: India and the Politics of Postcolonial Nationalism*, Durham, NC: Duke University Press.

Ruparelia, S. (2008) 'How the Politics of Recognition Enabled India's Democratic Exceptionalism', *International Journal of Politics, Culture and Society*, 21(1–4): 39–56.

Sarkar, S. (1996) 'Indian Nationalism and the Politics of Hindutva', in D. Ludden (ed.) *Contesting the Nation: Religion, Community and the Politics of Democracy in India*, Philadelphia, PA: University of Pennsylvania Press.

Searle-Chatterjee, M. (1994) 'Urban "Untouchables" and Hindu Nationalism', *Immigrants and Minorities*, 13(1): 12–25.

—(2008) 'Attributing and Rejecting the Label "Hindu" in North India', in N. Green and M. Searle-Chatterjee (eds) *Religion, Language and Power*, New York, NY: Routledge.

Sen, R. (2007) *Legalizing Religion: The Indian Supreme Court and Secularism*, Washington, D.C.: The East–West Center.

Sharma, J. (2003) *Hindutva: Exploring the Idea of Hindu Nationalism*, Delhi: Penguin.

Sunderrajan, R. and Needham, A. (eds) (2006) *The Crisis of Secularism in India*, Durham, NC: Duke University Press.

Teltumbde, A. (2010) *The Persistence of Caste: The Khairlanji Murders and India's Hidden Apartheid*, London: Zed Books.

Viswanath, R. (2010) 'Spiritual Slavery, Material Malaise: "Untouchables" and Religious Neutrality in Colonial South India', *Historical Research*, 83(219): 124–45.

—(2014) *The Pariah Problem: Caste, Religion and the Social in Modern India*, New York, NY: Columbia University Press.

Webster, J.C. (1992) *Dalit Christians: A History*, New Delhi: ISPCK.

Zelliot, E. (2010) *From Untouchable to Dalit: Essays on the Ambedkar Movement*, 3rd edn, New Delhi: Manohar.

16

Re-imagining Balkan diversity beyond and 'straight through' the ethno-national

Jelena Tosic

From a long-term perspective, the most recent developments in the Balkans rather give the impression of the destruction of diversity and are usually read as a revival of violent ethno-nationalism. Apart from the dramatic case of Former Yugoslavia, one can indeed easily trace the evolution of ethno-nationalist genealogies in Albania, Greece, Bulgaria and Romania in the late/post-imperial context up to the present day.

Nevertheless, the hegemonic representation of Balkan states – by media, politicians and 'experts' in and outside of the Balkans – can be characterized as quite simplistic. Aside from, for example, economic decline, crime and corruption or 'masses' of potential immigrants, the ethno-nationalist implosion of the Balkans eroded by 'ancient hatreds', Islamophobia and genocide is also the subject of endless accounts. The 'positive' accounts have been equally Balkanist and teleological: prosperity due to free markets and privatization, citizens embracing and 'learning democracy' or brave activists fighting ethno-nationalism as the main social 'evil'.

Without denying the salience of ethno-nationalist mobilization, and by no means disrespecting those who tragically lost their lives and homes – is that all there is? Is the predominant way of dealing with difference in the Balkans to vote for (ultra)-nationalists, discriminate against and securitize minorities, marginalize, expel and kill people because of the 'other' they are thought to embody? Are citizens of the Balkans led foremost by ethno-national sentiments as opposed to a 'democratic' consciousness of diversity 'naturally' embodied in a European future?

By drawing on anthropological and transdisciplinary 'destabilizations' of this ethnocentric and neoliberal gaze on the Balkans on the one hand, and fieldwork conducted in various parts of the region on the other, in this chapter I aim at a simultaneously exploratory and systematizing engagement with the issue of diversity in the Balkans. Thereby my line of thought follows a dialectic movement between two theoretical–empirical perspectives, both of which I regard as indispensable and interwoven.

The first takes seriously the tenacity of ethno-nationalism as one of the dominant dimensions of conceptualizing diversity in the Balkans. Inseparable from the first, the second perspective engages with looking 'beyond' ethno-nationalism (Verdery 1994) by in fact seeing 'straight through' it – 'diversifying' simplified readings of the Balkans by exploring its interdependence with and occlusion of other dimensions of social differentiation (such as the urbanity–rurality, economy, kinship, mobility, citizenship or gender) and their intersections throughout history.

Thus, this chapter aims to contribute to an exhaustive and stimulating perspective on the manifold ways difference was and is conceived, represented and lived in the south-eastern parts of Europe.

Tracing legacies of diversity in the Balkans

Even a very brief account focusing 'merely' on the Ottoman, Austro-Hungarian and socialist legacies in the Balkans reveals the stunning multidimensionality of diversity later infused by the ideology and political reality of the nation-state.

Although it can be argued that the Ottoman institution of the 'millet' may have provided a sound basis for a later articulation of nationalism, first and foremost its function was to regulate diversity along confessional lines beyond the realm of the state (see Lafi, this volume). Precisely those two dimensions – religion (being a Muslim or not) and the state (being a state-governing 'professional Ottoman' or not), and not ethno-national affiliation – were the main axes of differentiation in the Ottoman Empire (Sugar 1996 [1977]: 31f.), which had started incorporating the Balkans by the end of the fourteenth century. Apart from this core structure – clearly privileging Muslims and state-officials as opposed to non-Muslims and the 'flock' (*reaya*) – there existed an everyday realm comprising a huge number of other dimensions of differentiation. Namely, diversity in the Ottoman context was also crucially structured, for example, according to *language* (language was more associated with social class than with 'nation', multilingualism was very common and intersected with mobility, etc.); the *socio-spatial-migration dimension* (e.g. the specificities of urban–rural dynamics, borderlands, the vanishing 'Muslim' character of cities); or the intersection of *social class and profession* (beyond religious affiliation, individuals were 'grouped' and interacted according to their profession as, e.g., peasants, military land-administrators or urban craftspeople).

Perhaps the most striking aspect of the Ottoman legacy is the simultaneity of the order-obsession on the one hand and a pronounced flexibility on the other. Namely, a complex system of titles and functions 'co-existed' with processes of flexible 'negotiation' of identity and belonging. Apart from the millet system itself being marked by pronounced processuality, boundary management and internal diversity (see Barkey 2008), the dynamics of Ottoman frontiers is a prime example of how a highly regulated diversity regime (Grillo 2010) was very compatible with flexibility. Namely, the frontier legacy, or 'frontier code' (Sugar 1996 [1977]), of continuous mobility, conversion, religious tolerance, 'flexible loyalties' and nationalism-unsettling ambiguity (e.g. Bartov and Weitz 2013) has had a profound effect on local diversity patterns up to the present day (see Tošić forthcoming b).

The Habsburg/Austro-Hungarian way of accommodating difference was marked by a hierarchization based on the, essentially non-border-challenging, notion of 'historical rights' (e.g. Brubaker 2006). Accordingly, 'historical nations' (Germans, Italians, Poles and Hungarians) were distinguished from 'people without history' (such as the Slovaks, Ruthenians or Serbs), who were thought of as lacking ruling power, a nobility and a bourgeoisie. However, facing revolt framed in the language of national liberation, the empire reacted with flexibility. The new dual monarchy (1867) embodied a legally anchored equality of nationalities and state-approved multilingualism in schools and administration. Following Ernest Gellner, the responsiveness to circumstances led an – essentially absolutist – entity to become 'a patron of a pluralistic and tolerant society' (Gellner 1998: 12).

Accommodating religious diversity in the Balkans – with the focus on Islam in particular – was one of the prime concerns of the monarchy's diversity regime. While appropriating Ottoman religious tolerance and even stimulating the emergence of a tri-confessional Bosnian nation,

Austro-Hungarian colonial involvement in Bosnia featured a specific and enduring central European 'frontier orientalist' (Gingrich 1998) grammar of incorporating Islam based on the dual register of the 'civilizable', hence 'good', Bosnian Muslim, as opposed to the 'Turk', who represented the eternally different and 'bad' Muslim.

The late imperial emergence of nationalism – eventually resulting in the dissolution of the empires into nation-states accompanied by the process of the 'unmixing' of peoples (e.g. Brubaker 1996) – gave rise to the post World War I international regime of maintaining peace and regulating diversity according to the notion of minority rights. However, due to its final collapse marked by World War II, the minority rights regime was replaced by the liberal-individualistic idiom of human rights (Brubaker 2006; Falk 2000), which was strongly opposed by the project of socialist modernity itself stressing collective rights and national self-determination.

The extensive early Marxist engagement with the late imperial politics of national liberation (e.g. Hobsbawm 1987) – including the hierarchical differentiation between 'nations' and 'nationalities' – had a strong impact on the Soviet and subsequently the Yugoslav diversity regime of hierarchical and institutionalized multinationality (Bringa 1995, Brubaker 1996). In spite of socialism's ambivalence – simultaneously 'enshrining' nationality on the one hand and 'folklor-izing' and persecuting it on the other – precisely the ethno-national represented the main, if not the only, 'legitimate' difference as long as it did not become political. In spite of evoking the Marxist dictum of 'self-realization', the social practices of real-socialism actually produced uniformity rather than diversity.[1] All-pervading and 'difference-flattening' regimes of expropriation, surveillance and social engineering (Verdery 2011) 'cleansed' individual life of, for example, kinship, gender, religious or class difference by means of an ideological language reform (ibid.) and idealized 'normal' biographies (Niedermüller 2004). Staying securely put in a workplace and enthusiastically participating in the collective modernity project were supposed to make up the main elements of one's identity and sociality. Still, social engineering and the economy of shortage (Verdery 2001) produced new differentiations, inequalities and interest groups – some of whom easily 'picked up' the readily available ethno-national card in pursuing their economic and political goals (Verdery 1994).

Although representing merely one variation of the socialist implosion in the Balkans, the Yugoslav 'Balkan Tragedy' served as an excellent basis for Balkanist media and 'bestseller' accounts (Bougarel et al. 2007) of the 'outburst' of ancient ethno-national hatred thereby occluding the complexity and multidimensionality of social differentiation in this part of Europe.

Finally the ongoing process of EU integration – often featuring a normative rather than a grass-roots multidimensional discourse on diversity around the notion of anti-discrimination (Blagojević 2011) – blends in well with the latest international 're-institution' of the minority regime (Brubaker 2006) framed primarily in one-dimensional, that is, ethno-national, terms. Moreover, the dominant neoliberal idiom of rights (Falk 2000) enhances not only primarily civil and political rights, but also the implicit view that one should frame difference along one dimension at a time, rather than encouraging potentially 'solidary' intersectional imaginaries of (super)-diversity (Vertovec 2007) that imply that everyone simultaneously embodies different dimensions of difference.

'Unpacking' diversity in the Balkans 'straight through' the ethno-national

The challenge of viewing the Balkans 'beyond' 'parochial ethno-national terms' (Blumi 2011: 2) and 'ethnic bias' (Bougarel et al. 2007) can be met by taking a nuanced look 'straight through' the ethno-national – simultaneously allowing for its salience as well as its historical complexity and conditionality, and finally exposing the occlusion of other fundamental aspects of social differentiation (Verdery 1994).

In spite of the fact that the nationalist option was and still is simply a deliberate choice by a substantial fragment of the Balkan population (Hayden 2007), violent ethno-nationalism is neither an irrational Balkan 'trait' nor a mere 'Western' representational distortion of the peaceful Balkan cultural 'mosaic'. Rather, the different historical instances of 'ethnic unmixing' in the Balkans (Duijzings 2003) can indeed be viewed as 'modern' and 'European' (ibid.) and comprise diverse transnational socio-economic influences, most notably the spread of capitalism and the nation-state model (Verdery 1994). The latter represents the ground for the state/kin-state minorities constellation and hence the 'securitization' of the minority issue (Kymlicka 2002), which again led to perceiving nationalism in the Balkans along lines of 'ethnicity' rather than citizenship (Brubaker 2004; Verdery 1994). Although this potentially ethnocentric and teleological binary understanding is not sufficient to capture the complexity of identification and diversity in the Balkans, it reveals one important historical aspect of the salience of ethno-nationalist rhetoric and identification.

Exemplified by the diversification of citizenship regimes in the post-Yugoslav space, ethnocentric and multi-ethnic *citizenship* regimes clearly 'beat' the civic model (Shaw and Štiks 2013). However, as, for example, post-war Bosnia shows, civic citizenship also is a desired option of identification and belonging for a sizable number of individuals. In this case, however – rather than 'inherent' ethno-nationalism – it is precisely the internationally installed Dayton 'multi-ethnic citizenship' regime that de facto prescribes ethnically based political participation (Štiks 2011) and hence excludes the constitutional categories of 'others' and 'citizens' from enjoying full political rights[2] (Štiks 2011; Tošić 2009).

Although in a different way, as in the west European context characterized by colonialism and extensive work migration, *mobility* crucially diversified the Balkans through history up to the present (e.g. Roth and Hayden 2009). Notwithstanding its potential to strengthen ethno-national identification – in intersection with other factors such as socio-legal exclusion in the host country (e.g. Dahinden 2010) – migration also unsettles ethno-nationalism in the Balkans. For example, the intersection of generation, legal status and forced migration is of significance here. Namely, often precisely those *generations* that have experienced war, flight and emigration in their youth – as my first ethnographic example (on p. 155) will show – tend to take a more cosmopolitan, civic and multidimensional stance towards identity and belonging.

Socio-economic factors – for example, personal ties based on ethno-national belonging in the context of the economy of shortage – can contribute to the salience of ethno-nationalism (Verdery 1994). Furthermore, the *urban–rural dynamics* in the Balkans shows how socio-economic and migration-related differences become 'culturalized' and 'ethnicized' and at worst are manifested in 'ethno-national' violence as, for example, in Bosnia or Kosovo (e.g. Bougarel 1999; Duijzings 2003). Simultaneously, other cases exemplify crucially different, if not directly opposing, urban–rural diversity and integration patterns. Hence, legacies of urban diversity regimes in north Albania incorporating (rural) migrants along a middle-class discourse of 'urbanity' rather than ethno-nationalism or religion (Tošić forthcoming a) or the re-appropriation of cosmopolitan urban diversity patterns by young artists and entrepreneurs opposing the top-down 'nationalization' of urban space in Skopje (Janev 2012) highlight the importance of temporality and multidimensionality of diversity practices in the Balkans.

Notwithstanding the patriarchal and homophobic *gender* regime grounding the provincial (Blagojević 2011) nationalist (e.g. Verdery 1996) ideology, reframing difference and inequality along gender crucially disturbs one-dimensional readings of diversity in the Balkans. As, for example, the case of new social movements in Serbia shows (see p. 156) – in synergy with anti-war feminist interventions – different groups of activists (alterglobalist, anarcho-syndicalist, LGBT, student, anti-militaristic, urban, etc.) do not only oppose ethno-nationalism, but also unmask it as a political manoeuvre to distract the citizen's attention away from neoliberal reforms. By opposing all forms of discrimination and exploitation and encouraging social solidarity on a regional and global scale, these initiatives advocate a multidimensional conception of diversity and a trans-ethnic and anti-authoritarian society (Grubačić 2012).

Powder kegs, mosaics, salads . . . unsettling the hegemonic images of diversity in the Balkans

It comes as no surprise that anthropological engagements with the Balkans – combining the ethnographic focus on the multi-level complexity of everyday life and a critical stance towards hegemonic discourses and metaphors – unsettle both negative and positive Balkanist stereotypes. Hence, both the metaphors of 'Balkanization' and the 'powder keg' can simultaneously be read as synonyms for 'barbarianism' and the expression of 'ultimate Europeanization' (Todorova 2009: 13). Similarly, images such as the 'mosaic' or the 'Macedonian salad' reveal the dominant (Jansen 2005), yet essentialist (Green 2005: 128), perceptions of diversity patterns in the Balkans, occluding dimensions such as urbanity, rurality, gender, class, generation and occupation in favour of ethno-national identification (Bougarel et al. 2007: 2).

While engaging with the Balkans from myriad perspectives, anthropologists are critically thinking through alternative imaginaries. As a common way to challenge essentialist and primordial concepts of identity, and thus a useful conceptual tool for capturing a wide range of cases in the Balkans, the notion of 'hybridity', however, is also inextricably interwoven with discourses of purity and can thus produce essentialist frameworks of exclusion (Ballinger 2004). Another way of refuting the primordialist 'ancient hatreds' stereotype and highlighting common patterns of peaceful co-existence in diversity is the use of the notions of 'ambiguity' and 'fluidity' (Duijzings 2003). Through the metaphor of the 'fractal', the ambiguous, fluid and 'chaotic intermingling' of peoples and territories in the Balkans (Green 2005: 132) becomes abstractly tangible as a process of 'relational fragmentation' into ever smaller 'utterly relational' and 'endlessly recomposing' parts (ibid.: 130).

Concluding ethnographic outlooks: among refugees, borderers and activists

I will conclude with three ethnographic 'screen shots' on how the focus on the views and social practices of subaltern and counter-hegemonic social actors – whose lives are also crucially marked by different forms of mobility – can contribute to moving further towards a nuanced and multidimensional approach to diversity in the Balkans. The following ethnographic vignettes 'unpack' diversity in the Balkans, its prominent dimension of ethno-nationalism included, along the intersections of forced migration, urbanity and generation; socio-spatiality (at a borderland), kinship, multilingualism and citizenship; and socio-political identification and transnational mobility.

New Belgrade, 1998

'This war displaced me back into the fourteenth century. I, a young urban sneaker-wearing guy, a cineaste and rock music fan was suddenly supposed to be Milos Obilić.'[3] So said Darko in a perfect Belgrade slang, as if he had always lived in the capital of his 'mother-land' to which he had fled from war-torn Croatia three years earlier. In our countless conversations at the Belgrade flea-market – where he tried to make a living alongside, for example, cosmopolitan unemployed teachers, ultra-nationalist youngsters from Zemun, former university professors and street sellers from diverse Roma settlements – Darko was criticizing the nationalist project pursued by segments of the Serbian intellectual and political elite. Identifying as a cosmopolitan, an anti-militarist and a child of the 'trans-ethnic' 'golden years' of Yugoslav Rock Music – which have perished with the rise of ethno-nationalist mobilization – Darko was primarily longing to see the world. For him – as for innumerable young people in 1990s Serbia – forced immobility due to citizenship was even harder to bear than the threat of mobilization or the harsh winters at the open-air flea-market.

Surroundings of Tuzi, close to the Montenegrin–Albanian border, 2012

'We are real Montenegrins according both to origin and citizenship, but now we feel like Muslim Albanians. While living in Albania, however, we never thought of giving up our Yugoslav citizenship.' This paraphrase illustrates how the two brothers Safet and Husein – whose bio-graphies and family history are marked by bilingualism, repeated migration within the Montenegrin–Albanian borderland and conversion to Islam – kept stressing the 'implicitness' of their pluri-national identity. Beyond the latter – intersecting with mobility, confession, citizenship and bilingualism – their main dimension of belonging is kinship, which itself is actually 'grounding' their 'hybrid' and 'fluid' identification. Namely, the Sarapa family – to which the brothers belong – exemplifies a highly inclusive and borderland-specific genealogy-based kinship practice spanning all local ethno-national and religious categories. The common occurrence of such inclusive kinship networks and practices in the Montenegrin–Albanian borderland can be considered as one important factor in the absence of ethno-national violence in this part of the Balkans (Tošić forthcoming b).

Belgrade Old Town, 2003, and Jajinci (outskirts of Belgrade), 2004

'We oppose the false dichotomy between neoliberal globalization on the one hand and nationalism and patriarchy on the other!', stressed Marija, a feminist and anti-war activist at a conference entitled 'Globalization of Social Justice and Equality', which had brought together a number of activists, NGO representatives, anarchists, academics and other citizens from Belgrade and other parts of Serbia and former Yugoslav republics. While introducing the conference theme – universal values of justice and equality – Marija notably pointed out that 'universality for us does not mean uniformity, but precisely diversity'. A year later, a number of the conference participants reassembled at the third European People's Global Action (PGA) Conference in a school building in Jajinci (Belgrade). Apart from representing the first large-scale event of this sort in 'Post-Yugoslavia', this local meeting of a transnational social movement not only gathered together activists from all over Europe (and beyond), but also included highly diverse social actors: trade union, minority and NGO representatives; anti-militarist, anarchist, LGBT, feminist and other activists; and the local population. While mingling and being amazed by the unprecedented diversity of languages, clothing styles, food and activities in their neighbour-hood, the locals of this Belgrade suburb could read the following programmatic lines on the conference flyer:

> Together we are working on the establishment of a new political space – both beyond political parties and the so-called non-governmental sector. . . . We delimit ourselves from

the concept of 'civil', which we replace by the notion of a 'solidary society'. We insist upon a veritable and equitable dialogue among all members of society, many of which are forgotten both by political parties and the 'civil society's' NGOs – the workers, the unemployed, the refugees, the Roma, the peasants, the activists and many more.

Notes

1   A considerable degree of realization of equality and social justice (e.g. reducing illiteracy, free education, social security, gender equality) must, however, not be glossed over.
2   Persons not belonging to one of the three official ethnicities (Bosniak, Croat and Serb) cannot run for presidency and other ethnically defined positions (Štiks 2011: 259).
3   The Serbian mythic-historical figure of the assassin of Sultan Murad I in the background of the battle of Kosovo in 1389.

References

Ballinger, P. (2004) '"Authentic Hybrids" in the Balkan Borderlands', *Current Anthropology*, 45(1): 31–60.
Barkey, K. (2008) *Empire of Difference: The Ottomans in Comparative Perspective*, Cambridge, UK: Cambridge University Press.
Bartov, O. and Weitz, E.D. (eds) (2013) *Shatterzone of Empires: Coexistence and Violence in the German, Habsburg, Russian, and Ottoman Borderlands*, Bloomington, IN: Indiana University Press.
Blagojević, J. (2011) 'Between Walls: Provincialism, Human Rights, Sexualities and Serbian Public Discourses on EU Integration', in R. Kulpa and J. Mizielinska (eds) *De-centering Western Sexualities: Central and Eastern European Perspectives*, London: Ashgate.
Blumi, I. (2011) *Reinstating the Ottomans: Alternative Balkan Modernities, 1800–1912*, New York, NY: Palgrave Macmillan.
Bougarel, X. (1999) 'Yugoslav Wars: The "Revenge of the Countryside" Between Sociological Reality and Nationalist Myth', *East European Quarterly*, 33(2): 157–75.
Bougarel, X., Helms, E. and Duijzings, G. (eds) (2007) *The New Bosnian Mosaic: Identities, Memories and Moral Claims in a Post-war Society*, London: Ashgate.
Bringa, T. (1995) *Being Muslim the Bosnian Way: Identity and Community in a Central Bosnian Village*, Princeton, NJ: Princeton University Press.
Brubaker, R. (1996) *Nationalism Reframed: Nationhood and the National Question in the New Europe*, Cambridge, UK: Cambridge University Press.
—(2004) *Ethnicity Without Groups*, Harvard, MA: Harvard University Press.
—(2006) *Nationalist Practices and Everyday Ethnicity in a Transylvanian Town*, Princeton, NJ: Princeton University Press.
Dahinden, J. (2010) '"Are You Who You Know?" A Network Perspective on Ethnicity, Gender and Transnationalism', in C. Westin, J. Bastos, J. Dahinden and P. Gois (eds) *Identity Processes and Dynamics in Multi-ethnic Europe*, Amsterdam: Amsterdam University Press.
Duijzings, G. (2003) 'Ethnic Unmixing under the Aegis of the West: A Transnational Approach to the Breakup of Yugoslavia', *Bulletin of the Royal Institute for Inter-faith Studies*, 5(2): 1–16.
Falk, R. (2000) *Human Rights Horizons: The Pursuit of Justice in a Globalizing World*, London: Routledge.
Gellner, E. (1998) *Language and Solitude: Wittgenstein, Malinowski and the Habsburg Dilemma*, Cambridge, UK: Cambridge University Press.
Gingrich, A. (1998) 'Frontier Myths of Orientalism: The Muslim World in Public and Popular Cultures of Central Europe', in B. Baskar and B. Brumen (eds) *MESS Mediterranean Ethnological Summer School Piran/ Pirano, vol. II*, Ljubljana: University of Ljubljana.
Green, S.F. (2005) *Notes from the Balkans: Locating Marginality and Ambiguity on the Greek–Albanian Border*, Princeton, NJ: Princeton University Press.
Grillo, R. (2010) 'Contesting Diversity in Europe: Alternative Regimes and Moral Orders', *MMG MPI Working Paper* 10–02.
Grubačić, A. (2012) 'Balkanization of Politics, Politics of Balkanization', *Globalizations*, 9(3): 439–49.
Hayden, R.M. (2007) 'Moral Vision, Impaired Insight: The Imaginings of Other Peoples' Communities in Bosnia', *Current Anthropology*, 48(1): 105–31.

Hobsbawm, E.J. (1987) *The Age of Empire: 1875–1914*, London: Abacus.

Janev, G. (2012) 'What Happened to the Macedonian Salad? Ethnocracy in Macedonia', in K. Roth and J.L. Bacas (eds) *Southeast European (Post)modernities: Changing Practices and Patterns of Social Life*, Berlin: Lit.

Jansen, S. (2005) 'National Numbers in Context: Maps and Stats in Representations of Post-Yugoslav Wars', *Identities: Global Studies in Culture and Power*, 12(1): 45–68.

Kymlicka, W. (2002) 'Multiculturalism and Minority Rights: West and East', *Journal on Ethnopolitics and Minority Issues in Europe*, 4(1): 1–27.

Niedermüller, P. (2004) 'Arbeit, Identität, Klasse: der Sozialismus als Lebensentwurf', in K. Roth (ed.) *Arbeit im Sozialismus – Arbeit im Postsozialismus: Erkundungen zum Arbeitsleben im Östlichen Europa*, Berlin: Lit.

Roth, K. and Hayden, R. (2009) *Migration in, from and to Southeastern Europe: Historical and Cultural Aspects*, Berlin: Lit.

Shaw, J. and Štiks, I. (2013) *Citizenship after Yugoslavia*, London: Routledge.

Štiks, I. (2011) 'Being Citizen the Bosnian Way: Transformations of Citizenship and Political Identities in Bosnia-Herzegovina', *Transitions*, 51(1–2): 245–69.

Sugar, P.F. (1996) [1977] *Southeastern Europe under Ottoman Rule, 1354–1804*, Seattle, WA: University of Washington Press.

Todorova, M. (2009) *Imagining the Balkans*, updated edn, Oxford, UK: Oxford University Press.

Tošić, J. (2009) '"Diversity" in the Balkans: Balkanism, Anthropological Approaches to the State, and the Political Realities of the Contemporary Balkans', *Irish Journal of Anthropology*, 12(3): 108–18.

—(forthcoming a) 'Shkodër, the "City of the Calm people": Urban Diversity and Migration Legacies in a Balkan Border Town', *MMG MPI Working Paper*.

—(forthcoming b) 'Travelling Genealogies – (Re)assessing Identities: The Reconstruction of Family Histories Across the Albanian-Montenegrin Border', in M. Hurd, C. Leutloff-Grandits and H. Donnan (eds) *Border Crossings, Border Moving*, Manchester, UK: Manchester University Press.

Verdery, K. (1994) 'Beyond the Nation in Eastern Europe', *Social Text*, 38: 1–19.

—(1996) *What Was Socialism and What Comes Next?*, Princeton, NJ: Princeton University Press.

—(2001) 'Socialist Societies: Anthropological Aspects', in N.J Smelser and P.B. Baltes (eds) *International Encyclopedia of Social & Behavioral Sciences*, Amsterdam: Elsevier.

Vertovec, S. (2007) 'Super-diversity and its Implications', *Ethnic and Racial Studies*, 30(6): 1024–54.

17

European Fascism
and its aftermath

Keith Lowe

Fascism took hold in Europe during a particularly turbulent period in history. In the aftermath of the First World War, a series of huge social and political changes hit the continent. The Russian Revolution in 1917 brought Communists to power for the first time, sparking not only a devastating civil war throughout the Russian Empire, but also years of political unrest across Europe. The collapse of the German, Austro-Hungarian and Ottoman empires after the war also precipitated various power struggles. Then, in the late 1920s, Europe was struck by one of the greatest economic crises the world has ever seen, which again resulted in widespread civil unrest. Life during this time was, as the aphorism goes, just one damn thing after another.

Attitudes towards diversity during this turbulent period – particularly racial, ethnic and religious diversity – were different depending on which part of the continent one considers. In most of the west, generally speaking, things were relatively simple. Western Europe was not as badly affected by the aforementioned crises as was Eastern Europe, where there was more scope for conflict between different groups fighting for power or scarce resources. Countries like Britain and France had single dominant cultures with long, stable histories: ethnic and religious minorities therefore tended not to court trouble and, since they rarely represented a significant threat to those who were in power, on the whole they were officially tolerated.[1]

In the east of the continent, by contrast, the relationship between different groups was rather more complicated. On the one hand, there was still a strong tradition of tolerance left over from the days of Europe's great empires. Over the preceding centuries, in the absence of any meaningful national borders, a huge variety of ethnic, religious, cultural and linguistic minorities had spread and intermingled, not only in the cities, but also across the countryside. In varying degrees, these different groups had learned, grudgingly, to accept life amongst and beside one another because under the imperial system there had been little choice but to do so.[2] To modern eyes, this produced all kinds of cultural confusion. For example, Poland's national poet, Adam Mickiewicz, was born in what would today be considered Belarus and was brought up speaking Lithuanian. His most celebrated poem, which Poles to this day regard as the most sublime expression of Polish national sentiment, actually begins with the words 'Lithuania! My fatherland!'.[3] But during the early decades of the twentieth century most Poles who learned this poem at school saw no contradiction between these multiple identities: indeed, it was quite common to regard oneself as, say, Polish by birth, Lithuanian by nationality, German by ethnicity and Jewish by religion. In other words, diversity was a concept so widely accepted that many people had internalised it (Davies 2005: 52–4).

On the other hand, the way that the empires had broken up after the First World War created situations where many such people felt forced to choose between these multiple identities, or at least to prioritise one above the rest. As the empires collapsed, the international community tried to parcel out territory along ethnic lines. Thus Czechs and Slovaks were granted their own homeland; areas mainly peopled by Poles were assigned to Poland; the frontiers of Italy were expanded to include Italian-speaking minorities from neighbouring lands; and so on. While this redrawing of the map was born of good intentions, it had some unfortunate effects. One of these was the elevation in the popular mind of language and ethnicity as the most important markers of citizenship (Kamusella 2009: 51; Pearson 1983: 131f.). This immediately caused problems: if Czechoslovakia was a country for Czechs and Slovaks, what place was there for its 3.3 million German speakers, who together represented almost 24 per cent of the population? And what about the million or so Hungarians, Ruthenians, Poles and others – another seven per cent of the population? In the end, even the relationship between the Czechs and Slovaks proved very delicate, with the Slovaks very quickly complaining that the partnership was less than equal.[4]

Such problems became commonplace in Eastern Europe during the 1920s and 30s. For example, the official name for Yugoslavia after the war was 'The Kingdom of the Serbs, Croats and Slovenes', which was hardly reassuring for the state's large Bosniak, German, Albanian, Hungarian, Romanian and Gypsy minorities. The ethnic melting pot in Yugoslavia was further complicated by class (many of the minorities resented becoming subjects of a Serbian king) and religion (since the country was home to a mix of Catholics, Orthodox Christians, Muslims and Jews). Elsewhere, the Poles managed to forge a state for themselves out of the ruins of three empires – German, Austro-Hungarian and Russian – but inherited sizeable ethnic and religious minorities from each of them. The Ukrainians, meanwhile, ended up without a homeland at all, but found themselves split, rather unsatisfyingly, between Poland and the Soviet Union.

Attitudes towards ethnic diversity therefore underwent a period of radical change between the wars. The international community had treated diversity in Eastern Europe not as a normal and unavoidable part of life but as a problem that needed to be solved, and in doing so they had created an environment of ethnic winners and losers. The winners, who were never in a strong enough position to consider themselves entirely safe, strove to impose their own national identity on their new countries. Minority groups, meanwhile, became correspondingly indignant and resisted assimilation – sometimes violently. For example, arguments between rival ethnic groups in Yugoslavia rose to such a pitch that in 1928 a Serbian member of parliament shot several of his Croat opponents in the assembly chamber. A few years later, the Serbian king, Alexander I, was also assassinated – this time by one of his ethnic Bulgarian subjects who wanted an independent Macedonia.

It was in this context that fascism began to take hold in Europe. Fascist and other far right movements proved adept at harnessing the indignant nationalism of ethnic groups who felt they had been wronged by their rivals. They portrayed the nation – whichever nation that might be – as a single, homogeneous group with historic rights to a particular homeland and way of life. Anyone whose loyalty to this national group might be compromised was to be excluded. In practice this meant that all other political systems were to be eschewed in favour of a fascist totalitarian state; all other ethnic or racial groups were to be shunned in favour of those who were ethnically 'pure'; and in some places, such as Catholic Croatia, religion was also seen as a fundamental part of one's nationality. In addition, most fascists embraced the notions of social Darwinism and eugenics, whereby disabled and other supposedly 'inferior' humans would be purged from the race. Fascist attitudes towards women and homosexuals was also non-inclusive, the former being relegated to the role of child-bearing, and the latter being criminalised. The sum of all these beliefs meant that diversity was almost always regarded as a kind of national sickness which needed to be purged from the state. The ultimate goal of fascism, particularly in Germany, was to create a political, racial, ethnic, religious, sexual and genetic monoculture.[5]

Perhaps the most disturbing feature of fascist ideology was its promotion of the legitimacy of violence to achieve this aim. Violence was often considered to be little more than the expression of a perpetual struggle that was entirely natural in human affairs. It was also considered a driver of social change: since only the fittest could survive in a violent world, it was the quickest and most effective way of purging society of weak and degenerate elements (Bessell 2004: 1; Davies and Lynch 2002: 114; Griffin 1991: 104f.). 'War alone', claimed Mussolini, 'keys up all human energies to their maximum tension and sets the seal of nobility on those peoples who have the courage to face it.' (Mussolini 2000: 53).

The Nazis in Germany were particularly wedded to this notion. They used violent methods against political targets long before they came to power, and mythologised this violence as a noble struggle ever afterwards. Once they had seized power in Germany they turned their sights on their racial and genetic 'inferiors', both through eugenics programmes and through the persecution of racial minorities, particularly of Jews and Gypsies.

Almost inevitably, this internal violence was eventually also directed externally. The ultimate test of the German nation was to engage it in a trial of strength against all the nations around it. Thus they embarked on the military conquest of Poland, which marked the beginning of the Second World War in Europe. This was followed by the invasion of Denmark, Norway, the Low Countries, France and eventually the Soviet Union. The Italian fascists followed suit, and launched an invasion of Yugoslavia, Albania and Greece. Ion Antonescu's far right Romanian regime also enthusiastically entered the conflict against the Soviet Union in order to win back 'historic' Romanian territory in modern-day Moldova and Ukraine.

Wherever the fascists went, they imposed their ideology upon the territories they invaded. Puppet nationalist and fascist governments were installed across Europe, and fascist policies – particularly regarding race – were pursued everywhere. The most obvious example of this was the universal rounding up of Jews and Gypsies for export to the Nazi extermination camps, but other races were treated almost as badly. In their plan to cleanse Eastern Europe, Nazi officials hoped to expel 80 per cent of the Polish population from their lands, followed by 64 per cent of the Ukrainian population and 75 per cent of Belarusians. Some high ranking Nazis openly talked of bringing about the deaths of between 20 and 30 million Poles and Slavs through starvation. It was hoped such policies would free up territory, which could then be repopulated by ethnically 'pure' Germans (Tooze 2007: 366, 467, 479f.). The Second World War was therefore never merely a conflict over territory. It was also a war of race and ethnicity. Some of the defining events of the war had nothing to do with winning and maintaining physical ground, but with imposing one's own ethnic stamp on ground already held.

It is important to note that while the Nazis were the main protagonists of ethnic cleansing throughout Europe, local nationalists and ultra-nationalists learned from their methods. In wartime Ukraine, for example, local people were recruited to help round up and exterminate Jews. Once this moral line had been crossed there was no reason why it could not be crossed again. For ultra-nationalists, who had long been campaigning for a 'Ukraine for Ukrainians', the final solution to their 'Jewish problem' would serve equally well when dealing with their 'Polish problem'. From 1943 onwards, therefore, Ukrainian partisans in the regions of Volhynia and Galicia embarked on a savage campaign of ethnic cleansing against Poles. Whole villages were targetted, and their entire populations – men, women and children – were rounded up and slaughtered. According to Polish sources, around 70,000 Poles were massacred this way, and hundreds of thousands were encouraged to flee the region. Unsurprisingly this produced a backlash, and groups of enraged Poles began to commit reprisal atrocities against Ukrainian villages (Snyder 2003: 205; Statiev 2010: 87f.).

A similar process occurred in Yugoslavia, where the Croatian Fascists murdered almost 600,000 Serbs, Muslims and Jews in an attempt to purge their entire country of racial, ethnic and religious minorities (Tomasevich 2001: 727f.). Other groups, particularly the Serbs, then retaliated in kind, sending the whole country into a spiral of ethnic cleansing whose echoes would be repeated half a century later. More localised massacres also occurred in other parts of Europe such as the Greek–Bulgarian borderlands. When taken together, these various instances of ethnic cleansing provide a terrifying picture. During the Second World War a vast number of people – perhaps ten million or more – were deliberately exterminated for no other reason than that they happened to belong to the wrong ethnic or racial group (Lowe 2012: 187).

Ironically, many of those who survived this huge culling managed to do so precisely because they had grown up in diverse communities. In the many thousands of memoirs and personal testimonies that have been published and collected since the Second World War, stories of people using their intimate knowledge of other cultures in order to escape death are common. Some Jews and Gypsies were able to disguise themselves as members of other racial or ethnic groups just by changing their clothes and behaviour. People who could easily switch between different languages managed to avoid being caught up in the ethnic cleansing by speaking fluently in the dialect of whichever nationalist militia they came across. In Yugoslavia and Poland/Ukraine, those of 'suspicious' ethnicity were often asked to recite certain Christian prayers, since these were rendered differently depending on whether one followed the Catholic, Uniate or Orthodox form of the religion. But once again, those from the most mixed communities often knew the prayers and rites of the neighbours they had grown up with, and were thus able to escape death.

The end of the Second World War in May 1945 sounded the official death knell for fascism in most parts of Europe, but it did not signal the end of the attack on diversity. Over the next two years the political climate across the whole of Europe – west as well as east – underwent a marked swing to the left. Buoyed by its many successes during the war, and its uncompromising stance against fascism, the Communist Party enjoyed a sudden and massive renaissance. By the middle of 1945, the Italian Communist Party had over two and a quarter million members – far more than any other political party. In the French and Czech elections of 1946 it was the Communists who won the highest percentage of votes: almost 29 per cent in France and 38 per cent in Czechoslovakia (Judt 2007: 79, 88; Rioux 1987: 110). In most of Eastern Europe, Communism was more or less imposed by the presence of the Red Army – but even so it was an enormously popular ideology among some sections of the population. The Romanian Communist Party, for example, increased from only 1,000 members in August 1944 to more than a million four years later; and membership of the Hungarian Communist Party swelled from 3,000 to half a million within the course of just a single year (Kontler 2002: 392; Tismaneanu 2003: 87).

In many respects, Europe's Communists were every bit as intolerant of diversity as the fascists had been. In the countries where they held power, they denied the right of other political parties to exist, and strove to indoctrinate the entire population with a single, Stalinist ideology (Applebaum 2012: 319–51). They were intolerant of religion, and strove to convert religious institutions into further mouthpieces for the Communist message (ibid.: 286–92). They regarded class, rather than the nation, as society's central battleground, and lionised working class people above all others. The aristocracy, capitalist businessmen, the middle classes, the intelligentsia – indeed any group who saw themselves as separate from the working masses – was regarded as inimical to the Communist cause. Like the fascists, they advocated radical methods to purge society of these elements, and thought nothing of persecuting individuals who did not conform to government approved norms.

At first glance, ethnic diversity might seem to have been the one form of diversity to be immune from communist interference, since it was irrelevant to the class struggle. As the closing sentences of the Communist Manifesto make clear, Karl Marx had envisaged a brotherhood of all nations, united by their opposition to bourgeois and aristocratic values. However, the persecution of ethnic or racial minorities certainly did not stop when the communists took control of Eastern Europe after the war; in fact, in some regions it worsened.

There were several reasons for this. First, in the chaotic aftermath of the war, it was virtually impossible to prevent outbreaks of violence: all the normal structures of society had been swept away, and no matter how much the new authorities might want to impose a sense of order, they were not yet strong enough to do so.

Second, it was impossible to reverse the effects of fascist and far right ideology overnight. The European population had been subjected to years of fascist propaganda, and by 1945 racial hatreds had become deeply ingrained – particularly those hatreds that had pre-existed fascism, such as anti-ziganism and anti-semitism. When Jews returned to Poland after the war, for example, they were often attacked by people who had become used to assaulting Jews with impunity. Sometimes the violence was communal. The most infamous incident was the pogrom at Kielce in July 1946, where a mob attacked a Jewish community centre and killed 42 Jews. But there were dozens of similar episodes, not only in Poland, but also in Hungary and Slovakia. From 1946 Jews began to flee these countries out of fear that their former countrymen intended to finish off the job that Hitler had started. It is estimated that around 300,000 Jews fled Eastern Europe in the five years after the war (Bauer 1970: 318–20).[6]

Third, there is much evidence to suggest that, in the immediate aftermath of the war at least, the Communist parties of Eastern Europe actually encouraged ethnic tension. Communist leaders recognised the strength of nationalist feeling in Eastern Europe, and rather than fighting it they tried to harness it. For example, Hungarian Communist leaders made anti-semitic speeches (despite many of them being Jewish themselves) because they recognised the potential for using Jewish stereotypes in their propaganda against capitalists and speculators (Pelle 1995: 206).[7] Polish Communists encouraged the expulsion of ethnic minorities from their borderlands because it gave them the opportunity to play Father Christmas: all the land that was freed up as a consequence of these expulsions could then be parcelled out to grateful Polish peasants. The Soviet Union was glad to promote the wholesale displacement of ethnic minorities from one Eastern European country to another because communities of refugees were much easier to control than communities with established hierarchies and power structures.[8] It is possible that even the massacre of certain groups was tolerated, because it sent an unequivocal message to those most likely to resist the Communists. The mass executions of some 50,000–60,000 Croatian nationalists in May and June 1945 certainly ripped the heart out of any potential Croatian separatist movement in Tito's Yugoslavia (see Lowe 2012: 264f.).

But perhaps the greatest reason for the continued assault on ethnic diversity after 1945 was the continent-wide desire for revenge and retribution. Since so much of the war had been conducted along racial and ethnic lines, many people sought communal retribution against those communities they regarded as culpable. The Czechs, for example, blamed the Sudeten Germans for the dismemberment of their country and for the harsh treatment of Czechs during the war. According to the postwar Czech Justice Minister, Prokop Drtina, the Sudeten Germans were a 'foreign ulcer in our body', which had to be removed (Schieder 1960: 66f.; see also Staněk 1991: 59). Over the next two years, the Czech authorities expelled around three million Germans from the country, often with great violence. The rest of Eastern Europe followed suit.

Ethnic Germans were expelled from almost every country – 11,730,000 of them in total – in what would become the greatest forced migration in history.[9]

It was not only German populations that were expelled from various countries after the war. Throughout Eastern Europe ethnic minorities were now deemed a threat to national security, and many of these were also expelled from their homelands. Thus Ukrainians were expelled from Poland and vice versa, Romanians were expelled from Hungary and vice versa, Hungarians were expelled from Slovakia, Albanians from Greece and Italians from Yugoslavia. As a result of all this forced population movement, Eastern Europe became far less multicultural than it had been at any time in modern history. In the space of only one or two years, the proportion of national minorities across the eastern half of the continent more than halved (Pearson 1983: 229). Gone were the old imperial melting pots where Jews, Germans, Magyars, Slavs and dozens of other races and nationalities intermarried, squabbled and rubbed along together as best they could. In their place was a collection of monocultural nation-states, whose populations were more or less ethnically homogeneous. Eastern Europe had cleansed itself on a massive scale.

The ruthless pursuit of fascist fantasies before and during the war, and the postwar backlash against fascism, brought a new and disturbing contrast between the eastern and western halves of Europe. In much of Western Europe, which had managed to avoid some of the worst excesses of the war, diversity flourished. Many of those who had been displaced westwards between 1939 and 1945 chose to stay there afterwards, and immigration from all over the world was actively encouraged – at least on an official level – as workers of all races and creeds were invited to help rebuild war damage.

In Eastern Europe, by contrast, the cosmopolitanism that had existed for centuries was partly – and in many areas entirely – destroyed. Without free movement between countries, this lack of diversity remained until the fall of Communism more than 40 years later. But even when diversity returned, it was a diversity of a different kind. The old diversity of the Russian and Austro-Hungarian empires had been lost forever.

Notes

1   Despite this, minorities in the west were regularly on the receiving end of *unofficial* violence; see Panayi (1996).
2   Broadly speaking, national minorities focused their frustration against empire, not against each other; see Pearson (1983: 112–13). Different minorities also banded together in both left-wing movements and right-wing partnerships (ibid. 119–25; Mazower 2012: 48–54).
3   Adam Mickiewicz's *Pan Tadeusz*, quoted in Snyder (2003: 28–9).
4   Census figures from 1930, quoted in Gyurgyík (1999: 38).
5   For the extremely complex debate over what exactly constitutes 'fascism', see Davies and Lynch (2002: 1–5; Griffin 1991: 4–14).
6   For higher estimates based on immigration statistics to Israel, see Proudfoot (1957: table 35).
7   Communists also wanted to shake off their image as a party of and for Jews see Kenez (2009: 156).
8   For the Soviet promotion of the expulsion of minorities between one country and another, see Snyder (2003: 186–7) and Janics (1982: 136–9).
9   German federal statistics quoted by De Zayas (2006: 156).

References

Applebaum, A. (2012) *The Iron Curtain: The Crushing of Eastern Europe, 1944–1956*, London: Allen Lane.
Bauer, Y. (1970) *Flight and Rescue: Brichah*, New York, NY: Random House.
Bessell, R. (2004) *Nazism and War*, London: Weidenfeld & Nicolson.
Davies, N. (2005) *God's Playground: A History of Poland, Vol. II: 1795 to the Present*, Oxford, UK: Oxford University Press.

Davies, P. and Lynch, D. (2002) *The Routledge Companion to Fascism and the Far Right*, London: Routledge.

De Zayas, A. (2006) *A Terrible Revenge: The Ethnic Cleansing of Eastern European Germans*, New York, NY: Palgrave Macmillan.

Griffin, R. (1991) *The Nature of Fascism*, London: Routledge.

Gyurgyík, L. (1999) *Changes in the Demographic, Settlement and Social Structure of the Hungarian Minority in (Czecho-)Slovakia between 1918–1998*, Budapest: Teleki László Foundation.

Janics, K. (1982) *Czechoslovak Policy and the Hungarian Minority, 1945–1948*, New York, NY: Columbia University Press.

Judt, T. (2007) *Postwar: A History of Europe Since 1945*, London: Pimlico.

Kamusella, T. (2009) *The Politics of Language and Nationalism in Modern Central Europe*, New York, NY: Palgrave Macmillan.

Kenez, P. (2009) *Hungary from the Nazis to the Soviets: The Establishment of the Communist Regime in Hungary*, New York, NY: Cambridge University Press.

Kontler, L. (2002) *A History of Hungary*, Basingstoke, UK: Palgrave Macmillan.

Lowe, K. (2012) *Savage Continent: Europe in the Aftermath of World War II*, London: Viking.

Mazower, M. (2012) *Governing the World*, London: Allen Lane.

Mussolini, B. (2000) 'Foundations and Doctrine of Fascism', in J.T. Schnapp, O.E. Sears and M.G. Stampino (eds) *A Primer of Italian Fascism*, Lincoln, NE: University of Nebraska Press.

Panayi, P. (1996) 'Anti-immigrant Violence in Nineteenth- and Twentieth-century Britain', in P. Panayi (ed.) *Racial Violence in Britain in the Nineteenth and Twentieth Centuries*, London: Leicester University Press.

Pearson, R. (1983) *National Minorities in Eastern Europe*, London: Palgrave Macmillan.

Pelle, J. (1995) *Az utolsó vérvádak*, Budapest: Pelikán.

Proudfoot, M.J. (1957) *European Refugees 1939–52*, London: Faber & Faber.

Rioux, J.P. (1987) *The Fourth Republic 1944–1958*, Cambridge, UK: Cambridge University Press.

Schieder, T. (1960) (ed.) *Documents on the Expulsion of the Germans from Eastern-Central Europe, vol IV: Czechoslovakia*, Bonn: Federal Ministry for Expellees, Refugees and War Victims.

Snyder, T. (2003) *The Reconstruction of Nations*, New Haven, CT: Yale University Press.

Staněk, T. (1991) *Odsun němců z Československa 1945–1947*, Prague: Academia Naševojsko.

Statiev, A. (2010) *The Soviet Counterinsurgency in the Western Borderlands*, New York, NY: Cambridge University Press.

Tismaneanu, V. (2003) *Stalinism for all Seasons*, Berkeley, CA: University of California Press.

Tomasevich, J. (2001) *War and Revolution in Yugoslavia: Occupation and Collaboration*, Stanford, CA: Stanford University Press.

Tooze, A. (2007) *The Wages of Destruction*, London: Penguin.

18

Diversity, xenophobia and the limits to the post-apartheid state

Alex Wafer

South Africa is a society that comprises many linguistic, racial and ethnic identities – differences which were exacerbated and exploited by the apartheid state, and which have been equally reified in a post-apartheid context with regards to racial quotas in sport, affirmative action legislation and Black Economic Empowerment policies, to name a few. It is perhaps not altogether surprising that institutions of state and civil society in post-apartheid South Africa have been largely preoccupied with national identity and social cohesion – rather than with the integration of foreigners – when confronted with the question of diversity. In a society whose recent history is characterised by racial segregation, it is ironic yet inevitable that the ending of apartheid would be accompanied simultaneously by a celebration of non-racial democracy and 'a resurgence of research into racial identities, attitudes and behaviour in South Africa' (Seekings 2008: 1). South African society remains obsessed with these categories, going so far as to aggregate census data in these terms. Despite the ceremonial flag-waving that accompanies events such as the hosting of the FIFA 2010 World Cup, South Africa remains a deeply divided society – although contours of division are neither the same, nor perhaps as obvious, as they once were.

Amidst continuing socio-economic inequalities that characterise South African society, largely across lines of apartheid-inherited racial categories, the presence within that society of other articulations of either belonging or difference is very seldom explicitly recognised – at least in policy-related terms (see e.g. Landau 2012a). Yet the more hidden and subtle practices of exclusion from the narrative of *unity in diversity* expressed in the constitution were most horrifically and tellingly exposed in May 2008, when sixty-seven people were killed in several weeks of xenophobic-inspired violence that flared up in predominantly under-serviced and indigent neighbourhoods in cities across South Africa. These events were a major shock to the political establishment of South Africa, which assumes itself to be a tolerant and caring society. It is both tragically ironic and yet highly significant that at least twenty of those killed were South African citizens, members of demographically and geographically less prominent ethnic groups.

The xenophobic violence was all the more sobering to South Africa's political and economic elite precisely because the violent eruption was the sharp end of a much more general hostility towards difference in society; not only towards 'foreigners', but also members of minority ethnic and sexual orientation groups within South African society. That this resentment was first so violent, and second directed towards vulnerable and marginalised groups rather than the privileged position of the elite or even against whites, is further suggestive of the disintegration of the narrative of *unity in diversity*. Far from the constitutional assertion of a tolerant and diverse society, the xenophobic violence of 2008 illustrated the reality of an increasingly polarised, suspicious and precarious society.

Explanations for the xenophobic violence have ranged from dismissal of the violence as merely 'opportunistic criminality' (see Valji 2003) to interpretations based on the continued socio-economic marginality of the poor (Sharp 2008) and concerns about the nature and efficacy of the institutions of state and civil society after apartheid (Pillay 2008). Certainly, the causes of violence against others (whether foreigners or less-deserving nationals) are complex and varied, and not easily related to deep-seated antipathy – many of the victims of xenophobic violence had been living among their perpetrators without conflict for years prior. This short essay is not able to explore these arguments in any great detail. Rather, it is concerned with the implications of xenophobic violence for the possibility of a post-apartheid subjectivity based on an ethics of diversity: not only because of the fact that violence undermines the hegemony of state (for indeed it does), but also because the geography of xenophobic violence in South Africa corresponds very closely to what can be termed a *lost* geography of state – the spaces in society where the state does not appear to penetrate easily.

Diversity and its limits

The preoccupation with questions of *diversity* in post-apartheid South Africa, though emerging out of a history of racial conflict and a more recent ethics of reconciliation, is not first and foremost a question of tolerance of difference, at least as a general category. Diversity in the South African context implies engaging with particular defined differences within an already constituted political landscape. Xenophobia, as either discourse or as actual violence, need not necessarily conflict with this notion of diversity: indeed, one could all too vividly imagine a context where the exclusion of 'others' proves politically useful to discourses of nation-building, even when such discourses are entrenched in apparent non-racism. For this reason, policy related to diversity in South Africa is (increasingly) framed in the language of social cohesion. The explicit concern with 'race relations' that characterised research in the 1960s and then again in the early 1990s (Seekings 2008), in which research was conducted into perceptions of racial groups of each other (largely defined by apartheid categories), emerges only infrequently in the popular media around specific news events, such as proposals for race quotas in national sporting codes. Of far greater concern for the South African political and economic elite – and reflecting the changed political economy of South African society since 1994 – is the threat of social disintegration based on a range of criteria that are the result of historical racialised inequalities, but are not questions of race per se. Most specifically, these relate to geography and economy: while people formerly classified as white no longer make up the majority of the middle classes (Unilever Institute 2013), nevertheless the vast majority of the poor are black South Africans. In addition, there is a particular geography of inequality, with the urban centres having more infrastructure investment, and the disparity within these urban centres remaining between former white suburbs and former black townships. Poor, rural parts of the country remain the most severely indigent (McLennan and Roberts 2013).

Although the issue of social cohesion has emerged as a major preoccupation in policy circles, there is little consistency in how the term itself should be defined – let alone what the implications should be for policy. For example, the *National Development Plan Vision 2030* argues for improvements in education and skills training, increased investment in science and technology, public infrastructure and urban development spending and a national health insurance scheme.

In contrast, the draft *National Strategy on Social Cohesion and Nation Building* drafted by the Department of Arts and Culture places emphasis on social mobilisation and the establishment of national identity, through defining shared values and symbols, and a shared constitutional democracy (Nyar 2013). The *National Development Plan* is clearly concerned with the sometimes poor relationship between institutions of state and particularly indigent sectors of society, with the emphasis being on growing the economy in order to create jobs and increase infrastructure spending, whereas the *National Strategy on Social Cohesion* is premised on reinvigorating a shared national identity.

Implicit in both of these conceptualisations of social cohesion – as with the notion of national identity in any context – is an imagination of the post-apartheid state as the central cohesive element within society. Whether as the provider of services, welfare and economic impetus, or as the guardian of the national identity, social cohesion implies – in the South African context – the construction of a political community through the redistributive, constitutionally obligated and democratic state. For Chipkin (2007), in the context of a racially discordant history, what binds a shared conception of the nation is precisely the celebration of democracy. That is to say, despite the inequalities that remain in society, the shared act of enacting a democratic right is the basis for what constitutes a sense of South African identity. In this sense, *unity in diversity* implies not a self-evident reality, but a political ideal that is enacted through the shared symbols of post-apartheid democracy.

As with all symbols of national identity, what the unity in diversity ideal implies is not a general inclusiveness, but an exclusivity of membership into a political community. The material symbol of this exclusive membership is the green identity document that all South Africans are issued with at birth, and that very actively defines one's participation in the democratic process. Voting in elections in South Africa requires a stamped and bar-coded green identity document. However, in a more perverse materialisation of this national (and nationalist) symbol, the green identity document has been used as a way to identify foreigners and South African nationals in more prosaic contexts. Applying for access to stalls in the inner-city market place, for example, requires a green identity document, and there are anecdotal cases of marriages between South Africans and foreign nationals, or even fronting by South Africans with identity documents, in order to secure access to the resources (Wafer 2011). The ability to engage actively with the diversity of post-apartheid South Africa is a privilege of those who are already incorporated. It is therefore not surprising that a healthy informal economy exists in most South African cities for green identity documents.

The work of Giorgio Agamben (1998) has been influential in thinking about the body of the foreigner in post-apartheid South Africa in a context where legal status as citizen has become the site of intense contestation. Despite the fact that the rhetoric of the state is tolerant – sometimes even welcoming – of foreigners, they are nevertheless largely outside of the institutions of democratic membership. Foreigners, whether legal or undocumented, are protected by the constitution in terms of their basic human rights (Dodson 2011), but this does not prevent the more informal modes through which foreigners are controlled (Vigneswaran *et al.* 2010). As access to citizenship has become the primary mechanism to access social and economic resources, this has resulted in the emergence of both formal and informal modes of social order, which include new discriminatory practices (Gordon 2010). In this context, foreign nationals – especially other African nationals – have emerged as a particularly vulnerable group.

Non-government and civil-society organisations that have mobilised against xenophobia have focussed their efforts largely on the rights and constitutional obligations of the state with regard to foreigners – itself a reversion to the hegemony of a narrative of a caring, tolerant society (see Monson 2010). Against the general hostility towards foreigners in South Africa, in both official policy and everyday xenophobia, many foreign nationals living in South Africa have adopted a disposition that does not align with the more hegemonic discourse of *unity in diversity*. This is a resistance to their condition as the *homo sacer* of South African democracy. Landau and Freemantle (2010), for example, have demonstrated how many foreign nationals adopt what they term an ethics of tactical cosmopolitanism in direct contrast to the discourse of diversity. While diversity implies recognition of difference, and is accompanied by charity and/or tolerance of difference, cosmopolitanism appeals to an ethics of what we might term indifference (Tonkiss 2003). In other words, cosmopolitanism appeals not to an acknowledgement of one's difference, but to an assumption that difference is the constitutive factor of society.

Xenophobia and the lost geography of the post-apartheid state

This recent history of explicit violence against identified 'others', and the emergence more generally of discourses of xenophobia in South Africa after apartheid, have been the subject of a number of recent – and perhaps belated – attempts to understand a phenomenon of exclusion in a society with a constitutional commitment to diversity (e.g. Charman and Piper 2012). Responses have ranged from what might broadly be referred to as political-economy explanations to more governmentality explanations, drawing for example on Agamben's (1998) concept of *bare life* to speak about the presence of the body of the foreigner as the site of political exclusion, or Pillay's (2008) reformulation of Chatterjee's (2001) notion of *political society*, the largely excluded masses, whose subjectivity amounts to a 'subaltern self-fashioning', which operate outside the normative frameworks of emancipatory or liberal politics and are often chauvinistic and violent in character. Xenophobic violence has been viewed differently in the recent literature. It has been seen variously as 1) violent attacks on foreigners within the context of the continued frustration of poor South Africans at inequality in service delivery – there exist various versions of xenophobia as an expression of quasi-fascist nationalism (Murray 2003); 2) the jealous protection of new-found rights by South Africans (Nyamnjoh 2006), or the broader construction of a xenophobic state discourse; and 3) a politics of violence in the history of apartheid and segregation (Valji 2003). Certainly, Dodson (2011) argues that there have been no real attempts to explain the propensity towards violence or towards anti-foreigner sentiment among South Africans. Although the majority of South Africans did not take part in the xenophobic violence of May 2008 – and the majority expresses abhorrence at the violence – Crush (2011) has shown compelling quantitative data to suggest that there is a strong anti-foreigner sentiment across all spheres of South African society.

Of course, it is not just foreigners who are the objects of exclusion in South African xenophobic violence. Perhaps of greater concern for the political and economic elite of South Africa than the threat of xenophobic violence, is the fact that some South Africans were also victimised in the violence of 2008. If the construction of the post-apartheid state requires that subjects inhabit an ethics of unity in diversity, then the victimisation of marginal ethnic groups within South Africa suggests that in many parts of the country subjectivity is still constituted by the ethnic divisions that colonial and apartheid regimes exploited. In this regard, it is perhaps not surprising that many from within the political elite have rejected the idea that xenophobia is nascent within South African society. The xenophobic violence of May 2008 has been labelled as criminal – an attempt to eschew the spectre of intolerance from the body politic of rejecting the idea that the hegemony of the state narrative of unity in diversity is here challenged.

Even where it is engaged, xenophobia is cast as a potential threat to social cohesion, not as a social problem in and of itself:

> Xenophobia is … the exclusion of many people from the mainstream of our society, regardless of claims as to whether the presence of foreigners is lawful or not in each particular instance. The phenomenon of 'othering' has real consequences in many respects, including shaping the response of those excluded in legitimating behaviour that is not desirable. To what extent this is prevalent in society is only known in a very limited sense
>
> *(Office of the Presidency 2013)*

Under the Mbeki Presidency, when the main impulse of social and economic policy was the expansion of the black middle classes and the broadening of economic access to those previously denied access to the mainstream economy, the question of social cohesion was hidden behind the increasingly multi-racial face of the South African middle class. Tragedies such as the August 2012 Marikana Massacre (where a wildcat strike by mine-workers turned violent, and forty-four mine-workers were shot dead – some in the back – by riot-police) raise the uncomfortable spectre that for many black South Africans the relations of domination and oppression remain unchanged. The desperately poor communities dependent upon mine-worker's wages, and the micro- and informal economies that these wages sustain, are spaces of deeply suspicious, fractured and precarious subjectivity. Certainly, in such spaces the substance of post-apartheid democratic citizenship remains elusive. The breakdown of what has been termed the labour/citizenship nexus after apartheid (Dubbeld 2013) has resulted in the dissipation of discourses of citizenship amidst the fluidity, informality and extreme anxiety about and/or antipathy towards state authority. These 'badlands', situated in the blind spots and on the peripheries of the post-apartheid state imagination, are notorious hotbeds for what have been termed service delivery protests (i.e. protests that make claims upon state infrastructure). These protests have been primarily explained in terms of legitimate and unrealised expectations of democracy; certainly, service delivery backlogs are identified by both civil-society and state institutions in South Africa as a key element undermining social cohesion.

The informal settlements and makeshift livelihood strategies that characterise the mining-belt to the north and west of Gauteng (the province that contains the cities of Johannesburg and Pretoria, and largely regarded as the economic heartland of the country) resonate in many ways with the sorts of spaces that Landau (2012b, 2013) refers to as esturial spaces: 'cities, or parts thereof, where varied migrant trajectories intersect to generate novel forms of social interaction and authority' (Landau 2012b: 2). For Landau, these esturial spaces are spaces of dynamism, of rich associational life and new articulations of subjectivity. Yet to the definition of estuary must be added other qualities implicit in Landau's use of the term: estuaries have a propensity to muddy, to divert and to stagnate. In other words, esturial spaces are also spaces of suspicion, immobility and precarity. Landau is mostly concerned with those peripheral and interstitial spaces of large South African cities such as Johannesburg, and with the trajectories and subjectivities of foreign migrants in South Africa. The communities that cling to the disappearing economy of waged labour in the mining-belt, and with it the disappearing politics of citizenship, might be implicated into far more controlled histories of (internal) labour migration, but the conditions that both these groups face in the present political-economy of South Africa is not dissimilar. The eruption, therefore, of xenophobic violence in May 2008, and the continued spectre of xenophobic sentiment among many communities in South Africa, is both horrifying and incredibly revealing about the status of citizenship in post-apartheid South Africa. It is no coincidence that the sites of sporadic service delivery protest and xenophobic violence in the last ten years tend to correspond to a geography of largely esturial spaces, i.e. spaces where the presence of the state is tenuous at best. It is in precisely these sites that the political project of social cohesion and unity in diversity appears least resonant.

Conclusion

This short commentary cannot attempt to cover in any great detail all the popular and academic discourse that the xenophobic violence of May 2008 has produced. There have been many fierce debates about the implication of the violence for the project of the democratic post-apartheid state. The political goal of unity in diversity is one that should contain an ethics of tolerance and empathy, and in reaction to the xenophobic violence there was an outpouring of compassion towards the victims. What the violence does highlight, however, is that diversity and xenophobia are not necessarily opposing ideas and that the geography of xenophobic violence articulates the potential contours and limits of the post-apartheid state.

References

Agamben, G. (1998) *Homo Sacer: Sovereign Power and Bare Life*, Stanford, CA: Stanford University Press.

Charman, A. and Piper, L. (2012) 'Xenophobia, Criminality and Violent Entrepreneurship: Violence Against Somali Shopkeepers in Delft South, Cape Town, South Africa', *South African Review of Sociology*, 43(3): 81–105.

Chatterjee, P. (2001) 'On Civil and Political Society in Postcolonial Democracies', in S. Kaviraj and S. Khilnani (eds) *Civil Society: History and Possibilities*, Cambridge, UK: Cambridge University Press.

Chipkin, I. (2007) *Do South Africans Exist? Nationalism, Democracy and the Identity of the People*, Johannesburg: University of the Witwatersrand Press.

Crush, J. (2011) *The Perfect Storm: The Realities of Xenophobia in Contemporary South Africa*, Cape Town: Southern African Migration Programme.

Dodson, B. (2011) 'South African Immigration Law: A Gender Analysis', Cape Town: Southern African Migration Programme.

Dubbeld, B. (2013) 'Envisioning Governance: Expectations and Estrangements of Transformed Rule in Glendale, South Africa', *Africa: The Journal of the International African Institute*, 83(3): 492–512.

Gordon, S.L. (2010) 'Migrants in a "State of Exception"', *Transcience Journal*, 1(1): 1–19.

Landau, L. (2012a) 'Review Article: Race Trouble', *Ethnic and Racial Studies*, 35(4): 789–90.

—(2012b) 'Hospitality Without Hosts: Mobility and Communities in Africa's Urban Estuaries', Paper presented at WISER, 19 March 2012, Johannesburg: University of the Witwatersrand. Online. Available HTTP: <http://wiser.wits.ac.za/system/files/seminar/Landau2012.pdf> (accessed 16 April 2014).

—(2013) 'Recognition, Community and the Power of Mobility in Africa's New Urban Estuaries', Working Paper, Johannesburg: University of the Witwatersrand. Online. Available HTTP: <http://papers.ssrn.com/sol3/papers.cfm?abstract_id=2253743> (accessed 16 April 2014).

Landau, L. and Freemantle, I. (2010) 'Tactical Cosmopolitanism and Idioms of Belonging: Insertion and Self-exclusion in Johannesburg', *Journal of Ethnic and Migration Studies*, 36(3): 375–90.

McLennan, D. and Roberts, B. (2013) 'Exploring the Relationship between Spatial Inequality and Attitudes to Inequality in South Africa', Presentation on 11 September 2012, Pretoria: The Human Sciences Research Council.

Monson, T. (2010) *Report on the SAHRC Investigation into Issues of Rule of Law, Justice and Impunity Arising out of the 2008 Public Violence Against Non-nationals*, Johannesburg: South African Human Rights Commission. Murray, M.J. (2003) 'Alien Strangers in our Midst: The Dreaded Foreign Invasion and "Fortress South Africa"', *Canadian Journal of African Studies*, 37: 440–66.

Nyamnjoh, F.B. (2006) *Insiders and Outsiders: Citizenship and Xenophobia in Contemporary Southern Africa*, New York, NY: Zed Books.

Nyar, A. (2013) 'Social Cohesion: A Critical Reflection', Wynberg: SA Reconciliation Barometer Blog. Online. Available HTTP: <http://reconciliationbarometer.org/newsletter/volume-eleven-2013/social-cohesion-a-critical-reflection/> (accessed 28 October 2013).

Office of the Presidency (2013) 'Social Cohesion and Social Justice in South Africa', Pretoria: South African Government. Online. Available HTTP: <http://www.thepresidency.gov.za/pebble.asp?relid=1103> (accessed 28 October 2013).

Pillay, S. (2008) 'Dangerous Ordinary Discourse: Preliminary Reflections on Xenophobia, Violence and the Public Sphere in South Africa', Paper presented at CODESRIA 12th General Assembly, Cameroon.

Online. Available HTTP: <http://codesria.org/IMG/pdf/Suren_Pillay.pdf> (accessed 16 April 2014).

Seekings, J. (2008) 'The Continuing Salience of Race: Discrimination and Diversity in South Africa', *Journal of Contemporary African Studies*, 26(1): 1–25.

Sharp, J. (2008) '"Fortress SA": Xenophobic Violence in South Africa', *Anthropology Today*, 24(4): 1–3.

Tonkiss, F. (2003) 'The Ethics of Indifference: Community and Solitude in the City', *International Journal of Cultural Studies*, 6(3): 297–311.

Unilever Institute (2013) '4 Million and Growing', Rondebosch: University of Cape Town. Online. Available HTTP: <http://www.unileverinstitute.co.za/Research.aspx?ProjName=4%20Million%20 and%20Rising> (accessed 28 October 2013).

Valji, N. (2003) 'Creating the Nation: The Rise of Violent Xenophobia in the New South Africa', unpublished masters thesis, York University.

Vigneswaran, D., Araia, T., Hoag, C. and Tshabalala, X. (2010) 'Criminality or Monopoly? Informal Immigration Enforcement in South Africa', *Journal of Southern African Studies*, 36(2): 465–81.

Wafer, A. (2011) 'Informality, Infrastructure and the State in Post-apartheid Johannesburg', doctoral thesis, Open University.

19

Situating diversity in the global city

Emerging challenges and possibilities in Singapore

Junjia Ye

Singapore is changing rapidly because the world is changing rapidly. With increasing globalisation, many people from different parts of the world may choose to come to Singapore to work together with us or study together with us. Most of us will probably have a colleague, classmate, schoolmate or neighbour from another country. These are opportunities for us to interact and build new friendships across even more diverse cultures, and make each of us a more tolerant and cosmopolitan Singapore citizen.

(*Heng Swee Keat 2011, Singapore's Minister of Education*)

This chapter sets out the case for the idea of situated diversity. It puts forward a critical way of understanding diversity through the ways in which increasing mobility contributes to changing experiences of co-existing with difference. By referring to diversity as situated, I make reference to its historic and geographic specificities. This is in response to much of existing literature on urban diversity that is expressed in a Western context. I resist the urge to draw upon European and North American models of 'assimilation', 'integration' and 'multiculturalism' by delineating configurations of diversity in Asia, specifically Singapore. This is largely because of Singapore's distinct post-colonial geographies, histories of migration and economic development strategies. In Singapore, as in other Asian cities, human diversity, as led by newer waves of migration, presents myriad challenges and possibilities within the already existing varied socio-spatial landscapes. Rather than a descriptive focus on state responses to diversity, this chapter is an exercise in drawing linkages between processes of migration and the emergence of new forms of diversity.

Taking the opening quote of this chapter both as a source of critique and hope, I approach these linkages through a discussion of the strong role of the state before moving on to talk about more prosaic ways in which people negotiate difference in everyday life – ways that challenge official measures that contour diversity. I illustrate how the Singaporean state shapes the contours of diversity by discussing its means of administering diversification through its historical measures that mediate everyday forms of co-existence with difference. Moving on to more recent forms of migration and diversity, I examine the realities of the city-state's cosmopolitan aspirations through which the social experience of living with difference is rapidly changing. I highlight the emergent limits and possibilities to co-existence in diverse spaces specifically through fleeting social encounters by offering two concepts with which to understand diversity in more situated ways. By using the term 'emergent' here, I not only draw attention to the empirical transformations taking place in Singapore as a result of newcomers, but also, more crucially, I suggest the pressing need to theorize differently and distinctly about human relationships with diversity in a non-Western context.

Approaching diversity in Asia

Diversification processes are taking place across Asia at a rapid pace and are largely led by migrants, not only of different ethnicities, but also of varied legal statuses, language backgrounds and religions, and holding different understandings of social norms. Existing research, however, does not reflect the volume, velocity and variations of these transnational flows and their resulting socio-spatial circuits. Indeed, much of the recent work on urban diversity has paid great attention to Western European contexts such as the United Kingdom (e.g. Amin 2012) and 'immigrant' countries such as Canada, Australia and New Zealand (e.g. Pearson 2001). Terms such as 'multiculturalism', 'social cohesion' and indeed 'diversity' have become part of both political and academic discourse in describing and prescribing social relations in contexts peopled by individuals of different backgrounds. In contrast, processes, patterns and meanings of diversification in Asia have received far less scholarly attention (see Lai *et al.* 2013). By using the example of Singapore, I suggest new directions in conceptualizing the processes of living with diversity that are attentive to the city-state's historic and geographic particularities.

Historicizing diversity in Singapore

By the time Stamford Raffles landed on the island in 1819, Singapore was already a trade emporium with extraterritorial linkages to the region. Indeed, from its pre-colonial history, Singapore was already a multicultural entrepôt aided by its natural deep harbour. In becoming a British colony, Singapore's economy and labour supply reached further and in greater volume (Chew and Lee 1991). The history of Singapore's diversity, therefore, is founded upon its economic development. During the colonial period, it was the combination of immigration and geographical advantage that shaped the economic development of Singapore, and it remains one of the features of Singapore's economic development today. Colonial labour policies were largely responsible for the massive inflow of immigrant workers from China, India and Java to the Malayan hinterland and their concentration in separate-by-ethnicity work niches in Malaya and Singapore. In the rapidly growing economic environment, the division of labour was structured along ethnic lines – a pattern which went on to shape the opportunities of future immigrants (Lai 1995). By the time it achieved self-governance from the British in 1959, Singapore's diversity of immigrants, paired with its comparative advantage in terms of geographic location along the trade routes, provided the platform for its future development strategies through migration and economic growth.

Managing a historically multiethnic state

With independence, there was also a shift in the way the governing body related to its people. The governing body had to face the challenge of imagining a common objective as a nucleus of nationhood. Socially and politically, building a nation-state out of an ethnically diverse population with a complex background of economic, political, social and cultural differences has resulted in the People's Action Party's (PAP) attempt to produce an overarching national identity and an ideology of 'multiracialism' (Lai 1995: 17). This ideology officially gives separate but equal status to the Chinese, Malays, Indians and 'Others'[1] (or CMIO, for short) and informs official policies on various issues related to the economy, language, culture, religion and community life (Lai 1995, Perry *et al.* 1997). CMIO became part of the national ideology, so that Singaporeans of various backgrounds can imagine themselves as a multiracial people. English was adopted as a convenient language of trade and is the first language of the country, tying the different ethnic groups together.

The insecurity of Singapore's regional geopolitics was, and often continues to be, another dimension affecting ethnic relations and management in the city-state. Situated in the Malay Archipelago that has a large 'indigenous' Malay population and an 'immigrant' Chinese minority, Singapore's ethnic composition created an arguably disadvantageous fit to its surrounding region. It was because of its ethnic differentiation and dominance of its Chinese people that many viewed Singapore as a Chinese place, or even state (Lai 1995). To some extent, the ethnic identities of the Chinese and Malays in Singapore are shaped by the comparison of their economic and political positions with those of the Chinese and Malays in Malaysia. Further, the position of the Chinese in Singapore is structured by the historical experiences of the Chinese immigrant minorities in Southeast Asia (Tan 2004); conversely, however, some viewed the Malays' social position in Singapore as a disadvantaged indigenous minority (Lai 1995). Finally, among both Chinese and Malays, the ethnically differentiated development during the colonial period has mutually resulted in limited interaction, the maintenance of rigid ethnic boundaries, strong stereotyping and an underlying sense of insecurity and fear of dominance by Chinese and Malays of each other. These fears culminated in three violent riots prior to Singapore's independence.

The construction of the local multiethnic community must be understood against this background. Until the 1960s, Singapore's population mostly lived in separate ethnic settlements established by the colonial administration. Large-scale resettlement into self-contained public housing estates, implemented through the Housing and Development Board (HDB), was one of the ways in which the ideology of multiracialism materialized spatially. Through the construction of publicly administered, largely ownership-based, housing projects, the HDB has been able to provide Singaporeans with affordable shelter and spaces to facilitate interaction among different ethnicities. These include neighbourhood schools, markets, community centres, playgrounds, void decks and walkways that link one block of flats to another (Chua 1995; Lai 1995; Perry *et al.* 1997). There are also ethnic quotas enforced to ensure each housing block reflects Singapore's ethnic composition. From a strategic level, then, public housing in Singapore is a powerful tool in managing ethnic diversity and relations – a crucial issue that must be addressed in the creation of a national identity. Singapore's planners also saw the HDB as an efficient way of providing improved living conditions that are necessary for the city-state's economic success (Perry *et al.* 1997). The state also manages ethnic relations via the school curriculum, where the ethnicity of the student determines his or her 'mother tongue' – for example, a Malay student must study Malay, an Indian student must study Tamil. Ethnic identity also continues to be clearly denoted on every Singaporean's identity card. Hence, the notion of multiracialism is conveyed and experienced in the everyday living spaces of Singaporeans. There are also softer measures of managing diversity through national festivals, such as the Chingay and Racial Harmony Day, that celebrate particular forms of multiculturalism (Goh 2011).

State-led cosmopolitanism as diversification

Economic restructuring measures since the early 1970s illustrate configurations of state, capital, labour and commodity production within a changing international division of labour of which Singapore has always been keen to be a part. While I argue that these measures are by no means limited to practices of the state and are instead conditioned by the dynamics of global restructuring, the Singaporean state has particularly strong control over its strategies of development through its purposefully shaped processes of diversification (Olds and Yeung 2004). The integrated development processes of export-orientation and foreign investment driven developmental strategies – perceived to attract desirable 'global capital' – requires the import of human capital, with both high- and low-waged labour.

While other transnational sojourners, such as marriage and student migrants, are also contributing to growing social diversity, the sharp increase in immigration to Singapore in the past two decades has been propelled by the urgent economic need to fortify Singapore's labour force. The turn of century saw an increasing share of non-citizen population – a direct consequence of the city-state's restructuring policies to attract and rely on foreign labour (Yeoh 2004). The deliberate and strategic reliance on 'foreign manpower' is part and parcel of the dominant neoliberal discourse of globalization as an 'inevitable and virtuous growth dynamic' (Coe and Kelly 2002: 348). Indeed, as former Prime Minister Goh said during the 1997 National Day Rally: 'Singapore must become a global, cosmopolitan city, an open society where people from many lands can feel at home.'[2]

Today, foreigners make up 33 per cent of the total workforce in Singapore.[3] As elsewhere, the transmigrant population grows in tandem with restructuring processes to render labour more 'flexible' in relation to capital (Yeoh 2004). The workforce was strategically and rigorously configured to incorporate a significantly large foreign labour pool, which can be broadly divided into two strands: foreign talent and foreign workers. Both strands of workers are brought into Singaporean space strategically and they are administered very differently (Yeoh 2006). Foreigners' access to rights and privileges is mainly differentiated by skills status and by the perceived desirability of these skills to the achievement of national goals. Differentiated access is institutionalized by the issuance of a range of work passes and permits that fall broadly into the employment pass and work permit categories (Yeoh 2004). Building a nation in the image of a 'cosmopolis' requires selectively inclusionary projects to entice 'foreign talent' – highly skilled professional workers, entrepreneurs and investors who are part of the face of cosmopolitanism in Singapore (Yeoh 2004). This group of migrants holds a form of the employment pass that enables them to apply for dependants' passes and gain access to greater job mobility. Far greater in number, however, are the work permit holders, most of whom are concentrated in the manufacturing, construction, shipbuilding and domestic industries. This pool is also broken down further by nationalities, with rules and regulations set by the Ministry of Manpower (MOM), permitting only certain nationalities to access work in particular industries (Ye 2013).

The bulk of the increase in foreigners in the city-state comes from the increase of temporary migrant labourers who hold work permits (Ye 2013, 2014). Of this group that holds work permits, the largest percentage increase comes from foreign construction workers, many of whom are from Bangladesh, China, India and Myanmar. A large number of workers from the Philippines also take on work in the low-paying service sector outside of domestic work. These social divisions manifest tangibly in the segregated landscapes inhabited by temporary migrant workers compared to other populations in Singapore. Shipyard and construction jobs entailing shift-work require that Bangladeshi male migrants may work in the day or at night, and they generally work on sites that preclude interactions with the public. There is also a high degree of spatial constraint in the daily lives of the Bangladeshi workers as the everyday lives of migrant workers are highly reliant upon their employers. As stipulated in MOM guidelines for employers who hire foreign workers, low-waged male migrant workers in Singapore should be housed in state-approved, employer-provided accommodation. These come in the form of purpose-built dormitories that are commercially run, industrial and/or warehouse premises that have been partly converted to house workers, temporary quarters on worksites, harbourcrafts (such as ships and marine vessels) and, to a lesser extent, HDB flats (MOM website[4]). The majority of such accommodation is segregated from residential areas where locals live.

Accommodating new migrants

It should be noted that these newer waves of migration into Singapore have incited new social tensions and discrimination, expressed most prominently online (Yeoh and Lin 2013). The Indicators of Racial and Religious Harmony – put together by the Institute of Policy Studies and OnePeople.sg, the national body for racial harmony – showed that Singaporeans are not comfortable with having new immigrants making up the majority of people in the country. Only about 50 per cent of respondents are comfortable with that idea, with most preferring the status quo when it comes to Singapore's current racial mix (Channel News Asia 2013[5]). In response to this unhappiness, the government has set up various organizations to address and mediate these tensions (such as the National Integration Council and various grassroots organizations such as the People's Association and Onepeople.sg). Campaigns that seek to teach co-existence are also common, such as the 'Love Thy Neighbour' campaign to 'promote good neighbourliness' amongst residents. Also prominent are official discourses on the need to integrate, such as the following quote by Teo Chee Hean, Deputy Prime Minister of Singapore[6] in 2013:

> Even as we maintain an open environment in Singapore, foreigners working here must understand that they too bear a responsibility to the local community, and should respect Singaporean values and norms. This also applies to the group of foreign workers who are here to provide us a service, such as those in construction and estate maintenance. They too have to abide by our social norms and values. At the same time, we should treat them with respect, and appreciate the work they do and the services that they provide for us.

While these campaigns are not solely directed towards newcomers, they do condition the contours of what is locally acceptable behaviour and what is not. These state responses are efforts to manage relations and interactions between new diversities and long-time residents; however, they are interpreted and manifest in everyday ways that may not neatly square with official intentions. Indeed, I have found that, embedded within everyday co-existence between migrants and locals, there are highly nuanced forms of situating and organizing multiplicity in Singapore.

Everyday narratives of co-existing with diversity

As we have seen, there are various state-led socio-spatial measures in place to manage these newer waves of diversity in Singapore, such as housing and job allocation and the attempt to manage tensions between the new and old waves of diversity. In spite of these, there are sites that remain and also emerge as places of contact. Indeed, the realities of such official visions of diversification cannot only be seen as segregated from everyday urban life but are, crucially, situated in and transforming the social fabric of mundane encounters. Shared spaces such as schools, workplaces, buses, community events and food centres remain sites where long-time multicultural residents must both co-exist and interact with newcomers in highly prosaic and constantly evolving ways.

Yeoh and Huang (1998) draw attention to the way Filipina domestic workers use public spaces, such as Orchard Road's Lucky Plaza, during their rest days. The temporary but regular appropriation of these spaces by female domestic workers, as well as the ways in which they are accommodated, reflect, reinforce and sometimes circumvent larger unequal power relations at these public spaces. Similarly, Bangladeshi male migrants also assert their presence within different public spaces in the Singaporean landscape in complex and contentious ways (Ye 2013). By appropriating spaces that are overlooked by other urban residents as socializing spaces, these migrants are circumventing official policy and marking their presence in the city. In other words, while their use of such spaces is largely a result of exclusion from other urban areas, such as within shopping malls, their act of appropriation reconfigures the dynamics of specific urban spaces. While these instances of appropriation do not directly or permanently challenge broader inequalities, such practices of appropriation are important precisely because they allow for spontaneity away from the constraints faced by migrants in much of their daily lives. There are spaces, for example, where Bangladeshi male migrants congregate that suggest a co-presence with other urban residents without neglecting the broader power inequalities that are unfolded across space. Diversity in practice in such sites contains both challenges and possibilities to the project of living with difference. There are multiple modes of negotiating, including and excluding diversity that become patterns of socially organizing difference in everyday life; these can, in effect, produce new ways of discriminating as well as accommodating difference. I offer the notion of *gui ju* (规矩) as one such mode of social organization.

Gui ju

Gui ju is a localized code of conduct that mediates and governs people's fleeting and more sustained encounters with migrants in different public spaces. This term was used repeatedly by Chinese-Singaporean respondents in my work. To these respondents, having *gui ju* generally means that one is civil and behaving in the appropriate way. I argue that the discursive practice of *gui ju* is a significant way of mediating encounters amongst strangers in public and, more recently, of introducing a filter between migrants and locals. To 'integrate' in the Singaporean context, therefore, means to have *gui ju*. Within socio-spatial patterns of co-existence, *gui ju* is a form of normative, social classificatory set of values that forms local notions of civility, in which locals are deemed to know how to behave in public, whereas migrants do not. Yet, crucial to this form of civility is the element of restraint which negotiates encounters with difference where people hold themselves back from direct confrontations. *Gui ju* hence prevents this tension from bubbling over into more violent conflict and becomes a mundane way in which urban diversity is encountered and governed in the everyday. The violation of *gui ju* by people – who are, according to my informants, newcomers – exposes dominant orderings in space: those who know how to behave and those who do not, those who belong and those who do not. Civility and norms then become highly nuanced tools with which to judge who belongs and who does not in ways that go beyond simply ethnicity, nationality and gender.

The theoretical impetus for *gui ju* is largely twofold. The first is to consider critically the ways in which studies on diversity in an Asian setting – in this case, Singapore – can engage with notions and processes of global mobilities without the ingrained impulse to refer to Western models of co-existence. The second impetus is a response to much of the recent writings on cosmopolitanism, which celebrates openness and willingness to engage the other without recognizing the contradictions within such dispositions and attitudes.

Concluding notes

This chapter has addressed the ways in which diversity management in Singapore emerged, developed and continues to be reproduced. As Singapore was already multicultural as a pre-colonial trading port, the management of diversity during this time established the first traces of institutionalized co-existence. Diversification also intensified during the colonial period, with the arrival of migrants from China and India who eventually settled in Singapore. The policies of multiracialism through the CMIO framework after independence in 1965 thus reinforced the existing diversity. The overarching creed of multiculturalism in Singapore is most clearly institutionalized through the pervasiveness of the CMIO. This framework became a part of everyday life in Singapore through housing, education, religious and language policies. There are also softer measures of incorporating a citizenry of diverse backgrounds to co-existence in close proximity through various social campaigns. It can therefore be argued that older waves of diversity in Singapore have been socialized to accept particular ways of co-existence with difference. Diversification in recent years has been state led, with the majority of newcomers being international labour migrants. This incorporation of new diversity has been met with unhappiness and tensions from older groups of diversity. Rather than being conceived simply along racial and ethnic lines, I would argue that the unhappiness stems from the ways in which newcomers violate subtle, tacit cultural norms, values and behaviours because of their lack of local knowledge. Through the concept of *gui ju*, I argue that it is this highly nuanced, internalized cultural filter that enables people to judge who belongs and who does not in a place which has historically adopted and continues to reinforce a particular understanding of diversity.

Notes

1 This is a group comprising other ethnic minorities in Singapore – Eurasians, Jewish, Armenians, British, etc.
2 STARS, online archive of ministerial speeches. Website <http://www.moe.gov.sg/media/speeches/1997/240897.htm> (accessed 4 July 2014).
3 'Our Population, Our Future', Website. Available HTTP: <http://population.sg/resources/workforce-composition/#.UoMtcI3HQuU> (accessed 11 October 2013).
4 MOM Website. Online. Available HTTP: <http://www.mom.gov.sg/foreign-manpower/passes-visas/work-permit-fw/before-you-apply/Pages/overview.aspx> (accessed 1 November 2013).
5 Channel News Asia (2013) 'Study Confirms Discomfort between Singaporeans and New Immigrants', Online. Available HTTP: <http://www.channelnewsasia.com/news/singapore/study-confirms-discomfort/809784.html> (accessed 11 September 2013).
6 Speech at National Community Engagement Programme. Online. Available HTTP: <http://www.singaporeunited.sg/cep/index.php/Our-News/Speech-by-DPM-Teo-Chee-Hean-at-the-National-CEP-Dialogue-2013> (accessed 13 April 2013).

References

Amin, A. (2012) *Land of Strangers*, Cambridge, UK: Polity.
Chew, E. and Lee, E. (1991) *A History of Singapore*, Singapore: Oxford University Press.
Chua, B.H. (1995) *Communitarian Ideology and Democracy in Singapore*, New York, NY: Routledge.
Coe, N.M. and Kelly, P.F. (2002) 'Languages of Labour: Representational Strategies in Singapore's Labour Control Regime', *Political Geography*, 21(3): 341–71.

Goh, D.P. (2011) 'State Carnivals and the Subvention of Multiculturalism in Singapore', *British Journal of Sociology*, 62(1): 111–33.

Heng Swee Keat (2011) 'Speech on Racial Harmony Day', Singapore: Ministry of Education. Online. Available HTTP: <http://www.moe.gov.sg/media/speeches/2011/07/21/speech-by-mr-heng-swee-keat-at.php> (accessed 7 November 2013).

Lai, A.E. (1995) *Meanings of Multiethnicity: A Case-Study of Ethnicity and Ethnic Relations in Singapore*, Oxford: Oxford University Press.

Lai, A.E., Collins, L.F. and Yeoh, B.S.A. (2013) *Migration and Diversity in Asian Contexts*, Singapore: Institute of Southeast Asian Studies.

Olds, K. and Yeung, H.W.C. (2004) 'Pathways to Global City Formation: A View from the Developmental City-state of Singapore', *Review of International Political Economy*, 11(3): 489–521.

Pearson, D. (2001) *The Politics of Ethnicity in Settler Societies: States of Unease*, Houndmills, UK: Palgrave Macmillan.

Perry, M., Kong, L. and Yeoh, B. (1997) *Singapore: A Developmental City State*, Chichester, UK: Wiley.

Tan, E. (2004) 'The Majority's Sacrifices and Yearnings: Chinese Singaporeans and the Dilemmas of Nation-building', in L. Suryadinata (ed.) *Ethnic Relations and Nation-Building in Southeast Asia*, Singapore: Institute of Southeast Asian Studies.

Ye, J. (2013) 'Migrant Masculinities: Bangladeshi Men in Singapore's Labour Force', *Gender, Place and Culture*. Online. Available HTTP: http://dx.doi.org/10.1080/0966369X.2013.817966 (accessed 5 June 2014).

—(2014) 'Labour Recruitment and its Class and Gender Intersections: A Comparative Analysis of Workers in Singapore's Segmented Labour Force', *Geoforum*, 51, 183–90.

Yeoh, B.S.A. (2004) 'Cosmopolitanism and its Exclusions in Singapore', *Urban Studies*, 41(12): 2431–45.

—(2006) 'Bifurcated Labour: The Unequal Incorporation of Transmigrants in Singapore', *Tijdschrift voor Economische en Sociale Geografie*, 97(1): 26–37.

Yeoh, B.S.A. and Huang, S. (1998) 'Negotiating Public Space. Strategies and Styles of Migrant Domestic Workers in Singapore', *Urban Studies*, 35(3): 583–602.

Yeoh, B.S.A. and Lin, W. (2013) 'Chinese Migration to Singapore: Discourses and Discontents in a Globalizing Nation-state', *Asian and Pacific Migration Journal*, 22(1): 31–54.

20

Racial boundaries and persistent inequality

The case of African Americans

Jessica S. Welburn

Du Bois famously argues that "the problem of the Twentieth Century is the problem of the colorline" (Du Bois 1986: 359). Du Bois focuses specifically on the negative impact that racial boundaries in the United States can have on opportunities and outcomes for African Americans. Although he writes at the turn of the twentieth century, the colorline continues to have an impact on all aspects of life for members of stigmatized groups in the USA and abroad. This chapter will use the case of African Americans in the US post-Civil Rights Era to explore the ways in which racial boundaries can shape life circumstances. First, I briefly explore the persistence of racial boundaries in the USA. I argue that while African Americans have made progress in the post-Civil Rights Era, racial boundaries have an impact on interactions, opportunities and outcomes. Second, I review some of the most significant barriers facing African Americans in the post-Civil Rights Era, which include neighborhood circumstances, health outcomes, incarceration rates and racial discrimination. Third, I review research on how African Americans interpret and respond to their position in the USA. I focus specifically on African Americans' attitudes about inequality. Throughout this chapter I also emphasize the ways in which class can intersect with race to shape African Americans' experiences. Finally, I conclude with a brief discussion of research on racial and ethnic boundaries outside of the USA.

Racial boundaries and African Americans: an overview

Lamont and Molnar (2002) argue that "The concept of boundary has been central to the study of ethnic and racial inequality as an alternative to more static cultural or even biological theories of ethnic and racial differences" (ibid.: 174). Racial and ethnic boundaries are shaped by a combination of in-group and out-group processes. It is often argued that the USA has one of the more rigid systems of racial classification; Patterson (2005) claims that the USA has a binary system of racial classification, namely that racial groups are divided into two categories: black and white. Even as the country diversifies, Patterson argues that Americans often make distinctions between blacks and non-blacks. Non-blacks include whites and some other minorities who have assimilated with whites. In contrast, the black category includes a segregated population of African Americans and other racial and ethnic minorities who have not assimilated with whites. A number of scholars have worked to explain the persistence of racial boundaries in the USA

(Feagin and Sikes 1994; Fleming *et al.* 2012; Omi and Winant 1994). For example, Omi and Winant (1994) argue that race operates separately from other social categories in the USA and shapes interactions and institutions. They argue specifically that racial and ethnic boundaries are often politically constructed and contested. They emphasize that the state plays an important role in the formation and persistence of racial and ethnic boundaries.

Data on interpersonal relationships between African Americans and out-group members sheds light on the strength of racial boundaries in the USA. For example, survey data has shown that, while African Americans tend to prefer living in integrated neighborhoods, they are viewed as the least desirable neighbors by out-group members. Charles (2000) uses data from the Los Angeles Survey of Urban Inequality to examine the neighborhood preferences of whites, African Americans, Latinos and Asians. She finds that whites, Latinos and Asians all list African Americans as their least preferred neighbors. However, when African Americans are asked to describe their ideal neighborhood, it is on average only 37.41 per cent African American. African Americans are also more likely to be close friends with other African Americans (Massey *et al.* 2003). This can be attributed to feeling closer to other in-group members (ibid.) and living in closer proximity to other in-group members (Mouw and Entwisle 2006). Acceptance for interracial marriage has grown significantly since the mid-twentieth century. In 1985 only 48 per cent of Americans approved of intermarriage between African Americans and whites, compared to 83 per cent in 2010. Yet, African Americans have more positive attitudes toward interracial marriage than whites. In 2010 40 per cent of whites reported believing that increased interracial marriage rates are positive for society, compared to 51 per cent of African Americans (Wang 2012). In addition, African Americans are also more likely to marry interracially than whites – in 2010 9 per cent of whites intermarried compared to 17 per cent of African Americans (ibid.). However, African Americans are less likely than other racial minorities to intermarry. Wang (ibid.) finds that in 2010 26 per cent of Hispanics and 28 per cent of Asians married interracially. This may suggest that racial boundaries remain more rigid for African Americans than for other racial groups in the USA.

Racial boundaries in the USA are important because they shape opportunities and outcomes for African Americans in the post-Civil Rights Era. Thus, exploring the current circumstances of African Americans in more detail is key to understanding the role that race continues to play in the USA.

African Americans in the post-Civil Rights Era

The US Civil Rights movement brought about significant changes for African Americans. For example, the Civil Rights Act of 1964 made discrimination on the basis of "race, color, religion, sex or national orientation" illegal in the USA. The Voting Rights Act of 1965 worked to end the disenfranchisement of African American voters by putting in place significant federal voting laws and outlawing a number of discriminatory practices such as literacy tests for voters. The Civil Rights Act of 1968 was enacted to curb housing discrimination. These and other measures served essentially to abolish legalized Jim Crow segregation and to curb legalized racial discrimination in the USA (Brooks 2009).

A number of social scientists have pointed to progress made by African Americans in the post-Civil Rights Era. For example, Patterson (1998b) argues that circumstances for African Americans have improved significantly in the post-Civil Rights Era. He argues that given the history of slavery and legalized racial discrimination in the USA, "the achievements of the American people over the past half century in reducing racial prejudice and discrimination and in improving the socioeconomic and political condition of Afro-Americans are nothing short of astonishing" (ibid.: 15). Wilson (1980) famously argues that class has become a more significant determinant of life outcomes for African Americans than race. While Wilson does not argue that race no longer shapes the experiences of African Americans, he emphasizes that, particularly for middle-class African Americans, opportunities have improved since the mid-twentieth century.

Data on the circumstances of African Americans in the post-Civil Rights Era do reveal significant improvements in position. For example, educational attainment rates have improved significantly for African Americans since the passage of Civil Rights legislation in the mid-twentieth century. Overall incomes have improved for African Americans and overall poverty rates have also declined. The 2008 election and 2012 reelection of President Barack Obama has sparked further debate about racial progress in the USA. On the one hand, the election of an African American president may suggest that racial boundaries are becoming less rigid in the USA (Reed and Louis 2009). On the other hand, while circumstances for African Americans have improved, racial disparities in the USA persist.

Education and employment

Educational attainment rates have improved significantly for African Americans since the mid-twentieth century. Yet, their educational attainment rates remain lower than for whites. For example, in 1960 43.2 per cent of whites completed high school diplomas compared to 21.7 per cent of African Americans. In contrast, in 2012 the figures were 92.5 per cent of whites compared to 85.7 per cent of African Americans. In 1960 8.1 per cent of whites had earned a bachelor's degree or higher compared to 3.5 per cent of African Americans. In 2012, 34.5 per cent of whites earned college degrees, compared to 21.4 per cent of African Americans (Digest of Education Statistics 2012).

Unemployment rates for African Americans have been consistently higher for African Americans than for whites. For example, in 1975 7.8 per cent of whites were unemployed compared to 14.8 per cent of African Americans. Unemployment rates for African Americans fell to a low of 7.6 per cent in 2000. Yet, unemployment rates for whites were only 3.5 per cent in 2000. In 2010, at the height of the global recession, 8.7 per cent of whites were unemployed compared to 16 per cent of African Americans (Bureau of Labor Statistics 2012).

Income and wealth

Economic circumstances have also improved slightly for African Americans. In 1966 41.8 per cent of African Americans were living below the poverty line compared to 25.8 per cent in 2011 (Macartney et al. 2013). Yet poverty rates remain much higher for African Americans than for whites – in 2011 11.6 per cent of whites lived below the poverty line (ibid.). In 1967 the median household income for African Americans was $25,996 compared to $50,544 for whites. The gap had narrowed slightly by 2012 but remained large – the median income for African American households was $33,321 compared to $57,009 for whites (DeSilver 2013).[1] Income disparities persist even with increases in educational attainment. For example, 2011 American Community Survey data shows that while whites who hold at least a bachelor's degree earn a median annual income of $65,252, African Americans who hold at least a bachelor's degree earn a median annual income of just $49,435 (American Community Survey 2011). Gaps in income only provide partial insights into economic disparities between African Americans and whites.

When looking more closely at financial assets such as savings, stocks, bonds and property ownership, African Americans remain far behind whites. Oliver and Shapiro (2013) argue that this is the result of a combination of factors, including exclusion from government policies that increased wealth for white Americans, persistent racism and discrimination, and relatively low entrepreneurship rates for African Americans. Income and wealth gaps between African Americans and whites in the USA have only widened since the 2008 global recession (Kochhar 2011). In 2009 the median net worth of white households was $113,149 compared to just $5,677 for African American households (ibid.).

Oliver and Shapiro (2013) emphasize that, even for African Americans who earn middle-class incomes, limited wealth remains a significant obstacle. Oliver and Shapiro draw upon in-depth interviews with middle-class white and African American families to compare their everyday financial experiences. They find that, because of limited wealth, middle-class African Americans are more likely than whites to feel the negative impact of sudden changes to their economic circumstances. For example, African Americans who divorce are more likely to experience economic instability because of a limited access to financial assets (ibid.: 125). In addition, African Americans experience more job instability than whites. This may include having to work more than one job to maintain middle-class status (ibid.: 124). Middle-class African Americans are also more likely than middle-class whites to experience intergenerational downward mobility.

Using data from the Panel Study of Income Dynamics, Isaacs *et al.* (2008) find that the majority of whites who grew up in middle-income households are able to exceed their parents' socioeconomic status. In contrast, fewer than half of African Americans who grew up in middle-income households are able to do so. Lacy (2012) argues that it is important to take into account income differences *within* the African American middle class when assessing their economic position. Upper-middle-class African Americans experience more financial stability than other middle-class African Americans. For example, upper-middle-class African Americans have experienced fewer foreclosures than lower-middle-class African Americans since the 2008 recession.

The following sections explore several factors that contribute to disparate outcomes for African Americans, including neighborhood circumstances, incarceration rates, family instability and persistent racism and discrimination.

Neighborhood circumstances

Racial residential segregation has a significant impact on the life experiences of African Americans.

> Residential segregation is not a neutral fact; it systematically undermines the social and economic well-being of the United States. Because of racial segregation, a significant share of black America is condemned to experience a social environment where poverty and joblessness are the norm, where a majority of children are born out of wedlock, where most families are on welfare, where educational failure prevails, and where social and physical deterioration abound.
>
> *(Massey and Denton 1993: 2)*

Massey (2004) argues that "a majority of all African Americans, and the large majority of urban African Americans, continue to experience high levels of residential segregation in U.S. cities" (ibid.: 11). Massey estimates that approximately 40 per cent of African Americans are hypersegregated.[2] African Americans experience racial residential segregation across income levels (Marsh and Iceland 2010; Massey 2004). Neighborhood segregation is important because it shapes access to opportunities, including jobs and good schools.

Wilson (1997) argues that mid- to late-twentieth century deindustrialization led to a decline in availability of low-wage, low-skilled jobs for African Americans living in inner cities. Factories and other businesses located in cities closed in large numbers. Some businesses relocated to the suburbs, making it difficult for low-income inner-city residents to access job opportunities. Isolation can also limit access to the networks needed to learn about job opportunities.

Neighborhood disadvantage can also shape interactions between individuals. Wilson (1997) argues that a lack of job opportunities in low-income neighborhoods can lead to increased criminal activity. Specifically, he argues that "the process of inner-city neighborhood deterioration has been clearly related to the growth of the inner-city drug industry. The decline of legitimate employment opportunities among inner-city residents increases the incentive to sell drugs" (ibid.: 58). Drug activity can in turn lead to increased violence and gang-related crime. Anderson (2000) explores the dynamics of a poor, predominantly African American neighborhood in Philadelphia. Through ethnographic observations, Anderson finds that neighborhood residents must navigate persistent poverty, high crime rates and limited educational and employment opportunities. Navigating these circumstances becomes a daily project for neighborhood residents. As a result, Anderson argues that a "code of the street" has developed in the neighborhood. He argues that this code serves as "a set of informal rules governing interpersonal public behavior, particularly violence" (Anderson 2000: 33). He explains (ibid.):

> The rules prescribe both proper comportment and the proper way to respond if challenged. They regulate the use of violence and so supply a rationale allowing those who are inclined to aggression to precipitate violent encounters in an approved way.

Anderson argues that African American families in this neighborhood can be divided into two categories: "decent and street." The decent families are those who subscribe to "mainstream" American values, including hard work, educational attainment and strong family. In contrast, "street" families do not subscribe to these mainstream values and are more likely to become involved in criminal activity. Anderson documents the constant tension between street and decent families in the neighborhood.

In the post-Civil Rights Era, middle-class African Americans have moved out of some of the most disadvantaged neighborhoods in the USA. Yet, the neighborhoods that they live in are still not on par with the neighborhoods that middle-class whites live in. In fact, middle-class African Americans are more likely to live in racially segregated neighborhoods and in close proximity to economic disadvantage than whites (Pattillo 2000). This can have important consequences for their social interactions and access to resources. For example, in an ethnography of a mixed-income, predominantly African American neighborhood in Chicago, Pattillo-McCoy (1999) finds that middle-class (and particularly lower-middle-class) families often struggle to separate themselves from negative social situations including crime and drug activity. Similarly, Wilson and Taub (2011) argue that middle-class African Americans living in mixed-income neighborhoods must navigate "manifestations of social disarray." It is important to note that Lacy (2007) argues that upper-middle-class African Americans face a different set of circumstances. With access to more financial resources than their lower-middle-class counterparts, upper-middle-class African Americans tend to reside in more stable neighborhoods.

Incarceration

Incarceration rates have climbed significantly in the USA since the mid-twentieth century. However, incarceration rates for African Americans are higher than for any other group.

Incarceration rates are particularly high for African American males. Using data from the Public Safety and Mobility Project, Western and Pettit (2010) find that African American men born between 1975 and 1979 have a 26.8 per cent chance of being incarcerated during their lifetime. In contrast, white men born during the same period have only a 5.4 per cent chance of being incarcerated. Alexander (2012) argues that the criminal justice system serves to preserve the American racial hierarchy in the post-Civil Rights Era. While legalized segregation has ended, mass incarceration in the USA serves to restrict the social and economic options of many African Americans (ibid.: 13). Incarceration can have an impact on all dimensions of an individual's life, including their employment opportunities and family relationships. Incarceration can also have an impact on health outcomes (Western and Pettit 2010). For example, Schnittker *et al.* (2011) find that individuals who have been incarcerated are more likely to have asthma, diabetes or hypertension.

Family circumstances

Marriage rates have declined for all groups in the USA since the mid-twentieth century. Social scientists have attributed this decline to a number of factors, including increased participation of women in the workforce and increasingly less restrictive divorce laws (Cherlin 2010). Yet, Gross (2005) argues that the idea of "lifelong, internally stratified marriage" remains an important norm guiding relationships in the USA. While we have witnessed a rise in alternative relationship arrangements, evidence shows that many individuals still hope to get married (ibid.). However, the decline in marriage rates has been much more severe for African Americans than for whites. In the USA disproportionately high incarceration rates, high mortality rates, high unemployment rates and low educational attainment rates for African American men may restrict the availability of desirable partners for African American women (Anderson 2000; Darity and Myers 1984; Marsh *et al.* 2007; Massey *et al.* 2003; Wilson 1987). Social scientists have also argued that unstable gender relations contribute to low marriage rates for African Americans (Collins 2008; Patterson 1998a). Some have argued that since slavery, African American men in the U.S. have been deprived of the role of provider. This has continued as African American men face persistent structural barriers. As a result African American women have often been forced to take on the role of provider and consequentially have struggled to combat stereotypes of being overly independent and aggressive (Collins 2008; Patterson 1998a).

Declining marriage rates can have a number of important consequences for African Americans. First, married individuals are more likely to be financially stable and often have access to more financial resources than individuals who are not married. Thus, marriage is a critical part of class reproduction (Marsh *et al.* 2007). Second, as marriage rates have declined, rates of single parenthood have gone up. Children who grow up in single parent homes are more likely to grow up in poverty, face academic troubles, and become single parents themselves.

Racism and discrimination

Previous research has demonstrated that African Americans continue to believe that racial inequality has a negative impact on the outcomes of members of their group (e.g. Bobo 2011; Bobo and Charles 2009; Hochschild 1996; Hunt 2007). For example, using data from the General Social Survey, Bobo (2011) finds that African Americans are more likely than whites to believe that discrimination contributes to the persisting socioeconomic status (SES) gap between African Americans and whites. Surveyed between 2000 and 2008, 30 per cent of whites and 59 per cent of African Americans attribute the SES gap to discrimination. These findings illustrate African Americans' continued awareness of racial discrimination.

Research shows that African Americans continue to face racism and discrimination in a number of contexts. Experiences are both overt and covert. For example, a number of studies have documented the impact that job market discrimination can have on African Americans (Darity and Mason 1998; Feagin and Sikes 1994; Mong and Roscigno 2010; Wilson 1997). Wilson (ibid.) draws upon in-depth interviews with 179 employers in the Chicago metropolitan area to explore the impact that race can have on hiring practices. He finds that employers may stereotype low-income African American workers (especially males) as "uneducated, unstable, uncooperative, and dishonest" (ibid.: 111). Pager and Western (2012) compare the experiences of white and African American men aged 21 to 24 applying for low-wage jobs in New York City and Milwaukee. Following job interviews, white applicants in both cities received callbacks and job offers approximately twice as often as African American applicants. Other forms of discrimination across occupations can range from disparities in wages to failing to be promoted at the same rate as whites (Feagin and Sikes 1994; Fleming *et al.* 2012; Mong and Roscigno 2010; Roscigno 2007).

Housing audit studies also show that African Americans often experience discrimination when looking for properties to rent or buy (Yinger 1995). Ross and Turner (2005) explore housing discrimination in the rental and sales markets using data from the 2000 HDS. They randomly selected housing advertisements in the Sunday newspapers and submitted applications from African American and white applicants to selected units. They compare their results with Yinger (1995) and argue that discrimination in the housing market has declined since 1989, but remains persistent. African Americans report racism and discrimination in a number of other contexts, including getting service in public places. For example, Fleming *et al.* (2012) recount the story of an African American man who experienced covert discrimination while traveling in an elevator in a public building. He recalled that, as soon as he entered the elevator, a white woman who was also in the elevator immediately clutched her purse. To him, this signaled that she believed as an African American male he might be a dangerous criminal.

Class can shape how African Americans perceive and manage experiences with racism and discrimination (Lamont and Fleming 2005; Young 2004). Young (ibid.) argues that African Americans in racially segregated, economically disadvantaged neighborhoods may have fewer experiences with racism and discrimination. In contrast, middle-class African Americans are more likely to live, work, and spend leisure time in integrated environments. As a result, they may be more aware of the negative impact that racism and discrimination can have on opportunities for members of their group. In contrast, Feagin and Sikes (1994) argue that for middle-class African Americans managing persistent racism and discrimination is a part of daily life. The experiences of the African American middle class led Hochschild (1996) famously to argue that members of this group are "succeeding more but enjoying it less."

Drawing upon in-depth interviews, Fleming *et al.* (2012) explore how working-class and middle-class African Americans navigate persistent racism and discrimination. Their respondents experience racism and discrimination in a number of contexts, including at school, in the workplace, and in public places. Respondents' experiences with racism and discrimination include being misunderstood, over-scrutinized, and disrespected. They argue that African Americans have a repertoire of destigmatization strategies for navigating these experiences. Strategies include confronting, educating the discriminator, and walking away. Destigmatization strategies can depend upon what respondents believe is at stake in a particular situation. Thus, they argue that African Americans engage in "management of the self," which "has to do with (1) projecting an image of oneself that is positive or conform to out-group norms, so as to gain recognition, and (2) self-protection and the development of various aspects of identity" (Fleming *et al.* 2012: 144). Lamont *et al.* (2013) argue that neoliberalism shapes responses to discrimination for African Americans. Drawing upon in-depth interviews with 150 working-class and middle-class African Americans, they find their respondents emphasize the importance of individualistic destigmatization strategies such as hard work, educational attainment, and personal responsibility. They argue "More than ever, many African Americans may have become convinced that self-reliance, economic success, individual achievement, and consumption are the best response to stigmatization" (ibid.: 144).

Weighing structural- and individual-level explanations for racial inequality in the USA

Literature on racial attitudes sheds light on how African Americans and whites weigh structural- and individual-level explanations for persistent racial inequality in the post-Civil Rights Era. Social scientists have argued that whites' explanations of racial disparities have shifted. In general, whites have become less likely to believe that African Americans are biologically inferior and more likely to believe that the remaining racial disparities between African Americans and whites are caused by what they perceive to be a lack of effort on the part of African Americans (Byrd 2011). Henry and Sears (2002) define symbolic racism as a "coherent belief system" that includes the belief that African Americans are responsible for their own circumstances and the belief that any demands that African Americans make to improve their situation are not valid. Bobo and Smith (1998) argue that "laissez-faire racism blames African Americans themselves for the black-white gap in socioeconomic standing and actively resists meaningful efforts to ameliorate America's racist social conditions and institutions" (ibid.: 186). They argue that laissez-faire racism is a more nuanced theory than symbolic racism because it explains the change in whites' racial attitudes in the post-Civil Rights Era. Bonilla-Silva (2001) defines whites' attitudes about racial inequality in the post-Civil Rights Era as colorblind racism. He defines colorblind racism as the belief that in the post-Civil Rights Era the USA has eliminated barriers that deny African Americans the same opportunities as whites. As a consequence, colorblind racism holds African Americans responsible for any remaining barriers that their group faces. He identifies three specific frames of colorblind racism: "abstract liberalism," "biologization of culture," and "naturalization of matters that reflect the effects of white supremacy."[3]

Understandings of persistent inequality are more complex for African Americans. Because of their experiences, African Americans are more likely to believe that racial inequality shapes opportunities to get ahead in the USA. However, an emerging body of research suggests that African Americans may be increasingly likely to believe that individual-level *and* structural-level factors contribute to their group's position. Hunt (2007) draws upon General Social Survey (GSS) data to explore how African Americans explain the persistent economic gap between their group and that of whites. He finds that while only 19.6 per cent of whites attribute the black/white socioeconomic gap to a combination of structural and motivational factors, 33.2 per cent of African Americans combine structural and motivational explanations. He also finds that between 1977 and 2004 African Americans became less likely to attribute the black/white SES gap solely to structural factors and are more likely to employ motivational explanations. Similarly, Bobo *et al.* (2012) use GSS data to show that African Americans may be becoming increasingly individualistic in their explanations of persistent inequality. In addition, they find that African Americans are becoming less likely to support affirmative action policy. This suggests further gravitation toward individualistic explanations of inequality. Welburn and Pittman (2012) draw upon 45 interviews to explore how middle-class African Americans think about the election of

US President Barack Obama. They find that, for the majority of their respondents, Obama's election serves as evidence that in the post-Civil Rights Era African Americans can get ahead if they work hard enough. While respondents acknowledge the persistence of racism and discrimination, they also believe that African Americans should take more responsibility for their outcomes. More research is needed on how African Americans explain persistent racial inequality in the post-Civil Rights Era and the impact that it might have on their sense of group identity and their navigation of racial boundaries in the USA.

The US case demonstrates the ways in which racial boundaries shape the experiences of African Americans in the post-Civil Rights Era. Civil Rights Era legislation helped to create new opportunities for African Americans. As a result, life circumstances for African Americans improved on a number of dimensions. However, research also shows that African Americans continue to face a number of obstacles, including limited access to economic resources, challenging neighborhood circumstances, and persistent racism and discrimination. Thus, the US case demonstrates that strong racial boundaries can have an important impact on inequality.

Minorities abroad

While this chapter focuses on African Americans in the USA, exploring how national context shapes the experiences of racial and ethnic minorities is essential to unpacking the role of race in the twenty-first century. National context may shape the permeability of racial boundaries; it can also shape how racial and ethnic minorities perceive and respond to their position (Lamont and Molnar 2002). For example, through in-depth experiences, Lamont (2000) compares the experiences of working-class African Americans and North African immigrant men in France. She focuses on the strategies they use to combat racism and discrimination. Both groups emphasize their sense of morality and humanity to demonstrate equality with the dominant groups in their countries. However, in contrast to African Americans, North African immigrants may find responses constrained by their immigrant status. In addition, they are more likely than African Americans to place blame on members of their own group for racism. In addition, North African immigrants are less likely than African Americans to believe that earning money is a way to demonstrate equality to the dominant group. Mizrachi and Zawdu (2012) explore the destigmatization strategies of Ethiopian Jews in Israel. They find that Ethiopian Jews use religion to seek equality with the dominant group while downplaying racial discrimination. In contrast, Mizrachi and Herzog (2012) argue that Arab Israelis use a shared sense of humanity as a destigmatization strategy. Thus, they focus less on religious differences and more on the common human experience that they share with Jews in Israel. Silva and Reis (2012) explore the destigmatization strategies of working-class and middle-class Afro-Brazilians. They find that the majority of their respondents focus on Brazil's history of racial mixing to argue that all groups are equal. Research should continue to explore the extent to which national context shapes the experiences of racial and ethnic minorities. This will enhance our understanding of how racial and ethnic boundaries are formed and negotiated.

Conclusion

This chapter has explored the impact that racial boundaries in the USA have on the experiences of African Americans. I have shown that, while African Americans have made progress since the mid-twentieth century, they face persistent barriers in the USA. Thus, navigating and making sense of persistent racial inequality is central to the African American experience. Navigating racial and ethnic boundaries is also central to the experience of stigmatized groups outside of the USA. Research in a number of countries, including France, Brazil and Israel, shows that national context can have an impact on the salience of racial and ethnic boundaries and the ways in which these boundaries are navigated. Future research should continue to focus on how racial and ethnic boundaries shape the life circumstances of members of stigmatized groups in the USA and abroad.

Notes

1   All income figures are in 2012 dollars.
2   Massey and Denton (1993) use a dissimilarity index to measure racial residential segregation. This index measures the "unevenness of Black and White settlement across neighborhoods" (Massey 2004: 9). Dissimilarity index scores range from 1 to 100. High segregation is considered a dissimilarity index of 60 or higher. African Americans are hypersegregated if they have a dissimilarity index score of 60 or higher on five established dimensions of segregation: evenness, isolation, clustering, centralization, and concentration.
3   Bonilla-Silva (2001) argues that "abstract liberalism" is defined as a belief in egalitarian principles, that "biologizaton of culture" is defined as the use of culture to explain persistent racial disparities, that "naturalization of racial matters" is defined as the belief that persistent racial inequality is a natural occurrence, and that "minimization of racism" is defined as the denial of persistent racism and discrimination (ibid.: 142).

References

Alexander, M. (2012) *The New Jim Crow: Mass Incarceration in the Age of Colorblindness*, New York, NY: The New Press.

American Community Survey (2011) Online. Available HTTP: <https://www.census.gov/acs/www/about_the_survey/2011_acs_improvements/> (accessed June 1, 2014).

Anderson, E. (2000) *Code of the Street: Decency, Violence, and the Moral Life of the Inner City*, New York, NY: Norton & Company.

Bobo, L.D. (2011) "Somewhere Between Jim Crow and Post-racialism: Reflections on the Racial Divide in America Today," *Daedalus*, 140(2): 11–36.

Bobo, L.D. and Smith, R.A. (1998) "From Jim Crow Racism to Laissez-faire Racism: The Transformation of Racial Attitudes," in W.F. Katkin, N. Landsman and A. Tyree (eds) *Beyond Pluralism: The Conception of Groups and Group Identities in America*, Urbana, IL: University of Illinois Press.

Bobo, L.D. and Charles, C.Z. (2009) "Race in the American Mind: From the Moynihan Report to the Obama Candidacy," *The Annals of the American Academy of Political and Social Science*, 621(1): 243–59.

Bobo, L.D., Charles, C.Z., Krysan, M. and Simmons, A.D. (2012) "The Real Record on Racial Attitudes," in P.V. Marsden (ed.) *Social Trends in American Life: Findings from the General Social Survey since 1972*, Princeton, NJ: Princeton University Press.

Bonilla-Silva, E. (2001) *White Supremacy and Racism in the Post-civil Rights Era*, Boulder, CO: Rienner.

Brooks, R.L. (2009) *Racial Justice in the Age of Obama*, Princeton, NJ: Princeton University Press.

Bureau of Labor Statistics (2012) Online. Available HTTP: <http://data.bls.gov/search/query/results?cx=0137380361959193776442%3Aih0hfrgl50&q=2012> (accessed April 25, 2014).

Byrd, C.W. (2011) "Conflating Apples and Oranges: Understanding Modern Forms of Racism," *Sociology Compass*, 5(11): 1005–17.

Charles, C.Z. (2000) "Neighborhood Racial-Composition Preferences: Evidence from a Multiethnic Metropolis", *Social Problems*, 47(3): 379–407.

Cherlin, A.J. (2010) *The Marriage-go-round: The State of Marriage and the Family in America Today*, New York, NY: Vintage Books.

Collins, P. (2008) *Black Feminist Thought: Knowledge, Consciousness, and the Politics of Empowerment*, New York, NY: Routledge.

Darity, W.A. and Myers, S.L. (1984) "Does Welfare Dependency Cause Female Headship? The Case of the Black Family," *Journal of Marriage and the Family*, 46(4): 765–79.

Darity, W.A. and Mason, P.L. (1998) "Evidence on Discrimination in Employment: Codes of Color, Codes of Gender," *Journal of Economic Perspectives*, 12(2): 63–90.

DeSilver, D. (2013) "Black Incomes Are Up, But Wealth Isn't," Washington, D.C.: Pew Research Center. Online. Available HTTP: <http://www.pewresearch.org/fact-tank/2013/08/30/black-incomes-are-up-but-wealth-isnt/> (accessed 19 December 2013).

Digest of Education Statistics (2012) "Table 8: Percentage of Persons Age 25 and over with High School Completion or Higher and a Bachelor's or Higher Degree, by Race/Ethnicity and Sex: Selected Years, 1910 through 2012." Online. Available HTTP: <http://nces.ed.gov/programs/digest/d12/tables/dt12_008.asp> (accessed 19 December 2013).

Du Bois, W.E.B. (1986) *W.E.B. Du Bois: Writings*, New York, NY: Viking.

Feagin, J.R. and Sikes, M.P. (1994) *Living with Racism: The Black Middle-Class Experience*, Boston, MA: Beacon.

Fleming, C.M., Lamont, M. and Welburn, J.S. (2012) "African Americans Respond to Stigmatization: The Meanings and Salience of Confronting, Deflecting Conflict, Educating the Ignorant and 'Managing the Self'," *Ethnic and Racial Studies*, 35(3): 400–17.

Gross, N. (2005) "The Detraditionalization of Intimacy Reconsidered," *Sociological Theory*, 23(3): 286–311.

Henry, P.J. and Sears, D.O. (2002) "The Symbolic Racism 2000 Scale," *Political Psychology*, 23(2): 253–83.

Hochschild, J.L. (1996) *Facing up to the American Dream: Race, Class, and the Soul of the Nation*, Princeton, NJ: Princeton University Press.

Hunt, M.O. (2007) "African American, Hispanic, and White Beliefs about Black/White Inequality, 1977–2004," *American Sociological Review*, 72(3): 390–415.

Isaacs, J.B., Sawhill, I.V. and Haskins, R. (2008) *Getting Ahead or Losing Ground: Economic Mobility in America*, Economic Mobility Project, Washington, D.C.: Brookings Institution and Pew Charitable Trusts. Online. Available HTTP: <http://www.pewtrusts.org/uploadedFiles/wwwpewtrustsorg/Reports/Economic_Mobility/Economic_Mobility_in_America_Full.pdf> (accessed 16 April 2014).

Kochhar, R. (2011) "A Recovery No Better than the Recession: Median Household Income, 2007–2011," *Pew Social and Demographic Trends*, Washington, D.C.: Pew Research Center. Online. Available HTTP: <http://www.pewsocialtrends.org/files/2012/09/median-household-incomes-2007–2011.pdf> (accessed 16 April 2014).

Lacy, K.R. (2007) *Blue-chip Black: Race, Class, and Status in the New Black Middle Class*, Berkeley, CA: University of California Press.

—(2012) "All's Fair? The Foreclosure Crisis and Middle-class Black (In)stability," *American Behavioral Scientist*, 56(11): 1565–80.

Lamont, M. (2000) *The Dignity of Working Men: Morality and the Boundaries of Race, Class, and Immigration*, New York, NY: Russell Sage Foundation.

Lamont, M. and Molnar, V. (2002) "The Study of Boundaries in the Social Sciences," *Annual Review of Sociology*, 28: 167–95.

Lamont, M. and Fleming, C.M. (2005) "Everyday Antiracism: Competence and Religion in the Cultural Repertoire of the African American Elite," *Du Bois Review: Social Science Research on Race*, 2(1): 29–43.

Lamont, M., Welburn, J.S. and Fleming, C. (2013) "Responses to Discrimination and Social Resilience under Neo-liberalism: The United States Compared," in P.A. Hall and M. Lamont (eds) *Social Resilience in the Neoliberal Age*. Cambridge, UK: Cambridge University Press. Online. Available HTTP: <http://dash.harvard.edu/handle/1/10718376> (accessed 25 July 2013).

Macartney, S., Bishaw, A. and Fontenot, K. (2013) "Poverty Rates for Selected Detailed Race and Hispanic Groups by State and Place: 2007–2011," American Community Survey Briefs, Washington, D.C.: United States Census Bureau. Online. Available HTTP: <http://www.census.gov/prod/2013pubs/acsbr11–17.pdf> (accessed 16 April 2014).

Marsh, K. and Iceland, J. (2010) "The Racial Residential Segregation of Black Single Living Alone Households," *City & Community*, 9(3): 299–319.

Marsh, K., Darity, W.A., Cohen, P.N., Casper, L.M. and Salters, D. (2007) "The Emerging Black Middle Class: Single and Living Alone," *Social Forces*, 86(2): 735–62.

Massey, D.S. (2004) "Segregation and Stratification: A Biosocial Perspective," *Du Bois Review: Social Science Research on Race*, 1(1): 7–25.

Massey, D.S. and Denton, N.A. (1993) *American Apartheid: Segregation and the Making of the Underclass*. Cambridge, MA: Harvard University Press.

Massey, D.S., Charles, C.Z., Lundy, G. and Fischer, M.J. (2003) *The Source of the River: The Social Origins of Freshmen at America's Selective Colleges and Universities*, Princeton, NJ: Princeton University Press.

Mizrachi, N. and Herzog, H. (2012) "Participatory Destigmatization Strategies among Palestinian Citizens, Ethiopian Jews and Mizrahi Jews in Israel," *Ethnic and Racial Studies*, 35(3): 418–35.

Mizrachi, N. and Zawdu, A. (2012) "Between Global Racial and Bounded Identity: Choice of Destigmatization Strategies among Ethiopian Jews in Israel," *Ethnic and Racial Studies*, 35(3): 436–52.

Mong, S.N. and Roscigno, V.J. (2010) "African American Men and the Experience of Employment Discrimination," *Qualitative Sociology*, 33(1): 1–21.

Mouw, T. and Entwisle, B. (2006) "Residential Segregation and Interracial Friendship in Schools," *American Journal of Sociology*, 112(2): 394–441.

Oliver, M. and Shapiro, T. (2013) *Black Wealth/White Wealth: A New Perspective on Racial Inequality: 10th Anniversary Edition*, 2nd edn, New York, NY: Routledge.

Omi, M. and Winant, H. (1994) *Racial Formation in the United States: From the 1960s to the 1990s*, New York, NY: Routledge.

Pager, D. and Western, B. (2012) "Identifying Discrimination at Work: The Use of Field Experiments," *Journal of Social Issues*, 68(2): 221–37.

Patterson, O. (1998a) *Rituals of Blood: Consequences of Slavery in Two American Centuries*, Washington, D.C.: Civitas/CounterPoint.

—(1998b) *The Ordeal of Integration: Progress and Resentment in America's 'Racial' Crisis*, Washington, D.C.: Civitas/CounterPoint.

—(2005) "Four Modes of Ethno-somatic Stratification: The Experience of Blacks in Europe and the Americas," in G.C. Loury and T. Modood (eds) *Ethnicity, Social Mobility, and Public Policy: Comparing the USA and UK*, Cambridge, UK: Cambridge University Press.

Pattillo-McCoy, M.E. (1999) *Black Picket Fences: Privilege and Peril Among the Black Middle Class*, Chicago, IL: University of Chicago Press.

Reed, W.L. and Louis, B.M. (2009) "'No More Excuses': Problematic Responses to Barack Obama's Election," *Journal of African American Studies*, 13(2): 97–109.

Roscigno, V.J. (2007) *The Face of Discrimination: How Race and Gender Impact Work and Home Lives*, Lanham, MD: Rowman & Littlefield.

Ross, S.L. and Turner, M.A. (2005) "Housing Discrimination in Metropolitan America: Explaining Changes between 1989 and 2000," *Social Problems*, 52(2): 152–80.

Schnittker, J., Massoglia, M. and Uggen, C. (2011) "Incarceration and the Health of the American Community," *Du Bois Review: Social Science Research on Race*, 8(1): 133–41.

Silva, G.M.D. and Reis, E.P. (2012) "The Multiple Dimensions of Racial Mixture in Rio de Janeiro, Brazil: From Whitening to Brazilian Negritude," *Ethnic and Racial Studies*, 35(3): 382–99.

Wang, W. (2012) "The Rise of Intermarriage," *Pew Social and Demographic Trends*, Washington, D.C.: Pew Research Center. Online. Available HTTP: <http://www.pewsocialtrends.org/2012/02/16/the-rise-of-intermarriage/> (accessed 19 December 2013).

Welburn, J.S. and Pittman, C.L. (2012) "Stop 'Blaming the Man': Perceptions of Inequality and Opportunities for Success in the Obama Era among Middle-class African Americans," *Ethnic and Racial Studies*, 35(3): 523–40.

Western, B. and Pettit, B. (2010) "Incarceration and Social Inequality," *Daedalus*, 139(3): 8–19.

Wilson, W.J. (1980) *The Declining Significance of Race: Blacks and Changing American Institutions*, Chicago, IL: University of Chicago Press.

—(1987) *The Truly Disadvantaged: The Inner City, the Underclass, and Public Policy*, Chicago, IL: University of Chicago Press.

—(1997) *When Work Disappears: The World of the New Urban Poor*, New York, NY: Vintage Books.

Wilson, W.J. and Taub, R.P. (2011) *There Goes the Neighborhood: Racial, Ethnic, and Class Tensions in Four Chicago Neighborhoods and Their Meaning for America*, New York, NY: Vintage Books.

Yinger, J. (1995) *Closed Doors, Opportunities Lost: The Continuing Costs of Housing Discrimination*, New York, NY: Russell Sage Foundation.

Young, A.A. Jr (2004) *The Minds of Marginalized Black Men: Making Sense of Mobility, Opportunity, and Future Life Chances*, Princeton, NJ: Princeton University Press.

21

The question of sectarianism in Middle East politics

Sami Zubaida

Sectarianism seems to be central to current Middle East politics, with its internal divisions and regional alignments. It has led many commentators to see this situation as another manifestation of a historical schism between Sunnis and Shi`is going back to early Islam and perennial in the conflicts of the 'Muslim world' over the centuries. This is not entirely correct: sectarian differences change and mutate over the centuries, and they are politicised in diverse fashions and situations when they become political. I try here to trace the determinants of the current forms of politicisation.

The schism dates to contentions and battles in early Islam, relating to the succession to the leadership, the caliphate or imamate, of the Muslim community at the death of the Prophet. The Shi`a are those who favoured Ali bin Abi Taleb, the Prophet's cousin, husband to his daughter and father of Hassan and Hussein, the only male issue in the Prophet's line. The imamate, henceforth, was to be in this line of succession. The Sunnis are those who accepted the legitimacy of imams/caliphs designated by consensus of the community. In reality, very soon after the Prophet's death, the caliphate became hereditary and dynastic. The dynasties in Muslim history were predominantly Sunni, with the exception of the Fatimid, Shi`i/Ismaeli Caliphate (909–1171), brief periods of Shi`i sultanic dynasties, and the Zaydi Imamate in Yemen. The major exception was the rise of the Safavid dynasty in Iran in 1500, which established Shi`ism as the religion of the country, which continues to the present day.

This is the bare bones of the story. Over the centuries there have been many variations and mutations in the 'orthodox' as well as the sectarian formations, and the divisions only broke into conflicts when they were politicised in struggles for power or resources. For the most part, various Shi`ite sects lived quietly under Sunni rule, and were, mostly, left alone. Like elsewhere in the pre-modern world, communities were, typically, isolated in separate localities, except in the main cities where they often occupied different quarters. Politicisation came with social conflicts, rebellions and geopolitical confrontations. Some rebellions borrowed legitimist claims to holy lineage from Ali and the Prophet. Confrontation and battles between the Ottomans and the Safavids over the centuries involved sectarian symbols. Iraq, with its Shi`ite population and holy shrines, was often the battleground between the two. On the eve of modernity it fell to the

Wahhabis of Arabia to wage a jihad against Shi`a, in the Peninsula and in Iraq, and their hostility continues to the present.

From the outset, Shi`ism and the adulation of Ali split into many sects, cults and parties, with esoteric, mystical, militant and shamanic variants. Some of these survive to the present day, as we shall see presently. Imami or 'twelver' Shi`ism emerged as the established majority Shi`ism, enhanced by its establishment in the holy shrine cities of Iraq and in the Safavid state of Iran. It traces the imamate through twelve descendants from Ali, through Hassan and Hussein, till the mystical 'disappearance' of the twelfth Imam al-Mahdi in 941, in Samurra in Abbasid Iraq. He continues to be the Hidden Imam, whose eventual manifestation is awaited by the faithful as a messianic event. Clerics and mystics hint at some form of communication with the Imam: ex-president Ahmadinejad more than hinted. Messianic claimants appeared throughout that history, heading cults or social movements, the most recent significant being Babism in nineteenth-century Iran, culminating in modern-day Baha`ism.

Ismailism was one of the early offshoots, following the dispute over the succession to the sixth Imam in 765. Another early offshoot over succession was Zaydism, now existing mainly in Yemen and other parts of Arabia. Ismailism played a central part in the politics and wars of medieval Islam, and was embraced by the Fatimid Caliphate in Egypt and North Africa. It also split into many fragments; the notable surviving sects include the Druze of Syria/Lebanon/Palestine and the Nizari branch of the Agha Khan community from India, which is now worldwide. There were many other Alid (veneration of Ali) religions which emerged in different parts of the Middle East and the Balkans, with various syncretistic amalgams with local folk religions, old Persian religions and even elements of Christianity. Prominent examples involved in the present sectarian conflagration in the region are the Alawites of Syria and the Alevis of Anatolia.

'Mainstream' twelver Shi`ism (as well as Zaydism) is quite distinct from these other forms, and considers them heretical. In religious belief, ritual and law, twelver Shi`ism is more akin to Sunni Islam: they share the pillars of worship of the Quran, prayer, fasting, alms and pilgrimage, and differ in detail over the law/shari`a. The principal divergence is in religious authority, culture and ritual. The Shi`ite rituals and calendar revolve around the cult of martyrdom of Hussein and his family and companions, and the commemoration of births and deaths of the other members of the holy lineage. Oddly, this veneration of the holy lineage is shared by some Sufi orders, who are formally Sunni.

The other offshoots of Shi`ism are more or less remote from what is considered the core of Islam. The Quran is marginal or absent for most, some, like the Druze, having a different scripture of their own; they follow different patterns of prayer and fasting; they do not attend mosques, but have their peculiar locations of worship and ritual. Crucially, these religions are typically esoteric, with their scriptures and 'inner' truths only accessible to a class of the initiated, a class which is often hereditary. The Druze have a hereditary caste of 'sages', *uqqal*, who are the exclusive keepers of the book. The Alawites of Syria and the Alevis of Turkey were typically peasant, mostly illiterate, communities in mountain areas who were led by their elders and holy men. General literacy, coming with modernity, has posed challenges to these religions: typically, they have been re-shaped as ethnic communities of solidarity, especially in the face of Sunni hegemony and hostility. In Syria, it was this previously marginal and poor Alawite community which acquired power and rule through recruitment and rise in the army, through policies first initiated by the French Mandate regime that promoted minorities.

These differences have important implications for the conception of sectarianism and politics. The concept of the 'Shi`ite crescent' from Tehran to Lebanon, first raised as a warning to the Sunni world by the Jordanian King Abdullah, appears to include the Alawites of Syria, allied to

Iran, and the Lebanese Hizbullah. Yet this inclusion is not in terms of common faith: Alawite religion is just as alien to and disapproved of by twelver Shi`a as it is by Sunnis. Yet, the official Iranian ruling, by Khomeini himself, is that they are included in the Shi`ite fold, a judgement more to do with geopolitics than with religion. Equally to do with geopolitics are the fluctuating policies of the Sunni states of Saudi Arabia, the Gulf and Turkey towards Syria. Until the start of the rebellion in 2011, all these states were more or less friendly towards Syria. Turkey was especially friendly, establishing close diplomatic and trade relations. Saudi, at various points, had been a financial benefactor of the regime, despite its Iranian alliance, having a degree of influence over its actions in the region, especially in Lebanon. The Syrian Sunni bourgeoisie had, for the most part, supported or acquiesced in the Assad regime, benefitting from the stability and economic climate it provided. It seems, then, that it was not sectarianism that led to the hostilities, but rather the events themselves and the geopolitics of the region which have politicised sectarian divisions.

Another interesting aspect in this respect is the attitude of the Turkish Alevis (with an estimated population of 10 to 15 million) to the alignments in Syria and the policy of their government in supporting the opposition there, especially the Islamic elements. Alevis have long been marginalised and subordinated. Many supported Kemalist secularism, partly as a counter to Sunni hegemony. Yet, even under a secular constitution, the implicit qualification of full citizenship identity included Sunni Islam, and Alevis continued to be marginalised, with episodes of persecution, notably a massacre in Sivas in 1993. Many embraced liberal and leftist politics. Their marginalisation became more open under the pro-Islamic Adalet ve Kalkinma Partisi (AKP) government. The naming of the projected third Bosphorus Bridge after Yavuz Sultan Selim (1465–1520) has been particularly controversial in this regard. The said Selim, nicknamed 'the Grim', conducted a notorious massacre of Alevis in 1514, which claimed 40,000 victims, as part of the establishment of Sunni hegemony against 'infidels'. Many Alevis have been vocal in their opposition to AKP support for the Syrian opposition. Syrian-style Alawites do exist in southwestern Anatolia, close to the border with Syria, and they have been vocal in their opposition to government policy. But, while there may be overlaps of sectarian groups in Anatolia, the mainstream Alevis are geographically and doctrinally distinct from Alawites. Yet, they see the battle against Alawites as part of a Sunni hegemonic campaign to which they are common victims. Again, these alignments are not based on religious belief or sentiment on the part of Alevis or Alawites, but on political fears of communal victimisation. This is not always the case on the Sunni side.

The Sunni sectarian antagonism to Shi`is, especially in its Salafi and Wahhabi forms, does derive from a deep conviction that the Shi`a are heretic dissidents and a danger to the realm of Islam and its unity. These sentiments were politicised into action by key developments in the region: the first was the Iranian Revolution of 1979; the second was the allied invasion of Iraq in 2003 and the removal of the Sunni ruling clique in favour of the majority Shi`a of the country.

Iran was always a geopolitical rival to Iraq and Saudi. But under the Shah this rivalry was with a secular and West-friendly Iran, its Shi`ism muted in regional relations. This was totally transformed under Khomeini and the Islamic Republic. Khomeini's call was pan-Islamic, revolutionary and populist, and it appealed to many radical Arabs, nationalist and Islamist. It also emboldened the considerable Shi`i population in Iraq and Arabia into political claims against their subordination. Iran was rightly perceived as a threat and a challenge in both geopolitical and religious terms. It sharpened and activated the anti-Shi`i ire of the Sunni sectarians. The Iran–Iraq war of 1980–9 exacerbated these sentiments and actions, with Sunni sectarianism superimposed on Arab nationalism. Saddam was never popular with Saudi and the Gulf, but when it came to confrontation with Iran he was fully supported. Only Syria among the Arabs became an Iranian ally and was its conduit to the Lebanese Shi`a, and eventually to Hizbullah. Saddam's next adventure, the invasion of Kuwait in 1990–1 was a blow to his erstwhile Arabian allies, who appealed to the USA and the West, leading to the allied rescue of Kuwait and the first destruction of much of Iraqi wealth and infrastructure. In Iraq it gave a further twist to the sectarian divide.

Iraq

The sectarian division in Iraq has had various social and political expressions over the course of its history. For the most part, the tensions, when they existed, were political and religious, with mutual denigration at times, but mostly mild. Classes, ideas, institutions and cultures which emerged in the processes of modernity from the Ottoman reforms of the later nineteenth century, reinforced with the formation of the modern state, fostered a sense of common identity – national, pan-Islamic, pan-Arab or liberal/secular – which rejected sectarian, tribal or communalist solidarities. Shi`i clerics declared jihad on the side of the Sunni Ottomans during World War I, then led southern tribes in the 1920 uprising against British occupation, alongside Sunni nationalists. Iraqi Shi`i intellectuals were prominent in the Arab cultural renaissance, and were participants in the common national struggles. The modern, educated middle classes participated in a common milieu of civil society and cultural fields, education, media and the arts. Within these classes cross-sect intermarriage was not uncommon. The Iraqi Communist Party played an important part in the creation of this common milieu, with generalised participation of members from different religious and ethnic backgrounds. This situation continued in the early days of the Ba`th regime, through the 1970s, despite the violent repression of dissent and the Sunni nature of the ruling clique. It started to shift after the 1979 Iranian Revolution, and continued to do so after the war with Iran, 1980–9. It was then that the Shi`i political organisation challenged the regime, which responded with characteristic total violence. The public ideological discourse was rarely an attack on the Shi`a as such, but always expressed through a denunciation of enemies with Iranian connections. Saddam did not target the Shi`a as such (though there was plenty of sectarian prejudice and discrimination). The regime was dominated by Sunni clans because those were Saddam's kin and allies: they did not represent the Sunni totality, which, in any case, did not exist. Individual Shi`a held high positions in the regime, though not in the sensitive security apparatus. It was the Shi`ite institutions and organised activity, especially those with political import, that were the particular targets for regime pressure and violence. The Ba`th had succeeded in eliminating or incorporating all centres of power, organisation and revenue in Iraqi society. The Shi`ite institutions of *mujtahids*, schools, pilgrimage, *husseiniyas* (prayer and assembly halls) and rituals are all financed via independent channels of religious revenues, some of which originate from outside the country (Iran, the Gulf, India). While under constant pressure, surveillance and harassment, these institutions have never been successfully eliminated.

Many prominent Shi`a figures, notably Baqer al-Sadr and his sister, were imprisoned and executed in 1980. Large numbers of Shi`a communities and families were rounded up and expelled into the desert borders with Iran in several waves, while their young men were incarcerated. The ideological rationale of these persecutions was phrased in terms of combating the Persian enemy: the Shi`a victims were Iranians, not Arabs or Iraqis, and not even Muslim. The racist abuses against Persians included questioning their faith and calling them '*majus*', 'magians' and fire-worshippers. These designations related to their Shi`ism, and could be (and was) read as including all Shi`a. The explicit attack on Shi`a, however, was to come during the uprisings in the south following the Iraqi defeat in the Kuwait war in 1991. The tanks that entered Karbala and attacked the shrines, massacring countless inhabitants, bore the slogan *la shi'a ba'da al-yawm* ('no Shi'a after today').

The 1990s through to the 2003 invasion were years of great hardship for Iraqis, and of weakening regime grip on society. It was then that the initially secular Ba'th and Saddam turned to tribe and religion to reinforce social control. Saddam launched *hamlet al-iman*, the faith campaign, which favoured Sunni ulama and institutions. Iraqis, in their distress, turned increasingly to religion, with a sharpening of the sectarian lines. Salafi networks, influences and finances played an important role in this re-Islamisation, and was sectarian in character, connecting Iraqi sentiments with those in the region with increasing polarisation relating to Iranian power and the increasing confidence and activism of the Shi'a in Saudi Arabia and the Gulf, as well as the rise and prestige of Hizbullah in Lebanon. This sectarianism was to be enhanced and sharpened after the American invasion, the removal of the Sunni regime and the rise of Shi'a power. We are now familiar with the sectarian carnage that followed the invasion.

The standard view of many commentators was that the removal of authoritarian control exposed the sectarian and ethnic fault lines of Iraq. I, and many others, have argued that it was precisely the authoritarian regime, its violence and impoverishment of many Iraqis under the sanctions regime that drove those Iraqis to seek security and livelihood in local and communal networks and authorities, which were patriarchal, religious and sectarian. The civil society of earlier decades had withered, millions of its surviving personnel had been dispersed in neighbouring countries or in the West, and those that remained were isolated and impoverished. These were the progenitors of the equivalent of the current Tahriri generation that has emerged in many Arab countries that has been largely absent in Iraq. Iraq is now in a desperate state of sectarian, corrupt and failing government: large oil revenues are shared out between ministries and contractors, the lion share under the control of Prime Minister Maliki, consolidating his personal power. He is instrumentalising sectarian sentiments and fears to maintain control over a Shi'i population, most of whom are poor, lacking basic facilities and services and threatened by daily violence and random killing. Poor people continue to seek security and livelihood in survival units of kin, religion and patronage, all of which reinforce sectarian solidarity in the face of regular attacks by Sunni jihadis. A similar quest for survival drives Sunni sectarian solidarity in the face of an openly sectarian government. The Sunni regions of western Iraq are now finding common cause with their Syrian neighbours, thus adding to the sectarian confrontations on a regional scale. Iraqi Shi'a fighters have also entered the Syrian civil war alongside Hizbullah, some, ostensibly, to defend the Shi'i shrines.

Sociological aspects

An important aspect of the sociology of sectarianism is that of communitarianism, revived and reinforced by the withdrawal and fragmentation of state institutions and services in the latter decades of the twentieth century. The transformations of the second half of the twentieth century can be seen through the changes in what may be called the 'survival unit'. Historically the survival unit was that of particularistic attachments and solidarities of kin, tribe, religion and community and the networks of patronage and dependence. Every man/woman had a master and patron, and his/her security and livelihood depended on the units in which these relations were embedded. The processes of modernity, to various extents, liberated individuals from this collective dependence, through the creation of impersonal labour markets, forms of association and solidarity deriving from interests and ideologies and socio-political movements in the manner already elaborated. These processes of course were more or less limited, depending on time and place, and the role of primary solidarities continued to play a part, but were often transformed and reconstructed by the new processes.

Survival was now related to different spheres and units, in which the modern state, especially in its welfare phase, played an important part, insofar as its organs ensured a degree of physical security, providing education, employment and social goods and services. These provisions were sometimes dependent on informal connections and patronage, but they nevertheless functioned more or less individually. The effect of neo-liberal economic policies, state withdrawal from social provision and intensified repression and corruption was to push back many individuals and families into survival units consisting of new or reconstructed communal and personalistic networks, in which religion and sect often played an important part.

Nowhere is this process clearer than in Iraq. The 1970s was a relatively favourable decade for the country. The barbarity of the Ba`th repression at the inception of the regime in 1968 had moderated, and, indeed, Saddam drew the communists into a coalition government (which was to be a great disaster for that party a few years later when they had outlived their usefulness for the regime, and were massacred again). The hike in oil prices multiplied revenues and allowed generous avenues of welfare services, education, health, housing and elevated pay for the middle classes and the intelligentsia, all within a developmentalist and nationalist rhetoric. Legislation and policy favoured women in the family and society, amid measures to curb religious authority and patriarchal controls, part of the Ba`th programme to control social allegiances and life chances. Repression of any dissent or challenge continued to be violent and arbitrary, but those who kept within the system, including, for a while, the communists, were relatively secure. For considerable sectors of the population the state became an important source of survival, for livelihood, status and public services. The regime explicitly attacked primordial units of tribe, kinship and religious community: except, that is, for the ruling clan and its entourage.

All this came to an end with the decades of military adventures of the regime, starting with the Iran war in 1980, then the Kuwait war in 1990/1, followed by the UN sanctions, lasting till the US invasion of 2003. During these decades, the regime, with increasing scarcity of resources and the devastation of war, drastically reduced its public services, impoverished the population, including the middle classes and the intelligentsia, and intensified its violent repression. It became ever more sectarian and tribal. Resources were channelled ever more in the direction of control and loyalty. People were pushed increasingly into the protection of communities, networks and bosses, and lines of patronage to the regime and the party became avenues of survival. In the process, the state and the party were hollowed out and bypassed by personalistic networks of clan and faction. Even the lines of military command were subordinated to informal links: low ranking officers with the right connections could defy their superiors. The 'secularism' of the regime was reversed into an official 'faith campaign', *hamlet al-iman*. Family legislation was ignored in favour of communal and religious authority; 'honour crimes' were recognised and treated leniently if at all. Under those conditions, the only possible politics were those of kinship and connections, with a heavy dose of religion. Shi`ites were targetted largely because their religious institutions and revenues could not be totally eliminated, despite much violence and assassinations, and Shi`ite institutional and personal networks went beyond the borders of Iraq, notably to Iran. When the regime was removed by the invasion, this politics of community and religion was the only one to have popular constituencies and resources. The ideological politics of the earlier decades of the twentieth century had been all but eliminated: the once popular Iraqi Communist Party (ICP) had been reduced to the shadows, and was mostly in exile, especially after the collapse of the Soviet world.

It would seem, then, that 'tribal' and religious politics are not peculiar to the region, but are historically general. Political modernity was engendered in the Middle East, and, like in most other regions, this co-existed with reconstructed forms of patrimonialism and religion. The dominance of the latter forms is not an aspect of some essential character of the region, but the product of particular social and political conditions. During their statist 'socialist' phase, the totalitarian nationalist regimes eliminated or incorporated all political organisations and socio-economic centres of power. With their decadence into dynastic rule and crony capitalism, their ideological pretences and populist appeals became hollow and they depended increasingly on repression and personalistic networks of patronage, kinship and religion. The removal of these regimes, notably in post-invasion Iraq, creates a political vacuum in the absence of organisations and institutions that can step into the breach. Communal, tribal and religious bosses and authorities step into the vacuum, aided by the invading power desperate for a native leadership, and exploited by neighbouring states for their own ends. Groups and individuals working for political programmes of citizenship and economic reforms have little or no constituency, organisation or resources. In Iraq, government and economy is divided between contending sectarian parties, each in control of ministries, engaged in an open process of pillaging the country and its petrolic revenues. The challenge from political groups, media and protestors have so far made little impression, and these bodies are precariously holding on to the free spaces established after the invasion that are now under constant threat and harassment.

It is important to note that 'democracy' defined in terms of elections, however free, contributes to the legitimacy of this situation. Elections mobilise primordial and sectarian constituencies and legitimise the sharing of power and resources between corrupt politicians presiding over ministries which become resource centres for the factions and networks. Elections without institutional frameworks and legal safeguards reinforce communal and majoritarian authoritarianism.

Arab transformations

The generation that started (and continue) the Arab uprisings in 2011 are not sectarian, and their demands are for universal values of bread, liberty and dignity. Everywhere they have been confronted by entrenched vested interests of old regimes and its associates, the so-called 'deep state' in Egypt, and by Islamist populism. They have been most successful in Tunisia, which features no sectarian divisions. Egypt, another largely Sunni country, with a Christian minority, has seen limited success, threatened by ongoing struggles and turbulence. In Syria and the other countries, this 'Tahriri' generation has been thwarted and sidelined by sectarian and jihadi forces with opposite objectives. The alignment of regional powers, following geopolitical interests, has sharpened the sectarian lines. I have argued that these alignments are not somehow essential in the history and society of the region, but are the product of particular situations and interests.

Part III

Policies and politics of diversity

22

Governing diversity

Brendan O'Leary

A mere sketch of the modes of governing diversity is provided here. One way to manage the subject is by level of analysis. The state-wide goals of governments provide a macro-perspective; how governments regulate associational life provides a meso-perspective; and how they manage individual citizens, metics, migrants and refugees provides a micro-perspective. Governing diversity may also be approached by focusing on the 'substance' of the relevant diversity. The governing of national, ethnic, linguistic and religious diversity is briefly indicated in this chapter, and, for the sake of brevity, examples are mostly confined to Europe.

Macro-perspectives

Governments may try to eliminate or manage diversity (McGarry and O'Leary 1993; O'Leary 2001; O'Leary and McGarry 2012). Eliminationists 'right-people' the state, through extermination, expulsion or homogenization. Or they 'right-size' the state's territory. Or they try to do both – see Table 22.1. Exterminist and expulsionist responses to diversity have figured heavily in Europe's past, and have not gone away. The motives for such extremism have often been expressed in ideals of national, ethnic, linguistic or religious purity (Semelin 2007), or justified by alleged security imperatives (Naimark 2001). To govern diversity excludes these appalling options.

Homogenization, however, is a coherent response to diversity, with normative defenders. 'Voluntary' assimilation has exponents. Policies of assimilation aim to make people alike: under acculturation, group B is expected to conform to the culture of another group, A, and then be fully admitted to it: $B + A = A'$, where A' is an expanded version of A; under fusion, B and A merge to form a new group $C: A + B = C$. Nineteenth century Jewish migrants from Eastern Europe acculturated into German and British identities; in colonial Ireland, the Old English fused with the Gaelic Irish to form Irish Catholics – the fusion resulted from both groups being excluded from citizenship by New English Protestants. Acculturation and fusion may occur without government promotion, but usually require long-time horizons – they are projects across generations.

Assimilation is promoted by 'nation-builders'. France's Third Republic is the European paradigm. Not only did it make peasants into Frenchmen, but also Poles, Russian Jews, Italians

Table 22.1 Macro-strategies for the regulation of national, ethnic and religious differences

A. END Eliminate diversity	B. MeND Manage diversity
1. GENOCIDE Goals: Purity and security Means: Right-peopling through exterminating 'others'	1. CONTROL Goals: Preserve hierarchical dominance Means: Organize the dominant, disorganize the dominated (e.g. settler colonialism, Herrenvolk democracy, hegemonic control, ethnic democracy; established churches, tithes and taxation of subordinated sects or other religions; linguistic privileges)
2. HOMOGENIZATION Goals: Security, solidarity, coordination, efficiency Means: a. *Assimilation* (fusion or acculturation); often accomplished through 'Jacobin' democracy; religious or cultural uniformity or b. *Integration* (public homogenization with privatization of differences); implicit ideal of normal majoritarian democracy; laicism, secularism	2. ACCOMMODATION a. *Centripetalism* Goals: Coexistence based on moderating the majority Means: Separation of powers (functional and territorial) and 'vote pooling' Or b. *Consociation [corporate versus liberal forms]* Goals: Co-existence based on equality of partner groups and equal stakes in security Means: Inclusive power-sharing, autonomy, proportionality and veto-rights
3. EXPULSION Goals: Purity and security Means: Right-peopling through 'cleansing' territory	3. ARBITRATION Goals: Co-existence based on equality of partner groups, security; state equidistant from all religions, as mediator Means: Mediation or adjudication (permanent or transitional); may include territorial adjustments
4. TERRITORIAL MONISM Goals: Purity, security or avoiding the costs of accommodation Means: a. Decolonization b. Down-sizing partition c. Uniform administrative 'rationalism': eradicating particularistic differences and historical homelands	4. TERRITORIAL PLURALISM Goals: Management of diversity through territorial power-sharing Means: a. Particular deals: federacies [manage their own religions and languages] b. State-wide: union-state, federal state [regions manage their own cultures] c. Extra-state: cross-border institutions and external representation of multiple nationalities (or ethnicities or religions or languages) sanctioned

and Spaniards became French citizens *and* French (Horowitz and Noiriel 1992; Weber 1979). Assimilationists emphasize the virtues of solidarity and efficient co-ordination around one culture, one language and one citizenship; they believe that equality is best accomplished through removing the salience of ethnic, linguistic and religious difference: 'we have no minorities, only citizens'.

Integrationists do not compel the fusion of peoples, though they do not oppose it, and, indeed, may celebrate its voluntary emergence. They confine acculturation to the public

Table 22.2 Diversity among integrationists

	Republicans	*Liberals*	*Socialists*
Preferred image of the state	Centralized & unitary	Decentralized (but non-ethnic)	Centralized to achieve egalitarian outcomes
Public & private spheres	Public sphere strongly homogenized	Public homogenization in language; privatization of cultural differences	Public homogenization in language; class unity
Key socialization mechanisms	By state, especially through schools and military service	Language socialization through schooling	Social mixing (in education and housing policies) & unification of the working class
Model of democracy	Majoritarian	Majority rule with bill of rights and separation of powers	Majoritarian
Public sector	Meritocratic	Meritocratic	Affirmative class action

domain – particularly the joint acquisition of a common public language through education. They have no objections to many cultures; indeed, 'inter-culturality' is their current slogan – in contrast to multiculturalism, which they demonize as segregation. But 'privatizing' cultural, ethnic, racial, linguistic and religious difference is the integrationist creed. The territorial recognition of ethnic or cultural difference is rejected, as is using public resources to subsidize ethno-cultural or religious differences. Publicly funded religious school systems are frowned upon. A simplified taxonomy of integrationist governing strategies found in Europe is presented in Table 22.2.

In decolonizing, many European regimes (e.g. Great Britain, Denmark, the Netherlands, Spain, Portugal, France, Italy and Russia) down-sized their empires, reducing their 'core states' to rumps, thereby making the peoples they governed less diverse. But they often encouraged immigration from their former colonies, and thereby reversed previous patterns in the flow of peoples, and, in consequence, became more diverse at home. Some European polities, by contrast, were forcibly down-sized, by losses in war, notably Germany and Hungary. Others were forced to negotiate their reductions: the United Provinces accepted the departure of Belgium; Sweden had to accept the departure of Norway; Serbia may be getting used to the exit of Montenegro and Kosova. The United Kingdom was a reluctant decolonizer in Ireland, partitioning the island, creating and keeping Northern Ireland and negotiating the Irish Free State's secession after war. All these shrinkages had homogenizing effects, tempered by subsequent new waves of migration.

Governments that overtly accept and manage diversity may not necessarily be more tolerant of difference, or more humane, than those who pursue homogenization. Through 'control' (Lustick 1979) they may disorganize subordinate nationalities, ethnicities, religious communities or linguistic groups for extractive purposes. They may be suffused with hierarchical, racist, religious or caste-based notions of the pure and the impure. Serb-dominated governments exercised control over Albanians in the twentieth century (Ron 2003); and Northern Ireland governments exercised control over Irish Catholics and nationalists between 1920 and 1972 (O'Leary and McGarry 1993). These regimes had few homogenizing ambitions. The post-Soviet treatment of Russian minorities in the Baltic states have often been feared as reverse examples, of natives controlling settlers (Lieven and McGarry 1993). Fortunately, however, there are benign forms of diversity-management, including

  (i) multiculturalism (Kymlicka 2007; Vertovec and Wessendorf 2009a,b);
 (ii) centripetalism (Horowitz 1989; Reilly and Reynolds 1999);
(iii) consociation (Lijphart 1977; O'Leary 2005); and
(iv) federalism, devolution, home rule, autonomy, that is, multiple modes of territorial pluralism (McGarry and O'Leary 2009, 2011; Requejo 2005).

These four accommodationist ways recognize, publicly as well as privately, differences in language use, in religions, in ethnicity and sometimes in nationality. They modify the symbols, institutions and practices of the state so it does not overtly or solely express the ethos of the historically dominant group. We can think of (i)–(iv) as distinct policies on a spectrum of policy choices, and of movement from (i) to (iv) as a shift toward more accommodationist and less integrationist approaches to governing diversity. Differently put, dominant groups prefer (i) and (ii), whereas national minorities tend to prefer (iii) and (iv).

Multiculturalism has ambiguous meanings, but as a governing strategy it is generally adopted toward immigrants, and may be conceived as temporary, pending integration or assimilation, or as permanent. Its key themes are recognizing collective identities beyond those of the existing nation and its historically constituted minorities (if any), ensuring that those from all recognized cultures are represented in key public institutions and supporting group self-organization to enable autonomous cultural reproduction. There is little uniformity in multicultural practice, but variations on this strategy have been adopted for immigrants and refugees in Scandinavian countries, the Netherlands and the UK, though all are currently under challenge from anti-immigrant movements (Vertovec and Wessendorf 2009a). Centripetalism, as its name suggests, promotes political convergence on the centre, assumed to be a site of moderation. As a governing strategy it seeks to incentivize politicians from the majority or dominant bloc to become more moderate to attract the votes of ethnic, religious and linguistic minorities. It has few obvious successes in divided places (McCulloch 2013), did not work in Bosnia and has no other clear European illustrations, but it may have some merits in new states before collective identities have hardened.

Consociations are inclusive power-sharing arrangements in which executive, legislative and security power is organized to achieve a cross-community consensus of representative politicians from the consociated partners. Principles of proportionality, group autonomy and veto-rights apply throughout the state and sometimes associational life. 'The most important element of cultural autonomy in consociational democracies is usually the right of each group to establish and run its own religious or linguistic schools' (Lijphart 2000: 231). The Netherlands, Belgium, Northern Ireland, Bosnia and Macedonia have been or are consociational; the current negotiations over divided Cyprus include consociational components. This governing strategy can work well with ethnic, linguistic or religious groups who have a common national identity. On its own it rarely works with groups divided by national allegiance or colonial divisions, but it can be combined with territorial pluralism to ensure a more workable and inclusive political pluralism (McGarry and O'Leary 2009). Consociations may recognize the 'personal law' of religious communities. Liberal consociations are less likely to recognize religious law that clashes with standard bills of human rights (e.g. over divorce or the equality of women and men), whereas corporate consociations delegate authority to the designated legal systems of each community. Both types of consociation are likelier to permit religious exemptions than other kinds of governments, e.g. regarding military service or in following other presumptively universal laws (e.g. permitting

Sikh males to wear turbans rather than otherwise mandatory motorcycle helmets, or to carry their ritual daggers despite laws against the carrying of dangerous weapons in public places) (see Shachar, this volume). Liberal consociations protect the rights, representation and influence of 'others' (who identify with no religion, are of mixed or hybrid origins or who belong to micro-religious minorities that are not large enough to benefit from standard ways of achieving power-sharing and proportional representation) and insist that the rights of women cannot be compromised by rights of religious autonomy.

Variations in territorial pluralism are extensive. Confederations, federations, decentralized union states, decentralized unitary states, autonomy and asymmetric autonomy arrangements all have their distinctive characteristics, which may be illustrated by the European Union, Switzerland, Denmark, Italy, the Aaland Islands, and the United Kingdom, respectively. The modes of governing diversity all combine elements of territorial self-rule and shared rule. Belgium and Switzerland combine federal and consociational principles, as, arguably, do the European Union and Bosnia (McCrudden and O'Leary 2013).

The macro-goals of governments in Table 22.1 are not mutually exclusive. Governments may homogenize some groups but manage others. They may also manage different groups in different ways, e.g. multiculturalism for migrants and federalism for national peoples. Within the UK, Northern Ireland has internal consociational arrangements and cross-border institutions both with Ireland and with Great Britain (and its devolved and dependent governments). Scotland and Wales have different powers under different devolution statutes. Variations on control, inte-grationist and multiculturalist approaches are applied to immigrants throughout Europe. Guest-workers are controlled, with variations in their de jure and de facto rights. Some ethnic (Northern Ireland nationalists, Basques) and religious groups (Muslims) have been securitized, i.e. subjected to much greater surveillance and application of emergency powers than others.

Meso-perspectives

Governments shape associational life as well as inter-group and inter-personal communications. When intent on homogeneity, they may oblige all major organizations to assimilate or to integrate citizens. They may promote 'national' political parties, and ban ethnic or religious parties, as Turkey has done throughout most of its modern history. Local, city and regional governments and enterprises, public or private, may be encouraged to resemble the relevant governmental unit's full spectrum of diversities among citizens.

Governments have sometimes sought to homogenize religious differences: to make all citizens or subjects conform to one religion – or to one sect within one religion. Statutes of uniformity, fines and taxes, and exclusion from office and contracts, encouraged the recalcitrant; and criminal sanctions and, in extremis, death applied to those who did not conform. The analogue in governmental regulation of religious diversity to policies of 'integration' in ethnic relations is the attempted separation of the state (or the public realm) from religion: the de-theification of the state, the disestablishment and disendowment of particular religions and the privatization of religious differences. The integrationist today seeks a religion-free public realm and seeks to ban expressly religious political parties.[1] Just as the integrationist state proclaims itself ethnically neutral, leaving cultural differences to the private sphere, so public space is to be formally freed from religious creeds or clerisies. Some argue that liberalism arose from the effort to privatize religious differences and fear the extension of multiculturalism to religion (e.g. Barry 1991, 2001). Under the sharpest version of separating the state and religion, public forums, executives, legislatures, courts, militaries, hospitals, schools and their symbols and ceremonials are formally prevented or discouraged from displaying any religious identifications. Organizations of the godly, by contrast, are left to compete for souls or roads to nirvana in the marketplace of religious ideas and practices. Provided they obey the criminal and civil law, they are to be left alone, free to proselytize, but not to public officials, or in political and public institutions. Public officials must leave their creeds at home while performing their duties.

The ideal of the separation of religion and state faces similar challenges to the integration of ethnic differences. Critics claim that the state (or public space) is not neutral. Every secularism represents the residues of the previously established religion (or defines religion by those standards). Since religions vary in the extent to which their adherents are expected to port their beliefs into the public realm (or indeed to distinguish public and private realms), impartiality is impossible. The state cannot be equidistant from all religions because all religions are not equally distant from the state: many religions are mission committed to having the right rule determined by the right faith; many maintain versions of natural law deemed to supersede the obligations of positive law; and so on. While separating church from state is the ideal of liberal intellectuals in much of Europe, it is remarkable how rarely the full programme has been implemented (Stepan 2001: 213–54). Banning religious parties in Europe would require the outlawing of Christian democratic parties, currently contributors to the largest bloc in the European Parliament, and the leading party in Germany.

In managing religious diversity, control has arguably been the most frequent and recurrent political strategy. An official religion was privileged; whereas other religions ranged from being 'tolerated' near-equals to those that survived at the margins of the law, while yet others were expressly outlawed.[2]

After the Reformation and Counter-Reformation, throughout what had been Latin Christendom penal laws and civil disabilities were applied to Catholics by Protestant states, and to Protestants by Catholic states (MacCulloch 2003). Even within the same religion, doctrinal codification and uniform ritual were regularly attempted in the interests of one sect. Neither equality nor equal respect for difference applied.

Outlaw or pariah status for excluded religions slowly gave way to tolerance in Europe. Emancipation, in the sense of entitlement to citizenship and public office, took longer: Jews were not emancipated in most parts of Europe until the nineteenth century. Even today, five European Union member states which are not majority Roman Catholic have established churches: Greece, Denmark, Finland, Sweden and Great Britain. The Church of England (Anglican) has the monarch as its Supreme Governor, whereas the Church of Scotland (Presbyterian) is Scotland's national church without an official head (the Moderator of its General Assembly is not an official head), but whose constitution is specified in the Act of Union and updated by act of parliament of 1921 (which proclaims it free of state interference).[3] The Scandinavian Lutherans, the Greek Orthodox, Anglicans and Scots Presbyterians have government-sponsored churches, supported by general taxation, but are no longer empowered to oppress other Christians.

'Arbitration' is a distinct way of regulating diversity in associational life. Key decisions and adjudications are made by a person or institution deemed sufficiently impartial to make credibly binding determinations. Emperors, kings and sultans often presented themselves as such. Constitutional and supreme courts frequently present themselves as equidistant from the rival religions or ethnicities in their jurisdictions and as suitably placed to adjudicate cases in which values and beliefs clash.

Amid territorial pluralism, it matters which tier of government exercises sovereignty over ethnic or religious matters (or whether the relevant powers are jointly held, and if so in what way). The federal government may be constitutionally obligated to separate church and state (not to endow or establish any religion), whereas the regions may be free to have established religions, or to allow particular religions to shape law and public policy. A federal constitution, by contrast, may recognize an official religion that binds the federal government but leaves the regions free to determine religious matters in their own domains. In a union-state, such as the United Kingdom, quasi-federal management of religion prevails. In the Union of Great Britain of 1707 the Church of Scotland was recognized as Presbyterian in form and as the national church of Scotland, and its autonomy was respected. By contrast, the Church of England and the Church of Wales (both Anglican) were established and endowed; so was the (Anglican) Church of Ireland when the Union of Great Britain and Ireland came into force in 1801. In 1869 the Church of Ireland was disestablished, and Ireland thereafter had no established church, the position inherited by Northern Ireland and the Irish Free State in 1921–2. Between 1914 and 1921 the Church in Wales (as it was called) was disestablished and disendowed. So two parts of the successor UK (Wales and Northern Ireland) have no established church, whereas two other parts (Scotland and England) have different official Protestant churches.

Micro-perspectives

Two key sets of regulatory rules deeply affect the politics of diversity. One is the rules, rights and duties governing citizenship and residency. Here the key political issue is whether the state permits dual or more allegiances. The European Union's constituent units accept the duality of European and member-state citizenship, but many have seen the former as entirely derived from the latter, and not all have permitted their citizens to hold two passports. Citizenship also covers a bundle of rights, which may sometimes be differentiated according to ethnic origin, linguistic community or religion. Some governments make the acquisition of citizenship easy – if not cheap; others do not. Governments vary in the rights they grant residents. Europe has permanent and temporary residents, tax-haven metics and guest-workers, with intermittent efforts to make these codes consistent with the freedom of movement proclaimed by the Union. Governments also vary in how they respond to asylum seekers. Governments may apply different policies to different components of the same group, e.g. by granting citizenship to some while deporting others.

The other set of rules comprises electoral laws – including those rules that govern party organization and funding. Which electoral formulae are chosen (proportional or otherwise), and the districts, tier or constituencies within which they are applied, have major effects on the ease with which minority candidates will be elected. A review of the major electoral formulae and their repercussions for national minorities may be found in O'Leary (2010). Whether affirmative action or quotas are applied by parties to increase the nomination of minority candidates profoundly shapes the opportunities for individuals from minorities to become elected representatives.

The scale and substance of diversities

States, in principle, at one limit are completely homogeneous – everyone in the nation is mono-lingual in the same language, believes they have the same ethnic descent and conforms to the same religion. At the other limit is the hyper-diverse state, N^4, where N is the total population and each individual within it differs from every other individual in the four dimensions of nationality, language, ethnicity and religion. The homogenous state, of course, would have no problem in governing diversity, but no such entities exist. The hyper-diverse state is even more implausible – there are no 'groups' of any kind in this imaginary world. In the real world the degree of politically relevant diversity is always a lot less than N^4 but never zero. Numbers and proportions matter, but their demographic salience is not well understood. They are always mediated in a democracy by the effects of electoral, party and constitutional arrangements. Not all potential groups mobilize, and not all cleavages are equally salient to individuals. Very small groups quickly acculturate or fuse. When there is 'super-diversity', e.g. in immigrant or 'cosmopolitan' cities, rapid conformity to one lingua franca, at least, may be quickly expected.

Do we know whether some forms of diversity are more difficult to manage than others? There is no scholarly consensus. Social constructionists seem to believe that cleavages based on nationality, ethnicity, language and religion are equally fluid, malleable and capable of rapid change. This conviction is ideological, not empirical. After all, it takes time, even for the most apt, to learn new languages. One can change oneself, but not the DNA of one's parents. Or the nation(s) into which one was born. Serious religions differ from Paris fashion shows; they are for all seasons. This is not a plea for primordialism, merely for common sense: bargaining over resources is easier than bargaining over identity change. The rigidity of identities may or may not matter in governing diversity, but beliefs held about other groups, and how they shape politics and life-chances certainly shape governability. Are diverse identities believed antagonistic or complementary? Is there polarization or heterogeneity? It matters whether group encounters are framed by native–settler (antagonistic) or homeland–immigrant (negotiable) relations (Esman 1994); it matters whether life-chances, equality of status and opportunity are shaped by nationality, ethnicity, religion and language. Broadly speaking, though the hypothesis cannot be proved here, managing linguistic diversity may be easier than managing religious diversity; religious diversity may be easier than managing ethnic diversity; and ethnic diversity may be easier than managing national diversity. Bi-lingual and multi-lingual states function (Laitin 1992); though life is easier with a lingua franca. Religious diversity may be managed in conditions of shared ethnicity – though religious civil wars occur. Ethnic diversity may underpin competitive nations, but different ethnicities can have a shared and complementary nationhood. Multiple nations competing over the same affirmed homeland, by contrast, is a known, though not certain, recipe for conflict and war. Multi-national states exist, as do multi-ethnic, multi-religious and multi-lingual states, and exploring their conditions of survival remains a key enquiry in political science (Anderson 2012; McGarry and O'Leary 2009).

This précis has so far avoided defining the national, ethnic, religious and linguistic – or the complexity of their inter-relationships. Notoriously, for example, there is no scholarly unanimity in defining the ethnic or the religious. Broader definitions of ethnicity often include religious markers and religiosity and treat some religious groups as ethnic groups (e.g. Glazer and Moynihan 1975: 18). Caste and race are sometimes included within conceptions of ethnic groups as those 'defined by ascriptive differences, whether the indicium of group identity is color, appearance, language, religion, some other indicator of common origin, or some combination thereof' (Horowitz 2001: 17–18). Yet, many religions have claimed to be universal, supra-ethnic, open to all humanity. Moreover, many religions preceded the nation-state, while others have remained disconnected from it. Historians have identified functional linkages between imperial cosmopolitanism and monotheism in late antiquity (e.g. Fowden 1993), hinting that multi-ethnic empires benefit from universal religions, but there have been numerous polytheistic multi-ethnic empires, as Rome was before Constantine's conversion (see Heather, this volume).

Religions vary in their relations to languages as well as ethnic groups. For centuries the Catholic mass was celebrated in Latin, the language of Rome, and not in Hebrew or Aramaic, the language of Christ and his apostles. The 'critical' versions of the New Testament were written in Greek, the lingua franca and language of government of the Eastern Roman Empire (Millar 2006). However, while religions may aspire to be pan-ethnic and multi-lingual, even if worship or prayer occurs through one sacred language, ethnic groups may contain multiple religious differences or cleavages. Kurds include Sunni (including Sufi) and Shiite (including Alevi)

Muslims, Yezidis, Jews and a variety of Christians, as well as nonbelievers. The typical Kurd is a Sunni Muslim, but no significant Kurdish nationalist party since the 1920s has confined its constituency to this group. Religiously diverse ethnic groups and supra-ethnic religions therefore suggest that there are good reasons not to conflate the ethnic and the religious. In certain famous cases, however, e.g. Jews and Sikhs, it seems difficult to parse the two categorizations.

Formulae to differentiate the ethnic and the religious do not always succeed. That is not just because it may really matter which god(s) you do not believe in (as with 'Catholic' and 'Protestant' atheists in Northern Ireland). Many religious convictions are inherited, if not with one's mother's milk then perhaps with one's relatives' and schoolteachers' whips. Equally, beliefs about ancestry may matter more than the truths about the origins of particular groups revealed by DNA evidence. The prevalence of endogamous marriage may be a necessary condition of the reproduction of an ethnic group qua ethnic group, yet it may be difficult to tell whether such marriage is maintained by ethnic norms, religious taboos, their conjunction or through mere happenstance (the low availability of other types of partner), or complex permutations of these and other possibilities. Ethnic groups may have particular (ethnic) gods, in which case the relevant religion is a distinctive expression of that group's culture. Yet ethnic groups may adhere to universal religions, in which case their religious culture is at least partly assimilated with that of others. We cannot, however, say the same about the rest of such groups' culture without investigation. Anthropologists insist that all (or most) cultures are borrowed and hybridized. If ethnic groups adhere to universal religions, they may ethnicize their relationship to that religion, and declare that they have an elect, special or chosen relationship to the universal deity or doctrine; and that belief may be functional for group cohesion or survival (Smith 1992).

Occidental social science has certainly shared one presumption in the last two centuries. It expected both ethnicity and religion to wither away – through the consolidation of nation-states or of cosmopolitanism, and through secularization. They would cease to be problems for governments. Today it is not possible to sustain such convictions amid both ethnic and religious revivals. Some claim certain religions have been gathering in strength, notably Islam (Gellner 1992); others claim to identify a ubiquitous spread of 'fundamentalism' (Marty and Appleby 1991, 1994, 1995).

But if it is not always easy to differentiate the ethnic and the religious – especially given the propensities to ethnicize the religious and to sanctify the ethnic – we should nevertheless distinguish them analytically. Etymologically, ethnicity comes from the Greek ὄθνος (just as nation is from the Latin *natio*), which simply meant a group (or herd) of common descent. Its recent widespread usage in numerous languages is explained by the discrediting of racism and racial science (and the word 'race'), which characterized the era of European and Japanese imperialism, and culminated in (but was not confined to) the atrocities of the Nazis. Its currency reflects the search for a neutral term that avoids presuming that descent-based human groups are in a ranked hierarchical order of normative (or evolutionary) significance, or that all such groups are clearly differentiated by typical differences in physical appearance (phenotypes).

To describe the ethnic, or ethnic groups, and to treat them as a question of government, entails no commitment to ontological 'groupism' – the belief that (only) groups exist and are holistic agents. But it does, however, require the recognition that humans may act and think in group-focused ways (at least on some occasions), and that they may judge and treat individuals as being 'representative' of groups. Such recognition should not be confused with full-blown methodological holism. The most famous methodological individualist of the last century, Max

Weber, had no difficulty in including ethnic groups within the ambit of social science concepts, and there are no compelling reasons not to follow him:

> We shall call 'ethnic groups' those human groups that entertain a subjective belief in their common descent because of similarities of physical type or of customs or of both, or because of memories of colonization and migration; this belief must be important for the propagation of group formation; conversely, it does not matter whether or not an objective blood relationship exists. Ethnic membership (Gemeinsamkeit) differs from the kinship group precisely by being a presumed identity.
>
> *(Weber 1978: 389)*

Weber's definition is as good as many available, though there is no need to limit the sources of belief in common ancestry to shared phenotypes, customs, colonization or migration. Weber also helps distinguish nations from ethnic groups. A nation may be based on an ethnic group, or it may be based on the fusion or alliance of several such groups, or it may claim (often implausibly) to have no ethnic foundations. Nations are political collectivities: they have institutions of political self-government *or* they are politically mobilized to achieve national self-determination. Ethnic groups, by contrast, need not seek self-government – once they do, they are nationalizing themselves. Differently put, nations are politically self-conscious; ethnic groups need not be (Connor 1994 *passim*, especially ch. 4): 'The essence of the nation ... is a matter of *self-awareness* ...'. Connor has argued that the nation necessarily has ethnic foundations:

> It is this group-notion of kinship and uniqueness that is the essence of the nation, and tangible characteristics such as religion and language are significant to the nation only to the degree to which they contribute to this notion or sense of the group's self-identity and uniqueness.
>
> *(ibid.: 104)*

Not all agree. Nations certainly have (or seek) homelands; ethnic groups need not, partly because their members may have left their homeland of origin. Nations are modern (understood as post-sixteenth century) political phenomena, integrally linked to the discourses of national self-determination and democracy, whereas ethnic groups are perennial, recorded throughout human history (Connor 1994; Gellner 1983; Hall 1998). Differently put, nations are legitimated through nationalism, whereas ethnic groups have no such universal discourse of justification. 'Ethnicism' is not a doctrine – ethnic groups are particularist, though the globally diffused charters of 'minority rights' (and the idea of 'cultural rights') are now available for their use and defence.

In one respect, defining religion is just like defining ethnic groups or nations. As anthropologists say, we must distinguish *etic* (i.e. outsiders') from *emic* (i.e. insiders') accounts of the phenomenon. The emic approach to defining religion has clear problems. Unless the relevant believers are relativists they will usually regard most of the rest of the world as followers of false prophets or false religions, i.e. as not properly religious. They may insist that others lack a correct ontology, epistemology, theology or account of revelation, and may have explanations for why the rest of us are not (yet) believers. There are, however, monistic and pluralistic emic perspectives. In the former, there is one true religion (*extra ecclesiam nulla salus* as the Catholic catechism still has it). In the latter, many pathways and destinations somehow share a common core. By contrast, ethnicity and nationality are necessarily pluralistic in emic conceptions; debates over where boundaries should be drawn occur, but the multiplicity of the groups is inherent in popular accounts.

Conclusion

This exploratory note has suggested that the governing of national, ethnic, religious and linguistic diversity may be approached as both common and distinct subjects. The propensities to discriminate unjustly, by nationality, ethnicity, language and sect, and to trigger thereby violence and civil war, are critical subjects of politics. Governments intent on eliminating differences behave in broadly similar ways. Questions of status, recognition, representation and access to decision-making (shared and autonomous) pose similar problems for accommodationist governments and those intent on control. So do the questions of the extra-state allegiances of citizens and resident subjects.

Where the regulation of religion most obviously differs from the regulation of ethnicity and nationality is on substantive matters, notably, today in many states, on matters of science, especially science which shapes policy on women's rights. Science, both its procedures and outcomes, challenges (and sometimes renders ludicrous) religious claims to knowledge, in ways which seem much less true of the claims of ethnicity and nationality (though myths on these subjects are also challenged by scientific inquiry and discovery). Governments often have to choose whether to be guided by science or by religion(s). Liberal states, even those with established religions, are generally guided by science, and have generally beaten back religious claims to alternative knowledge. All governments regulate relations between men and women (and their children). Liberal states insist on the equality of women, and have granted women significant rights over the control of their own bodies and rights of and in divorce. In freeing women from patriarchy, they have generally legislated against most of the world's religions. A similar pattern may be repeating itself regarding the rights of gay people. Liberal states insist on education systems, and educational curricula, in which every religious dogma may be questioned in the market place of ideas, and, where freedom of expression is strongly protected, they may also insist on the right to ridicule religious beliefs, even though it may not be prudent, and even though marches and demonstrations may be regulated (O'Leary 2006). It is rare for liberal states to extend the freedom to ridicule to ethnic (or racial) relations. Where inter-communal tensions are high, however, prudent liberal states enforce rules against expressions of religious hatred that are likely to lead to breaches of the peace. The policing of diversity, however, has to be addressed elsewhere.

Notes

1 For a discussion of the banning of religious (and ethnic) parties, see Bogaards (2008).
2 Many states face the difficulty of accepting historically formed religions, but then being called upon to outlaw (or to free forcefully those persuaded by) new 'cults'. The latter are alleged to practise brain-washing, to be embezzlement schemes or not to be authentic religions. The difficulty, of course, is that no religion can be free of accusations of brain-washing, embezzlement or inauthenticity.
3 'Articles Declaratory of the Constitution of the Church of Scotland', http://www.churchofscotland.org.uk/about_us/church_law/church_constitution. For observations on Europe's deviations from the separation of church and state model, see Stepan (2001).
4 One author fears that this strange conviction is widespread, whence the anxious title of his book (Brubaker 2006).

References

Anderson, L. (2012) *Federal Solutions to Ethnic Problems: Accommodating Diversity*, New York, NY: Routledge.
Barry, B. (1991) 'How Not to Defend Liberal Institutions', in B. Barry (ed.) *Liberty and Justice: Essays in Political Theory I*, Oxford, UK: Clarendon.

—(2001) *Culture and Equality: An Egalitarian Critique of Multiculturalism*, Oxford, UK: Polity.

Bogaards, M. (2008) 'Comparative Strategies of Political Party Regulation', in B. Reilly and P. Nordlund (eds) *Political Parties in Conflict-prone Societies: Regulation, Engineering and Democratic Development*, New York, NY: United Nations University Press.

Brubaker, R. (2006) *Ethnicity Without Groups*, Cambridge, UK: Cambridge University Press.

Connor, W. (1994) *Ethnonationalism: The Quest for Understanding*, Princeton, NJ: Princeton University Press.

Esman, M. (1994) *The Stakes in Ethnic Conflict*, Ithaca, NY: Cornell University Press.

Fowden, G. (1993) *Empire to Commonwealth: Consequences of Monotheism in Late Antiquity*, Princeton, NJ: Princeton University Press.

Gellner, E. (1983) *Nations and Nationalism*, Oxford, UK: Blackwell.

—(1992) *Postmodernism, Reason and Religion*, London: Routledge.

Glazer, N. and Moynihan, D.P. (1975) 'Introduction', in N. Glazer and D.P. Moynihan (eds) *Ethnicity: Theory and Experience*, Cambridge, MA: Harvard University Press.

Hall, J.A. (1998) *The State of the Nation: Ernest Gellner and the Theory of Nationalism*, New York, NY: Cambridge University Press.

Horowitz, D.L. (1989) 'Making Moderation Pay: The Comparative Politics of Ethnic Conflict Management', in J.P. Montville (ed.) *Conflict and Peacemaking in Multiethnic Societies*, Lexington, MA: Heath.

—(2001) *Ethnic Groups in Conflict*, 2nd edn, Berkeley, CA: University of California Press.

Horowitz, D.L. and Noiriel, G. (eds) (1992) *Immigrants in Two Democracies: French and American Experiences*, New York, NY: New York University Press.

Kymlicka, W. (2007) *Multicultural Odysseys: Navigating the New International Politics of Diversity*, Oxford, UK: Oxford University Press.

Laitin, D.D. (1992) *Language Repertoires and State Construction in Africa*, Cambridge Studies in Comparative Politics, Cambridge, UK: Cambridge University Press.

Lieven, D. and McGarry, J. (1993) 'Ethnic Conflict in the Soviet Union and its Successor States', in J. McGarry and B. O'Leary (eds) *The Politics of Ethnic Conflict Regulation: Case Studies of Protracted Ethnic Conflicts*, London: Routledge.

Lijphart, A. (1977) *Democracy in Plural Societies: A Comparative Exploration*, New Haven, CT: Yale University Press.

—(2000) 'Varieties of Nonmajoritarian Democracy', in M.M.L. Crepaz, T.A. Koelbe and D. Wilsford (eds) *Democracy and Institutions: The Life Work of Arend Lijphart*, Ann Arbor, MI: University of Michigan Press.

Lustick, I.S. (1979) 'Stability in Deeply Divided Societies: Consociationalism versus Control', *World Politics*, 31(3): 325–44.

McCrudden, C. and O'Leary, B. (2013) *Courts and Consociations: Human Rights versus Power-sharing*, Oxford, UK: Oxford University Press.

McCulloch, A. (2013) 'The Track Record of Centripetalism in Deeply Divided Places', in J. McEvoy and B. O'Leary (eds) *Power-sharing in Deeply Divided Places*, Philadelphia, PA: University of Pennsylvania Press.

MacCulloch, D. (2003) *Reformation: Europe's House Divided 1490–1700*, London: Allen Lane.

McGarry, J. and O'Leary, B. (1993) 'Introduction: The Macro-political Regulation of Ethnic Conflict', in J. McGarry and B. O'Leary (eds) *The Politics of Ethnic Conflict Regulation*, London: Routledge.

—(2009) 'Must Pluri-national Federations Fail?', *Ethnopolitics*, 8(1): 5–26.

—(2011) 'Territorial Approaches to Ethnic Conflict Settlement', in K. Cordell and S. Wolff (eds) *The Routledge Handbook on Ethnic Conflict*, London: Routledge.

Marty, M.E. and Appleby, R.S. (1991) *Fundamentalisms Observed*, The Fundamentalism Project, Chicago, IL: University of Chicago Press.

—(1994) *Accounting for Fundamentalisms: The Dynamic Character of Movements*, The Fundamentalism Project, Chicago, IL: University of Chicago Press.

—(1995) *Fundamentalisms Comprehended*, The Fundamentalism Project, Chicago, IL: University of Chicago Press.

Millar, F. (2006) *Rome, the Greek World, and the East*, Chapel Hill, NC: University of North Carolina Press.

Naimark, N.M. (2001) *Ethnic Cleanisng in Twentieth-century Europe*, Cambridge, MA: Harvard University Press.

O'Leary, B. (2001) 'The Elements of Right-sizing and Right-peopling the State', in B. O'Leary, I.S. Lustick and T. Callaghy (eds) *Right-sizing the State: The Politics of Moving Borders*, Oxford, UK: Oxford University Press.

—(2005) 'Debating Consociational Politics: Normative and Explanatory Arguments', in S.J.R. Noel (ed.) *From Power-sharing to Democracy: Post-conflict Institutions in Ethnically Divided Societies*, Toronto: McGill-Queens University Press.

—(2006) 'Liberalism, Multiculturalism, Danish Cartoons, Islamist Fraud and the Rights of the Ungodly', *International Migration*, 44(5): 23–33.

—(2010) 'Electoral Systems and the Lund Recommendations', in M. Weller and K. Nobbs (eds) *Political Participation of Minorities: A Commentary on International Standards and Practice*, Oxford, UK: Oxford University Press.

O'Leary, B. and McGarry, J. (1993) *The Politics of Antagonism: Understanding Northern Ireland*, London: Athlone.

—(2012) 'The Politics of Accommodation and Integration in Democratic States', in A. Guelke and J. Tournon (eds) *The Study of Politics and Ethnicity: Recent Analytical Developments*, Opladen, Germany: Budrich.

Reilly, B. and Reynolds, A. (1999) *Electoral Systems and Conflict in Divided Societies*, Papers on International Conflict 2, Washington, D.C.: National Academy Press.

Requejo, F. (2005) *Multinational Federalism and Value Pluralism: The Spanish Case*, London: Routledge.

Ron, J. (2003) *Frontiers and Ghettos: State Violence in Serbia and Israel*, Berkeley, CA: University of California Press.

Semelin, J. (2007) *Purify and Destroy: The Political Uses of Massacre and Genocide*, New York, NY: Columbia University Press.

Smith, A.D. (1992) 'Chosen Peoples: Why Ethnic Groups Survive', *Ethnic and Racial Studies*, 15(3): 436–56.

Stepan, A. (2001) *Arguing Comparative Politics*, Oxford, UK: Oxford University Press.

Vertovec, S. and Wessendorf, S. (2009a) 'Assessing the Backlash against Multiculturalism in Europe', in S. Vertovec and S. Wessendorf (eds) *The Multiculturalism Backlash*, London: Routledge.

—(2009b) *The Multiculturalism Backlash*, London: Routledge.

Weber, E. (1979) *Peasants into Frenchmen: The Modernization of Rural France, 1870–1914*, London: Chatto and Windus.

Weber, M. (1978) *Economy and Society: An Outline of Interpretive Sociology*, Berkeley, CA: University of California Press.

23

Equality for whom?

Sarah Spencer

Equality is invariably presented as an inclusive principle. The Universal Declaration of Human Rights speaks of 'the equal and inalienable rights of all members of the human family'. The European Union, mindful that its diversity agenda now extended beyond race and gender to other categories of difference, designated 2007 the 'Year of Equal Opportunities for All'; and the British Conservative party raised no eyebrows in 2010 with a pre-election commitment to equality of opportunity for 'every single individual in this country'.[1]

In that assertion of inclusivity, it is invariably overlooked that there is one section of society for whom equality of opportunity is not the intention of any government, a group for whom the law itself sets out the terms of their inequality: immigrants.[2] The global experience of immigrants, in differing forms and to differing degrees, is that their conditions of entry to a state variously include restrictions on entitlements to access the labour market, public services, welfare support, family reunion and participation in elections.

These restrictions are not perceived by governments as discrimination but rather as the legitimate exercise of immigration control. For migrants, as the American scholar Linda Bosniak (2006) has neatly phrased it, 'the border effectively follows them inside', and the contradiction this creates with the equality principle raises the question that this article addresses: when is it legitimate for a government to restrict the rights of migrants as part of its sovereign right to control its territorial borders, and when should that capacity be curtailed by a competing principle: equality for all those living within the territory, regardless of immigration status? (ibid.: 2–4, 14). If it is legitimate to restrict some of the rights of immigrants in some circumstances, what are those circumstances, and when can it be said that those restrictions go too far and constitute illegitimate discrimination?

As Bosniak has observed, while it is common in the literature to come across 'laundry lists of the vectors of subordination', such as race, gender, class, sexual orientation and disability, the literature invariably fails to mention immigration status: it focuses on inequality among those who are *entitled* to equality while ignoring the more problematic category of those who by law are denied the full enjoyment of social, political and civil rights (Bosniak 2006: 4). Few argue that immigrants should enjoy full access to all rights on the same basis as citizens from the day they arrive: to vote, for instance, or to receive contributory benefits. Yet there are rights, such as freedom from torture and to a fair trial, where equal treatment with citizens is, in a liberal democracy, taken for granted (Carens 2005: 32). On what basis is this distinction made? If not equality for all, equality for whom, in what circumstances and on what grounds?[3]

Equality: on what grounds?

Scholars who have explored this question have not all seen the equality principle as the default position from which departures need to be justified. Rather, they have asked 'on what grounds should immigrants acquire equal rights with citizens?' and suggested various grounds on which steps toward that entitlement might be justified. As in policy discourse, some have argued that the strength of an individual's affiliation to the country should be the basis on which, over time, they acquire equal rights. The greater the individual's ties to the society, the more enmeshed their social relations and identification with it, the stronger their claim to be treated as an equal member by their neighbours and the state. Joseph Carens (2005), while arguing that any departure from equal rights requires justification, has taken that view. Arguing that tourists may legitimately be denied certain rights because they are not members of society but visitors, and hence subject to the state's authority only on a temporary basis, he continues:

> But what about immigrants who have a right of ongoing residence? They are in a very different category. Living in a society on an ongoing basis makes one a member of that society. The longer one stays, the stronger one's connections and social attachments. For the same reason, the longer one stays the stronger one's claim to be treated as a full member. At some point a threshold is reached, after which one simply is a member of society, *tout court*, and one should be granted all the legal rights that other full members enjoy.
>
> *(ibid.: 33)*

We see this emphasis on social ties reflected in discourse on access to scarce local resources: that long term residents in a locality, for instance, should have priority in the queue for public housing. A related view, in academic theory and policy discourse, is that rights should reflect the contribution an individual has made (Cox and Hosein 2012: 9).

As criteria for determining rights, however, affiliation and contribution have flaws. The individual may be motivated to participate in society and to contribute but be excluded, facing discrimination or other barriers (such as a husband who does not allow his wife to attend language classes) beyond their control. Denial of equal rights on that basis would thus be reinforcing their exclusion rather than supporting their efforts to overcome it. Affiliation, moreover, prioritises length of residence or belonging over the individual's needs, or their capacity to contribute in future should equality of opportunity be enjoyed. Moreover, even if affiliation or contribution were legitimate grounds on which to justify calibrating the path to equality, it is by no means clear how they should be measured or the differing value of indicators of attachment and contribution assessed.

'The affiliation view', Cox and Hosein (2012) argue, 'has it that your interactions with individual members of society change what the state owes you. But it's more plausible to think that what the state owes you should depend on your interactions with the state itself' (ibid.: 13). Struggling to find a justification for the common sense view that immigrants should enjoy fewer rights, they advocate an approach based on social contract theory. People give up a level of their autonomy, they argue, and accept a degree of state control over their lives, for which in return it provides some protection and access to resources. While that relationship applies in equal measure among citizens, hence equal rights, immigrants do not have the same relationship. If they are in the country for a short period, like tourists, the state has little impact on their lives so the state owes little back in return. Whereas the state's impact on refugees, for instance, is great because they will make their future lives in the country, and have no alternative country to which they can return, the impact on temporary skilled workers will be limited. Restrictions in autonomy come in degrees, they argue, and the converse is that access to rights should too: 'So what matters crucially in the autonomy view is the amount of time someone is in a country for and, perhaps, their ability to pursue their life elsewhere' (ibid.: 17)

Baubock (1994), in his rejection of the related argument that migrants knowingly enter into a social contract that grants fewer rights when they gain admission to a country, rightly pointed out that refugees are not the only migrants who may effectively have no choice in their country of residence (ibid.: 203). It is also difficult to say that the significance of restricted rights on the life of, say, a temporary worker who is desperate to save for her family's future, is more or less than the impact on a professional person migrating permanently for family reunion (who may nevertheless, in the event, not remain long term). Nor does this approach, like the affiliation criterion, take into account differing levels of need, or provide a clear means through which the impact of the state on the migrant's autonomy could be measured.

Equality principle in liberal democracy

Baubock (1994) argued that states should put migrants on a trajectory toward equal rights because of the importance of the equality principle in the legitimacy of the liberal democratic state, not least in relation to the entitlement to vote. Denying the right to vote to those affected by its decisions undermines the legitimacy of the state. Tomas Hammar (1990) had earlier argued the case for voting rights for long term residents ('denizens') on the same grounds. While Baubock acknowledged it would be possible to develop a range of indicators which could be deemed grounds for inclusion in the franchise, such as birth in the country or payment of taxes, nothing other than residence could satisfy the democratic principle that all those who are subject to the jurisdiction of the state should be able to participate in elections. Extending his case beyond voting rights, he argued that there ought to be a general presumption in favour of equal treatment and rights for immigrants resident within the territory unless inequality is expressly provided for by legislation. In most European states he judged the opposite presumption to apply (Baubock 1994: 222).

The vast majority of states have signed up to international and regional human rights instruments in which the equality principle features large. Soysal (1994) foresaw this new legal framework leading to a universal concept of citizenship based on universal personhood rather than national belonging. Rights and privileges once reserved for citizens were, through the international human rights instruments, being codified and expanded as personal rights, undermining the national order of citizenship (ibid.: 1). Hollifield (2004) and others have indeed since noted that the extension of the international human rights legal framework and liberal ethic it reflects have to an extent constrained Western states' capacity to limit future migration; according migrants rights to settlement and family reunion, for instance, which they do not enjoy elsewhere.

Soysal's prediction nevertheless proved over-optimistic in the protection it would provide. International human rights norms have not prevented the imposition of restrictions on immigrants' entitlements. This is in part because the restrictions can fall below the high threshold required to bring those safeguards into play. Thus, as Benhabib (2004) has argued, 'a series of internal contradictions between universal human rights and territorial sovereignty are built into the logic of the most comprehensive international law documents in the world' (ibid.: 11).

In Europe, at least, that assessment is unduly pessimistic as the European Convention on Human Rights (ECHR), binding on Council of Europe member states, does provide some protection from discrimination on grounds of nationality, immigration and residence status, and that protection is increasingly coming into play (De Schutter 2009: 78). Not only are governments being called to account for some of the restrictions they impose on immigrants, but also the test which the Convention sets down for determining whether its rights have been infringed provides the intellectual yardstick that is needed to answer our question: when is it legitimate to restrict rights and when should the equality principle prevail? In so doing, it also sets a new research agenda to address the paucity of evidence and analysis needed to apply the test.

Discrimination on grounds of nationality and immigration status

It is well known that Article 14 of the ECHR provides protection from discrimination 'on any ground such as sex, race, colour, language, religion, political or other opinion, national or social origin, association with a national minority, property, birth or other status'. That protection is only invoked where it relates to one of the rights contained in the Convention, but that includes any right which a state has voluntarily decided to provide which falls within the scope of any Articles of the Convention.[4]

Not every difference in treatment amounts to discrimination. It has to be established that other people in a similar situation enjoy preferential treatment, and that the difference in treatment has no objective and reasonable justification. That means that for less favourable treatment to be non-discriminatory, it must pursue a legitimate aim *and* there must be a reasonable relationship of proportionality between the means employed and the aim that it is intended to achieve.[5]

A series of decisions of the European Court of Human Rights in Strasbourg has established that differential treatment on the basis of nationality status may violate Article 14. In considering, first, whether non-nationals are deemed to be in a comparable position to citizens of the country, the Court takes into account the factual bonds that an individual has to the state, such as payment of taxes and length of residence. It then looks to see if the treatment has objective and reasonable justification. The denial of unemployment benefit to a tax-paying Turkish national in Austria on the basis of his nationality was, for instance, found to be discrimination in the enjoyment of his right to property. Significantly, the Court emphasised that 'weighty reasons would have to be put forward before the Court could regard a difference of treatment based exclusively on the ground of nationality as compatible with the Convention'.[6]

The Court requires weighty reasons when it considers the grounds for discrimination to be suspect. Discrimination on grounds of birth out of wedlock and sexual orientation, for instance, are treated in the same way (De Schutter 2011: 16–19). In the context of nationality the Court has thus made clear in a series of cases that the need to 'balance . . . the state's welfare income and expenditure', to 'protec[t] . . . the country's economic system' and to 'curtai[l] the use of resource-hungry public services' (Pobjoy and Spencer 2012: 167) do not in themselves justify a state's less favourable treatment of immigrants than of its own citizens.

Significantly, the Court has also found restricting rights on the grounds of a person's immigration and residence status to be discriminatory. In 2005 it found that the absence of a stable residence permit was not sufficient reason to deny access to child benefits in Germany[7] (De Schutter 2011: 15), while in 2012 immigration status was found to be insufficient grounds for denying the right to family reunion to one category of migrant with temporary residence (a refugee whose marriage post-dated his arrival) when allowing other temporary residents (workers and students) to be joined by their spouses. As the only difference between these categories of migrants was the timing of their marriage, the Court considered them to be in an analogous position. The UK government argued that the less favourable treatment was justified because it needed to provide an incentive to workers and students to come to the country. The Court accepted that this was a legitimate aim but did not consider the difference in the treatment of refugees to be justified and proportional on those grounds.[8]

Implications for restrictions on immigrant rights

This means that European governments can indeed cite immigration control as a legitimate aim for restrictions on the rights of immigrants after they have entered the country. However, that government must *also* show that there is a reasonable and objective justification for the particular restriction in question: that there is evidence demonstrating that the restriction is necessary in order to achieve that aim; and that it is proportional, not a proverbial sledge-hammer to crack a nut.

This test surely provides us with much more than arguments for lawyers to debate in court. Intellectually, it provides us with an operational yardstick which we can use to consider, on the basis of evidence, when it is legitimate for rights to be restricted and when the equality principle should prevail. In making that judgement, significantly, it is not just the migrant's relationship with neighbours or the state which has to be considered, as in alternative approaches, nor indeed their needs or the impact of exclusion. Rather, a broad range of economic and social considerations may come into play in weighing up the necessity and proportionality of the restriction. In considering whether undocumented children should have access to education in the United States, for instance, the courts considered not only the impact on the child, but also the potential fiscal burden on the state, whether denying access would help to deter future undocumented migrants and the social costs if the individuals concerned were, as a result, unable to read and write (Bosniak 2006: 65).

European governments have hitherto not felt any great need to spell out any justification for restrictions on the rights of migrants and the evidence on which they are based. A recent study had considerable difficulty tracking down any rationale for many restrictions in place on migrants in the UK, except where, retrospectively, they had been challenged through the parliamentary process or in court (Pobjoy and Spencer 2012, Spencer and Pobjoy 2011). In legislation enacted in 2010 to strengthen protection from discrimination, the Equality Act, sweeping exemptions were allowed for restrictions on migrants' rights without any requirement that they be objectively justified or proportional.[9] The government's use of the argument that the risk of 'health tourism' was sufficient justification for exclusion of many immigrants from AIDS treatment was an example of a justification later found by parliamentarians to lack a sufficient evidence base. In the face of overwhelming public health evidence on the benefits of inclusive access to AIDS treatment, that decision was reversed in 2012.

Recent court judgements challenging restrictions on immigrants' rights are likely to lead to a stronger 'culture of justification' (Steyn 2000: 552) in which governments feel the need to spell out the rationale for restrictions, and the evidence on which they are based, to forestall legal challenge. Yet they may find this a challenging task because of the paucity of research evidence on the restrictions currently in place. Where is the evidence on the socio-economic and personal impact of denial of family reunion, of exclusion from recourse to public funds or restrictions on access to sections of the labour market? Do we know sufficient to be able to say authoritatively whether those restrictions are proportional to the policy aim to which they are directed? With many variables at play, those questions will never be easy to answer. Nevertheless, they provide a rich ground for new research and analysis that would enable us to argue where a line might be drawn between 'invidious discrimination and appropriate differentiation' (Fredman 2001: 9, 30). Armed with evidence addressing that question, we could attempt to answer with more justification than in the past: Equality for whom, when and why.

Notes

1 Teresa May, Shadow Home Secretary, Second Reading Equality Bill, 11 May 2009. Col 565.
2 I use immigrant and migrant interchangeably to refer to those who are foreign born and have not subsequently acquired the nationality or permanent residence of their country of current residence.
3 In this analysis I draw significantly on the work I have done with Jason Pobjoy at the Faculty of Law, University of Cambridge, published in Spencer and Pobjoy (2011) and Pobjoy and Spencer (2012) and acknowledge with gratitude his contribution.
4 *Hode and Abvi v. UK* (Appl. No. 22341/09), judgement of 6 November 2012 at [42]. If a government decides, for instance, to confer a right on certain categories of immigrant to be joined by spouses it must not discriminate between comparable categories of migrant when allocating that right.
5 *Weller v. Hungary* (Appl. No. 44399/05), judgement of 31 March 2009 at [27].
6 *Gaygusuz v. Austria* (Appl. No. 17371/90), judgement of 16 September 1996 at [42].
7 ECHR (4th sect.) *Niedzwiecki v. Germany* (Appl. No. 58453/00), judgement of 25 October 2005 (final on 15 February 2006).
8 *Hode and Abvi v. The United Kingdom* (Appl. No. 22341/09), judgement of 6 November 2012. *Bah v. The United Kingdom* (Appl. No. 56328/07, 2011) also found less favourable treatment on grounds of immigration status to be discriminatory.
9 Equality Act 2010, Schedule 3 Point 4 Para 17, which allows discrimination on grounds of nationality, ethnic or national origins in relation to public services; and Schedule 23, allowing discrimination (through legal provision or ministerial decision) on the grounds of place and length of residency, for instance in access to the labour market for different categories of labour migrant and international student.

References

Baubock, R. (1994) 'Changing the Boundaries of Citizenship: The Inclusion of Immigrants in Democratic Politics', in R. Baubock (ed.) *From Aliens to Citizens: Redefining the Status of Immigrants in Europe*, Aldershot, UK: Avebury.

Benhabib, S. (2004) *The Rights of Others: Aliens, Residents and Citizens*, Cambridge, UK: Cambridge University Press.

Bosniak, L. (2006) *The Citizen and the Alien: The Dilemmas of Contemporary Membership*, Princeton, NJ: Princeton University Press.

Carens, J. (2005) 'The Integration of Immigrants', *Journal of Moral Philosophy*, 2(1): 29–46.

Cox, A.B. and Hosein, A. (2012) 'Immigration and Equality', *New York University Public Law and Legal Theory Working Papers*, paper no. 308. Online. Available HTTP: <http://lsr.nellco.org/cgi/viewcontent.cgi?article=1309&context=nyu_plltwp> (accessed 19 March 2014).

De Schutter, O. (2009) *Links between Migration and Discrimination*, Luxembourg: European Commission.

—(2011) *The Prohibition of Discrimination under European Human Rights Law: Relevance for the EU Non-discrimination Directives: An Update*, Luxembourg: European Commission.

Fredman, S. (2001) 'Combating Racism with Human Rights: The Right to Equality', in S. Fredman (ed.) *Discrimination and Human Rights: The Case of Racism*, Oxford, UK: Oxford University Press.

Hammar, T. (1990) *Democracy and the Nation State: Aliens, Denizens and Citizens in a World of International Migration*, Aldershot, UK: Avebury.

Hollifield, J. (2004) 'The Emerging Migration State', *International Migration Review*, 38(3): 885–912.

Pobjoy, J. and Spencer, S. (2012) 'Equality for All? The Relationship between Immigration Status and the Allocation of Rights in the United Kingdom', *European Human Rights Law Review*, 2012(2): 160–75.

Soysal, Y. (1994) *Limits of Citizenship: Migrants and Postnational Membership in Europe*, Chicago, IL: University of Chicago Press.

Spencer, S. and Pobjoy, J. (2011) 'The Relationship between Immigration Status and Rights in the UK: Exploring the Rationale', Compas Working Paper no. 86, Oxford: Centre on Migration, Policy and Society. Online. Available HTTP: <http://www.compas.ox.ac.uk/fileadmin/files/Publications/working_papers/WP_2011/WP1186%20Spencer-Pobjoy.pdf> (accessed 19 March 2014).

Steyn, L. (2000) 'The New Legal Landscape', *European Human Rights Law Review*, 5(6): 549–54.

24

Fundamental rights and minorities

Kristin Henrard

This contribution on minorities and fundamental rights is structured around the foundational principles of minority protection, namely the right to equal treatment on the one hand and the right to (respect for one's separate minority) identity on the other.

The right to equal treatment is important to persons belonging to minorities in two respects. Such persons certainly seek an effective protection against discrimination (disadvantageous treatment without reasonable and effective justification) related to their separate identity. In addition they seek (positive) recognition of their separate identity and 'special' rights aimed at its protection and promotion, which also further substantive or real, genuine equality. In other words, there is a need to protect persons belonging to minorities from both oppression masquerading as difference and assimilation masquerading as equal treatment (Jackson-Preece 2012: 528). The discussion of the right to identity follows the fundamental rights perspectives of the three dimensions of population diversity usually distinguished, namely cultural diversity, linguistic diversity and religious diversity.

First, the scene is set with a section on the concept of minority, as well as typical characteristics and categories of fundamental rights.

Setting the scene: minorities, migrants, state integration concerns and (the interpretation of) 'fundamental rights'

Minorities make for an obvious angle of analysis in a handbook on diversity studies, as one of the essential characteristics of a minority is its separate ethnic, religious or linguistic identity. The lack of a generally agreed upon definition of the concept 'minority' goes hand in hand with a broad understanding of a range of essential characteristics, including a separate identity, numerical minority position, non-dominance and wish to hold on to the separate identity. It is exactly the ensuing vulnerable position of minorities which explains why the right to equal treatment in both its dimensions and the right to a separate minority identity are the overriding concerns of minorities and the foundational principles of minority protection.

Traditional discussions of the concept of minority included a nationality requirement and/or the requirement of long lasting ties with the state concerned. Considering the extensive similarities in terms of reality, needs and concerns, it is increasingly accepted that *migrant* groups can qualify as (new) minorities and thus are entitled to minority rights. At the same time, arguments are put forward that migrant groups have less strong (minority) rights compared to traditional minorities, since duration of residence and traditional ties are among the relevant parameters for the sliding scale which is inherent in the formulation of these rights (Medda-Windischer 2009).

While explicit state integration policies focus on migrant groups, *integration concerns* also exist towards traditional minorities. State reluctance to acknowledge the existence of minorities, and the extensive discretion left to states in international agreements on minority rights attest to this. While state concerns regarding traditional minorities are ultimately related to the fear of the emergence of secessionist movements, migrant integration is supposed to counter (the emergence of) parallel societies with different values than the receiving society. In the end, similar questions about the appropriate balance between unity and diversity, about promoting social cohesion, peace and stability are raised concerning migrants and traditional minorities alike (see also Henrard 2011, Pentikainen 2008).

Two features of *fundamental rights* need to be highlighted. First, human rights law is determined not only by the text of the legal provisions, but also by the interpretation of these norms by the official supervisory bodies. Furthermore, this interpretation tends to be teleological and evolutive, which implies that the interpretation of the text is coloured by its (ultimate) objective, while taking into account changes in society over time. Second, most fundamental rights are not absolute but subject to 'legitimate limitations': states can limit the effective enjoyment of fundamental rights provided particular conditions are met. Since limitations need to be proportionate to the legitimate aim invoked, the analysis whether limitations are legitimate implies a weighing of the respective interests at stake, each time taking into account all relevant circumstances of the case (Christoffersen 2009). Notwithstanding this case-by-case analysis, particular trends can be identified.

In relation to persons belonging to minorities, two types of fundamental rights need to be distinguished: general rights (as rights for everyone) and minority specific rights (as rights for persons belonging to minorities). This distinction is clearly visible in UN and Council of Europe standards.[1] Traditionally, the interpretation of general fundamental rights did not embrace substantive equality, and supervisors were reluctant to address identity claims of minorities. However, since the mid-1990s a shift in interpretation has entailed a gradual change in these respects (Henrard and Dunbar 2009). Minority specific rights are all about substantive equality and the right to identity. However, these rights seem very weak because of their formulation, which is replete with conditional clauses. Also, the interpretation by the supervisory bodies has brought a qualitative change, this time by de facto reducing the discretion left to states (Kymlicka 2007; Ringelheim 2010).

The right to equal treatment: formal and substantive equality

This paragraph on the right to equal treatment is structured around the two ways in which the right to equal treatment is important to minorities: (a) an effective protection against discrimination and (b) a right to differential treatment aimed at substantive or real equality in relation to their right to identity.

Regarding the *protection against (invidious) discrimination* in the sense of unreasonable disadvantageous treatment, the evaluation whether a particular differential treatment amounts to a prohibited discrimination crucially depends on whether the differential treatment is considered to be proportionate to the legitimate aim pursued. The outcome of this proportionality review depends largely on how demanding and intense this review is: the more intense the review, the higher the level of protection against discrimination (Henrard 2007). A history of discrimination on a particular ground makes that ground 'suspect' and raises the intensity of the review. Grounds that are particularly relevant for minorities are race/ethnicity, language and religion. Race/ethnicity is generally recognized as a suspect ground, as is also visible in the fact that at the UN level an entire convention is dedicated to outlawing racial discrimination. While language and religion are usually regarded as components of ethnicity,[2] the supervisory practice does not yet denote them (clearly) as suspect (ibid.: 102,108). Regarding religion, the situation is more ambiguous: the intensity of the review in cases of invidious discrimination is de facto rather high, but the supervisors are reluctant explicitly to qualify religion as a suspect ground of differentiation. This reluctance appears related to the broad discretion that states are granted concerning decisions about religion–state relations (Henrard 2012a: 73–5; see infra under 'Religious diversity').

Traditionally, the prohibition of discrimination was meant to root out differential treatment and was thus focused on formal or mathematical equality. Over time, various shifts in the interpretation of the prohibition of discrimination occurred which allow or even necessitate differential treatment, thus opening towards real or substantive equality. These duties of differential treatment are particularly important for persons belonging to minorities, considering their wish to maintain their separate identity.

Most explicit argumentations in terms of duties of differential treatment are found in the jurisprudence of the European Court on Human Rights (ECtHR), which decided in its seminal *Thlimmenos* judgment that states also violate the prohibition of discrimination when they fail to treat differently persons that find themselves in substantively different situations, unless there is a reasonable and objective justification not to do so.[3] While this is a very promising theoretical development, the case law of the Court has so far not yielded many examples of *duties of differential treatment* that would directly benefit the separate identity of minorities (Henrard 2007: 124–6). The UN treaty bodies (supervisors of human rights conventions) similarly acknowledge that the prohibition of discrimination encompasses duties 'to take affirmative action measures [= differential treatment] in order to diminish or eliminate conditions which cause or help to perpetuate discrimination prohibited by the Covenant'.[4]

Special attention is warranted for *duties of reasonable accommodation* as a specific type of duties of differential treatment (Howard 2013: 363–6; Jackson-Preece 2012: 529, 533). Duties of reasonable accommodation are about realizing equal opportunities (substantive equality), by evening out barriers to full participation, including (de facto) unequal access to employment, to public services, to education and to social services more broadly. Due to the overlap with duties of differential treatment as a dimension of the prohibition of discrimination, duties of reasonable accommodation are conceivable for all possible grounds of differentiations (Jackson-Preece 2012: 534), and thus also for religion (Waddington 2011: 190f.), ethnicity and language.

When considering the explicit international law standards, however, duties of reasonable accommodation have only been identified for persons with a handicap.[5]

Although minority specific rights are not framed in terms of duties of reasonable accommodation, and are not as such related to (a particular dimension of) the prohibition of discrimination, many can surely be understood in that way. This is confirmed by the supervisory practice of minority specific rights, which is replete with accommodation language and references to substantive equality (Henrard 2012b: 81).

The supervisory practice under general human rights conventions has not yet developed explicit duties of reasonable accommodation. Nevertheless, the UN treaty bodies (supervisory bodies of UN human rights conventions) do impose obligations on states, in terms of the prohibition of discrimination, to adopt special measures aimed at substantive or real equality, which take into account and accommodate the cultural distinctiveness of particular groups. Examples include granting a special legal status to indigenous peoples, entitling them to special rights and protection,[6] and requiring that minority languages are used in the educational system to an extent commensurate to the proportion of the different ethnic communities represented in the student body so as to enable equal access to education.[7]

The ECtHR has so far only once hinted at duties of reasonable accommodation in terms of the prohibition of discrimination in a case of a person with a handicap who was not allowed to do his military service but still needed to pay tax for not fulfilling this duty.[8] In addition, the Court is increasingly using reasonable accommodation lingo and reasoning in cases under the freedom of religion, while still refusing to examine the discrimination claim separately. Furthermore, the Court is so far only willing to identify a violation of the freedom of religion due to a failure to accommodate in cases where the refusal to accommodate is clearly unreasonable and does not fundamentally interfere with state discretion regarding religion–state relations (Henrard 2012b: 76f.). For example, the refusal to accommodate the religiously inspired dietary needs of a prisoner, where this only involved leaving the meat out of the meals, constitutes a violation of the freedom of religion.[9] The Court is much more reserved regarding religiously inspired demands in the work environment, such as wearing the Christian cross at work,[10] or rescheduling a hearing of a case to enable the lawyer to respect a religious holy day.[11]

These duties of differential treatment (including duties of reasonable accommodation) can furthermore be related to the prohibition of indirect discrimination, targeting measures or practices that seem neutral on the face of it but that impact disproportionately on particular groups, without objective and reasonable justification (Henrard 2007: 113 and references therein). Since these apparently neutral criteria de facto favour the dominant culture, the prohibition of indirect discrimination tends to further the accommodation of diversity and benefits with regard to persons belonging to minorities (see also Fredman 2001: 24). Duties of differential treatment can be considered the other side of the coin of the prohibition of indirect discrimination, since differential treatment is needed to avoid the disparate impact (Jackson-Preece 2012: 529). While supervisory bodies now in principle sanction indirect discrimination, the practice used to be rather uneven.[12]

Separate minority identity: the right to respect

One's separate minority identity can be protected directly, through minority specific rights, or indirectly, through the interpretation of general fundamental rights pertaining to a separate culture (Horvath cited in Francioni and Scheinin 2008: 190f.), a separate language (May 2008) or a separate religion (Henrard 2012b; Van der Ven 2008).

Each sub-section first considers the minority specific rights, then the general rights.

Cultural diversity

Generally, the minority specific rights (at the UN and Council of Europe level) do not contain many explicit references to culture. Still, these rights are infused by the recognition of the right to identity of minorities, making them overall relevant for cultural diversity.

At the UN level, the individual complaints procedure under article 27 ICCPR (International Covenant on Civil and Political Rights) – the 'Grundnorm regarding minority rights' (Henrard 2000: 156) – has so far mainly concerned indigenous peoples and their own way of life. It has clarified that the right to an own way of life also encompasses traditional economic activities

(Scheinin 2008: 32–5). However, the broad discretion left to states implies that a violation of article 27 is seldom found (ibid.: 34f.).

In Europe, the Framework Convention for the Protection of National Minorities does not define the concept national minority, but the supervisory body confirms its applicability to indigenous groups, while inviting states also to consider migrants, at least on an article-by-article basis (Ringelheim 2010). Traditional economic activities that are intrinsically related to minority culture are also protected. Furthermore, the supervisory practice exhibits a recognition of the interrelation between the right to identity of minorities and their socio-economic participation rights. In addition, state duties to promote intercultural dialogue and understanding yield cultural diversity lingo.

General human rights conventions contain only a few cultural rights: some pertaining to education and a right to participate in cultural life. At the UN level, the state duty to ensure that education should promote understanding, tolerance and friendship amongst all nationals and all racial and religious groups[13] promotes the related population diversity, albeit rather indirectly (Martín Estébanez 2008: 220). This theme of multicultural education, promoting respect of all cultures within the state, is actually visible in the supervisory practice of several UN treaty bodies.[14] Traditionally, the right to take part in cultural life[15] seemed to be understood as a right of participation in a general culture (Horvath 2008: 172). Nevertheless, the reference to culture can also be interpreted as encompassing minority cultures (Martín Estébanez 2008: 225). This inclusive vision of culture is visible where the supervisory practice underscores that effective access to socio-economic rights is only realized where this is culturally appropriate (Henrard 2013: 57–62). It should be highlighted that also the supervisory practice under the UN Convention against racial discrimination identifies several state duties to protect and promote the separate culture and identity of minority groups, including migrant minorities. For example, Roma should not be evicted without providing them with alternative, culturally appropriate housing,[16] and indigenous peoples should be provided with culturally sensitive health care.[17]

Early on, UNESCO actively promoted a right to cultural identity (Horvath 2008: 172f.). Three older instruments contain several references to cultural identity, while two more recent ones engage with issues related to cultural identity.[18] In the end, cultural identity is not enshrined as a right, rather as a general value. Nevertheless, it has been argued that contracting parties 'accept a responsibility to take positive measures in relation to the promotion and protection of cultural diversity' (Donders 2008: 338).

In Europe, the ECtHR has interpreted the right to respect for private life, family life and home as enshrining a right to a traditional (minority) way of life. The Court has even stipulated that states have a positive obligation to facilitate the Gypsy (minority) way of life. However, at the same time states are granted an extensive discretion in the way in which and the extent to which they fulfil this positive obligation, entailing a rather limited de facto protection (Brems 2010: 671–5; Henrard 2008: 343–5). It seems unlikely that the Court would extend this right to a traditional way of life to migrant minorities.

Linguistic diversity

The intrinsic relation between linguistic and cultural diversity is common knowledge. Consequently, not sufficiently protecting, promoting and revitalizing minority languages so that they can be kept has implications for the preservation of the related minority cultures (Eide 1999). As the Expert Mechanism on the Rights of Indigenous Peoples highlighted in its 'Study on the role of languages and culture in the promotion and protection of the rights and identity of indigenous peoples': 'language is the main mechanism in the intergenerational transmission of indigenous knowledge and is one of the signs of life of indigenous peoples' cultures. It is one of the essential elements of the identity of indigenous peoples'.[19] This close relation between language and minority identity arguably explains why language is the identity feature which is most prevalent in minority specific rights instruments.

It was only in 2009 at the UN level that a case on language rights was decided under article 27 ICCPR.[20] The refusal to register a newspaper in the minority Tajik language, containing inter alia educational materials, amounted to an interference with an essential element of the Tajik minority's culture, and effectively constituted a denial of the right to enjoy minority Tajik culture and thus was a violation of article 27. The case also clarified that 'in the context of article 27 education in the minority language is a fundamental part of minority culture'. The supervisory practice furthermore reveals a broader concern with a reported decline of minority languages while recognizing the importance, to counter this trend, of teaching in the minority languages, as well as the use of the minority language at the local government and administration level, and also in court proceedings, if need be with the help of translators and interpreters.[21]

At the European level, there is extensive attention for the use of minority languages, not only in the Framework Convention for the Protection of National Minorities, but also in the European Charter for Regional or Minority Languages. The latter's primary focus is the protection and promotion of cultural diversity with special attention for the use of minority (and regional) languages (Dunbar 2008: 155f.). Its focus on state obligations concerning the use of these languages is complementary to the individual rights approach of the Framework Convention.

The supervisory practice of both conventions significantly reduces the state discretion, which seems very wide in the provisions themselves. Under the Framework Convention[22] the supervisory mechanism aims to address linguistic obstacles that impede effective access to services, employment and education. Numerical thresholds for linguistic rights should not be set too high and should not be applied rigidly. The importance of mother tongue education is valued so highly that states are even requested to stimulate demands for education in minority languages through awareness-raising among parents. At the same time, bi-lingual education models are promoted to secure and improve the knowledge of the official languages. Furthermore, public service broadcasting should reflect the linguistic diversity existing within a society. More generally, it is argued that

> language policies should ensure that all languages that exist in society are audibly and visibly present in the public domain, so that every person is aware of the multilingual character of society and recognizes him- or herself as an integral part of society
>
> *(Thematic Commentary on Language Rights, para. 33)*

The European Language Charter aims at promoting the use of minority languages in six broad areas of public life, namely education, administrative authorities and public services, judicial authorities, media, cultural activities and facilities and economic and social life. For each of these areas states should select, from a menu of obligations ranging from rather weak to very strong, the obligation level which matches as closely as possible the particular context of each minority language (Dunbar 2008: 170).

Particularly problematic is the exclusion of migrant languages from the field of application of the Charter, especially in the current era of globalization and high migration levels. Notwithstanding the explicit exclusion by article 1, the supervisory practice demonstrates that there is room for flexibility in the application of the Charter, also because the exclusion is limited to languages of 'recent' migration (Dunbar 2008: 164f.).

The UN Conventions show that linguistic rights of minorities can be and are also dealt with in terms of general fundamental rights. It is striking that several cases pertaining to linguistic rights of minorities have not been decided under article 27 ICCPR. In the complaint brought by English-speaking businessmen in the province of Quebec that the prohibition on advertising in English violated the freedom of expression,[23] article 27 was not considered applicable because the English speakers in Quebec (being the majority country-wide) could not qualify as a minority. The complaint by Afrikaners in Namibia about the explicit prohibition to civil servants not to use Afrikaans in communications with the public, not even when they were able to speak Afrikaans, constitutes a prohibited discrimination.[24] The imposition of a Latvian spelling of a surname, after decades of using the original form, entailed a disproportionate interference with and thus a violation of the right to respect for one's privacy.[25] These cases show that it appears preferable to decide a case in terms of general rights, without having recourse to minority specific rights.

In addition, state obligations concerning the use of minority language in the public sphere are identified in terms of economic, social and cultural rights. Concern is expressed about the lack of possibilities for minorities to use their language in dealings with public authorities,[26] and about the absence of minority languages in the public media (Martín Estébanez 2008: 244), while education in the minority language is strongly recommended.[27] Under the UN Convention against Racial Discrimination similar concerns are expressed.[28] Furthermore, states are regularly called upon actively to preserve minority languages, which are part of the national cultural heritage.[29]

At the European level, the ECtHR has very few specific language rights, and then only pertaining to arrest and criminal court procedures. Traditionally this induced the ECtHR to give little or no protection to minority languages in terms of the other convention rights, such as freedom of expression and the right to education (Brems 2008: 680–2). More recently, though, the Court seems willing to protect language rights in order to follow its own teleological interpretation method and its concern for fundamental rights to be real and effective. The Court hinted at a denial of the substance of the right to education when pupils are deprived of education in the mother tongue (ibid.: 683).[30] Similarly, it accepted that the choice of the medium of instruction concerns philosophical convictions of the parents that need to be respected by the state.[31]

Religious diversity

In terms of norms pertaining to religious diversity, the absence of a convention outlawing discrimination on grounds of religion is mirrored by the paucity of minority specific rights concerning religion and religious diversity (Henrard 2012b). The supervisory practice of both general fundamental rights and minority specific rights strengthens this image of 'relative neglect' of religious diversity.

At the UN level, it is quite striking that cases on religious minorities are not considered on the merits under article 27 ICCPR, but rather under the prohibition of discrimination[32] or under the freedom of religion. The UN treaty bodies have only dealt with a handful of cases concerning religious diversity, leaving various matters undecided, especially regarding the scope of positive state obligations. Protection is clearly provided against the criminalization of particular religious activities, especially when that leads people to convert to the dominant religion.[33]

At the European level, the Framework Convention does not merit discussion, since no provision of that Convention elaborates on religious minority rights, while the supervisory practice does not add significant additional protection to persons belonging to religious minorities.

The jurisprudence of the ECtHR is rather promising for religious minorities in several respects, but also has numerous and ongoing problematic features, questioning the degree to which religious diversity is effectively protected (Henrard 2012b: 51–78). The guiding principle of interpretation for the freedom of religion is religious pluralism, while the state has a duty of neutrality towards the distinctive religions in its jurisdiction, ultimately aimed at religious tolerance and harmony. The Court furthermore acknowledges the importance of religious identity in the framework of the protection of human rights. However, at several stages of analysis of an alleged violation of the freedom of religion, the actual protection of religious minorities and religious diversity is not that strong. Ultimately this is related to the Court's reluctance to meddle in choices of states regarding religion–state relations, issues that are uniquely sensitive and potentially explosive (Brems 2008: 656; Henrard 2012b: 56f.).[34] This reluctance to take a stance also translates into the Court imposing, in comparison with other fundamental rights, only few positive obligations on states aimed at the effective enjoyment of the freedom of religion (Brems 2008: 680; Henrard 2012b: 55f.). The reluctance is also visible in the grant of a wide discretion to states when they limit the manifestation of a religion because of the lack of a common European standard regarding 'church–state relations'.

Conclusion

Minorities are a case of population diversity that certainly merit consideration in a handbook on diversity studies. Fundamental rights perspectives on 'minorities' and the related diversity are logically structured in relation to the foundational principles of minority protection: an effective protection against discrimination, the realization of real or substantive equality and the right to (respect for the own, separate minority) identity. While only the latter are directly geared towards the diversity (separate identity) aspect, the former are at least indirectly relevant, since they have an enabling and facilitating function towards the related diversity.

In relation to both respects in which the right to equal treatment is important for minorities, several positive assessments and developments go hand in hand with shortcomings and flaws. The effective protection against discrimination for persons belonging to minorities (in relation to their minority status and related separate identity) is improved when the minority identity characteristics qualify as 'suspect' grounds of discrimination. Race/ethnicity are generally recognized as 'suspect', but this is not (yet) the case for religion or language. Increasingly, the prohibition of discrimination is interpreted as implying duties of differential treatment and thus duties to adopt special measures. However, this has not yet developed in any significant way in relation to persons belonging to minorities.

When discussing the rights that more directly protect and promote minority separate identity, general fundamental rights and minority specific rights reinforce and complement one another, while standards directly promoting cultural diversity (including linguistic diversity) also merit consideration. The preceding analysis has demonstrated that separate ways of life of minorities are protected in theory, but only minimally so in practice due to the extensive discretion left to states. Rights pertaining to religion and religious diversity are in several ways underdeveloped in the legal texts, while the interpretative practice of most supervisors is rather thin. The more extensive jurisprudence of the ECtHR recognizes religious pluralism as a guiding principle, but its grant of an extensive discretion to states in religious matters entails a sub-optimal protection of religious diversity. Rights pertaining to linguistic diversity are not only most elaborated and thus most visible, but also interpreted in ways that strengthen the rights concerned.

The jurisprudence of the ECtHR is rather the exception in this respect, since it remains restrictive overall.

Formulating an overall conclusion for this rich tapestry of standards that pertain to minorities and the related diversity is virtually impossible. Arguably important developments in terms of principles tend to go hand in hand with restrictive de facto protection and promotion of the population diversity concerned.

Notes

1 Although the EU may become an ever more powerful player in Europe in the field of fundamental rights, its competencies concerning culture, religion and language have not been increased (and stay very weak). The EU Charter of Fundamental Rights enshrines in article 22 the Union's obligation to respect cultural, religious and linguistic diversity, but this does not translate easily into concrete minority protection standards (De Witte 2004: 115) and has not yet translated into policies and concrete action reflecting the conviction that the 'diversity' that the Union needs to respect encompasses diversity not only between but also within states.

2 The practice of the treaty body of the UN Convention outlawing racial discrimination clearly reviews language rights, such as rights to mother tongue education, as relevant for the prohibition of discrimination: inter alia conclusions and recommendations of the Committee on the Elimination of Racial Discrimination (CERD/C), Concluding Observations on Albania 2003, para 16; on Ghana 2003, para 20; on Moldova 2008, para 19; on Sweden 2008, para. 18.

3 ECtHR, *Thlimmenos v. Greece*, 6 April 2000, para. 44 (Appl. no. 34369/97).

4 Human Rights Council (HRC), General Comment no. 18, para. 10; CERD, article 2, 2 and related practice.

5 UN Convention on the Rights of Persons with a Handicap and EU Directive 2000/78 article 5.

6 HRC, Concluding Observations on Japan 2008, para. 32.

7 CERD/C, Concluding Observations on Pakistan 2009, para. 22.

8 ECtHR, *Glor v. Switzerland*, 30 April 2009 (Appl. no. 13444/04).

9 ECtHR, *Jakobski v. Poland*, 7 December 2010 (Appl. no. 18429/06).

10 ECtHR, *Eweida e.a. v. UK*, 15 January 2013 (Appl. no. 48420/10).

11 ECtHR, *Fransesco Sessa v. Italy*, 3 April 2012 (Appl. no. 28790/08).

12 The treaty bodies of the UN Conventions against Racial Discrimination and on Economic, Social and Cultural rights embraced indirect discrimination from the beginning, whereas the UN treaty body on Civil and Political Rights and its European counterpart (ECtHR) were traditionally very reluctant to engage with the idea of 'indirect discrimination'. The former did so in 2001 (see *Althammer* v. *Austria* and *Derksen* v. *The Netherlands*), whereas the ECtHR only began in 2007 in the Grand Chamber judgment in *D.H. et al.* v. *Czech Republic* (Appl. no. 57325/00).

13 Article 13, International Covenant on Economic, Social and Cultural Rights.

14 HRC Concluding Observations on Hong Kong 2006, para. 3, CERD/C Concluding Observations on Finland 2009, para. 15. See also CESCR/C, General Comment on the Right to Education, para. 50. Similar support for multicultural education is visible in the supervisory practice under the Convention on the Rights of the Child (Henrard 2013: 57).

15 Article 15, International Covenant on Economic, Social and Cultural Rights.

16 CERD/C, Concluding Observations on the UK, 2011, para. 28.

17 CERD/C, Concluding Observations on Colombia 2009, para. 22.

18 Declaration of the Principles of International Cultural Co-operation (1966); Recommendation on the Participation by the People at Large in Cultural Life and their Contribution to it (1976); Declaration on Race and Racial Prejudice (1978); Universal Declaration on Cultural Diversity (2001); UNESCO Convention on the Protection and Promotion of the Diversity of Cultural Expressions (2005).

19 A/HRC/21/35 2012: 9.

20 HRC, *Mavlonov and Sa'di v.Uzbekistan*, 19 March 2009.

21 HRC, Concluding Observations on the Former Yugoslav Republic of Macedonia (FYROM) 2008, para. 17.

22 See the Thematic Commentary on Language Rights by the Advisory Committee on the Framework Convention for the Protection of National Minorities (FCNM).

23 HRC, *Ballantyne et al. v. Canada*, 31 March 1993.
24 HRC, *Diergaardt v. Namibia*, 25 July 2000.
25 HRC, *Raihman v. Latvia*, 28 October 2011.
26 CESCR/C, Concluding Observations on Estonia 2002, para. 57; Concluding Observations on Denmark 2013, para. 27.
27 CESCR/C, Concluding Observations on Japan 2001, para. 60; Concluding Observations on Iran 2013, para. 29.
28 CERD/C, Concluding Observations on Ghana 2003, para. 20; Concluding Observations on Algeria 2013, para. 14; Concluding Observations on Albania 2011, para. 16; Concluding Observations on Australia 2010, para. 21.
29 CERD/C, Concluding Observations on New Zealand 2013, para. 17; Concluding Observations on Lao 2012, para. 21.
30 ECtHR, *Cyprus v. Turkey*, 10 May 2001, para. 278 (Appl. no. 25781/94).
31 ECtHR, *Catan et al. v. Moldova and Russia*, 19 October 2012, paras 143–4 (Appl. nos. 43370/04, 8252/05, 18454/06).
32 HRC, *Waldman v. Canada*, 5 November 1999.
33 HRC, Concluding Observations on Algeria 2007, para. 23; CERD/C, Concluding Observations on Pakistan 2009, para. 19.
34 This controversial nature of state–religion relations was clearly noticeable in the case on crucifixes in Italian public classrooms: ECtHR, *Lautsi v. Italy*, 3 November 2009 and *Lautsi v. Italy*, 18 March 2011 (Appl. no. 30814/06).

References

Brems, E. (ed.) (2008) *Conflicts Between Fundamental Rights*, Antwerp: Intersentia.
—(2010) 'Human Rights as a Framework for Negotiating/Protecting Cultural Differences: An Exploration of the Case-Law of the European Court on Human Rights', in M.C. Foblets, J.F. Gaudreault-Desbiens and D. Dundes Renteln (eds) *Cultural Diversity and the Law: State Responses from Around the World*, Brussels: Bruylant.
Christoffersen, J. (2009) *Fair Balance: Proportionality, Subsidiarity and Primarity in the European Convention on Human Rights*, Leiden: Nijhoff.
De Witte, B. (2004) 'The Constitutional Resources for an EU Minority Protection Policy', in G.N. Toggenburg (ed.) *Minority Protection and the EU: The Way Forward*, Budapest: Local Government and Public Service Reform Initiative & Open Society Institute.
Donders, Y. (2008) 'A Right to Cultural Identity in UNESCO', in F. Francioni and M. Scheinin (eds) *Cultural Human Rights*, Leiden: Nijhoff.
Dunbar, R. (2008) 'The Council of Europe's European Charter for Regional or Minority Languages', in K. Henrard and R. Dunbar (eds) *Synergies in Minority Protection*, Cambridge, UK: Cambridge University Press.
Eide, A. (1999) 'The Oslo Recommendations Regarding the Linguistic Rights of National Minorities: An Overview', *International Journal on Minority and Group Rights*, 6(3): 319–28.
Francioni, F. and Scheinin, M. (eds) (2008) *Cultural Human Rights*, Leiden: Nijhoff.
Fredman, S. (2001) 'Introduction', in S. Fredman (ed.) *Discrimination and Human Rights: The Case of Racism*, Oxford, UK: Oxford University Press.
Henrard, K. (2000) *Devising an Adequate System of Minority Protection – Individual Human Rights, Minority Rights and the Right to Self-Determination*, The Hague: Martinus Nijhoff.
—(2007) 'Non-discrimination and Full and Effective Equality', in M. Weller (ed.) *Universal Minority Rights: A Commentary on the Jurisprudence of International Courts and Treaty Bodies*, Oxford, UK: Oxford University Press.
—(2008) 'The Added Value of the Framework Convention for the Protection of National Minorities: The Two Pillars of an Adequate System of Minority Protection Revisited', in A. Verstichel (ed.) *The Framework Convention for the Protection of National Minorities: A Useful Pan-European Instrument?*, Antwerp: Intersentia.
—(2011) 'Tracing Visions on Integration and/of Minorities: An Analysis of the Supervisory Practice of the FCNM', *International Community Law Review*, 13(4): 333–60.
—(2012a) 'A Critical Appraisal of the Margin of Appreciation Left to States Pertaining to "Church-State Relations" under the Jurisprudence of the ECtHR', in K. Alidadi, M.C. Foblets and J. Vrielink (eds)

A Test of Faith? Religious Diversity and Accommodation in the European Workplace, Farnham, UK: Ashgate.

——(2012b) *The Ambiguous Relationship between Religious Minorities and Fundamental (Minority) Rights*, The Hague: Eleven International.

——(2013) 'Minorities, Identity, Socio-Economic Participation and Integration: About Interrelations and Synergies', in K. Henrard (ed.) *The Interrelation between the Right to Identity of Minorities and their Socio-Economic Participation*, Leiden & Boston, MA: Brill.

Henrard, K. and Dunbar, R. (eds) (2009) *Synergies in Minority Protection*, Cambridge, UK: Cambridge University Press.

Horvath, E. (2008) 'Cultural Identity and Legal Status: Or the Return of the Right to Have (Particular) Rights', in F. Francioni and M. Scheinin (eds) *Cultural Human Rights*, Leiden: Nijhoff.

Howard, E. (2013) 'Reasonable Accommodation of Religion and other Discrimination Grounds in EU Law', *European Law Review*, 38(3): 360–75.

Jackson-Preece, J. (2012) 'Positive Measures and the EU Equality Directives: Closing the Protection Gap between "New" and "Old" Minorities through the Reasonable Accommodation of Religion', *European Yearbook of Minority Issues 2010*, 9(1): 519–48.

Kymlicka, W. (2007) 'Rights to Culture, Autonomy and Participation: The Evolving Basis of Minority Rights in Europe', in O.A. Payrow Shabani (ed.) *Multilingualism and Law: A Critical Debate*, Cardiff, UK: University of Wales Press.

Martín Estébanez, M.A. (2008) 'The UN International Covenant on Economic, Social and Cultural Rights', in K. Henrard and R. Dunbar (eds) *Synergies in Minority Protection*, Cambridge, UK: Cambridge University Press.

May, S. (2008) *Language and Minority Rights: Ethnicity, Nationalism and the Politics of Language*, New York, NY: Routledge.

Medda-Windischer, R. (2009) *Old and New Minorities: Reconciling Diversity and Cohesion: A Human Rights Model for Minority Integration*, Baden Baden: Nomos.

Pentikainen, M. (2008) 'Creating an Integrated Society, Managing Diversity and Human Rights in Europe', *European Yearbook on Minority Issues 2006/7*, 6(1): 329–68.

Ringelheim, J. (2010) 'Minority Rights in a Time of Multiculturalism: The Evolving Scope of the Framework Convention on the Protection of National Minorities', *Human Rights Law Review*, 10(1): 99–128.

Scheinin, M. (2008) 'The UN ICCPR: Article 27 and Other Provisions', in K. Henrard and R. Dunbar (eds) *Synergies in Minority Protection*, Cambridge, UK: Cambridge University Press.

Van der Ven, J. (2008) 'Religious Rights for Minorities in a Policy of Recognition', *Religion and Human Rights*, 3(2): 155–83.

Waddington, L. (2011) 'Reasonable Accommodation: Time to Extend the Duty to Accommodate Beyond Disability?', *NJCM Bulletin*, 36(2), 186–98.

25

When law meets diversity
Implications for women's equal citizenship

Ayelet Shachar

We live in an age of diversity, as Steven Vertovec eloquently articulates in the introduction to this Handbook (Vertovec, this volume) – but ours is also the age of equality. And both diversity and equality are open to multiple and potentially competing interpretations by those seeking social change. While it is now commonplace in the social sciences and humanities to emphasize the fluidity and malleability of collective identities, rejecting reified notions of culture and religion and instead placing a "cosmopolitanized" individual at the heart of the analysis (Beck 2006), the law has traditionally had a hard time dealing with intersectionist, dynamic identities (e.g. Nussbaum 2012). It tends to pin them into fixed boxes. This is true for individuals, and it is true for collectives such as religious, ethnic, or linguistic minorities. This raises several important questions: who can, and should, speak for a minority community in inter- and intra-communal legal disputes? How are we to define "culture" and "religion" for the purposes of crafting legal policies of reasonable accommodation or exemption, and according to what criteria? Who gets silenced when the state "takes sides" in disputes concerning membership demarcation or the distribution of rights and powers among group members?

In recent years, arguments over the recognition that ought to be afforded to religious faiths and practices have risen to the forefront of public debate. This is evidenced by the controversy in Europe about the issue of veiling, an issue that has been considered in the European Court of Human Rights several times over the last decade (Howard 2011; Laborde 2008), and we may well see a new wave of controversy and litigation with the coming into force of face-covering laws and regulations. As if these charged debates over the boundaries of recognition (or, increasingly, restriction) of the expression of religious-identity markers in the public sphere – what I shall refer to as the terms of *fair inclusion* – do not present enough of a challenge, we are also starting to see a second, related type of claim by advocates of *privatized diversity* (Shachar 2008, 2013). Unlike fair inclusion, privatized diversity captures the growing pressure exerted by the more conservative elements within religious minority communities to promote a whole new kind of politics, one that invites members of the faith community to turn to private, religious dispute-resolution processes in lieu of the ordinary institutions of the state with its human-enacted constitution (Hirschl and Shachar 2009). Privatized diversity, in its extreme variants, represents a call for insulation from the general law of the land, and possibly also from international human rights standards, in effect asking members of minority communities to engage in "private ordering," potentially at the risk of losing established protections under public law. This new trend raises weighty justice issues, such as whether reliance by individuals and communities on alternative dispute mechanisms established by contract and consent can absolve the state from responsibility if these non-state mechanisms breach an individual's hard-earned rights and protections as an equal citizen. The jurisprudence on this question has been mixed, but recent years have seen a shift in both regional and international law jurisprudence toward a view that holds the state accountable for human rights violations even if they are perpetuated by non-state actors (Quane 2013: 682–3).

The situation is more ambiguous under domestic law, however. There is a wide spectrum of response to this issue across different countries, with their varying state–religion models and varying degrees of legal pluralism (Adhar and Leigh 2005; Barro and McCleary 2005; Shachar 2001; Stone 2008). That said, there are important dilemmas at play even under the most favorable conditions. The most difficult challenge for advocates of greater recognition of cultural diversity in societies committed to the separation of state from religion has always been that of line drawing. Clearly, not every claim that is grounded in "culture" or "religion" should be respected by the state and the wider society (Kymlicka 1995; Parekh 2002). But what precise set of principles or guidelines ought to be used to distinguish between those situations that merit recognition, exemption or accommodation from those that do not? When conflicts arise, for example, between group autonomy and individual rights, who, or what entity, should have the authority to determine how to resolve them – and on what basis? These hard questions evade any neat and simple answers. Indeed, they linger as a source of charged and ongoing debate in the world of scholarship and public policy making even among those committed to a multicultural vision of citizenship and human rights; among those who oppose and reject such a vision, they obviously provide ample fodder.

Addressing with a clear moral voice the actual cases where conflicts between claims for equality and of respect for diversity are concrete and proven is imperative in a just society. At the same time, it is equally important that new ways be crafted to identify those situations where diversity and equality can be seen as mutually reinforcing rather than conflicting and incompatible. The trickier task is that of finding ways to translate these values into applicable measures that make inclusive membership a reality that counters the marginalization of non-dominant minorities, both *within* and *across* different communities and affiliations. For women caught in the knots of secular and religious legal orders, especially in the context of marriage and divorce, such a new approach holds the promise of averting the "your culture or your rights" dilemma, instead giving them recognition and protection as *both* religious believers and equal citizens.

Exploring hot-button issues ranging from denial of access to citizenship, to *niqab*-wearing women, to the display of crucifixes in state-run public schools, to the rise of private religions arbitration tribunals, my discussion will draw upon comparative constitutional law and jurisprudence in order to elucidate some of the most pressing challenges and dilemmas we face today in our diverse societies. I will then offer several ideas about how it might be possible to mitigate the potential strains between diversity and equality, before turning to chart the still unresolved and puzzling dimensions of these dilemmas which are ripe for critical analysis and innovative multidisciplinary research.

The "cultural turn" in citizenship

The worldwide backlash against multiculturalism (Banting and Kymlicka 2013; Vertovec and Wessendorf 2010) gives new impetus to reflect on the relation between diversity and equality. This new political reality has placed female members of religious minorities at the epicenter of larger debates about "civilization" and progress, membership and its "others." A compelling contemporary example of this trend can be found in the fierce controversies surrounding legislation that bans the public wearing of head-to-toe veiling and particularly the more extensive forms of face covering (the *niqab* and *burka*). France was the first country in Europe to implement such a ban, which it did with legislation that prohibits the wearing of any clothing that conceals the face while in public spaces, except when worshipping in a religious place. A woman wearing a face veil in defiance of the law risks a fine; this can also be accompanied or replaced by compulsory citizenship classes. Such state action purports to advance the goals of gender equality, secularism and public order, but it may stand in tension with protected principles of religious freedom, as well as with individual choice and autonomy. Generalized bans of this nature, and their compatibility with constitutional principles and human rights norms, will surely occupy domestic and regional courts in the years to come. At present, it is undisputed that the relentless attention paid to Muslim women's veiling has only further politicized the matter. In the current charged environment, every act of veiling (or refusing to veil) is interpreted by multiple actors as a statement about one's "loyalty" and "belonging." What is often lost in the discussion is a recognition that immigrant women who belong to minority or marginalized religious communities are constantly negotiating their *multiple* affiliations (to their gender, their faith, their families, their new and old home countries, and so on) while operating within a tight space for action. Nevertheless, these women and their attire have become visual markers of far broader struggles over power and identity, secularism and the expression of "difference," the blurring of once-fixed lines distinguishing the metropolitan from the rest of the (once-colonized) world, and the ability to "speak" for oneself rather than being artificially placed in predefined boxes and categories. The situation has also reinforced the majority culture as the norm and thereby marked certain communities as implicitly "foreign."

Many of these themes came to a head in the *Faiza M.* ruling. In *Faiza M.*, the Conseil d'État upheld a decision to decline a naturalization request submitted by a Muslim female immigrant named Silmi, who was legally admitted to France, spoke fluent French, was married to a French citizen, and had three French children, because "she had adopted a radical practice of her religion, incompatible with the essential values of the French communaté, especially the principle of equality between the sexes". This decision was grounded in article 21–4 of the Civil Code as it applied in 2005, which states that "[b]y decree in the Conseil d'État, the Government may, on grounds of indignity or lack of assimilation other than linguistic, oppose the acquisition of French nationality by the foreign spouse".

The formal legal basis for the denial was not the religious attire per se, but rather the government's conclusion that Silmi had shown "insufficient assimilation" into the French Republic. In reality, however, as one astute legal observer noted, it remains uncertain whether Silmi was denied citizenship due to "her beliefs, or her conduct, or both" (Orgad 2010: 64). If we think of a country's immigration and citizenship law and policy as a porous membrane that reflects and discloses the qualities it values in its members-to-be, then the *Faiza M.* decision tells us something important about the state of citizenship today and the direction in which we may be heading. By denying an immigrant woman access to citizenship, the Conseil d'Etat left her in a dependent position vis-à-vis her husband, who already had a secure legal status in the state, and further politicized the debate over the "compatibility" of certain Islamic practices with both women's rights and the laïcité predominant in France's vision of citizenship – all while placing a substantial burden on women's (covered) heads and bodies (Nussbaum 2012; Volpp 2007).

This logic of incompatibility relies on an inflated dichotomy between culture ("them") and citizenship ("us"), and between symbols of subordination ("veiling") and of emancipation (the "naked face"), paradoxically reflecting a secular-absolutist vision of feminism that may end up leaving precisely those individuals it purports to defend in a vulnerable and dependent position, giving them only restricted access to the settlement and governmental services that new immigrants need most. A related debate, this one about the wearing of visible religious symbols – crosses, veils, turbans, and yarmulkes – during the provision or receipt of government services, is now brewing in Quebec. The view of those in favor of such a ban is informed by a particular vision of state neutrality that is then translated into a governmental prohibition of the personal display of religiosity in the public sphere. This vision rallies the identitarian claims of many members of the majority, while at the same time disproportionately burdening the religious freedoms of minorities and ignoring the intersection of overlapping affiliations in individuals' lives.

Is there a more fruitful approach that overcomes this predicament? I believe the answer is in the affirmative, although reaching it will require a healthy dose of hard-nosed imagination as well as innovative strategies for building the political will required to address the momentous challenge we face – namely, the challenge of determining how to nourish pathways to membership in both minority communities and the larger societies to which individuals belong in ways that will allow women, sexual minorities, and other historically vulnerable individuals to enjoy full and equal protection of their rights to cultural expression and substantive equality (Henrard, forthcoming; Shachar 2013). There are already promising developments that can guide us in thinking about how to get from here to there, but elaborating and fleshing these out is a task for the next generation of scholars and jurists.

Fair inclusion in the public sphere

No state is an island. And no state can be regarded as a *tabula rasa*. Each society makes collective choices about its official language(s), public holidays, and national symbols, choices that lead to some members feeling more welcome than others. Claims of fair inclusion are designed to overcome the "burdens, barriers, stigmatizations, and exclusions" that occur under laws and institutions that "purport to be neutral ... [but] are in fact implicitly tilted towards the needs, interests, and identities of the majority group" (Kymlicka and Norman 2000: 4). These are claims for equal respect and equal opportunity for members of non-dominant minority cultures in a diverse society, as well as calls to renegotiate the tripartite relationship between the state, the group, and the individual.

In the legal arena, fair inclusion refers to a wide range of exemption or accommodation measures which are designed to make it possible for religious and other minorities, if they so wish, to "express their cultural [or religious] particularity and pride without it hampering their success in the economic and political institutions of the dominant society" (Ryder 2008: 87). In the American tradition, the US Supreme Court's decision in *Sherbert*, termed a "high water mark" in the constitutional protection of minority religions, provides a textbook example. In that case, the Court held that a Seventh-day Adventist who was fired for refusing to work on her Sabbath could not be denied unemployment compensation. Under the *Sherbert* approach, religious freedoms may only be curtailed to further a compelling state interest, and only as a last resort. Even in last resort situations, the least restrictive means must be adopted.

Another illustration of fair inclusion is drawn from Canada, from a Supreme Court of Canada (2006) case called *Multani*. This case involved an 11-year-old Sikh immigrant, Gurjab Singh Multani, who was enrolled in a public school in Quebec. The Court considered whether the boy should be allowed to carry a *kirpan* (a ceremonial dagger) in accordance with his beliefs, even though his doing so created potential safety hazards and led to an apparent conflict with the school board's prohibition on weapons and dangerous objects. Indeed, the categorization of the *kirpan* as either a prohibited weapon (as the school board claimed) or an important religious symbol (the position of the pupil, his parents, and the interveners on behalf of the Sikh community) was at the heart of the dispute. In Canada, judges addressing a constitutional case of this nature will look to whether the state body being challenged curtailed the plaintiff's religious freedom in the "least drastic" way possible. A decision to ban the *kirpan* universally, the Court ruled, was not the least drastic means to address the rather limited potential of harm, especially considering the sincerity of the pupil's religious beliefs. The Court thus held in favor of Multani, the pupil, and in the process provided a resounding articulation of the fair inclusion vision of human rights and equal citizenship:

> The argument that the wearing of kirpans should be prohibited because the kirpan is a symbol of violence and because it sends the message that using force is necessary to assert rights and resolve conflict must fail. Not only is this assertion contradicted by the evidence regarding the symbolic nature of the kirpan, it is also disrespectful to believers in the Sikh religion and does not take into account Canadian values based on multiculturalism.
>
> *(Multani, para. 71)*

Translating this commitment into a social reality is, of course, a major challenge. But it typically begins by placing an obligation on various public and private institutions to create fair conditions of inclusion for those once excluded and marginalized (often under the color of state law) from equal membership in our shared public spaces and the realm of citizenship. Moving beyond the traditional anti-discrimination measures that focus on the removal of formal and official barriers, proponents of this vision of substantive equality before the law also advocate anti-subordination interpretations of our social relations and human rights protections (Balkin and Siegel 2003; Fiss 1976), envisioning "a heterogeneous public, in which persons stand forth with their differences acknowledged and respected" (Young 1990: 119).

Many other distinguished courts (whether national or supranational) have taken a less favorable view to minority-based fair inclusion claims than the Supreme Court of Canada, instead facilitating the "re-appropriation" of culture by members of dominant *majorities*. The *Lautsi* decision recently handed down by the Grand Chamber of the European Court of Human Rights (ECtHR), which sits in Strasburg at the apex of the European human rights system, offers a powerful illustration. In *Lautsi*, the Grand Chamber rejected the human rights claim of a Finnish-born mother residing in Italy who objected to the mandatory display of crucifixes in her sons' public school. Using the "margin of appreciation" technique, the Court held that there is no consensus among the contracting parties on the issue of religious symbols in public space, so that it is up to individual signatory states to determine whether or not to display the crucifix in schools. The Strasbourg Court did clarify, however, that the Italian tradition of display "confer[s] on the country's majority religion preponderant visibility in the school environment" (*Lautsi*, para. 71), though it held that such visibility did not reach the prohibited level of indoctrination of young pupils. In effect, this meant that non-Christian children and those professing no religion will continue to be educated under the cross – literally – in Italian state schools. In earlier stages of this legal dispute, Italy argued that in a non-religious context like a school, the crucifix carries a different meaning: it is not a religious emblem (as it would be in a place of worship) but a universal and inclusive symbol of tolerance. This reversal of meanings – a majoritarian religious icon being turned into a national symbol of tolerance and "the foundation of our civil life" (as Italy put it) – not only reaffirms the standing and privilege of the dominant majority, but also turns the minority claimants into the "intolerant" ones by implying that they have failed to understand the inclusive intent of the majority.

Privatized diversity in family law

The bulk of the literature on citizenship, multiculturalism, and human rights has focused on the aspirations of fair inclusion, while almost completely ignoring the challenges raised by privatized diversity, which are most actually manifested in the fields of education and family law. A dramatic example of this trend is found in the acrimonious and globally important debates that broke out in Canada during the opening decade of the twenty-first century over the possibility of using faith-based principles to resolve, in a binding fashion, a range of family and inheritance disputes among consenting parties by turning to extralegal, alternative sources of authority and identity. In their most extreme variants, demands for privatized diversity amount to a call for the secular state (through its manifold institutions and agencies) to adopt a hands-off approach whereby private religious arbitration tribunals give parties an unrestrained choice of forum and choice of law, and operate, as it were, in a completely unregulated and parallel domain of service provision "untouched" by established legal norms and values. On this account, respect for religious freedom or cultural integrity does not require inclusion in the public sphere, but *exclusion* from it.

This potential storm-to-come must be addressed head on. Privatized diversity involves a mix of three inflammatory components of today's political environment: religion, gender, and the rise of the neoliberal state. The volatility of these issues is undisputed; they require a mere spark to ignite. In England, a scholarly and nuanced lecture by none other than Rowan Williams, the former Archbishop of Canterbury (the head of the Church of England/Anglican Church), which explored the relations between civil and religious law and proposed further accommodation of the latter within the former (Williams 2008), has provoked zealous criticism from across the political spectrum. In the United States the debate has taken a different twist: recently, a slew of state legislatures passed amendments that "preempt" and prevent the use of religious principles in courts, arbitrations, or mediations, specifically singling out both Shari'a law and international law as competing normative orders that must be avoided (Helfand 2010).

With this background in mind, we can see why Rowan Williams's lecture and the Shari'a tribunal debate in Canada provoked such uproar. These proposals were seen as challenging the normative and juridical authority, not to mention the legitimacy, of the state's asserted mandate to represent and regulate the interests and rights of *all* its citizens in their family-law affairs, as well as its liberal democratic telos to protect their rights more generally, irrespective of communal affiliation. In this respect, the turn to religious private ordering raises profound questions concerning hierarchy and lexical order in law and citizenship: which norms *should* prevail? And who, or what entity, ought to have the final word in resolving value conflicts between equality and diversity, should they arise? The regulatory state retains an interest in marriage and divorce for public policy reasons, including its interest in promoting gender equality and children's welfare and in lessening the impact of family breakdown on third parties. But it is no longer, if it ever has been, the only force that matters. Historically, of the conflicting claimants to authority in family law, it is the state, not the church, that is the newcomer. Gaining the upper hand in regulating matters of the family has always been significant both politically and jurisdictionally. It represented the solidification of power in the hands of secular authorities, a symbol of modern state-building. As historian Nancy Cott observes, "For as long as the past millennium in the Christian West, the exercise of formal power over marriage has been a prime means of exerting and manifesting public authority" (Cott 1995: 108).

Even today, the family remains a crucial nexus where both collective identity and gendered relations are manifested (Cott 2000; Shachar 2001; Yuval-Davis and Anthias 1989). The stakes are particularly high for women. Marriage and divorce rules govern matters of status and property, as well as a woman's right to divorce and remarry, and her legal relationship with her children. At the same time, the approach taken to marriage and divorce is crucially important to minority communities that wish to maintain their communal definition of membership boundaries. Religious minorities in secular societies are typically non-territorial entities; unlike certain national or linguistic communities (think of the Québécois in Canada, the Catalans in Spain, and so on), they have no semi-autonomous subunit in which they constitute a majority or have the power to define the public symbols that manifest, and in turn help preserve, their distinctive national or linguistic heritage. These minority communities are thus forced to find other ways to sustain their distinct traditions and ways of life. With no authority to issue formal documents of membership, to regulate mobility, or to raise revenues through mandatory taxes, religious family laws that define marriage, divorce, and lineage come to play an important role in regulating membership boundaries. They demarcate a pool of individuals as endowed with the collective responsibility to maintain the group's values, practices, and distinct ways of life (if they maintain their standing as members in that community). This is family law's demarcating function (Shachar 2001). As an analytical matter, secular and religious norms may lead to broadly similar results, may coexist despite tensions, may point in different directions, or may directly contradict each other. It is the last of these possibilities that is seen to pose the greatest challenge to the authoritativeness of the modern state.

The contours of dynamic interaction

Instead of asking women caught in the knots of these potentially rivalrous legal orders to leave their cultural worlds behind, the lessons of the new age of diversity and its social imaginary (Vertovec 2012) encourage us to consider respecting a woman's agency and choice if she voluntarily turns to non-binding religious sources for advice so long as nothing is then asked of her that would breach the basic rights and protections she has as a member of the larger society to which she belongs as an equal. We can think of such joint-governance arrangements as facilitating freedom for individuals to turn to communal authorities to assist them with the removal of religious barriers to remarriage (e.g. the *get*, the Jewish divorce decree, or the *khula*, a divorce proceeding that can be initiated by the Muslim wife), while turning to a family judge or secular arbitrator to resolve any related property, child custody, or support obligations. This approach discourages an underworld of unregulated religious dispute resolution and offers a path around the either/or choice between culture and rights, family and state, citizenship and group membership. The next step in my analysis is to investigate whether a carefully regulated recognition of multiple legal affiliations – and the subtle interactions among them – can permit devout women to benefit from the protections offered by the secular order without abandoning the tenets of their faith.

The ambition, easier to define than to implement, is to find a more fruitful approach that overcomes the predicament by placing the interests of women – as citizens, mothers, human-rights bearers, and members of a faith, to mention but a few of their multiple responsibilities and affiliations – at the center of the analysis. Arguably, the obligation to engage in just such renegotiation is pressing in light of the growing demands to reevaluate the relations between state and religion the world over. From the perspective of women caught in the web of overlapping and potentially competing systems of secular and divine law, the almost automatic rejection of any attempt to establish a forum for resolving standing disputes related to the religious dimension of their marriage might respect the protection-of-rights dimension of their lived experience, but does little to address the cultural or religious affiliation issue. The latter may well be better addressed by attending to the removal of religious barriers to remarriage, which does not automatically flow from a civil release of the marriage bond. This is particularly true for observant women who have solemnized their marriage relationship according to the requirements of their religious tradition, and who may now wish – or feel bound – to receive the blessing of that tradition for the dissolution of that relationship.

In a world of increased mobility across borders, these pressures also acquire a transnational dimension. In Great Britain, for example, many Muslim families with roots in more than one country (e.g. the UK and Pakistan) perceive a divorce or annulment decree that complies with both the demands of the faith (as a non-territorial identity community) and those of the secular state in which they reside as somehow more "transferable" across different Muslim jurisdictions. In technical terms, this need not be the case: private international law norms are based on the laws of states, *not* of religions (Carrol 1997). But what matters here is the *perception* that an Islamic council dealing with religious release from marriage may provide a valuable legal service to its potential clientele, a service that the secular state – by virtue of its formal divorce from religion – simply cannot provide.

These acute challenges cannot be fully captured by our existing legal categories. They require a new vocabulary and a fresh approach. In the space remaining I will briefly sketch the contours of such an approach, *dynamic interaction*, by asking what is owed to those women whose legal dilemmas (at least in the family-law arena) arise from the fact that their lives have *already* been affected by the interplay between overlapping systems of identification, authority, and belief – in this case, religious and secular law. The Jewish test case of the *agunah* (pl. *agunot*), a woman whose marriage is functionally over but whose husband refuses to issue or grant a writ of Jewish divorce (a *get*), will serve as an illustrative example. In contrast with privatized diversity, the alternative I develop invites both the state and the faith community to accommodate individuals who are already entangled in both secular and religious bonds. Many jurisdictions permit the solemnization of marriage by recognized religious, tribal, or customary officials, and thereby allow a degree of regulated interaction between state and non-state traditions at the point of entry into marriage. At least in theory, there is no reason not to implement a similar kind of coordination at the point of *exit* from such a relationship. Indeed, this is already a reality in some jurisdictions. English law, for example, now permits collaboration between family courts and Rabbinical tribunals (*beth din*, pl. *battei din*) to ensure the removal of religious barriers to remarriage, as does the famous New York "*get* law." Such engagement and coordination across the secular–religious divide is informed by a commitment to substantive (rather than merely formal) equality. It is designed to allow individuals with multiple belongings the same freedoms as other citizens – in this context, the right to be released from a dead marriage and to build a new family if they so wish. Taken to its logical conclusion, engagement in dynamic interaction can be understood as a form of fair inclusion that tames and resists the opposing centrifugal and harmful tendencies of privatized diversity.

The motivation for this kind of interaction is the need to integrate diversity *with* equality. This is not a prescription likely to be favored by advocates of privatized diversity, who claim authority to define and enforce a "pure" or "authentic" manifestation of a distinct cultural or religious identity in the face of real or imagined threats. Such self-proclaimed "guardians of the faith" wish to impose rigid readings of what are arguably more flexible and malleable traditions, and threaten to stifle interpretative debates within the religious community itself about the potential adoption of more gender-friendly readings of sacred texts and the tradition that evolved from them. For those advocating variants of "retro-traditionalism" (Moghadam 1994), it is convenient to portray the constitutional state as an external "enemy," a foreign intruder that has no interest in truly recognizing or accommodating the special needs of the faithful. Such hyperbolic arguments, whether falsifiable or not, then serve as a pretext for encouraging community members to "contract out" of the kind of protections they are guaranteed as citizens and human-rights bearers, all as part of an agenda to establish unofficial and privatized "islands of jurisdictions" that lie outside the governance of such secular orders. No less significant, such pressures can also be utilized within minority communities to legitimize strict readings of traditional rules and practices that breach women's hard-earned rights with respect to marriage, divorce, property, and a host of other issues. In the process, these pressures obscure a critical reality: traditions are always contested, but marginalized women rarely have a say in shaping them.

The alternative approach I propose can break the cycle of silencing and radicalization that privatized diversity facilitates. Adherents of the faith are simultaneously citizens of the state and members of the larger family of humanity. Even religious communities that seek to build walls around their members find that a diffusion of human-rights ideas and resources is already occurring. Indeed, constructivist understandings of culture submit that such interactions are a major reason for the rise of "retro" and more radical interpretations of traditions that claim to purify it from the corrosive effects of the outside world (Benhabib 2002; Moghadam 1994; Shachar 2001; Song 2007). Assuming that such direct and indirect influences are ongoing, there is "no neutral position for the state here: action and inaction both have consequences for the distribution of power and [authority] inside the cultural community" (Williams 2011: 71). Given that cultural and religious traditions are never as uncontested or as inflexible as advocates of privatized diversity would like us to believe, there is, inevitably, a need for minority communities, as well as dominant majorities, to find creative answers to the ongoing challenges of interacting with the multiple pressures around them, whether above or below the state level. For those *within* the community who reject the wholesale option of privatized diversity but wish to uphold the most precious aspect of personal status law from the perspective of their faith (such as the ability to define the community's membership boundaries and avoid a breach of a strict prohibition), a vision of dynamic interaction offers a viable alternative.

Entertaining just such possibilities, courts and legislatures have recently broken new ground by adopting what we might refer to as "intersectionist" or "joint governance" remedies. One example is found in *Bruker* v. *Marcovitz*, in which the Supreme Court of Canada explicitly rejected the simplistic "your culture or your rights" formula. Instead, the Court developed a nuanced and context-sensitive analysis, which begins from the ground up by seeking to identify who is harmed and why and then proceeds to find a remedy that satisfies, as much as possible, the commitment to diversity and equality. Such an approach, the Court held, is consistent with, not contrary to, public order. Moreover, it harmonizes with Canada's approach to religious freedom, to equality rights, and to divorce and remarriage generally, and it has been judicially recognized internationally. In England, the recent decision in *AI* v. *MT* exhibits a similar logic and represents another step in the direction of finding compatibilities among different sources of law and identity that already intersect in women's lived experience and that matter greatly for their sense of self and their membership in the multiple communities to which they are attached as rights and culture bearers.

Despite persistent, and at times oppressive, attempts by the modern state to monopolize the power to regulate law and identity, other relations and values have retained a hefty influence in this significant realm of life. The resulting issues are among the most complex and sensitive matters that need to be addressed in today's diverse societies. Alas, the almost automatic response of insisting on the disentanglement of state and church (or mosque, synagogue, and so forth) in the regulation of the family may not always work to the benefit of female religious citizens who are deeply attached to, and influenced by, *both* systems of law and identity. Their complex claim for full inclusion in both the state and the group is grounded in their multilayered connections to both systems. Empowering the once voiceless has always been a central mission of human rights. To reach this goal, we sometimes require fresh ideas and innovative institutional designs that challenge settled conventions. The assumption that it is impossible to grant consideration to religious diversity and gender equality at the same time is one convention that ought to be so challenged.

References

Adhar, R. and Leigh, I. (2005) *Religious Freedom in the Liberal State*, Oxford, UK: Oxford University Press.

Balkin, J.M. and Siegel, R.B. (2003) 'The American Civil Rights Tradition: Anticlassification or Anti-subordination', *Issues in Legal Scholarship*, 2(1): article 11.

Banting, K. and Kymlicka, W. (2013) 'Is There Really a Retreat from Multiculturalism Policies? New Evidence from the Multiculturalism Policy Index', *Comparative European Politics*, 11(5): 557–98.

Barro, R.J. and McCleary, R.M. (2005) 'Which Countries Have State Religions?', *The Quarterly Journal of Economics*, 120(4): 1331–70.

Beck, U. (2006) *The Cosmopolitan Vision*, Cambridge, UK: Polity.

Benhabib, S. (2002) *The Claims of Culture: Equality and Diversity in the Global Era*, Princeton, NJ: Princeton University Press.

Carrol, L. (1997) 'Muslim Women and "Islamic Divorce" in England', *Journal of Muslim Minority Affairs*, 17(1): 97–115.

Cott, N.F. (1995) 'Giving Character to our Whole Civil Polity: Marriage and the Public Order in the Late Nineteenth Century', in L.K. Kerber, A. Kessler-Harris and K. Kish Sklar (eds) *U.S. History as Women's History: New Feminist Essays*, Chapel Hill, NC: University of North Carolina Press.

—(2000) *Public Vows: A History of Marriage and the Nation*, Cambridge, MA: Harvard University Press.

European Court of Human Rights (2011) *Lautsi v Italy*. Online Available HTTP: <//www.echr.coe.int/echr/en/hudoc> (accessed 25 April 2014)

Fiss, O.M. (1976) 'Groups and the Equal Protection Clause', *Philosophy and Public Affairs*, 5(2): 107–77.

Helfand, M.A. (2010) 'Religious Arbitration and the New Multiculturalism: Negotiating Conflicting Legal Orders', *New York University Law Review*, 86(5): 1231–305.

Henrard, K. (forthcoming) 'Minorities', Oxford, UK: Oxford University Press.

Hirschl, R. and Shachar, A. (2009) 'The New Wall of Separation: Permitting Diversity, Restricting Competition', *Cardozo Law Review*, 30(6): 2535–60.

Howard, E. (2011) *Law and the Wearing of Religious Symbols: European Bans on the Wearing of Religious Symbols in Education*, London: Routledge.

Kymlicka, W. (1995) *Multicultural Citizenship: A Liberal Theory of Minority Rights*, Oxford, UK: Oxford University Press.

Kymlicka, W. and Norman, W. (2000) 'Citizenship in Culturally Diverse Societies: Issues, Contexts, Concepts', in W. Kymlicka and W. Norman (eds) *Citizenship in Diverse Societies*, Oxford, UK: Oxford University Press.

Laborde, C. (2008) *Critical Republicanism: The Hijab Controversy and Political Philosophy*, Oxford, UK: Oxford University Press.

Moghadam, V.M. (ed.) (1994) *Identity Politics and Women: Cultural Reassertions and Feminism in International Perspectives*, Boulder, CO: Westview.

Nussbaum, C.M. (2012) *The New Religious Intolerance: Overcoming the Politics of Fear in an Anxious Age*, Cambridge, MA: Harvard University Press.

Orgad, L. (2010) Illiberal Liberalism Cultural Restrictions on Migration and Access to Citizenship in Europe, *American Journal of Comparative Law*, 58(1): 53–105.

Parekh, B. (2002) *Rethinking Multiculturalism: Cultural Diversity and Political Theory*, Cambridge, MA: Harvard University Press.

Quane, H. (2013) 'Legal Pluralism and International Human Rights Law: Inherently Incompatible, Mutually Reinforcing or Something in Between?', *Oxford Journal of Legal Studies*, 33(4): 675–702.

Ryder, B. (2008) 'The Canadian Conception of Equal Religious Citizenship', in R. Moon (ed.) *Law and Religious Pluralism in Canada*, Vancouver: University of British Columbia Press.

Shachar, A. (2001) *Multicultural Jurisdictions: Cultural Differences and Women's Rights*, Cambridge, UK: Cambridge University Press.

—(2008) 'Privatizing Diversity: A Cautionary Tale from Religious Arbitration in Family Law', *Theoretical Inquiries in Law*, 9(2): 573–607.

—(2013) 'Entangled: Family, Religion and Human Rights', in C. Holder and D. Reidy (eds) *Human Rights: The Hard Questions*, Cambridge, UK: Cambridge University Press.

Song, S. (2007) *Justice, Gender, and the Politics of Multiculturalism*, Cambridge, UK: Cambridge University Press.

Stone, S.L. (2008) 'Religion and State: Models of Separation from Within Jewish Law', *International Journal of Constitutional Law*, 6(3–4): 631–61.

Supreme Court of Canada (2006) *Multani v. Commission Scolaire*. Online. Available HTTP: <://www.law. yale.edu/documents/pdf/Intellectual_Life/Multani_v._Comm._scolaire_Marguerite-Bourgeoys.pdf > (accessed 25 April 2014).

Vertovec, S. (2012) '"Diversity" and the Social Imaginary', *European Journal of Sociology*, 53(3): 287–312.

Vertovec, S. and Wessendorf, S. (eds) (2010) *The Multiculturalism Backlash: European Discourses, Policies, and Practices*, London: Routledge.

Volpp, L. (2007) 'The Culture of Citizenship', *Theoretical Inquiries in Law*, 8(2): 571–602.

Williams, R. (2008) 'Archbishop of Canterbury Lecture at the Royal Court of Justice, Civil and Religious Law in England: A Religious Perspective'. Online. Available HTTP: <http://www. archbishopofcanterbury.org/1575> (accessed 7 February 2008).

Williams, S.H. (2011) 'Democracy, Gender Equality, and Customary Law: Constitutionalizing Internal Cultural Disruption', *Indiana Journal of Global Legal Studies*, 18(1): 65–85.

Young, I.M. (1990) *Justice and the Politics of Difference*, Princeton, NJ: Princeton University Press.

Yuval-Davis, N. and Anthias, F. (1989) *Woman-Nation-State*, London: Palgrave Macmillan.

26

Diversity and social welfare

To restrict or include?

Jenny Phillimore

Diversity is, to a greater or lesser extent, a feature of all societies. Originating in the biological sciences, and used initially predominantly in relation to biodiversity – the degree of variation of life forms – the term is now used in many different fields. In the social sciences, diversity discourse emerged from the US minority rights movement in the 1960s, and while its use has been extended from race and ethnicity to include gender and disability it is still mainly associated with ethnicity and migration (Vertovec 2012), the focus of this chapter. Although in the biological sciences there is broad agreement that high levels of biodiversity signify a healthy ecosystem, there is much debate about the extent to which diversity is good for society. In recent times the debate about the relative positives and negatives of diversity has featured within the field of social policy. Both within social policy as a discipline that concerns itself with the study of social issues and their causes and resolutions, and the development of policies aimed at achieving social purposes, the nature, role and impact of diversity are receiving increasing attention. This has particularly been the case over the past 20 years as globalisation has amplified levels of integration in societies through communication, transportation and trade and the speed and scale of population movement has increased.

In particular, concerns about the impact of increasing population diversity have played out around access to social welfare: the arrangements made by states for 'coping with collective risks and reducing inequality' (Mau and Burkhardt 2009: 213). Welfare states and the regimes that underpin them are generally associated with the nation state and meeting the needs of those who are seen as both belonging and to be deserving of support. It is possible to trace a connection between fears about increased diversity, immigration control and denial of social rights over a century; for example, in the 1905 Aliens Act in the UK it was intended to deny entry to paupers or criminals – in reality at the time of high levels of Jewish immigration from Eastern Europe – who were deemed both ethnically and religiously diverse (Humphries 2004). However, the majority of political attention to diversity, social policy and the welfare state has occurred since the 1950s as migration increasingly became a feature of life in Europe and Black Americans' demands for equal rights began to attract attention.

Growing political attention to, and policy focus on, diversity and access to social welfare have not been matched in the discipline of social policy. Introducing critical social policy, Fiona Williams (1989) highlighted the neglect of both race and gender and the uncritical acceptance of assumptions about the breadwinner role, whiteness and the responsibility of culture for unequal outcomes in both the design of social policies and academic analysis of their development, operation and impact. She and several others note the lack of attention paid to diversity in social policy as 'the welfare state was assumed to be colour blind and so already an engine of equality' (Fitzpatrick 2005: 299) and the study of ethnicity treated as a specialism (Vickers *et al.* 2012), neglected in comparative welfare research (Sainsbury 2006) or undertaken only at a local level (Bhopal 2012; Cochrane *et al.* 2001), thus failing to focus on structural underpinnings of inequality. Some commentators even consider that social policy analysts have compounded the development of racist and sexist social policy by failing to examine power differentials, reifying culture and problematising minorities as being responsible for their own exclusion. While efforts such as equalities legislation in the UK and Civil Rights laws in the USA compel researchers to ensure the use of diverse samples, overly simplistic ideas of ethnicity and biology and associated sampling techniques have over-emphasised biology, particularly in quantitative research, while failing to look at structural and social characteristics and their role in determining social outcomes (Epstein 2008).

Much effort has been made by social policy analysts to categorise social welfare regimes (see Esping-Anderson 1990). Welfare regimes tend to over-simplify the influences on policy development but do provide useful categories for comparing social welfare provision at a national level. While the theory around these regimes neglects diversity and provision for minority groups, the key fault lines around what determines provision, rights based upon need, citizenship or work, provide a basis with which to consider the relationship between diversity and social welfare. Liberal and Conservative regimes offer the lowest levels of provision, often relying on contributions made by those in employment. Such regimes are thought to be the least generous for migrants and minorities who make lower levels of contribution than the general population because of their vulnerability to unemployment or low paid employment (Avato *et al.* 2010). Social-democratic regimes are based upon the idea of universalism with generous state benefits available based upon citizenship which may not be available to all minorities or migrants despite length of residence. Mediterranean models rely heavily on the extended family for provision of social support, which may be problematic for those whose family live overseas.

Whether rights to welfare are granted to migrants also depends on the immigration policy regime that is operating. Castles and Miller (2009) point to exclusionary, assimilationist and multicultural approaches each with its own set of expectations about the role of migrants in society and the extent to which social needs, sometimes seen as relating specifically to language and culture, should be met by welfare providers. Access to, and outcomes from, social welfare for minority ethnic groups and migrants are argued to be influenced by a combination of national welfare regime and immigration policy regime (Sainsbury 2006) and the moral justifications made by policymakers in introducing and seeking support for associated policies (Dean 2011). There is little work that has considered the interaction between welfare and immigration regimes (see Sainsbury 2006), largely resulting from the general neglect of diversity in welfare research (as already outlined) but also due to the complexity of creating categories and typologies by over-generalising characteristics that are themselves highly complex and variable at regional, national and supra-national levels.

Perhaps the main area of focus for social policy researchers in relation to diversity is that of deservingness. In the USA, Gilens (1996) shows there is a racial dimension to deservingness, with the majority population believing that black people are lazier and less responsible than white people and more likely to be welfare recipients. Meanwhile, with these beliefs being held, support for welfare provision is low and services are restricted for all. In the EU there has been much debate about whether increasing diversity will lead, or has led, to reduced social solidarity.

The presence of solidarity – the willingness to contribute to welfare systems, providing a safety net for the general population – is said to be critical to the preservation of the welfare state and avoidance of a US type situation. Goodhart (2004) argues that people want to share with those who share their values, while Putnam (2007) argues that trust is critical to solidarity. Without the belief that people are sufficiently similar to ourselves, and equally deserving, it is argued that moral commitment to the welfare state will be undermined. In particular, research has focused on the role of immigration in relation to support for welfare provision. Analyses of the European Social Survey demonstrate that there is considerable evidence to suggest that immigrants are seen as the least deserving of all groups (Van Oorschot 2006). Certainly there are signs of widespread public anxiety about the impact of immigration on public services, with concerns about infectious disease, strain on services and housing and job shortages played out in the media and agitated by emerging new right political parties (Arai 2005). Attitudes to redistribution are mediated by public discourse and politicisation. Carmel and Cerami (2011) point to the emotive language used by both journalists and politicians in relation to policymaking around migration and welfare states, with a 'siege mentality' promoted by the media (Schierup *et al.* 2006: 22).

Yet other evidence shows that, rather than diversity undermining the welfare state, people want to see the emergence of a dual welfare system with immigrants demonstrating a commitment to their new country through gaining employment and seeking naturalisation (Miller 2006). There is no clear evidence that immigration reduces commitment to redistribution (Burgoon *et al.* 2012) or that perceived religious, ethnic or cultural differences lead to lack of solidarity. Instead it is clear that solidarity can emerge from economic integration and political citizenship (Myles and St-Arnaud 2006). Certainly, experience in Canada, which has enjoyed both increased immigration and an expanding welfare state, provides evidence that increased immigration and diversity do not necessarily undermine welfare states. Canada's largely contributory welfare system, celebration of immigration and strong naturalisation programme may be explanatory factors (Soroka *et al.* 2006).

In the past decade, austerity and associated workfare regimes have emerged in many states as they seek to reduce welfare expenditure while a shift to social cohesion promotes a move from social citizenship to civic citizenship, wherein long term migrants have civic and political rights but not full nationality, and different categories of migrants have differential access to welfare (Banting 2000). With the general population prepared to include working migrants and workfare making benefits available to those in need, or to those who have made contributions, in theory it should be possible for migrants to access welfare on the same basis as the general population and for established minorities to have equal access to welfare. However, the increased use of welfare as a tool of restrictionalism has impacted upon access. Several authors have outlined the use of welfare as a tool of restrictionalist migration policy (Bloch 2000; Geddes 2000; Lewis 2003; Sales 2002). Restrictionalism, also labelled welfare chauvinism, emerged from political concern about the availability of benefits acting as an incentive and attracting migrants (Geddes 2000; Home Office, UK 2007) and also that the voting public viewed migrants as scroungers (Law 2009). It has subsequently proliferated in the form of

> . . . internal differentiation of migration types [which] means that the relation of immigrants to the welfare state is internally highly differentiated dependent on their legal/residential status and labour market position.
>
> *(Ryner 2000: 67)*

A whole range of different measures, including no recourse to public funds for those joining families, the detention of asylum seekers or their accommodation in camps, exclusion of unsuccessful asylum seekers from some secondary health care, preventing asylum seekers from accessing employment and exclusion of economic migrants from some benefits, serve as but a few examples of restrictionism. Law (2009) points to the re-racialisation of welfare, as welfare benefits increasingly have conditions attached to them stating the ineligibility of persons subject to immigration control. In addition, the complexity of regulations and eligibility has put service providers under great pressure and led, it is argued, to those unable to prove their status being excluded from services (Maffia 2008; Mir 2007). Restrictionism is said to have culminated in poor welfare outcomes for migrants and immigrants experiencing high levels of unemployment, poor housing conditions, low levels of educational attainment and poor health outcomes as exclusion has become tinged by ethnification (Schierup et al. 2006). The FRA (2011) points to differential access to healthcare, particularly for undocumented migrants and failed asylum seekers, contradicting WHO guidance and European Human Rights legislation and the desires of welfare professionals. Such approaches are argued to reduce cost-effectiveness of health services and potentially damage public health, and are evident even in countries such as Sweden with its generous social-democratic welfare regime and multicultural immigration regime.

With civic citizenship all important to belonging and acquiring full access to social welfare and, as we have seen, to acceptance by the general population, naturalisation might be argued to be critical to ensuring that migrants can settle in countries of migration. Yet accessing citizenship has become increasingly difficult as countries raise the bar for those who wish to naturalise. In the last decade eligibility criteria for naturalisation have toughened in many countries (MIPEX 2013) and look set to become increasingly dependent on language ability and income.

While migrants have limited access to social welfare services, which depend upon their immigration and employment status, established minorities who have gained access to citizenship or were born in their country of residence have full access to labour markets and the welfare state, yet poor outcomes are observed in many social policy areas with what Atkin and Chattoo (2007: 378) describe as 'depressing familiarity'. Analysis of survey data such as the European Social Survey and the US General Social Survey have evidenced poor outcomes in education, health and housing (Craig 2007), higher unemployment, residential segregation and discrimination in access to finance (Ahmad and Craig 2003). Little research has explored how minority groups use services (Arai 2005) and why inequalities exist. It is widely acknowledged that in the early days of migration to Europe social welfare services were colour blind. There is evidence of a lack of recognition of the needs of minority groups in policy and of widespread use of myths about biological characteristics that make some ethnic groups either more or less likely to experience problems or provide social support to each other, thereby sidelining the state (Chahal 2004). The tendency to blame the victim for poor outcomes – either their culture or perceived biological characteristics – while failing to recognise or question racism, is commonplace (Atkin and Chattoo 2007; Craig 2007).

In countries such as the UK and Sweden multicultural social policies have, at least until recent austerity cuts and the backlash against multiculturalism, been relatively widespread in urban areas. Such approaches, wherein culturally specific services such as interpretation and translation were offered and ethnic minority staff employed (Chahal 2004), were made available on the basis that special services, outside of the mainstream, could help meet the specific needs of minority groups. However services were not universally available. They could only practically be provided where a critical mass of people from one ethnic background was present. Furthermore they did nothing to address the wider structural problems and institutionalised racism that shape access to, and experiences of, key social policy resources: employment, housing, education and health services. Thus, ethnic minority and migrant groups continue to be among the core poverty groups in Europe (Van Oorschot 2006), while Black and Hispanic Americans are three times more likely to be impoverished than white Americans (NPC 2013). Although many countries have introduced anti-discrimination and race-relations legislation, this tends to operate at local or community levels, and the taken for granted assumptions that lead to discriminatory outcomes combined with the uncritical application of social policy and procedures mean that many problems endure despite repeated initiatives (Vickers *et al.* 2012).

Minorities and migrants continue to experience poor social policy outcomes, yet they are the main providers of social welfare at both an institutional and a domestic level (Kofman *et al.* 2000). Much of the labour migration to Europe between the 1950s and the 1970s commenced in response to labour shortages in emerging welfare states, and this migration continues today, with established minority groups continuing to play important roles in the provision of social welfare (Lewis 2003). A clear racialised and gendered division of labour is in evidence, with low paid work almost exclusively undertaken by minorities (Cochrane *et al.* 2001) and migrants imported as units of labour rather than people with needs of their own (Clarke *et al.* 2001). Women's entrance to the labour market in the developed world has seen the shift of domestic caring responsibilities from the home to informally or privately provided child or elder care, much of which is dependent upon female migrant labour working at, or below, minimum wage level (Kofman *et al.* 2000).

With the gradual realisation that ethnic diversity is a permanent feature of societies in the developed world, a new field of social policy has emerged focusing upon migrant settlement and acculturation and inter-ethnic relations. There has been much academic debate about the nature of integration and the extent to which it is a means of assimilation or encourages social cohesion, the key features (Ager and Strang 2004) or measurements of integration (Phillimore and Goodson 2008), whether it is a process (Bhatia and Ram 2009) and what migrants should integrate into (Hall 1990). In policy terms there appears to be a consensus that both new and old migrants and their descendants should become integrated through being economically active, adopting the mother tongue of their country of migration, adapting to behave in culturally appropriate ways and socially mixing with the mainstream population.

As integration continues to dominate national debates around migration and ethnic diversity, little consideration is given to the incremental approach to integration that occurs when migrants and minorities have different rights according to status and length of residence (Schierup *et al.* 2006) and minorities fail to achieve their potential. The role of the state or the general population is a much neglected dimension in the debate around integration (Phillimore 2012), where ever more emphasis is placed upon migrants to integrate or build social cohesion with majority communities. Furthermore, as attitudes to migrants and minorities harden amongst the public and politicians, greater emphasis has been placed on welfare professionals to act as gatekeepers. Social workers, doctors and others are increasingly expected to adopt an authoritarian stance and shift from being care-givers to de facto immigration officials obliged to ascertain individuals' migration status before offering services and to contact the immigration authorities to report identified 'offenders' (Duvell and Jordan 2002; Humphries 2004).

In the face of such regimes, minorities and migrants are increasingly turning to the voluntary sector for help, setting up their own voluntary organisations and acting as mediators in their own welfare by establishing services to help themselves and others (FRA 2011; Kofman *et al.* 2000). Thus, migrant, refugee and community groups have taken a key role in the provision of, or brokering of access to, welfare, providing services with low levels of funding accessed from local, national or supra-national resources (FRA 2011). These organisations have tended to be viewed by welfare professionals as repositories of knowledge about minority communities, and much pressure has been placed on over-stretched small, voluntary or community organisations to meet the needs of growing numbers of migrants and minorities. While there is some evidence that they are able to meet needs more effectively than core services, they are marginal to policy development (Chahal 2004), lacking the time, resources and influence to bring their specialist knowledge to help reshape mainstream social policies based around taken for granted assumptions that lead to discriminatory outcomes (Phillimore and Goodson 2010; Vickers *et al.* 2012).

Despite 50 years of migration in Europe, the Black rights movement in the USA, the acceptance and celebration of ethnic diversity in Australia and Canada and the recognition of, and in some cases attempt to meet the needs of, diversity in social policies across the developed world, extensive ethnic or racial inequalities endure. Although there is no doubt that the politics of recognition have led to the acknowledgement, and perhaps the simultaneous essentialisation, of specialist needs (Atkin and Chattoo 2007; Taylor 1994), and there have been improvements in outcomes for some ethnic groups, it is clear that social policy has failed ethnic, racial and migrant minorities. As we enter an era of superdiversity, the unresolved problems of the last half a century are likely to be amplified. The remainder of this chapter will explore some of the challenges and opportunities that superdiversity has brought for social policy and how they might be addressed.

Vertovec (2004) coined the term 'superdiversity' to describe the emergence of diversity that supersedes anything experienced before. The key features of superdiversity – its scale, spread, speed of change, complexity, fragmentation and multi-layering – all represent challenges and opportunities for social policy provision. Much of the developed, and many developing, countries are seeing far greater numbers of arrivals, from many more countries than ever before. Furthermore these new arrivals often come in small groups, do not live in ethnic or country of origin communities (as has often been the case in earlier migrations), often move around their country of migration or supra-national region and have different immigration statuses and associated rights and entitlements to social welfare. Emergent superdiverse communities are thus not fixed, less likely than longer-established groups to establish organisations to meet their needs, or seek to influence policy, and have languages, cultures and social problems that are both novel and complex (see Phillimore, forthcoming).

The mechanisms employed previously if, and when, social policy providers have sought to meet the needs of diverse communities – specialist services based around perceived cultural needs of minorities – are no longer feasible in places like Birmingham, UK (arrivals from 187 countries), Toronto (over 200 ethnic groups) and Sao Paulo (over 100 countries of origin). The absence of a critical mass of migrants or minorities sharing at least a language and some knowledge of the workings of welfare states means that newcomers lack a source of information about institutional cultures. With movement and increased transnationality becoming increasingly common, change rather than stability has become the norm. In the absence of fixedness, welfare professionals are increasingly expected to police access to the welfare state by understanding and implementing rights of access to services that are dependent on migration status, while they are struggling to understand and provide for need (Phillimore 2011). While such transiency and complexity is particularly an issue in urban escalator areas (Travers *et al.* 2007) where it is demonstrated that administrative costs associated with movement are onerous; superdiversity and change are becoming part of life in smaller urban, and rural, areas.

Governments have attempted to use immigration policy to reduce pressures on social welfare by toughening entry requirements or increasing welfare restrictionalism, but have failed spectacularly and have perhaps even compounded problems around complexity. The ways that we have traditionally sought to plan welfare services at the local and regional level have depended upon knowing who resided in those areas, using knowledge based upon previous trends to make predictions about likely need, seeking to consult service users and designing services accordingly about their needs. We lack much of this information. It might be argued that previous research undertaken by social policy analysts has done little to resolve unequal outcomes perpetuating the problematising of minorities and reinforcing stereotypes (Atkin and Chattoo 2007). In addition, emphasis in social policy on exploring the impacts of migration or ethnicity on social welfare provision or the health outcomes of diverse groups has depended upon over-generalised categories consisting of a handful of ethnic groups, with migrants defined as those born overseas, and a growing category of 'other' ethnicity that now makes up 25 per cent of ethnic minorities in some UK cities. These approaches cannot and do not capture the complexity associated with superdiversity and mean that social problems experienced by individuals outside key ethnic groups or along other dimensions are not identified, let alone addressed.

We cannot prevent at national level global forces of movement and change. So we need to plan for change and complexity and to introduce new approaches to understanding the nature of need and creating social policies appropriate for a superdiverse society. The answers to these challenges are not currently available, which offers huge scope for the development of a research agenda bringing together social policy analysts and race, ethnicity and migration researchers. A key starting point is changing ethnic monitoring systems, which were designed before the emergence of superdiversity, to include data about key variables such as country of origin, immigration status and language. Collecting data will help us to understand which combinations of variables are important in influencing outcomes and will allow us to target limited resources. Qualitative research examining why outcomes are poor is also necessary. This will need to concentrate on variables associated with poor outcomes and will require a shift from approaches focusing on ethnicity to perhaps those examining experiences of locations, newness, transiency or status, or combinations of those or other variables. A clear priority is to understand what works in achieving equitable social welfare outcomes. There is a need for comparative research looking at the governance of immigration, diversity and social policy in countries with more/less favourable outcomes, possibly using welfare and migration regimes to develop a conceptual framework. Also important is research that focuses on the micro level to examine the processes through which migrants and minorities as agents secure access to welfare across the sectoral boundaries (public/private/third) within, but not between, which social policy analysis is generally undertaken, and to look at the ways individuals use cross-sector hybrids in conjunction with informal, transnational and virtual provision. Much could be learned from exploring the strategies adopted by migrants and minorities to help shape provision to meet their needs and those of the general population better. Given that inequality in access to social welfare is experienced across the globe and has sustained for decades, perhaps the time has come to re-imagine completely social policy and models of welfare delivery so we can better meet the needs of all in an era of mobility and change.

References

Ager, A. and Strang, A. (2004) *Indicators of Integration: Final Report*, Home Office Development and Practice Report 28, London: Home Office.

Ahmad, W. and Craig, G. (2003) '"Race" and social welfare', in P. Alcock, A. Erskine and M. May (eds) *The Student's Companion to Social Policy*, Oxford, UK: Blackwell.

Arai, L. (2005) *Migrants and Public Services in the UK: A Review of the Recent Literature*, Oxford, UK: Compas. Online. Available HTTP: <http://www-dev.compas.ox.ac.uk/fileadmin/files/Publications/Research_Resources/Welfare/Lisa_Arai_Migrants_public_services_in_the_UK.pdf> (accessed 19 March 2014).

Atkin, K. and Chattoo, S. (2007) 'The Dilemmas of Providing Welfare in an Ethnically Diverse State: Seeking Reconciliation in the Role of a "Reflexive Practitioner"', *Policy and Politics*, 35(3): 377–93.

Avato, J., Koettl, J. and Sabates-Wheeler, R. (2010) 'Social Security Regimes, Global Estimates, and Good Practices: The Status of Social Protection for International Migrants', *World Development*, 38(4): 455–66.

Banting, K. (2000) 'Looking in Three Directions: Migration and the European Welfare State in Comparative Perspective', in M. Bommes and A. Geddes (eds) *Immigration and Welfare: Challenging the Borders of the Welfare State*, London: Routledge.

Bhatia, S. and Ram, A. (2009) 'Theorizing Identity in Transnational and Diaspora Cultures: A Critical Approach to Acculturation', *International Journal of Intercultural Relations*, 33(2): 140–9.

Bhopal, R. (2012) 'Research Agenda for Tackling Inequalities Related to Migration and Ethnicity in Europe', *Journal of Public Health*, 34(2): 167–73.

Bloch, A. (2000) 'Refugee Settlement in Britain: The Impact of Policy on Participation', *Journal of Ethnic and Migration Studies*, 26(1): 75–88.

Burgoon, B., Foster, K. and van Egmond, M. (2012) 'Support for Redistribution and the Paradox of Immigration', *Journal of European Social Policy*, 22(3): 288–304.

Carmel, E. and Cerami, A. (2011) 'Governing Migration and Welfare: Institutions and Emotions in the Production of Differential Integration', in E. Carmel, A. Cerami and T. Papadopoulos (eds) *Migration and Welfare in the New Europe: Social Protection and the Challenges of Integration*, Bristol, UK: Policy.

Castles, S. and Miller, M. (2009) *The Age of Migration: International Population Movements in the Modern World*, Basingstoke, UK: Palgrave Macmillan.

Chahal, K. (2004) *Experiencing Ethnicity: Discrimination and Service Provision*, York, UK: Joseph Rowntree Foundation.

Clarke, J., Langan, M. and Williams, F. (2001) 'Remaking Welfare: The British Welfare Regime in the 1980s and 1990s', in A. Cochrane, J. Clarke and S. Gewirtz (eds) *Comparing Welfare States*, London: Sage.

Cochrane, A., Clarke, J. and Gewirtz, S. (eds) (2001) *Comparing Welfare States*, London: Sage.

Craig, G. (2007) 'Cunning, Unprincipled and Loathsome: The Racist Tail Wags the Welfare Dog', *Journal of Social Policy*, 36(4): 605–23.

Dean, H. (2011) 'The Ethics of Migrant Welfare', *Ethics and Social Welfare*, 5(1): 18–35.

Duvell, F. and Jordan, B. (2002) 'Immigration, Asylum and Welfare: The European Context', *Critical Social Policy*, 22(3): 498–517.

Epstein, S. (2008) 'The Rise of "Recruitmentology": Clinical Research, Racial Knowledge and the Politics of Inclusion and Difference', *Social Studies of Science*, 38(5): 801–32.

Esping-Anderson, G. (1990) *The Three Worlds of Welfare Capitalism*, Cambridge, UK: Polity Press.

Fitzpatrick, T. (2005) 'Alternative Approaches to Social Policy', in H. Bochel, C. Bochel, R. Page and R. Sykes (eds) *Social Policy: Issues and Developments*, Harlow, UK: Pearson.

FRA, European Agency for Fundamental Rights (2011) *Migrants in an Irregular Situation: Access to Health care in 10 European Union Member States*, Vienna: FRA.

Geddes, A. (2000) 'Denying Access: Asylum Seekers and Welfare Benefits in the UK', in M. Bommes and A. Geddes (eds) *Immigration and Welfare: Challenging the Borders of the Welfare State*, London: Routledge.

Gilens, M. (1996) 'Race and Poverty in America: Public Misconceptions and the American News Media', *Public Opinion Quarterly*, 60(1): 515–41.

Goodhart, D. (2004) 'Too Diverse?', *Prospect Magazine*, 95: 1–6.

Hall, S. (1990) 'Cultural Identity and Diaspora', in J. Rutherford (ed.) *Identity and Difference*, London: Sage.

Home Office, UK (2007) *A Strategy to Ensure and Enforce Compliance with our Immigration Rules*, London: UK Home Office.

Humphries, B. (2004) 'An Unacceptable Role for Social Work: Implementing Immigration Policy', *British Journal of Social Work*, 34(1): 93–107.

Kofman, E., Phizacklea, A., Raghuram, P. and Sales, R. (2000) *Gender and International Migration in Europe: Employment, Welfare and Politics*, London: Routledge.

Law, I. (2009) 'Racism, Ethnicity, Migration and Social Security', in J. Millar (ed.) *Understanding Social Security*, Bristol: Policy.

Lewis, G. (2003) 'Migrants', in P. Alcock, A. Erskine and M. May (eds) *Social Policy*, Oxford, UK: Blackwell.

Maffia, C. (2008) *Health and Migration in the North West of England: An Overview*, Manchester, UK: North West Strategic Partnership.

Mau, S. and Burkhardt, C. (2009) 'Migration and Welfare State Solidarity in Western Europe', *Journal of European Social Policy*, 19(3): 213–19.

Miller, D. (2006) *Multiculturalism and the Welfare State: Theoretical Reflections*, Bristol, UK: Policy.

MIPEX, Migrant Integration Policy Index (2013) 'Homepage of the Migration Integration Policy Index'. Online. Available HTTP: <http://www.mipex.eu/> (accessed 13 July 2013).

Mir, G. (2007) *Effective Communication with Service Users*, London: Race Equality Foundation.

Myles, J. and St-Arnaud, S. (2006) 'Population Diversity, Multiculturalism, and the Welfare State: Should Welfare State Theory be Revised?', in K. Banting and W. Kymlicka (eds) *Multiculturalism and the Welfare State: Recognition and Redistribution in Contemporary Democracies*, Oxford, UK: Oxford University.

NPC, National Poverty Center (2013) *Poverty in the United States*, Ann Arbor, MI: NPC. Online. Available HTTP: <http://www.npc.umich.edu/poverty/> (accessed 26 June 2013).

Phillimore, J. (2011) 'Approaches to Welfare Provision in the Age of Super-diversity: The Example of Health Provision in Britain's Most Diverse City', *Critical Social Policy*, 31(1): 5–29.

—(2012) 'Implementing Integration in the UK: Lessons for Theory, Policy and Practice', *Policy and Politics*, 40(4): 525–45.

—(forthcoming) 'Delivering Maternity Services in an era of Superdiversity: The Challenges of Novelty and Newness', *Journal of Ethnic and Racial Studies*.

Phillimore, J. and Goodson, L. (2008) 'Making a Place in the Global City: The Relevance of Indicators of Integration', *Journal of Refugee Studies*, 21(3): 305–25.

—(2010) 'Failing to Adapt: Institutional Barriers to RCOs Engagement in Transformation of Social Welfare', *Social Policy & Society*, 9(2): 1–12.

Putnam, R. (2007) '*E Pluribus Unum*: Diversity and Community in the Twenty-first Century: the 2006 Johan Skytte prize lecture', *Scandinavian Political Studies*, 30(2): 137–74.

Ryner, M. (2000) 'European Welfare State: Transformation and Migration', in M. Bommes and A. Geddes (eds) *Immigration and Welfare: Challenging the Borders of the Welfare State*, London: Routledge.

Sainsbury, D. (2006) 'Immigrants' Social Rights in Comparative Perspective: Welfare Regimes, Forms in Immigration and Immigration Policy regimes', *Journal of European Social Policy*, 16(3): 229–44.

Sales, R. (2002) 'The Deserving and the Undeserving? Refugees, Asylum Seekers and Welfare in Britain', *Critical Social Policy*, 22(3): 456–78.

Schierup, C., Hansen, P. and Castles, S. (2006) *Migration, Citizenship, and the European Welfare State*, Oxford, UK: Oxford University Press.

Soroka, S., Johnston, R. and Banting, K. (2006) 'Ethnicity, Trust and the Welfare State', in K. Banting and W. Kymlicka (eds) *Multiculturalism and the Welfare State: Recognition and Redistribution in Contemporary Democracies*, Oxford, UK: Oxford University Press.

Taylor, C. (ed.) (1994) *Multiculturalism: Examining the Politics of Recognition*, Princeton, NJ: Princeton University Press.

Travers, T., Tunstall, R., Whitehead, C. and Pruvot, S. (2007) *Population Mobility and Service Provision: A Report for London Councils*, London: London School of Economics and Political Science.

Van Oorschot, W. (2006) 'Making the Difference in Social Europe: Deservingness Perceptions Among Citizens of European Welfare States', *Journal of European Social Policy*, 16(1): 23–42.

Vertovec, S. (2004) 'The Emergence of Super-Diversity in Britain', Compas Working Paper no. 25, Oxford, UK: Centre on Migration, Policy and Society. Online. Available HTTP: <https://www.compas.ox.ac.uk/fileadmin/files/Publications/working_papers/WP_2006/WP0625_Vertovec.pdf>.

—(2012) '"Diversity" and the Social Imaginary', *European Journal of Sociology*, 53(3): 287–312.

Vickers, T., Craig, G. and Atkin, K. (2012) 'Addressing Ethnicity in Social Care Research', *Social Policy and Administration*, 47(3): 310–26.

Williams, F. (1989) *Social Policy: A Critical Introduction, Issues of race, Gender and Class*, Bristol, UK: Policy.

27

Diversity management

John Wrench

Diversity management is an organizational strategy which emphasizes the need to recognize ethnic, cultural, gender and other differences between groups of employees and clients and make practical allowances for these in organizational policies. The 'main message' of the approach is that organizations must see the human diversity within them as a strength rather than as a problem.

Private sector companies and public sector organizations alike have become increasingly interested in techniques of the management of diversity. The increasing demographic diversity of populations and labour markets, and political demands for equality and fairness in employment, have stimulated organizations to experiment with new human resource policies. In this context diversity management has come to the fore as a strategy to get excluded minorities and under-represented social groups, including women, better represented in employment. The term diversity management came commonly into use in the 1980s in the USA; the practice was adopted first in the USA, Canada and Australia, and started to be considered seriously in some countries of Europe in the 1990s.

Diversity management is said to be significantly different from previous employment equity approaches, such as equal opportunity policies and affirmative action, in a number of ways. For one thing, its rationale is primarily one of improving organizational competitiveness and efficiency, driven by business purpose and market advantage. One definition of diversity management is as follows:

> The basic concept of managing diversity accepts that the workforce consists of a diverse population of people. The diversity consists of visible and non-visible differences which will include factors such as sex, age, background, race, disability, personality and workstyle. It is founded on the premise that harnessing these differences will create a productive environment in which everybody feels valued, where their talents are being fully utilised and in which organisational goals are met.
>
> *(Kandola and Fullerton 1998: 8)*

New metaphors

Advocates of diversity management have a tendency to draw on positive metaphors to explain its advantages, and these metaphors differ from those of previous approaches. For example, the old idea of an organization as a 'melting pot', with its overtones of assimilation and 'sameness', is replaced with that of the 'mosaic', where 'Differences come together to create a whole organization in much the same way that single pieces of a mosaic come together to create a pattern. Each piece is acknowledged, accepted and has a place in the whole structure' (Kandola and Fullerton 1998: 8). Metaphors such as 'the salad bowl' and 'the patchwork quilt', like 'the mosaic', are all part of what one American critic called the 'celebratory and harmonious imagery' and aim to convey how the whole is 'enriched by the differences of its component parts' through a diversity approach (Kersten 2000: 242).

Primary and secondary dimensions

There are differences as to which particular dimensions of diversity are perceived as important by practitioners. Some use narrow definitions which reflect equal employment laws, and define diversity in terms of 'race', gender, ethnicity, age, national origin, religion and disability, whereas others define diversity more broadly as simply 'All the ways in which we differ' (Hayles 1996: 105). Griggs (1995) classifies diversity into primary and secondary dimensions. Primary dimensions of diversity are those human differences that are inborn and/or that exert an important impact on early socialization and have an ongoing impact throughout life. The six primary dimensions are seen as:

1. age,
2. ethnicity,
3. gender,
4. physical abilities/qualities,
5. race,
6. sexual/affectional orientation.

According to Griggs, these primary dimensions are unchangeable; they shape our basic self-image and have great influence on how we view the world. Secondary dimensions of diversity are defined as those that can be changed, and these might include educational background, income, marital status, parental status, religious beliefs and so on (Wentling and Palma-Rivas 1997a: 2). Whilst diversity management is by definition multi-dimensional, the dimensions of gender and 'race'/ethnicity have generally been near the top in priority for managers in US organizations, and were also the dimensions which stimulated the original interest in the subject by practitioners and policy makers in Europe.

Differences from earlier approaches

There are differences between managing diversity approaches and equal employment opportunity/affirmative action (EEO/AA) approaches, common in the USA. In a managing diversity approach, top management plays a leading role, it is a strategic element of the business plan, it is linked to managerial performance evaluations and rewards, it is long term and it is inclusive of all employees, rather than simply focusing on excluded groups (Wentling and Palma-Rivas 1997a). Diversity management implies a systemic transformation of the organization as opposed to the singular emphasis on recruitment/selection that was characteristic of earlier equality approaches. It is presented as a voluntary effort on the part of the organization, and justified with economic rather than legal arguments (Kersten 2000).

An advantage of diversity management is said to be its more positive approach, rather than the negative one of simply avoiding transgressions of anti-discrimination laws. It is said to avoid some of the 'backlash' problems associated with affirmative action, as, unlike previous equality strategies, diversity management is not presented as a policy directed solely towards the interests of excluded groups or under-represented minorities. Rather, it is seen as an inclusive policy, which therefore encompasses the interests of all employees, including white males.

The benefits of diversity management

Across the diversity management literature, case studies of private companies and public sector organizations describe the benefits that diversity initiatives have provided to their organization. The most commonly stated can be summarized as follows (Wrench 2007: 10f.):

- using the skills and talents of the workforce appropriately, and ensuring that recruitment and selection decisions are based on rational criteria;
- avoiding internal problems such as conflicts and misunderstandings, grievances, higher absenteeism, greater staff turnover and damage to staff development;
- making products or services more attractive to multi-ethnic customers and clients;
- increasing creativity, innovation and problem solving through the inventiveness of diverse work teams;
- stimulating more flexible working practices through responding to the needs of a diverse workforce. This flexibility itself can enhance the creativity and efficiency of the organization;
- accessing international markets with more success, in particular when a diverse workforce allows a company to draw on the skills or connections of employees to reach new markets;
- avoiding the costs of racial discrimination, such as damage to the organization's image through adverse publicity and/or the financial penalties resulting from legal cases;
- enhancing the likelihood of winning contracts in situations where national or local government authorities operate a system of 'contract compliance' regarding equality and anti-discrimination issues;
- enhancing the likelihood of winning contracts through the positive image of a diverse sales team, or winning sales from corporate clients who themselves put a high priority on the diversity policies of their suppliers or partners;
- improving the image of the company in the eyes of potential investors who choose to invest in companies demonstrating practices of corporate social responsibility.

The origins of diversity management in the USA

American accounts generally agree on the factors which caused the shift in thinking towards diversity management at the end of the 1980s.

Demographic developments

One of the most cited references in this respect has been Johnston and Packer's (1987) book *Workforce 2000: Work and Workers for the 21st Century*. This and other reports made it clear that dramatic changes were to be expected in the composition of the US workforce over the coming decades:

> ... the demographic change will be away from the European-American male and more towards an increasingly diverse and segmented population. This population will include women and men of all races, ethnic backgrounds, ages, and lifestyles. It will include people of diverse sexual/affectional orientations, religious beliefs, and different physical abilities, who will need to work together effectively.
>
> *(Wentling and Palma-Rivas 1997a: 3)*

Thus it was argued that if managers did not find some way to accommodate this change, by recruiting, managing and retaining a diverse body of employees, the competitiveness of their organization would suffer.

The growth in minority communities as markets

As the workforce is becoming more heterogeneous, so is the domestic market becoming more ethnically diverse. The implication for businesses and service providers is that the employment of a diverse workforce and the proper management of this diversity will be increasingly necessary in order to be able to compete effectively in selling goods and services in these markets.

The growth in the service sector

The shift from a manufacturing-based economy to a service economy and the fact that the majority of jobs in the USA are now in the service sector provides a stimulus to diversity management practices. This is because, in the service area, interpersonal skills of employees have a greater intrinsic importance, with potential direct effects on the quality of service provision, and interactions between employees and clients have a direct bearing on business success.

Globalization and the increasing importance of foreign markets

US companies have been increasingly buying companies in other parts of the world, and foreign companies are increasingly buying US companies. The North American Free Trade Agreement, the consolidation of the European Union single market and the disintegration of the former Soviet Union all had implications in the 1990s for the internationalization of organizational practices in the context of new opportunities for foreign links, investments and markets. The increasingly international way that organizations operate means that companies are faced with the need to manage diversity both at home and with their global partners (Kandola and Fullerton 1998: 30). Amongst other things, this means that US corporations need a more multicultural perspective to be able to relate to employees, suppliers and customers abroad, and must develop appropriate human resource practices to reflect this.

Two further factors were suggested by a telephone survey of diversity experts from across the United States (Wentling and Palma-Rivas 1997b). One was the growth in 'identity politics' in the USA, whereby in the increasingly diverse US workforce, people are 'more comfortable being different'. In the words of the authors of the report:

> These people bring to the workplace a variety of experiences, values, cultures, physical abilities, religions, work styles, and so forth. They are no longer willing to deny their differences in order to assimilate into the organization's mainstream.
>
> *(Wentling and Palma-Rivas 1997b: 4)*

A second mentioned factor was the pressure of US equal employment opportunity and affirmative action programmes. As Mor Barak (2005) observes: 'Equal rights legislation and affirmative positive action policies are prerequisites for the development of diversity management because they create the social, legal, and organizational environment on which diversity management initiatives can be based' (ibid.: 212).

Over the 1990s and 2000s, surveys pointed to the growing 'normality' of diversity management in the USA. In 1992 a Conference Board survey found that three-quarters of America's biggest firms had a diversity manager, and by 1994 more than two-thirds of Fortune 50 companies had diversity initiatives. In a 2002 survey of 829 US firms, the number with 'diversity performance evaluations for managers' grew from 4 per cent in 1985 to nearly one in five by 2002 (Kalev *et al.* 2006). Diversity innovations were spearheaded by the biggest firms in the US, later spreading to smaller companies. In a national sample of US firms, 40 per cent of medium sized and large firms had a diversity mission statement by 2002 (Dobbin 2009: 144).

The first diversity management policies were seen in European countries during the 1990s. Two EU reports in the early 2000s found evidence of a growing awareness of the strategy among employers, with 'good practice' examples identified in the UK, Germany, Spain, Belgium, France, the Netherlands and Sweden. The reported business benefits included overcoming labour shortages, reducing absenteeism, attracting and retaining qualified staff, improving staff motivation, enhancing customer satisfaction, improving innovation and creativity and accessing new markets (European Commission 2003, 2005).

Critiques of diversity management

The logic of diversity management would seem to imply that workplace struggles for equality are set to become a thing of the past. Organizations now have the motivation voluntarily to mainstream policies for the fair and equal inclusion of female, minority ethnic and immigrant workers, for reasons of self-interest and business efficiency. No longer will they need to be persuaded by arguments of morality, or threatened by anti-discrimination laws. However, not everyone has been convinced by this logic, and many have raised critical questions on a number of grounds regarding the growing popularity of diversity management strategies in business. Examples of such critiques are as follows.

Diversity benefits overstated

One claim of diversity management practitioners which has come under critical focus is the assumption that a diverse workforce automatically brings benefits to the organization in terms of, for example, increased productivity or creativity. An American review of the literature (Williams and O'Reilly 1998) concluded that the 'diversity is good for organizations' mantra has been overstated. They argue that, in contrast, the preponderance of empirical evidence suggests that diversity is just as likely to impede group functioning, and they conclude:

> Simply having more diversity in a group is no guarantee that the group will make better decisions or function effectively. In our view, these conclusions suggest that diversity is a

mixed blessing and requires careful and sustained attention to be a positive force in enhancing performance.

(ibid.: 120)

The implication is that diversity management techniques need to be applied to counteract these effects, given the evidence that, by itself, diversity may have negative rather than positive effects on group performance. Yet the evidence for the effectiveness of diversity management techniques themselves has been called into question by some critics. In theory, an evaluation of beneficial effects for an organization could include an analysis of measurable variables such as levels of job satisfaction, labour turnover, absenteeism, productivity and profitability. However, in reality it is very difficult to attribute tangible changes in these indicators to be primarily the result of the introduction of diversity management, because of all the other factors and variables which affect an organization over the time period studied (Fischer 2009: 103). Most commonly, the evidence on the benefits of diversity management is rooted simply in qualitative data, often taken from interviews with managers, carried out in company case studies.

There have been studies examining whether particular diversity strategies increase workforce diversity. For example, a study of 708 private sector organizations in the US (Kalev *et al.* 2006) concluded that affirmative action plans, diversity committees and diversity staff positions are more effective in increasing diversity than, for example, training programmes that target managerial bias, because the former initiatives assign responsibility for change (Benschop 2011: 24). Nevertheless, as Dobbin notes, although the workplace has become markedly more diverse since the early 1960s, it is still not possible to say how much of that is due to the particular programmes initiated by the human resources profession (Dobbin 2009: 232).

Diversity management as a sectional interest

In the view of Dobbin (2009), the reason diversity management was so readily adopted in the USA, despite the paucity of tangible and reliable evidence on benefits, was that it served the interests of a particular occupational group. Kelly and Dobbin (1998) trace the development of diversity management in the USA in the 1980s in the context of the political assault on equal employment opportunities/affirmative action (EEO/AA). They outline four stages in American employers' response to AA and EEO law. First, in the 1960s, the ambiguity and weak enforcement of these laws led to few changes in employers' practices. Then, between 1972 and 1980, increased federal enforcement led employers to pay closer attention to anti-discrimination law, and during this period they started to hire EEO/AA specialists to devise strategies to comply with the law. In so doing, 'employers created internal constituencies that championed EEO/AA measures'. The third stage was a time of 'backlash' in the early 1980s when the Reagan administration began to criticize EEO/AA programmes and curtail enforcement. However, despite this undermining of EEO/AA, many employers continued with the anti-discrimination practices that they already had in place, and EEO/AA specialists began to emphasize the efficiency gains that had followed the adoption of these practices. Fourth, after 1987, when the legal future of affirmative action remained uncertain and courts continued to 'chip away' at the law, EEO/AA specialists transformed themselves into diversity managers and promoted a range of human resource practices aimed at maintaining and managing diversity in the workforce (Kelly and Dobbin 1998: 963).

Diversity management is a soft option

One reason why equal opportunities activists are sometimes suspicious of diversity management has been the fear that diversity management might be used to prioritize 'soft' rather than 'hard' equal opportunities practices. The problem is that diversity management in practice can mean many things. It can be little more than a desire to celebrate cultural diversity, or it can incorporate the full range of previous equal employment opportunities and affirmative action measures. We can conceive of a range of different levels of anti-discrimination and equal opportunities measures in organizations, with at the 'soft' end measures such as the recognition of cultural differences at work, and at the 'harder' end the setting of targets, the use of positive action or even the adoption of some forms of preferential treatment. It is possible that diversity management could be used to give the impression that an organization is doing something for excluded groups whilst avoiding many of those aspects of anti-discrimination and equal opportunities activities which are likely to be less popular with employers. For example, employers might be more receptive to the provision of 'cultural awareness training' and less receptive to positive action measures such as targets to produce a workforce which reflects the ethnic make-up of the locality, anti-discrimination training to modify the behaviour of white managers and employees or strong internal anti-harassment initiatives. If a diversity management approach consists of little more than celebrating cultural diversity, it will sidestep many of the 'harder' elements which have existed within a broader equal opportunities and affirmative action approach.

Diversity management dilutes the ethnicity/gender focus

Another concern amongst some equal opportunities activists has been that diversity management dilutes policies against ethnic and gender discrimination by mixing them with policies relating to too many other groups. Sometimes the extension and inclusiveness of the diversity concept is taken so far that it becomes almost meaningless. Mor Barak (2005) notes that many diversity trainers as well as human resource managers have readily embraced the 'broad' approach 'because it allows them to pull everyone in the organization under the "diversity umbrella", thus avoiding the controversial process of identifying groups with or without power, those who are discriminating and those who are discriminated against ...' (ibid.: 130). Mor Barak describes how, during a diversity seminar in California, she observed a diversity trainer enthusiastically encouraging participants to identify the qualities that made them 'diverse', which included not only characteristics such as race, gender, age, sexual orientation and disability, but also attributes such as the region where they grew up, the high school they attended and even their hair colour and taste in clothing and foods (ibid.: 121). For Mor Barak, this approach represents a common confusion between benign differences and differences that have practical or even detrimental consequences in people's lives. By including all types of individual differences as 'diversity', the implication is that *all* differences are equal. Mor Barak argues for the importance of employing categories of distinction that have a perceived commonality within a given cultural or national context and that have an impact on potentially harmful or beneficial employment outcomes such as job opportunities, treatment in the workplace and promotion prospects, irrespective of job-related skills and qualifications. Such a definition emphasizes the *consequences* of the distinction categories, which overcomes the problem of over-broad definitions of diversity that include 'benign and inconsequential' characteristics in their diversity dimensions (ibid.: 130, 132).

The reliance of diversity management on business arguments

One of the most profound criticisms of diversity management is that it removes the moral imperative from equal opportunities actions. Arguments for the introduction of equal opportunities and affirmative action policies relate to equality, fairness and social justice. Critics argue that diversity management has moved equal opportunities away from a moral and ethical issue to a business rationale. Whilst this development is seen as an advantage by many people, in that it increases the likelihood of the adoption of the policies by employers, others see it as a long-term weakness. The problem is that fighting racism and discrimination will now only be seen to be important if there is seen to be a business reason for doing it. With a diversity management approach, racism is indeed argued to be unacceptable, but only when it is recognized that the outcome of such racism leads to inefficiency in the utilization of human resources. If a change in market conditions means that racism and discrimination do not lead to inefficiency, then there will be no longer any imperative to combat it. In the American context, Kelly and Dobbin warn:

> Perhaps diversity management will succeed in winning over middle managers because it embraces an economic, rather than political, rationale. But precisely because it is founded on cost-benefit analysis rather than on legal compliance, perhaps diversity management will come under the ax of budget-cutters when America faces its next recession.
>
> *(Kelly and Dobbin 1998: 981)*

For some critics, serious questions must be raised about whether individuals within organizations pursuing private preferences constrained by the market can be left to be the custodians of employment equity practice. Noon (2007: 776–9) warns that the 'business case' relies on a cost-benefit analysis to indicate the advantages of investing in equality initiatives, and yet such advantages might not be readily apparent – managers might judge the costs of pursuing equality initiatives to be greater than the benefits. It may be that the true benefits of equality initiatives are only evident five or ten years in the future, whereas managers are required to focus on short-term benefits. This is a particular problem since, as discussed earlier, the benefits of diversity management are not easily measured. Noon concludes:

> The traditional moral case for equality remains the strongest foundation for underpinning equality of opportunity. The business case might rest upon this by providing an additional economic rationale, but in the absence of such a rationale ... the moral base remains firm. The argument for the moral case based on the human rights of all employees and job seekers must not be abandoned for the current fashion of diversity and the business case.
>
> *(Noon 2007: 781)*

In conclusion, it is clear that diversity management can take different forms. Some forms may operate with a singular emphasis on the business rationale coupled with an individualizing view of human diversity, which can thus be criticized for sidestepping the consequences of prejudice and discrimination experienced on a group basis, and defusing the stronger forms of equality struggles. However, there is no necessary contradiction between the business and moral arguments for diversity management. Other diversity management policies may emphasize the primary dimensions of diversity, encompassing those groups which have historically suffered exclusion and under-representation, operating with a genuine desire to increase both business efficiency and equality and human dignity at the workplace. It is quite possible for diversity management policies to grow from and strengthen existing equality strategies rather than replace them.

References

Benschop, Y. (2011) 'The Dubious Power of Diversity Management', in S. Gröschl (ed.) *Diversity in the Workplace: Multi-disciplinary and International Perspectives*, Farnham, UK: Gower.

Dobbin, F. (2009) *Inventing Equal Opportunity*, Princeton, NJ: Princeton University Press.

European Commission (2003) *The Costs and Benefits of Diversity*, Luxembourg: Office for Official Publications of the European Communities.

—(2005) *The Business Case for Diversity: Good Practices in the Workplace*, Luxembourg: Office for Official Publications of the European Communities.

Fischer, M. (2009) 'Diversity Management and the Business Case', in K. Kraal, J. Roosblad and J. Wrench (eds) *Equal Opportunities and Ethnic Inequality in European Labour Markets: Discrimination, Gender and Policies of Diversity*, Amsterdam: University of Amsterdam Press.

Griggs, L.B. (1995) 'Valuing Diversity: Where From . . . Where To?', in L.B. Griggs and L.L. Louw (eds) *Valuing Diversity: New Tools for a New Reality*, New York, NY: McGraw-Hill.

Hayles, V.R. (1996) 'Diversity Training and Development', in R.L. Craig (ed.) *The ASTD Training and Development Handbook*, New York, NY: McGraw-Hill.

Johnston, W. and Packer, A. (1987) *Workforce 2000: Work and Workers for the 21st Century*, Indianapolis, IN: Hudson Institute.

Kalev, A., Dobbin, F. and Kelly, E. (2006) 'Best Practices or Best Guesses? Diversity Management and the Remediation of Inequality', *American Sociological Review*, 71(4): 589–617.

Kandola, R. and Fullerton, J. (1998) *Diversity in Action: Managing the Mosaic*, London: Institute of Personnel and Development.

Kelly, E. and Dobbin, F. (1998) 'How Affirmative Action Became Diversity Management', *American Behavioral Scientist*, 41(7): 960–85.

Kersten, A. (2000) 'Diversity Management: Dialogue, Dialectics and Diversion', *Journal of Organizational Change Management*, 13(3): 235–48.

Mor Barak, M.E. (2005) *Managing Diversity: Toward a Globally Inclusive Workplace*, Thousand Oaks, CA: Sage.

Noon, M. (2007) 'The Fatal Flaws of Diversity Management and the Business Case for Ethnic Minorities', *Work Employment and Society*, 21(4): 773–84.

Wentling, R.M. and Palma-Rivas, N. (1997a) *Diversity in the Workforce: A Literature Review*, Diversity in the Workforce Series Report no.1, Berkeley, CA: National Center for Research in Vocational Education.

—(1997b) *Current Status and Future Trends of Diversity in the Workplace: Diversity Experts' Perspective*, Diversity in the Workforce Series Report no. 2, Berkeley, CA: National Center for Research in Vocational Education.

Williams, K.Y. and O'Reilly, C.A. (1998) 'Demography and Diversity in Organizations: A Review of 40 Years of Research', *Research in Organizational Behavior*, 20(1): 77–140.

Wrench, J. (2007) *Diversity Management and Discrimination: Immigrants and Ethnic Minorities in the EU*, Aldershot, UK: Ashgate.

Part IV
Encounters and diversity

28

Diversity unpacked

From heterogeneities to inequalities[1]

Thomas Faist

Diversity and heterogeneities

No matter which words we use – integration, assimilation, incorporation, or insertion – all of these normatively loaded terms hold the promise of equality for immigrants. Nonetheless, the other side of the coin reveals manifold inequalities, such as high unemployment, residential segregation, or religious extremism. Diversity, along with assimilation, has been one of the main paradigms of integration and of policy aimed at addressing such inequalities. And even though diversity may mean many different things – a demographic description, an ideology, a set of policies, or a political theory of modern society – one can discern a core tenet in its normatively oriented intellectual lineage: to overcome social inequalities based on cultural markers (heterogeneities) by shaping cultural, civic, political, and economic relations via public policies. In essence, diversity as a concept and a set of – not necessarily coherent – policies, programmes, and routines straddles several worlds: it appeals to those who emphasize individual economic competence and self-reliance of migrants ('neoliberals'), those who cherish the public competence of immigrants in public affairs ('republicans'), as well as those, like the European Commission, who push for structural reforms to turn incorporation into a two-way process. In particular, the adaptation of organizations to 'cultural' factors, the economic use of soft skills, and the delivery of service to a culturally heterogeneous clientele come to the forefront. While the focus of assimilation is on individual migrants passing into mainstream society and of multiculturalism, in some varieties, on the rights of migrants as a means to increase their sense of recognition and belonging and also overall national unity, the emphasis of diversity approaches can be seen to lie on the level in between – on organizations. The problem is that diversity as a management technique in organizations does not address issues of social inequality. Therefore, we need to go beyond an understanding of diversity as an organizational technique and start with considering diversity in the sense of heterogeneities along the boundaries of, for example, class, gender, religion, ethnicity, age, and transnationality. This understanding will allow the tracing of the mechanisms of how differences or diversity turn into social inequalities (Diewald and Faist 2011).

Here, heterogeneity is used to denote markers such as gender, class, ethnicity, or nationality because the term seems to be more neutral compared to the alternatives of diversity and difference. The term diversity already contains within itself that which is to be explained, namely the perception and valuation of difference, and often in a quite positive sense, such as in 'diversity management' (see Wrench, this volume). In notions of diversity management or managing diversity, the issue of inequality is almost absent. It is not part of the concern. Instead, in the private sector it is hitherto 'private' competencies, such as knowledge of languages useful for the company, which come to the fore. In the public sector, such as in hospitals, schools, or the police, the main goal in serving groups with migrant or minority backgrounds is improving service delivery (Faist 2010). Furthermore, the terms diversity and difference mostly refer to cultural markers. Yet such a limitation is already part of the problem because cultural markers (e.g. ethnicity or religion) interact with non-cultural ones (e.g. class, see Gordon's (1964) early concept of 'ethclass'). In order to avoid policy valuations as much as possible, it is helpful to return to a sociological use of the term heteroge-neity (Blau 1977: 77). We can distinguish various sorts of heterogeneities: they can (a) be ascriptive, as with age, ethnicity, nationality, or gender; (b) refer to cultural preferences, dispositions, or worldviews; (c) relate to competencies or qualifications as societally legitimated mechanisms of attributing life chances; and finally (d) refer to activities, such as wage and household labour.

Inequalities arise from categorizations of heterogeneities. Such categorizations generate unequal access to resources (redistribution), to status (recognition), and to decision-making (power). Rewards based upon the categorizations of heterogeneities are differential, such as gendered wage differences. In short, inequalities are those categorizations of difference based upon heterogeneities which generate unequal returns and have been institutionalized (using somewhat different terms: Tilly 1998). Resulting inequalities then refer to both statistical distributions of resources (objective positions) and the perceptions of inequalities.

Social mechanisms: from heterogeneities to inequalities

Social mechanisms can be defined as 'a delimited class of events that alter relations among specified sets of elements in identical or closely similar ways over a variety of situations' (McAdam et al. 2001: 24) and '[p]rocesses are frequently occurring combinations or sequences of mechanisms' (Tilly 2005: 28). The term social mechanism thus refers to recurrent processes or pathways, linking specified initial conditions (not necessarily causes in the strict sense) and specific outcomes, the latter of which can be effects produced or purposes achieved. Formally, one can thus define a social mechanism (M) as a link between initial conditions (input I) and effect (outcome O). M explicates an observed relationship between specific initial conditions and a specific outcome. The short formal expression then is: I-M-O.

A social mechanism-based kind of explanation aims toward causal reconstruction of processes leading to defined outcomes. Mechanism-based statements – not to be confused with mechanistic statements, since most social mechanisms are not mechanical, as in machines – are generalizations about recurrent processes (Mayntz 2004). Mechanism-based explanations do not look for statistical relationships among variables (Bunge 2004) but seek to explain a given social phenomenon – an event, structure, or development – by identifying the processes through which it is generated. There is no necessary claim that such mechanisms are akin to covering-laws. A social mechanism-based explanation would claim that certain outcomes occur sometimes. Mechanisms can be analyzed on various levels of aggregation – for example, socio-psychological mechanisms such as agenda-setting or stereotyping, social-relational ones such as opportunity-hoarding, or macro-structural mechanisms such as 'structural violence' (Galtung 1969).

Examples of social mechanisms significant for the (re-)production of inequalities are – in addition to boundary-making – exclusion, opportunity-hoarding, exploitation, and hier-

Table 28.1 General and specific mechanisms in the genesis of inequalities out of heterogeneities

General social mechanisms	Specific social mechanisms (examples)
Boundary-making	Distantiation (e.g. nationality → religion); stereotyping (e.g. status matters)
Exclusion	Human and political rights (e.g. restriction of dual citizenship)
Opportunity-hoarding	Corrosion (de-solidarization)
Exploitation	Informal and irregular work (e.g. household and care work)
Hierarchization	Genderization; ethnicization; hiring rules

archization (see Table 28.1), while inclusion, redistribution, de-hierarchization, and 'catching up' constitute mechanisms which can further equality between categories of persons and groups (see Table 28.2). The following discussion sketches selected general and specific social mechanisms. The preliminary list of general mechanisms presented here draws on old and new classics in the social sciences, such as inclusion and exclusion and opportunity-hoarding (Tilly 1998) as variations of social closure (Weber 1972 [1922]), exploitation (Karl Marx) and redistribution, and hierarchization and de-hierarchization (Therborn 2006: 13). These general mechanisms are specified by concrete mechanisms in order to link them to empirically observable processes.

In addition to the general social mechanisms just mentioned, there is another general mechanism that should not be forgotten, namely boundary-making. The perception and evaluation of heterogeneities is important, as heterogeneities are always perceived and evaluated, and actors use such valuations in the process of producing inequalities.

One pattern of boundary-making is of particular relevance here, namely boundary-shifting. In Germany, for example, data from the General Survey in the Social Sciences (*Allgemeine Bevölkerungsumfrage der Sozialwissenschaften*, ALLBUS) suggest that between 1996 and 2006 significant shifts took place in boundaries between migrant groups and the dominant group ('German-Germans'). The dominant group in 2006 clearly perceived certain migrant groups – Italians, Spaniards, and Greeks – as being part of its own. Rapprochement seems to have taken place (see Table 28.2). However, there were also categories for which no change occurred or which even experienced an increase in dissimilarity, namely 'Muslims' (Fincke 2009). In the case of this category, there is evidence of greater social distance, and the mechanism of distantiation (see Therborn 2006: 12) seems to have been at work. In a way, one could even speak of a new boundary, as 'Turks' have during this time metamorphosed into 'Muslims'. This mechanism of distantiation has created social distance between the dominant group and minority groups by way of defining the 'other' as culturally distinct in religious ways. Social distance has probably been reinforced by mechanisms such as stereotyping, but also by thematization and agenda-setting: the 'Muslim' has variously served not only as an object of social integration, but also as the 'other' in the context of terrorism, securitization, and an impending 'clash of civilizations'.

An intersectional analysis is necessary to overcome unjustified simplifications. The changes just explained by the shifting of boundaries and the concrete mechanisms involved do not yet serve to answer the question of which interactions are regarded by the various groups as equal or unequal. Social status, among other markers of heterogeneity, makes a difference in how, for example, ethnic or religious categories are evaluated by dominant groups. Field experiments – quasi-experimental research regarding hiring in labour markets – suggest that discrimination is starkly reduced if the interaction partners are perceived to be equals with respect to social status. Socio-economic positions and majority group language skills are strong predictors (see de Beijl

2000 on discrimination in recruitment processes). We thus encounter intersections of ethnic belonging, status, and language competencies.

Since it is usually much easier to exit from groups, organizations, and states than to enter them, mechanisms of closure assume an important role in accounting for the genesis of inequalities. One of the central questions involved is: Who belongs to 'us'? At least part of the answer can be found in rules of admission and membership. For admission on the state level, immigration policies make the differential inclusion and exclusion of categories quite obvious. In most Western immigration countries nowadays, the so-called highly skilled are bound to experience a fast track to residence and citizenship, while the low-skilled service population is expected to rotate. Again, this is pushed one step further in neoliberal, populist discourses of boundary-making: it is only the economically active segment of the population – high achievers in formal labour markets – which is valued (Sarrazin 2010). For membership on the state level, citizenship rules constitute a rather mixed bag and point to contradictory developments. On the one hand, the liberalization of rules has been quite visible in the past few decades (e.g. eased access to citizenship in terms of requirements such as length of stay, shorter waiting times). On the other hand, the requirements for those 'wanted but not welcome' (Zolberg 1987) have been stepped up, as can be seen, for example, in labour market activation policies. The latter are clearly exclusionary and have led from a social right to welfare to workfare. Interestingly, this broader pattern applies not only to immigrants, but also to those dependent on subsidies from the welfare state.

Opportunity-hoarding, in the words of Charles Tilly (1998), occurs 'when members of a categorically bounded network acquire access to a resource that is valuable, renewable, subject to monopoly, supportive of network activities, and enhanced by the network's modus operandi' (Tilly 1998: 91). In a way, even (international) migration could be labelled an overall strategy of opportunity-hoarding. There are numerous examples in the literature of migrant groups who have successfully occupied and monopolized economic niches (e.g. Light *et al.* 1990). Nonetheless, by bringing in co-villagers or co-ethnics, dependencies are also established, such as indebtedness, which can lead to increasing hierarchization within such groups.

Another concrete mechanism of opportunity-hoarding is brokerage, namely migrants serving to fill structural holes by connecting persons and organizations which have no direct links. As the new 'mantra' of migrants-as-development-agents suggests, international migrants' financial remittances are greater than the funds for Official Development Aid (ODA) (though reverse remittances flowing from developing to developed countries are conveniently forgotten). It is clear that opportunity-hoarding occurs when organizations in the development cooperation sector try to co-opt migrant associations to serve their need to ensure a constant flow of public resources for their own work (Faist *et al.* 2011). Of interest in this case is not only opportunity-hoarding, but also a 'new' kind of heterogeneity usually not regarded as such: transnationality. Transnationality, that is, persons, groups, or organizations building and maintaining relatively continuous cross-border transactions, is not – contrary to many claims – simply a resource which is either positive (e.g. enhancing educational careers by shifting children to the most appropriate location) or negative (e.g. transfers from one educational system to another as a dead end). Instead, we need to account for how transnationality *becomes* a positive or negative resource, i.e. how it turns from a heterogeneity marker to a characteristic of social inequality.

Normally we speak of exploitation when powerful persons command resources from which they draw significantly increased returns. These dominant agents pool these returns so that they exclude those outside their group from the full value the latter add to the effort (Tilly 2005). Exploitation occurs, for example, in the case of employment of migrant women in irregular conditions through the imposition of rules (e.g. working hours and the working schedule;

Orozco 2007). In particular, in irregular care work, power asymmetries between employer and employee have repercussions for family relations of the employer and employees. The employers' labour market participation is enhanced, whereas for the migrants problems arise in managing transnational families.

Hierarchization (Therborn 2006: 13) refers to the existence of positions in formal organizations differentially endowed at least with rights, duties, and resources, as seen in informal systems of roles and cultural hierarchies. Not only do organizations themselves create hierarchies through the layering of positions, reward and remuneration systems, and career ladders; there is also an interplay of organizations and informal networks. For instance, if children of labour migrants compete with German youth on the basis of equal educational (high school) credentials, informal hiring networks assume importance. For many young persons of Turkish descent (so-called second generation), parental networks no longer function because of de-industrialization. Their parents' employment concentration in a small number of economic sectors, such as the manufacturing and steel industries, has become disadvantageous over time, as there are often no informal networks reaching into new and attractive sectors of the labour market (Faist 1995). Again, an intersectional approach becomes relevant. For example, in organizational hierarchies in firms or even labour markets, the confluence of ethnic and occupational or class hierarchies can be decisive. In 'split labour markets', a concept which has been usefully applied to white settler colonies with slavery in the nineteenth and early twentieth centuries (e.g. the American South or South Africa), labour markets are divided along ethno-racial lines. Ethnic antagonism and ethno-racial hierarchies resulted from this kind of hierarchization, as did outright exclusion of groups from certain labour market segments (Bonacich 1972).

Social mechanisms: the production of equalities

Multicultural citizenship promoting equalities is very much tied to the public policies of an intervening welfare state. This relationship is a complex one because we are dealing not only with negative rights ('freedom from'), but also so-called positive rights ('freedom to'), and thus the enabling aspect of citizenship. As in the preceding analysis, we also need to consider a universe of policies and politics that is broader than those imagined by multiculturalism. Networks of trust, such as rotating credit associations, mutual aid societies, and homeland associations, are also important.

On the societal level, inclusion points toward formal equality and substantive equality (equality of outcomes). Opportunities for resident migrants to achieve legal equality, such as the

Table 28.2 General and specific social mechanisms in the production of equalities out of heterogeneities

General social mechanisms (selection)	Specific social mechanisms (examples)
Boundary-making	Rapprochement
Inclusion	Liberalization of citizenship acquisition (e.g. dual citizenship); human rights enforcement; denizenship
Redistribution	Subsidies for public institutions (e.g. child care, educational institutions)
Catching up	Anti-discrimination, affirmative action
De-hierarchization	Special representation rights in political parties, unions, etc. (claim-making) → de-intersectionalization

Source: Mayntz (2004)

possibility of acquiring citizenship, seem to have improved. Citizenship rules have been liberalized; for example, some European countries complemented *ius sanguinis* with *ius soli* laws for persons born in the country; reduced the time of residence required for application for citizenship; and/or have increased toleration of dual citizenship. Another example is the introduction of far-reaching social rights for resident immigrants (denizenship). Still, inclusion in the legal sphere does not necessarily imply inclusion in substance, as the example of informal networks for obtaining access to organizations in the labour market suggests. Organizations may take account of equality explicitly in applying anti-discrimination rules, or may simply pretend to do so, or ignore it altogether.

Positive rights usually demand redistribution through taxes. Intervention in schooling, such as the provision of comprehensive schools or day-long instruction, requires additional resources. These universal policies are most often 'colour blind', however, and it is an empirical question whether certain universal policies favour privileged groups (e.g. the child allowance in Germany). While most policies that address heterogeneities require state intervention, they do not depend heavily on redistribution via tax resources (income redistribution), as, for example, in the case of affirmative action.

Another general mechanism advancing equality is that of 'catching up'. Again, in this case we need to consider not only official public policies, such as affirmative action, but also trust networks, such as professional networks and cliques. Affirmative action explicitly takes heterogeneities such as gender, ethnicity, religion, or sexual orientation as a point of departure. The basic idea is that there has been a historical injustice which calls for remedial action and/or there is empirical evidence that (institutional) discrimination along the lines of such heterogeneities is still prevalent. In its weak form, such as the EU directive dealing with anti-discrimination, the idea of 'catching up' is not fiercely contested in public debates. It is implemented into national law and often upheld by the respective courts. Nonetheless, there is wide latitude in implementing the directive and corresponding national legislation, and questions revolve around whether such legal instruments advance the goal of anti-discrimination effectively. In addition to public policies, trust networks are decisive in helping less represented categories to catch up with established and dominant ones (see also opportunity-hoarding). Even if anti-discrimination policies contribute to a higher degree of equality for historically underrepresented groups, the effects of public contention are worth considering. The strong claim by the critics of multiculturalism is that cultural pluralism and the perception of cultural relativism may undermine solidarity with certain groups; one has only to think of the charges against affirmative action as 'reverse discrimination'.

De-hierarchization as a general mechanism is certainly very much connected to claims-making of immigrants. Two classic examples are unionization and the setting up of political organizations to achieve political empowerment. The mechanism of de-hierarchization is particularly important because it reminds us that debates on multiculturalism need to look not only at redistribution and recognition, but also at participation in political decision-making as a third dimension of equalities and inequalities. Mobilization around religion, religious freedom, and representation in public life is a prominent current example of efforts at de-hierarchization on the part of certain immigrant groups. The example of the category 'Muslim' discussed on p. 267 on the production of inequalities through boundary-making and social distantiation is illustrative. It is around this category that substantial mobilization has occurred in European countries. In Germany, for example, one of the central issues has been the representation of Muslim organizations in the corporatist system of interest articulation. Note that this mobilization has been paralleled in public discourses by a seminal shift of the marker of heterogeneity from ethnicity/nationality to religion. Quite a few Muslim organizations have tried to become incorporated as a 'corporation of public law' (*Körperschaft des öffentlichen Rechts*), thus entitling them to practices of inclusion such as the state collection of taxes by the state from registered believers, representation on the boards of public mass media, and extension of religious instruction in public schools.

Yet, and this is leading us to the duality of mechanisms producing equalities and inequalities, de-hierarchization may go along with essentialization and identity politics. The *Deutsche Islamkonferenz* (DIK) is a convenient lens through which one may analyze de-hierarchization through the inclusion of groups, in this case through religious organizations (cf. Modood 2007), and the possible re-essentialization of collective identities. Obviously, the inclusion of Muslim organizations refers not only to the legal–political inclusion of Islamic groups and organizations into the corporatist system, which has been an ongoing concern for state and religious associations and established churches alike. Through DIK, religion is co-constituted as the main axis of immigrant integration politics and policy (Tezcan 2013). The focus on Islam in the context of a specific corporatist mode of religious institutionalization denotes an entire population of persons, namely those who (allegedly) hold Muslim belief. As a result, in public debates the individuals in question are not Muslims who have a religious identity in addition to their class, gender, or ethnic identity. Rather, their entire collective identity is defined by religious belonging. We could call this process one of de-intersectionalization. It is well worth studying the actual effects of specific interfaces such as the DIK. The question would be whether members of the category in question withdraw their commitment from other boundaries, for example those defined along class or national lines, as they focus increasingly on allegiance to the boundary defined in religious terms.

Outlook: transnationality as a heterogeneity

We need to make a clear distinction between heterogeneities and inequalities. It is only by means of a close examination of how initial conditions of heterogeneities turn into equalities and inequalities that we can begin to understand the social mechanisms involved. Needless to say, the distinction between heterogeneities and (in)equalities is an analytical one since heterogeneities such as gender and ethnicity always come with a history and are loaded with meaning and valuation in one form or another. It should also be emphasized that we are dealing with recursive processes. The perceptions of heterogeneities are also a product of inequalities and equalities, and heterogeneities are the basis for boundaries between categories. Nonetheless, the differentiation allows us to specify the claims of critics and defenders of multicultural citizenship.

The approach roughly outlined here allows us to bring in 'new' heterogeneities such as transnationality. It connotes the social practices of agents – individuals, groups, communities, and organizations – across the borders of nation-states. The term denotes a spectrum of cross-border ties in various spheres of social life – familial, socio-cultural, economic, and political – ranging from travel, through sending financial remittances, to exchanging ideas. Seen in this way, agents' transnational ties constitute a marker of heterogeneity, akin to other heterogeneities, such as age, gender, citizenship, sexual orientation, cultural preferences, or language use. In short, transnational ties can be understood as occupying a continuum from low to high – that is, from very few and short-lived ties to those that are multiple and dense and continuous over time. For example, migrants may remit varying sums of money or none at all. This is also to say that, for our purposes, migrants and non-migrants should not be considered simply as transnational or not, but as being transnational to different degrees. Transnationality is characterized by transactions of varying degrees of intensity and at various stages of the life course; it is not restricted to geographical mobility. For example, non-mobile family members of migrants may engage in transnational practices.

Transnationality has implications for other heterogeneities and raises the question whether and to what extent markers such as ethnicity, nationality, religion, gender, and sexual orientation are all (also) constituted across borders of national states. If the question is answered affirmatively, we arrive at a transnational puzzle: cross-border transactions among categories such as migrants (both mobile and non-mobile) constitute a significant part of overall ties and practices. Yet public resources and institutions such as redistribution and institutional regulation intended to address the implications of diversity are mainly national.

Note

1   The main ideas of this contribution are based on Faist (2013).

References

Blau, P.M. (1977) *Inequality and Heterogeneity: A Primitive Theory of Social Structure*, New York, NY: The Free Press.

Bonacich, E. (1972) 'A Theory of Ethnic Antagonism: The Split Labor Market', *American Sociological Review*, 37(5): 547–59.

Bunge, M. (2004) 'How Does It Work? The Search for Explanatory Mechanisms', *Philosophy of the Social Sciences*, 34(2): 182–204.

de Beijl, R.Z. (ed.) (2000) *Documenting Discrimination Against Migrant Workers in the Labour Market: A Comparative Study of Four European Countries*, Geneva: International Labour Organization (ILO).

Diewald, M. and Faist, T. (2011) 'Von Heterogenitäten zu Ungleichheiten: Soziale Mechanismen als Erklärungsansatz der Genese Sozialer Ungleichheiten', *Berliner Journal für Soziologie*, 21(1): 91–114.

Faist, T. (1995) *Social Citizenship for Whom? Mexican Americans in the United States and Turks in Germany*, Aldershot, UK: Ashgate.

—(2010) 'Cultural Diversity and Social Inequalities', *Social Research*, 77(1): 257–89.

—(2013) 'Multiculturalism: From Heterogeneities to Social Inequalities', in P. Kivisto and Ö. Wahlbeck (eds) *Debating Multiculturalism in the Nordic Welfare States*, Houndmills, UK: Palgrave Macmillan.

Faist, T., Fauser, M. and Kivisto, P. (eds) (2011) *The Migration-Development Nexus: Transnational Perspectives*, Houndmills, UK: Palgrave Macmillan.

Fincke, G. (2009) *Abgehängt, Chancenlos, Unwillig? Eine Empirische Reorientierung von Integrationstheorien zu MigrantInnen der Zweiten Generation in Deutschland*, Wiesbaden: VS.

Galtung, J. (1969) 'Violence, Peace and Peace Research', *Journal of Peace Research*, 6(2): 167–91.

Gordon, M. (1964) *Assimilation in American Life: The Role of Race, Religion and National Origins*, New York, NY: Oxford University Press.

Light, I., Parminder, B. and Stavros, K. (1990) 'Migration Networks and Immigrant Entrepreneurship', California Immigrants in World Perspective Working Paper, Los Angeles, CA: Institute for Social Science Research. Online. Available HTTP: <http://escholarship.org/uc/item/50g990sk> (accessed 16 September 2013).

McAdam, D., Tarrow, S. and Tilly, C. (2001) *The Dynamics of Contention*, New York, NY: Cambridge University Press.

Mayntz, R. (2004) 'Mechanisms in the Analysis of Social Macro-phenomena', *Philosophy of the Social Sciences*, 34(2): 237–59.

Modood, T. (2007) *Multiculturalism*, Oxford, UK: Polity.

Orozco, A.P. (2007) 'Global Care Chains', Gender, Remittances and Development Series, Working Paper no. 2, Santo Domingo: United Nations Instraw.

Sarrazin, T. (2010) *Deutschland Schafft Sich Ab: Wie Wir Unser Land aufs Spiel Setzen*, Munich: Deutsche Verlags-Anstalt (DVA).

Tezcan, L. (2013) *Das Muslimische Subjekt: Verfangen im Dialog der Deutschen Islam Konferenz*, Konstanz: Konstanz University Press.

Therborn, G. (ed.) (2006) *Inequalities of the World: New Theoretical Frameworks, Multiple Research Approaches*, London: Verso.

Tilly, C. (1998) *Durable Inequality*, Berkeley, CA: University of California Press.

—(2005) *Identities, Boundaries and Social Ties*, Boulder, CO: Paradigm.

Weber, M. (1972) [1922] *Wirtschaft und Gesellschaft*, 5th edn, Tübingen: Mohr.

Zolberg, A.R. (1987) '"Wanted but not Welcome": Alien Labor in Western Development', in W. Alonso (ed.) *Population in an Interacting World*, Cambridge, MA: Harvard University Press.

29

Discrimination, diversity, and work

Vincent J. Roscigno and Jill E. Yavorsky

Discrimination, diversity, and inequality, especially as they pertain to the workplace, have become core social science foci over the prior three decades due to political pressures, legal oversight, and social movements surrounding equal access and opportunity. Significant transformation has certainly occurred when it comes to greater institutional access and compositional diversity by race/ethnicity and sex within organizations. Inequalities, however, persist. Relative to the workplace, for example, research continues to note persistent group level disadvantages in status, rewards and mobility despite greater diversity, formalized and bureaucratic rules, and clear-cut civil rights mandates. This has pushed some to question the extent to which conceptualizations and methods for studying inequality and diversity are themselves adequate. Indeed, it has become all too clear that there remains a "black box" surrounding how and why such inequality persists, the extent to which discrimination is playing a role, and whether focusing solely on compositional diversity, also often referred to as "organizational demography," is enough. Take, for instance, the following conclusions from recent work:

> Thus, discrimination is not observed, but must be inferred as a residual significant effect, once presumably meritocratic factors have been statistically accounted for. It seems unlikely that we will ever advance knowledge of discrimination mechanisms with data collected in a human capital or status-attainment framework.
>
> *(Tomaskovic-Devey et al. 2005: 85)*

> Do employers engage in reasonable evaluation practices that accurately distinguish productive from less productive workers, or do they make such distinctions on the basis of informal criteria, which allow more leeway for the influence of stereotypes based on race and class background? ... The large residual raises the possibility that unmeasured discrimination accounts for differential rates of employment exit and, again, intra-firm processes would shed light on the issue.
>
> *(Reid and Padavic 2005: 1257)*

In this article, we provide theoretical guideposts for scholars interested in the "black box" of discrimination, inequality, and diversity alluded to in the quotes. We do so by first offering a brief overview of influential research on workplace inequality and discrimination. Such literature is useful, to be sure, but it is restricted in its conception of discrimination and the relational processes that undergird it. By relational, we mean a "recognition of inequality's complexity, the role of actors, and multiple social forces at structural, cultural and interactive levels." Seeing discrimination in such a way, we argue, extends and moves us beyond the typical demographic compositional focus that permeates much inequality and diversity scholarship. Indeed, it provokes novel questions surrounding substantive diversity, or the extent and manner in which categorical distinctions, such as race and sex, are meaningful and enacted within organizational contexts and in the course of everyday interactions.

Workplace diversity, inequality, and discrimination in the contemporary era

Despite decades of civil rights oversight and higher levels of compositional diversity relative to the past, inequality remains a key feature of the employment context, intricately woven into organizational practices and interpersonal relations. Such inequality is particularly evident when examining attainment outcomes between disadvantaged and advantaged groups, using statistical or aggregate modeling. In this vein, we find persistent inequalities for women (Blau and Devaro 2007), sexual minorities (Antecol et al. 2007), mothers (Budig and England 2001), aging workers (Roscigno et al. 2007), and non-whites (Tomaskovic-Devey and Skaggs 2002) even when pertinent background attributes are accounted for. Similar disparities are observed when examining promotion and firing. Compared to white males, for instance, women and minorities who have comparable human capital are less likely to obtain promotions, and race/ethnic minorities are also more likely to be involuntarily terminated (Byron 2010). While such patterns may be a function of non- or poorly measured variations in worker attributes (i.e. human capital, personality, or social skills), many contend that remaining gaps are more likely the result of discrimination (Alon and Haberfeld 2007).

Along with the aforementioned disadvantages, we also know that, despite compositional diversity at the firm level, segregation within workplaces and across occupations persists and has implications for workplace opportunities and rewards (e.g. Mouw and Kalleberg 2010; Stainback and Tomaskovic-Devey 2012). Recent work highlights the importance of sorting and social closure mechanisms in stratifying workers into different, and unequal, jobs across and within workplaces (e.g. Kmec 2003; Pager et al. 2009; Semyonov and Herring 2007). Several core mechanisms are alluded to, including: (1) the cutting off of subordinate access to higher-status, higher-paying jobs (Huffman and Cohen 2004; McBrier and Wilson 2004); (2) the hoarding by superordinates of valued positions or advantages in job networks (McDonald et al. 2009; Royster 2003); (3) biased appraisals of performance and merit (Castilla 2012; Shwed and Kalev 2014); and (4) supervisory evaluations that err toward homophily (Maume 2011). Importantly, such inequalities persist despite compositional diversity. Scholars, constrained by methodological and data limitations, are often left speculating as to why or how.

Research regarding the role of cognitive bias offers a compelling starting point for filling some of these gaps. This work suggests that stereotypes and biases, conscious or unconscious, tend to influence employment-related decisions. Much research in this vein, drawing on experimental designs, indeed indicates that women are evaluated less favorably and as less capable when it comes to leadership (Eagly and Karau 2002). Moreover, they are also evaluated more harshly for displaying agentic qualities than men (Gill 2004); mothers are viewed as less competent than non-mothers (Correll et al. 2007); blacks are judged as having fewer "soft skills," being less competent, and less able to be effective leaders than non-whites (Rosette et al. 2008); and older people are seen as less competent and responsible than younger people (Cuddy *et al.* 2005). Not only can this affect mobility decisions, but it can also shape subtle verbal and non-verbal cues in a manner that taints group dynamics and interpersonal relationships (Quillian 2008).

Audit studies, like experimental designs, have allowed researchers to capture more directly evidence of bias and the discrimination that oftentimes ensues. Results show formal patterns of hiring discrimination on the basis of sex (Riach and Rich 2004), race (Pager *et al.* 2009), motherhood (Correll *et al.* 2007), age (Lahey 2005), and sexual orientation (Tilcsik 2011). Hebl *et al.* (2002), for instance, found that candidates portrayed as gay were treated more negatively in interactions and allotted less time with the employer than non-gay applicants. In an audit study on race, Pager *et al.* (2009) highlight ways in which employers use shifting standards to disqualify African Americans from jobs that white applicants are considered qualified for, and they also tend to steer blacks into lower-authority and lower-paying jobs. This type of methodology also provides a window onto the ways in which stereotypes operate. In an audit study testing sexual orientation discrimination, Tilcsik (2011) found that employers who posted job descriptions that consisted of male-typed characteristics (e.g. rational, competitive) were less likely to call back gay-signaled applicants, likely due to stereotypes that link gay men with effeminacy. Although such audit designs are illuminating, it is also the case that they are limited to the point of hire. Thus, various other dimensions of workplace discrimination, which can be as or even more pernicious, including firing, mobility, wages, and interactional harassment on the job, are overlooked.

It is important to recognize that the patterning of discrimination often coalesces with formal divisions of labor, leading employers to steer women and minorities into poorly rewarded jobs (Stainback *et al.* 2010). Indeed, contemporary organizations are structured in such a way that, even in the contemporary era, managers and supervisors continue to exert significant discretion, oftentimes with limited organizational oversight or effective accountability (Roscigno 2007). Petersen and Saporta (2004) refer to this discretion as the "opportunity structure" that allows inequitable decisions to be made. And, notably, we typically find similar disparities even in organizations with more formalized and bureaucratic merit-based systems (Castilla 2008). This suggests either that formalized procedures are somehow bypassed or that bias may exist within formalized procedures themselves – two points we return to shortly.

The potential for bias, discriminatory tendencies, and uneven allocations of individuals and groups to distinct and differentially rewarded positions in diverse workplaces has been and continues to be important. No less significant is recognition that these are not merely individual attitudes or actions about which we speak, but rather are processes that are forged in a broader, cultural milieu and that also operate at the structural level of organizations. Feminist scholars have been on the forefront here, outlining how broader cultural stereotypes and discriminatory potentials become inscribed and institutionalized in business practices and policies (Williams *et al.* 2012). Acker's (1990) discussion of "gendered organizations" and Martin's (2004) argument surrounding "gender as an institution" capture this, highlighting that, while proximate processes of interaction and social closure are certainly relevant, there is something more fundamental about the structures individuals and groups traverse that creates, or at least allows to persist, the unequal outcomes we find. Similarly, while state-structured and sponsored racism is less pronounced than it was in the past, ideological and structural dynamics that allow race/ethnic discrimination to permeate workplaces remain (Bonilla-Silva 2010). Broad insights such as these have provoked a new relational conception of discrimination – a relational conception that we now outline.

A relational framework for understanding discrimination, diversity, and inequality

The literature on discrimination, diversity, and inequality has witnessed fresh theoretical developments recently – theoretical developments surrounding the inherently relational nature of inequality production within otherwise (compositionally) diverse environments. The push here is not on statistical differences relative to the increasing, decreasing, or variable nature of workplace composition, but rather substantive diversity – that is, the ways in which workplace interactions (including discrimination) are conditioned by and constitutive of the organizational structures and cultures within which they are enfolded (in this regard, see especially Ridgeway 2011). Our conception of a more relational approach to understanding discrimination is displayed in Figure 29.1.

Such a conception challenges prevailing top-down depictions of structural constraint and/or neutrality in organizations while being explicit about the constitutive interplay of structure, culture, and interaction when it comes to discrimination and inequality in otherwise diverse contexts (Wilson *et al.* 2013). In this regard, "relational" entails the joint interplay of external and internal organizational structures and culture with hierarchical workplace interactions in which discrimination is often enacted. Conceiving of how and why discrimination emerges and persists using such a framework has generated at least four pertinent foci regarding substantive diversity and inequality within contemporary organizations. Each offers important insights on discrimination. Taken together, they bridge the processes outlined in Figure 29.1 and offer an orienting relational framework for understanding discrimination and its implications for diversity and inequality.

Discrimination and the enabling/constraining impact of structure

Legal and political environments, structures, and exerted pressures, are perpetually subject to change, and they constrain the abilities and opportunities of employers to engage in discrimination. In America, the passage of the Civil Rights Act of 1964 and the subsequent creation of the Equal Employment Opportunity Commission (EEOC) and the Office of Federal Contract Compliance Programs (OFCCP) have been instrumental in halting overt and blatant forms of discrimination and segregation so commonplace during the pre-civil rights era. Integrative gains, however, have stalled since the 1980s, especially in higher-level positions (Stainback and Tomaskovic-Devey 2012). Significant legal and political changes over the past few decades – changes that included the waning public sentiment and political advocacy for affirmative action programs and the federal deregulation of EEO organizations – are partly to blame for stalled progress given the implications they have had for regulation and enforcement. Further, the ways in which legal systems address discrimination (i.e. based largely on individual claims, rather than

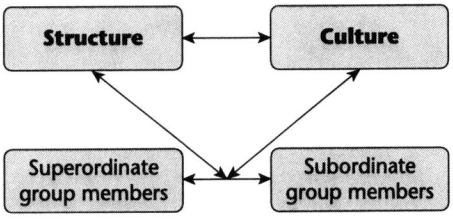

Figure 29.1 Relational conception of discrimination and its structural, cultural, and interactional foundations

collective harm) is limited and problematic inasmuch as the burden of proof is usually placed on the victim (Hirsh 2014).

Despite its limited impact, scholars have nevertheless identified two primary ways in which laws still influence organizations to diversify their workforces and/or decrease discriminatory practices: (1) direct coercion and (2) indirect coercion (Skaggs 2009). Direct coercion occurs when organizations are compelled to change organizational policies or practices either due to lawsuits or in response to compliance reviews of their firms. When they do so, according to some research, discrimination decreases and managerial diversity increases (Kalev *et al.* 2006; Skaggs 2009). However, deleterious effects, specifically backlash and increases in segregation, may also occur (Hirsh 2009; Roscigno 2007). Indirect coercion or constraint, in comparison, is the pressure exerted by legal and political environments that spurs firms to align organizational practices to culturally normative standards. Litigation against other firms in the same industries or legal contexts may, for example, motivate firms to reprioritize or restructure their own diversity efforts to avoid similar legal intervention or negative publicity (Hirsh 2009). As Skaggs notes, "inconsistencies with the institutional environment are likely to jeopardize legitimacy," thereby introducing subtle prodding that incentivizes companies to more carefully monitor and sanction discriminatory behavior (Skaggs 2009: 227).

Importantly, and worth highlighting, is the fact that much of the focus on federal EEO agencies and companies themselves has centered on increasing compositional diversity rather than the broad array of discriminatory processes and mechanisms embedded within workplaces and/or substantive diversity on the shop floor. Although one might argue that human resources and diversity offices are set up to perform this function, rigorous and relatively representative recent work suggests that their effectiveness is limited at best. At worst, they provide legitimacy or window dressing to ensure legal compliance. This is due, at least in part, to the fact that such internal offices are seldom given tangible powers to oversee and enforce (Kalev *et al.* 2006). The same could be said for EEO federal agencies and policies, which, as Stainback and Tomaskovic-Devey (2012) and other scholars purport, act largely as symbolic offerings rather than change-oriented measures that achieve substantive, meaningful results for disadvantaged groups.

Bureaucratic processes and discrimination

How do we explain, in the face of developments such as civil rights law and, more generally, formalization and bureaucratic development, persistent workplace discrimination? One possibility, of course, surrounds simple cognitive biases and the possibility that "bad apples" circumvent bureaucratic constraints in the course of interactions and when undertaking discriminatory behaviors. It is difficult to deny that this is at least partially true, in which case scholarship on discrimination might reasonably and simply focus on the interactions between subordinate and dominant actors, represented at the bottom of Figure 29.1. Yet, at least two dominant strands of contemporary work – strands that challenge the assumption of bureaucratic neutrality itself – call for a more comprehensive relational focus that includes attention to structure and culture within the process. Indeed, although organizations may be bureaucratically rational on the face of it and seemingly immune from hierarchical abuses, such structures are a product of the histories and cultures in which they were formed (Dobbin 1994; Morrill 2008). What this means is that historically and culturally proscribed hierarchies become inscribed in bureaucratic structures, practices, and internal power dynamics, and with relevance for discrimination, diversity, and inequality.

Pertinent here, as well as several other general strands of theory (e.g. Acker 1990), is the work of Alexandra Kalev surrounding inequality and its roots in formalized organizational practices.

Kalev (2009) suggests that otherwise neutral appearing workplace policies may be part of the problem through the fostering of internal segregation and hierarchical interactions – segregation and interactions that essentially allow cognitive biases and biased evaluations to go unchecked. When organizations deformalize and allow for cooperative group interaction through self-directed teams and cross-training programs, on the other hand, the visibility of women and minorities improves, thus undermining the potential for stereotyping. Further work (Kalev 2014) on workplace downsizing suggests that formalized and indeed bureaucratic processes themselves disadvantage and discriminate against women and minorities unless legal oversight is introduced. In both cases, bureaucratic formalization is part and parcel of the discriminatory process.

A second, non-mutually exclusive, insight has to do with the malleability of bureaucratic structures and constraints themselves – structures and constraints that are typically seen in the social sciences as neutral and more or less applicable to all of those in the workplace environment. Through the analyses of thousands of workplace discrimination lawsuit filings, Roscigno *et al.* (2007) find that not only do employers and supervisors apply differential criteria when assessing women and minorities, but they also invoke otherwise neutral policies and organizational mandates in a discretionary manner to ostracize, penalize and remove minority, female, and aging employees. This is consequential for discrimination and the reification of hierarchy in workplaces, to be sure. It also challenges dominant conceptions and, specifically, the assumption that the bureaucratic character of contemporary organizations necessarily constrains power and its malicious manifestations, as predicted by Weber (see Weber and Eisenstadt 1968). Instead, formal bureaucratic rules and procedures can be used to discriminate and ultimately shape, constrain, and enable more proximate interactions where discrimination is often most evident. Whether through biased formalization or the malleability and use of bureaucratic tools, it is clear that understandings of discrimination must account for, and indeed integrate, attention to the structures within which inequality and diversity manifest.

Discrimination, legitimation, and culture

It is not simply external forces and bureaucratic structures that are consequential. Culture is also meaningful. Classic sociological theory makes this point straightforwardly: inequality, when and if maintained effectively, requires not only reifying structures and behaviors, but also normative frameworks, values, and systems of belief that are consistent with and legitimating of such structures and actions. Until recently, however, and with the exception of ethnographic work denoting the realities of internal cultures (e.g. Goffman 1961), organizational research, including that pertaining to the workplace, has remained loyal to acultural, universalistic assumptions and has neglected questions of legitimacy and the broader cultural foundations of organizational life. We now know, however, from neo-institutional research, that actors, institutions, and organizations draw from the cultures within which they are embedded to legitimate their existence and operations (Meyer and Rowan 1991; Powell and DiMaggio 1991; Zucker 1988).

Dominant cultural formulations permeate organizational settings in at least two key ways relative to discrimination. First, culture matters for actors' cognitions, evaluations of others, and differential treatment – a fact now well established by recent experimental and audit designs (noted on p. 276), which demonstrate rather convincingly biases toward less powerful status groups, including assumptions of their lower levels of dependability and/or effort and commitment (Pager *et al.* 2009). Second, culture and the beliefs that it proliferates, which include values regarding merit and bureaucratic neutrality, help legitimate discriminatory actions as somehow justifiable (Castilla 2008). Indeed, cultural frameworks offer a construction of social reality wherein present arrangements are portrayed as natural or evident. This occurs through the often simultaneous and two-pronged process of *symbolic vilification*, wherein less powerful actors are discursively deemed as less worthy, problematic, or in some regard dangerous, and *symbolic amplification*, which involves discursive processes that imbue and elevate certain elements of cultural and institutional/organizational life (e.g. business necessity, meritocracy, formality) to a place of almost sacred reverence (Roscigno 2011).

Interaction and the production of inequality in structural/cultural contexts

The structural and cultural contexts discussed in the preceding section, and their implications for discrimination, inequality, and diversity, have significant implications for day-to-day and face-to-face interactional processes in everyday work life. That is, inequality and its roots in discrimination are best understood as an unequal relation, or inequality, based on personal attributes, institutional positioning, and statuses that are defined, codified, and acted upon within historical, structural, and cultural contexts (Ridgeway *et al.* 2009). Structural and cultural contexts enable and legitimate hierarchical interactions and decision-making, while interactions and decision-making reify structures and cultural interpretations. Without recognizing such complexities, compositional diversity may be achieved but substantive diversity within everyday work life and interactions will remain problematic.

This conception extends to insights regarding workplace interactions and bias as well as dominant formulations surrounding social closure by highlighting the interactional nature of discrimination (represented toward the bottom of Figure 29.1). Yet, it also makes explicit: (1) the ways in which culture and structure confer statuses on actors – statuses that shape valuations, treatment, interactions, and leverage; (2) how discrimination, beyond interaction and interpersonal power differentials, often also entails the invoking (or not) of seemingly neutral bureaucratic structures; and (3) the ways in which culture, broadly, confers status differentials and biases while also offering legitimizing cover for acts of discriminatory malfeasance, often through discursive processes of vilification and amplification. Importantly, especially in the case of biased formalization as previously discussed, the degree to which interpersonal interactions are even necessary for discrimination to occur may not be obvious as formalized structures themselves do the dirty work.

Conclusions

A relational approach to understanding workplace discrimination, diversity, and inequality, as we have outlined, offers several important guideposts and directions for future work. Indeed, it encourages scholars interested in these topics to: (1) move beyond overly simplistic, reductionist accounts of bias and cognition; (2) recognize the centrality of status dynamics and interaction, to be sure, but within structural and cultural contexts that enable and constrain interactions, the salience of statuses, and the leverage actors exert; and (3) acknowledge that compositional diversity rarely automatically equates to either substantive diversity or equality within organizational processes themselves. We believe that doing so will generate a more comprehensive understanding of inequality (Wilson *et al.* 2013) while also revealing potential points wherein issues of substantive diversity and inequality might be effectively, if not more directly, addressed.

To follow through effectively on a dynamic, multi-layered conception of discrimination and study it, of course, will necessitate creative analytic designs. Such designs might include, for instance, multi-level data that effectively capture the ways in which the compositional diversity of workplace environments impacts not simply levels of inequality but rather the more proximate processes wherein discrimination (be it through formalized rules, face-to-face interactions, or bureaucratic manipulations and discretion) play out. Case studies and various qualitative methodologies may be especially effective in this regard, though quantitative and comparative techniques are necessary as well to establish the extent to which processes, trends, and patterns are representative. Finally, analyses of discourses pertaining to discrimination, diversity, and inequality – discourses by employers, workers, as well as those within the broader socio-legal environment – are equally necessary, if not fundamental, for capturing the cultural scaffolding of discrimination, including actors' cognitions but also organizational legitimacy claims. It is only through such work and an accumulated body of such work, we believe, that adequate understandings and effective remediation can be realized.

References

Acker, J. (1990) 'Hierarchies, Jobs, Bodies: A Theory of Gendered Organizations', *Gender and Society*, 4(2): 139–58.

Alon, S. and Haberfeld, Y. (2007) 'Labor Force Attachment and the Evolving Wage Gap Between White, Black, and Hispanic Young Women', *Work and Occupations*, 34(4): 369–98.

Antecol, H., Jong, A. and Steinberger, M. (2007) 'Sexual Orientation Wage Gap: The Role of Occupational Sorting and Human Capital', *Industrial and Labor Relations Review*, 61(4): 518–43.

Blau, F.D. and Devaro, J. (2007) 'New Evidence on Gender Differences in Promotion Rates: An Empirical Analysis of a Sample of New Hires', *Industrial Relations*, 46(3): 511–50.

Bonilla-Silva, E. (2010) *Racism Without Racists: Color-blind Racism and the Persistence of Racial Inequality in the United States*, Plymouth, UK: Rowman & Littlefield.

Budig, M.J. and England, P. (2001) 'The Wage Penalty for Motherhood', *American Sociological Review*, 66(2): 204–25.

Byron, R.A. (2010) 'Discrimination, Complexity, and the Public/Private Sector Question', *Work and Occupations*, 37(4): 435–75.

Castilla, E.J. (2008) 'Gender, Race, and Meritocracy in Organizational Careers', *American Journal of Sociology*, 113(6): 1479–1526.

—(2012) 'Gender, Race, and the New (Merit-based) Employment Relationship', *Industrial Relations*, 51(4): 528–62.

Correll, S.J., Benard, S. and Paik, I. (2007) 'Getting a Job: Is there a Motherhood Penalty?', *American Journal of Sociology*, 112(5): 1297–339.

Cuddy, A.J.C., Norton, M.I. and Fiske, S.T. (2005) 'This Old Stereotype: The Pervasiveness and Persistence of the Elderly Stereotype', *Journal of Social Issues*, 61(2): 267–85.

Dobbin, F. (1994) 'Cultural Models of Organization: The Social Construction of Rational Organizing Principles', in D. Crane (ed.) *The Sociology of Culture. Emerging Theoretical Perspectives*, Oxford, UK: Blackwell.

Eagly, A.H. and Karau, S.J. (2002) 'Role Congruity Theory of Prejudice Toward Female Leaders', *Psychological Review*, 109(3): 573–98.

Gill, M.J. (2004) 'When Information Does Not Deter Stereotyping: Prescriptive Stereotyping Can Foster Bias Under Conditions That Deter Descriptive Stereotyping', *Journal of Experimental Social Psychology*, 40(5): 619–32.

Goffman, E. (1961) *Asylums: Essays on the Social Situation of Mental Patients and Other Inmates*, Garden City, NY: Anchor.

Hebl, M.R., Foster, J.B., Mannix, L.M. and Dovidio, J.F. (2002) 'Formal and Interpersonal Discrimination: A Field Study of Bias Toward Homosexual Applicants', *Personality and Social Psychology Bulletin*, 28(6): 815–25.

Hirsh, C.E. (2009) 'The Strength of Weak Enforcement: The Impact of Discrimination Charges, Legal Environments, and Organizational Conditions on Workplace Segregation', *American Sociological Review*, 74(2): 245–71.

—(2014) 'Beyond Treatment and Impact: A Context-oriented Approach to Employment Discrimination', *American Behavioral Scientist*, 58(2): 256–73.

Huffman, M.L. and Cohen, P.N. (2004) 'Racial Wage Inequality: Job Segregation and Devaluation across U.S. Labor Markets', *American Journal of Sociology*, 109(4): 902–36.

Kalev, A. (2009) 'Cracking the Glass Cages? Restructuring and Ascriptive Inequality at Work', *American Journal of Sociology*, 114(6): 1591–643.

—(2014) 'How You Downsize is Who You Downsize: Biased Formalization, Accountability and Managerial Diversity', *American Sociological Review*, 79(1): 109–35.

Kalev, A., Dobbin, F. and Kelly, E. (2006) 'Best Practices or Best Guesses? Assessing the Efficacy of Corporate Affirmative Action and Diversity Policies', *American Sociological Review*, 71(4): 589–617.

Kmec, J.A. (2003) 'Minority Job Concentration and Wages', *Social Problems*, 50(1): 38–59.

Lahey, J. (2005) *Age, Women, and Hiring: An Experimental Study*, Cambridge, MA: National Bureau of Economic Research.

Martin, P.Y. (2004) 'Gender as Social Institution', *Social Forces*, 82(4): 1249–73.

Maume, D.J. (2011) 'Meet the New Boss . . . Same as the Old Boss? Female Supervisors and Subordinate Career Prospects', *Social Science Research*, 40(1): 287–98.

McBrier, D.B. and Wilson, G. (2004) 'Going Down? Race and Downward Occupational Mobility for White-collar Workers in the 1990s', *Work and Occupations*, 31(3): 283–322.

McDonald, S., Lin, N. and Ao, D. (2009) 'Networks of Opportunity: Gender, Race, and Job Leads', *Social Problems*, 56(3): 385–402.

Meyer, J.W. and Rowan, B. (1991) 'Institutionalized Organizations: Formal Structure as Myth and Ceremony', in W.W. Powell and P.J. DiMaggio (eds) *The New Institutionalism in Organizational Analysis*, Chicago, IL: University of Chicago Press.

Morrill, C. (2008) 'Culture and Organization Theory', *The Annals of the American Academy of Political and Social Science*, 619(1): 15–40.

Mouw, T. and Kalleberg, A.L. (2010) 'Occupations and the Structure of Wage Inequality in the United States 1980s to 2000s', *American Sociological Review*, 75(3): 402–31.

Pager, D., Western, B. and Bonikowski, B. (2009) 'Discrimination in a Low-wage Labor Market: A Field Experiment', *American Sociological Review*, 74(5): 777–99.

Petersen, T. and Saporta, I. (2004) 'The Opportunity Structure for Discrimination', *American Journal of Sociology*, 109(4): 852–901.

Powell, W.W. and DiMaggio, P.J. (eds) (1991) *The New Institutionalism in Organizational Analysis*, Chicago, IL: University of Chicago Press.

Quillian, L. (2008) 'Does Unconscious Racism Exist?', *Social Psychology Quarterly*, 71(1): 6–11.

Reid, L.L. and Padavic, I. (2005) 'Employment Exits and the Race Gap in Young Women's Employment', *Social Science Quarterly*, 86(1): 1242–60.

Riach, P.A. and Rich, J. (2004) 'Deceptive Field Experiments of Discrimination: Are they Ethical?', *Kyklos*, 57(3): 457–70.

Ridgeway, C.L. (2011) *Framed by Gender: How Gender Inequality Persists in the Modern World*, Oxford, UK: Oxford University Press.

Ridgeway, C.L., Backor, K., Li, Y.E., Tinkler, J.E. and Erickson, K.G. (2009) 'How Easily does a Social Difference Become a Status Distinction? Gender Matters', *American Sociological Review*, 74(1): 44–62.

Roscigno, V.J. (2007) *The Face of Discrimination: How Race and Gender Impact Work and Home Lives*, Lanham, MD: Rowman & Littlefield.

—(2011) 'Power, Revisited', *Social Forces*, 90(2): 349–74.

Roscigno, V.J., Mong, S., Byron, R. and Tester, G. (2007) 'Age Discrimination, Social Closure and Employment', *Social Forces*, 86(1): 313–34.

Rosette, A.S., Leonardelli, G.J. and Phillips, K.W. (2008) 'The White Standard: Racial Bias in Leader Categorization', *Journal of Applied Psychology*, 93(4): 758–77.

Royster, D.A. (2003) *Race and the Invisible Hand: How White Networks Exclude Black Men from Blue-collar Jobs*, Berkeley, CA: University of California Press.

Semyonov, M. and Herring, C. (2007) 'Segregated Jobs or Ethnic Niches? The Impact of Racialized Employment on Earnings Inequality', *Research in Social Stratification and Mobility*, 25(4): 245–57.

Shwed, U. and Kalev, A. (2014) 'Are Referrals More Productive or More Likeable? Social Networks and the Evaluation of Merit', *American Behavioral Scientist*, 58(2): 288–308.

Skaggs, S. (2009) 'Legal-political Pressures and African American Access to Managerial Jobs', *American Sociological Review*, 74(2): 225–44.

Stainback, K. and Tomaskovic-Devey, D. (2012) *Documenting Desegregation: Racial and Gender Segregation in Private Sector Employment since the Civil Rights Act*, New York, NY: Russell Sage Foundation.

Stainback, K., Tomaskovic-Devey, D. and Skaggs, S. (2010) 'Organizational Approaches to Inequality: Inertia, Relative Power, and Environments', *Annual Review of Sociology*, 36(1): 225–47.

Tilcsik, A. (2011) 'Pride and Prejudice: Employment Discrimination Against Openly Gay Men in the United States', *American Journal of Sociology*, 117(2): 586–626.

Tilly, C. (1998) *Durable inequality*, Berkeley: University of California Press.

Tomaskovic-Devey, D. and Skaggs, S. (2002) 'Sex Segregation, Labor Process Organization, and Gender Earnings Inequality', *American Journal of Sociology*, 108(1): 102–28.

Tomaskovic-Devey, D., Thomas, M. and Johnson, K. (2005) 'Race and the Accumulation of Human Capital Across the Career: A Theoretical Model and Fixed-Effects Application', *American Journal of Sociology*, 111(1): 58–89.

Weber, M. and Eisenstadt, S.N. (1968) *On Charisma and Institution Building: Selected Papers*, Chicago, IL: University of Chicago Press.

Williams, C.L., Muller, C. and Kilanski, K. (2012) 'Gendered Organizations in the New Economy', *Gender and Society*, 26(4): 549–73.

Wilson, G., Roscigno, V.J. and Huffman, M.L. (2013) 'Public Sector Transformation, Racial Inequality and Downward Occupational Mobility', *Social Forces*, 91(3): 975–1006.

Zucker, L.G. (1988) 'Where do Institutional Patterns Come From? Organizations as Actors in Social Systems', in L.G. Zucker (ed.) *Institutional Patterns and Organizations: Culture and Environment*, Cambridge, MA: Ballinger.

30

Contact and prejudice

Ben Fell and Miles Hewstone

Although mixed social environments can provoke conflict, such diversity can also promote positive intergroup contact and the reduction of prejudice. At the psychological level, increasing proximity to, and therefore salience of, social 'outgroups' has been associated with numerous negative psychological effects (e.g. intergroup anxiety, see Stephan and Stephan 1985; ingroup favouritism, see Mullen *et al.* 1992; prejudice, see Allport 1954). Concomitant to this, however, diversity provides opportunities for resolution of conflict through contact between opposing groups; contact which, under the right circumstances, can have a significant and lasting positive effect on intergroup relations. Since its formulation by Gordon Allport (1954), the 'contact hypothesis' has embodied this potential positive effect in the field of social psychology, and has produced a significant body of research into its conditions, processes, and outcomes. This chapter will outline the progression of intergroup contact research over the last 50–60 years, provide a summary of the current state of the field, and discuss some of the recent criticisms levelled against contact theory. It will conclude that, despite the challenges to its claims and principles, the position of contact as an evidentially sound and integrated theory of intergroup relations renders it an invaluable tool in the study of diversity.

Allport and the early years of contact theory

In his book *The Nature of Prejudice*, Allport (1954) writes, 'It has sometimes been held that merely by assembling people without regard for race, color, religion, or national origin, we can thereby destroy stereotypes and develop friendly attitudes. The case is not so simple' (Allport 1954: 261.) According to this assertion, the fallacy against which Allport cautions might be termed 'mere contact' or indeed 'mere diversity': diversity and opportunities for contact are not, in and of themselves, sufficient to improve group relations. In his chapter on the effects of contact, Allport provided examples of intergroup contact in various settings, and, by evaluating the factors which might have contributed to the success (or otherwise) of these interventions, concludes with four optimal conditions under which prejudice is likely to be reduced. According to these criteria, contact is most likely to be effective if the groups involved are given equal status and work collaboratively towards common goals. Furthermore, the contact itself should receive institutional support and encourage perceptions of common group interests and identity.

As the oft-credited source of intergroup contact theory, Allport's work paved the way for an extensive body of research elaborating upon the precise nature of his proposed conditions and extending its principles to a wide range of cultural contexts and social groups. Subsequent studies reported by other authors have replicated the positive influence of contact on intergroup relations outside of the USA (e.g. Black and White workers in South Africa, see Bornman and Mynhardt 1991), on non-ethnic outgroups (e.g. homosexuals, see Herek and Capitanio 1996; the disabled, see Anderson 1995), and using a wide variety of research designs beyond archival or survey data (e.g. experimental, see Cook 1978; neuroimaging, see Walker *et al.* 2008). The majority of these studies confirmed the ameliorating influence of contact on various aspects of prejudice, and several subsequent reviews attest to the general consistency of benefits of contact (e.g. Hewstone and Brown 1986). In addition, a large-scale meta-analysis by Pettigrew and Tropp (2006) revealed that across 515 studies and over 250,000 participants, contact produced a modest but significant effect on prejudice (Pearson's r between -0.205 and -0.214). Furthermore, this effect was found to be larger for the subset of studies that designed their contact scenarios to uphold Allport's conditions ($r = -0.287$) than those that did not ($r = -0.204$). As a result of this broad consensus, the contact hypothesis has become relatively well confirmed.

Limits of the conditional approach

In his review of contact theory, Pettigrew (1998) outlined several limitations of the research that followed Allport's introduction of the contact hypothesis, including the failure to establish the causal sequence of contact (i.e. whether contact reduces prejudice or prejudice reduces contact), a lack of evidence for the generalization of the effects of contact with an outgroup individual to the outgroup as a whole, and the dangers of focusing solely on cataloguing the optimal conditions for contact. As Pettigrew asserts, research conducted after Allport's introduction of the contact hypothesis produced an ever-growing 'laundry list' of conditions which threatened to deny the contact hypothesis any degree of parsimony, undermining its generalizability as the line between 'facilitating' versus 'essential' conditions became blurred. Though it may be practically useful to establish that contact works best when, for example, conducted in a common language or under a prosperous economy (Wagner and Machleit 1986), or when outgroup stereotypes are disconfirmed (Cook 1978), such findings contribute relatively little to our understanding of the *process* (or processes) by which contact reduces prejudice.

Mediators and moderators

Contact research in the twenty-first century has seen increased focus on determining *how* contact works (rather than merely establishing *that* it works), and this has largely been reflected in the emphasis on the statistical concepts of mediation and moderation (for a detailed discussion, see Baron and Kenny 1986). The first of these (i.e. mediators) represents a direct response to the question: By which processes does intergroup contact exert its effects? Indeed, the terms 'mediator' and 'process' are usually somewhat synonymous. For example, a key mediator of the effect of contact on prejudice is anxiety, in that contact has been shown to reduce prejudice through the *process* of reducing anxiety towards the outgroup (Stephan and Stephan 1985). The second concept, moderation, is exemplified in Allport's notion of optimal conditions. In simple terms, a moderator is some factor which changes the nature of the relationship between a predictor and outcome variable. For example, the salience of one's group identity is a well-established moderator of the relationship between contact and prejudice, in that the ameliorative effect of contact on prejudice is increased when identity salience is high.

Brown and Hewstone's (2005) 'An Integrative Theory of Intergroup Contact' provides a review of many of the established mediators and moderators of contact, and attempts to synthesize these into what is essentially an updated expression of the contact hypothesis. In doing so their model embodies several key elements of contemporary contact research. First, the authors draw a distinction between the role of cognitive and affective mediators of contact. Much of the early work on contact, including that of Allport himself, conceptualized intergroup relations at a primarily cognitive level, emphasizing the effects of factors such as knowledge about the outgroup (Allport 1954), or the individuation of its members (Brewer and Miller 1984). Although the effects of these cognitive variables have been replicated (Pettigrew and Tropp 2008), their effect sizes are generally rather small compared to those of the affective factors that have risen to prominence in recent years. Factors such as anxiety, intergroup threat, empathy, and perspective taking (ibid.) are now generally considered more instrumental in the contact process (Pettigrew 1998) and have been shown to exert a greater influence over intergroup behaviour (Stangor et al.1991). It must be noted, however, that the effectiveness of any mediator is highly dependent on the nature of the outcome variable being measured; just as with mediators, dependent variables can be cognitive (e.g. stereotypes) or affective (e.g. intergroup emotions, see Tropp and Pettigrew 2005).

The Role of Friendships

Although Allport's focus on the importance of outgroup knowledge has been largely superseded in recent years, the renewed emphasis on building affective ties with outgroup members does confirm one of the central tenets of his original hypothesis – the importance of cross-group friendships (see meta-analysis by Davies et al. 2011). By their very nature, friendships satisfy many of the classic conditions for optimal contact (equal status, common identity, see Pettigrew 1997), and promote the positive mediators of intergroup contact (e.g. self-disclosure, see Turner et al. 2007) whilst reducing its negative processes (e.g. anxiety, see La Greca and Lopez 1998). Cross-group friendships are now seen as something of a 'special case' of contact, and their effects are generally treated separately from more traditional non-affiliative contact experiences. Research into the role of friendship networks has also led to a further diversification of the *types* of contact under consideration by psychologists. Along with direct contact and cross-group friendship, much attention has been given to the role of extended contact, that is, the knowledge that one's ingroup friends are having contact with members of the outgroup (Wright et al. 1997). Cross-sectional, experimental, and longitudinal research into extended contact has revealed significant positive effects on outgroup attitudes (as well as mediators such as anxiety, see Paolini et al. 2004) even when controlling for the effects of direct contact. Extended contact also has the unique advantage of providing an indirect means of reducing prejudice. In their discussion of intergroup anxiety, Stephan and Stephan (1985) caution that in direct contact scenarios participants are likely to feel a certain amount of apprehension towards outgroup members (due to threatening stereotypes, lack of familiarity, etc.), which can undermine the contact process. Extended contact neatly sidesteps this issue, by avoiding potentially anxiety-inducing face-to-face interactions, whilst still allowing participants to reap the benefits of intergroup contact. Similarly, extended contact provides a form of contact that can retain its effectiveness even in the face of pronounced segregation.

Multiple outcomes of contact

Although the majority of contact literature focuses on the reduction of prejudice, the array of dependent variables linked with intergroup contact has grown over the years, and now provides an extremely rich tapestry of social indicators. The first seeds of this diversification have been present since the foundation of the contact hypothesis, with early analyses emphasizing its effects on stereotypes as an alternative outcome to attitudes (e.g. Rothbart and John 1985). More recent research has investigated the effects of contact on a wide array of dependent variables, finding significant effects on action tendencies (e.g. Tam *et al.* 2003), trust (e.g. Tam *et al.* 2009), forgiveness (e.g. Hewstone *et al.* 2006), infrahumanization (the denial of complex, uniquely human emotions to outgroup members, see Leyens *et al.* 2000), and attitude strength (e.g. Christ *et al.* 2010). The development of data-collection techniques beyond traditional self-report questionnaires has opened up the scope of contact research to include implicit or unconscious attitudes (e.g. Maass 1999), physiological responses (e.g. Blascovich *et al.* 2001), and neural activity (Walker *et al.* 2008). The consistent replication of the basic positive effect of contact at the cognitive, affective, behavioural, and physiological level represents some of the strongest evidence for its value as a robust theory of intergroup relations.

As mentioned previously, one of the key criticisms of early contact research was the failure to generalize its effects to the outgroup as a whole. Although this particular issue has largely been resolved, the question of generalization has seen a resurgence in recent years. Specifically, Pettigrew (1997) hypothesized that the beneficial effects of contact with one particular outgroup might generalize to members of other, distinct outgroups. This process was later dubbed the 'secondary transfer effect' (Pettigrew 2009) and has now received substantial evidential support. Tausch *et al.* (2010) found that the direct contact-induced positive attitude changes towards the primary outgroup did indeed generalize to secondary outgroups, even when controlling for direct contact with the secondary outgroup and other factors such as socially desirable responding.

Critics of contact

Although the principle that positive intergroup contact generally reduces prejudice remains relatively unchallenged, a number of authors have expressed criticisms of certain elements of contact theory. Serious consideration of such critiques is of great potential value to contact research as a whole. The empirical response it demands results in either the strengthening of the theory when challenges are rebuffed, or identification of limits on the effectiveness of contact when they are upheld. This section will include a discussion of four challenges to elements of contact theory which have emerged in recent years: Putnam's (2007) claim that diversity reduces trust and 'social capital'; the so-called 'leading the horse to water' problem that although groups may be given opportunities for contact, contact theory speaks little to their inclination to seek out interactions with outgroup members of their own volition (Dixon *et al.* 2005); Reicher's (2007) concern that contact has little impact on social policy and may in fact discourage disadvantaged minority groups from taking collective action; and finally the call by Pettigrew (2008) and others to give greater consideration to the effects of negative contact.

Putnam and the 'downside' of diversity

Of all the criticisms of contact, Putnam's attack on the concept of diversity has probably received the most mass-media attention, thanks to its controversial claim that 'social capital' (essentially an index of trust towards one's neighbours) is reduced in communities with high interethnic mixing. Putnam (2007) based this claim on a national survey of communal trust and social behaviour in 41 American communities, from which he concluded not only that diversity reduces social capital, but also that those with low trust in ethnically diverse areas demonstrate 'hunkering down' behaviour, characterized by reduced political engagement and confidence in local government, fewer friendships, increased television viewing, and less self-reported happiness. Contrary to the fairly misrepresentative media coverage of his report, Putnam did concede that these toxic effects of diversity were likely limited to the short term. Indeed, he asserted that, in the long term, diverse societies tend to overcome the struggles of interethnic tension and reach a state of increased social solidarity.

Caveats aside, however, there are several significant methodological flaws with Putnam's research that reduce its capacity to undermine contact theory. Chief among these is the fact that although Putman explicitly targets contact theory in his report, his analyses did not include actual measures of intergroup contact. Instead, he uses the overall level of ethnic heterogeneity for each of the 41 communities as the 'diversity' variable in his analyses. At the very best, this could be considered a measure of *opportunity* for contact, which, although a strong predictor of actual contact experience, is by no means the same construct. Furthermore, using a high-level contextual variable like community homogeneity to infer individual-level experiences is highly questionable, particularly when the report included no measure of self-reported segregation. Finally, since Putnam's (2007) publication, several authors have found that the effect of neighbourhood diversity was significantly reduced in a subset of individuals who had regular, face-to-face contact with outgroup members (Stolle *et al.* 2008). Rothwell (2009) found that the effects of local desegregation actually reversed the 'diversity' effect such that higher neighbourhood-level mixing increased intergroup trust. It would therefore seem that, at least for the purposes of contact theory, Putnam's findings are limited to a re-treading of ground already covered by Allport himself when he asserted that the case of contact was 'not so simple' as merely bringing groups into close proximity. In this case, diversity certainly has the potential to reduce trust, but only when combined with high levels of segregation at the local level. When intergroup mixing is permitted, or indeed encouraged, the beneficial effects of intergroup contact appear and counteract the potential negative impact of diversity (Schmid *et al.* 2014).

Leading the horse to water

Another conclusion that may be drawn from Putnam's work is the importance of appropriate scale of analysis. Putnam's results are undermined by the fact that they place too much emphasis on relatively coarse, high-level representations of group dynamics. However, some authors, notably Dixon *et al.* (2005), argue that much of the research into contact theory is guilty of a similar failing of analytic scale (though in the opposite direction). Dixon *et al.* point out that the vast majority of contact research fails to address the issue of group behaviour in realistic settings. With a few exceptions, the majority of contact studies utilize either self-report questionnaires or rather artificial experimental settings to induce and record behaviour. Dixon *et al.* caution that in social contexts marked by protracted and entrenched conflicts, self-reports and lab experiments may misrepresent the true levels of actual contact experienced by the group members involved. As an illustration of both the problem and a potential means of solving it, Tredoux and Dixon (2009) report a study in which they observed patterns of seating for different racial groups in Cape Town bars and nightclubs. They analysed the seating patterns at four levels: the establishment as a whole, its subsections, their separate tables, and finally individual interactions between patrons. They found that the degree of ethnic segregation increased with the resolution of their analysis – that is it was greatest at the level of individual interactions, and lowest at the level of the nightclub as a whole.

Although the complete 'reorientation' of contact research that Dixon *et al.* (2005) recommend is probably unnecessary, their call for a greater application of qualitative, observation-based measures of intergroup behaviour to assess the 'true' effects of contact is one which should be wholeheartedly accepted by the field. As previously mentioned, contact theory today includes a wide range of dependent variables, but there is certainly a need for more *in situ* behavioural data to address the outstanding question of self-driven contact behaviour. This being said, it is likely that part of the reason for the relative lack of such data is the difficulty of explicitly linking observed naturalistic behaviour to the more traditional metrics of contact. For example, if Tredoux and Dixon (2009) had attempted to gather self-reported attitude data from the customers in their bars and nightclubs, not only would they have likely ruined a lot of people's evenings, but also they would almost certainly have disrupted the very behavioural patterns they sought to record. This methodological impediment to linking self-report and behavioural data poses a significant challenge for contact researchers, and, although some existing techniques have the potential to provide some degree of synthesis (e.g. diary studies, see Shook and Fazio 2008; agent-based modelling, see Neal and Neal 2014), resolution of this issue should be a high priority for contact theorists.

Collective action and social change

Reicher (2007) voiced concerns that the ameliorative effects of contact on minority groups' attitudes towards the dominant majority might have the potential to reduce minority members' drive to carry out collective action to redress inequalities in their social environment. This claim is backed up by significant evidential support drawn from self-report surveys of various disadvantaged groups (e.g. Dixon *et al.* 2010) and from experimental data (Saguy *et al.* 2009). In one clear example of the importance of numerical status, Durrheim and Dixon (2010) report that although White South Africans who experienced contact with Black South Africans showed increased support for 'transformative' social policies, Black South Africans themselves displayed the opposite effect, with contact reducing their support for such policies. Although this demobilization may be somewhat attributable to the diminished effect of contact on minority members in general (Pettigrew and Tropp 2005), Pettigrew and Tropp (2011) assert that this overlap is only partial. They also argue that minority action is not the only driving force behind social change, citing weakening support for the group hierarchy amongst majority members, institutional collapse, economic hardship, and natural disasters as additional potential instigators. However, based on the empirical evidence it would seem that minority demobilization represents a real and present concern for the use of contact as a social intervention.

In response, Pettigrew and Tropp propose two possible factors which could preserve the benefits of contact whilst encouraging political mobilization: first, targeting the majority group in an attempt to weaken their resolve to preserve the unfair hierarchy; second, using contact as a means of highlighting status discrepancies between majority and minority groups, as well as to give minority members an opportunity to identify any weaknesses in the majority position that might be exploited to their benefit. In addition, Dixon *et al.* (2010) propose a third process, wherein contact *between* minority groups might encourage unity against the common majority oppressor. Although the latter of these processes appear quite antithetical to the 'stated aim' of contact (i.e. the reduction of prejudice and the promotion of intergroup harmony), it could very well be argued that collective action should be the priority for social interventions, since it has at least the potential to redress the status differential between minority and majority groups. For contact theory as a whole, the value of investigating negative experiences and outcomes is an oft-overlooked yet vital component of any complete model of intergroup process.

Negative contact

Pettigrew (2008) points out that the body of contact research in its entirety suffers from a marked positivity bias. Diversity provides opportunities for both positive and negative experiences with outgroup members. Yet, despite the enormous body of literature detailing the conditions, processes, forms, and outcomes of positive intergroup contact, very little has been said on the subject of negative contact. In discussing this issue, it is important to avoid the pitfall of treating negative contact as the mere absence of positive contact. In the first study of their 2012 paper on the relative effects of positive and negative contact, Barlow *et al.* amalgamated several studies which used bipolar measures of contact valence (in which, for example, a high score would represent high positive contact and a low score would mean high negative contact). Barlow *et al.* themselves note that such measures fail to convey the independence of positive and negative contact experiences, and in their second study employ two separate unipolar measures, with which they show that, although negative contact occurred less frequently in their sample, it was nonetheless a stronger predictor of racism and outgroup avoidance than was positive contact.

The paucity of negative contact studies makes it difficult to conclude with any certainty as to the relative effects of positive and negative contact, as Barlow *et al.* sought to do. A previous experimental study by Wilder (1984), in which participants were assigned to conditions of positive or negative contact with typical or atypical outgroup confederates (as well as a control condition with no contact), found that *only* positive interactions with a typical outgroup member significantly altered the participants' evaluation of the outgroup. Other studies have investigated factors such as which contact conditions are most likely to cause contact to be perceived as negative (Pettigrew and Tropp 2011) and the effect of positive and negative (or 'valenced') contact on attitude strength (Christ *et al.* 2008). The fact that negative contact has remained relatively untested during the past 60 years of contact research leads to the somewhat overwhelming situation where there are almost as many questions to ask about negative contact as have been answered about positive contact. What processes mediate or moderate the effects of negative contact? What outcome measures does it influence, and is it possible to experience negative extended contact, or negative secondary transfer effects? As with most of the challenges to contact theory discussed here, the omission of negative contact does not necessarily undermine the findings of the literature to date. It does, however, demand attention because, as it stands, contact theory is arguably missing its other, 'worse', half.

Conclusions

In their review of contact research celebrating 50 years of the *British Journal of Social Psychology*, Hewstone and Swart (2011) put forth the argument that over the course of that half-century, intergroup contact had grown from a simple 'hypothesis' into a fully fledged 'theory'. In this chapter we have adopted Hewstone and Swart's terminology in the hope that it will serve to emphasize not only how far contact research has progressed, but also, more importantly, the fact that contact theory represents an invaluable tool for the social scientist interested in the psychological processes of diversity. As evidenced by the fact that roughly half the content of this review has involved significant challenges to the principles of intergroup contact, it is clear that the theory is far from complete. However, these very challenges provide the inspiration for the next generation of contact research; research which, if the last 60 years are any indication, will have a widespread and significant impact on the field of diversity studies.

References

Allport, G.W. (1954) *The Nature of Prejudice*, Cambridge, MA: Perseus.

Anderson, L.S. (1995) 'Outdoor Adventure Recreation and Social Integration: A Social Psychological Perspective', Unpublished Doctoral Dissertation, University of Minneapolis.

Barlow, F.K., Paolini, S., Pedersen, A., Hornsey, M.J., Radke, H.R., Harwood, J., Rubin, M. and Sibley, C.G. (2012) 'The Contact Caveat: Negative Contact Predicts Increased Prejudice More Than Positive Contact Predicts Reduced Prejudice', *Personality and Social Psychology Bulletin*, 38(12): 1629–43.

Baron, R.M. and Kenny, D.A. (1986) 'The Moderator–Mediator Variable Distinction in Social Psychological Research: Conceptual, Strategic, and Statistical Considerations', *Journal of Personality and Social Psychology*, 51(6): 1173–82.

Blascovich, J., Mendes, W.B., Hunter, S.B., Lickel, B. and Kowai-Bell, N. (2001) 'Perceiver Threat in Social Interactions with Stigmatized Others', *Journal of Personality and Social Psychology*, 80(2): 253–67.

Bornman, E. and Mynhardt, J.C. (1991) 'Social Identity and Intergroup Contact in South Africa with Specific Reference to the Work Situation', *Genetic, Social, and General Psychology Monographs*, 117(4): 439–62.

Brewer, M. B. and Miller, N. (1984) 'Beyond the Contact Hypothesis: Theoretical Perspectives on Desegregation', in N. Miller and M.B. Brewer (eds) *Groups in Contact: The Psychology of Desegregation*, Orlando, FL: Academic Press.

Brown, R. and Hewstone, M. (2005) 'An Integrative Theory of Intergroup Contact', *Advances in Experimental Social Psychology*, 37: 255–343.

Christ, O., Ulrich, J. and Wagner, U. (2008) 'The Joint Effects of Positive and Negative Intergroup Contact on Attitudes and Attitude Strength', Paper Presented at the General Meeting of the European Association of Experimental Social Psychology, Opatija, Croatia.

Christ, O., Hewstone, M., Tausch, N., Wagner, U., Voci, A., Hughes, J. and Cairns, E. (2010) 'Direct Contact as a Moderator of Extended Contact Effects: Cross-sectional and Longitudinal Impact on Outgroup Attitudes, Behavioral Intentions, and Attitude Certainty', *Personality and Social Psychology Bulletin*, 36(12): 1662–74.

Cook, S.W. (1978) 'Interpersonal and Attitudinal Outcomes in Cooperating Interracial Groups', *Journal of Research and Development in Education*, 12(1): 97–113.

Davies, K., Tropp, L.R., Aron, A., Pettigrew, T.F. and Wright, S.C. (2011) 'Cross-group Friendships and Intergroup Attitudes: A Meta-analytic Review', *Personality and Social Psychology Review*, 15(4): 332–51.

Dixon, J., Durrheim, K. and Tredoux, C. (2005) 'Beyond the Optimal Contact Strategy: A Reality Check for the Contact Hypothesis', *American Psychologist*, 60(7): 697–711.

Dixon, J., Durrheim, K., Tredoux, C., Tropp, L., Clack, B. and Eaton, L. (2010) 'A Paradox of Integration? Interracial Contact, Prejudice Reduction, and Perceptions of Racial Discrimination', *Journal of Social Issues*, 66(2): 401–16.

Durrheim, K. and Dixon, J. (2010) 'Racial Contact and Change in South Africa', *Journal of Social Issues*, 66(2): 273–88.

Herek, G.M. and Capitanio, J.P. (1996) '"Some of My Best Friends". Intergroup Contact, Concealable Stigma, and Heterosexuals' Attitudes Toward Gay Men and Lesbians', *Personality and Social Psychology Bulletin*, 22(4): 412–24.

Hewstone, M. and Brown, R. (1986) 'Contact is Not Enough: An Intergroup Perspective on the "Contact Hypothesis"', in M. Hewstone and R. Brown (eds) *Contact and Conflict in Intergroup Encounters*, Oxford, UK: Blackwell.

Hewstone, M. and Swart, H. (2011) 'Fifty-odd Years of Inter-group Contact: From Hypothesis to Integrated Theory', *British Journal of Social Psychology*, 50(3): 374–86.

Hewstone, M., Cairns, E., Voci, A., Hamberger, J. and Niens, U. (2006) 'Intergroup Contact, Forgiveness, and Experience of "The Troubles" in Northern Ireland', *Journal of Social Issues*, 62(1): 99–120.

La Greca, A.M. and Lopez, N. (1998) 'Social Anxiety Among Adolescents: Linkages with Peer Relations and Friendships', *Journal of Abnormal Child Psychology*, 26(2): 83–94.

Leyens, J.P., Paladino, P.M., Rodriguez-Torres, R., Vaes, J., Demoulin, S., Rodriguez-Perez, A. and Gaunt, R. (2000) 'The Emotional Side of Prejudice: The Attribution of Secondary Emotions to Ingroups and Outgroups', *Personality and Social Psychology Review*, 4(2): 186–97.

Maass, A. (1999) 'Linguistic Intergroup Bias: Stereotype Perpetuation through Language', *Advances in Experimental Social Psychology*, 31: 79–121.

Mullen, B., Brown, R. and Smith, C. (1992) 'Ingroup Bias as a Function of Salience, Relevance, and Status: An Integration', *European Journal of Social Psychology*, 22(2): 103–22.

Neal, Z.P. and Neal, J.W. (2014) 'The (in) Compatibility of Diversity and Sense of Community', *American Journal of Community Psychology*, 53(1–2): 1–12.

Paolini, S., Hewstone, M., Cairns, E. and Voci, A. (2004) 'Effects of Direct and Indirect Cross-group Friendships on Judgments of Catholics and Protestants in Northern Ireland: The Mediating Role of an Anxiety-reduction Mechanism', *Personality and Social Psychology Bulletin*, 30(6): 770–86.

Pettigrew, T.F. (1997) 'Generalized Intergroup Contact Effects on Prejudice', *Personality and Social Psychology Bulletin*, 23(2): 173–85.

—(1998) 'Intergroup Contact Theory', *Annual Review of Psychology*, 49(1): 65–85.

—(2008) 'Future Directions for Intergroup Contact Theory and Research', *International Journal of Intercultural Relations*, 32(3): 187–99.

—(2009) 'Secondary Transfer Effect of Contact: Do Intergroup Contact Effects Spread to Noncontacted Outgroups?', *Social Psychology*, 40(2): 55–65.

Pettigrew, T.F. and Tropp, L.R. (2005) 'Allport's Intergroup Contact Hypothesis: Its History and Influence', in J. Dovidio, P. Glick and L.A. Rudman (eds) *On the Nature of Prejudice: Fifty Years after Allport*, Oxford, UK: Blackwell.

—(2006) 'A Meta-analytic Test of Intergroup Contact Theory', *Journal of Personality and Social Psychology*, 90(5): 751–83.

—(2008) 'How Does Intergroup Contact Reduce Prejudice? Meta-analytic Tests of Three Mediators', *European Journal of Social Psychology*, 38(6): 922–34.

—(2011) *When Groups Meet: The Dynamics of Intergroup Contact*, Hove, UK: Psychology Press.

Putnam, R.D. (2007) 'E Pluribus Unum: Diversity and Community in the Twenty-first Century', *Scandinavian Political Studies*, 30(2): 137–74.

Reicher, S. (2007) 'Rethinking the Paradigm of Prejudice', *South African Journal of Psychology*, 37(4): 820–34.

Rothbart, M. and John, O.P. (1985) 'Social Categorization and Behavioral Episodes: A Cognitive Analysis of the Effects of Intergroup Contact', *Journal of Social Issues*, 41(3): 81–104.

Rothwell, J.T. (2009) 'Trust in Diverse, Integrated, Cities: A Revisionist Perspective', Unpublished Paper, Princeton: Woodrow Wilson School of Public and International Affairs.

Saguy, T., Tausch, N., Dovidio, J.F. and Pratto, F. (2009) 'The Irony of Harmony: Intergroup Contact can Produce False Expectations for Equality', *Psychological Science*, 20(1): 114–21.

Schmid, K., Al Ramiah, A. and Hewstone, M. (2014) 'Neighborhood Ethnic Diversity and Trust: The Role of Intergroup Contact and Perceived Threat', *Psychological Science*, 25(3), 665–74.

Shook, N.J. and Fazio, R.H. (2008) 'Interracial Roommate Relationships: An Experimental Field Test of the Contact Hypothesis', *Psychological Science*, 19(7): 717–23.

Stangor, C., Sullivan, L.A. and Ford, T.E. (1991) 'Affective and Cognitive Determinants of Prejudice', *Social Cognition*, 9(4): 359–80.

Stephan, W.G. and Stephan, C.W. (1985) 'Intergroup Anxiety', *Journal of Social Issues*, 41(3): 157–75.

Stolle, D., Soroka, S. and Johnston, R. (2008) 'When Does Diversity Erode Trust? Neighborhood Diversity, Interpersonal Trust and the Mediating Effect of Social Interactions', *Political Studies*, 56(1): 57–75.

Tam, T., Hewstone, M., Kenworthy, J.B., Voci, A., Cairns, E. and Geddes, L. (2003) 'The Mediational Role of Empathy and Intergroup Emotions in Contact Between Catholics and Protestants in Northern Ireland', Paper presented at Conference on Social Exclusion, University of Kent at Canterbury.

Tam, T., Hewstone, M., Cairns, E., Tausch, N., Maio, G. and Kenworthy, J.B. (2007) 'The Impact of Intergroup Emotions on Forgiveness in Northern Ireland', *Group Processes and Intergroup Relations*, 10(1): 119–35.

Tam, T., Hewstone, M., Kenworthy, J.B. and Cairns, E. (2009) 'Intergroup Trust in Northern Ireland', *Personality and Social Psychology Bulletin*, 35(1): 45–59.

Tausch, N., Hewstone, M., Kenworthy, J.B., Psaltis, C., Schmid, K., Popan, J.R. and Hughes, J. (2010) 'Secondary Transfer Effects of Intergroup Contact: Alternative Accounts and Underlying Processes', *Journal of Personality and Social Psychology*, 99(2): 282–302.

Tredoux, C.G. and Dixon, J.A. (2009) 'Mapping the Multiple Contexts of Racial Isolation: The Case of Long Street, Cape Town', *Urban Studies*, 46(4): 761–77.

Tropp, L.R. and Pettigrew, T.F. (2005) 'Differential Relationships Between Intergroup Contact and Affective and Cognitive Dimensions of Prejudice', *Personality and Social Psychology Bulletin*, 31(8): 1145–58.

Turner, R.N., Hewstone, M. and Voci, A. (2007) 'Reducing Explicit and Implicit Outgroup Prejudice via Direct and Extended Contact: The Mediating Role of Self-disclosure and Intergroup Anxiety', *Journal of Personality and Social Psychology*, 93(3): 369–88.

Wagner, U. and Machleit, U. (1986) '"Gastarbeiter" in the Federal Republic of Germany: Contacts Between Germans and Migrant Population', in M. Hewstone and R. Brown (eds) *Foundations of Stereotypes and Stereotyping*, Oxford, UK: Blackwell.

Walker, P., Silvert, L., Hewstone, M. and Nobre, A.C. (2008) 'Social Contact and other Race-Face Processing in the Human Brain', *Social Cognitive and Affective Neuroscience*, 3(1): 16–25.

Wilder, D.A. (1984) 'Intergroup Contact: The Typical Member and the Exception to the Rule', *Journal of Experimental Social Psychology*, 20(2): 177–94.

Wright, S.C., Aron, A., McLaughlin-Volpe, T. and Ropp, S.A. (1997) 'The Extended Contact Effect: Knowledge of Cross-group Friendships and Prejudice', *Journal of Personality and Social Psychology*, 73(1): 73–90.

31

Diversity and social cohesion

Allison Harell and Dietlind Stolle

Increasing levels of ethnic and racial diversity in industrialized democracies have given rise to growing concerns about community and social cohesion in Europe and North America. There are worries that ethnic diversity may threaten the ties that bind civil society together (Putnam 2007). Sceptics of diversity seem to believe that diverse societies create problems. Accordingly, the assumption is that they are more likely to breed ethnic conflict, less likely to develop into stable democracies, less likely to enact a solidaristic social welfare system and less likely to foster widespread generalized trust. While some of these earlier concerns have been refuted, pessimism continues to linger, especially within the broader public debate. Indeed, the acceptance of cultural diversity is relatively low across Europe, and the rise of far-right parties in some European countries has been partly fuelled by widespread anti-immigrant sentiment (Sniderman *et al.* 2000).

Concerns about the potentially negative impact of diversity have also emerged in academic debates. Levels of generalized trust, for example, are lower not only among minorities themselves, but also among majority populations living in diverse surroundings (Alesina and La Ferrara 2002). Robert Putnam (2007) has recently argued that in the short run racial and ethnic diversity is likely to reduce various aspects of social capital, defined as the norms of trust and reciprocity that characterize healthy communities. His study finds that in racially diverse areas in the USA, citizens tend to trust each other less and are less able to cooperate with one another to address shared problems. He even finds that trust in one's own group members (e.g. the trust of Blacks in other Blacks) is reduced when facing social diversity. Several other studies confirm these insights in the US context (Alesina and La Ferarra 2000, 2002; Hero 2003). This kind of research leaves the impression that changing demographic realities in the USA are going to make democratic politics more difficult.

This chapter summarizes this debate and examines why it has recently stagnated. Some of the issues to be addressed include the one-sided focus on neighbourhood or regional ethnic diversity, and the related lack of integrating actual measures of inter-ethnic contact, and the little attention paid so far to considering the broader context in which diversity is experienced. We also propose a new approach to studying social cohesion that is relevant in diverse societies, discuss examples of research and end with suggestions for a research agenda.

The state of the research on diversity and social cohesion

The research on the consequences of ethnic diversity seems to create some puzzling results. According to some studies, when different ethnic or racial groups are brought together, the result is heightened intergroup conflict (Blumer 1958; Giles and Buckner 1993). According to this view, conflict results in part because ethnic or racial groups struggle over the same socio-economic resources or for cultural dominance. Thus majorities see out-groups as a threat to their own in-group, and as a result both in-group favouritism and out-group prejudice arise (Tajfel and Turner 1979). The 'conflict' or 'threat' hypothesis suggests that, as localities become increasingly diverse, out-group hostilities are likely to emerge. This phenomenon is found especially in less privileged areas and in the absence of meaningful contact (Oliver and Mendelberg 2000).

The empirical evidence for this thesis, however, is mixed. While some studies indicate that the ethnic diversity in areas is accompanied by lower levels of trust, out-group attitudes and social solidarity (Soroka *et al.* 2007a), other research turns up no relationships (Hooghe *et al.* 2009) or even positive effects (Stolle and Harell 2013). A recent meta-analysis that examines 90 articles on the topic finds that about 26 articles tend to support Putnam's findings; however, the same number of studies reject his findings (25), and 39 studies provide mixed or neutral findings (Van der Meer and Tolsma 2014). In short, the results do not seem to show any consistency and cannot really be generalized. We believe that there are several reasons for this unstable result, and these are discussed below.

Measuring diversity

One of the fundamental challenges to the study of the relation between diversity and social cohesion is related to the theorizing about which aspect of diversity actually matters. For example, in many of the discussed studies, diversity is tapped at various levels, at the contextual level, sometimes in countries, regions, states or provinces, counties, cities and census tracts. Clearly the variance in these contextual units of analysis will cause some of these diverging and inconsistent results (Dinesen and Sønderskov 2012). Moreover, studying diversity in these geographical units means that diversity should work mostly based on its visibility and its perception. Such measures of diversity do not take into account actual social interactions. While diverse regions or contexts usually offer more opportunities for inter-ethnic contact (Joyner 2000), this opportunity for contact is not always pursued or, in some cases, even likely. In other words, the puzzle about diversity may not be as much about the presence or absence of minority groups as such, but about the level of segregation in each area (Uslaner 2012) and variance in inter-ethnic social interaction patterns. If the most diverse areas and neighbourhoods are also the most segregated, then the potential for intergroup contact to counteract group conflict is minimized. Therefore, including inter-ethnic contact into the analyses is a fundamental goal.

Studies on the relationship between diversity and social capital, however, have not sufficiently integrated the insights of the contact hypothesis, which claims that positive interactions between people of different ethnic backgrounds can help to establish inclusive intergroup feelings (see Hewstone 2009). This is particularly surprising as the essence of the social capital literature has been that social relationships have value. In its early formulation by Putnam (2000), there were high hopes for so-called bridging contacts with people who are different from oneself. These beneficial contacts between people of different backgrounds were expected to happen, for example, in voluntary associations where people also learn to cooperate and trust each other. In turn, these experiences of positive interaction across lines of difference were hoped to generalize to the broader society.

Contact theory is obviously not an invention of social capital scholars. It has a long history and has provided extensive evidence that inter-ethnic contact matters for lowering prejudice and negative out-group attitudes (Allport 1954; Hewstone 2009). Yet, the psychological literature on the contact hypothesis has not received the attention it deserves in this debate.[1]

Research so far has shown that the inclusion of contact does not fundamentally change the overall effect of neighbourhood diversity (Stolle and Harell 2013), however, it can overpower the weak and unstable effects of neighbourhood diversity on trust in some contexts (Semyonov and Glikman 2009). For example, people with inter-ethnic contact are not susceptible to negative effects of increasing contextual diversity (Stolle *et al.* 2013). Clearly, considering just neighbourhood diversity cannot possibly capture the myriad ways in which diversity is actually experienced. There is promising research, then, that intergroup contact can, at least to a degree, counteract the negative effects of living in a diverse context.

One of the major challenges of taking contact more seriously, of course, are issues of endogeneity. There is a strong correlation between prejudice (or lack thereof) and having diverse friendships, but the direction of causation presents a real problem. While the relationship is almost certainly reciprocal, researchers need to invest in designs that attempt to capture the direction of effects. Longitudinal and experimental studies are promising avenues for this (as an experimental example, see Veit and Koopmans 2014).

We also need to make sure we do not neglect the substance of interaction. Not all interaction is equal. Some interactions occur in hierarchical relationships (e.g. a citizen and a police officer) while others are between relative equals (e.g. between neighbours). Other interactions include shared commitment to an outcome (e.g. working together in a sports team or on a community project), while yet others may be more adversarial (e.g. competing for community resources or those in a court of law). Without research that includes both measures of contact and context, we cannot begin to disentangle the effects, and this is key in making sense of the conflicting results that plague the current debate.

The importance of the broader context

While we believe strongly that we need to dig down into the nature and quality of contact that occurs in diverse contexts, we also think that it is equally important to look up into the broader context in which such interaction is embedded. Two societies with equal proportions of immigrants distributed in similar ways across regions may still vary greatly in terms of how such diversity is experienced. One society may have a long history of living with such diversity, with policies in place that promote a positive view of diversity and a relatively friendly discourse in favour of diversity animating public debates. Another may have recently experienced large and new waves of immigration and a hostile political climate. Such contexts can matter greatly to how the average citizen thinks about others in society and how she experiences diverse interactions. In a society where diversity is normalized in everyday life, interactions with people from various backgrounds are more likely to be positive, and hence more likely to promote positive outcomes for social cohesion.

In other words, diversity is not experienced in a vacuum. There is a political discourse and nation-wide (or at least region-wide) value system that influences and shapes whether and how diversity might affect social cohesion (Laxer 2013). One particularly promising avenue for exploring such political discourses is by looking at how political parties are framing the issue of diversity. An article by Helbling *et al.* (2013) examines party discourses on national and immigration issues. The analysis shows that diversity on its own does not have a negative effect on generalized trust. Rather, it is the combination of the higher proportion of foreigners and the political mobilization of immigration in national party discourses which diminish generalized trust. The more often political parties mentioned the topic of immigration in a diverse country, the more this became threatening to trust in society.

Party discourses are not the only way to examine the context in which diversity is experienced. Policy contexts also provide important evidence about the larger norm environment, especially in countries that have a longer history of managing diversity. Canada is a good example. While it is often considered unique when compared to the European context because of the perceived success of multiculturalism, we cannot simply dismiss it as an outlier. Rather, it provides a good case for studying just how much the norm environment can matter. Canada has a very diverse population, with about one in five of its residents (20.6 per cent) being foreign born, the highest percentage in the G8 (Statistics Canada 2013: 6f.). The population is ethnically diverse and relatively young, meaning that in the past 40 years, the ethno-cultural makeup of Canada has changed drastically, largely due to immigration. While it would be a mistake to argue that there has not been any tension, the official discourse has largely been welcoming and open to diversity and immigration, which is reflected in both the policy climate and in public opinion. The principle of multiculturalism was adopted by the Canadian government in 1971, enshrined in the constitution in 1982, and, since the 1990s, Canadians have been increasingly supportive of immigration and ethnic diversity (Harell and Deschâtelets 2014). Today, then, we expect a very different norm environment than, say, what existed in the 1960s or even the 1980s, and this should condition the diversity–social cohesion nexus, especially for the youngest generation.

This assumption is based on the idea that diversity can become normalized and that, when it does, diverse interactions are less likely to evoke threat and distrust. While Putnam's (2007) work is often cited to show the negative effects of diversity, he also suggests that, over time, these effects may diminish. This may be particularly true for younger generations that come of age in such environments. Younger generations in diverse and multicultural societies should be more immune to increasing diversity around them compared to generations who were socialized into a homogeneous time period with little government policy in place that supports immigrant integration and recognition of ethnic diversity.

Our previous work speaks directly to this generational effect by looking at how diverse social networks affect younger Canadians compared to the older generations (Stolle and Harell 2013). We argue that the different norm environment in which young people have grown up creates more opportunities to experience positive inter-ethnic contact and, as a result, will promote the generalization of positive intergroup experiences that can be measured by variables such as generalized trust. We find that, for older generations, contextual diversity and even diverse social networks have negative effects on trust. In contrast, diverse social networks among the younger generation consistently benefit them in terms of trust. In other words, we find asymmetrical effects with young Canadians not experiencing the adverse effects of diversity in their surroundings and benefiting positively from their inter-ethnic contacts. Again, such an approach combines contextual diversity with actual contact and considers how both can influence attitudes across generations. Furthermore, it embeds these findings within a specific norm environment in the Canadian context that we argue may not necessarily be generalized to other countries where the broader norm environment is not favourable.

Taking the norm environment more seriously may also help to account for the variance in country-level findings. As we discussed before, the negative effects of increasing diversity are not found everywhere, although they seem more likely in the United States compared to other areas of Western democracies.

These conclusions, however, are challenged by other recent work. With data spanning three decades, Dinesen and Sønderskov (2012) find that immigration-related diversity at the munici-pality level depresses generalized social trust in Denmark; and so does Schaeffer (2013) with data from 55 cities and regions in Germany. Similar findings are reported for the Netherlands by Lancee and Dronkers (2011) for contact with neighbours. In Canada, results are mixed. While Canadians who live in ethnically diverse environments are also less trusting overall (Soroka *et al.* 2007a), their attitudes of social solidarity are completely unaffected (Soroka *et al.* 2007b). Overall the tally collected by van der Meer and Tolsma (2014) shows that 50 per cent of US studies, but only 25.6 per cent of European studies (and only 11.1 per cent of European cross-national studies) and 16.7 per cent of Anglo-Saxon studies outside of the USA and Europe support the negative relationship between diversity and trust.

In sum, there is not only variation in the results for the relationship between diversity and social cohesion based on contextual data, but also this variation is unequally distributed between North America and Europe. While US neighbourhood studies often find that diversity nega-tively shapes the views of others and out-groups, the results from European cases and in Canada are less homogeneous.[2] This calls for a more nuanced consideration in cross-national research that does not rely simply on aggregate percentages of foreign-born statistics. This nuance can be achieved by looking at how diversity emerged over time and how both the public and the state have reacted to it at key periods. Our analyses of the divergent effects of diversity on different generations suggest the potential for such an approach. More generally, we see several ways to contextualize aggregate measures of diversity. One way, as Putnam (2007) himself has suggested, is to look at changes in rates of diversity rather than simply the proportion. Another avenue of research is to focus more on heterogeneity (defined as the presence of multiple groups) rather than simply the White–other dichotomy. Along with changing rates of immigration, understand-ing what makes up a given country's diversity may be equally important. Countries in which immigrants originate in a particular place (especially when those immigrants tend to have lower socio-economic status than the receiving country and are more culturally distinct), might expe-rience more negative reactions compared to a situation where diversity is spread out over mul-tiple groups (and when these groups are not socially disadvantaged). Finally, the types of immigrants who enter the host countries matter (e.g. whether they be primarily family re-unification, asylum seekers or economic class immigrants), as does the level of illegal immigra-tion into a country. This is especially important because we know people perceive immigrants differently based on where they come from and their socio-economic status, and to a lesser extent whether they are bringing families with them (Iyengar *et al.* 2013).

Revising the measure of social cohesion: the way forward

Another major reason for the divergent results is the use of different dependent variables across various studies. While they all are meant to capture some aspect of social cohesion, social capital or social solidarity, they range from various types of trust, out-group attitudes and neighbour-hood feelings, to problem solving in the neighbourhood. While these are certainly relevant aspects of cohesion, the literature on the concept of social cohesion has not yet addressed how to redefine social cohesion in a time of immigration and diversity. Early work tended to view social cohesion very narrowly, and it was almost synonymous with the idea of a community defined by shared characteristics, often of an ascriptive nature (such as blood ties, ethnicity or some inherent national identity) (Harell and Stolle 2011).

There is little room for diversity in such conceptions, making ethnic and racial minorities a priori a challenge to community, or at best placing the burden to conform unfairly on their shoulders, with little consideration of how majority values or culture may need to change to incorporate new groups of citizens. While a minimal set of shared liberal democratic values may be necessary (Stanley 2003), serious discussion and caution is required to make sure that the values set up as desirable do not exclude those who are perceived to be visibly or culturally different from the dominant society.

Social cohesion must, therefore, be defined in such a way that it includes larger attitudes that are not assimilationist in nature. One way to do this is to extend the concept of social cohesion to include larger attitudes such as generalized trust and tolerance rather than focusing on adoption of majority culture, which some of the literature in this area has done. It may also require focusing more closely on network actors such as the density of social networks in an area. The questions that arise in this context are related to the equal access to these beneficial networks, as well as to a focus on how equally spread values such as generalized trust are. A focus on the spread of values is all the more salient, given recent concerns that it may be inappropriate (or impossible) to expect generalized trust from marginalized members of society toward members of the dominant majority (Arneil 2006). In short, while measures of generalized trust and out-group trust have been widely used in studies on social cohesion, we suggest that the gaps of trust between minority and majority groups are of equal if not higher importance.

For these reasons, we believe that future work needs to be careful not only in defining the nature of diversity (level of analysis, causal mechanisms and norm environment in which it occurs), but also in how we define and operationalize the concept of social cohesion. Social cohesion, in effect, is about how well people get along with each other and, importantly, on what terms interaction between people take place. Many social arrangements may lead to an equilibrium which may define a somewhat stable set of social relationships that could be considered a community, but in our view social cohesion should be defined by a set of social relations that are characterized by people's ability to collaborate with one another to solve collective issues and to conduct dialogue in a way that does not privilege one social group's identity or perspective over another. Given the limitations with current conceptualizations of social cohesion, we propose a refined definition of social cohesion as *cooperative relations among individuals and groups of individuals that are based on mutual recognition, equality and norms of reciprocity*. We see such relationships as defining a socially cohesive community and necessary for both the peaceful and democratic functioning of localities, states and even supranational communities. This relational view of social cohesion takes as a starting point that for a political community to be cohesive, it must be inclusive.

Social cohesion as primarily a relational concept can be observed at two key levels of analysis. At the macro-level, we argue that socially cohesive societies are characterized by structural equality across salient social groups. At the micro-level, socially cohesive societies are characterized by extensive and overlapping networks among individuals. We view the two levels as being causally related, and we argue that a society characterized by large structural gaps among groups is unlikely to foster extensive and overlapping networks. When both the relationship among groups is relatively equal and relationships among individuals are extensive and bridge salient social cleavages, we assume that people from various social groups are likely to hold a number of facilitative values that support and reinforce these relationships. We argue that the focus should be specifically on facilitative attitudes that reinforce non-hierarchical relationships and the capacity for shared conversations about issues facing the political community. Instead of promoting a totally shared normative framework or identity, we suggest that certain values are embedded in egalitarian relationships and are required in order for differently situated social groups to be able to cooperate and communicate with each other to address shared issues. In particular, we focus on norms of mutual recognition, democratic equality and reciprocity.[3]

Such a definition of social cohesion puts the emphasis on how social diversity is experienced, and the norms and values – at both the micro- and macro-level – which are required for these interactions to be positive. By recognizing the limits and contradictions in the current research agenda, we believe that moving forward with a theoretically rich account of diversity and social cohesion is the only way to proceed.

Notes

1   There are exceptions, for example see Semyonov and Glikman (2009).
2   Of course, when contact is taken into account, more positive effects emerge overall.
3   We have developed this framework in more detail elsewhere (see Harell and Stolle 2011).

References

Alesina, A. and La Ferrara, E. (2000) 'Participation in Heterogeneous Communities', *The Quarterly Journal of Economics*, 115(3): 847–904.
—(2002) 'Who Trusts Others', *Journal of Public Economics*, 85(20): 207–34.
Allport, G.W. (1954) *The Nature of Prejudice*, Cambridge, MA: Addison-Wesley.
Arneil, B. (2006) *Diverse Communities: The Problem with Social Capital*, Cambridge, UK: Cambridge University Press.
Blumer, H. (1958) 'Race Prejudice as a Sense of Group Position', *The Pacific Sociological Review*, 1(1): 3–7.
Dinesen, P.T. and Sønderskov, K.M. (2012) 'Trust in a Time of Increasing Diversity: On the Relationship between Ethnic Heterogeneity and Social Trust in Denmark from 1979 until Today', *Scandinavian Political Studies*, 35(4): 273–94.
Giles, M.W. and Buckner, M.A. (1993) 'David Duke and Black Threat: An Old Hypothesis Revisited', *The Journal of Politics*, 55(3): 702–13.
Harell, A. and Stolle, D. (2011) 'Reconciling Diversity and Community? Defining Social Cohesion in Democracies', in M. Hooghe (ed.) *Social Capital and Social Cohesion: Interdisciplinary Theoretical Perspectives*, Brussels: Royal Flemish Academy of Belgium for Science and the Arts.
Harell, A. and Deschâtelets, L. (2014) 'Political Culture(s) in Canada: Orientations to Politics in a Pluralist, Multicultural Federation', in A.G. Gagnon and J. Bickerton (eds) *Canadian Politics*, 6th edn, Toronto: University of Toronto Press.
Helbling, M., Reeskens, T. and Stolle, D. (2013) 'Political Mobilization, Cultural Diversity and Social Cohesion: The Conditional Effect of Political Parties', *Political Studies*. First published Online. Available HTTP: <http://onlinelibrary.wiley.com/doi/10.1111/1467-9248.12087/pdf> (accessed 24 April 2014).
Hero, R.E. (2003) 'Social Capital and Racial Inequality in America', *Perspectives on Politics*, 1(1): 113–22.
Hewstone, M. (2009) 'Living Apart, Living Together? The Role of Intergroup Contact in Social Integration', *Proceedings of the British Academy*, 162(2009): 243–300.
Hooghe, M., Reeskens, T., Stolle, D. and Trappers, A. (2009) 'Ethnic Diversity and Generalized Trust in Europe', *Comparative Political Studies*, 42(2): 198–223.
Iyengar, S., Jackman, S., Messing, S., Valentino, N., Aalberg, T., Duch, R., Soroka, S., Harell, A. and Kobayashi, T. (2013) 'Do Attitudes about Immigration Predict Willingness to Admit Individual Immigrants? A Cross-National Test of the Person-Positivity Bias', *Public Opinion Quarterly*, 7(3): 641–65.
Joyner, K. (2000) 'School Racial Composition and Adolescent Racial Homophily', *Social Science Quarterly*, 81(2000): 810–25.
Lancee, B. and Dronkers, J. (2011) 'Ethnic, Religious and Economic Diversity in Dutch Neighbourhoods: Explaining Quality of Contact with Neighbours, Trust in the Neighbourhood and Inter-Ethnic Trust', *Journal of Ethnic and Migration Studies*, 37(4): 597–618.
Laxer, E. (2013) 'Integration Discourses and the Generational Trajectories of Civic Engagement in Multi-Nation States: A Comparison of the Canadian Provinces of Quebec and Ontario', *Journal of Ethnic and Migration Studies*, 39(10): 1577–99.
Oliver, J. E. and Mendelberg, T. (2000) 'Reconsidering the Environmental Determinants of White Racial Attitudes', *American Journal of Political Science*, 44(3): 574–89.

Putnam, R. (2000) *Bowling Alone: The Collapse and Revival of American Community*, New York, NY: Simon and Shuster.

—(2007) 'E Pluribus Unum: Diversity and Community in the Twenty-First Century', *Scandinavian Political Studies*, 30(2): 137–74.

Schaeffer, M. (2013) *Ethnic Diversity and Social Cohesion*, Aldershot, UK: Ashgate.

Semyonov, M. and Glikman, A. (2009) 'Ethnic Residential Segregation, Social Contacts, and Anti-Minority Attitudes in European Societies', *European Sociological Review*, 25(6): 693–708.

Sniderman, P.M., Crosby, G.C. and Howell, W.G. (2000) 'The Politics of Race', in D.O. Sears, J. Sidanius and L. Bobo (eds) *Racialized Politics: The Debate about Racism in America*, Chicago, IL: University of Chicago Press.

Soroka, S., Helliwell, J.F. and Johnston, R. (2007a) 'Measuring and Modelling Trust', in F. Kay and R. Johnston (eds) *Social Capital, Diversity and the Welfare State*, Vancouver: University of British Columbia Press.

Soroka, S., Johnston, R. and Banting, K. (2007b) 'Ethnicity, Trust and the Welfare State', in F. Kay and R. Johnston (eds) *Diversity, Social Capital and the Welfare State*, Vancouver: University of British Columbia Press.

Stanley, D. (2003) 'What Do We Know about Social Cohesion: The Research Perspective of the Federal Government's Social Cohesion Research Network', *Canadian Journal of Sociology*, 28(1): 5–18.

Statistics Canada (2013) 'Immigration and Ethnocultural Diversity in Canada: National Household Survey 2011', Ottawa: Ministry of Industry.

Stolle, D. and Harell, A. (2013) 'Social Capital and Ethno-racial Diversity: Learning to Trust in an Immigrant Society', *Political Studies*, 61(1): 42–66.

Stolle, D., Petermann, S., Schmid, K., Schönwälder, K., Hewstone, M., Vertovec, S., Schmitt, T. and Heywood, J. (2013) 'Immigration-related Diversity and Trust in German Cities: The Role of Intergroup Contact', *Journal of Elections, Public Opinion and Parties*, 23(3): 279–98.

Tajfel, H. and Turner, J. (1979) 'An Integrative Theory of Intergroup Conflict', in W.G. Austin and S. Worchel (eds) *The Social Psychology of Intergroup Relations*, Monterey, CA: Brooks-Cole.

Uslaner, E.M. (2012) *Segregation and Mistrust: Diversity, Isolation, and Social Cohesion*, Cambridge, UK: Cambridge University Press.

Van der Meer, T. and Tolsma, J. (2014) 'Ethnic Diversity and Its Supposed Detrimental Effects on Social Cohesion', *Annual Review of Sociology*, 40. First published Online. Available HTTP: <http://www.annualreviews.org/doi/abs/10.1146/annurev-soc-071913-043309> (accessed 24 April 2014).

Veit, S. and Koopmans, R. (2014) 'Thinking about Ethnic Diversity: Experimental Evidence on the Causal Role of Ethnic Diversity in German Schools and Neighbourhoods', in R. Koopmans, B. Lancee, M. Schaeffer (eds) *Social Cohesion in Diverse Societies: Mechanisms, Conditions and Causality*, London: Routledge.

32

Diversity in United States and British higher education

Natasha Warikoo

While the United States and Britain are commonly understood as multicultural capitalist democracies, they differ in the role that diversity has played in the popular imagination as well as on university campuses. In what follows I discuss the history of diversity as it is commonly understood in the United States and Britain, with particular attention to how the national contexts have shaped cultures of diversity in higher education, comparing the cases throughout. I show that while both countries have dealt with critiques of diversity and multiculturalism in the civic sphere, in the United States these debates have often spilled onto high-status university campuses, while similar British campuses have not seen the same level of public critique related to diversity and multiculturalism. At low-prestige universities, in both contexts minority students are overrepresented. On the one hand, the expansion of this sphere may be a source of increased opportunities for ethnic minority students in higher education; on the other hand, the lower completion rates and levels of prestige suggest that minority students are not benefitting from the just rewards of university education when shunted to lower-level institutions. I conclude with some areas for further research and refinement in the literature on diversity in higher education in comparative perspective.

The United States

Prior to the 1950s, racial segregation and legally enforced inequality were the norm in the United States, rooted in the former slave economy that legally ended in the nineteenth century. While southern African Americans moved to northern industrial cities for work in large numbers during the early twentieth century's Great Migration in search of a less oppressive racial system as well as economic opportunities, they continued to face many hardships, experiencing racial discrimination far beyond that experienced by European immigrant groups (Lieberson 1980). Further, federal social support policies systematically excluded them while providing mechanisms for poor whites to experience social mobility, such as the policies of red-lining that prevented African Americans from obtaining loans for housing; the GI Bill that enabled working class whites to enter college during the era of higher education expansion; and more.

Although African Americans experienced systematic oppression and exclusion, the United States has been a nation of immigrants, both demographically with waves of immigrants since its inception, and in its identity as a nation. Foner (2005) has documented the historical and contemporary construction of the ideal immigrant forefathers of the United States, in contrast to European erasure of immigration history in the popular imagination.[1] More than 40 years ago, Milton Gordon (1964) wrote *Assimilation in American Life*, in which he suggested that the country had shifted from an ideology of assimilation – the American "melting pot" – to one of "cultural pluralism." This shift was from a model in which immigrants and their children would blend into a uniquely American culture, to one in which ethnic communities would maintain their ethnic cultures. Immigrants and their descendants in the United States have benefited from the hard-earned victories of the African American-led Civil Rights Movement. Even more so today than when Gordon wrote his famous book, the United States is understood to have largely accepted diversity and multiculturalism under the model of cultural pluralism, at least in a soft sense.[2] This history has led contemporary Americans broadly to support ethnic identities: when asked if it is better for America for different racial and ethnic groups to maintain their cultures or for them to change so that they blend into the larger society, 32 per cent of Americans support the maintenance of cultures (GSS 2000); when Britons were asked the same question, just 20 per cent supported the maintenance of cultures (Park 2003). Furthermore, 54 per cent of Britons preferred that minorities adapt and blend, in contrast to just 37 per cent of Americans. Recent research demonstrates that in fact many Americans define what it means to be American as diverse or multicultural (Schildkraut 2011), and that in fact part of identity as a modern, moral self in the United States is to be multicultural (Voyer 2011). To be sure, immigrants and their children have experienced systematic discrimination and racism in the United States, whether at the turn of the last century (Alba and Nee 2003) or today (Telles and Ortiz 2008). Scholars should thus pay attention to the deep complexity of race, ethnicity, immigration, and social exclusion in the United States.

When the 1954 *Brown v. Board of Education* US Supreme Court decision forbidding segregated schools was made, US higher education was undergoing massive expansion, and the 1944 GI Bill allowed many working class whites to take advantage of the increased availability of higher education. Eventually, in the post-segregation era, minority students would be overrepresented in community colleges. Today, African Americans and Latinos comprise 33 per cent of the US college-age population, but 15 per cent of students at selective colleges and 37 per cent of students at non-selective two- and four-year colleges (Carnevale and Strohl 2013). Some see this development as evidence that community colleges are an important means for social mobility among racial minorities, while others lament the "diverted dream" of lower-level education and resources available to students at non-selective institutions, many of whom eventually drop out altogether (Brint and Karabel 1989).

The 1960s witnessed federal legislation to end legally racial discrimination and segregation, while also providing for social mobility for middle class blacks through affirmative action policies and federal financial aid for college. The 1960s Civil Rights Movement had a profound influence on college campuses. Open admissions to the City University of New York resulted in 1970 from protests led by black and Puerto Rican students over the underrepresentation of minority students on the CUNY campuses. This led to significant increases in diversity on those campuses. On four-year campuses with selective admissions, affirmative action policies initiated in the 1960s increased the percentage of black and Latino students on campus. Unlike solutions to the problem of underrepresentation in other national contexts in which quotas are used (e.g. Brazil and India), the holistic admissions process already in place at elite US universities allowed for race to become part of a larger evaluation of individuals' merit using a holistic view (Chen and Stulberg 2008).[3]

The landmark *Regents of the University of California* v. *Bakke* Supreme Court case in 1978 established the legality of diversity as a "compelling interest" for universities, allowing for some (limited) types of affirmative action.[4] This decision established the goal of expanded world views through racial diversity as a compelling state interest in the United States.[5] In addition, the post-Civil Rights Era led to student demands for African American studies and ethnic studies departments; institutional support for black and Latino student groups; and minority student centers (Chen 2000). Most of these institutions endured – today, 9 per cent of four-year colleges have a department of African American studies, as do all Ivy League universities. These courses are attended by minority and white students alike: 41 per cent of college seniors report having taken an ethnic studies course in college, and it is just as common for undergraduates to participate in an ethnic or racial student organization as it is to join a sorority/fraternity (Saenz and Barrera 2007). Campus cultures subsequently changed. For example, by 2005 a majority of undergraduates in the United States favored prohibitions on racist or sexist speech on campus (ibid.). Overall, college professors tend to be more liberal than other Americans (Gross and Fosse 2012), leading some conservatives to claim that faculty views contribute unwarranted support for identity politics and diversity-related programming among their students.

A new and growing body of research studies the impact of campus diversity and other diversity-related campus programming on students' racial attitudes, academic outcomes, and more (e.g. Sidanius *et al.* 2008). These studies generally find positive impacts, supporting Allport's (1954) contact hypothesis that, under the right conditions, intergroup contact will reduce prejudice.

Overall, the discourse on diversity on US university campuses has expanded beyond race, to include ethnicity, gender (including transgender identities), class, sexuality, learning (dis)ability, political identity, and more. On the one hand, the expansion can lead to a more inclusive university. On the other hand, it may equate the resource and power differences between, for example, white and black Americans as similar to those between liberal- and conservative-identified students. That is, the "diversity" rationale for affirmative action bases race-based considerations in admissions on the need for a diverse learning environment, while downplaying the resource and power differences between race groups (Berrey 2011), preventing students from easily understanding structural racism or other forms of racial injustice that continue to plague American society. Students at elite universities espouse the "diverse learning environment" justification for a value for diversity as important to the university experience. This is because it leads to a better learning environment for the majority-group individual, rather than for its attention to the rights of and disadvantages faced by minority groups. It signals a shift from diversity as highlighting inequality between groups in society to diversity as a cosmopolitan celebration of individual differences.

University campuses have also been a major site for the so-called "culture wars," in which debates about racial justice, affirmative action, multiculturalism, free speech, and more have played themselves out, often on the national stage (Arthur and Shapiro 1995). These debates have manifested themselves in discussions over university curricula (Rojas 2007), affirmative action in admissions (Moore and Bell 2011), conceptions of merit, and more (for the most prominent critiques, see D'Souza 1991). This has been especially true on elite campuses, and the most high-profile controversies over multiculturalism often take place on elite campuses (Bryson 2005). Today, national conservative organizations contribute significant financial resources to conservative student groups, in an effort to foreground conservative perspectives on, among other things, multiculturalism and diversity (Binder and Wood 2013).

Anti-diversity backlash has not been confined to college campuses. In the United States Hispanic immigrants have been targeted as a major social problem, often perceived to be collectively undocumented. Samuel Huntington (2004) has suggested that the large number of Hispanics in the United States, their cultural impact, and significant undocumented migration from Latin America are leading to a fracturing of American national identity, in part due to the growing use of Spanish in some areas. In 1996, voters in California passed Proposition 209, which banned affirmative action, leading to a precipitous decline in the percentage of black and Latino students on University of California campuses; other states followed with similar state referenda.[6] Some studies are starting to evaluate the impact of the end of affirmative action on campuses in those states, beyond the dramatic decline in numbers of black and Latino students (e.g. see Beasley 2011); still, the long-term impact of the increasing number of affirmative action bans on college campuses remains to be seen.

Great Britain

Similar to the United States, Britain identifies as a multicultural society.[7] Britain's ethnic and racial diversity is rooted in migration from the Commonwealth, especially South Asia and the Caribbean. Low-skilled workers came in large numbers during the 1950s to fulfill jobs in industry, while many professionals came to take up roles in the newly formed National Health Service; this wave of immigration from the former Empire became increasingly restricted, starting in the 1960s. Because of this early history, a significant third generation exists in Britain, while the third generation in the United States from the post-1965 wave of immigration is still quite young.

British multiculturalism stemmed from a 1950s government decision to allow immigrant communities – especially those relating to Indians, Pakistanis, and Bangladeshis – to continue their cultural practices that sometimes conflicted with dominant British society. This agreement began to unravel during the "Rushdie affair," when Muslim protesters burned copies of Salman Rushdie's *Satanic Verses*, while British writers fiercely defended Rushdie's right to satirize Islam without threats to his life. Over time, the implicit link between Islam and terrorism has grown in the public eye in Britain, fueled by the World Trade Center attacks in 2001 and especially the London Underground bombings of 2005. Due to anti-Muslim sentiments rooted in perceptions of cultural difference, Modood (1996) argues that the American model of race discourse, focusing on skin color, does not suit the British context, where, for example, discrimination can be stronger towards white Muslims than towards black West Indians.

In the past few years Britain has undergone a backlash against multiculturalism, in favor of policies of "community cohesion" (Vertovec and Wessendorf 2010). According to some politicians, journalists, and public opinion, policies of multiculturalism – allowing ethnic minorities to maintain their distinct cultures – have led to a fractured society, and one in which cultural practices antithetical to democracy, such as gender inequality and radical preaching in mosques, have been allowed to continue. Some suggest that the 7/7 London Underground bombings (and subsequent attempts) are in fact results of the lack of Muslim integration and consequent radicalization.[8] The perceived British "multiculturalism" mode of incorporation has led to concern about the need to define a uniquely British identity and to calls for parameters for assimilation expected of immigrant communities to be defined. These calls have come not only from the right end of the political spectrum, but also from the left, including from former Prime Minister Gordon Brown and the former Chair of the Equality and Human Rights Commission, Trevor Phillips. In 2005–6, the Labour Government changed Britain's citizenship laws, instituting requirements that naturalizing residents demonstrate a command of English and pass an exam on "Life in the UK."

British public opinion has also moved toward assimilation and away from multiculturalism, even among politically liberal groups. Since the mid-1990s, this is evident in successive years of the British Social Attitudes Survey (see www.natcen.ac.uk). The number of British citizens in favour of the maintenance of immigrants' customs has declined, while the proportion supporting immigrant adaptation has increased; at the same time, general British attitudes have become more skeptical of immigrants' positive contributions to the economy, and survey respondents have been more prone to thinking that immigrants increase crime. Since 2002, Britons increasingly feel that ethnic minorities need to "demonstrate a real commitment to [Britain] before they can be considered British" (Ipsos MORI 2006).

In 1992 the landscape of British higher education changed, with the transformation of Britain's former polytechnics into universities; this increased the number of universities in Britain by over 50 per cent. Although this was an attempt to democratize higher education, the most recent research on diversity and higher education in Britain finds that, while racial minorities are overrepresented in the "new" universities (former polytechnics), which have lower status, they are underrepresented in the high-prestige "Russell Group" universities. The former polytechnics share with US community colleges their relatively low prestige, relatively high numbers of minority students, and relatively high dropout rates (Modood 2006). While their transformation into fully fledged universities allowed for greater numbers of minority students to obtain university degrees, like associated degree-granting community colleges in the United States, some argue that this is the mechanism by which the same students are systematically excluded from more prestigious British universities.

In terms of elite "Russell Group" universities in Britain, black Britons and some Asian groups are underrepresented, and recent research suggests a bias in favor of white students in admissions among students with similar qualifications who apply (Boliver 2013). Although they employ very different criteria in admissions, in both Britain and the United States elite universities have often been criticized for the underrepresentation of both working class students (Vasagar 2010; Vasagar et al. 2010) and US- and UK-born racial minorities (Lammy 2010). While Teles (1998) explains the lack of affirmative action overall in Britain, the collegiate structure of Oxford and Cambridge (Oxbridge) in particular may prevent these universities from adopting policies such as affirmative action. Nevertheless, new British government legislation requires universities to enter into "widening participation" agreements with the government if they want to maintain federal funding (UK Office for Fair Access 2012). These agreements are explicit plans for diversifying the student body, and they most often consider geographic representation as well as social class, as measured by type of high school (state versus private). Universities are also starting to utilize "contextual" information on applicants, such as the average GCSE scores in the applicant's secondary school, or the percentage of families living in poverty in an applicant's neighborhood. Hence, British universities may be moving toward greater emphasis on ensuring that students of all backgrounds are represented on campus, regardless of their prior educational opportunities. The new widening participation agreements may quicken the pace of change toward more access and inclusion that began 50 years ago at Oxford.

Overall, perhaps because British universities, whether old or new, have not experienced the race-related protests that US universities did, little infrastructure related to diversity exists on British university campuses. In contrast to the United States, where high-profile attacks on multiculturalism often target higher education, high-profile public attacks on diversity and multiculturalism in Britain have not targeted British university campuses during times of criticism of multiculturalism. In comparison, attacks on multiculturalism in the United States seem inevitably to turn to the liberal leanings of university professors, affirmative action in selective universities' admissions, and other practices in higher education. Amidst numerous politicians calling for the scaling back of British multiculturalism in recent years, the one parliamentary attack on higher education came from David Lammy (Member of Parliament for Tottenham since 2000), who cited the very low numbers of British Afro-Caribbean students on Oxford's campus (in 2010), sparking a public debate about the roots of the underrepresentation, and whose responsibility it was to change it.

What explains this difference? Elite British universities, despite their public funding, continue to be "socially buffered" to a large extent, whereas elite US universities, mostly private, tend to be "socially embedded" (Ramirez 2006). That is, while, for example, Oxford transformed during the mid-twentieth century from an institution serving the artistocratic elite to one that is "democratic elitist" with an emphasis on meritocracy in a narrow sense, it has retained its raison d'être as an intellectual center. In contrast, even the most elite US universities have always thought of themselves as playing a more civic role, perhaps most clearly demonstrated by the early history of professional schools at many of them. Thus, for example, students at elite US universities frequently expect their universities to address inequality of educational opportunities when making admissions decisions, while their counterparts at elite UK universities most often express concern that this type of consideration would compromise the status and role of their universities.

Conclusion

I have synthesized the literature on diversity in higher education in the United States and Britain, with particular attention to the development of diversity in a national context. Overall, comparing diversity-related practices, understandings, and policies reveals important contextual forces that shape diversity work in education and beyond. Unexpected findings arise when comparing educational institutions and the role that diversity has played and continues to play within them. Future research should examine the impact of social contexts around diversity in higher education institutions across other national boundaries, with an eye toward promoting equity in education. That is, by looking outside of national contexts, researchers may be able to identify promising practices and mechanisms for promoting access to higher education for non-traditional students. Further, the interplay between national discourses around diversity and university practices, protests, and structures is understudied, yet revealing, as I have shown. The junction between national cultures of diversity and institutional practices around diversity also allows researchers to see how national ideologies and rhetoric are engaged by individual actors.

Notes

1 Glazer (1997) has suggested that in fact a desire to distance the majority from African Americans has led to the valorization of immigrants in the United States.
2 There is some revival of the notion of assimilation among American academics, with the key question of "assimilation to what?" driving debates (Alba and Nee 2003; Portes and Zhou 1993). Still, these debates take into account the influence of ethnic groups on the majority and on American society more broadly.
3 During the 1920s, in an effort to limit the numbers of admitted Jewish students, Ivy League universities added "character" to their admissions criteria. This exclusionary practice, ironically, paved the way for holistic admissions, which takes race into consideration.
4 Given the recent decision in *Fisher* v. *Texas*, the future of race-based affirmative action in higher education admissions remains to be seen.
5 Some have critiqued this "diversity rationale" for its inattention to resource differences between groups (Berrey 2011; Yosso et al. 2004).

6 Note that the US Supreme Court has recently agreed to hear a challenge to the Michigan state ban on affirmative action; the decision in this case may affect bans in other states.

7 Many also describe Britain as a class-based society, in contrast to the United States being race based (for example, see Foner 2005; Katznelson 1973; Modood 1996). Still, there is a significant literature in Britain on racial exclusion (Gilroy 1987; Majors *et al.* 2001) and cultural/ethnic exclusion (Modood 2005).

8 These concerns are not limited to Britain, and indeed can be found in France (Bowen 2007), the Netherlands (Sniderman and Hagendoorn 2007), and elsewhere in Europe.

References

Alba, R.D. and Nee, V. (2003) *Remaking the American Mainstream: Assimilation and Contemporary Immigration*, Cambridge, MA: Harvard University Press.

Allport, G.W. (1954) *The Nature of Prejudice*, Reading, MA: Addison-Wesley.

Arthur, J. and Shapiro, A. (1995) *Campus Wars: Multiculturalism and the Politics of Difference*, Boulder, CO: Westview.

Beasley, M.A. (2011) *Opting Out: Losing the Potential of America's Young Black Elite*, Chicago, IL: The University of Chicago Press.

Berrey, E.C. (2011) 'Why Diversity Became Orthodox in Higher Education, and How It Changed the Meaning of Race on Campus', *Critical Sociology*, 37(5): 573–96.

Binder, A. and Wood, K. (2013) *Becoming Right: How Campuses Shape Young Conservatives*, Princeton, NJ: Princeton University Press.

Boliver, V. (2013) 'How Fair is Access to More Prestigious UK Universities?', *British Journal of Sociology*, 64(2): 344–64.

Bowen, J.R. (2007) *Why the French Don't Like Headscarves: Islam, the State, and Public Space*, Princeton, NJ: Princeton University Press.

Brint, S.G. and Karabel, J. (1989) *The Diverted Dream: Community Colleges and the Promise of Educational Opportunity in America 1900–1985*, New York, NY: Oxford University Press.

Bryson, B.P. (2005) *Making Multiculturalism: Boundaries and Meaning in U.S. English Departments*, Stanford, CA: Stanford University Press.

Carnevale, A.P. and Strohl, J. (2013) 'Separate and Unequal: How Higher Education Reform Reinforces the Intergenerational Reproduction of White Racial Privilege', Georgetown: Georgetown Public Policy Institute. Online. Available HTTP: <http://www9.georgetown.edu/grad/gppi/hpi/cew/pdfs/Separate%26Unequal.FR.pdf> (accessed 12 September 2013).

Chen, A.S. and Stulberg, L.M. (2008) 'Beyond Disruption: The Forgotten Origins of Affirmative Action in College and University Admissions 1961–1969', Ann Arbor: Gerald R. Ford School of Public Policy. Online. Available HTTP: <http://www.fordschool.umich.edu/research/pdf/chen-stulberg.pdf> (accessed 1 June 2012).

Chen, S.L. (2000) *Debates over Third World Centers at Princeton, Brown and Harvard: Minority Student Activism and Institutional Responses in the 1960s and 1970s*, Cambridge, MA: Harvard Graduate School of Education.

D'Souza, D. (1991) *Illiberal Education: The Politics of Race and Sex on Campus*, New York, NY: The Free Press.

Foner, N. (2005) *In a New Land: A Comparative View of Immigration*, New York, NY: New York University Press.

Gilroy, P. (1987) *'There Ain't No Black in the Union Jack': The Cultural Politics of Race and Nation*, London: Hutchinson.

Glazer, N. (1997) *We Are All Multiculturalists Now*, Cambridge, MA: Harvard University Press.

Gordon, M.M. (1964) *Assimilation in American Life: The Role of Race, Religion, and National Origins*, New York, NY: Oxford University Press.

Gross, N. and Fosse, E. (2012) 'Why are Professors Liberal?', *Theory and Society*, 41(2): 127–68.

GSS (2000) *General Social Survey*. Chicago: National Opinion Research Center.

Huntington, S.P. (2004) *Who Are We? The Challenges to America's National Identity*, New York, NY: Simon & Schuster.

Ipsos MORI (2006) 'Race Relations 2006', London: Ipsos MORI.

Katznelson, I. (1973) *Black Men, White Cities; Race, Politics, and Migration in the United States, 1900–30 and Britain, 1948–68*, London: Institute of Race Relations, Oxford University Press.

Lammy, D. (2010) 'The Oxbridge Whitewash', *The Guardian*, 6 December. Online. Available HTTP: <http://www.guardian.co.uk/commentisfree/2010/dec/06/the-oxbridge-whitewash-black-students> (accessed 23 May 2011).

Lieberson, S. (1980) *A Piece of the Pie: Blacks and White Immigrants Since 1880*, Berkeley, CA: University of California Press.

Majors, R., Gillborn, D. and Sewell, T. (2001) 'The Exclusion of Black Children: Implications for a Racialised Perspective', in R. Majors (ed.) *Educating Our Black Children: New Directions and Radical Approaches*, London: Routledge.

Modood, T. (1996) 'The Limits of America: Rethinking Equality in the Changing Context of British Race Relations', in B. Ward and T. Badger (eds) *The Making of Martin Luther King and the Civil Rights Movement*, New York, NY: New York University.

—(2005) *Multicultural Politics: Racism, Ethnicity, and Muslims in Britain*, Minneapolis, MN: University of Minnesota Press.

—(2006) 'Ethnicity, Muslims and Higher Education Entry in Britain', *Teaching in Higher Education*, 11(2): 247–50.

Moore, W.L. and Bell, J.M. (2011) 'Maneuvers of Whiteness: "Diversity" as a Mechanism of Retrenchment in the Affirmative Action Discourse', *Critical Sociology*, 37(5): 597–613.

Park, A. (ed.) (2003) *British Social Attitudes, 20th Report*. London: Sage.

Portes, A. and Zhou, M. (1993) 'The New Second Generation: Segmented Assimilation and its Variants', *Annals of the American Academy*, 530(1): 74–96.

Ramirez, F.O. (2006) 'Growing Commonalities and Persistent Differences in Higher Education: Universities between Global Models and National Legacies', in H.D. Meyer and B. Rowan (eds) *The New Institutionalism in Education*, Albany, NY: State University of New York Press.

Rojas, F. (2007) *From Black Power to Black Studies: How a Radical Social Movement Became an Academic Discipline*, Baltimore, MD: Johns Hopkins University Press.

Saenz, V.B. and Barrera, D.S. (2007) *Findings from the 2005 College Student Survey (CSS): National Aggregates*, Los Angeles, CA: Higher Education Research Institute.

Schildkraut, D.J. (2011) *Americanism in the Twenty-First Century: Public Opinion in the Age of Immigration*, New York, NY: Cambridge University Press.

Sidanius, J., Levin, S., van Laar, C. and Sears, D.O. (2008) *The Diversity Challenge: Social Identity and Intergroup Relations on the College Campus*, New York, NY: Russell Sage Foundation.

Sniderman, P.M. and Hagendoorn, A. (2007) *When Ways of Life Collide: Multiculturalism and its Discontents in the Netherlands*, Princeton NJ: Princeton University Press.

Teles, S.M. (1998) 'Why is There No Affirmative Action in Britain?', *American Behavioral Scientist*, 41(7): 1004–26.

Telles, E.E. and Ortiz, V. (2008) *Generations of Exclusion: Mexican Americans, Assimilation, and Race*, New York, NY: Russell Sage Foundation.

UK Office for Fair Access (2012) 'Introducing Access Agreements,' retrieved 27 September 2012, from http://www.offa.org.uk/universities-and-colleges/Introducing-access-agreements/

Vasagar, J. (2010) 'Tears for State Pupils as Top Universities Insist on A* at A-level', *The Guardian*, 2 August 2010. Online. www.theguardian.com/education/2010/aug/02/universities-state-schools-a-levels.

Vasagar, J., Shepherd, J. and Stratton, A. (2010) 'Elite Universities Welcome Flexibility to Triple Students' Fees', *The Guardian*, 3 November 2010. Online. www.theguardian.com/education/2010/nov/03/universities-welcome-flexbility-triple-fees.

Vertovec, S. and Wessendorf, S. (eds) (2010) *The Multiculturalism Backlash: European Discourses, Policies and Practices*, London: Routledge.

Voyer, A. (2011) 'Disciplined to Diversity: Learning the Language of Multiculturalism', *Ethnic and Racial Studies*, 34(11): 1874–93.

Yosso, T.J., Parker, L., Solarzano, D.G. and Lynn, M. (2004) 'From Jim Crow to Affirmative Action and Back Again: A Critical Race Discussion of Racialized Rationales and Access to Higher Education', *Review of Research in Education*, 28(1): 1–25.

33

Xenophobia

The role of political articulation

Jens Rydgren

Xenophobia may be characterized as the belief that it is "natural" for people to live among others of "their own kind," along with a corresponding hostility toward people of "another" kind. However, this hostility need not necessarily be activated until "strangers" come too close to the ingroup (in geographical or social space) and are believed to threaten the identity (consensual beliefs and practices, mores, and traditional values) or the material interests of the ingroup. Strangers at a distance are not likely to meet with the same hostility or be as feared. A major part of xenophobia in Europe is supposedly directed against immigration and immigrants. However, we should keep in mind that there are important forms of xenophobia that are not necessarily related to immigration and immigrants, such as prejudice against indigenous ethnic minorities.

Previous research has tried to explain xenophobia and related phenomena in several ways, of which most take a bottom-up perspective. This is true for, e.g., realistic group conflict theory (Blalock 1957, 1967; Olzak 1992; Pettigrew 1957), the group position hypothesis (Blumer 1958; Bobo and Tuan 2006; Quillian 1995), and the contact hypothesis (Allport 1954; Pettigrew and Tropp 2006; see Fell and Hewstone, this volume). However useful these perspectives and explanations are, I will argue that they need to be complemented by a top-down perspective, which is why this chapter will focus on the role of political articulation for explaining variation in xenophobia. This is a theme that so far has received considerably less attention in the literature.

More specifically, in this chapter I will discuss how an emerging anti-immigrant party, such as a radical right-wing party (Rydgren 2007), under certain conditions may cause an increase in xenophobia. Papers by Semyonov *et al.* (2006) and Wilkes *et al.* (2007) strongly indicate that the presence of successful radical right-wing parties affect the level of immigration scepticism, and Rydgren (2003) indicates that the salience of immigration-negative attitudes increases after the emergence of electorally successful radical right-wing parties, so that the relationship between immigration-negative attitudes and radical right-wing parties can be described as a vicious circle. In this chapter, therefore, I will identify and discuss various mechanisms that link the event of an emerging anti-immigrant party to increases in the level of xenophobia. These mechanisms can be divided into two main categories: the first deals with how the emergence of a radical right-wing party, or another anti-immigrant party, changes the structure of the political space and influences other political actors; the other deals with the influence an emerging radical right-wing party has on people's frames of thought. The former category of mechanisms is of importance because it (1) may influence the way other political actors talk about immigrants (and other ethnic minorities), which in turn may influence people's frames of thought, and/or (2) because it sometimes results in an increasing legitimization of xenophobic attitudes. As a result of the legitimization effects, xenophobic beliefs may spread to groups of individuals that previously stayed away from them because of the stigma associated with them. The latter category of mechanisms is of importance mainly because they provide a means to reduce negative emotions and affections (e.g. fear, frustration, anxiety, and resentment). Taken together, these mechanisms illustrate how already existing popular xenophobia may be lifted to a manifest level by the intrusion of an anti-immigrant party in the political space. Once at a manifest level, xenophobic attitudes are more likely to spread, because manifest xenophobes are more inclined than latent xenophobes to try to persuade others.

Radical right-wing parties

Radical right-wing parties have emerged in Western and Eastern Europe during the past two and a half decades, and have gained substantial voter support in several countries. These parties share an emphasis on ethno-nationalism rooted in myths about the distant past. Their program is directed toward strengthening the nation by making it more ethnically homogeneous, and by returning to traditional values. They generally view individual rights as secondary to the goals of the nation. They also tend to be populists in accusing elites of putting internationalism ahead of the nation, and of putting their own narrow self-interests, and various "special interests," ahead of the interest of the people. Hence, the new radical right-wing parties share a core of ethno-nationalist xenophobia and anti-establishment populism (see Rydgren 2007).

People's frames of thought

The presence of a radical right-wing party, or another anti-immigrant party, of significant size may influence people's frames of thought. This point is well acknowledged within social movement theory, where these kinds of processes are discussed in terms of "framing" and "frame struggle" (e.g. Benford and Snow 2000). For Goffman (1986), frames are those basic elements that organize people's experience and govern their "definition of a situation." In other words, for Goffman, frames or frameworks are equivalent to schemata and other schemes of interpretation. In this way, what Goffman calls frames and what cognitive psychology calls cognitive schemas (e.g. Augoustinos and Walker 1998) are strongly overlapping concepts, denoting the importance of socially mediated a priori forms for people's perception and understanding of the surrounding world.

In this chapter it will be argued that the ideology and propaganda of anti-immigrant parties, or similar xenophobic movements, offer a frame in which some people's more or less unarticulated stock of xenophobic attitudes (which may be no more than gut feelings of attraction or repulsion) can be articulated in a more comprehensive way. Hence, similar to Bourdieu's (1984) argument on political taste, people's beliefs and attitudes are not always thoroughly articulated until they are confronted with the "already-made-explicit" line of thought presented by the political supply side or by other elite actors. Put differently, the "ethos of popular xenophobia" may not find its form until an articulated and (sufficiently) comprehensive program of ideas (but also slogans etc.) is offered by the supply side of the social/political production of opinion. In this perspective, the articulation of the demand side is never prior to the offered alternatives of opinion. Yet, at the same time, the ideology and propaganda offered by the supply side have to be sufficiently attuned to people's preconceptions of reality if it is not to fall flatly. Differently stated, in order to be successful, offered frames have to be sufficiently culturally resonant. With the emergence of an electorally successful radical right-wing party, or a similar anti-immigrant party, and the attention it attracts, a new alternative frame of thought is offered, which may help people articulate their previously more or less unarticulated xenophobic attitudes, especially if the offered frame is in line with their psychological wants (Merton 1968: 572–3). This, one may argue, can lift the latent popular xenophobia to a manifest level.

More specifically, there are three partly overlapping reasons why people, consciously or not, may find politicized xenophobia an attractive frame of thought.

First, to start with the most general reason, the ideology of a radical right-wing party may offer a theory of guidance in black-box situations, i.e. a way to make the complex social and political reality meaningful. In this way, it may provide a means to reduce fear and anxiety. This is most likely to attract people who have little knowledge of society and politics and/or who have low trust and confidence in political institutions (most notably, political parties) and established information sources. For these people the level of uncertainty is higher, at least in this context. There are also reasons to assume that the need for such a theory of guidance is most acute in periods of rapid social change (e.g. post-industrialization), when established traditions, ideologies, and identities are dissolving. In such "unsettled times" (Swidler 1986) people are more open to alternative belief systems. Moreover, as will be discussed further on p. 313, there are reasons to assume that more people will adopt a xenophobic ideology as a theory of guidance, if it is sufficiently legitimized.

The second reason, which will be discussed further on p. 314, is that the xenophobic political ideology of the radical right-wing parties is a powerful tool in its ability to reframe political problems. In fact, it offers a "cardinal solution" to any conceivable social problem or ill. As Winock (1998) argues, in the case of the French Front National party, for the radical right-wing parties "everything comes from immigration, everything goes back to immigration" (e.g. unemployment, personal insecurity, the financial problems of the welfare state, AIDS, etc.). Such social and political problems, representing issues that affect people in a very direct and fundamental way, lead to negative emotions and affections in two ways. They are not only a cause of frustration for people who are subjected to these problems, and of worry and anxiety for those who are not affected, but they may also lead to distrust in and dissatisfaction with political institutions because of the perceived inability of these institutions to cope with these essential problems. The ideology of the radical right-wing parties may offer a way to reduce – or at least canalize – these kinds of negative emotions and affections. In the case of feelings of increasing personal insecurity (whether caused by criminality or diseases), it may provide a means to reduce the diffuse fear and anxiety arising from not knowing what or who to fear. Since a belief that immigrants are criminal, for instance, may result in a reduced level of self-perceived uncertainty (i.e. "you know who you should look out for"), it may have positive effects for individuals living under this kind of stress. In the case of negative emotions and affections resulting from unemployment, it may reduce the frustrating feeling that you yourself (or your relatives, friends, etc.) lack the qualifications needed to find a job (i.e. "it is the immigrants' fault, not ours").

The third mechanism may be found in these latter kinds of psychological factors. The ideology of the radical right-wing parties may also offer a way to reduce the level of personal frustration, e.g. by offering themes of *ressentiment*, a theme particularly likely to attract people who feel impotent (i.e. unable to satisfy their wants), who are excluded from society, and/or whose discrepancy between ambition and reality has become acute (i.e. people in situations of relative deprivation). Themes of *ressentiment* have in common that they aim at a re-valuation, i.e. at a negation, of the established value order (Scheler 1998: 49). If ethno-nationality, for instance, were valued higher than social class and/or education, this would have positive effects for people of the lower classes with low education. Similarly, those who do not possess flexibility, knowledge of languages, computer skills, etc., which are depicted as important values and qualities in the post-industrial society, may be attracted by an ideological program that stresses the supreme values of tradition, authority, and, not least, of ethno-national belonging.

Influence on other political actors

We now turn to a discussion on mechanisms that have to do with radical right-wing parties' influence on other political actors; an influence that may have certain effects on the level of manifest xenophobia in a society. More specifically, in accordance with Bourdieu (2000), I will argue that the supply side of the political space (which Bourdieu calls the political *field*) is characterized by the symbolic struggle over the legitimate principles of division, and ultimately over the power of categorization (and, hence, over how to perceive and apprehend the socio-political reality). The intrusion of a new political actor into this field may have consequences on the dynamics of the field.

(A) The intrusion of a radical right-wing party may increase the salience of the socio-cultural cleavage dimension. If this dimension is gaining in importance, it will be more important for the other political actors to talk about politics in terms of categories and division lines belonging to the socio-cultural dimension. There are always several cleavage dimensions existing simultaneously (e.g. Rydgren 2012), most of them ultimately based on social identity or interests. Most contemporary West European democracies are dominated by two major cleavage dimensions: the socio-economic cleavage dimension, which puts workers against the capital, and which concerns the degree of state involvement in the economy, and the socio-cultural cleavage dimension, concerning values and identities and containing issues such as immigration, law and order, abortion, etc. (e.g. Kriesi *et al.* 2006). Together, these two cleavage dimensions constitute the basic contours of the political space; and, as Converse (1966) observes, two dimensions represented in a Cartesian space can always be perceived as three different shapes: one where the x and y axes are equal, one where the x axis is seen as more important, and one where the y axis is seen as more important.

Hence, at a voter level, it is not uncommon that people at the same time endorse anti-immigrant and redistributive attitudes. However, the *salience* of these cleavage dimensions is historically contingent. Although the socio-cultural cleavage dimension has existed throughout the twentieth century, the economic cleavage dimension has structured most of the political behavior in many countries since the Second World War. Yet, by being mainly concerned with the socio-cultural cleavage dimension (most notably about the division between ethnic natives and immigrants, or other ethnic minorities), the intrusion of a radical right-wing party into the political space has challenged this major cleavage dimension. Partly as a result of the emergence of radical right-wing parties, the salience of the socio-economic cleavage dimension has decreased, which means that many who previously defined themselves (as well as their adversaries) in terms of economic position, now instead define themselves and their adversaries in terms of ethnicity and nationality.

There are important differences between the West European countries regarding the dealignment or realignment processes, however. Most importantly, cleavage structures may be of different degrees of complexity. For example, France has a much more complicated cleavage structure than Sweden, dominated by the economic dimension. In France, other cleavage dimensions (e.g. religious, ethnic, regional) have for a long time cut through economic class bonds and loyalties, which has reduced the impact of social class on political behavior (Lipset in Mair *et al.* 1999: 313). It is probable that stronger bonds of class loyalties evolve in countries that have been strongly dominated only by the economic cleavage dimension, such as Sweden, which delays the realignment process.

(B) An emerging radical right-wing party may politicize the immigration issue, i.e. "translate" the social phenomenon of immigration into political terms. In order to deem an issue politicized in the full sense of the term, this translation process should embrace the level of political actors as well as the level of the voters, i.e. both voters and political actors should talk about immigration in political terms (Campbell *et al.* 1960: 29–32). A politicization of the immigration issue permits people to think and talk of immigration as being *caused by* political processes, as well as being the *cause to* other political and social phenomenon. In particular, the latter may have an impact on the level of racism and xenophobia in a society.

(C) By being considered as a relevant political actor (by, at least, significantly large groups of the electorate), a successful radical right-wing party is entitled to take part in the frame struggle over how to define social and political issues. Such parties have occasionally been successful in these frame struggles, which is indicated, for instance, by the way many established political actors, in several West European democracies, have accepted the general diagnostic frame that immigration and immigrants (or other ethnic minority groups) are *problems*. Accordingly, the debate has occasionally been more about the prognostic frame, i.e. how the problem should be solved (on the notions of "diagnostic" and "prognostic" frames, see McCarthy *et al.* 1996).

(D) We are now turning to mechanisms that do not just involve the supply side of the political space: an emerging radical right-wing party may "force" the established political parties to adjust their position in the political space in a more xenophobic direction. Since one or several of the already established parties within each party system have lost parts of their electorate as a result of the emergence of the radical right-wing parties, they have an incentive to adjust their position in the political space. One way of doing this is to approach, or even adopt, policy propositions from the newly emerged radical right-wing party, especially one or several of the core issues (i.e. anti-immigration and law and order). By aiming at the core issues, they hope to capture dissident issue voters as well as those who based their vote for a radical right-wing party on its party image. This phenomenon, which can be observed in several West European countries, may legitimize xenophobic attitudes. As a consequence, xenophobic attitudes may spread to wider groups of people within a society; groups that had previously stayed away from these attitudes, at least in their more manifest and elaborate forms, because of the stigma associated with them. Of course, this legitimization effect will be stronger in cases where established parties are in a position to legislate on, and implement, policy propositions influenced by, or adopted from, a radical right-wing party.

Concluding remarks

To sum up, I have argued that increases in popular xenophobia in a society may (partly) be understood from a top-down perspective, putting focus on political articulation and mobilization. More specifically, the presence of a radical right-wing party, or another anti-immigrant party, may cause an increase in xenophobia because it has an influence on people's frames of thought, and because it has an influence on other political actors.

In the first case, the emergence of a radical right-wing party offers a frame in which people's more or less unarticulated stock of xenophobic beliefs and attitudes can be articulated in a more comprehensive way, because it presents a new alternative political ideology, or "line of thought." The ideology of the radical right-wing parties may also offer a "schema of perception" or a "theory of guidance" which reduces the feeling of uncertainty, as well as other negative emotions and affections (such as fear, anxiety, and resentment). Hence, in this way the emergence of a radical right-wing party may lift the latent popular xenophobia to a manifest level. Once at a manifest level, the popular xenophobia is more likely to diffuse, because manifest xenophobes (which have gained in number) are more likely than latent xenophobes to propagate and to try to persuade others.

In the second case I have discussed how the emergence of a radical right-wing party may cause increases in the level of xenophobia in a society: because it may increase the salience of the socio-cultural dimension at the expense of the socio-economic cleavage dimension (which makes people more inclined to define themselves, others, and important political problems in terms of ethnicity and nationality, rather than in terms of social class); because it may be successful in the frame struggle over how to define the immigration issue (i.e. it may impose its diagnostic frame that immigrants are "problems" on other political actors); and because it may "force" established parties to adjust their position in the political space in a more xenophobic direction, which leads to a legitimization of xenophobic attitudes. This, in turn, may make these attitudes spread to wider groups of people within a society – groups that had previously stayed away from these attitudes, at least in their more elaborate form, because of the stigma associated with them.

References

Allport, G.W. (1954) *The Nature of Prejudice*, Reading, MA: Addison-Wesley.

Augoustinos, M. and Walker, I. (1998) *Social Cognition: An Integrated Introduction*, London: Sage.

Benford, R.D. and Snow, D.A. (2000) 'Framing Processes and Social Movements: An Overview and Assessment', *Annual Review of Sociology*, 26(1): 611–39.

Blalock, H.M. (1957) 'Percent Non-white and Discrimination in the South', *American Sociological Review*, 22(6): 677–82.

—(1967) *Toward a Theory of Minority-group Relations*, New York, NY: Capricorn.

Blumer, H. (1958) 'Race Prejudice as a Sense of Group Position', *Pacific Sociological Review*, 1(1): 3–7.

Bobo, L.D. and Tuan, M. (2006) *Prejudice in Politics*, Cambridge, MA: Harvard University Press.

Bourdieu, P. (1984) *Distinction: A Social Critique of the Judgement of Taste*, London: Routledge.

—(2000) 'Conférence: Le Champ Politique', in P. Bourdieu (ed.) *Propos sur le Champ Politique*, Lyon: Presses Universitaires de Lyon.

Campbell, A., Converse, P.E., Miller, W.E. and Stokes, D.E. (1960) *The American Voter*, New York, NY: John Wiley & Sons.

Converse, P.E. (1966) 'The Problem of Party Distances in Models of Voting Change', in K.M. Jennings and L.H. Zeigler (eds) *The Electoral Process*, Englewood Cliffs, NJ: Prentice-Hall.

Goffman, E. (1986) *Frame Analysis: An Essay on the Organization of Experience*, Boston, MA: Northeastern University Press.

Kriesi, H., Grande, E., Lachat, R., Dolezal, M., Bornschier, S. and Frey, T. (2006) *West European Politics in the Age of Globalization*, Cambridge, UK: Cambridge University Press.

McCarthy, J.D., Smith, J. and Zald, M.N. (1996) 'Accessing Public, Media, Electoral, and Governmental Agendas', in D. McAdam, J.D. McCarthy and M.N. Zald (eds) *Comparative Perspectives on Social Movements: Political Opportunities, Mobilizing Structures, and Cultural Framings*, Cambridge, UK: Cambridge University Press.

Mair, P., Lipset, S.M., Hout, M. and Goldthorpe, J.H. (1999) 'Critical Commentary: Four Perspectives on the End of Class Politics?', in G. Evans (ed.) *The End of Class Politics? Class Voting in Comparative Context*, Oxford, UK: Oxford University Press.

Merton, R.K. (1968) *Social Theory and Social Structure*, New York, NY: The Free Press.

Olzak, S. (1992) *The Dynamics of Ethnic Competition and Conflict*, Stanford, CA: Stanford University Press.

Pettigrew, T.F. (1957) 'Demographic Correlates of Border-state Desegregation', *American Sociological Review*, 22(6): 683–9.

Pettigrew, T.F. and Tropp, L.R. (2006) 'A Meta-analytic Test of Intergroup Contact Theory', *Journal of Personality and Social Psychology*, 90(5): 751–83.

Quillian, L. (1995) 'Prejudice as a Response to Perceived Group Threat: Population Composition and Anti-immigrant and Racial Prejudice in Europe', *American Sociological Review*, 60(4): 586–611.

Rydgren, J. (2003) 'Meso-level Reasons for Racism and Xenophobia', *European Journal of Social Theory*, 6(1): 45–68.

—(2007) 'The Sociology of the Radical Right', *Annual Review of Sociology*, 33(1): 241–62.

—(ed.) (2012) *Class Politics and the Radical Right*, London: Routledge.

Scheler, M. (1998) *Ressentiment*, Milwaukee, WI: Marquette University Press.

Semyonov, M., Raijan, R. and Gorodzersky, A. (2006) 'The Rise of Anti-foreigner Sentiment in European Societies 1988–2000', *American Sociological Review*, 71(3): 426–49.

Swidler, A. (1986) 'Culture in Action: Symbols and Strategies', *American Sociological Review*, 51(2): 273–86.

Wilkes, R., Guppy, N. and Farris, L. (2007) 'Right-wing Parties and Anti-foreigner Sentiment in Europe', *American Sociological Review*, 72(5): 831–40.

Winock, M. (1998) *Nationalism, Anti-semitism, and Fascism in France*, Stanford, CA: Stanford University Press.

34

Conviviality

(Re)negotiating minimal consensus

Tilmann Heil

Conviviality directs our focus on the everyday process of how people live together in mundane encounters, of how they (re)translate between their sustained differences and how they (re)negotiate minimal consensuses. This seems more pressing than ever because of continued diversification, the failure of the integration and multiculturalism paradigms and the restless competition and ongoing marginalisation due to unfavourable economic conditions in times of crisis.

Unlike the obvious tendencies that such difficult conditions might entail, conviviality points at phenomena different from ethnic absolutism, cultural racism and nationalism. It references the forms of sociality, generally understood as the entire field of someone's social relations, which are characterised by a minimal, yet sufficient, engagement with diversity and difference. Homogenising and cleansing tendencies which are rife in the political discourse on belonging and autochthony (Geschiere 2009) hinder the constructive engagement with differences. The perspective of conviviality is different from processes in which imagined communities continue to play a large role for integration and which suggest homogenisation. Similarly, the scenarios of cultural hybridity and mixing should be considered as distinct from conviviality since they are not concerned with the translation and negotiation of sustained differences; rather, they stress processes in which cultural differences have become unrecognisable. Different from Gilroy (2005: xv), who argues that ethnic differences in the form of 'multiculture' have become ordinary or unremarkable, I maintain that cultural differences remain meaningful in times of enhanced diversification (Vertovec 2007b), especially when they combine with situations of hierarchy and social inequality. These cultural differences challenge the idea of living peacefully with difference and contribute to the uncertainties of convivialities.

The conceptual notion of 'conviviality' needs to be set apart from its commonplace English meaning. In accordance with Overing and Passes (2000: xiii) conviviality conceptually 'eschews … [and] transcends the particular English sense of simply having a good (and, it is implicit, slightly inebriated) time in the company of others'. I shall show that tension, conflict and frustration form part of a conceptual notion of conviviality as well as situations of consensus, consideration and respect. On analysing cooperative *and* conflictual situations in negotiation and translation processes, convivialities emerge as fragile and changing and only able to lead to minimal forms of sociality.

Local policies as well as emic discourses in neighbourhoods use various terms to address the everyday living together which, under the conditions of diversification, is pragmatically reformulated as living *with* differences. It is the diversification of a local population and the perceived failure of integration and multiculturalism (Vertovec and Wessendorf 2010) that raise questions of conviviality in the first place. As one of the earliest relevant examples, the Castilian term *convivencia* makes reference to Andalusia and the Middle Ages when Jews, Muslims and Christians simultaneously resided there (see Mann *et al.* 1992; Suárez-Navaz 2004: 191f.)[1]. Similarly, Catalonia uses the term *convivència* in migration-related policy documents to describe ways of dealing with difference, and in Senegal *cohabitation* is used to address the living together of the different faith communities (Erickson 2011; cf. Heil 2014). All of these emic notions – similar but not identical with the English term – address the process of conviviality that this contribution will outline. As political terms, however, they have a normative connotation which conviviality as a concept does not assert.

Since I am concerned with social encounters, including the most fleeting, which happen between people who perceive one another as different, urban spaces – which in principle are accessible to all – are the logical arena of conviviality. As Goffman (1966: 4) argues, parks, streets and squares, generally referred to as public spaces, 'tell us a great deal about [the] most diffuse forms of social organization'. Unable to pay a great deal of attention to the spaces of conviviality, I proceed here in three steps. First, I take inspiration from the discussion of cosmopolitanism to state why conviviality seems better suited as an analytical term to study living with sustained differences. In the second section I enquire into the various modes of everyday interactions and their absence to understand what kind of sociality conviviality evokes and which other dynamics, such as avoidance and uncertainty, can be at play in encounters with difference. Finally, I explore the limits of the processes leading to convivialities as they consist of situations of agreement and others of conflict. I conclude that conviviality highlights processes that remain fragile due to the interplay of people who remain culturally and socially different with normative, pragmatic and tactical motives at stake.

Beyond cosmopolitanism

To start, I shall situate my interest in conviviality in relation to concepts that address living *with* difference. Often, social situations characterised by the participants' engagement with diversity and difference have been dealt with under the heading of cosmopolitanism (e.g. Delanty 2012; Skrbiš and Woodward 2013).

Closest to my interest in conviviality are those notions of cosmopolitanism that have been refined as working class, vernacular, everyday or in another way mundane (e.g. Noble 2009; Werbner 1999). Such a refinement appears necessary, since these authors are interested in practices of 'ordinary' people including migrants and their activities. Due to its suggestive links to the life worlds and concerns of a small elite of upper middle class people aspiring to world citizenship, cosmopolitanism has been continuously critiqued for being a Western elite project and derived from a Kantian global humanism (see Delanty 2006[2]). Qualified cosmopolitanism, however, describes everyone's everyday practices, attitudes and competencies that cope just fine with difference. Providing some more detail, many authors maintain that a certain openness to difference is key – a classical cosmopolitan value (e.g. Skrbiš and Woodward 2013: 2) – while others argue that people act strategically to get something done (e.g. Noble 2009: 51), or mainly are pragmatic and unable to react to the multiple differences encountered in super-diverse situations.

Conviviality as derived from emic concepts of living with difference does not carry the same elitist and normative baggage of cosmopolitanism. Rather, it delineates a process which describes aspects of the everyday life in neighbourhoods where local residents engage in practices and discourses of living together, engaging with, confronting and embracing differences. It thereby additionally draws from a number of locally available discourses and concepts such as *teranga* (Wolof: hospitality), *siñooyaa* (Mandinka: neighbourliness), 规矩 (*gui ju*, a Singaporian code of conduct), hierarchical incorporation, multilingualism, respect and, as one among many, a cosmopolitan self-representation.[3] Conviviality, I hold, addresses an engagement with cultural diversity across social classes. Surely, there are differences of whether one belongs to a working class family or has received an elite education abroad which has bestowed one with cultural capital, including some kind of cosmopolitan self-understanding. However, speaking of conviviality as minimal sociality, it remains universally applicable as a form of human interaction in which differences are negotiated and translated.

Clearly, it would be too easy to stop here, since inequality, conflict, depreciation, social stratification and status differences persist everywhere alongside cultural differentiation. Despite increased cultural globalisation, many contemporary social situations continue to be characterised by cultural essentialism and closure (Wimmer 2013). Inevitably, cosmopolitanism carries the risk of representing the positively perceived counterpart of such developments. Conviviality conceptually embraces both since it ties in with the everyday and the ordinary. In this domain of people's lives, both agreement and conflict concerning living with difference can be found.

Despite this argument for the general analytical value of conviviality, it has most strongly been attributed to specific ethnographic fields and cultural practices. For example, Overing and Passes (2000: 2) suggest in their introduction that conviviality is key to Amazonian sociality. Gilroy (2005) perceived conviviality among youths in postcolonial cities. I myself embraced a West African migrant perspective to study conviviality, asking whether there was something specific to their pre-migration socialisation with diversity in Casamance, Senegal, that explained their participation in conviviality in Catalonia. Indeed, they had been habituated into ways of living with sustained differences despite processes of homogenisation and closure.

Conviviality should not, however, be disregarded as a culture-specific way of socialisation. Apart from the specific convivialities practised in certain parts of the world and their corre-sponding emic notions, the level of minimal sociality that conviviality addresses is a crucial one which, I hold, has been frequently neglected. In my understanding, conviviality neither addresses community cohesion and solidarity, nor is it concerned with indifference and neglect. It addresses the in-between, the fleeting, the superficial and the unremarkable. This can be studied well by taking cases into account that show the historical rootedness of living with dif-ference. It will become clear that these processes are not mainly concerned with normative ideals but rather with working consensuses in the everyday. Next, I further develop the everyday focus of conviviality as part of the realm of minimal, yet sufficient, sociality.

Focusing on the everyday

The aspects of ordinary social relations in the everyday are diverse and include openness, civility, avoidance, vigilance, dispute, indifference, curiosity, etc. In encounters, many nuances of living with difference are perceptible, showing, apart from respect, consideration and a certain easiness with difference, silent forms of domination and marginalisation, tactical alliances and careful responses to negative potentialities emanating from neighbours and strangers alike. All of these dimensions of sociality manifest in convivialities as forces perpetually constitute, change and challenge social relations. Analytically, they play out in interactions and ensuing (re-)negotiations and (re)translations of social and cultural differences, which are ongoing in everyday conviviality.

In particular, conviviality shares an interest in ordinary, pragmatic and potentially partial and fleeting aspects of sociality with the scholarship on (in)civility, which refers to interactions with strangers in public spaces (Boyd 2006; Sennett 2005). Emphasising the challenge of 'finding ways to knit the city together without homogenising it' (Sennett 2005: 2), civility, as 'the capacity of people who differ to live together' (ibid.: 1), directly addresses a central concern of conviviality. Concerning the quality of interactions, Vertovec (2007a: 32) sees civility in 'cordial but distant relations', and Boyd (2006: 867) defines being civil to strangers as 'treating them with an "easy spontaneity" that demonstrates both a willingness to look past differences and that communicates equal respect.' Implying that everyone is a respected equal, civil relations thus neither refer to just living side by side described by pragmatism and indifference, nor do they imply ties relying on strong obligations, expectations and solidarity common to group specific sociability. Contrary to the perceived risk of civil relations being overlooked as meaningless, conviviality substantiates their relevance in diverse settings. This scholarship has raised several issues of importance to understanding convivialities, for example questions of equality, indifference, respect, social distance and spontaneity. Some of these dimensions go beyond that which the focus on civility can provide and which is relevant for delineating the sphere of conviviality. Put differently, it would be too simple only to qualify people's behaviours towards others, who are different (or not), as either civil or not.

Sustained differences, which at times might result in civil encounters, can also foster mutual avoidance. Early on, studies concerned with plural societies observed that 'groups of differing race and culture liv[e] side by side in economic symbiosis and mutual avoidance' (Smith 1974: vii). Smith thus opposed consensual theory and blamed it for 'begin[ning] by assuming the normative consensual integration of all social systems' (ibid.: xiii). The juxtaposition of avoidance and consensus raises the question of whether conviviality is founded on common values and willing submission to them, unwilling submission and coercion, or avoidance. This is of utmost importance, since Goffman (2008 [1967]) leaves no doubt that in face-to-face interactions mutual avoidance is a key strategy of people fearing to lose face by acting inappropriately, a heightened risk if cultural differences complicate the communication process.

In contrast to utter avoidance or indifference, which can both run the risk of leading only to indispensable exchange or mere co-presence, engaged encounter or face-to-face interaction is a crucial practice of conviviality (Gilroy 2005: xv). In a similar vein, social contact and encounter are necessary ingredients of local liveability. In convivial interactions, I suggest that cultural differences and degrees of social inequality are continuously maintained in stressing the relevance of negotiation and translation. Thus, Noble (2009: 51) notes that 'unpanic' in situations of diversity 'emerge[s] out of sustained practices of accommodation and negotiation'. However, rather than mainly heralding relatively stable relations, as Noble does, negotiation is ongoing and the limits of negotiation need to be explored. This inevitably re-introduces the fragility of conviviality and its being in-process. The same holds true for translation between distinct, but concurring, systems of meaning. Translation can be understood 'as a continuous process of re-articulation and re-contextualization, without any notion of a primary origin' (Hall and Chen 2005: 394). The practice of translation is also part of 'cosmopolitan conviviality' for Gilroy (2005: 8), which he juxtaposes to ethnocentrism as untranslatability. To translate references the acts of comparing, connecting and understanding processes and practices that at first seem irreconcilably different. The importance of these three basic practices of conviviality has been frequently noted by scholars who studied living *with* difference.

Intentions and acts of greeting and mutually acknowledging the presence of the other may serve as obvious examples of the processes of conviviality. In my own fieldwork, Senegalese immigrants to Spain regularly emphasised the need to show respect to and recognition of those encountered by spending time greeting them and enquiring into the whereabouts of their close ones. Furthermore, they regularly found themselves in social situations where greeting was reduced to almost nothing, something like a nodding of heads or an 'hola'. In situations, however, in which no interaction took place at all, Senegalese immigrants felt that conviviality was non-existent, which would lead to uncertain social situations with unknown social consequences. Greetings reduced this uncertainty by gaining some initial insights into who the other one is. The differences encountered in conceptions of greeting at times required translation justifying that an 'hola' could indeed be an acceptable replacement for long chats. Exposing of various forms of 'truncated multilingualism' (Blommaert et al. 2005: 199), the knowing of just enough of the other's language to get by, also falls into the realm of translation. The disjuncture over how to engage one another causes uncertainty and conflict, which requires negotiation. As a consequence, in conviviality both normative and tactical considerations combine in many ways. Greeting is presented as a moral obligation which enhances the need for negotiation. Addressing someone unknown in his own mother tongue and finding out about them are tactical choices. Whether consciously lived or habitually accommodated, differences continue to matter in such circumstances and are a central element of conviviality.

Leading on from these insights into micro-interactions, the spectrum between avoiding and seeking interaction needs to be closely evaluated since social settings always bear the potential of negative social consequences. Choosing extreme examples, Vigh (2011) traces the origins of people's hyper-vigilance to the negative potentiality of ubiquitous long-term conflict and uncertainty in Guinea Bissau and Belfast. Lacking predictability, Vigh (ibid.: 99) defines social hyper-vigilance as 'characterized by a constant awareness and preparedness toward the negative potentialities of social figures and forces.' I suggest that everyday life among people who differ to various degrees is equally in flux and full of uncertain outcomes, even if violence does not penetrate everyday life to the same extent. Thus, people observe and enquire into the processes and people around them, trying to 'tell' from where risks will emanate. As an alternative to keeping a distance, interaction and greetings are a preferred way of local residents to find out about new arrivals while at the same time establishing rapport (Goffman 2008 [1967]: 41, note 30). This analysis falls into the domain of conviviality since it encompasses phenomena that are in between set categories and which lack clear-cut signs that could provide orientation.

In complex social situations, in which multiple differences overlap and the intentions of those encountered can stem from various sources, being prudent and sometimes trying to avoid encounters is part of the everyday. Such behaviours may cast a doubt on people's commitment to interaction, but at the same time they offer a nuanced reading of minimal forms of sociality as they spring from the processes of conviviality. Furthermore, they raise the questions of whether and to what extent avoidance and even indifference can play a role in conviviality, especially if we think of the increasing number of people in precarious conditions in current societies. This also importantly affects the relationship of agreement and conflict in the processes of conviviality. It is to this last aspect that I devote the remainder of this discussion.

Between agreement and conflict

Authors who use conviviality in its literal sense – referring to generally friendly but superficial relations – would most likely not disagree with the idea that conviviality delineates minimal sociality (e.g. Gandhi and Hoek 2012). As we have seen, however, they limit their analysis to agreeable aspects of living together. However, the minimal and fleeting kind of sociality, not least in relation to difference, seems full of uncertainty, discontinuities and ruptures that emerge from translating between differences and negotiating minimal consensuses in conviviality. Such processes are often conflictual when they are lived in interaction. Rather than juxtaposing conviviality and conflict, I suggest that conviviality encompasses both cooperative and conflictual social situations.

The example of greeting on p. 321 has revealed how conviviality relies on everyday practice. Reciprocal greeting which manifests mutual respect can be described as happening in mutual agreement. In contrast, passing without greeting can be interpreted as avoidance, disregard or indifference, which in the view of some may border on exclusion and open discrimination, or at least evoke such feelings. Clearly such encounters are bound to provoke conflictual situations. Mutual accusations of not cohering to social consensuses, which some perceive to be locally valid, reveal a disquieting facet of conviviality. Local residents who stick to various views concerning greeting practices may accuse each other of falling short of their expectations. Yet in more or less open negotiations they will either re-constitute a former consensus or eventually formulate a different one. Conviviality understood as social process inevitably encompassed such conflictual episodes as well. Trying to understand enough about differences – a practice observable among migrant populations – further deescalates the negotiation process by way of conceptual translation.

Normative, tactical and pragmatic considerations play out in translation and negotiation practices of local residents who try to address their differences in conviviality. Tactical and pragmatic solutions gain centrality in circumstances when cultural differences are linked to questions of relative (in)equality, hierarchy and status differences. Well-known examples of this in contexts of migration and cultural diversity are the differentiations between first-comers and late-comers, hosts or landlords and strangers, autochthons and allochthons (e.g. Geschiere 2009). In such configurations, cultural differences mark important social distinctions and valuations. The processes of a guest's reception under the heading of hospitality and a stranger's social incorporation are clearly marked by the power differentials between patrons (hosts, landlords) and clients (strangers, guests, immigrants). Tensions and contradictions arise from an array of possible practices, which range from granting strangers respect and thus social recognition to their potential marginalisation and exclusion. As a consequence, I suggest that, apart from negotiating cultural differences, conviviality faces the challenge of contesting and accommodating power hierarchies and status differences. In such cases, conviviality risks being hampered by people's mutual avoidance and vigilance.

On the other hand, hierarchical but reciprocal relations are omnipresent and commonplace. In everyday encounters, negotiations and translation do not need to result in equality. All that is up for negotiation are ways to live with difference. Quite often, this also implies living with some level of hierarchy and stratification that is perceived to be acceptable; only a sufficient equality can be achieved. The latter actually can form part of the negotiated shared understandings, especially if the consensus found is a reciprocal one.

The tactical engagements with local configurations of difference and power on the one hand can aim at achieving a minimal consensus to regain peaceful interaction. On the other hand, their intention can also be both to increase the individual autonomy of expression and to subvert dominant discourses. Interaction therefore necessarily encompasses both cooperative and conflictual elements, keeping outcomes uncertain. Following de Certeau (1988), the tactics of those in relatively less powerful positions are their creative ways to engage with and contest dominant institutionalised structures. Conviviality can raise our awareness of such negotiations in times of pervasive status and power differences due to increased diversification, which includes a plurality of legal statuses and migration control. However, outcomes also remain uncertain since the processes of conviviality may fail and result in uncertainty and open confrontation.

The extent to which conflictual interactions are part of convivialities can be discerned in the light of ongoing negotiations and translations. Perceiving differences in interaction is potentially conflictual, yet it may be embraced in negotiation and, conceivably, translation. For example, upon arrival in a new place, migrants learn different everyday practices in their encounters with other local residents. Differences in greeting are a case in point. If everyday practices and the understanding of how things are habitually done vary, the various participants in the encounter will potentially try to translate between the differences. Alternatively, a social negotiation process is bound to start to which the conflicting views will be subjected. The latter does not have to imply hostility and escalation; a situation may result in which everyone follows different but relatively compatible ways of interacting. An understanding of how and why practices differ reveals the local populations' translation efforts; however, the level of tension or conflict in such processes of conviviality remains unpredictable. Where the limits of the capacity of convivialities to embrace social inequalities lie remains an empirical question. Yet, I suggest that physical violence in encounters as well as fundamentalist beliefs are incompatible with convivialities. Both foreclose the forming of consensus in the processes of interacting and negotiating, and of making differences mutually intelligible by way of (cultural) translation.

Conclusion: fragile convivialities

We have seen that living with cultural and social differences comes to the fore in various ways and at the intersection of a set of social practices. It raises the crucial question of how people's everyday practices mediate cultural differences as well as power relations and (in)equality structures in diverse societies. Defining conviviality as the field of such processes and setting it in relation to complementary concepts, I suggested looking into practices like interaction, negotiation and translation since they are relevant in both cooperative and conflictual situations. Despite challenges to the feasibility of interaction due to mutual avoidance and exclusion, I have upheld that these basic practices are part of the process from which minimal local consensuses can emerge. Their raison d'être is the sharing of urban spaces peacefully in diversity and with difference. It is a mode of sociality that builds on difference, rather than trying to erase or subjugate it. By relying on various processes and forms of interaction, consensuses are changing and convivialities remain malleable and alive.

People enter the processes which constitute conviviality with various, sometimes conflicting, intentions. Normative convictions combine with, and are juxtaposed to, those that are tactical and creative, as well as purely pragmatic considerations concerning the ways of engaging with social situations characterised by diversity. The interplay of situational and uncertain, as well as habitual and predictable, responses to changing configurations of diversity is equally characteristic of convivialities. Whether people move or stay put, static conceptions of living with difference increasingly seem inapplicable to contemporary conditions of diversification. Whether urban spaces are designed as spaces of encounter or not, people are bound to partake in the processes of conviviality while also living up to their distinctiveness. Maybe more than ever, we need to study those everyday aspects of sociality that are about living together with sustained differences.

Notes

1   This plays down the fact that the three faith communities never lived together on equal terms (Kamen 1998).

2 Nevertheless, people from everywhere practise cosmopolitanism (e.g. Breckenridge *et al.* 2002).
3 For the exemplary concepts from Senegal (Wolof, Mandinka), see Heil (2014); for 规矩 (*gui ju*), see Ye (this volume).

References

Blommaert, J., Collins, J. and Slembrouck, S. (2005) 'Spaces of Multilingualism', *Language & Communication*, 25(3): 197–216.

Boyd, R. (2006) 'The Value of Civility?', *Urban Studies*, 43(5/6): 863–78.

Breckenridge, C.A., Bhabha, H.K., Pollock, S. and Chakrabarty, D. (eds) (2002) *Cosmopolitanism*, Durham, NC: Duke University Press.

de Certeau, M. (1988) *The Practice of Everyday Life*, Berkeley, CA: University of California Press.

Delanty, G. (2006) 'The Cosmopolitan Imagination: Critical Cosmopolitanism and Social Theory', *The British Journal of Sociology*, 57(1): 25–47.

—(ed.) (2012) *Routledge Handbook of Cosmopolitanism Studies*, New York, NY: Routledge.

Erickson, B. (2011) 'Utopian Virtues: Muslim Neighbors, Ritual Sociality, and the Politics of Convivència', *American Ethnologist*, 38(1): 114–31.

Gandhi, A. and Hoek, L. (2012) 'Introduction to Crowds and Conviviality: Ethnographies of the South Asian City', *Ethnography*, 13(1): 3–11.

Geschiere, P. (2009) *The Perils of Belonging: Autochthony, Citizenship, and Exclusion in Africa and Europe*, Chicago, IL: University of Chicago Press.

Gilroy, P. (2005) *Postcolonial Melancholia*, New York, NY: Columbia University Press.

Goffman, E. (1966) *Behavior in Public Places: Notes on the Social Organization of Gatherings*, New York, NY: The Free Press.

—(2008 [1967]) 'On Face-work', in E. Goffman (ed.) *Interaction Ritual: Essays in Face-to-face Behavior*, 4th edn, New Brunswick, NJ: Aldine Transaction.

Hall, S. and Chen, K.H. (2005) 'Cultural Studies and the Politics of Internationalization: An Interview with Stuart Hall', in D. Morley and K.H. Chen (eds) *Stuart Hall: Critical Dialogues in Cultural Studies*, London: Routledge.

Heil, T. (2014) 'Are Neighbours Alike? Practices of Conviviality in Catalonia and Casamance', *European Journal of Cultural Studies*. Published online. Available HTTP: <http://ecs.sagepub.com/content/early/2014/03/13/1367549413510420> (accessed 27 March 2014).

Kamen, H. (1998) *The Spanish Inquisition: A Historical Revision*, London: Phoenix.

Mann, V.B., Glick, T.F. and Dodds, J.D. (eds) (1992) *Convivencia: Jews, Muslims, and Christians in Medieval Spain*, New York, NY: Braziller.

Noble, G. (2009) 'Everyday Cosmopolitanism and the Labour of Intercultural Community', in A. Wise and S. Velayutham (eds) *Everyday Multiculturalism*, Basingstoke, UK: Palgrave Macmillan.

Overing, J. and Passes, A. (eds) (2000) *The Anthropology of Love and Anger: The Aesthetics of Conviviality in Native Amazonia*, London: Routledge.

Sennett, R. (2005) 'Civility', *Urban Age*, Bulletin 1: 1–3.

Skrbiš, Z. and Woodward, I. (2013) *Cosmopolitanism: Uses of the Idea*, Los Angeles, CA: Sage.

Smith, M.G. (1974) *The Plural Society in the British West Indies*, Kingston: Sangster's Book Stores.

Suárez-Navaz, L. (2004) *Rebordering the Mediterranean: Boundaries and Citizenship in Southern Europe*, Oxford, NY: Berghahn.

Vertovec, S. (2007a) *New Complexities of Cohesion in Britain: Super-diversity, Transnationalism and Civil-integration*. London: Commission on Integration and Cohesion.

—(2007b) 'Super-diversity and its Implications', *Ethnic and Racial Studies*, 30: 1024–54.

Vertovec, S. and Wessendorf, S. (2010) *The Multiculturalism Backlash: European Discourses, Policies and Practices*, London: Routledge.

Vigh, H. (2011) 'Vigilance: On Conflict, Social Invisibility, and Negative Potentiality', *Social Analysis*, 55(3): 93–114.

Werbner, P. (1999) 'Global Pathways: Working Class Cosmopolitans and the Creation of Transnational Ethnic Worlds', *Social Anthropology*, 7(1): 17–35.

Wimmer, A. (2013) *Ethnic Boundary Making: Institutions, Power, Networks*, New York, NY: Oxford University Press.

35

Locality and diversity

The city as arena of ethnic expression and accommodation

William Safran

Most scholarly analyses of ethnic politics focus on the national level because the ethnie is juxtaposed to the nation. The national is said to overwhelm and supersede the ethnic; ethnic politics therefore struggles to contain and, if possible, to reverse this process. The modern nation is transethnic and the national government is supraethnic because, in its most advanced form, it has merged ethnic minorities into a larger community.

According to an American maxim, however, "all politics is local." Life is lived in cities; they are places where the needs of subcommunities have to be addressed. Neighborly relations develop in the city in recognition of differences. Ethnic identity is expressed and mobilized on the local level. This is especially true of large cities; these are often marked by segregation along ethnic lines, and the cultures, languages, and religions of ethnic groups are best maintained there (Lieberson 1971). With its network of ethnic institutions and community services, the city fosters a local pride that goes beyond topophilia and distinguishes it from other places and from the national territory.

The city is the most feasible ethnic site because of its concentrated space: there are no "national" Chinatowns, barrios, Black ghettoes, or Little Italies. Large cities have multilingual street signs and store marquees, a profusion of mosques, temples, ethnically specific churches, and networks of ethnic establishments (Heldman 2006). The typical metropolis is a collection of ethnopoles, where ethnic groups are most apt to thrive and resist the melting pot. It applies in particular to immigrants, whose ethnic identity is preserved by a relocalization of their homeland culture (Argun 2003: 20). This process involves what Appadurai (1996) has called the "transnational construction of imaginary landscapes" (ibid.: 31). Such construction needs opportunity structures – demographic density, a welcoming environment, and global communication facilities – which are usually found in large cities.

Nevertheless, the translation of Old-Country patterns is selective. It is easier to reconstitute an experienced and remembered Old-Country community than an imagined one. The place that is remembered most clearly is a homeland *city* with its particular features, including "iconic sites alongside more personal places of memory" (Blunt *et al.* 2012: 34). These features are more likely to be reproduced in a hostland urban setting than in a provincial space where pressures to conform to the majority are more intrusive. That explains the existence of Turkish Berlin, Jewish New York, and Greek Toronto (Centner 2010). The city is a testing ground of multiculturalism;

but some ethnic traditions, like honor killings or cliterectomies, cannot be easily maintained in the hostland, because they are impractical or forbidden.

Occasionally, however, minorities may behave in a more ethnic manner in a large hostland city than do their kin in the homeland. Turkish women in Berlin may wear the Islamic veil in public, which in Turkey was, until recently, banned. German culture was maintained more freely in New York than in Nazi Germany, and Iranian culture is pursued with fewer constraints in Los Angeles than in ayatollah-dominated Iran. Tibetan culture and religion are supported more openly in Dharamsala, India, than in Lhasa. At the same time, exile culture incorporates experiences of the hostland and represses the concerns of the homeland. For Armenians and Sikhs in Paris and London, the memory of oppression looms larger than for their kin in the homeland, who are preoccupied with national politics and quotidian problems (Safran 2007: 50).

The creation of ethnic cultural, social, and religious space is easier on a local level than a national one, especially in metropoles, which often escape direct control by national governments. Yet local ethnically specific patterns and policies may serve as prototypes and be adopted nationally. In the USA this has happened in teaching English as a second language and in the accommodation of ethnic and religious needs in schools and hospitals. Cities are training grounds of ethnic minorities for political leadership; for example, African Americans in Chicago, Latinos in Los Angeles, and Beurs[1] in French cities often begin their political careers as community organizers.

The local and the global

Large cities engage in transnational interactions. They are the sites of consulates, which provide information about the homeland and facilitate cultural exchanges (Laguerre 2000: 20–4, 53). Hostland city governments use the ethnic community as "an anchor for globalizing processes" such as tourism and trade (Kwok 2008: 469f.). The homeland tries to preserve the ethnic identity of expatriate communities by sending imams and cultural agents. In large cities ethnic diasporas organize for lobbying and paradiplomacy, and hostland governments use them to influence homeland policies. Ethnic elites and entrepreneurs flourish in cities. The former have an ideological stake in defending the ethnic identity of their clientele; the latter instrumentalize it for their own political advancement.

The city is the port of entry of ethnic replenishments. Many immigrants remain there because it contains elements of a recreated homeland – a fact that underscores the city's ethnopolitan character.[2] The metropolis contains schools providing ethnic-language instruction[3] and churches where sermons are given in the homeland language. But the German-language schools in Midwestern cities were not copies of the Swabian *Bauernschulen*; and the language taught in schools in India is not always pure Tibetan.

Certain behavior patterns sometimes found among ethnic minorities in large cities that are associated with exclusion and poverty, such as drug dealing and prostitution, become stereotypes of the culture (Body-Gendrot 1993). It is also in large cities that endogamy is more common than in small provincial towns, which lack an adequate pool of ethnic cohorts.

The city constitutes an exception to the national space because it is more self-sufficient and sometimes more narcissistic, and therefore ethnic identity is more robust on the urban level than the national one. This is found above all in cities where special conditions prevail due to their history, location, or ethnolinguistic mixture. The reconstitution of an ethnic community in a hostland metropolis such as New York, London, Paris, and Toronto is not necessarily based on *national* homeland patterns; the identitarian point of reference may be a particular city. This applies especially to border cities such as Vilnius, Cernauti, and Brussels.[4] They contain multiple ethnic groups; they have come under periodically changing jurisdictions due to boundary changes; and they do not have stable national identities because they are located in weak states. For these reasons they have enjoyed relative autonomy vis-à-vis central governments.

Jews settling in North America have been nostalgic for Odessa but not Soviet Russia, and for Vilnius but not Poland (Lipphardt 2010). Immigrants from Hong Kong identify specifically with that city while remaining hostile toward Communist China. Cuban refugees in Miami have pined for Havana but not for Castro's Cuba. In building their communities in hostland cities, immigrants from the Mezzogiorno did not attempt to recreate Italy but rather a more narrowly focused "agrotown," in particular certain elements of it – the extended clan, the authority of the paterfamilias, and the church (Gabaccia 1984: 100). The culture of the Dominicans reconstituted in Manhattan is a mixture of Santo Domingo idiom, music, and religion, as well as American Latino culture (Hoffnung-Garskof 2008).

Collaboration, competition, and conflict

A relocated community cannot preserve its antecedent character in pure form. Collective identities are modified by local conditions and influences. It is not always clear how the position of one ethnic minority is affected by the presence of others, and how that presence affects their relationship with the urban population at large.

In the nineteenth century, Irish Catholics of New York were hostile to Jews, while Anglo-Saxon Protestants were hostile to both the Irish and the Jews, regarding them equally as foreigners. Subsequently, the Irish were considered more "American" than the Italians or the Jews. After a sustained migration of African Americans from the South to the North and the end of immigration from Eastern and Southern Europe, previously settled whites muffled their antagonism to new white immigrants and shifted it toward Blacks (Wilson 1984: 95). In the second half of the twentieth century, Jews were no longer considered a minority. This development contributed to their assimilation and weakened their ethnic identity. A similar situation occurred in France. Before World War II, Jews were often regarded as an alien presence on the Parisian urban landscape. But after the massive influx of Muslims, Jews became more acceptable to the majority of French society, and their culture came to be seen as part of "Judeo-Christian civilization" (Club de l'Horloge 1985: 205). In Berlin, the image of immigrants from Eastern Europe improved with the arrival of "guest workers" (*Gastarbeiter*) from Turkey.

Ideally, the existence of several ethnic minority groups generates interethnic solidarity in the face of dominant, and often hostile, majority. In the 1940s and 1950s, Jewish and Catholic groups in large American cities collaborated with the Urban League and the National Association for the Advancement of Colored People in promoting civil rights for African Americans (Glazer 1983: 24f.). But interethnic collaboration collapsed due to disagreements over affirmative action and the administration of the school system. Because the urban power relations between Jews and African Americans were unequal, the African-American image of Jews became a negative one: they were the heartless shopkeepers and slumlords of Black neighborhoods of New York and Detroit. In Los Angeles, Korean shopkeepers projected a similar image.

Interethnic relations have national and transnational dimensions. African Americans and Jews in the USA, and Indians and Pakistanis in the UK, may support one another on local socioeconomic issues, but not necessarily on issues beyond the local setting. In New York, African Americans have not shared the Jews' sympathy for Israel; conversely, Jews and other white ethnics have not shared the collective pride of Blacks in the rise of sovereign states in Africa. In Paris, Jews and Muslims collaborate in fighting racism and xenophobia; but that collaboration tends to break down over disagreements about the Middle East. In some cases, interethnic rivalries are reenactments of homeland patterns. Polish–Jewish business relations in Chicago were recapitulations of relations in pre-war Poland (Gold 2012: 53); and relations between Turks and Kurds in Western cities echo those prevailing in Turkey.

Relations between ethnic groups may reflect self-perceptions regarding their relative positions within society at large. In the USA many white ethnics have entered the middle class, and their ethnic consciousness is no longer tied to poverty but to a misty cultural nostalgia. They are not particularly interested in improving the lot of Blacks and Latinos lest it destroy their own status advantage, bring Blacks into white neighborhoods, and lower the value of housing and the quality of the public schools. Such attitudes have led to the growth of private schools that are often ethnically specific.

The improvement of the status of an ethnic minority can serve to de-ethnicize it. Thus, urban political machines such as Tammany Hall in New York had a strong preference for the Irish in political appointments. That preference helped to integrate the Irish into the American system, but in the process Irish identity became attenuated and emptied of cultural content, so that most New York Irish relate to the American urban scene rather than to Ireland. There are still many Irish priests, but since most officiate at non-Irish churches they represent the Catholic priesthood rather than the Irish subculture.

Metropoles are particularly exposed to ethnocultural mixing, as in couscous-pommes frites in Paris, Creole cooking in New Orleans, and Chinese–Cuban cuisine in New York. Ethnic interchange is also attested by the African American clad in green who marches in the annual Saint Patrick's Day parade in New York, and by the Cinco de Mayo parade in Los Angeles, which has been influenced by African-American cultural styles (Rogers 1995). Such interchanges give rise to these questions: Do they suggest genuine cultural sharing and interethnic comity, or do they dilute ethnic culture and reduce it to kitsch? If they are associated with ethnic rivalries, do they generate hostility toward multiculturalism? In many cases, laws affecting immigration, multiculturalism, and religious ritual have been responses to negative perceptions of ethnically mixed cities, such as "Londonistan," "Judapest,", and "Havana in Florida."

Identitarian Aggregations and reconfigurations

The differentiations within ethnic groups in their ancestral homeland are not necessarily replicated abroad, where they are often treated as single categoric groups for statistical or public-policy purposes. In the USA, one sees more references to Hispanics than to Puerto Ricans, to Chicanos than Cubans, and to Indians rather than Bengalis, Punjabis, or Sikhs. In London, Indians, Pakistanis, and Chinese are often collectively labeled as Asians.

Members of minority ethnic groups may reconfigure or relabel their identities in response to social pressure or influences by other minorities. This occurs often in large cities, where ethnic groups can live "under the radar" of census-takers. Black immigrants from the West Indies to New York undergo a process of "Haitization" – inter alia, by introducing Creole elements into their language – in order to fit in with a well-established Haitian community (Morin 1990). Moroccan Jews who immigrated to Montreal before the 1980s tended to reshape their Sephardic culture toward the Ashkenazic one because it was dominant (Elbaz 1990). In principle, there are no race distinctions in France; but Black neighborhoods in Paris have produced a Black identity called "Parisianism." Based on feelings of exclusion and exile, it emphasizes racial bonds, negates attachment to France, and minimizes distinctions between Blacks from Africa and the Antilles (Jules-Rosette 2000). Most residents of the casbah in Marseilles are Francophone and secularized, but perceptions of socioeconomic disprivilege have re-Arabized and re-Islamized them. In the Parisian and other French conurbations, poor housing conditions of immigrants have exacerbated feelings of relative deprivation and sharpened ethnic identity. In the USA, residents of impoverished and densely populated Black neighborhoods have developed a distinctive ghetto consciousness.

The constitutional–institutional context

The local viability, legitimacy, and articulation of ethnic identity depend heavily on the overall national political context, because that is where conditions of categoric belonging are determined, including the legal relationship of the ethnic community to the city, and of the city to the state. These relationships vary according to the division of jurisdictions between the central government and subnational units. Federal systems grant the greatest decision-making authority to regional and local authorities, and especially to large cities, which have greater resources than small towns and villages. In the USA, institutional pluralism, marked by territorial and functional distribution of power, is paralleled by cultural pluralism, a multidimensional approach to being American. This is reflected in a distinction between citizenship and nationality, and has accommodated itself easily to the retention of ethnic identities and institutions.

In the unitary system of France, subnational units have no a priori decision-making authority; its Jacobin ideology conceives of the republic as a nation-state relating directly to the amorphous citizen. France frowns upon ethnic cultural expression, which is regarded as reactionary or (in the case of non-territorial minorities) denounced as *communautarisme*, an orientation marked by the turning inward of an *ethnie*. The culture of indigenous minorities, expressed in regional costumes, Breton bagpipes, and Occitan harvest festivals, is viewed as harmless folklore. But regional languages cannot be used publicly in a country whose constitution stipulates that "the language of the republic is French." France has refused to ratify the European charter on minority languages.

Jacobin ideology, however, is competing with "the right to be different" (Giordan 1982). This right is increasingly accepted; it is expressed in the teaching of regional languages that are considered part of the national patrimony and in the official support of cultural centers and programs of regional and non-territorial ethnic minorities (Safran 1989: 138–44, 2003: 443f.). The authorities in Paris and other large cities sponsor Armenian, Chinese, Jewish, Russian, and Vietnamese cultural festivals.

Several categoric groups that had not been recognized since the Revolution of 1789, but whose members were seen only as individual adherents of religious cults, are gradually being acknowledged as *ethnic communities*. Jews in France, who had been de-ethnified two centuries ago, have become re-ethnified; this development is manifested in networks of ethnic educational and philanthropic organizations, mostly concentrated in the Paris metropolitan area. Armenians, Greeks, Muslims, and Blacks have followed the Jewish model by forming umbrella organizations based on ethnicity.

The ethnic identity of Armenians in Paris is expressed in social and cultural clubs, mutual-aid societies, and churches; but since most of them do not speak Armenian and many no longer attend church, their ethnic identity is increasingly confined to keeping alive their national narrative, including the memory of genocide, and to economic support of the homeland. Transnational solidarity becomes particularly important during special events, such as an earthquake in the homeland (Hovanessian 1992: 95f.).

These activities have been selectively supported by politicians, especially in cities with large ethnic minority populations. Politicians have appeared before Jewish and Maghrebi audiences in Paris, Marseilles, and Lyons, especially before elections. In 2012 French political leaders lent their support to a mass demonstration by Armenians in favor of a government bill to criminalize the denial of the genocide of Armenians committed by Turkey a century ago.

In Germany, the maintenance of ethnic identity has been difficult. Traditionally, membership in the German nation was based on ancestry (*jus sanguinis*), and those who did not share it would seldom become part of the German political community. Non-German residents were regarded as "guest workers" – for the most part Turks – who would eventually be returned to their countries of origin. This situation encouraged them to maintain their ethnic culture. But immigrants can now become naturalized; as a result, Germany has become much more ethnically mixed. While increasingly open to non-German cultural influences, some German authorities have been wary of multiculturalism and insisted that its ethnic minorities adhere to the country's majority culture (*Leitkultur*). Although formally accepted as citizens, ethnic Turks are not quite regarded as Germans; they continue to organize along ethnic lines, especially where their numbers are large enough (Laguerre 2006). This condition usually obtains only in big cities. A prime example is the Kreuzberg section of Berlin, which is often referred to as "Little Turkey."

Other countries have more specific approaches to ethnicity, which often reflect the multiethnic reality at the founding of their polities. Owing to the settlement of Canada by two major ethnolinguistic groups, the concept of citizen coexists with a pluralistic approach to national identity: a Canadian may belong to some minority community and also attend a municipally supported ethnic school. This bicultural approach was extended to ethnics of more recent immigrant origin, particularly in cities where they constitute a critical mass. A similar situation obtains in Belgium, where the various constitutional and institutional changes keep pace with the evolving position of two dominant ethnonational communities. It is manifested in a parallel system of education, civil-service recruitment, and the media on both national and municipal levels.

Although the United Kingdom is a unitary country, it is composed of several ethnoregions that enjoy considerable autonomy. Furthermore, local governments are responsible for education and social services; in Greater London, this has been reflected in an array of institutions run by ethnic communities.

In several other countries, political authority has been delegated to subnational units, for the most part urban, both to maintain closer ties between citizens and their representatives and to relieve national governments of financial burdens. In countries whose citizens are divided along linguistic lines, as in Belgium, Spain, and South Africa, subnational units are in charge of education, and they pay particular attention to the cultural claims of ethnic minorities. There are cities where special regimes exist for language use in public offices, social services, and education due to the polyglot character of their inhabitants, such as bilingual Brussels and trilingual Vilnius.

The presence of concentrated ethnic communities is inevitably reflected in the political arena. In London, New York, Paris, and Toronto these communities make up a significant electoral element. They use their demographic weight to make demands through bloc voting; and politicians instrumentalize this weight to further their own political ambitions by securing financial support for schools, community centers, and other municipal projects, and distributing public-service jobs on an ethnic basis.

It may be true that the lack of formal participation in urban politics sharpens the feeling of ethnic exclusion. It is not certain, however, whether ethnically based recruitment institutionalizes the participation of minorities and thereby strengthens their ethnic identity or weakens it by cooptation. Urban ethnic patterns do not automatically translate into "mesogovernments" (Moreno 2000: 69), but they contribute to functional autonomy in selective areas. In cities with large ethnic concentrations, this autonomy has a political dimension, involving lobbying, rainbow coalitions, and balanced tickets.[5] Ethnic minorities are a most concrete political force on a municipal level because it is only in cities where they are numerous enough to constitute a significant electorate (Laguerre 2006: 37). In Sydney and other Australian cities, political parties have formed "contribution networks" with Chinese communities, in which the latter become clients and their official participation legitimizes them as political actors (Kwok 2008). This is often accomplished by means of fundraising banquets.

Yet it is unclear what political consequences result from a concentration of ethnics in urban communities that are strong enough to elect ethnic representatives to national and regional legislatures. Minority candidates for public office have a vested interest in emphasizing their own ethnicity and in maintaining the ethnic identity of their electorate; but the success of that electorate helps to identify it with the political system as a whole and instill in its members the values of that system, and serves as an incentive to assimilation. As a result, the political position of ethnic politicians may be undermined. The very success of Irish politicians in New York – a success originally due to ethnic electoral solidarity – blunted Irish-American distinctiveness, in terms of culture, language, and sociopolitical aspirations, from the "generic" urban American so that, in the end, the Irish influence on urban political machines weakened.

One of the instruments of modernizing nation-builders has been the claim of superiority of the national over the ethnic culture, which has been regarded as parochial. This claim has been made with respect to the immigrants who came to North America from Southern Italy, many of whom were semi-illiterate members of extended peasant families, and whose first important opportunity to obtain education, and hence to gain upward mobility, was provided in the hostland city. Immigrants were also attracted by the political environment of the hostland, which compared favorably to the oppressions they had suffered in their countries of origin. Another magnet was the range of socioeconomic benefits provided by the hostland national government.

Public policy

The multiple offerings of national governments of the host society have been effective in "nationalizing" the orientation of minorities and persuading them to relinquish their ethnic identities. Under the New Deal legislation of the 1930s, the federal government of the USA assumed responsibility for numerous social and economic services that had once been provided by voluntary associations, including ethnic organizations, thereby powerfully stirring the melting pot.

Selected local policies sustain subcommunities and the ethnic consciousness on which they are based. In New York City, municipal governments have financed welfare programs that benefited the Puerto Rican community, and facilitated the maintenance of Latino culture by issuing public announcements in Spanish and encouraging public employees to learn that language (Glazer and Moynihan 1970: 101). This official benevolence reduced the pressure on ethnic community organizations; and it also benefited middle-class Latinos who could afford to maintain them. In France, social, cultural, and educational organizations of both immigrant and indigenous ethnics have been encouraged by national government subsidies (especially since 1981) as well as by municipal governments, which have made agreements with ethnic neighborhood associations (Safran 1989: 127, 142).

The retrenchments in the federal safety net and other redistributive measures that began in the USA several years ago have forced educational and welfare services to rely increasingly on local resources, which are often private. The services they offer tend to be more community oriented, i.e. more "ethnic." A current example is provided by many cities in the USA, where, due to steadily declining budgets for education, public schools have begun to deteriorate. In consequence, the number of private schools, many run by ethnic and religious minority communities, has mushroomed. This development has reinforced ethnic identity.

Yet it has not made the ethnies more cooperative; rather, it has sharpened interethnic rivalries and hostilities. In Brooklyn, New York, in the 1980s, members of certain orthodox Jewish sects organized the Jewish Defense League in response to increasing violence on the part of members of the Black community and in the conviction that the municipal police was unable or unwilling to halt that violence. The riots of Latinos in a Washington, D.C. neighborhood in 1991 stemmed from their belief that they were victimized by other minority groups: Black police officers who harassed them and Asian merchants who overcharged them. Similar riots by African Americans in Los Angeles were aimed at Koreans.

The relationship between class and economic condition on the one hand, and ethnicity on the other, is a matter of controversy; meanwhile, the city is where particular occupations have been identified with particular ethnic groups: Irish policemen in New York and Boston; Jewish garment workers and Black porters in New York; and sanitation workers in the Paris metro system hailing from Central Africa. In many cases, the *locus operandi* of these occupations is viewed as the "turf" of the ethnic group in question.

Urban public policies may be more advanced than national ones. This applies in particular to New York, Boston, and other American cities where public policies have reflected the cultural influences and political pressures of ethnic minorities. But there has been an unanticipated consequence: the very existence of such policies has weakened the ethnic identity and cohesion of these minorities by reducing the relevance of ethnic social and charitable organizations on which such identity depends. To many Chinese, Greeks, and Jews such dependence justifies the retention of the institutions of the ethnic sub-community and the culture they express. For many Black leaders, however, such institutions are reactionary because they allow the government to shirk its responsibilities and help to maintain ethnic inequalities (Glazer 1983: 41–2; Patterson 1977).

Conclusion: bones of contention

This study suggests an ambiguous causal relationship. On the one hand, large cities *weaken* ethnic ties because they provide networks of social services that are available to all residents – *so long as these services last*; on the other hand, large cities *strengthen* ethnic ties because of (a) the existence of ethnic enclaves and organizations that maintain ethnic culture and attract newcomers; (b) the adequate size and density of the ethnic population; (c) the depersonalized nature of urban relationship, which impels minorities to seek *Gemeinschaft*-based relations. This applies especially to ethnic groups that come from rural backgrounds, such as Vietnamese and Hmong; or that are subject to discrimination, such as Blacks and Latinos in the USA, Beurs in France, and Turks in Germany. Black and Latino leaders defend the existence of ethnic institutions on local levels – but not necessarily for the sake of maintaining ethnic culture as an end in itself. In the 1820s, Blacks in Cincinnati, Ohio, were forced to create their own protective organization because the municipal police refused to protect them adequately (Wade 1990). In this case ethnic identity maintenance was a by-product of communal self-help efforts.

The mere existence of a network of organizations in a city densely inhabited by ethnic minorities does not mean that members of these minorities will join in large numbers. Many upwardly mobile African Americans focus on their personal ambitions and are uninvolved in specifically Black concerns, although their racial identity is a permanent reality. The proportion of Jews joining synagogues is much greater in small towns or suburbs than in urban areas. In New York City, it is not necessary for a Jew to join a synagogue in order to feel Jewish. The large number of Jews in that city makes it possible for Jews to be "free riders" – to remain Jewish by osmosis, as it were – because Jewishness is present in sufficient measure to nourish Jewish identity for individuals.

A note of caution: demographic density is necessary but not sufficient for the retention of diaspora identity; the fact that Chicago has more stores in which kielbasa is sold than in other American cities is not an indicator of Polish cultural reproduction. This is even truer of expressive ethnicity, such as Columbus Day parades and celebrations of Cinco de Mayo, which are exercises in demonstrative or "performance" ethnicity. These require a participating audience that only cities can provide.

A recent example of demonstrative ethnicity was a two-day celebration of the investiture of the regional chief of the Ashanti tribe of Ghana for the New York metropolitan area. The event, held in the Bronx, brought together scores of participants representing more than 20,000 members of the Ghanaian diaspora. The responsibilities of the chief include mediation in family disputes and efforts at finding jobs, housing, and medical care for members of the community as well as maintaining links with the homeland. His appeal, however, has been limited, especially among younger members of the Ghanaian diaspora, many of whom are American born (Semple 2012).

The maintenance of community networks may be impeded by family structure and other factors. Mexican Americans, for example, have smaller social networks and less contact with network members than non-Hispanic whites; they are more likely to have relatives, but not friends (Golding and Baezconde-Garbanati 1990).

The metropolis is the arena in which all sorts of ethnic identities, attitudes, and behavior can be found in addition to the "natural" ethnicity of the homeland, where it developed in a majoritarian context subject to little outside influence. Among these are the following:

(1) Adaptive ethnicity – ethnic culture heavily modified by conditions of the host environment. This applies to the religious culture of Greeks, Armenians, and Indians in the USA, Britain, and France. The culture of the Polish *shtetl* survived for many years in the form of Yiddish-language schools and theater in New York and other large American cities; but it was a deracinated culture expressed in an Americanized Yiddish. Similarly, Chinese customs are kept, but in English.

(2) Vestigial ethnicity – an indistinct ethnic identity marked by nostalgia, a receding collective memory, and a legacy largely confined to ethnic foods and family customs, as in the case of Italian-American or Irish-American culture. The Irish (Gaelic) language was not imported into New York City because it had ceased long ago to be a crucial element of Irish identity. In the nineteenth century, Irish Americans, like their ethnic kin in Dublin, had been intensely concerned with the Irish fight against the British; but the Irish-American distinction was progressively detached from concern with the ancestral homeland; what remained were residual cultural patterns that fitted easily into New York, such as wakes, church-sponsored social events, and a more or less distinct pronunciation (Glazer and Moynihan 1970: 245).

(3) Vicarious ethnicity – an ethnic identification displayed in support of ethnic institutions by those who do not use them. This applies to urbanized Native Americans who have adopted Anglo lifestyles. They prefer to live in the city, but they have a highly developed ethnocultural cognition: they care about preserving native arts and crafts and tribal traditions, and they keep their ethnic consciousness alive by making frequent trips to their reservations and participating in powwows (Deloria 1981). It also applies to secular Jews who support orthodox religious seminaries because they are regarded as most effective in helping to preserve

an authentic Jewish community. These types of ethnicity are not static. The consciousness of members of ethnic groups may change from one type to another in response to public policies or the behavior of the host society.

To be sure, minority cultures adapt to the surrounding community. However, living together in a locality even for generations has not always been sufficient to foster a cultural identity in common with the majority. The identity of ethnic minorities tends to persist in part because the majority is *less modern* than they are (as, in the past, in the case of the Greek minority in the Ottoman Empire, the Jewish minority in Poland, and the Chinese minority throughout Southeast Asia); because, conversely, the majority is *too modern* and its values are so different from those of the ethnic minority that the two cannot be easily reconciled; or because the minority culture is reinforced by external linkages. During the period between the two world wars, Lithuanians, Poles, and Jews shared municipal space and services in Vilnius; yet these communities remained distinct because they had different external points of reference: the Lithuanians had the newly independent republic next door; the Poles had the reborn Polish state to which they were annexed and which shared a Polish cultural tradition identified with that city for several centuries; and the Jews had a sizable transnational Yiddish-speaking region. During the same period, Christian residents of Warsaw defined their identity in terms of Catholic saints and a collective memory of Polish national independence, while to most of that city's Jewish proletariat "the Vistula spoke in Yiddish," as the writer I.B. Singer put it. Living together has not led to a common political identity for the Protestants and Catholics in Belfast; they share a language, yet each community has a separate identity; there are separate residential neighborhoods, social and political organizations, schools, and churches, and there is little intermarriage (Schmitt 1988: 34f.).

New York has been the place where Jews from selected cities of the Russian Empire could "rebuild the homeland in the Promised Land" – by means of community centers, synagogues, benevolent associations, and burial societies (Kobrin 2010: 69f.). One example is the Bukharan Jewish diaspora in the USA, almost all of whose members live in Queens, New York. They rebuilt a semblance of their former community, once centered in Uzbekistan, by establishing Bukharan synagogues, cultural centers, and specialized shops and performing traditional rites of passage. Such a phenomenon may apply to entire towns. The residents of Kiryas Joel and New Square, "ethnoburgs" outside New York City, identify more with defunct Jewish communities in Hungary and Ukraine than with the USA (Logan *et al.* 2002).

These examples suggest a successful ethnic identity maintenance through mimetic reproductions of Old-Country patterns in hostland metropoles. But the realism and durability of these reproductions vary: some fit into the context of the dominant culture, while others are untenable in the long run. In New York, the ethnic identity of Jewish immigrants from Eastern Europe was expressed importantly in terms of socialism (which clashed with American ideology) but survived in the form of trade unionism (which gradually lost its ethnic flavor) and secular Yiddish culture (whose societal basis had been destroyed). As indicated earlier, the rural foundation of the Italian immigrant community could not be replicated in the American metropole, and its extended family structure could not easily maintain itself in the face of the *Gesellschaft*-oriented pressures of the hostland society. The ethnic identity of the Italian immigrant community, which lacked a cultural elite, expressed itself largely in Catholic religious terms. But since Catholicism in the typical American city has been transethnic, the Italian specificity has been progressively diluted.[6]

It is an open question how the identity of ethnic communities will maintain itself faced with the abandonment of urban neighborhoods for the suburbs, a development that already covers a quarter of ethnic minorities (Scheffer 2011). The ethnic identity of members of this category, most of whom have entered the middle class, will be attenuated. The ethnic identity of those left behind – the "core" ethnics – may remain strong, but, since they are likely to be poorer than the ethnic kin who abandoned them, their financial and organizational means of community cohesion will have been curtailed.

Notes

1　French-born descendants of Arab immigrants from North Africa.
2　Ethnic minorities living in villages seldom have the facilities for such re-creation; their social relations are mostly with their neighbors, and, since these are often warmer compared with the functional relations in large cities, ethnic community support is needed less and ethnic identity weakens.
3　In the thirteenth arrondissement of Paris, most public *collèges* provide bilingual classes in Chinese, English, German, and/or Spanish; several arrondissements stage ethnic folk festivals annually.
4　Brussels is not a border city in the "national" sense, but it straddles a linguistic border.
5　In New York City, a typical distribution of candidacies for political office has included an Irish person, an Italian, a Jew and, more recently, a Latino and an African American.
6　One Italian feature that was successfully transplanted to American metropoles is the mafia, but it is no longer purely Italian.

References

Appadurai, A. (1996) *Modernity at Large: Cultural Dimensions of Globalization*, Minneapolis, MN: University of Minneapolis Press.

Argun, B.E. (2003) *Turkey in Germany: The Transnational Sphere of Deutschkei*, London: Routledge.

Blunt, A., Bonnerjee, J. and Hysler-Rubin, N. (2012) 'Diasporic Returns to the City: Anglo-Indian and Jewish Visits to Calcutta', *South Asian Diaspora*, 4(1): 25–43.

Body-Gendrot, S. (1993) 'Migration and the Racialisation of the Post-modern City', in Keith, M. (ed.) *Racism, the City, and the State*, New York, NY: Routledge.

Centner, R. (2010) 'Cities and Strategic Elsewheres: Developments in the Transnational Politics of Remaking Urban Space', *New Global Studies*, 4(1): 1–7.

Club de l'Horloge (1985) *L'identité de la France*, Paris: Albin Michel.

Deloria, V. (1981) 'The Native Americans: The American Indian Today', *Annals of the American Academy of Political and Social Science*, 454(1): 139–49.

Elbaz, M. (1990) 'Figures de l'identité et de l'altérité: Les Juifs dans le Système Urbain et Ethnique Montréalais', in I. Simon-Barouh and P.J. Simon (eds) *L'étranger dans la Ville: Le Regard des Sciences Sociales*, Paris: L'Harmattan.

Gabaccia, D.R. (1984) *From Sicily to Elizabeth Street*, Albany, NY: Suny.

Giordan, H. (1982) *Démocratie Culturelle et Droit à la Différence*, Paris: Documentation Française.

Glazer, N. (1983) *Ethnic Dilemmas 1964–1982*, Cambridge, MA: Harvard University Press.

Glazer, N. and Moynihan, D.P. (1970) *Beyond the Melting Pot: The Puerto Ricans, Jews, Italians, and Irish in New York City*, Cambridge, MA: MIT Press.

Gold, S.J. (2012) *The Store in the Hood: A Century of Ethnic Business and Conflict*, Lanham, MD: Rowman & Littlefield.

Golding, J.M. and Baezconde-Garbanati, L.A. (1990) 'Ethnicity, Culture, and Social Resources', *American Journal of Community Psychology*, 18(3): 465–86.

Heldmann, M.E. (2006) 'Creating Sacred Space: Orthodox Churches of the Ethiopian American Diaspora', *Diaspora*, 15(2/3): 285–302.

Hoffnung-Garskof, J. (2008) *A Tale of Two Cities: Santo Domingo and New York after 1950*, Princeton, NJ: Princeton University Press.

Hovanessian, M. (1992) *Le Lien Communautaire*, Paris: Armand Colin.

Jules-Rosette, B. (2000) 'Identity Discourses and Diasporic Aesthetics in Black Paris: Community Formation and the Translation of Culture', *Diaspora*, 9(1): 39–58.

Kobrin, R. (2010) *Jewish Bialystok and its Diaspora*, Bloomington, IN: Indiana University Press.

Kwok, J.T. (2008) 'Clientelism in the Ethnopolis: Ethnic Contribution Networks and Political Fundraising under Late Multiculturalism', *Journal of Australian Studies*, 32(4): 467–79.

Laguerre, M.S. (2000) *The Global Ethnopolis: Chinatown, Japantown and Manilatown in American Society*, New York, NY: St.Martin's.

—(2006) *Diaspora, Politics, and Globalization*, New York, NY: Palgrave Macmillan.

Lieberson, S. (1971) 'Residential and Language Maintenance in a Multilingual City', *Plural Societies*, Summer (1): 63–73.

Lipphardt, A. (2010) *Vilne: Die Juden aus Vilnius nach dem Holocaust: Eine Transnationale Beziehungsgeschichte*, Paderborn: Ferdinand Schöningh.

Logan, J., Zhang, W. and Alba, R.D. (2002) 'Immigrant Enclaves and Ethnic Communities in New York and Los Angeles', *American Sociological Review*, 67(2): 299–322.

Moreno, L. (2000) 'Local and Global: Mesogovernments and Territorial Identities', in W. Safran and R. Maíz Suárez (eds) *Identity and Territorial Autonomy in Plural Societies*, London: Frank Cass.

Morin, F. (1990) 'Des Haitiens à New York: De la Visibilité Linguistique à la Constructions d'une Identité Caribéenne', in I. Simon-Barouh and P.J. Simon (eds) *L'étranger dans la Ville: Le Regard des Sciences Sociales*, Paris: L'Harmattan.

Patterson, O. (1977) *Ethnic Chauvinism: The Reactionary Impulse*, New York, NY: Stein & Day.

Rogers, A. (1995) 'Cinco de Mayo and 15 January: Contrasting Situations in a Mixed Ethnic Neighbourhood', in A. Rogers and S. Vertovec (eds) *The Urban Context: Ethnicity, Social Networks and Situational Analysis*, Oxford, UK: Berg.

Safran, W. (1989) 'The French State and Ethnic Minority Cultures: Policy Dimensions and Problems', in J.R. Rudolph and R.J. Thompson (eds) *Ethnoterritorial Politics, Policy, and the Western World*, Boulder, CO: Lynne Rienner.

—(2003) 'Pluralism and Multiculturalism in France: Post-Jacobin Transformations', *Political Science Quarterly*, 118(3): 437–65.

—(2007) 'Comparing Visions of the Nation: The Role of Ethnicity, Religion and Diaspora Nationalism in Armenian, Jewish and Sikh Relations to the Homeland', in M. Young, E. Zuelow and A. Sturm (eds) *Nationalism in a Global Era*, London: Routledge.

Scheffer, P. (2011) *Immigrant Nations*, Cambridge, UK: Polity.

Schmitt, D.E. (1988) 'Bicommunalism in Northern Ireland', *Publius*, 18(2): 33–45.

Semple, K. (2012) 'With Fanfare, Ashanti People from Ghana Install their New York Chief', *New York Times*, 4 June.

Wade, R.C. (1990) 'The Enduring Ghetto: Urbanization and the Color Line in American History', *Journal of Urban History*, 17(1): 4–13.

Wilson, W.J. (1984) 'The Urban Underclass', in L.W. Dunbar (ed.) *Minority Report: What Has Happened to Blacks, Hispanics, American Indians, and other Minorities in the Eighties*, New York, NY: Pantheon.

36

Segregation, mixing and encounter

Deborah Phillips

The growing diversity of cities has been simultaneously conceptualised as economically productive, socially creative and nurturing of tolerance of difference (Florida 2005) and problematic, as evidenced through socially and spatially segregated populations, persistent inequalities, weak social capital, informal trust and co-operation and heightened prejudices towards 'otherness' (Amin 2012). Threaded through these debates has been the politicisation of residential segregation as an indicator of minority adaptation, social integration and intercultural relations (Phillips 2006). Whilst the meaning and measurement of residential segregation have long been contested in the scholarly literature, urban policies that aim to manage diversity through the promotion of spatial, social or ethnic mixing abound. At the forefront of such initiatives has been a concern across many European cities with the promotion of migrant integration and harmonious group relations through intercultural mixing, particularly at the neighbourhood scale (Phillips *et al.* 2014).

This chapter focuses on shifting conceptualisations of minority ethnic segregation and their implications for policy interventions designed to manage ethnic diversity and difference. Whilst traditional models of migration, settlement and urban change envisage relatively smooth pathways to integration for many groups, largely through processes of acculturation and spatial dispersal, newer understandings seek to complicate this transition through a greater appreciation of individualised identities and differences within groups, the contextualised experience of negotiating diversity and difference and the power of structural factors to undermine policy efforts to build good relations in diverse social settings. Underpinning such concerns is the vexed question of the link between segregation, isolation and social mixing, and the value of interventions that commonly aim to build 'communities of place' through a focus on neighbourhood-based encounters with difference. This chapter argues for a more sensitive appreciation of the complexities of new migrants' and established minorities' sense of identity and belonging, greater understanding of the specificity of place and the contingent outcomes of negotiated differences. This has methodological implications for research, which offer a challenge to the quantitative–qualitative divide that besets much of the existing scholarship in this field and strategic implications for policy.

Residential segregation contested

Residential segregation has long been seen as a marker of diversity and difference. The meanings, indicators and implications of persistent social and spatial separation are, however, contested. A significant body of scholarly literature has variously conceptualised ethnic minority segregation as a signifier of newcomer status, weak bridging social capital, strong cultural/religious differences and structural inequalities associated with minority discrimination and 'otherness' (e.g. Bolt *et al.* 2012). Intertwined with such debates are questions about temporality, causal mechanisms (i.e. is segregation voluntary or forced?), 'good' versus 'bad' segregation (Peach 1996) and the responsibilities (and culpability) of minority ethnic citizens that may appear unwilling to mix with other social groups. Political discourses on the interconnections between growing diversities, faltering multiculturalism, good citizenship and national belonging have sharpened the debate on the meaning of persistent minority ethnic residential segregation across European Union states (Phillips 2010). Anxieties about the apparent failure of some minority ethnic groups to follow the usual pathways towards social and spatial integration has brought a raft of policy interventions designed to enhance contact, promote mixing and minimise the potentially damaging effects of living with 'too much' cultural difference at the local and national scales.

A hegemonic discourse that associates levels of minority ethnic integration with degrees of spatial mixing raises a number of areas for critical enquiry. A large body of scholarly work has sought to measure the intensity of ethnic, racialised and religious segregation, using a range of statistical indicators (see, for instance, Musterd 2012). Policy makers, keen to quantify the dynamics of diversity, have found such statistical outputs appealing. Such research is, however, underpinned by contentious issues that relate to the validity of different indices, the interpretation of outputs and the appropriate geographical units for measurement. There has also been a tendency for researchers to present the results of such analyses in ways that emphasise segregation as group outcome, rather than an ongoing process that is individualised, politicised and contextualised. Demographers and population geographers, amongst others, have spent considerable energy computing indices from large data sets, such as census wards or tracts, or, where data permit, smaller output areas. Whilst this can apparently offer valuable comparative insights into changing trends in segregation and mixing, the administrative units chosen for analysis may have little bearing on people's everyday lived experiences at the street or neighbourhood scale.

Critical voices, such as those of the Radical Statistics Group in the UK, have offered incisive critiques of statistical analyses used (and misused) in 'race' and segregation debates. Ludi Simpson (2007), for example, has exposed the way in which erroneous inferences can be drawn about the trajectories of minority ethnic groups through the neglect of wider demographic processes of population change. Meanwhile, Finney and Simpson (2009) have challenged dominant segregationist discourses by interrogating a series of racialised myths surrounding immigration, integration and settlement through a far-reaching re-interpretation of statistical data. These authors have also called for greater insights into segregating processes through research that crosses the quantitative–qualitative divide. The work of Stillwell and Phillips (2006) in Leeds and McGarrigle (2010) in Glasgow provides examples of research that has combined statistical analyses of population diversity and change with qualitative data on the processes at work in these localities, but detailed studies that use qualitative research to ground findings emerging from quantitative analyses are relatively rare.

Our understanding and conceptualisation of segregation, diversity and difference is furthermore reflected in, and shaped by, the socially constructed data categories available to us in large quantitative data sets. Critical commentaries by scholars such as Alexander (2002) and Howard (2006) have exposed the politics of group representation in census data, for example, and how this serves to recognise, and underline, certain diversities and differences, whilst rendering others invisible. The powerful historical effects of such official encodings are most evident in the ideological census classifications employed in the legally enforced segregation of Jim Crow Laws in the USA and apartheid South Africa. Approaches to data categorisation in democratic societies nevertheless still have the power to shape scholarship, through the nature of research questions we ask, and can answer, on the integration and settlement of diverse populations, as well as policy interventions in this field, and thus deserve further critical evaluation.

The rigidity of ethnic and national labels can also serve to fix people's identities according to their group affiliations, effectively masking complex intra-group diversities that arise through individual attributes, personalised biographies and contextualised experiences. Wright and Ellis (2006) alert quantitative researchers concerned with computing segregation indices to the particular challenges of reflecting growing diversity within households, for example. Drawing on research in the USA, they point to the distinctive geographies of households characterised by mixed-race partnerships, and suggest that this field is ripe for further investigation. Meanwhile, studies drawing on post-structuralist scholarship, which recognises the fluidity, complexity and hybridity of people's identities, and, more specifically, sociological work on 'new ethnicities' that cross ascribed ethnic boundaries (Back 1996), highlight the complexity and diversity of identities, life-styles and interaction patterns embedded within and across officially encoded populations. Greater attention to such diversities, particularly using ethnographic methods, has the potential to open up debate about what we expect from the integration process. Geographers such as Hopkins (2007) and Dwyer (1999), for example, reveal how gender, class and religious difference intersect to produce multiple ways of being British Muslim over time and space. Their work challenges popular discourses and undifferentiated representations of these minorities as segregating, unpatriotic and inward looking – commonly ascribed group characteristics that are perceived to impede good intercultural relations and traditional pathways to social and spatial integration for these citizens.

Narrow concerns with charting changing patterns of residential segregation are increasingly giving way to qualitative studies that explore the dynamics of migration through everyday experiences of living with diversity and difference (e.g. Wise and Velayutham 2009). These studies disclose the social, political and material connections of urban spaces, and reveal the complexity of associations, contextuality of experience and situatedness of prejudice, with clear implications for the development of locally grounded policy agendas. A growing body of research on trans-locality reminds us that migrant (and non-migrant) experiences are not only a product of the local, but also a multiplicity of imaginations, discourses and practices at a range of nested scales (Brickell and Datta 2011). This has implications for how we might conceptualise social and spatial integration in an era of growing mobility and transnational connections and points to multiple expressions of citizenship and belonging. As Nagel and Staeheli (2008) remind us, integration is a complex socio-political process, involving a dialogue between diverse groups as they negotiate a social membership that may well rest on multiple loyalties in sending and receiving countries as well as locally embedded encounters.

Segregation, encounters and mixing – managing diversity

If living with growing diversity and difference is one of the most pressing questions of the twenty-first century, as Hall (1993) contends, then the management of that diversity has been one of the greatest challenges for politicians and policy makers. Positive perspectives on the creative advantages and economic potential of new migration are commonly outweighed by the immediacy of concerns associated with everyday tensions, spatially segregated minorities, popular prejudices, welfare rights and wider anxieties about the construction of national identity, social cohesion and citizenship. A range of policies, across European cities, has been designed with the aim of creating more liveable, cohesive and harmonious spaces in the face of growing diversity (Arapoglou 2012). Integral to these has been a concern with breaking down the social and spatial segregation of ethnic and religious minorities through the promotion of social and intercultural dialogue and mixing. The efficacy of such policies is, however, uncertain and raises questions about the meaning of segregation, expectations of integration and belonging and the potential for change through social contact.

Scholarly interest in such interventions has focused attention on varying scales of interaction from the city to the body. Fincher and Iveson (2008), for example, drawing inspiration from literature on both urban planning and social encounters, examine how urban policy makers might best respond to growing diversity through interventions designed to create a 'just city'. Their argument rests on the productive intersection of strategies for re-distributional justice, in the face of inequality, the political recognition of unheard voices and the value of opportunities for social encounter between diverse groups for breaking down (unequal) social and spatial segregation. Crucially their work recognises the contextuality of experience and outcomes, but also, through the use of a range of case-studies, opens up a conversation on the key elements (or 'social logics') of diverse and socially just urban living that can be missing from more narrowly focused studies. A closer evaluation of initiatives designed to engineer physical mixing between diverse groups, however, points to limited evidence of success (Bolt *et al.* 2012). Housing and regeneration schemes, for example, incorporating minority ethnic household quotas, mixed tenure developments or mobility initiatives appear to have had little impact on residential segregation levels, because of selective out-migration, and can undermine ethnic minority housing choice and community building. What emerges is a need for more attention to the impact of structural inequalities on positive outcomes, the contingent effects of the characteristics and histories of migrant populations and the local politics of place.

As new diversities arising from migration continue both to enrich and complicate the dynamics of urban community, a renewed interest in places of potential intercultural encounter has emerged. A burgeoning literature on hospitality, urban citizenship and cosmopolitanism has sought to explore how a co-presence in public spaces might facilitate the negotiation of social and cultural difference and break down preferences for separation (e.g. Koutrolikou 2012). Inspired by social contact theory (see Fell and Hewstone, this volume), and the apparent promise of mundane interactions to erode prejudices, weaken stereotypes and help to build conviviality, scholars have turned their attention to the multicultural capacities of encounters in, for example, streets, parks, buses, markets and the everyday spaces of the neighbourhood. In policy circles, the politicised 'parallel lives' discourse, which associates ethnic residential segregation with poor social integration, cohesion and citizenship, has focused particular attention on the neighbourhood as a site of 'everyday multiculturalism' and bridge-building between divided groups. Although a raft of social initiatives has been implemented across European cities, and wide-ranging claims about the positive effects of social engagement have been made, we know relatively little about the impact of these on those involved (Phillips *et al.* 2014). It is unlikely, as Vertovec (2007) points out, that fleeting encounters between strangers in public spaces will do more than promote basic modes of civility. Meanwhile, Amin (2002) amongst others has warned that social interactions played out against a backcloth of racist discourse and unchallenged prejudice may serve only to exacerbate divisions. Encounters, Ahmed (2004) observes, can re-open particular histories so that some bodies are read in more hostile ways than others.

We thus still know relatively little about how diversity is constructed and shifts, how it is imagined and performed in different places and the implications of this for policy interventions that seek to erode social and spatial segregation. As Anne-Marie Fortier (2007) has argued, social interventions in the management of diversity not only find spatial form through social and spatial engineering and place-based cohesion initiatives, but also invoke 'specific emotional and ethical injunctions', such as 'embracing the other' and 'loving thy neighbour' (ibid.: 107). This opens up questions about shifting constructions of imagined differences, the engineering of affect and the management of 'multicultural intimacy' that deserve further exploration. Negative discourses on the uncertain place of Muslim minorities in the national imaginaries of non-Muslim nation-states, for example, highlight the selective and politicised nature of the national embrace. Gendered and embodied constructions of the good Muslim citizen versus the feared Muslim 'other' expose further uncomfortable questions about 'acceptable' diversity and whether, as Amin (2012) questions, we can really work towards a 'civility of indifference' to difference.

Drawing on research with new and established migrants in Bradford, Phillips *et al.* (2014) suggest that structured, mediated forms of intercultural dialogue around shared neighbourhood and community concerns may well have greater transformative power than fleeting casual encounters, where deep differences (perceived or real) tend to remain unspoken. Intercultural dialogue that directly challenges tensions, they argue, presents an opportunity to negotiate socially constructed group boundaries and unsettle stereotypes that underpin everyday animosities and present barriers to social and spatial mobility. They caution, however, that the capacity for negotiation appears to differ within and between groups, reflecting individualised complexities of identification, affiliation and belonging. Women with children living in areas undergoing rapid change through new migration, for example, seem more willing to reach out to bridge divides than, say, young, single men who readily project their own insecurities on to the incoming 'other'. Perceived and real inequalities in power and resources between diverse residents may also undermine policy-driven bridge-building efforts to open up dialogue and forge new associations.

Conclusion

Scholars concerned with urban residential segregation, mixing and its consequences in the context of growing diversity face a range of conceptual and methodological challenges. Deeper critical understandings of the meaning and implications of residential segregation rest on more nuanced insights into different ways of negotiating difference in the light of politicised discourses that problematise some forms of segregation and not others. The conceptual challenge lies in marrying the appeal for greater attention to relational, dynamic and performed identities that are sensitive to people's multiple biographies, attachments and experiences with how these translate into broader understandings of compositional, contextual and structural effects. At the local scale, we might do well, following Valentine (2007), to prioritise research into the operation of intersectionality, which seeks not only to acknowledge the complexity of identification, but also to expose how diversity is entangled with intersecting 'grids of power' that infuse gender, class, ethnic, 'race' and other relations. This may also help us to gauge how to move beyond the learned 'grammars of sociability' (Buonfino and Mulgan 2009: 16) that characterise the convivialities associated with many everyday multicultural encounters, but do little to diffuse more deeply rooted tensions. Meanwhile, the global picture calls for more comparative research, and there have been some notable contributions in this respect. Maloutas and Fujita (2012), for example, move beyond the universalisation of the Anglo-American experience to explore urban (mainly class-based) segregation in different historical, socio-economic and political contexts. Glick Schiller and Çağlar (2009) offer a comparative theoretical perspective on locality to reveal different pathways of migrant incorporation and how migrants contribute differentially to the (re)making of post-industrial cities. Cross-national comparisons, however, bring their own challenges. As Harrison *et al*.'s (2005) review of ethnic minority statistics in 15 EU countries makes clear, the accuracy of data, the descriptors used and the ideological premises underpinning the construction of data categories vary considerably between countries.

Research into migration, segregation, mixing and encounter has brought cross-fertilisation across a wide spectrum of intellectual disciplines, ranging from migration and refugee studies to demography, geography, anthropology, sociology, etc. Nevertheless, there is room for interdisciplinary methodological innovation. The field has long been fractured by divisions between quantitative studies of ethnic isolation, integration and settlement, on the one hand, and qualitative research encompassing ethnographic insights into, for example, the enactment of diversity and difference on the other. Despite a growing interest in mixed methods studies, which combine quantitative and qualitative approaches, truly interdisciplinary research that moves beyond an 'additive model' remains nascent. As Bracken and Oughton (2009) highlight, the everyday challenges of engaging in interdisciplinary scholarship remain considerable, and can be hampered by differences in ontology, epistemology, working practices, publishing strategies and the differential value accorded to particular data outputs by disciplinary scholars. There are certainly examples of enthusiasm for new forms of engagement, including from participants in the aforementioned Radical Statistics Group, but there is also a frequent retreat into the safety of empiricism, and therefore there are relatively few examples of real theoretical advancements. One possibly fruitful avenue rests with methodological innovation in pursuit of the co-production of research, which involves quantitative as well as qualitative researchers working with research subjects rather than 'on' them or distant from them. The challenge for scholars is to capture the dynamic, individualised and multiple trajectories associated with migration and settlement without fixing them in time and space, as well as to uncover the deeply embedded structural inequalities in 'race', class, gender, etc. that underpin enduring divisions and open up new ones.

Academic contributions to the field of ethnic segregation and mixing, such as those by Alba and Nee (2003), have established that social integration cannot simply be read off from patterns of residence, and that there is no simple pathway to ethnic minority incorporation into the nation-state. One of the key challenges for scholars is to communicate this more effectively beyond the academy. My own experience of engagement in the UK and wider European policy sphere suggests, despite lip-service to the recognition of diversity, the prevalence of a fairly undifferentiated view of migrant groups by practitioners. This is all too often accompanied by an uncritical adherence to the 'parallel lives' discourse that sees residential segregation as inextricably linked to weak social integration in ways that may have little meaning for the everyday lives of either newcomers or longer established citizens that they seek to support.

References

Ahmed, S. (2004) 'Collective Feelings: or, the Impressions Left by Others', *Theory, Culture and Society*, 21(2): 25–42.

Alba, R. and Nee, V. (2003) *Remaking the American Mainstream: Assimilation and Contemporary Immigration*, Cambridge, MA: Harvard University Press.

Alexander, C. (2002) 'Beyond Black: Rethinking the Colour/Culture Divide', *Ethnic and Racial Studies*, 25(4): 552–71.

Amin, A. (2002) 'Ethnicity and the Multi-cultural City: Living with Diversity', *Environment and Planning A*, 34(6): 959–80.

—(2012) *Land of Strangers*, Cambridge, UK: Polity.

Arapoglou, V. (2012) 'Diversity, Inequality and Urban Change', *European Urban and Regional Research*, 19(3): 223–37.

Back, L. (1996) *New Ethnicities and Urban Culture: Racisms and Multiculture in Young Lives*, New York, NY: St. Martin's.

Bolt, G., Ozuekren, S. and Phillips, D. (eds) (2012) *Linking Integration and Residential Segregation*, London: Routledge.

Bracken, L. and Oughton, E. (2009) 'Interdisciplinarity Within and Beyond Geography: Introduction', *Area*, 41(4): 371–3.

Brickell, K. and Datta, A. (eds) (2011) *Translocal Geographies: Spaces, Places, Connections*, Farnham, UK: Ashgate.

Buonfino, A. and Mulgan, G. (2009) *Civility Lost and Found*, London: Young Foundation.

Dwyer, C. (1999) 'Veiled Meanings: Young British Muslim Women and the Negotiation of Difference', *Gender, Place and Culture*, 6(1): 5–26.

Fincher, R. and Iveson, K. (2008) *Planning and Diversity in the City: Redistribution, Recognition and Encounter*, New York, NY: Palgrave Macmillan.

Finney, N. and Simpson, L. (2009) *Sleepwalking to Segregation? Challenging Myths about Race and Migration*, Bristol, UK: Policy.

Florida, R. (2005) *Cities and the Creative Class*, London: Routledge.

Fortier, A.M. (2007) 'Too Close for Comfort: Loving thy Neighbour and the Management of Multicultural Intimacies', *Environment and Planning D*, 25(1): 104–19.

Glick Schiller, N. and Çağlar, A. (2009) 'Towards a Comparative Theory of Locality in Migration Studies: Migrant Incorporation and City Scale', *Journal of Ethnic and Migration Studies*, 35(2): 177–202.

Hall, S. (1993) 'Culture, Community, Nation', *Cultural Studies*, 7(3): 349–63.

Harrison, M., Law, I. and Phillips, D. (2005) *Migrants, Minorities and Housing: Exclusion, Discrimination and Anti-discrimination in 15 Member States of the European Union*, Vienna: EU Monitoring Centre for Racism and Xenophobia.

Hewstone, M. and Brown, R. (eds) (1986) *Contact and Conflict in Inter-group Encounters*, Oxford: Blackwell.

Hopkins, P. (2007) 'Young People, Masculinities, Religion and Race: New Social Geographies', *Progress in Human Geography*, 31(2): 163–77.

Howard, K. (2006) 'Constructing the Irish of Britain; Ethnic Recognition and the 2001 UK Censuses', *Ethnic and Racial Studies*, 29(1): 103–23.

Koutrolikou, P. (2012) 'Spatialities of Ethno-cultural Relations in Multicultural East London: Discourses of Interaction and Social Mix', *Urban Studies*, 49(10): 2049–66.

McGarrigle, J. (2010) *Understanding Processes of Ethnic Concentration and Dispersal: South Asian Residential Preferences in Glasgow*, Amsterdam: Amsterdam University Press.

Maloutas, T. and Fujita, K. (eds) (2012) *Residential Segregation in Comparative Perspective: Making Sense of Contextual Diversity*, Farnham, UK: Ashgate.

Musterd, S. (2012) 'Ethnic Residential Segregation; Reflections on Concepts, Levels and Effects', in D. Clapham, W. Clark and K. Gibb (eds) *The Sage Handbook of Housing Studies*, London: Sage.

Nagel, C.R. and Staeheli, L.A. (2008) 'Integration and the Negotiation of "Here" and "There": The Case of British Arab Activists', *Social & Cultural Geography*, 9(4): 415–30.

Peach, C. (1996) 'Good Segregation, Bad Segregation', *Planning Perspectives*, 11(4): 1–20.

Phillips, D. (2006) 'Parallel Lives? Challenging Discourses of British Muslim Self-segregation', *Environment and Planning D*, 24(1): 25–40.

—(2010) 'Minority Ethnic Segregation, Integration and Citizenship: A European Perspective', *Journal of Ethnic and Migration Studies*, 36(2): 209–25.

Phillips, D., Athwal, B., Robinson, D. and Harrison, M. (2014) 'Towards Inter-cultural Engagement: Building Shared Visions of Neighbourhood and Community in an Era of New Migration', *Journal of Ethnic and Migration Studies*, 40(1): 42–59.

Simpson, L. (2007) 'Ghettos of the Mind: The Empirical Behaviour of Indices of Segregation and Diversity', *Journal of Royal Statistical Society Series A*, 170(2): 405–24.

Stillwell, J. and Phillips, D. (2006) 'Diversity and Change: Understanding the Ethnic Geographies of Leeds', *Journal of Ethnic and Migration Studies*, 32(7): 1131–52.

Valentine, G. (2007) 'Theorising and Researching Inter-sectionality: A Challenge for Feminist Geography', *Professional Geographer*, 59(1): 10–21.

Vertovec, S. (2007) *New Complexities of Cohesion in Britain, Superdiversity, Transnationalism and Civil Integration*, London: Commission on Integration and Cohesion.

Wise, A. and Velayutham, S. (eds) (2009) *Everyday Multiculturalism*, Basingstoke, UK: Palgrave Macmillan.

Wright, R. and Ellis, M. (2006) 'Viewpoint; Mapping Others', *Progress in Human Geography*, 30(3): 285–8.

Part V
Fusions of diversity

37

Assimilation, diversity, and change

Nancy Foner

Understanding immigration and diversity has long been a major concern in the social sciences in the United States. This is not surprising. As a classic settler society, immigration has played a central role in the United States since its inception. Moreover, important social science works on immigration were written in the wake of the last great wave of immigration in the early twentieth century. Indeed in 1910, the US population was nearly 15 per cent foreign born, a height it still has not reached again, though at 13 per cent in 2010 it is coming close.

A guiding concept in the immigration literature for many years has been assimilation, which was elaborated a century ago in the context of classic studies of the Chicago School of Sociology (at the University of Chicago, the nation's first sociology department); assimilation has continued to be a central theoretical concept even as it has been critiqued, reworked, and reformulated (Alba *et al.* 2012; Foner and Lucassen 2012; Waters 2000).

Classic assimilation theory as it developed in the United States has focused on how immigrants and their children become part of American mainstream society, and the newest conceptions of assimilation have continued this emphasis. Despite its main title, *Remaking the American Mainstream: Assimilation and Contemporary Immigration* (Alba and Nee 2003), which has played an important role in the field of immigration studies, is almost entirely concerned with how immigrants and the second generation assimilate to American society rather than the other side of the equation – how they remake it.

It is time, I believe, to shift gears to put more emphasis on how immigration, and the diversity it has brought, have transformed – and continue to transform – American society itself. What follows offers some reflections on these processes. I begin with a brief background on various approaches emphasizing assimilation, before turning to the heart of the matter: some of the ways that immigration has affected cultural and social patterns in American society. A key issue is how the continuous inflow of immigrants has been an engine of change in the United States over the past 100 years, introducing new kinds of diversity and transforming American institutions and culture and the very "model of integration" implicated in how immigrants are incorporated into the nation today. The focus is mainly on ethnic and religious diversity – and on developments in the past that have shaped the context for present-day newcomers and their children. Not only do we know the outcomes of developments that took place in the past, but also a historical perspective brings out, in a powerful way, how ideas about diversity are not fixed or static but change over time. I come back in the conclusion to some comments about changes afoot today and about some additional aspects of diversity.

Assimilation approaches

Until recently, assimilation in the United States, at least in sociological circles, was largely synonymous with William Lloyd Warner, Leo Srole, and Milton Gordon. In their study of Newburyport, Massachusetts, in the 1930s, Warner and Srole (1945) described the intergenerational progression of ethnic groups from the residential and occupational segregation of the first generation to the residential, occupational, and identificational integration and Americanization of later generations. In what has been called a "canonical synthesis" (Alba and Nee 2003: 23), Gordon (1964) in *Assimilation in American Life* set out several stages of the assimilation process, beginning with identification with cultural patterns of the host society. Once structural assimilation, or integration into primary groups, occurred, then other types of assimilation would follow, including intermarriage, the waning of a separate ethnic identity, and decline not only of prejudice and discrimination against the group, but also of ethnic distinction.

Over the years, American sociologists and historians have raised many objections to these conceptions, among them that assimilation is presented as inevitable; that middle-class whites of British ancestry set the norm by which other groups are assessed; that minority groups are assumed to change in order to assimilate while the majority culture remains unaffected; and that there is no room for the positive role of ethnic and racial groups (for a summary of the objections, see Alba and Nee 2003: 3–5).

Most prominent among the new conceptions of assimilation is Richard Alba and Victor Nee's (2003) revised theory which is laid out in *Remaking the American Mainstream*. Based on a detailed analysis of, among other things, intermarriage and linguistic acculturation, they argue that not only was assimilation the master trend for the children and grandchildren of the earlier European immigration, but also it is the most likely path for most descendants of the post-1965 immigration. Although assimilation remains a powerful force, they argue, it also needs to be reconceptualized. (Assimilation, as they define the term, is the decline – or attenuation in salience – of an ethnic distinction and its corollary cultural and social differences so that an individual's ethnic origins become less relevant in relation to members of other ethnic groups.) In their view, ethnicity does not inevitably disappear or weaken as assimilation takes place – many ethnic markers and features of ethnic culture may persist. Moreover, immigrants and their descendants may change the mainstream culture at the same time as they are incorporated into it (ibid.: 11).

What has been presented as an alternative to the "conventional assimilation model" – segmented assimilation – takes diversity into account in a different way, yet keeps the focus on the incorporation of the second generation, with little concern for the impact of immigrants and their descendants on the wider society. As elaborated by Alejandro Portes and his colleagues, segmented assimilation, as the term implies, asks what segment of American society a group assimilates into. "Instead of a relatively uniform mainstream whose mores and prejudices dictate a common path of integration," segmented assimilation presumes "several distinct forms of adaptation," including integration into the white middle class, into the minority underclass, or advancement through preservation of the immigrant community's values and tight solidarity (Portes and Zhou 1993: 82). Much of the controversy over segmented assimilation concerns how widespread downward assimilation actually is, but the point here is that this perspective sees the children of immigrants as being affected by existing ethno-racial divisions – not changing them.

Immigration as an engine of change

Important as it is to understand how immigrants and their children become incorporated into American society, we also need to appreciate how the very process of incorporation has the potential to change significant elements in American society, including the structure of and attitudes to diversity. Throughout American history, immigrant inflows have not only introduced individuals with new ethnic, cultural, and religious features – or new diversity. These inflows, and the way they are incorporated in each period, also alter the social, economic, political, and cultural context that greets – and affects the experiences of – the next wave of inflows (Foner 2006, 2013, 2014). Immigration itself can thus be viewed as generating new forms of diversity and, over time, leading to new conceptions of diversity. Often, the new groups initially have been scorned and stigmatized but, owing to a wide range of factors, including processes of social and economic assimilation, generally they have come to be more accepted, and the diversity they represent has, in many ways, become "normalized."

Religion

One example concerns religion, in particular the incorporation of Catholicism and Judaism into the system of American pluralism. Immigrants today enter a society in which Catholicism and Judaism, along with Protestantism, are seen as the three main American religions, but 100 years ago this was certainly not true.

It was the massive immigration of the Irish, Italians, and Jews in the nineteenth and twentieth centuries that dramatically changed the religious composition of the US population in the first place, of course. And it was the integration of nineteenth- and twentieth-century immigrants and their children that led to an eventual acceptance of Judaism and Catholicism as American religions so that, by the end of World War II, "the Judeo-Christian tradition as the American way had become ubiquitous" (Gerstle, forthcoming).

For much of US history, mainstream America had a decidedly Christian, even Protestant, character – and anti-Catholicism and anti-Semitism have been threaded throughout that history.[1] In the late nineteenth and early twentieth centuries, Protestant denominations were more or less "established" in that they dominated the public square, crowding out Catholicism and Judaism, both associated with disparaged Southern and Eastern European immigrants and seen by nativist observers as incompatible with mainstream institutions and culture. Even earlier in the nineteenth century, Irish immigrants, who constituted the first mass immigration of Catholics to the United States, were the target of deep-seated and virulent anti-Catholic nativism. Many native Protestants viewed the assimilation of the Irish as blocked by what was seen as a fanatical and unholy devotion to the Catholic Church and a foreign, anti-republican pope. The fear that a Catholic president would be beholden to papal influence helped defeat Democratic Irish Catholic nominee Al Smith in 1928. Even in 1960, John F. Kennedy, who would become the nation's first Catholic president, had to appear before a group of Protestant ministers in Texas to prove that his election would not make the Vatican the ruler of Washington (Gerstle, forthcoming). In the nineteenth and early twentieth centuries, non-Protestant religions had either separated from the dominant society to create their own institutions – Catholic parochial schools and universities are a major example – or, as was true for much of American Judaism, confined their religious beliefs and practices to the private realm and "thus acceded to Protestant domination in the public realm" (Wolfe 2006: 159).

Eventually, however – by the middle of the twentieth century – Catholics and Jews were incorporated into the system of American religious pluralism. Or, as Richard Alba has put it, the boundary dividing Catholics and Jews from the Protestant majority moved to include alternative models of religious belief and practice (Alba 2005: 31). One reason was that the descendants of the immigrants became part of the American mainstream – in terms, for example, of economic and educational achievements. The legal separation of church and state in the United States also played a role in enabling the religions imported by earlier immigration streams to achieve parity with Protestant versions of Christianity (Foner and Alba 2008). Whatever the reasons, Americans came to think in terms of a tripartite perspective – Protestant, Catholic, and Jew – with Judaism treated as a kind of branch or denomination within the larger Judeo-Christian framework, a religion of believers who just happened to attend churches called synagogues (Wuthnow 2005). By the late twentieth and early twenty-first century, opponents of multiculturalism were even referring to "our Judeo-Christian heritage" in upholding the value of Western civilization (Alba 2005: 30).

The very transformation of America into a "Judeo-Christian" nation – and Protestant, Catholic, and Jew into the three main denominations in American religious life – has meant that post-1965 immigrants enter a more religiously open society than their predecessors did 100 or 150 years ago. Today, the encounter of immigrant religions with American society benefits from the awareness of and legal context deriving from the earlier incorporation of Jewish and Catholic immigrant groups. In the mid-1990s, President Bill Clinton proclaimed in a Rose Garden ceremony that "Islam is an American religion," and George W. Bush confirmed this by making a point of visiting a mosque in the wake of the September 11 attacks. In the midst of heated debates about the building of the Muslim community center near the World Trade Center site in the summer of 2010, President Obama hosted the annual Iftar Ramadan dinner at the White House, a tradition, he noted, "that goes back several years just as we host Christmas parties, seders, and Diwali celebrations" (*Los Angeles Times* 2010). This does not necessarily mean that the new religions, most notably Islam, will eventually attain the charter status now occupied by Catholicism and Judaism. It is important to stress this point. The outcomes of the current encounter between non-Western religions and the American mainstream are not predictable; at least so far, anti-Muslim sentiment is unfortunately alive and well among sectors of the US population. What it does mean, however, is that today's immigrants benefit from an acceptance that is the result of the difficult integration of Catholicism and Judaism into mainstream America, and they enter a society more tolerant of non-Protestant religions than the one that confronted newcomers 100 years ago.

Hyphenated Americans

Immigrants in the United States today are also living in a society that is more open to diversity in another way: Americans are generally comfortable with hyphenated identities. This openness is part of what has been called a "national integration model," and it contrasts markedly with the melting-pot model that dominated a century ago (Foner 2012). In the contemporary United States, holding onto earlier identities and cultures is viewed as acceptable as long as these are additions to a fundamentally American core. New Americans can retain what they wish of the old country, but, as Waldinger (2007: 141) has put it, they need to "master the native code." Ethnicity, in short, is not a barrier to integration, but reconcilable with acquiring a new American identity.

Whereas in present-day Europe the second generation tends to feel more pressured to express an exclusive national identity, you can be an American and "ethnic" at the same time. In the United States today, moreover, it is not just the children of immigrants who often embrace hyphenated identities. So do many long-established natives, at least some of the time. Being a hyphenated American, one might say, is the American way and not something that makes the second generation stand out as a group apart. Just as there are Chinese-Americans and Mexican-Americans with immigrant parents, so, too, there are millions of Irish-Americans and Italian-Americans, well established in the mainstream whose immigrant ancestors go much further back. To borrow from Glazer (1997), we are all or – virtually all – hyphenated Americans.

This acceptance of hyphenated identities is not an inherent American characteristic; far from it. "Life on the hyphen" (Perez Firmat 1994) was hardly de rigueur 100 years ago. In the midst of the massive Eastern and Southern European immigration a century ago, hyphenated Americanism, as the historian Matthew Frye Jacobson (2006: 9) observes, even "amounted to *un*-Americanism" to some. Indeed, then the emphasis was on "100 percent Americanism." As former president Theodore Roosevelt proclaimed in a 1915 speech: "There is no such thing as a hyphenated American who is a good American. The only man who is a good American is the man who is an American and nothing else." (Roosevelt cited in Foner 2012.)

What explains the dramatic change from then to now? The cessation of Eastern and Southern European inflows after the 1920s meant that immigration aroused less anxiety, and white ethnic communities were no longer being replenished with Old World cultures. The European second generation's economic successes and assimilation to American ways also contributed to greater comfort with ethnic identities (Foner 2005). So did the second generation's patriotic embrace of America during World War II. As the children of European immigrants fought together, the image of the "multi-ethnic platoon with its Protestant, Irish, Polish, Italian and Jewish soldiers fighting side by side to preserve American democracy and freedom" became, in Gary Gerstle's words, an "honored image of the nation" (Gerstle, forthcoming).

In the post-war period, the American national narrative was refashioned to elevate immigration to a central role in the country's myth of origin. By the 1940s, the notion that America was a "melting pot" had entered the majority of American history textbooks (Fitzgerald 1979). In the next two decades, "Ellis Island identities" began to replace "Plymouth Rock ones" (Jacobson 2006) as the ideal of Anglo-Conformity was dethroned and the mainstream opened up; at the same time, the phrase "nation of immigrants" became widely and popularly used as a celebration of the United States (Alba 2009).

Also of critical importance was another dimension of diversity in the United States that has not yet been mentioned: the huge African-American population. The struggle for civil rights by African Americans, to be free of legal segregation, ghettoization, and subordination, and the "minority rights revolution" (Skrentny 2002) that the civil rights movement brought about had enormous implications for all ethnic groups in the country. The acknowledgment of racial and ethnic group experiences in the dominant discourse in national civic life that followed the civil rights legislative successes of 1964 and 1965, as one historian writes, was "electrifying" (Jacobson 2006: 19f.).

Policy and legislative changes begun in the civil rights era to combat discrimination and open up opportunities for African Americans in schools, workplaces, and at the ballot box were extended to other racial minorities and thus to many immigrants and their children. One result was to move decisively "the discourse on integration in the United States beyond a singular focus on Americanization" and change "the cultural idiom of American national identity" (Bloemraad, forthcoming). Ethno-racial diversity was not only tolerated but also often celebrated as part of America's founding principles, and, by the 1990s, it had become central to a program of national belonging. Following the Black is Beautiful movement, immigrant groups, both old and new, adopted a similar stance in regard to their own ethnic cultures, in this way "broadening and intensifying the effort to locate America's vitality in its ethnic and racial diversity" (Gerstle, forthcoming). Ethnic hyphenation became a "natural idiom of national belonging," and, as the history textbooks make clear, the United States, once conceived as male and Anglo Saxon, became filled with blacks, white ethnics, Latinos, native Americans, and Asians.

Concluding comments: looking ahead

If, as we have seen, the incorporation of earlier immigrations in the United States played a role in creating a more receptive context for present-day newcomers and their children in some ways, then a host of issues arises about possible changes in the future. How will the incorporation of today's first-generation immigrants and the second generation change the nature and perceptions of diversity – and its impact on American society as a whole? Predicting the future is, of course, risky, but let me end by raising some questions about what may lie ahead as well as aspects of diversity that I have not yet considered.

Immigrants, because of cultural traditions they bring, almost invariably change – indeed, we can say, diversify – the tastes and cuisines that are dominant in the receiving society, or at least this has been the case in the United States. Bagels and pizza, to name a Russian Jewish and an Italian import in the past, are now as American as apple pie. Today, salsa outsells ketchup, and Chinese restaurants outnumber all the McDonald's, Burger Kings, and Kentucky Fried Chickens in the United States combined. Immigrants have added new art and music styles (hip hop among them) to the American landscape. A main theoretical issue is whether cultural change occurs as the mainstream expands to accommodate cultural alternatives, usually after being "Americanized" to some extent (Alba and Nee 2003) – or if some cultural changes reflect a "creolization" process, with elements from the cultures of immigrant and native-born groups blending into something new (Foner 1997).

Then there is the impact of immigration, and the diversity it brings, on community institutions. Do these institutions undergo changes in form and function as they adjust to the needs and demands of newcomers who have new, and diverse, cultural and linguistic backgrounds? Many US schools and health-care facilities, for example, have introduced new programs to serve immigrant populations, including modern bilingual education in schools and translation services in hospitals, which have become "normal" features of these institutions. Altogether new institutions have emerged, such as newcomer schools with language and cultural training programs for new student arrivals from abroad. So have new kinds of neighborhoods, including neighborhoods which are home to native whites and racial minorities as well as multiple immigrant groups.

Earlier European immigrants pioneered – and established – ethnic politics as an accepted feature of the American urban landscape. The Irish, and later Southern and Eastern Europeans, in the late nineteenth and early twentieth centuries rallied voters, built coalitions, and gained political influence by appealing to voters on ethnic grounds. The civil rights movement reinforced and strengthened this pathway to political influence for non-white groups. Today, candidates of all colors and ethnicities in presidential and local elections eat tacos on the campaign trail and sprinkle their speeches with Spanish in the quest for the large and growing Latino vote. A more basic question, currently the subject of much debate in the United States, is whether the rising electoral power of immigrants and their children, especially Latinos who are now the nation's largest minority group, will lead to more fundamental political and policy shifts, potentially changing the electoral balance between the two major parties. Political pundits are now asking whether the Republican Party is in jeopardy, at least in presidential elections, if it continues to be indifferent, and sometimes downright hostile, to the country's diverse constituencies – blacks, women, Latinos, Asians, and gays (Tanenhaus 2013).

Finally, there is the matter of race. This is an essential topic in any discussion of diversity in the United States because of its fundamental role in inequality since the nation's very founding as a country is based on chattel slavery, but it is also intrinsic to discussions of earlier European immigrations. The historical literature on immigration has been concerned with the racialization of earlier European immigrants – and how the second- and third-generation descendants of Jewish and Italian immigrants, who were initially considered racial inferiors and whose status as whites was often doubted, came to be considered part of an all-encompassing white racial majority. Among the many factors involved were the economic successes of the second and third generations in the context of post-war prosperity and educational expansion; the end of massive immigration from Southern and Eastern Europe in the late 1920s; the role of the Nazi genocide in making anti-Semitism less respectable; the struggles of the groups themselves to eliminate exclusionary barriers; and the physical resemblance of those of Eastern and Southern European descent to members of older Northern and Western European groups (Foner 2000, 2005).

Social scientists are now asking whether any of the factors responsible for enabling Jews and Italians to meld into the white majority will operate in changing ethno-racial boundaries confronting descendants of contemporary Latino, Asian, and black immigrants. Will any groups currently thought of as non-white, as well as non-black, come to be seen as white? Will ethno-racial boundaries and meanings shift in an altogether different way? Given how prominent color is in today's racial discourse, will intermarriage be a more important agent of racial change than in the past (Perlmann and Waters 2007)? Will, as Alba (2009) argues, members of the second generation in racial minority groups be able to take advantage of non-zero sum mobility – ascending socially without adversely affecting the life chances of the established majority – as happened among Jews and Italians in the past?

The study of immigration, in short, raises some fundamental questions about diversity and change in American society. An emphasis on assimilation puts the spotlight on how immigrants and their children change as they adapt to the society where they now live – processes that are, to be sure, of the utmost importance and relevance, which is why they have been the subject of so much study. Yet, we need to also pay attention to how immigrants themselves, with the particular kinds of diversity they bring, are agents of change who continually remake and transform their societies. Understanding how immigrants and their descendants are bringing about these transformations in the contemporary period is a topic that deserves to be at the top of our research agenda.

Note

1   The following paragraphs on religion in American society draw on Foner and Alba (2008).

References

Alba, R. (2005) 'Bright vs. Blurred Boundaries: Second-Generation Assimilation and Exclusion in France, Germany and the United States', *Ethnic and Racial Studies*, 28(1): 20–49.

—(2009) *Blurring the Color Line: The New Chance for a More Integrated America*, Cambridge, MA: Harvard University Press.

Alba, R. and Nee, V. (2003) *Remaking the American Mainstream: Assimilation and Contemporary Immigration*, Cambridge, MA: Harvard University Press.

Alba, R., Reitz, J.G. and Simon, P. (2012) 'National Conceptions of Assimilation, Integration, and Cohesion', in M. Crul and J. Mollenkopf (eds) *The Changing Face of World Cities: Young Adult Children of Immigrants in Europe and the United States*, New York, NY: Russell Sage Foundation.

Bloemraad, I. (forthcoming) 'Re-imagining the Nation in a World of Migration: Legitimacy, Political Claims-Making and Membership in Comparative Perspective', in N. Foner and P. Simon (eds) *Fear, Anxiety and National Identity*.

Fitzgerald, F. (1979) *America Revised*, Boston, MA: Little Brown.

Foner, N. (1997) 'The Immigrant Family: Cultural Legacies and Cultural Changes', *International Migration Review*, 31(4): 891–904.

–(2000) *From Ellis Island to JFK: New York's Two Great Waves of Immigration*, New Haven, CT: Yale University Press.

—(2005) *In a New Land: A Comparative View of Immigration*, New York, NY: New York University Press.

—(2006) 'Then *And* Now or Then *To* Now: Immigration to New York in Contemporary and Historical Perspective', *Journal of American Ethnic History*, 25(2–3): 33–47.

—(2012) 'Models of Integration in a Settler Society: Caveats and Complications in the US Case', *Patterns of Prejudice*, 46(5): 486–99.

—(2013) 'Immigration Past and Present', *Daedalus*, 142(3): 16–25.

—(2014) 'Immigration History and the Remaking of New York', in N. Foner, J. Rath, J.W. Duyvendak and R. van Reekum (eds) *New York and Amsterdam: Immigration and the New Urban Landscape*, New York, NY: New York University Press.

Foner, N. and Alba, R. (2008) 'Immigrant Religion in the U.S. and Western Europe: Bridge or Barrier to Inclusion?', *International Migration Review*, 42(2): 360–92.

Foner, N. and Lucassen, L. (2012) 'Legacies of the Past', in M. Crul and J. Mollenkopf (eds) *The Changing Face of World Cities: Young Adult Children of Immigrants in Europe and the United States*, New York, NY: Russell Sage Foundation.

Gerstle, G. (forthcoming) 'The Contradictory Character of American Nationality: A Historical Perspective', in N. Foner and P. Simon (eds) *Fear, Anxiety and National Identity*.

Glazer, N. (1997) *We Are All Multiculturalists Now*, Cambridge, MA: Harvard University Press.

Gordon, M. (1964) *Assimilation in American Life: The Role of Race, Religion, and National Origin*, New York, NY: Oxford University Press.

Jacobson, M.F. (2006) *Roots Too: White Ethnic Revival in Post-Civil Rights America*, Cambridge, MA: Harvard University Press.

Los Angeles Times (2010) 'At Ramadan Iftar Dinner Obama Supports New Mosque on Private Property Near Ground Zero', 13 August. Online. Available HTTP: <Latimesblogs.latimes.com/ . . . /obama-ramadan-iftar-remarks-text.html> (accessed 23 April 2014).

Perez Firmat, G. (1994) *Life on the Hyphen: The Cuban-American Way*, Austin, TX: University of Texas Press.

Perlmann, J. and Waters, M.C. (2007) 'Intermarriage and Multiple Identities', in M.C. Waters and R. Ueda (eds) *The New Americans: A Guide to Immigration Since 1965*, Cambridge, MA: Harvard University Press.

Portes, A. and Zhou, M. (1993) 'The New Second Generation: Segmented Assimilation and its Variants among Post-1965 Immigrant Youth', *Annals of the American Academy of Political and Social Science*, 530(1): 74–98.

Skrentny, J. (2002) *The Minority Rights Revolution*, Cambridge, MA: Harvard University Press.

Tanenhaus, S. (2013) 'The Republicans: The Party of White People', *New Republic*, 25 February.

Waldinger, R. (2007) 'Transforming Foreigners into Americans', in M.C. Waters and R. Ueda (eds) *The New Americans: A Guide to Immigration Since 1965*, Cambridge, MA: Harvard University Press.

Warner, W.L. and Srole, L. (1945) *The Social Systems of American Ethnic Groups*, New Haven, CT: Yale University Press.

Waters, M.C. (2000) 'The Sociological Roots and Multidisciplinary Future of Immigration Research', in N. Foner, R. Rumbaut and S. Gold (eds) *Immigration Research for a New Century*, New York, NY: Russell Sage Foundation.

Wolfe, A. (2006) 'Religious Diversity: The American Experiment that Works', in M. Kazin and J. McCartin (eds) *Americanism: New Perspectives on the History of an Ideal*, Chapel Hill, NC: University of North Carolina Press.

Wuthnow, R. (2005) *America and the Challenges of Religious Diversity*, Princeton, NJ: Princeton University Press.

38

From creolization to syncretism
Climbing the ritual ladder

Charles Stewart

Syncretism has both an outside and an inside. The outside involves the actual situations of diverse social groups in contact. How and where do they meet, and under what economic and political terms? In cases of recent migration, the study of these interactions might fall into the analytical sphere of creolization, which refers to the adaptation of a person or a group in new surroundings. The inside of syncretism is the theological level, where new ideas or gods may be inserted into a pre-existing system, precipitating a reconfiguration of the pantheon or the form of rituals. This chapter discusses the respective spheres of creolization and syncretism, and it observes that mutual participation in rituals may be an important bridge leading from creolization to syncretism. Acceptance into the rituals of the host community can mark a momentous staging point on the way to the localization of migrants. This sharing of rituals gives an opportunity for newcomers to introduce novel elements, thus taking a step in the direction of syncretism. Rather than conflate creolization and syncretism, I see ritual as an avenue leading from creolization to syncretism.

Uncertain mixture

The social science vocabulary for cultural mixture is notoriously undertheorized, which is why researchers often use the terms syncretism, hybridity, creolization and fusion interchangeably, as virtual synonyms (Robbins 2011: 13). It seems that the idea of 'mixture' has been the common denominator encouraging conflation. While recognizing that creolization and syncretism belong to the creative flow of living theoretical vocabulary, and that they are often used evocatively (rather than analytically), I nonetheless present views on how to differentiate them. In order to disambiguate creolization and syncretism, I shift focus from mixture per se to the temporal dynamics of crystallization. When can it be said that a mixture has occurred such that a new entity has formed or an old one dissolved?

The historical semantics of creolization cover territory that does not involve mixture and thus serve to guide us away from a fixation on mixture. The earliest definitions of a 'creole' often insisted that this was a person of *pure* Old World descent. This was true in the French colony of Louisiana (Chaudenson 2001: 6), as well as in Spanish Gran Colombia (Palmié 2007). Although it is a complicated matter (Dominguez 1986), over the last two centuries in Louisiana the term 'creole' has generally referred to a white person, while people of mixed French and African ancestry have been called 'creoles of color'. What made early colonial creoles different from former compatriots in the Old World was the acclimatization, seasoning, indigenization, adaptation and loss undergone in the New World. Such restructuring can occur without genetic mixture, but via localization in a new environment and the acquisition of immunities, cultural practices and new goals. Anderson's (1991) account of Iberian settlers in Latin America, who at first identified with Spain but later saw themselves as indigenous inhabitants of the New World in rebellion against Spain, presents a classic example of creolization as adaptation after migration. People who were once Spanish came, after a few generations, to be non-Spanish. As their consciousness of themselves as Spanish ebbed away over the years, an established social entity fell apart. Japanese migrants to Brazil furnish a more recent example, to be considered later.

Figure 38.1 maps out the overlaps and differences between key terms for cultural mixture in contemporary theory. I take 'hybridity' and 'mixture' to be synonymous and thus coterminous in the area colored grey. This is the common denominator area or 'mixture' where all the terms overlap, although 'mixture' itself is not an unproblematic concept. Most importantly, the diagram highlights the areas where syncretism, creolization and mixture/hybridity do not overlap.

Theravada Buddhism as practised in Thailand, Burma or Sri Lanka presents a case where syncretism cannot be reduced to 'mixture'. It has long been noted that, theologically, Buddhism does not admit any supernatural beings. The Buddha was an exemplary human being and adherents follow his path to wisdom. In local Burmese communities, however, people also appeal to a variety of supernatural forces such as the *nat* spirits that survive from pre-Buddhist times (Spiro 1994: 194), while in Sri Lanka people resort to Hindu gods as well as local spirits (Gombrich 1971: 49). In Richard Gombrich's analysis, the Buddha and his path mediate other-worldly concerns of salvation, while people appeal to gods and spirits only to ameliorate this-worldly problems of disease and misfortune. He does not, therefore, consider Sri Lankan Buddhism syncretic, but rather as 'accretive' – i.e. as possessing two discrete modules attached to one another and operating complementarily. But one analyst's complementarity may be another's syncretism. Assessing the very same phenomenon, the German scholar Heinz Bechert (1978: 24) labelled Sri Lankan Buddhism 'syncretic'. This example suggests that two or more religions may be in unmixed relations of complementarity, accretion, proximity or 'convergence' (Vertovec 1998) and yet qualify as syncretic according to some opinions.

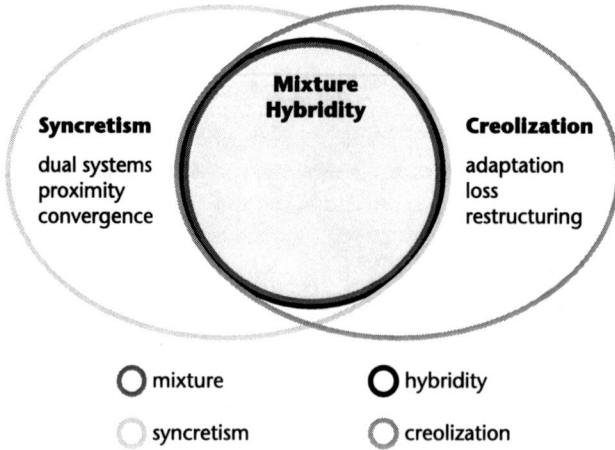

Figure 38.1   Spheres of syncretism, creolization, hybridity and mixture

Further limiting cases for syncretism as mixture are found in recently converted societies where people may be baptized and yet continue to practise their former religion in some contexts. The Urapmin of Papua New Guinea, who converted to Pentecostalism in the 1970s, sacrifice pigs to the ancestors. This could be regarded as syncretism, or as a novel facet of their particular Christianity, as Joel Robbins has contended (Robbins 2007: 16). In cases of mixed marriages, spouses may also find themselves practising two religions, complementarily, at two different moments. On the island of Naxos, where I have carried out field research, the Venetians gained control in 1204 and remained in power until the Ottomans displaced them in the seventeenth century. Over this long stay, Catholic Venetians and Franks occasionally intermarried with the local Orthodox Christians, although this usually meant that Orthodox women converted to Catholicism. In one case, a Catholic noble married an Orthodox woman but did not demand that she convert. On the premises of his fortified little castle, known as the Pyrgos tou Belloni, one may still see the small, double-vaulted family church with two entrances built by the noble. One door opens to a Catholic chapel, the other to an Orthodox chapel. Thus the couple could each pray, almost in the same place, but within their two different spheres of faith. Perhaps the couple prayed together on occasion, but architecturally the two denominations retained a membrane of separation. The theologian Robert Schreiter (1985) calls such arrangements 'dual systems' rather than syncretisms since the religions are practised in alternation. Yet, once two religions are brought into close proximity, the boundary between alternation and mixture might be fluid in practice, and difficult to legislate. Such cases point to the need for analyses of other dimensions of the syncretism phenomenon. The dimension of time would be one such possibility. How might yesterday's juxtaposition, or accretion, be a prelude to tomorrow's mixture?

Then there is the matter of religious spaces shared by Muslims, Christians and Jews in longstanding plural societies such as those found in the Mediterranean and Balkan areas (Bowman 2012; Couroucli 2012). The shrine (*turbe*) of the Sufi saint Hadir Bābā in Macedonia actually operates as an Orthodox church most of the time. When Muslims do worship there, they clear away some of the Christian paraphernalia so that they may spread out their prayer rugs, but the Orthodox icons nonetheless look down upon them from the walls (Bowman 2012). Their prayers are not mediated by these icons, but rather by the holiness of Hadir Bābā, who is thought to be buried below the floor. The two religions are not being mixed. The case is different at the Sveta Bogoroditsa Monastery, also in Macedonia, where Muslims visit the church alongside Christians (Bowman 2010). Like the Christians, the Muslims climb through a hole in the wall three times in order to be healed or protected from illness. Above this hole are suspended icons of Mary and Jesus. The Muslims do not kiss the icons or make the sign of the cross, but they appeal to the same holy power that the Christians do in crawling through the hole. Both Christians and Muslims alike also pass chains/beads over their bodies for good luck and protection against illness. Some analysts might judge this as a syncretic ritual, while others might consider it to be a one-off occasional practice, set apart in space and time from normal Muslim observance at home or in the mosque. Resorts to rosary chains or the hole in the wall do not have any impact on systematic practice or theology.

Rethinking mixture

The given examples expose the very poor social science criteria for mixture, and this is reflected in the vagueness and subjectivity of analysis. This state of affairs may be contrasted with the vocabulary of the hard science most directly concerned with mixture, namely chemistry, where we find clear distinctions into elements (irresolvable units), compounds (a distinctive combination of two or more elements that involves adding/generating energy) and mixtures (in which components retain their own properties and can be separated without adding/releasing energy). Indeed, the chemist's vocabulary is much more nuanced than this as it goes on to discriminate homogeneous from heterogeneous mixtures according to how intimately combined the components are and whether the constituent parts might be visibly distinguished. There is not the space here to consider properly the attributes of solutions, suspensions and colloids, but this much is sufficient to show that chemistry has a clear analytical vocabulary which differentiates various kinds of mixtures according to certain principles: variable versus fixed proportion; visibility or invisibility of elements; energy necessary for fusion or separation.

Chemistry focuses on units of nature that show universal consistency in properties. Furthermore, these units do not talk back. Chemical compounds do not read research reports, or change their minds about how to act. For Ian Hacking (1999: 105), they are 'indifferent' to how they are classified. In this respect, chemistry is fundamentally different from the social sciences and humanities. Although Durkheim (1982 [1895]) initially set out to create sociology as a science based on the study of 'social facts', his positivism cannot capture the 'looping effects' of classifications. As Hacking (1995: 239) explains: 'A new or modified mode of classification may systematically affect the people who are so classified, or the people themselves may rebel against their knowers, the classifiers, the science that classifies them.' Social science researchers may, for example, identify a situation and denominate it as 'syncretism'. The people so described may then agree or disagree with this analysis. They may celebrate their syncretism and use it to attract new members, or they may decide to stamp it out as an embarrassment. The classification itself precipitates social changes. This factor of consciousness becomes part of the field of study in the ethnography of syncretism. Syncretism takes on new force when the people involved explicitly recognize new elements and embrace or reject them. Until that happens (in local terms) syncretism is but an outside analytic, a scholastic classification of social phenomena.

Ritual, pluralism and social process

Syncretisms arise through cultural contact and it is instructive to look at recent examples of migration to see this process in its early stages. The flood of Albanian migrants into Greece since the early 1990s offers a case in point. Albanians come to villages like Arachova, near Delphi in central Greece, and take jobs as casual labourers, often waiting in the café on a daily basis for someone to employ them. Greek political unease over high levels of illegal immigration means that they are watched and periodically deported by police, and discriminated against by the locals.

Every year, Arachova celebrates its patron saint, Saint George, in a four-day festival (called *'panigyraki'*), which cleaves into sacred and profane sections as such festivals do in many parts of Greece (Stewart 1994: 220). The morning liturgy presided over by the priest inside the church stands at the pole of the sacred, while drink-fuelled dancing in the streets until late at night stands at the opposite extreme. Folkloric dancing in traditional costumes and the official athletic events and speeches of public officials form an intermediary point in a spectrum of ritual activities stretching between these two poles. The saint's day ritual thus offers various levels of controlled access to the community's *sacra*, spanning from Holy Communion in the church through widening popular involvement in athletics and folk dancing, through to a still more open and unscripted night-time celebration. One could view this festival from a Durkheimian perspective as a ritual of social solidarity and autochthony, where the community celebrates its cohesion and historical rootedness.

The influx of migrants might initially have reinforced this cohesive function by providing an audience of outsiders, whose presence validated the authentic belonging of the local community.

Indeed tourists and other visitors had long filled this role of the other as witness, excluded from participation. During the years after their arrival, Albanian migrants watched the saint's festival from the margins. Yet many of them had begun to reside permanently in Arachova, and they had begun to participate in civic life. They learned to speak Greek, sent their children to local schools and joined local football teams and marching bands.

The anthropologist Roland Moore (2003) reported that, after a decade, the Albanians began to join the evening dances alongside the Greek villagers. The Albanians had mastered a sense of what the occasion required and they had the spare cash to throw at the musicians to enter the dance by themselves. They even began to participate in the athletics and the folk dancing. Thus they joined the overall festival, starting at the profane end and progressing toward the higher level of formal secular ritual. Beyond its literal meaning, the expression 'to enter the dance' in Greek means to enter into the flow of things, to blend in through active participation – in this case, joining the dance was a step toward active involvement in local society, a step toward assimilation.

Something similar can be seen in the case of Japanese Brazilians. The Japanese who migrated to Brazil in the early twentieth century remained proficient in Japanese language in the first generation, but in succeeding generations they lost the ancestral language and they became Brazilian by formal citizenship, and self-identification, although as a minority group they embraced an ethnic tie to Japan. In short, they creolized in Brazil.

During the Japanese economic boom of the 1990s, many of these by then second- and third-generation Japanese Brazilians journeyed to Japan for work, settling in industrial cities such as Hamamatsu. At first, the Japanese locals kept apart and looked down upon them. Although, according to Japanese ideology, Japanese-ness flows from Japanese descent, people did not recognize these migrant workers as fully Japanese (Tsuda 2003: 117). As Joshua Roth (2007) observed:

> Nikkei [people of Japanese ancestry residing overseas, in this case Japanese Brazilians] for the most part looked Japanese, yet did not speak or behave like them. Their very body language betrayed a fundamental difference in sense of self. The public displays of affection among Nikkei couples, the use of *fio dental* (literally dental floss, that is, thong bikinis) by some Nikkei women at public swimming pools, the smells of barbecued beef and *linguiça* (Portuguese/Brazilian sausages), and the boisterous conversation and music that escaped the confines of cramped Nikkei apartments all presented Japanese with a jarring sensory presentation utterly different from what many had expected of the Japanese Brazilians returnees.
>
> *(ibid.: 207)*

Every year, the people of Hamamatsu hold a kite-flying festival over three days in May, a celebration of the patriline and of local rootedness and belonging. One of the central acts of the ritual is for a father to place his young son on his shoulders, and for him, in turn, to be raised on the shoulders of a strong young man – a pillar of manhood celebrating the generations. As in Arachova, this festival had multiple parts, ranging from formal parades with floats, through kite flying, to evening parties where revellers troop through the streets to various private homes which provide food and music. Visitors are generally only invited to watch the public parade.

Like the *panigyraki* in Arachova, the kite-flying festival operated as a ritual of locality, casting as audience those who were not local. Joshua Roth (2002: 132) found, however, that people in the working class neighbourhoods – some of whom worked alongside the Japanese Brazilians in the factories – showed more receptivity to the Brazilians. Some Japanese even became interested in samba drumming, and formed groups of Japanese and mixed Japanese and Brazilian samba drummers.

Eventually, at the home parties during the kite-flying festival, families began to play samba music, which 'mixed' with the whistle and drum of the traditional Japanese music. Two different rhythms and musical instruments of two previously discrete traditions alternated and played off each other to the enjoyment of the participants, who found the quicker samba beat exciting. As in Arachova, the entry point was the most informal part of the festival involving music, dance and alcohol consumption. It was the thin end of the syncretism wedge, but perhaps syncretisms often begin at such points. Migrant incomers climb up the ladder from spectators to profane participants, and it remains to be seen if they will ascend into the more exclusive official, and even sacred, parts of the ritual. If they do manage to scale those heights, they will have been fully localized.

The earlier view of these rituals as celebrations of autochthony and exclusive communal identity must therefore be modified to a consideration of them as but one moment in a longer temporal framework. As local society in Hamamatsu and Arachova became diversified, the role of ritual changed. In plural societies the presence of others can introduce new dynamics into old rituals (Baumann 1992: 111). Rather than reinforcing the boundaries of the core community by separating 'us' from 'them', as the Durkheimian view would have it, in plural societies rituals may bring 'others' into dialectical relationship with the established community. The ritual of static social solidarity can become a ritual of social change. Rituals such as the panigryaki and the kite-flying festival can catalyse the transformation of 'them' into 'us'; like the energy added to form a compound in chemistry.

The temporality of mixture

The foregoing examples highlight the dimension of time underlying the appraisal of mixture. Hybridity must be understood temporally as beginning at a particular moment when exogenous traditions encounter one another and appear different to each other. After hybrids are formed, they may, in time, become their own coherent entities. People may even claim that these cultural forms are 'pure'. Yesterday's hybrid thus becomes available as one of the progenitors of tomorrow's hybrid. It's hybrids all the way down. A cycle begins with the encounter between two mutually apparent zones of difference. Hybridization begins in these moments and the resulting mixtures have life cycles. People go from dynamic consciousness of their process of mixing to a situation of taking their own composition for granted. Bakhtin (1981: 358) labelled these respectively 'conscious' and 'unconscious' hybridity. A pidgin language spoken between speakers of two different mother tongues would carry with it a level of conscious realization that two different languages are being mixed, reinforced by the fact that those communicating retain mastery of different native languages. The children born speaking this pidgin as their exclusive native language do not reflect on it as a mixed language; it is just their language and this is how all 'natural' languages have been formed over time. The juxtaposition of Japanese whistle blowing music and samba drumming is a conscious hybrid. In time it may not be consciously perceived as hybrid but as a unitary phenomenon.

How do people become aware and reflect upon the moment when they no longer belong to one tradition or culture, but have crossed over into another? In the pidgin to creole situation this transition is made when the subsequent generation learn the pidgin as a first language. Culture and ethnicity are a bit more fluid and difficult to pin down. Creolization may begin to occur after relatively short periods.

While living and working in Japan, Japanese Brazilians endure a certain degree of exclusion and criticism from surrounding Japanese society. At the same time, they feel increasing nostalgia for Brazil, and imagine themselves returning with money and commodities from Japan. While living in Brazil they strongly embraced a sense of Japanese-ness and the idea of an ancestral homeland elsewhere. The trip to Japan convinces them, however, that they are really Brazilians and that they will never be Japanese (Tsuda 2003: 370). Instead of coming 'home' to Japan, or re-finding home there, indications are that the majority rapidly come to view it as just a place to sojourn as a migrant labourer. After their return to Brazil people continue to address them as *Japonês*, but they now know more surely than ever that they are *Brasileiros* (ibid.: 368).

Japanese Brazilians cannot easily decreolize upon return to their original mother culture. After two or three generations in Brazil, Japan became foreign. This example illustrates that over time creolization creates new zones of assumed, embodied identity, while simultaneously creating new zones of difference (Knörr 2010: 733). In this case one new zone of difference happens to be the original ancestral culture from which they departed sixty or eighty years earlier. The attempt to re-settle in Japan shows the limits of the concept of decreolization because a line of 'entification' has been crossed. The Japanese of Brazil had crystallized a new localized identity based on their set of situated practices and competencies. To become Japanese (again) would involve more than just reaching down and elaborating old abilities that were still there. It demanded, rather, a new creolization that would cross them over into a zone of difference. This is the circularity of hybridity. Every creolization is a re-creolization.

Instead of focusing exclusively on the components and proportions of 'mixture' – the concept which has been at the core of studies of syncretism and creolization – it might be illuminating to look at the formation and dissolution of 'zones of difference' or 'spaces of identification'. How do these come into being? How fast? And how do those involved perceive what is happening? To change our angle of study we might again take some inspiration from chemistry, but now we must look at the terms for analysing the formation and dissolution of discrete entities. The key term here would be 'nucleation', which takes place in familiar processes such as crystallization, congealing, condensation and gelling. This change in focus will allow us to highlight the crucial dimension of time in the formation, dissolution and reformation of identities and other bodies of cultural practice. Rather than fixating on mixture, which, as we have seen, may be difficult to define properly, the focus shifts to 'entitivity', the quality of forming a discrete entity. The study of ritual comes to the fore in this reorientation. The creolization of migrants in new surroundings is the precondition for their admission into ritual practices, and their participation may bring new elements into these rituals, resulting in syncretism.

References

Anderson, B. (1991) *Imagined Communities*, revised edn, London: Verso.
Bakhtin, M.M. (1981) *The Dialogic Imagination*, trans. C. Emerson and M. Holquist, Austin, TX: University of Texas Press.
Baumann, G. (1992) 'Ritual Implicates "Others"', in D. Coppet (ed.) *Understanding Rituals*, London: Routledge.
Bechert, H. (ed.) (1978) *Buddhism in Ceylon and Studies on Religious Syncretism in Buddhist Countries*, Goettingen: Vandenhoeck and Ruprecht.
Bowman, G. (2010) 'Orthodox-Muslim Interactions at "Mixed Shrines" in Macedonia', in C. Hann and H. Goltz (eds) *Eastern Christians in Anthropological Perspective*, Berkeley, CA: University of California Press.
—(ed.) (2012) *Sharing the Sacra: The Politics and Pragmatics of Inter-communal Relations around Holy Places*, Oxford, NY: Berghahn.
Chaudenson, R. (2001) *Creolization of Language and Culture*, London: Routledge.

Couroucli, M. (ed.) (2012) *Sharing Sacred Spaces in the Mediterranean: Christians, Muslims, and Jews at Shrines and Sanctuaries*, Bloomington, IN: Indiana University Press.

Dominguez, V. (1986) *White by Definition: Social Classification in Creole Louisiana*, New Brunswick, NJ: Rutgers University Press.

Durkheim, E. (1982) [1895] *The Rules of the Sociological Method*, trans. W.D. Halls, New York, NY: Free Press.

Gombrich, R. (1971) *Precept and Practice: Traditional Buddhism in the Rural Highlands of Ceylon*, Oxford, UK: Clarendon.

—(1995) *Rewriting the Soul: Multiple Personality and the Sciences of Memory*, Princeton, NJ: Princeton University Press.

—(1999) *The Social Construction of What?*, Cambridge, MA: Harvard University Press.

Knörr, J. (2010) 'Contemporary Creoleness; or, The World in Pidginization?', *Current Anthropology*, 51(6): 731–59.

Moore, R. (2003) 'Dancing in from the Shadows: Recent Albanian Immigrants in a Small Greek Town', Paper presented at the 18th Biennial Meeting of the Modern Greek Studies Association, Toronto, 17 October 2003.

Palmié, S. (2007) 'The "C-Word" Again: From Colonial to Postcolonial Semantics', in C. Stewart (ed.) *Creolization: History, Ethnography, Theory*, Walnut Creek, CA: Left Coast Press.

Robbins, J. (2007) 'Continuity Thinking and the Problem of Christian Culture: Belief, Time, and the Anthropology of Christianity', *Current Anthropology*, 48(1): 5–38.

—(2011) 'Crypto-Religion and the Study of Cultural Mixtures: Anthropology, Value, and the Nature of Syncretism', *Journal of the American Academy of Religion*, 79(2): 408–24.

Roth, J. (2002) *Brokered Homeland: Japanese Brazilian Migrants in Japan*, Ithaca, NY: Cornell University Press.

—(2007) 'Adapting to Inequality: Negotiating Nikkei Identity in Contexts of Return', in C. Stewart (ed.) *Creolization: History, Ethnography, Theory*, Walnut Creek, CA: Left Coast Press.

Schreiter, R. (1985) *Constructing Local Theologies*, London: SCM Press.

Spiro, M. (1994) 'Religion: Problems of Definition and Explanation', in M. Spiro, B. Kilborne and L.L. Langness (eds) *Culture and Human Nature*, New Brunswick, NJ: Transaction.

Stewart, C. (1994) 'Honour and Sanctity: Two Levels of Ideology in Greece', *Social Anthropology*, 2(3): 205–28.

Tsuda, T. (2003) *Strangers in the Ethnic Homeland: Japanese Brazilian Return Migration in a Transnational Perspective*, New York, NY: Columbia University Press.

Vertovec, S. (1998) 'Ethnic Distance and Religious Convergence: Shango, Spiritual Baptist, and Kali Mai Traditions in Trinidad', *Social Compass*, 45(2): 247–63.

39

Intersectionality
Assembling and disassembling the roads

Helma Lutz

Intersectionality is a concept of fusion, but it has a special message and a particular history which cautions against any kind of 'melting pot' idea where the elements dilute and become something new. In this essay I will first give an account of intersectionality's rapid spread from the USA to Europe and other continents; I will then distinguish between various strands and positions among those who use the concept; finally, I will outline open questions linked to the debates about intersectionality's scientific use and status.

Intersectionality's brilliant career

When in 2005 the American sociologist Leslie McCall wrote: 'One could even say that intersectionality is the most important theoretical contribution that women's studies, in conjunction with related fields, has made so far' (McCall 2005: 1771), she paid tribute to a concept that was coined in 1989 by the black US law expert Kimberlé Crenshaw and spread quickly beyond the United States, first and foremost in the field of gender studies. Notwithstanding the term's relatively short history, it does have a long past which is closely related to black women's fight for equality, human rights and recognition. Formerly discussed as the *gender, race and class nexus*, intersectionality has several forerunners and founding narratives. Some authors consider as an early reflection of black women's struggle against slavery, subordination and discrimination the speech from the year 1851 by Sojourner Truth, a former slave and anti-slavery activist:

> That man over there says that women need to be helped into carriages, and lifted over ditches, and to have the best place everywhere. Nobody helps me any best place. And ain't I a woman? Look at me! Look at my arm! I have plowed, I have planted and I have gathered into barns. And no man could head me. And ain't I a woman? I could work as much and eat as much as any man – when I could get it – and bear the lash as well! And ain't I a woman? I have borne thirteen children and seen them most all sold into slavery, and when I cried out with my mother's grief, none but Jesus heard me. And ain't I a woman?
>
> *(Sojourner Truth quoted in Brah and Phoenix 2004: 77)*

With these words, Truth addressed the exclusion of black women from the collective of *women* during a meeting of the burgeoning women's rights movement in Akron, Ohio. Her plea for the consideration of 'race' and 'racism' as important markers of difference and inequality between women has proved relevant for the women's movement up to this very day.

More than 100 years later, in 1977, the manifesto of the Combahee River Collective, a Boston-based black lesbian feminist organization, renewed this request. It highlighted the futility of privileging a single dimension of oppressive experience:

> We believe that sexual politics under patriarchy is as pervasive in Black women's lives as are the politics of class and race. We also often find it difficult to separate race from class from sex oppression because in our lives they are most often experienced simultaneously.
>
> *(Combahee River Collective 1981: 213)*

This is an early manifestation of challenging hetero-normativity, simultaneously in the women's movement and in the black movement. The demand for a 'development of integrated analysis and practice based upon the fact that the major systems of oppression are interlocking' (ibid.: 210) was followed, echoed and elaborated in black feminist scholars' work, for example in the famous book by Angela Davis (1981), *Women, Race and Class*. Strongly influenced by Marxism and the Frankfurt School, Davis insisted on the importance of 'class' as a crucial category for the analysis of black women's inequality, which intersects with gender and race. Davis revived a theme that had been fiercely discussed in the European women's movement at the beginning of the twentieth century, when Marxist feminists such as Clara Zetkin and Alexandra Kollontai (1918) clashed with the representatives of the bourgeois feminist movement over their disregard of class differences between women.[1] While these earlier concepts of race–class–gender in which the categories were portrayed as markers of difference and exclusion were added up to the 'triple oppression theory', intersectionality established a new agenda for women's and gender studies.

> Intersectionality is a conceptualization of the problem that attempts to capture both the structural and dynamic consequences of the interaction between two or more axes of subordination. It specifically addresses the manner in which racism, patriarchy, class oppression and other discriminatory systems create background inequalities that structure the relative positions of women, races, ethnicities, classes, and the like. Moreover, it addresses the way that specific acts and policies create burdens that flow along these axes constituting the dynamic or active aspects of disempowerment.
>
> *(Crenshaw 2002)*

Crucial for Crenshaw's framing of the concept is the interaction of the macro level (inequality structures functioning as social positioning) with the micro level (subjective experiences of discrimination and identity formation as an excluded group).

In summary, it was the analysis of the specific socioeconomic situation of black women in the USA which made it possible for the first time to speak of the simultaneity and mutual co-constitution of different categories of social differentiation, and to emphasize the specificity of the experiences shaped by these interactions. Crenshaw's term intersectionality, suggesting an imagery of black women being positioned in the very dangerous middle of an intersection, became a dazzling success; it was adopted in gender studies in more or less all English-speaking countries from the start (Davis 2008a: 68f.), and has made its journey into mainland Europe since the early 2000s.[2] Furthermore, it is now used by gender studies scholars from India, Africa and

Asia. In an effort to explain the eager adoption of the term in various regions of the world, Kathy Davis explains:

> Intersectionality takes up the political project of making the social and material consequences of the categories of gender/race/class visible, but does so by employing methodologies compatible with the poststructuralist project of deconstructing categories, unmasking universalism, and exploring the dynamic and contradictory working of power.
>
> *(ibid.: 74)*

Intersectionality clearly released new energy as an answer to the search for a satisfying theorization of the interactions between different social structures and identity positions.

Strands and positions

In her review of the intersectionality landscape, Leslie McCall (2005) distinguishes between three main approaches: the anti-categorical, the intra-categorical and the inter-categorical. The *anti-categorical* approach, strongly influenced by post-structuralism, focuses on the socially constructed nature of gender and other categories; its main interest lies in the deconstruction of categories which are unpacked as legitimization of essentialized/naturalized inequality. One example that comes to mind is Barack Obama's self-identification as a 'post-racial candidate' during the election campaign in 2008; his attempt can be interpreted as an act of resistance against coercive self-identification in one single category of race when, as a child of a black and a white parent, he could claim at least two. Ultimately, anti-categorialists completely reject (static) categories; they are rather sceptical intersectionalists (see Villa 2011).

While the proponents of the *intra-categorical* approach do not deny that categories are socially constructed, they argue that such categories are still needed; their aim is to fine-tune by marshalling the internal inconsistencies and complexities of these categories. Lastly, the advocates of an *inter-categorical* approach look for overlaps and mutual amplification of categories by reducing the analysis to one or two inter-group relations at a time. Their purpose is to focus on commonalities between the categories without falling back into simplistic deduction or the declaration of the primacy of one category. According to McCall's (contested) view, qualitative researchers favour the first and second approaches, while the inter-categorical approach is embraced by quantitative intersectionalists such as herself (McCall 2005: 1782).

Over the last 15 years a number of controversies have dominated the debate about intersectionality (see also Davis 2008b). First, various researchers contributed to the amendment of the categories beyond the race–class–gender triangle by adding nationality (Anthias and Yuval-Davis 1992), sexuality (McClintock 1995), able-bodied-ness/disability (Meekosha 1990) and age (Williams 1989). The plea for the recognition of differences such as religion, citizenship status (different 'belongings'), sedentariness (versus nomadism)[3] and geo-political location ('the West' versus 'the Rest') has led to further additions to the concept (Krüger-Potratz and Lutz 2002; Lutz 2001) and an attempt to summarize these categories as embodied, socio-spatial and economical diversifications (Lutz and Wenning 2001). This search for an *inclusive* conceptualization of multidimensional inequalities (open to further amendments) argues for the embedded consideration of more than one category (Leiprecht and Lutz 2005) by emphasizing the analysis of the categories' contradictory and conflicting relations to each other, instead of focusing on distinct and isolated realms of experience (see McClintock 1995). The amendment protagonists have been accused of arbitrariness (the 'etc.' reproach), and Anna Bredström (2006), justifiably, considers this multiplicity as the 'Achilles heel of Intersectionality'; indeed, the question of which differences are the most salient needs an answer, one of which is the present author's suggestion to consider 'race, class, gender' as a minimum standard to which other categories can be added, depending on the context and the research problem (Leiprecht and Lutz 2005).

Second, an ongoing dispute concerns the meaning of the categories 'race' and 'class' and the different conceptualizations in the USA and Europe (Knapp 2005; Marx Ferree 2011). Many European researchers regard 'ethnicity' as a more appropriate category than 'race' because, after the Holocaust, 'race' is first and foremost connected with Nazi racial ideology and is considered historical baggage that cannot be used in a positive way. In German mainstream sociology, this has resulted in not only avoiding the term but dismissing 'racism' as an analytical category altogether. However, a growing number of researchers inspired by anti-racist and post-colonial theory claim that 'ethnicity' carries a similar baggage of hierarchization and – in connection with 'culture' – has become a powerful tool of (symbolic, political and social) exclusion (Lutz *et al.* 2011: 10ff.). The question of whether the answer should be a reintroduction of 'race' into the European debate is the subject of heated discussions (see Crenshaw 2011; Lewis 2013). Likewise, researchers have warned against equating the meaning of 'class' in the US context with the European meaning of the term (Marx Ferree 2011). All in all, these debates mirror a genuine effort to deal with the travelling of theory and its adaptation in multiple geo-political societies and settings.

Third, the question has been asked: What exactly is intersectionality? A buzzword? A theory? A concept? A heuristic device? A method? An analytical tool for textual analysis? A living practice?

I shall restrict myself to mentioning a few contributions to these debates. Kathy Davis (2008a,b), for example, regards intersectionality as a theory that goes far beyond its appearance as a 'buzzword', as it offers new potential and perspectives for the connectivity of a broad range of social science scholars' approaches; she argues that its attraction lies in particular in its open-ness, ambiguities and contradictions. Katharina Walgenbach (2010) goes even further by con-sidering intersectionality as a *new paradigm* for the scientific community in that it offers a set of terms, theoretical interventions, premises, problem definitions and suggested solutions. Klinger and Knapp (2005) embrace intersectionality's potential for the building of 'grand' theory, but argue that on the structural level the term is unable to identify how and by what means race, class and gender as separate categories are constituted as social categories. Moreover, they are concerned with the intersectionalist tendency to let go of 'gender' as a master category (by declaring that no category is sacrosanct) because they fear a political backlash in academia: once gender is regarded as a decentred category it could easily be made superfluous. Others, like myself, consider the concept a heuristic device that is particularly helpful in detecting the over-lapping and co-construction of visible and – at first sight – invisible strands of inequality (Lutz 2001). In this context, I consider the proposal by Mary Matsuda to ask 'the other question' a helpful methodological tool.

> The way I try to understand the interconnection of all forms of subordination is through a method I call 'the other question'. When I see something that looks racist, I ask 'Where is the patriarchy in this?' When I see something sexist, I ask 'Where is the heterosexism in this?' When I see something that looks homophobic, I ask 'Where are the class interests in this?'
>
> *(Matsuda 1991: 1189)*

This may sound like an easy procedure, as it offers the tantalizing possibility of exposing multiple positions and power inequalities as they appear in any social practice, institutional arrangement or cultural representation; however, it requires a rather complicated analytical process and, given the openness of the invisible, it is not clear when one can stop (Ludvig 2006).

Recently, some intersectionalists (Cho *et al.* 2013) have argued that it is more important to ask what intersectionality *does* than to argue about what it is, pointing to the political legacy and goals of the founding 'mothers' in the USA. Insisting that intersectionality is first and foremost a tool for making visible various strands of discrimination, these authors reject the now popular use of intersectionality in a managerial context where it is purely considered as an addition to gender mainstreaming.

Fourth, another hotly debated subject is the question of the level on which intersectionality – considered as a methodology – does its work, i.e. on the structural or the individual level.

Floya Anthias (1998) has suggested a multi-level analysis that works on four levels: (a) the level of discrimination (experience); (b) the actors' level (inter-subjective praxis); (c) the institutional level (institutional regimes); and (d) the level of representation (symbolic and discursive) (see also the adaptation of this model by Winker and Degele 2011). Lutz and Davis (2005) shift attention from how structures of racism, class discrimination and sexism *determine* individuals' identities and practices to how individuals ongoingly and flexibly *negotiate* their multiple and converging identities in the context of everyday life. Introducing the term *doing intersectionality*, the authors explore how individuals creatively and often in surprising ways draw upon various aspects of their multiple identities as a resource to gain control over their lives. We show how 'gender' or 'race' are invariably linked to structures of domination, can also mobilize or deconstruct disempowering discourses, even undermine and transform oppressive practices. We thereby show that individuals are not always and in every situation multiply vulnerable, but they develop strategies of resistance by drawing on multiple identities. Nancy Fraser (2003) gives a good summary of this approach: 'Rather, individuals are nodes of convergence for multiple, cross-cutting axes of subordination. Frequently disadvantaged along some axes and simultaneously advantaged along others, they wage for recognition in modern regimes' (ibid.: 57). Here the stress is on the understanding of individuals not only as dominated by oppression in all fields of life but also as people who – under certain circumstances – can make use of privileged aspects of identity.

The concept of intersectionality is also used in the construction of the European Union's anti-discrimination law – see the picture gallery from *Tackling Multiple Discrimination: Practices, Policies and Laws* (European Commission 2007). This is an illustration of an understanding of identities as simultaneously merging advantaged and disadvantaged social positioning.

Challenges and future lines of investigation

Looking at the preceding example, it should be evident that intersectionality has long left the field of gender studies; it has been imported by sociology, education, anthropology, psychology, political sciences, law and literary studies, health studies and social work and many other (sub)disciplines dealing with social inequalities and identities. A myriad of divisions among intersectionalists have already been mentioned. In this final part I want to expand on other fields of application.

Agreeing with those critics who want to see intersectionality embedded in the broader theoretical frame of inequality research, I argue for the use of theoretical tools that go beyond a pure assessment of the overlap and co-construction of categories of difference. As a demonstration, I use the example from Steven Vertovec's introduction to this handbook, where he refers to a *New Yorker* cartoon which depicts a person replying to a doorstep pollster, saying: 'How would you like me to answer that question? As a member of my ethnic group, educational class, income group, or religious category?' While this cartoon mirrors the multitude of social identities that individuals can embody and shows that a uni-categorical identification is incommensurable in multi-ethnic societies, it is also evident that this person fails to mention gender or race as markers of diversity. This can be interpreted as an indication that the pollster has already recorded these two characteristics based on visual perception – an instance of the frequent implicit naturalization of these two social divisions while the other aspects are less obvious. Thus, not all categories of difference are equally salient; moreover, their impact on social positioning can be extremely dissimilar. It is, therefore, important to investigate diversity in the context of power relations and analyse in detail *which* of all possible differential facets makes the difference, creates unequal identities. The sociological theory of social stratification may be helpful here. Social stratification 'relates to the differential hierarchical locations of individuals and groupings of people on society's grids of power' (Yuval-Davis 2011: 162). The reduction of most social stratification theories being configured within the container of the nation state needs to be overcome by consideration of the continually shifting 'orders of stratification' on the global and the regional as well as on the national and the local level, and we should likewise 'reject the naturalisation of any construction of social divisions, and challenge the priorisation of any of them, such as class and gender' (ibid.: 166).

In her exemplification of such an approach, Nira Yuval-Davis writes:

> I find it problematic, for instance, that the construction of the 'black woman' is automatically assumed, unless otherwise specified, to be that of a minority black woman living in white Western societies. The majority of black women in today's world are black women in black societies. This has major implications for a global intersectional stratification analysis.
>
> *(ibid.: 162)*

Implicit in this statement is the conviction that debates about intersectionality and social inequalities can no longer reduce the analysis of gender, class and race to oppression and discrimination, but need to consider the 'privileged' positionings within and between them – a position that is deeply contested, as many intersectionality scholars implicitly and explicitly cherish a master category of oppression.

Another debate that is being conducted is the search for a more adequate metaphor. Many criticize 'intersection' as a too rigid visualization, one that ignores the fact that stratification is better depicted as a matter of relations rather than categories. Whether this can be Nina Lykke's botanical image of a 'rhizome', an underground plant stem that moves horizontally in all directions and bears both roots and shoots (Lykke 2011: 211), or her earlier idea of a nodal point, or something completely different, is still an open question.

Notes

1 Marxist–feminist theorists of the 1980s revisited this debate in their analysis (see Barrett and McIntosh 1982, Haug 1978).
2 For various adoptions, see Lutz *et al.* (2011: 4ff.).
3 See, for example, the current debate about the Roma people in Europe.

References

Anthias, F. (1998) 'Rethinking Social Divisions: Some Notes Towards a Theoretical Framework', *Sociological Review*, 46(3): 505–35.

Anthias, F. and Yuval-Davis, N. (1992) *Racialized Boundaries: Race, Nation, Gender, Colour and Class and the Anti-Racist Struggle*, London: Routledge.

Barrett, M. and McIntosh, M. (1982) *The Anti-Social Family*, London: Verso.

Brah, A. and Phoenix, A. (2004) 'Ain't I a Woman? Revisiting Intersectionality', *Journal of International Women's Studies*, 5(3): 75–86.

Bredström, A. (2006) 'Intersectionality: A Challenge for Feminist HIV/AIDS Research?', *European Journal of Women's Studies*, 13(3): 229–43.

Cho, S., Crenshaw, K. and McCall, L. (2013) 'Toward a Field of Intersectionality Studies: Theory, Applications, and Praxis', *Signs*, 38(4): 785–810.

Combahee River Collective (1981) 'A Black Feminist Statement', in C. Moraga and G. Anzaldúa (eds) *This Bridge Called My Back: Writings by Radical Women of Color*, New York, NY: Kitchen Table Women of Color Press.

Crenshaw, K. (2002) 'Background Paper for the Expert Meeting on the Gender-Related Aspects of Race Discrimination', *Revista Estudos Feministas*, 10(1): 171–88.

——(2011) 'Postscript', in H. Lutz, M.T. Herrera Vivar and L. Supik (eds) *Framing Intersectionality: Debates on a Multi-Faceted Concept in Gender Studies*, Farnham, UK: Ashgate.

Davis, A. (1981) *Women, Race and Class*, New York, NY: Random House.

Davis, K. (2008a) 'Intersectionality as a Buzzword: A Sociology of Science Perspective on What Makes a Feminist Theory Successful', *Feminist Theory*, 9(1): 67–85.

——(2008b) 'Intersectionality in Transatlantic Perspective', in C. Klinger and G.A. Knapp (eds) *ÜberKreuzungen Fremdheit, Ungleichheit, Differenz*, Münster: Westfälisches Dampfboot.

European Commission (2007) *Tackling Multiple Discrimination: Practices, Policies and Laws*, Luxembourg: Office for Official Publications of the European Communities. Online. Available HTTP: <http://ec.europa.eu/social/main.jsp?catId=738&pubId=51> (accessed 10 October 2013).

Fraser, N. (2003) 'Social Justice in the Age of Identity Politics: Redistribution, Recognition, and Participation', in N. Fraser and A. Honneth (eds) *Redistribution or Recognition? A Political-Philosophical Exchange*, London: Verso.

Haug, F. (1978) *Für eine Sozialistische Frauenbewegung*, Berlin: Argument.

Klinger, C. and Knapp, G.A. (2005) 'Achsen der Ungleichheit – Achsen der Differenz: Verhältnisbestimmung von Klasse, Geschlecht, "Rasse"/Ethnizität', *Transit*, 29: 72–95.

Knapp, G.A. (2005) '"Intersectionality" – ein Neues Paradigma Feministischer Theorie? Zur transatlantischen Reise von "Race, Class, Gender"', *Feministische Studien*, 1(2005): 68–82.

Kollontai, A. (1971) [1918] *The Autobiography of a Sexually Emancipated Communist Woman*, New York, NY: Herder and Herder.

Krüger-Potratz, M. and Lutz, H. (2002) 'Sitting at a Crossroads – Rekonstruktive und Systematische Überlegungen zum Wissenschaftlichen Umgang mit Differenzen', *Tertium Comparationis*, 8(2): 81–92.

Leiprecht, R. and Lutz, H. (2005) 'Intersektionalität im Klassenzimmer: Ethnizität, Klasse, Geschlecht', in R. Leiprecht and A. Kerber (eds) *Schule in der Einwanderungsgesellschaft*, Schwalbach: Wochenschau Verlag.

Lewis, G. (2013) 'Unsafe Travel: Experiencing Intersectionality and Feminist Displacements', *Signs*, 38(4): 869–92.

Ludvig, A. (2006) 'Differences Between Women? Intersecting Voices in a Female Narrative', *European Journal of Women's Studies*, 13(3): 245–58.

Lutz, H. (2001) 'Differenz als Rechenaufgabe? Über die Relevanz der Kategorien Race, Class und Gender', in H. Lutz and N. Wenning (eds) *Unterschiedlich Verschieden: Differenz in der Erziehungswissenschaft*, Opladen: Leske und Budrich.

Lutz, H. and Wenning, N. (2001) *Unterschiedlich Verschieden: Differenz in der Erziehungswissenschaft*, Opladen: Leske und Budrich.

Lutz, H. and Davis, K. (2005) 'Geschlechterforschung und Biographieforschung: Intersektionalität als Biographische Ressource am Beispiel einer außergewöhnlichen Frau', in B. Völter, B. Dausien, H. Lutz and G. Rosenthal (eds) *Biographieforschung im Diskurs*, Wiesbaden: VS.

Lutz, H., Herrera Vivar, M.T. and Supik, L. (2011) *Framing Intersectionality: Debates on a Multi-Faceted Concept in Gender Studies*, Farnham, UK: Ashgate.

Lykke, N. (2011) 'Intersectional Analysis: Black Box or Useful Critical Feminist Thinking Technology?', in H. Lutz, M.T. Herrera Vivar and L. Supik (eds) *Framing Intersectionality: Debates on a Multi-Faceted Concept in Gender Studies*, Farnham, UK: Ashgate.

McCall, L. (2005) 'The Complexity of Intersectionality', *Signs*, 30(3): 1771–800.

McClintock, A. (1995) *Imperial Leather: Race, Gender and Sexuality in the Colonial Contest*, New York, NY: Routledge.

Marx Ferree, M. (2011) 'The Discursive Politics of Feminist Intersectionality', in H. Lutz, M.T. Herrera Vivar and L. Supik (eds) *Framing Intersectionality: Debates on a Multi-Faceted Concept in Gender Studies*, Farnham, UK: Ashgate.

Matsuda, M. (1991) 'Beside My Sister, Facing the Enemy: Legal Theory out of Coalition', *Stanford Law Review*, 43(6): 1183–92.

Meekosha, H. (1990) 'Is Feminism Able-Bodied? Reflections from Between the Trenches', *Refractory Girl*, (August): 34–42.

Villa, P.I. (2011) 'Embodiment is Always More: Intersectionality, Subjection and the Body', in H. Lutz, M.T. Herrera Vivar and L. Supik (eds) *Framing Intersectionality: Debates on a Multi-Faceted Concept in Gender Studies*, Farnham, UK: Ashgate.

Walgenbach, K. (2010) 'Postscriptum: Intersektionalität – Offenheit, interne Kontroversen und Komplexität als Ressourcen eines gemeinsamen Orientierungsrahmens', in H. Lutz, M.T. Herrera Vivar and L. Supik (eds) *Fokus Intersektionalität – Bewegungen und Verortungen eines vielschichtigen Konzeptes*, Wiesbaden: VS.

Williams, F. (1989) *Social Policy: A Critical Introduction: Issues of Race, Gender and Class*, Cambridge, UK: Polity.

Winker, G. and Degele, N. (2011) 'Intersectionality as Multi-level Analysis: Dealing with Social Inequality', *European Journal of Women's Studies*, 18(1): 51–66.

Yuval-Davis, N. (2011) 'Beyond the Recognition and Re-distribution Dichotomy: Intersectionality and Stratification', in H. Lutz, M.T. Herrera Vivar and L. Supik (eds) *Framing Intersectionality: Debates on a Multi-Faceted Concept in Gender Studies*, Farnham, UK: Ashgate.

40

Cultural complexity

Thomas Hylland Eriksen

Since the study of complex societies is as old as the social sciences themselves, the use of the term 'cultural complexity' to denote a particular kind of situation requires some initial elaboration.

To begin with, it may be useful to distinguish between social and cultural complexity. The former may well refer to differentiation along the lines of class and occupation, but cultural diversity is not necessarily a cause or consequence of this. Cultural complexity, by contrast, refers to variations in cognitive and symbolic phenomena such as world-views, notions of personhood, domestic practices, religious beliefs and other aspects of ways of life.

As this book shows, it has long been recognised that societies are often diverse at the level of symbolic meaning and subjective world-structures, as well as being socially differentiated. Yet culture still tends to be conceptualised in terms of sharing, rather than in terms of communication. Although this perspective has produced genuine insights into the diversity of humanity, it always had its limitations, and has, in an era of accelerated globalisation, become theoretically obsolete. Clifford Geertz (1973), arguably the most influential theorist of culture in the latter decades of the twentieth century, initially compared the integration of culture to a fugue by Bach – a highly symmetrical, stringently integrated kind of composition – but later conceded that a more appropriate metaphor might be that of an octopus, a literally many-stranded organism with a weak central command system (Geertz cited in Shweder 1984). However, he still saw culture as something that could be pluralised and which was bounded. Ulf Hannerz (1992), in a major work entitled *Cultural Complexity*, refrains from defining the central concept of the book, but notes at the outset that the term 'complex' is 'about as attractive as the concept "messy"' (ibid.: 6). Like Anthony Wallace (1970) before him, Hannerz proposes to study culture as *the organization of diversity* rather than *the replication of uniformity*. In Hannerz's analyses of cultural flows in the contemporary world, which he often describes as cultural creolisation, symbolic processes of diverse origins may melt together or react through mutual repulsion or confrontation, but they never result in a permanent, uniform cultural form.

The concept of cultural complexity adds a necessary dimension to the intellectual toolbox needed for a full appreciation of human diversity in today's world. Rather than seeing society as composed either of a particular cultural group or of a finite number of such groups, cultural complexity takes the flows of meaning and their expressions in particular fields or situations as the main point of departure. This chapter first discusses the concept itself and its ramifications, before describing some empirical fields where it is needed, returning to the concept at the end.

Complex flows

Wallace's conceptualisation of diversity rests on a psychodynamic perspective where a relatively uniform social system gives rise to a wide range of individual world-views in societies with no ethnic variation (his ethnographic field was Native Americans). By contrast, most anthropologists working in this field approach complexity with the assumption that it resides not chiefly in the individual mind, but rather in the jungle of meanings and significant symbols in the socio-cultural domain itself. Complexity, thus, is a property of the public sphere.

Cultural complexity, as it is conceptualised here, is related to several of the other perspectives discussed in this book. It departs from the recognition that contemporary societies are far from uniform and seamlessly integrated, and characterised by variation along many lines. It may also be pointed out that the kind of variation characterising many if not most societies today is of a different order to that typified in historical cities and empires (see Grillo 1998). Although many anthropologists have written about culturally complex societies (see Banton (1966) for some early contributions), few have defined or operationalised complexity beyond the commonplace that it entails the coexistence of several culturally distinctive groups or categories within a shared social or political space. One interesting, largely ignored attempt to conceptualise social complexity was Fredrik Barth's (1972) typology of social forms, based on the distribution of statuses and allocation of tasks, ranging from the relatively undifferentiated band via caste societies to modern individualistic societies, where the number of statuses is almost unlimited. Regarding cultural as opposed to social complexity, an early, influential contribution was Lee Drummond's (1980) study from Guyana where he identified a 'cultural continuum' within which individuals were differently positioned, thereby showing empirically the inadequacies of approaches to multiethnic societies which presupposed cultural boundaries and similarity within each ethnic group.

The concept of super-diversity (Vertovec 2007) and its empirical foundation in research on early twenty-first-century London indicates the need for a view of cultural streams as highly mobile, shifting and partly overlapping, as does Rogers Brubaker's (2004) notion of ethnicity without groups. In both cases, the very idea of relatively bounded, stable ethnic groups becomes an obstacle to studying the facts on the ground, which turn out to be less tidy than census data may suggest.

What is distinctive about the present approach to complexity is that it is not based on an assumption about the existence of discrete groups based on cultural sharing. Cultural meaning varies along many lines, of which the ethnic is but one. Cultural complexity can, thus, be compared by analogy to the findings of Cavalli-Sforza and Cavalli-Sforza (1995) regarding the genetic landscape in Europe. Studying the frequencies and distributions of a significant number of genes, they draw a genetic map where the variation along different genes follows different lines. The explanation is that migrations into and within the continent have taken different courses (ibid.: 144–59). As a result, a German may share some genes with Bulgarians that he does not share with the French and vice versa, and, if one were to draw genetic boundaries between groups or categories, it would be necessary to specify the criteria. Similarly, in research on cultural worlds where complexity is part of the analytical apparatus, assumptions about cultural sharing or sameness have to be specific and precise, since the existence of relatively homogeneous groups sharing 'the same culture' cannot be taken for granted.

Complexity as a way of seeing

To a certain degree, scientific findings depend not only on empirical delineations and problem formulations, but also on the chosen concepts. If complexity is assumed from the outset, complex descriptions necessarily follow, rather than monocausal explanations or simplistic generalisations. This applies, in principle, to any cultural phenomenon, but the necessity of a complex gaze is most urgent in societies characterised by the partly overlapping confluence of several streams. Female circumcision, or genital mutilation, may be an example.

Highly politicised and almost universally seen as objectionable in Western societies, female circumcision is widespread in some parts of Africa, including Somalia. A common interpretation of the practice sees it as an expression of male control over female sexuality, and many Somali and Ethiopian men and women in diasporas support this view. It is nevertheless a fact that women tend to be responsible for the operation and ritual context surrounding it, and that many circumcised women claim that they would have been less 'whole' and less 'pure' if they had not been circumcised (Talle 2010). At least four approaches to female circumcision in the diaspora are necessary for a complex account to be possible: (a) within a context where virtually everybody is circumcised, it appears as necessary and natural; (b) within a diasporic context, uncertainty and disagreement around the practice emerge since migrant women are surrounded by native women as well as other minority women who are uncircumcised; (c) from a standard majority point of view, in the same diasporic context, genital cutting is seen as barbaric, and it is banned by the authorities; (d) in the frontier area between (b) and (c), a fourth perspective emerges, where negotiations take place regarding the possibility of removing the practice without violating the autonomy of the people concerned. All four perspectives (and doubtless others) need to be investigated for a complex analysis to be possible.

Edgar Morin, a major theorist of complexity, similarly exemplifies his position through a discussion of sacrifice (Morin 2001: 37ff.; see also Eriksen 2007). Although elegant Darwinist, structuralist, structural-functionalist and culturalist accounts of 'the true nature of sacrifice' abound, Morin distinguishes between no less than seven distinctive aspects of sacrifice that cannot be reduced to one another, ranging from the magical exploitation of the power of death to reciprocity between groups, a safe channelling of violent impulses and the strengthening of societal integration.

Drawing extensively on a different source of inspiration, namely the natural science literature on complexity, the sociologist David Byrne (1998) arrives at a mode of analysis, looking at phenomena such as the spread of tuberculosis, education and urban planning in England, with an applied social-engineering orientation. His main argument is that a complex analytical gaze leading to complex descriptions are to be preferred because of their naturalism, which makes policies more effective.

This point seemed to be confirmed as I was contacted, just as I had finished writing the preceding paragraph, by a journalist who wanted an account of the riots in Stockholm in May 2013. I explained that monocausal explanations were ultimately unhelpful, and that at least five interwoven stories were necessary to understand what had happened: the crisis in Europe leading to insecurity and loss of trust; the growth in youth unemployment in Sweden; the rise of anti-Western Islamic groups; the feeling of ethnic discrimination and exclusion experienced by many minority youths; and, finally, the warm weather, which had made the Swedish public spaces more inviting than usual for informal interaction. At the end of my monologue, the journalist meekly asked if aggression might have something to do with it. I agreed, but pointed out that aggression has to come from somewhere and be directed somewhere; in this case, both origin and destination were complex.

Concerning the kind of complexity primarily dealt with here, suffice it to say at this point that what matters is to view culture not in terms of sharing or sameness, but in terms of communication and diversity, not only at the level of the group or category, but also at the level of the individual and the situation. This approach presents a far less tidy picture of the social world than the notions of ethnic diversity associated with place which have been common in studies of contemporary ethnicity.

Finally, cultural complexity may well, and often does, coexist with ethnic boundedness. Ethnic diversity in itself says little about cultural variation since the former is about social organisation and networks, while the latter is about symbolic meaning. Culture varies in a continuous or analogue way, while identities are, at least in theory, discontinuous and digital (bounded). We now move from the conceptual and methodological work to considering some empirical areas where the concept of complexity has proved to be especially fruitful.

The empirical continuum

There is a very considerable academic literature on migration, diasporas and transnationalism, but one growing category of people seems to be largely neglected, namely those of mixed parentage. They rarely appear as separate statistical categories, and policies between countries vary as to their classification. In many schools in larger European cities, nevertheless, a significant proportion of the children have one native and one immigrant parent. Many of them seem to identify with the majority, but most have a complex social or ethnic identity. They are anomalies in societies based on the existence of unambiguous ethnic identities, but are neither more nor less anomalous than everybody else in a society where complexity is taken for granted. How people with mixed origins identify, and which cultural traditions they attach themselves to, is not only variable, but also unpredictable. In the coastal Sami areas of northern Norway, where cultural Norwegianisation has weakened Sami language, tradition and identity, and where intermarriage has led to the proliferation of 'halfies', intensified identity politics has encouraged especially the young to choose between a Sami or a Norwegian identity (Hovland 1996). Siblings may choose opposing identities, and there appears to be no simple causal explanation for why they do so, just as two Muslim sisters from Oslo's East End may choose piousness and radical feminism, respectively.

No facile assumptions about such aspects of culture as religious persuasions, political views, home language, gender relations or even concepts of personhood, can be made in a setting of cultural complexity. A few examples may illustrate this.

As in other European countries, controversies around the continuum love marriage–arranged marriage–enforced marriage are common in Norway, with Asian immigrants being the main target. Significantly, all the major positions on these controversies are represented within the Pakistani Norwegian category of citizens: defenders of tradition, defenders of liberal individualism, critical voices problematising assumptions of free choice in the majority and dissenting voices claiming that all arranged marriages are de facto enforced marriages. In order for the full diversity in perspectives and values of society to be represented in the debate, in other words, no participation from anybody but Norwegian Pakistanis would have been necessary.

That migrants from the same areas should hold different political views and different perspectives on their cultural traditions, including religion, comes as no surprise. However, it needs to be pointed out that the complexity in question bifurcates right down to the level of the individual: each person expresses a complex blend of diverse influences, and no two are identical. Groups or cultural communities only exist in particular respects, not in absolute terms.

Complexity and simplification

Cultural complexity and its challenges are intensified in the global information society. The almost unlimited number of possible combinations of statuses indicating social complexity in modern settings is now increasingly matched by a growth in the possible number of social identities and of cultural flows. In a culturally complex setting, mixing is endemic and difficult to avoid; moreover, no two individuals represent exactly the same kind of cultural mélange. During research in an ethnically mixed suburb of Oslo, we became acquainted with a young family of Vietnamese origin. Mapping out their allegiances and orientations, it quickly became apparent that they were particularly attached neither to the place (suburb, city or country) nor to the diasporic community of Vietnamese scattered across the city and country. Instead, their main social and cultural identity was religious: they belonged to a Protestant congregation and gravitated, in their spare time, towards its church, played its devotional music in their flat, read their publications and tried, in a modest way, to get their neighbours interested in this particular true faith.

Although a great number of Pakistani Norwegians celebrate the Pakistani national day, hosted by the Embassy every year on 23 March, those who gather for this occasion do not necessarily share more, in terms of world-view, values and way of life, than some of them do with their ethnic majority neighbours. At least this cannot be taken for granted.

Precisely because the forces leading to an unprecedented degree of cultural complexity are so strong, counter-reactions are growing in intensity and also visibility. It is important to understand ethnic nationalism, puritan religion and group-based attempts to withdraw wholly or partly from the cultural whirlwind of modernity in this context. In situations where social group boundaries remain intact, so that the primary identification of individuals is with bounded ethnic, national, religious or linguistic groups, attempts are often made to patrol the cultural boundaries in order to create congruence between the social group and its cultural content. This is far from easy, since group boundaries may be fixed, yet cultural flows continuously cross them and create new patterns and forms. When group boundaries are less clear cut because of a high incidence of people of mixed descent or other liminal or anomalous persons, the border work also entails the establishment of criteria for inclusion and exclusion from the group. This may be the case with some indigenous groups where intermarriage with outsiders has been common (however, in some groups mixed origins are a criterion for membership, such as the South African Griqua or the Canadian Métis), but the most publicised and consequential forms of boundary work along these lines concern citizenship and membership in national communities.

Attempts to purify, homogenise and standardise cultural content within a group follow the same general logic as the implementation of criteria for group membership, but should be distinguished from it. A clearly bounded group may yet be culturally diverse; conversely, sharing of cultural codes may well cut across group boundaries. The social and cultural processes of boundary-making nevertheless are not independent of each other. As Ernest Gellner (1983) showed in his *Nations and Nationalism*, a main aim of nationalism consists in creating a homogeneous culture within the territory of the nation, ideally encompassing all members of the nation. Gellner wrote chiefly of nineteenth-century nation-building in Europe. In today's more fragmented world, the logic of nationalism continues to function, but in murkier waters: the target groups for attempts to standardise culture and reduce inherent complexity are often not territorially based, politically sovereign or even clearly delineated. When, for example, Salafi clerics explain why their conservative and puritan brand of Islam should be the norm for all

Muslims, they neither have the support of a state nor the privilege of speaking to audiences that can a priori be assumed to share their world-view.

In contemporary identity politics, the tension between cultural complexity and simplification is a key feature. It is sometimes described as a conflict between modernity and tradition, where tradition is 'unscalable' and locally embedded (Tsing 2012) while modernity is standardised, but there is a paradox inherent in this view which is endemic in the ongoing debate about globalisation: does globalisation make people more similar or more different; does it chiefly lead to homogenisation or heterogenisation?

On the one hand, standardisation is a central aspect of globalisation (Eriksen 2013): the spread of a monetary economy, of English as the world's second language, of Facebook accounts and fast-food outlets seem to reduce complexity in the sense that formerly discrete and distinctive societies become more similar at the level of cultural values, consumption and ways of life (Ritzer 2004).

However, these very processes of globalisation also lead to the proliferation of new cultural forms – mixing, hybridisation and creolisation (Appadurai 1996; Hannerz 1996), migration resulting in unprecedented forms of diversity, diversification in ways of life, beliefs and world-views – precisely because so many more options are now available.

It is true that globalisation creates shared templates and a shared grammar, but they are often used to express difference and uniqueness at the level of the group or individual. The extent to which globalising processes affect local life-worlds should also not be exaggerated. It may sometimes appear more comprehensive than it actually is.

Cultural complexity and individualism

In a telling simile, Gellner (1983) compared the world before and after nationalism with the work of two painters. Oskar Kokoschka is known for his use of bright, often contrasting colours, sometimes depicted as overlapping, multicoloured dots – this was the world of a multitude of small identities before the advent of nationalism. The paintings of Amedeo Modigliani – often portraits of women – by contrast were characterised by large, single-colour surfaces which did not mingle; the world of nationalism. In a rejoinder to Gellner, Hannerz (1996) argues that contemporary cultural complexity seems to suggest 'Kokoschka's return', where the multicoloured dots have again taken over from the monochromatic surfaces. Although Hannerz is obviously right, it needs to be emphasised that the kind of cultural complexity witnessed in the globalising information society is of a qualitatively different order to the diversity typical of the pre-modern world. It is not a product of limited contact and historical uniqueness, but on the contrary the result of intensified contact and full participation in contemporary world history. In order to come fully to grips with contemporary cultural complexity, it should be understood as a product of individualism, or perhaps more accurately the tension between individualism and non-individualistic conceptualisations of personhood.

Individualism is associated with rights and self-determination at the level of the individual. De facto citizenship in a state and participation in a monetary economy today are almost ubiquitous and contribute to individualisation in crucial ways. Only in a society where individualism is broadly embedded in practices and world-views is the kind of cultural complexity described here possible. In complex caste societies, such as those in traditional India, statuses come in packages in the sense that caste membership and religion determine a person's place in society. In contemporary India, where the significance of both caste and religion is contested, a much broader palette of options and possible combinations of statuses is available.

The conflicts created by the tension between standardisation and complexity described here presuppose individualism: persons are asked to take a stance; the path they take is a result of personal decisions, not of obligations founded in tradition. Conflicts involving opposing views of personhood may appear to be of a different kind since they confront tradition and modernity openly. Individuals may be denounced as defectors if they take decisions deemed to be detrimental to group identity or tradition, for example by marrying outside of the group or declaring allegiance to values not associated with the group's traditions. The tension, in this case, is between views of personhood as being embedded in a cultural tradition or as being the product of free agency and personal decisions. However, resistance to modern individualism is also largely a result of individualism. In a post-traditional society, to use Giddens' (1991) term, traditions continue to exist, but they have ceased to 'go without saying' and have to be chosen actively. Resistance to individualism and secularism may be interpreted as a defence of group-based multiculturalism (or monoculturalism, if the group is dominant) and a rejection of cultural complexity the way it is defined here.

Cultural complexity should be seen simultaneously as a property of the contemporary world and as an analytical approach to its conceptualisation. It does not deny the existence of bounded groups founded on assumptions of shared culture, but neither does it take them for granted; and the question of cultural similarity within a society is asked in the most open-ended way possible: there is no a priori answer to the question of 'how much' or 'what' people need to have in common, culturally speaking, in order to keep a society going together. The question is an empirical one. Finally, it should be kept in mind, as pointed out by Edgar Morin (1994: 10) in one of his latest statements on complexity, that: 'Complexity is a problem word and not a solution word'.

References

Appadurai, A. (1996) *Modernity at Large*, Minneapolis, MN: University of Minnesota Press.

Banton, M. (1966) *The Social Anthropology of Complex Societies*, Tavistock: Auflage.

Barth, F. (1972) 'Analytical Dimensions in Comparison of Social Organizations', *American Anthropologist*, 74(1–2): 207–20.

Brubaker, R. (2004) *Ethnicity Without Groups*, Cambridge, MA: Harvard University Press.

Byrne, D. (1998) *Complexity Theory and the Social Sciences*, London: Routledge.

Cavalli-Sforza, L.L. and Cavalli-Sforza, F. (1995) *The Great Human Diasporas*, New York, NY: Basic Books.

Drummond, L. (1980) 'The Cultural Continuum: A Theory of Intersystems', *Man* 15(2): 352–74

Eriksen, T.H. (2007) 'Complexity in Social and Cultural Integration: Some Analytical Dimensions', *Ethnic and Racial Studies*, 30(6): 1055–169.

—(2013) *Globalization: The Key Concepts*, 2nd edn, London: Bloomsbury.

Geertz, C. (1973) *The Interpretation of Cultures*, New York, NY: Basic Books.

Gellner, E. (1983) *Nations and Nationalism*, Oxford, UK: Blackwell.

Giddens, A. (1991) *Modernity and Self-Identity*, Cambridge, UK: Polity.

Grillo, R. (1998) *Pluralism and the Politics of Difference: State, Culture and Ethnicity in Comparative Perspective*, Oxford, UK: Clarendon.

Hannerz, U. (1992) *Cultural Complexity: Studies in the Social Organization of Meaning*, New York, NY: Columbia University Press.

—(1996) *Transnational Connections*, London: Routledge.

Hovland, A. (1996) *Moderne Urfolk: Samisk ungdom i bevegelse*, Oslo: Cappelen Akademisk.

Morin, E. (2001) *L'identité Humaine: La Méthode*, Paris: Seuil.

—(1994) *La Complexité humaine*, Textes choisis, Paris: Champs Flammarion, coll. l'Essentiel

Ritzer, G. (2004) *The Globalization of Nothing*, London: Sage.

Shweder, R. (1984) 'A Colloquy of Culture Theorists', in R. Shweder and R.A. LeVine (eds) *Culture Theory*, Cambridge, UK: Cambridge University Press.

Talle, A. (2010) 'Getting the Ethnography "Right": On Female Circumcision in Exile', in M. Melhuus, J.P. Mitchell and H. Wulff (eds) *Ethnographic Practice in the Present*, Oxford, NY: Berghahn.

Tsing, A.L. (2012) 'On Nonscalability', *Common Knowledge*, 18(3): 505–24.

Vertovec, S. (2007) 'Super-diversity and its Implications', *Ethnic and Racial Studies*, 30(6): 1024–54.

Wallace, A.F.C. (1970) *Culture and Personality*, New York, NY: Random House.

41

Critical diversity literacy

Essentials for the twenty-first century

Melissa Steyn

The concept of critical diversity literacy (CDL) has been a work in progress for more than a decade.[1] It represents an attempt to distil into a single framework the analytic proficiencies I believe a qualification in diversity studies should provide. The particular framing is the outcome of a confluence of factors: the specific higher education context in post-apartheid South Africa where students enter a society characterized by an impetus towards transformation, integration and greater equity; the deepening of my own work on whiteness towards recognizing the family resemblances in how privilege and oppression operate along other axes of difference; and a serendipitous encounter with France Winddance Twine's concept of racial literacy,[2] which I recast, developed and extended along new lines for a different purpose.

In Twine's empirically grounded work, racial literacy describes a 'reading practice' acquired by the white partners of British interracial couples to manage the racial climate affecting the lives of their children. She helpfully casts racial literacy as 'a sociopolitical vision'. The framework of CDL, by contrast, synthesizes relevant trends in social theory pertaining to questions of diversity, difference and otherness. It is an ethical sociopolitical stance in a world increasingly characterized by heterogeneous spaces – organizational, social and public.

This chapter will briefly explicate the concept of 'critical diversity literacy' (CDL) before presenting the model, giving necessarily brief, broad-stroke comments on each of the criteria, which would obviously be further developed and nuanced when taught.[3]

Critical diversity literacy

The new context

It has become commonplace to note the complexity of the unfolding world attributable to its increasing diversity, the manner in which differences of many varieties increasingly co-exist – more or less functionally – as the globe 'shrinks'. The discrete national state belonging to a homogeneous population group has been recognized as a myth of modernity. Not all of the new complexity we call our diversity is the result of mobility within and across borders; it is also a function of the changing relationships between people who are differently positioned within the nation state. Under the changing social imaginary of our times described by Vertovec (2012), a more rights-based ethos has taken hold and some oppressed groups now claim the right to be visible, affirmed and included in how we think about ourselves as social collectivities.

It is obvious that such a changed environment requires new skills from the citizens that inhabit it. This is particularly true of those who have acquired a high level of education. Those who exercise leadership within their respective fields will need to be freer from the constraints of a single history, and understand human reality as multilayered and multiperspectival, shifting, ambivalent and open to yet unknown possibilities. In short, they need to be literate in reading the complex world of the twenty-first century.

Being socially literate

Conventionally, literacy has been regarded as a private accomplishment, a set of cognitive skills used to encode and decode written texts. However, since the 'social turn' (Gee 2005), literacy is seen as always already embedded in social and cultural contexts, involving the ability of an actor to engage with and respond to the world in which she exercises agency. 'Literacy' increasingly embraces an expanded and growing set of skills necessary for participation in technology rich and complex societies: information literacy, media literacy, computer literacy, health literacy, scientific literacy, emotional literacy and more. A lack of access to the means of gaining these capacities can be regarded as a disabling condition.

In line with this understanding, I suggest 'diversity literacy' is 'an enabled' mode of existence, congruent with the requirements of the emerging social imaginary of the twenty-first century.

Being critically literate

Any term gaining currency as a descriptor of social relations is subject to attempts to secure its use and meaning in ways that serve the interests of differently positioned groups. A term like 'diversity' could be regarded as a floating signifier (Laclau and Mouffe 1985) in the social imaginary, which contesting discourses attempt to secure, gaining most currency. 'Diversity' has at times encapsulated legal compliance, demographic representivity and neo-liberal inclusion, and has accommodated conservative, liberal and transformative impulses.

It can be argued that a normative conception of diversity as 'all the ways we differ' has emerged, especially prevalent in the corporate world. Epitomized in terms that lean towards the carnivalesque – 'embracing,' 'celebrating' diversity – all differences are grist to the merry diversity mill:

> Differences of all sorts, including cultural differences (as long as the cultures have money and can consume) are celebrated since they simply allow communities of practice to be infused with diverse knowledge and skills (any of which might eventually become a novel source of change and value), as well as allowing for the creation of more market niches with their distinctive consumer identities.
>
> *(Gee 2005: 184)*

Such a characterization divorces people from the power relations within society that advance or constrain the achievement of their full potential, moulding how others see us and how we see ourselves in relation to them. Apolitical, individualized conceptualizations of differences serve the interests of those who are already centred economically, socially and organizationally.

Dominant collectivities can be seen to be adjusting to the new diversity imperatives, while actually controlling, even stemming, the deeper, less comfortable aspects of these very imperatives.

It is into this normative space that the idea of critical diversity literacy speaks. The Critical school of social thought owes its intellectual debt to the Frankfurt School, and ultimately to Marx. Foregrounding unequal power relations, social inequities and fundamental contestations of situated interests in society, the tradition seeks to critique and not just to understand or explain society. The goal is a more socially just world. Embedded within this tradition, CDL shares the commitment to uncovering assumptions that obscure more penetrating understandings of historical and current social realities.

The CDL framework

'Critical diversity literacy' can be regarded as an informed analytical orientation that enables a person to 'read' prevailing social relations as one would a text, recognizing the ways in which possibilities are being opened up or closed down for those differently positioned within the unfolding dynamics of specific social contexts. The following section outlines ten criteria for CDL. Each of these requires much deeper explication than it is possible to provide in a short chapter; the comments therefore merely indicate one or two central concerns for each criterion.

(1) *An understanding of the role of power in constructing differences that make a difference.*

Far from reflecting a pre-given, natural order, all our categories for thinking about difference are socially constructed within unequal power relations. Some differences are constructed as those that make a difference (Hall 2007) while others remain unmarked. The implication is that difference is always (inter)relational, inessential, incomplete, fluid and destabilized. To retain the conceptual frameworks that support and maintain the appearance of a natural hierarchy requires constant ideological work. Paradigmatically this is achieved through the polarization of a range of human variation into mutually exclusive, binary opposites, such as man/woman; white/black; heterosexual/homosexual. In each case one side of the binary is valorized above the other. These binaries obscure and repress human variation along the axis in question, sedimenting social understandings into an ultimately self-fulfilling 'common sense'. Oppressive social structures maintain the categories, conferring or withholding rewards such as inclusion, belonging and acceptance, or conversely administering exclusion and censure.

Such inequitable social arrangements other those subordinated, and progressively develop systems of entitlement for the privileged; power and resources are sapped away from those disadvantaged. Social, economic and psychological rewards are amassed in the hands of the more powerful. We can thus rightfully talk about non-normative groups as oppressed by those in dominant positionalities. Young (1990) usefully identifies the 'faces of oppression' as exploitation, marginalization, powerlessness, cultural imperialism and violence. The presence of these, singly or in combination, indicates the presence of oppression. These dynamics operate both within nation states and transnationally, an important consideration in the experiences and conditions of migration.

Understanding and acknowledging the constitutive role of power in issues of diversity is the first principle of CDL. All the other criteria arise from the effects of underlying unequal power dynamics and how these are played out in relation to different differences – establishing normative orders, creating centres and margins, bringing about systems of privilege and disadvantage. Oppression on any vector obviously needs to be examined for the specificities affecting that oppression. Yet, sexuality, for example, requires analysis of the specific constructions and dynamics that pertain to bodily difference, sexual identities and expressions, as opposed to those that create, say, racial oppression; the deep systemic dynamics need to be understood as those of unequal power.

(2) *A recognition of the unequal symbolic and material value of different social locations. This includes acknowledging hegemonic positionalities and concomitant identities, such as whiteness, heterosexuality, masculinity, cisgender, ablebodiedness, middleclassness, etc. and how these dominant orders position those in non-hegemonic spaces.*

Some of the social fault lines created along particular axes of difference have proved to be enduring and wide ranging in their effects – they have long histories and wide reach. The divisions along lines of genders, 'races', ethnicities, sexualities and nationalities, for example, are entrenched and difficult to change (Payne 2006). These condition and shape knowledge formations, our sense of reality and self-understandings, collective and personal (Cesaire 2000 [1972]).

A critical approach to diversity names the ideological systems put in place by and for these positionalities as well as the hegemonic discourses that reproduce them, such as whiteness, heteronormativity, patriarchy, eurocentrism, etc. This does not imply that all people are identically placed in relation to the power structures that hold their positionalities in place. Social spaces include great disparities, and are riven with inconsistencies and contradictions. Not all people who are regarded as heterosexual, white and male will benefit equally from the privileges afforded to heteronormativity, whiteness and/or maleness. Some may be in quite weak positions within what is nevertheless a relationship of privilege when seen relative to the 'othered' groups.

Powerful forms of these centred positionalities are able to define the outside 'other' so that they retain their own psychological and material comfort. This applies also to non-dominant expressions – those that don't conform, or may be marked as less desirable. Patriarchal notions of masculinity, for example, constrain not only expressions of femininity, as the other, but also those of gay masculinities, or transgendered expressions of both masculinity and femininity. It is difficult for non-dominant and subordinated people to express their personhood in ways that challenge or fall outside of the 'admissible' ways of being endorsed within their societies, particularly in interactions with dominant groups or in public spaces (Biko 1987). A woman who performs her femininity within the parameters set for a 'good woman' will accrue the benefits, unlike those who step outside of these strictures. Disabled people are often constructed as recipients of charity if they accept their role as objects of sympathy, or as heroic if they exceed the expectations held for them. For the most marginalized in society the only way to perform their selfhoods so that the required ease of the dominant groups is retained may be to render the 'offending' self invisible, as with gay and trans people who simply do not risk coming out, either 'passing' or living a precarious life in fringe and alternative spaces.

Generally, those who are socialized into spaces of relative disadvantage are more likely to understand and recognize that these systemic odds are at play in their lifeworlds and are stacked against them. They contend with unearned barriers in the way of their advancement, being predominantly situated in positions of service and support for those who are advantaged, and with dominant versions of their realities superseding their own (DuBois 2008). But they also have to work through feelings of shame and humiliation and threats to their mental and physical health; they also have to confront the perils of nonconformity if they do challenge social expectations set for them. They may resist acknowledging relations or incidents of collusion and co-option, and the extent to which they may accept the prevailing narratives of the society.

Those socialized into positions of relative privilege tend to have less insight into the social dynamics that have created their advantages. The field of whiteness studies has drawn attention to the blindnesses and distortions that tend to infuse the spaces of racial privilege. Mills (1997) has eloquently described the epistemological contract that developed along with white racial domination through modernity:

> On matters related to race, the Racial Contract prescribes for its signatories an inverted epistemology, an epistemology of ignorance, a particular pattern of localized and global cognitive dysfunctions (which are psychologically and socially functional), producing the ironic outcome that whites will in general be unable to understand the world they themselves have made.
>
> *(ibid.: 18)*

At the heart of the subjectivities of entitlement that develop in such spaces is a sense of comfort with, and indeed commitment to, a world that is dominated by, centred upon and identified with their interests and the normalized unearned advantages that accrue to them (Johnson 2001). The way things are is experienced as ordinary, normal and ideal. Unsurprisingly, when the constructs that hold such a lifeworld in place are exposed or challenged, the tendency is often towards denial and an unwillingness to acknowledge how one benefits from the systems which continue to hoard advantage for those like oneself.

None of the above analysis should be read as denying people's agency, as clearly we adopt different personal stances towards how we find ourselves positioned by history and chance. But we are located within social relations, and this is a critical point, given the growing ethos that encourages us to think of ourselves simply as individuals who control our own destinies through our worthiness, entrepreneurship, self-belief and positive attitudinal toolkit.

My experience is that fully appreciating the import of how we are positioned within the relations of power that structure hierarchies is the most difficult part of acquiring CDL.

(3) *Analytic skill at unpacking how these systems of oppression intersect, interlock, co-construct and constitute each other, and how they are reproduced, resisted and reframed.*

Black feminist writers have been at the forefront of exposing how dominant formations do not act singly, and are not experienced discretely within people's lives (Collins 1993). A disabled woman's life will be shaped by the interaction of her disability and her gender in ways that are not simply an aggregate of the two lived separately or additively, and her racial location, yet again, will change her experience. Recent scholarship has taken the analysis further, showing not only that these axes intersect, but also that they are actually constructed through and mutually sustain one another (see Lutz, this volume). Othering processes on the basis of class and gender, gender and race, race and nation, masculinity and nation, sexuality and race, disability and race, gender and sexuality – all of these, for example, in different permutations and interactions, are implicated in one other. Given this mutual imbrication, theorists increasingly name composite hegemonic formations that capture some of these intersectional relations – such as heteropatriarchy, heteronationalism, europatriarchy, etc.

Intersectionality plays an important role in how systems of domination are reproduced. Oppressed groups often vie for advantage relative to one another; to create a hierarchy of oppressions would prioritize their interests above those oppressed differently. Intersectionality creates ambiguities in people's lives that may sustain such hierarchies. Black men who have historically experienced emasculating racial subordination may compensate through taking the advantages that a sexist order provides them; in the face of the ubiquitous power of whiteness, black women may be called upon to demonstrate racial solidarity, thus repressing gendered hardships within patriarchal communities. White women may take for granted the advantages of whiteness, contributing to black women's racial oppression, just as 'first world' disabled people may not see how their relative advantage is related to the deprivation of those in less privileged parts of the world. Class and race are often played off against each other, rendering one less visible than the other, rather than holding both simultaneously in analysis.

Recognizing the processes that allow the relatively smooth reproduction of existing power relations – such as those that invisibilize the norm, naturalize the status quo, construct ambiguities, promote patterns of forgetting and remembering, render some things unthinkable, discourage envisaging other possibilities – is essential for CDL. Included among these is the function of hegemony, through which the internalized oppression of dominated groups renders the overt violence of contradictory social relations indirect and obscure. Conforming oppressed people may develop positive self-images in order to form successfully their subjectivities in ways that bring them the rewards conferred upon those who bolster the system and weaken the position of others who may be more resistant. To the extent that the ideological machinery is able to reproduce a world in which whiteness is held to be the standard for all of us, systemic benefits along racial lines can be perpetuated, while the violence – physical, psychological and discursive – of the colonial conquests integral to shaping modern understandings of 'race' can be allowed to recede from memory.

The constructs of the powerful are invested in their own reproduction; however, this does not suggest that existing relations of power are inviolable. History is replete with examples of struggles against hegemonic orders that have yielded results. Members of non-dominant groups are not simply victims, and there are always resistances, refusals, oppositional memories, alternative knowledges and challenging sense makings. These provide resources for those who would open up different possibilities. A commitment to social justice requires being open to, and affirming of, such multiple realities: seeking out knowledges constructed from non-dominant positionalities, speaking out as a voice from a marginalized space, acknowledging the legitimacy of the organic experience of othered groups, recognizing value in alternative histories, putting in place and supporting affirmative programmes – these all work to counter the ways in which hegemonic orders would disqualify, discredit and undermine resistance.

(4) *A definition of oppressive systems such as racism as current social problems and (not only) a historical legacy.*

It is commonplace to hear that we now live in post-race societies; that we should focus on the future and not dwell on the injustices of the past. Discourses which (re)write the past so that the oppressive dynamics formative of current inequities are lost to memory construct epistemologies of ignorance and amnesia essential to continuing the gains of the past discriminatory practices without any moral accountability.

Struggles of memory and forgetting are about present social arrangements, as groups jostle for relative advantage. This has deep implications for what kind of practice we put in place, and how we set in motion options for the future. When we depoliticize the present by refusing a critical memory of the past, we render it impossible to understand the depth and scope of current challenges. We delegitimize the realities of the recipients of egregious effects of the past and their struggles for redress.

Far from simply accepting an ahistorical present, undertaking an archaeology of concepts can show the contingency, as opposed to the inevitability, of current understandings and determinations. Different possibilities for any of the axes of difference that shape social orders could have emerged under other power configurations and historical confluences, and often can be shown to have in fact existed in other contexts. Historical work on the construction of Africa through the colonial period, for example, shows that many achievements of the pre-colonial societies on the continent were actively undervalued (Davidson 2013). Misrepresentations of African creativity were integral to the construction of the idea of a 'dark' continent, a discursive strain that endures in representations of Africa as 'hopeless'. A sense of historical contingency, rather than historical inevitability, facilitates envisioning other possibilities for the future.

(5) *An understanding that social identities are learned and are an outcome of social practices.*

The four preceding criteria all facilitate an understanding of this one. The tendency to naturalize the positionings we have created is facilitated through essentialist notions of the groups simultaneously constructed within these spaces. This criterion of CDL requires recognition that there are no immutable characteristics attributable to a group of people that would be evident regardless of the historical processes of location, socio-economic conditions and other such social influences. Work on stereotypes has shown that often the characteristics that will be attributed to a group of people can be 'read off' how they are positioned in relation to the prevailing power dynamics in a context (Sidanuis 2001). Similar stereotypes have been held about such divergent groupings as the Irish, the English working class and Africans, for example. The social nature of what is regarded as innate personal characteristics also applies to the identities that people hold of themselves. Post-humanist understandings of selfhood deconstruct the bifurcation of the individual and the social, indicating the permeability and unclear nature of our personal boundaries. This constitutive porousness is reflected in the important processes of internalized domination and oppression and in our sense of how various intersectionalities 'land' within our sense of being.

(6) *The possession of a diversity grammar and a vocabulary that facilitates a discussion of privilege and oppression.*

As with any literacy, development of the lexicon in the area is key to fluency. An important indicator of CDL concerns the skill to engage the discourses that circulate within the contestations to define issues, people and events – placing them within dominant and oppressive understandings or challenging such attempts at closure. Being able to name these dynamics is often the first step in changing the power balances. A grasp of notions such as ideology, hegemony, oppression as well as commonly used notions in antiracist practice, such as 'blaming the victim', 'institutional racism' and 'internalized oppression' provides the tools to navigate difficult conversations. Having a language for CDL assists our agency not to be in the grip of dynamics that we cannot name; it enhances the capacity to recognize, point out and insist on the reality of the practices, strategies and effects of the operations of power on difference.

An example of how naming the operations of power has led to an empowering redefinition of a group has been the successful reframing of disability by the Disability Rights Movement. Once recognized as an othered social relation that affects people with impairments, disability can be shown to be created and maintained through the normalizing pressures of an ablest society. This shifts the struggle for better lives for disabled people from the discursive terrains of medicalization and charity to empowerment and rights (Charlton 2000; cf. Thomas, this volume).

(7) *The ability to 'translate' (see through) and interpret coded hegemonic practices.*

One of the key insights that frames CDL is that power never names itself as such. Rather, hegemonic language tends to obfuscate the ways in which social control is being exercised, how powerful groups may be benefiting or how the options of others are curtailed. So, for example, there is a tendency to create systems of explanation that attribute benefits to the virtue of those within the privileged group, to 'merit' or 'standards', rather than to unearned advantage. These discourses tend to be characterized by strategies of deflection, ambivalences and minimization of the adverse effects for those on the receiving end of social injustice and its legitimization.

Because dominant discourses are able to recast issues in ways that suit prevailing interests, they can co-opt, contain and curtail oppositional discourse. Dominant ways of talking about things may, for example, accommodate contradictions, keep shifting the terms of discourse or deflect attention away from how power is operating, holding the overall agenda in place. We can see how this has happened as the norms have become clearer for the emerging social imaginary as discussed. As a general disapproval of overt racist language has taken root in the contemporary world, the language that facilitates racial privilege has changed. Racial advantage is now advanced through 'colour blind' discourse, resulting in what Bonilla-Silva (2013) terms 'racism without racists' and through various forms of 'white talk' (Steyn and Foster 2008).

(8) *An analysis of the ways that diversity hierarchies and institutionalized oppressions are inflected through specific social contexts and material arrangements.*

While the fault lines of gender, for example, are evident across the globe, we need to understand how they play out within the intersectional webs of the politics of locations, the particularities of place, time and the specific ways in which people live within and through their material worlds. Gender is expressed and inflected under different historical processes and geographical influences. Assumptions arising from one context simply generalized to another can be misleading and imperializing in effect. Rather, it may be beneficial to think in terms of how hegemonic frameworks 'translate' between specific contexts, with differing outcomes (Drzewiecka and Steyn 2009). Similarly, constructs shift over time, and may mutate in different economic conditions and arrangements. An example is how the current neo-liberal economic system enables denial of the enduring salience of race and facilitates the belief that we live in a post-race era (Goldberg 2007).

The social and material worlds are inextricable. Objects, spatial arrangements, the built environment, all carry symbolic and emotional significance, and play a role in establishing, maintaining and/or subverting relationships between people. Inequitable distribution of wealth and fluency in accumulation and exchange of material assets and resources characterize the unequal relations created along social divisions. Disabled people, for example, tend to be the poorest people in every class of their societies. Oppressed people are often placed in positions of economic dependency on those who oppress them. Women have had to struggle, and continue to struggle, for the right to be economically active within a marriage relationship, and the work for which they are overwhelmingly held responsible, housekeeping, remains unpaid labour, widely institutionalized in the role of 'wife'. 'Things', commodities, even our tastes in these things, are often the vehicles through which relative positionalities are established and communicated (Dolby 2000). Through the constructions of certain diseases, even germs and viruses are vehicles for stigmatizing groups (Sontag 2001). The human immunodeficiency virus (HIV) has been a carrier of racism and homophobia, playing a role in configuring social arrangements. The most oppressed have literally themselves been reduced to material objects of exchange, as has been the case with black Africans who have been enslaved as chattel, women who have been the vehicle through which status and wealth have circulated and been preserved and children who are sold into the sex trade.

Spatial arrangements reveal a great deal about what is considered the proper relationships between people, and reflect the normative moral order. In apartheid South Africa physical distance between races was seen to reflect their moral distance (Mbembe 2004). Disabled children have often been placed in 'special' schools, often also physically removed, situated in semi-rural or rural areas, out of sight and largely out of mind.

(9) *An understanding of the role of emotions, including our own emotional investment, in all of the above.*

Recent social theory has emphasized the mutually constitutive nature of the social and the affective. Affect and emotions bind collectivities, circulating within what Sara Ahmed (2004) calls an affective economy. These economies provide bonding and belonging, and define the actual contours of our 'groupness'. The social construction of our emotions schools us into systems that tie in our affect in patterned ways: who we should move towards, who away from; who to connect to, who to separate from; who to protect, who to repulse. We are, literally, incorporated into this flow of feelings, into a sense of how we matter in relation to all other mattering objects: how and to what to give recognition and value; what lacks worth and deserves to be held in contempt; what should evoke our compassion or cause us outrage; what is lovable, desirable, joyful or repulsive; what gives us safety, what threatens us. All such flows of affect are operative within systems of power and have social effects.

How we are taken up within the circulation of affect is at least partly constitutive of our felt embodiment within particular locations, and of how we fashion a sense of identity in relationship to social power. CDL encourages a capacity for self-reflexivity and critical reflection on how our feelings are caught up in collectivities. How may we be encouraged to feel complacency or indignation towards specific experiences of social injustice? Which objects/issues are our feelings directed towards? What do we learn about our participation in processes of social formations? Processes of othering are crucially about impeding the current of positive affect towards those othered, and encouraging instead affective responses usually socially channelled to objects, those things regarded as less human, or less than human. To break these patterns, therefore, requires 'the education of the sentiments' (Rorty 2011) and sometimes uncomfortable emotional labour (Boler 2003).

(10) *An engagement with issues of the transformation of these oppressive systems towards deepening social justice at all levels of social organization.*

This final criterion raises the question of praxis, the willingness to bring together theory and practice in everyday life. It points to our imbrication in the dynamics outlined in the other nine criteria; our inevitable enmeshment in the social, with all its complex intersectional dynamics, constantly creates, recreates and redraws centres and margins. This criterion asks of us to recognize and interrogate these 'messinesses' and yet still to act into the world with a will to bring about more socially just arrangements: not only to understand them, but also to change them; to become an ally to those whose oppression would otherwise be further entrenched through conscious and unconscious assumptions of privilege.

Conclusion

These ten criteria are not intended to be exhaustive, or complete. Nevertheless, taken together, they provide a complex set of analytic skills with which to recognize, think about and interrupt prevalent relations of social oppression. No single person is likely to be equally or fully adept at all the criteria. They may represent directions for personal development as graduates, especially, the need to 'read', confront and engage with the increasing complexities of differences and otherness emerging in the twenty-first century, as they take on the challenges of the new social imaginary it births.

Notes

1 See, for example, Steyn (2010).
2 France Winddance Twine (2010) provides the following criteria for racial literacy: the definition of racism as a contemporary problem rather than a historical legacy; an understanding of ways that experiences of racism are mediated by class, gender inequality, and heterosexuality; a recognition of the cultural and symbolic value of whiteness; an understanding that racial identities are learned and are an outcome of social practices; the possession of a racial grammar and vocabulary to discuss race, racism and antiracism; the ability to interpret racial codes and racial practices.
3 For an open source version of a course based on this work, see http://opencontent.uct.ac.za/ Humanities/Diversity-Literacy.

References

Ahmed, S. (2004) 'Affective Economies', *Social Text*, 22 (2): 117–39.

Biko, S. (1987) *I Write What I Like*, Oxford, UK: Heinemann.

Boler, M. (2003) 'Discomforting Truths: The Emotional Terrain of Understanding Difference', in P. Trifonas (ed.) *Pedagogies of Difference: Rethinking Education for Social Change*, New York, NY: RoutledgeFalmer.

Bonilla-Silva, E. (2013) *Racism Without Racists: Color-Blind Racism and the Persistence of Racial Inequality in America*, 4th edn, Lanham, MD: Rowman & Littlefield.

Cesaire, A. (2000) [1972] *Discourse on Colonialism*, New York, NY: Monthly Review Press.

Charlton, J.I. (2000) *Nothing About Us Without Us: Disability, Oppression and Empowerment*, Berkeley, CA: University of California Press.

Collins, P.H. (1993) 'Toward a New Vision: Race, Class and Gender as Categories of Analysis and Connection', *Race, Class and Sex*, 1(1): 25–45.

Dolby, N.E. (2000) 'The Shifting Ground of Race: The Role of Taste in Youth's Production of Identities', *Race, Ethnicity and Education*, 3(1): 7–23.

Davidson, B. (2013) *Africa in History*, London: Hachette.

Drzewiecka, J. and Steyn, M.E. (2009) 'Discourses of Exoneration in Translation: Polish Immigrants in South Africa', *Communication Theory*, 19(2): 188–209.

DuBois, W. (2008) *The Souls of Black Folk*, Rockville, MD: Arc Manor.

Gee, J. (2005) 'The New Literacy Studies: From "Socially Situated" to Work of the Social', in D. Barton (ed.) *Situated Literacies: Theorising Reading and Writing in Context*, London: Routledge.

Goldberg, D.T. (2007) 'Neoliberalizing Race', *Macalester Civic Forum*, 1(1): 76–100.

Hall, S. (2007) 'Living with Difference: Stuart Hall in Conversation with Bill Schwarz', *Soundings*, 37(2007): 148–58.

Johnson, A.G. (2001) *Privilege, Power, and Difference*, Boston, MA: McGraw-Hill.

Laclau, E. and Mouffe, C. (1985) *Hegemony and Socialist Strategy: Towards a Radical Democratic Politics*, London: Verso.

Mbembe, A. (2004) 'Aesthetics of Superfluity', *Public Culture*, 16(3): 373–405.

Mills, C. (1997) *The Racial Contract*, Ithaca, NY: Cornell University Press.

Payne, G. (2006) *Social Divisions*, 2nd edn, Basingstoke, UK: Palgrave Macmillan.

Rorty, R. (2011) 'Human rights, Rationality and Sentimentality', in A.S. Rathore and A. Cistelecan (eds) *Wronging Rights?: Philosophical Challenges for Human Rights*, New Delhi: Routledge.

Sidanuis, J.L. (2001) 'Legitimizing Ideologies: The Social Dominance Approach', in J.T. Jost and B. Major (eds) *The Psychology of Legitimacy: Emerging Perspectives on Ideology, Justice, and Intergroup Relations*, Cambridge, UK: Cambridge University Press.

Sontag, S. (2001) *Illness as Metaphor and AIDS and its Metaphors*, 1st edn, New York, NY: Picador.

Steyn, M. (ed.) (2010) *Being Different Together: Case Studies on Diversity Interventions in Some South African Organisations*, Rondebosch: University of Cape Town. Online. Available HTTP: <https://vula.uct.ac.za/access/content/group/525e7b60-fc27-4a57-85e2-e673b9467714/being-different-together_9780620493826.pdf> (accessed 14 April 2014).

Steyn, M. and Foster, D. (2008) 'Repertoires for Talking White: Resistant Whiteness in Postapartheid South Africa', *Ethnic and Racial Studies*, 31(1): 25–51.

Twine, F. (2010) *A White Side of Black Britain: Interracial Intimacy and Racial Literacy*, Durham, MD: Duke University Press.

Vertovec, S. (2012) '"Diversity" and the Social Imaginary', *European Journal of Sociology*, 53(3): 287–312.

Young, I. (1990) *Justice and the Politics of Difference*, Princeton, NJ: Princeton University Press.

Index